A Chinese Reading
of
the *Daodejing*

SUNY series
in
Chinese Philosophy and Culture

David L. Hall and Roger T. Ames, editors

A Chinese Reading of the *Daodejing*

Wang Bi's Commentary on the *Laozi* with Critical Text and Translation

Rudolf G. Wagner

State University of New York Press

Published by
State University of New York Press, Albany

© 2003 State University of New York

For information, address the State University of New York Press,
90 State Street, Suite 700, Albany, NY 12207

Production by Michael Haggett
Marketing by Fran Keneston

Library of Congress Cataloging-in-Publication Data

Wagner, Rudolf G.
 A Chinese reading of the Daodejing : Wang Bi's commentary on the Laozi with critical
text and translation / Rudolf G. Wagner
  p. cm. — (SUNY series in Chinese philosophy and culture)
 Includes bibliographical references and index.
 ISBN 0–7914–5181–X (alk. paper) — ISBN 0–7914–5182–8 (pbk. : alk. paper)
  1. Laozi. Dao de jing. 2 Wang, Bi, 226–249. I. Title: Wang Bi's commentary on the
Laozi with critical text and translation. II. Laozi. Dao de jing. English. III. Wang, Bi,
226–249. Laozi wei zhi li lüe. English. IV. Title. V. Series.

BL1900.L35W28 2003
299'.51482—dc21
                                                              2002045257

10 9 8 7 6 5 4 3 2 1

Contents

Preface

It has taken many years, and several other books, to finish this study of which the present book is the second of three separate volumes. In fact, the writing of this study took as many years as Wang Bi, its subject, lived, namely, twenty-three. Debts of gratitude for spiritual and material support and critical discussion have accumulated. The core ideas were developed in 1971 in Berkeley, where I spent a wonderful year as a Harkness Fellow. The first of many drafts of an extrapolative translation of the *Laozi* through the Wang Bi *Commentary* was begun then and continued in the following year in Berlin with a habilitation grant from the German Research Association (DFG). A position as assistant professor at the Free University of Berlin began a long detour. My education had been exclusively in the field of classical Chinese studies; the focus of the Berlin Institute was modern China. While gaining some expertise in this new field, work on Wang Bi remained active, but on the back burner. After the job in Berlin had run its course in 1977, I finished the first full draft of this study, which I submitted in 1980 in German as a habilitation thesis. It was passed in 1981 with my late teacher Professor Wolfgang Bauer (Munich) and Professor E. Zürcher (Leiden) as external referees. Cornell University was generous enough to invite me as a fellow into its Society for the Humanities in the same year, which resulted in a book on Taiping religion. In the subsequent years I worked as a research fellow at Harvard University and as a research linguist at the University of California at Berkeley on two books about the politics of modern Chinese fiction.

Only small segments of my Wang Bi study were published in English during these years, among them earlier versions of Chapters 1 and 3 of this book. In 1987, I began to teach at the University of Heidelberg in Germany, an institute in urgent need of a major development effort. A stipend from the Stiftung Volkswagenwerk made possible another year at Harvard, working now on the English version of this study. In the meantime, scholarship had revived in mainland China, and a sizable amount of new work had emerged. I was relieved that my core arguments seemed solid enough to survive, and developed new sections, such as the analysis of Wang Bi's commentarial strategies contained in the first volume of this series, *The Craft of a Chinese Commentator*, a full critical edition of the *Laozi* text used by Wang Bi, as well as of his commentary, and an analysis of the textual transmission of Wang's commentary, both of which are contained in this volume; all the rest was reworked. In short bursts of feverish work between long stretches of other equally feverish work, the study finally was completed.

It is published in the following three independent volumes, of which the present is the second: *The Craft of a Chinese Commentator: Wang Bi on the Laozi*; A Chinese Reading of the *Daode jing*: Wang Bi's Commentary on the *Laozi*. With Critical Text and Translation; and *Language, Ontology, and Political Philosophy in China: Wang Bi's Scholarly Exploration of the Dark (Xuanxue)*.

Much of the emotional cost of such a study is not borne by the author but by those on whom this kind of work imposes painful deprivations. For my lovely daughters, Martha and Tina, this book had been a burden ever since they were born. I wish to thank them both, as well as their mother, for the many years of their bearing the burden of this work with me, and I apologize for the disruptions in their lives.

Catherine Vance Yeh, with her unflinching optimism and support, is thanked for the study's eventual completion—because of her efforts, this protracted, tumultuous, and often very frustrating work lost its grim colors and ended up enriching our lives.

My thanks to the foundations and universities that have generously supported this work at various stages, such as the DFG, the Stiftung Volkswagenwerk, and the universities of Cornell, Harvard, and Berkeley, which offered me research opportunities; to the members of the research group "Text and Commentary" in the Institute of Chinese Studies in Heidelberg, who gave much-needed spiritual support and critical advice; and to Dr. Johannes Kurz and Holger Kühnle who, during the last stages, helped as research assistants to finish the manuscript and the bibliography. In addition, Florence Trefethen eventually applied her firm and gentle pen in an effort to make my English more understandable and economical.

This book is dedicated to my daughters Martha and Tina Dohna as congratulations for completion of their own studies.

Introduction

During my work on early Chinese Buddhist thinkers, especially Shi Daoan 釋道安 (312–385) and Shi Huiyuan 釋慧遠 (334–416), I found that Buddhist arguments often were understood and expressed in a language originating in third-century Xuanxue 玄學, the "scholarly investigation of that which is dark," to use a cumbersome translation. Though the importance of Xuanxue in Chinese philosophy, including Chinese Buddhist philosophy and even Song-dynasty neo-Confucianism, is known, few detailed critical studies of particular texts and issues were available. It seemed natural to take up the study of Wang Bi (226–249), by all accounts the most brilliant of the Xuanxue philosophers.

There is a dearth of critical editions of Chinese texts and detailed studies of individual philosophical works. This is most pronounced for the works of commentators, even though China's best minds were working with this medium.

In studies of the Western classics, there has been a division of labor between scholars collating, editing, and perhaps translating texts and scholars mostly bent on analyzing the works thus made available. There were some scholars, however, such as Rudolf Bultman, in his work on the environment of the early Christian dispensation, who managed to span the entire breadth of the enterprise, from painstaking philological research, through broad analyses of religions, social, and political currents, to hermeneutical explorations of the internal logic of philosophical texts and religious beliefs. This model I set out to emulate, assisted by some years of studying hermeneutics with Hans-Georg Gadamer at the University of Heidelberg.

This volume is a workbook for the study of Wang Bi's writings on the *Laozi*. It includes studies on the textual history and available editions of Wang Bi's *Laozi* text, as well as Wang Bi's *Laozi* commentary, which show that the current editions are late, and very deficient; critical reconstructions and editions of both texts on the basis of internal evidence and new sources, including the new manuscript finds Mawangdui (1973) and

1

Guodian (1993); and fully annotated translations of Wang Bi's *Laozi* text, his *Commentary*, and his *The Structure of the Laozi's Subtle Pointers, Laozi weizhi lüeli.*

We have a great many translations of the *Laozi*, and even a few of Wang Bi's commentary. These *Laozi* translations are based on the privilege boldly claimed by the modern scholar to understand earlier Chinese philosophers better than anyone in the long tradition of Chinese commentaries. The present translation focuses on a Chinese reading of the *Laozi*, in particular on that by a young genius called Wang Bi, whose influence on later readings is unanimously and justly described as second to none other. It reads the *Laozi* through this commentary, and while this might arrive at a philosophical rather than historical reading, it certainly makes available an exciting contribution in terms of the sheer brilliance of the solutions it offers to many an enigmatic line in the *Laozi*. It is an even more exciting work in its own right by being a highly original philosophical approach that actively and philosophically engages with the giants of the past. The translation thus sets out to be extrapolative and to extract from Wang Bi's Commentary the exact way in which he read or constructed the *Laozi*.

For many things evident to Wang Bi's implied reader, a modern reader from whatever background—Chinese, Japanese or Western—will need an explicit hint. This might be an unannounced quotation from another part of the *Laozi* or from another text altogether, the implied subject of the entire chapter, or rhetorical information about the links between the different phrases. Mr. Haggett from SUNY Press has nicely matched Wang Bi's making sense of the *Laozi* phrases by putting on the cover of this volume a structure each node of which is in fact constituted by linkages to other nodes. The translation has tried to take seriously its duty of cultural mediation by supplying, in brackets, the relevant information. The purpose is to achieve a similar absence of ambiguity in the translation as Wang Bi managed to achieve through his commentary. The result is, I hope, a translation that is explicit enough to be falsifiable. In places that have remained hard to understand, I have gone out of my way to avoid the opaqueness of grammar, terminology, and rhetoric with which such passages often are rendered. A serious scholarly debate can only be based on translations that are in this sense falsifiable so that it can be proven that they are wrong where they are wrong.

Both the *Laozi* in Wang Bi's reading and Wang Bi himself turn out to be philosophers with important contributions to make. It is my hope to contribute to a deeper and more precise understanding of both through this critical edition, extrapolative reading, and falsifiable translation. It will be completed in the third volume through a study of the key philosophical issues treated in Wang Bi's writings on the *Laozi*.

Chapter 1

The Wang Bi Recension
of the *Laozi*

INTRODUCTION

Since[1] early Tang times, the *Laozi* was transmitted mainly over two commentaries, those of Wang Bi 王弼 (226–249) and Heshang gong 河上公. Most Tang excerpts, such as those included in the *Qunshu zhiyao* 群書治要 by Wei Zheng 魏徵 (580–643), on steles, and in manuscripts, are based on the Heshang gong text or, rather, on various Heshang gong texts.[2] By the early Tang, however, some scholars attempted to promote the Wang Bi text and *Commentary*, with Lu Deming 陸德明 (556–627), Fu Yi 傅奕 (554–639) and others making efforts to preserve it from distortions by the competing Heshang gong text. Lu Deming considered the latter text a fake, writing "Heshang ('s readings) are not those of the *Laozi*."[3]

Despite these efforts, the Heshang gong commentary continued to dominate and had practically replaced the Wang Bi version by the Song dynasty. During the Song, Lu Deming's efforts were taken up by scholars such as Fan Yingyuan 范應元, who published an edition explicitly comparing the various versions then circulating in an attempt to preserve the "old text."[4]

In recent decades, Professor Rao Zongyi (Jao Tsung-i) has published, along with an extensive commentary, two Dunhuang manuscripts of parts of the *Laozi*. The Suo Dan 索統 manuscript, Chapters 51–81, is dated C.E. 270 and is closely linked to the Heshang gong text, while the second, the Xiang Er 想爾 manuscript, which contains the first part of the *Laozi*, is dated by various scholars anywhere between the second and fifth centuries.[5]

3

Both of these manuscripts derive from the Celestial Master lineage of Taoism. The 1973 discovery of two *Laozi* manuscripts, in Mawangdui 馬王堆, near Changsha, both from tombs dating from the first decades of the Former Han, has in the main confirmed the stability of the *Laozi* text at that early date.[6] A 1993 discovery of three batches of *Laozi* segments in Chu 楚 script on bamboo slips in Guodiancun 郭店村 tomb No. 1 near Jingmen 荊門 in Hubei, dated by the editors to the "middle of the Zhan-guo period," around 300 B.C.E., has now been published.[7] The Guodian texts, again, are rather close to the Mawangdui versions, coming as they do from the Chu area.

These finds allow us to trace the history of the *Laozi* with greater precision and have confirmed readings in quotations from the *Laozi* in some pre-Qin, Qin, and Former Han texts. Some readings, however, have not been confirmed, and we have reason to assume that the Guodian and Mawangdui manuscripts belong to one among several textual lineages existing alongside each other.

These discoveries have come on the heels of textual studies by Yao Nai 姚鼐 (1732–1815) and Xu Dachun 徐大椿 (1693–1771), and more recently, Ma Xulun 馬敘倫 (1884–1970), who have all resumed the hearty denunciation of the Heshang gong text as a Taoist fake and have established the "Wang Bi version" as the "standard text."[8] This "Wang Bi standard text," however, is far from secure. The earliest available copies go back to Ming-dynasty editions, the earliest actual edition (in the *Zhengtong Daozang*) to the mid-Ming (1445). Scholars have noted discrepancies between quotations from the main text given in Wang Bi's *Commentary* and the very *Laozi* text to which this *Commentary* is attached. Ma Xulun mentioned this as early as 1924.[9] Similar comments have been made by D. C. Lau and William Boltz, but the "Wang Bi version" continues to be used and even translated.[10]

It is odd, too, that Hatano Tarō 波多野太郎 did not consider the problems of Wang Bi's *Laozi* text in his monumental compilation of the variant readings for the Wang Bi *Commentary*, and even the edition of Wang Bi's works by Lou Yulie 樓宇烈 never questions the *Laozi* text printed over current editions of Wang Bi's *Commentary*.[11]

As far as I know, the only scholar to have seriously worked at recon-structing the Wang Bi *Laozi* is Shima Kuniō 島邦男. His *Rōshi kōsei* (1973) has the great advantage of having been published before the Mawangdui manuscripts became known. This provides an independent check on the accuracy of his assumptions and conjectures. Sadly, the work basically went unnoticed at the time in the flurry after the Mawangdui discovery, and Lou Yulie did not make use of it for his Wang Bi edition.[12]

THE PROBLEM

There are various versions of the *textus receptus* of the *Laozi* text of Wang Bi, the oldest reproduced in the *Zhengtong Daozang*. These texts show only slight deviations, however, in all received versions of this Wang Bi *Laozi*, which will be referred to here as *Wang Bi Laozi Receptus*, there is a conflict between the *Laozi* text used in the *Commentary* and the text printed above that *Commentary*.[13]

This conflict appears in the following forms:

1. In his commentaries, Wang Bi frequently quotes the *Laozi* with formulae such as "that is why [the *Laozi*] says," or simply, "that is why." There are cases where the subsequent quotation deviates from the *Laozi* text printed immediately above this commentary. One such example is found in *Laozi* 6:

Wang Bi Laozi Receptus:	是謂天地　根
Wang Bi Comm.:	故謂 ″ ″之 ″

2. Wang Bi quotes one *Laozi* passage in his commentary to a different *Laozi* passage, with differences between *Wang Bi Laozi Receptus* and the wording in this commentary.

Wang Bi Laozi Receptus (2.2):	聖人處無爲之事
Wang Bi Comm. (on 17.1):	″ ″居 ″ ″ ″ ″

3. Wang Bi quotes the *Laozi* in his other writings, in words that differ from those in the received text of the Wang Bi *Laozi*. One such example comes from his *Commentary to the Zhouyi* (*Zhouyi zhu* 周易注).[14]

Wang Bi Laozi Receptus (58.6):	人之迷　其日固　久
Zhouyi zhu:	″ ″ ″也 ″ ″ ″ ″已 ″矣

4. Wang Bi's *Commentary* uses elements of the *Laozi* that imply wording in the main text different from the wording in the *Wang Bi Laozi Receptus*.

Wang Bi Laozi Receptus (1.2):	無名天地之始
Wang Bi Comm.:	道以無名無形始成萬物
Wang Bi Comm. (on 21.7):	以無名閱萬物之始

The expression *tiandi* 天地 of the received text of the *Laozi* neither occurs in the commentary to the passage itself nor in the reference to it in the commentary on Chapter 21. Both comments suggest, instead, that *wanwu* 萬物 was the reading in the *Wang Bi Laozi*. That sloppy quoting by Wang Bi accounts for these differences should be dismissed for two reasons. First, the readings suggested by the *Commentary* and the other texts by Wang Bi find strong support in the available "old manuscripts," including the Guodian and Mawangdui. Second, the philosophical authority of the text in the eyes of Wang Bi, who obviously took the exact wording very seriously, would seem to preclude sloppy quoting. We are thus left with the following preliminary conclusions: first, the *Wang Bi Laozi Receptus* is not identical to the *Laozi* text actually used by Wang Bi, the *Wang Bi Laozi*; second, another *Laozi* text has been superimposed over Wang Bi's *Commentary*, while the *Commentary* itself has not been changed to conform. That this reflects careless editing has to be dismissed as well. The extreme importance that the different traditions attached to "their" versions as being uniquely true and authoritative would seem to preclude this possibility, but why was the Wang Bi *Commentary* not changed? The only explanation seems to be that it had an authority of its own. While the *Laozi* text was adapted to fit the dominant school, Wang Bi retained his credentials as a philosopher in his own right, the text of his *Commentary* remaining untouched. Obviously, we are now called upon to reconstruct the *Wang Bi Laozi*, to try to figure out how the changes in the received text came about, and to establish the *Wang Bi Laozi* in its proper position within the *stemma codicum*.

WANG BI'S
ORIGINAL RECENSION OF THE *LAOZI*

Since it is possible that Wang Bi's *Laozi* differed greatly from all known *Laozi* texts, we will have to secure a fair number of firm readings of the *Wang Bi Laozi* before looking at other versions of the *Laozi* text. For evidence about the *Wang Bi Laozi*, we will draw on the following sources:

1. Wang Bi's quotations from the *Laozi* in his *Commentary* and other writings (with the provision that these might have problems in their transmission);
2. Inferences based on the wording in Wang Bi's *Commentary*;
3. Quotations of *Laozi* passages with Wang's commentary in pre-Tang and perhaps early Tang texts, on the assumption that in these cases the wording of the *Wang Bi Laozi* was used;

4. Explicit statements by Lu Deming in his *Laozi Daodejing yinyi* about the readings of the "Wang Bi text" available to him (a text, however, that might already have undergone some changes);[15] and
5. Explicit statements by Fan Yingyuan in his *Laozi Daodejing guben jizhu*, relating his Wang Bi *Laozi* manuscript to one or several "Old Manuscript(s)."

These are listed in a decreasing degree of reliability, however, the reliability of the external sources (quotations and explicit statements about the Wang Bi text) can be enhanced if they coincide with the internal evidence in many places.

In seventy-nine passages, the wording in Wang Bi's *Commentary* deviates from the *Wang Bi Laozi Receptus* (see Appendix A). In all but one, the reading suggested by the *Commentary* also can be found in the Guodian and Mawangdui manuscripts, texts such as the *Huainanzi* 淮南子, *Wenzi* 文子, or *Zhangguo ce* 戰國策, dated manuscripts such as the Suo Dan manuscript of C.E. 270, or the pre-Tang Xiang Er manuscript from Dunhuang, or the "Old Manuscripts" on which Fu Yi 傅奕 (554–639) and Fan Yingyuan based their own editions. In short, it can be assumed that these readings represent the text of the *Laozi* known to Wang Bi.

On the basis of these confirmed readings, we can proceed to check on the reliability of the other sources for the reconstruction of the *Wang Bi Laozi*. There are hundreds of phonetic glosses by Lu Deming, but only three deviate from the readings common to all strands of the received tradition. In those three cases, the deviant reading is corroborated by either Fu Yi's or Fan Yingyuan's "Old Manuscript" or by Wang Bi's own commentary.[16]

A number of Lu Deming's readings have to be discarded, however, because strong evidence supports other readings for the *Wang Bi Laozi*. It is apparent that Lu's text had already undergone some changes. Furthermore, as noted by Hatano Tarō, the difference between quotations of Lu Deming given in Fan Yingyuan's *Laozi Daodejing guben jizhu* and the *textus receptus* of Lu Deming's *Laozi Daodejing yinyi* indicates that the latter text also has been tampered with.[17]

In forty-seven places, Fan Yingyuan provides information about the relationship of the "Old Manuscript(s)" available to him with the *Wang Bi Laozi* in his hands (see Appendix B). We do not know the exact origin of Fan's "Old Manuscript" or the criteria that prompted him to mark the differences and coincidences in those places but not in others. From his remarks, we learn that the Wang Bi *Laozi* recension in his hands agreed with his "Old Manuscript" in all but three places; in each case, the deviation concerns only one character.[18]

The best extant version of the *Wang Bi Laozi Receptus* differs from the reading given by Fan in no less than thirty-seven places. In twenty cases (2.4, 10.4, 19.1, 20.5, 20.9, 21.6, 28.7, 34.4, 35.3, 38.2, 38.2, 41.15, 42.2, 45.2, 48.3, 49.4, 51.4, 57.3, 59.2, and 65.4) Wang Bi's own comments reveal unequivocally the original reading of the *Wang Bi Laozi*. In thirteen of these twenty cases, the reading given by Fan for his Wang Bi *Laozi* is the original one, while the received text is corrupt. In three cases (19.1, 42.2, and 65.4), both Fan's text and the received text are wrong. In only four cases is the received text supported by internal evidence (20.5, 20.9, 21.6, and 45.2). Indirect summaries by Wang Bi of the *Laozi*'s wording permit educated guesses about his text. These reveal twelve more places where Fan's Wang Bi *Laozi* is superior to the received text (see Appendix B). In the remaining places, there is either no clear evidence, or Fan's reading is improbable. We can conclude that the Wang Bi *Laozi* recension in Fan's hands was rather close to the original: twenty-five out of thirty-two verifiable places favor the reading in Fan's text. As for the quotations in late-Han and early-medieval material, they mostly occur in other commentaries such as Zhang Zhan's 張湛 (fourth century) *Commentary on the Liezi* 列子注, Li Shan's 李善 (d. 689) *Commentary on the Wenxuan* 文選注, or Yan Shigu's 顏師古 (581–645) *Commentary on the Hanshu* 漢書注. No unified conclusion can be reached about them, since some date from a period when the original Wang Bi text was already undergoing changes. Their readings can be accepted only if strongly buttressed by internal and supporting evidence. Shima Kuniō has collected many of these explicit quotations, however, such citations often are not explicit, so locating them can be a matter of serendipity.

We now have a great number of authenticated specifications of the *Wang Bi Laozi*. The high incidence of deviance from the received text suggests that it should be abandoned as the basis for a reconstruction of the *Wang Bi Laozi* if we find another text or textual family where the coincidence with authenticated passages of the *Wang Bi Laozi* is substantially higher. We can already conclude from the differences between the *Wang Bi Laozi* and Lu Deming's Wang Bi *Laozi*, and the even greater difference in Fan Yingyuan's Wang Bi *Laozi*, that the *Wang Bi Laozi* gradually has been superseded by other readings. A second question follows from this conclusion. Is there a text or group of texts that can be identified as having gradually superseded the *Wang Bi Laozi*? We can state from the outset that we do not have a text identical to the *Wang Bi Laozi* Urtext in all authenticated passages to use as a replacement for the received text. Furthermore, there is no extant text other than that including Wang Bi's *Commentary* that is identical to the *Wang Bi Laozi Receptus*. This excludes the possibility that, at some point, a completely different *Laozi* text had been superimposed over the old Wang Bi *Commentary*. Things are, as usual, messy. Where can we find the closest approximation to the *Wang Bi Laozi*?

The debate about the Mawangdui and now the Guodian manuscripts has practically obliterated the fact that the search for the "old" and true *Laozi* has been going on for some time. To the natural decay of books written on bamboo strips or silk, to the fires periodically destroying entire private or imperial libraries, to the worms happily feeding on the newly discovered repository for culture's written products, namely, paper, was added time and again the official destruction of books. Since the destruction during the Qin, this has continuously received unfavorable comments and has spurred and legitimized official and private efforts at book retrieval. Throughout Chinese history, scholars and rich and mighty men have chased and occasionally produced "old manuscripts." Of Prince Liu De 劉德 (d. 128 B.C.E.), Ban Gu 班固 (32–92) wrote:

> He honed his scholarship, was well versed in olden times, and sought truth from facts. When he received a good book from the common folk, he would inevitably make a fair copy for them while keeping the original, and would add presents of gold and cloth to attract them. The effect of this was that people from all directions who were versed in the arts did not consider a thousand miles too far [to come to him], and sometimes there were those who had old books from their forefathers which they often would proffer to the prince. Therefore, he got hold of a great many books, as many in fact as the Han Court itself. At the time, Liu An 劉安, the Prince of Huainan, was also fond of books, but what he attracted were for the most part empty babblers. The books that came into Prince Liu De's possession were all pre-Qin books in the old scripts. For the likes of the *Zhouguan* 周官, the *Shangshu* 尚書, the *Li* 禮, the *Liji* 禮記, the *Mengzi* 孟子 and the *Laozi*, he had all the classical texts, the transmissions (*zhuan* 傳), the explanations (*shuo* 說), and the records (*ji* 記), and what the seventy disciples [of Confucius] had to say [about them].[19]

We have no further record of his pre-Qin *Laozi* text that must have predated the Mawangdui manuscripts. Seven centuries later, Fu Yi was a fervent collector of *Laozi* manuscripts, eventually publishing his own *Daodejing guben* 道德經古本, a critical conflation of those that he had perused. He also wrote a short history of the discovery of these texts and their transmission. Although this is lost, it forms, along with Lu Xisheng's

陸希聲 (late ninth century) preface to his *Daode zhenjing zhuan* 道德眞經傳, the basis of Xie Shouhao's 謝守灝 *Hunyuan shengji* 混元聖紀, with a preface dated in the third month of 1191.[20] The excerpt given there of Fu Yi's report about the various *Laozi* manuscripts he had seen and perused is again quoted from Xie Shouhao in Peng Si's 彭耜 (fl. 1229) *Daode zhenjing jizhu zashuo* 道德眞經集註雜說. Peng Si seems to have had a better version of Xie Shouhao's text than that preserved in the Daozang, and he furthermore indicates that in his version Xie Shouhao mentioned the source from which he had taken this quotation, namely, Du Guangting's 杜廣庭 (850–933) now lost *The Precious Record of Lord Lao*, (*Laojun baolu* 老君寶錄).[21] I shall make use of Peng's text. What survives of Fu Yi's report deserves a translation in full.[22]

> Fu Yi of the Tang [dynasty] has carefully examined all manuscripts [of the *Laozi*] and has investigated the number of characters [each of them] had, and he said: "As to the Xiang Yu 項羽 (–202 B.C.E.) Concubine Manuscript, a man from Pengcheng [city in Shandong], who opened the tomb of a concubine of Xiang Yu's in the 5th year of the era *wuping* 武平 of [Northern] Qi [i. e. 574] found it. As to the Anqiu Wangzhi 安丘望之 [fl. 30 B.C.E.)[23] Manuscript [Xie Shouhao writes Wang An Qiu Zhi 望安丘之 here], [i. e. a *Laozi* text with a commentary by Anqiu Wangzhi], it came into the possession of the Daoist Kou Qianzhi 寇謙之 (363–448) during the *taihe* 太和 era of the [Northern] Wei (477–500).[24] As for the Heshang zhangren 河上丈人 Manuscript [i.e., the manuscript over the commentary by Heshang zhangren], the retired scholar from [Northern] Qi, Qiu Yue 仇嶽, handed it down.
>
> These three manuscripts all have 5,722 characters and are related to [the *Laozi* text which forms the basis of] the Hanfeizi 韓非子 chapter "Yu Lao" 喻老. Furthermore, there is also the Luoyang Official Manuscript (*guanben* 官本) with 5,635 characters. As for Wang Bi Manuscripts, there is one with 5,683 characters and one with 5,610. As for Heshang gong 河上公 Manuscripts, there is one with 5,355 [Xie Shouhao: 5,555] characters and one with 5,090 characters. The [manuscripts transmitted over] the various commentaries all have greater or lesser differences, but as time went on, each [school] believed only in [the manuscript] handed down [by their own people], or they mixed them up with manuscripts from other people. Therefore, there are errors and mistakes, and there is no unity.

In the *Shiji* 史記, Sima Qian 司馬遷 says that Laozi published a book that talks about the meaning of Dao and De, and has "five thousand plus words" (*wuqian yu yan* 五千餘言).[25] "Five thousand plus" means more than five thousand but less than six thousand. When the Daoists today say that the *Laozi* is a text with "five thousand characters," they refer to the general volume 大數 [but not to the text's having exactly 5,000 characters].[26]

Fu Yi's account shows that the endeavor to find the "original" *Laozi* has a long history. We do not know the exact basis of his own "Old MS" edition, but it is probable that it is an attempt to establish a critical text through the comparison with the seven "old MSS" that he managed to peruse. Lu Deming operated in much the same vein. His effort to establish the correct reading of the *Laozi* assumed that the notation in the manuscripts before the reform of writing was largely phonetic and that, given the large number of loan graphs in old manuscripts, the meaning would only become clear once the reading had been established. In his own (badly corrupted) notes, he refers to the *Laozi* texts given over different commentators, and also to a *Laozi* text on bamboo slips, *jian wen* 簡文, which must have been a Han or even a pre-Han dynasty manuscript.[27] Editors such as Fu Yi also made efforts to stabilize the text. Evidence of this attempt is to be found in the notation, in the Mawangdui B manuscript, of the number of characters in each of the two *pian* 篇.

Fu Yi read and compared these seven manuscripts, counting their characters in the process. The discovery of the Mawangdui manuscripts indicated that, at least since Qin-dynasty efforts at cutting off certain textual traditions altogether, the statement of the number of characters the copied text contained was a device both to enhance textual stability and to define textual lineage. The number of characters indicated to which kind of lineage a given manuscript belonged. *More sinico*, Fu Yi's narrative sequence gives us a chronological order for the writing (not the discovery or copy) of these manuscripts. The Xiang Yu Concubine Manuscript must be the oldest, as Xiang Yu died in 202 B.C.E. and must have still been alive for the concubine to receive such a lavish tomb. At least one of the texts from this tomb, a *Guwen Xiaojing* 古文孝經 manuscript survived to the early Song, where it formed one of the sources of reference for Xia Song's 夏竦 (985–1051) *Guwen sisheng yun* 古文四聲韻, a work completed in 1044 that provided under standard characters the forms in which they were written in a variety of old manuscripts and inscriptions.[28] Sadly, no work has hitherto been done on the texts in old script used in early Song handbooks that set out to provide help and guidance in the reading of old inscriptions and manuscripts to the rapidly growing number of scholars and officials fascinated with the "authentic" traces of China's past. Among the twelve "old texts" listed in the preface to Guo Zhongshu's 郭忠恕 (tenth century) *Han jian* 汗簡 as having been used by him, there is an "old *Laozi*" 古老子 or rather "*Laozi* in the old script," but I have not been able to locate a direct quotation from this *Laozi* edition in his work.[29] This is different with Xia Song's 夏竦 (985–1051) *Guwen sisheng yun*, a book that used the *Han jian* and many new materials.[30] Xia makes use of two old *Laozi* manuscripts, namely, a "*Laozi* in old script," 古文老子, and a *Daode jing* but does not seem to have had access to the *Laozi* manuscript from the tomb of Xiang Yu's concubine.[31] In his preface, Xia talks about the texts in old script, their discovery and transmission. Since the Wei and Jin dynasties the capacity to read these texts all but disappeared. However, among a few devotees, the interest and skill were preserved, as well as some texts. The son of Li Yangbing 李陽冰 (ca. 713–ca. 785), a relative of Li Bo's and a poet as well as seal script specialist in his own right,[32] had a Xiaojing 孝經 and another text in the old script in his family possession. Obviously unable to read it, he gave it to none other than Han Yu 韓愈 (768–824), but at this time Han Yu had not discovered his interest in rediscovering the "authentic" pre-Buddhist China and, seemingly unable to read it, he brought it to the attention of Master Gui 歸公 (Gui Deng? 登) who "loved antiquity and was able to understand it." The manuscript therefore was bequeathed to him. While nothing about the origin of Xia's "*Laozi* in the old script" is known, he details some of the transmission of the *Daode jing* in two *juan* written with lacquer on bamboo strips, a *qishu* 漆書, to which he had access. It had been in the possession of another great specialist in old script, the Heavenly Master Sima Chengzhen 司馬承禎 (647–735). A copy of this manuscript from the hands of another Taoist was stored on Tiantai shan and eventually retrieved during the Song dynasty's efforts to assemble reliable texts so that Xia had access to it.[33] Sadly, we still lack a critical study of these two texts, or rather of the individual characters quoted from them in Xia Song's book. It is possible that Fan Yingyuan's "Old MS" had a connection to either of these two texts.

We return to Fu Yi's list. The Xiang Yu Concubine Manuscript, it should be remembered, is thus older than both Mawangdui manuscripts, which date from the first decades of the second century B.C.E. Next comes a surprising lacuna in Fu Yi's holdings, namely, the absence of a Zhuang Zun 莊遵 (= Yan Zun 嚴遵) manuscript, the original of which would have predated his next manuscript, the late first century B.C.E. Anqiu Wangzhi manuscript that ended up in the hands of the famous Daoist Kou Qianzhi of the Northern Wei. The text here has an impossible era name. The *taihe*

太和 era began in 477, but Kou had died in 448. It must be the era *yanhe* 延和 (432–435) or *taiping* 太平 (440) under Taiwu di.[34] The Heshang zhangren manuscript first surfaced after the founding of the Northern Qi in 550. As it is mentioned before Wang Bi, Fu Yi dates this text into the later Han dynasty. He rejects the link between a Heshang zhangren of the Zhanguo period mentioned in the *Shiji*[35] and this text, which had been made by the Liang dynasty book catalogue.[36] Fu Yi noted the closeness of the three oldest manuscripts in his hands to the version used in the *Hanfeizi*. Their identical number of characters (5,722) points to a surprisingly high degree of standardization but is not close enough to the aggregate number given for the two parts of the *Laozi* in Mawangdui B, namely, 3,041 plus 2,426 = 5,467, to warrant an argument that the Mawangdui manuscripts represent a text close to these three manuscripts.

The Luoyang Official Manuscript again is mentioned before Wang Bi. As Luoyang was the capital of the Later Han dynasty, this Luoyang Official Manuscript must have been an uncommented Laozi manuscript from the Later Han imperial library. The Wang Bi texts come next, followed by the youngest and last of the manuscripts worthy of any consideration, that of Heshang gong. Here again, Fu Yi rejects the Liang dynasty book catalogue that dates this commentary to the time of the Han emperor Wen 文 (red. 179–156 B.C.E.).[37]

Since Fu Yi counted the number of characters in the Heshang zhangren manuscripts, and thus must have read them, it can be inferred that he saw a substantial difference both in age and structure between the Heshang zhangren and the Heshang gong manuscripts. The criticism voiced in the last section evidently refers to Ge Xuan's 葛玄 (164–244) actual reduction of the *Laozi* to exactly 5,000 characters, which Fu Yi considers an all too verbatim reading of the remark by Sima Qian. Fu Yi's own "Guben" or "Old Manuscript" does not fit any of the numbers mentioned above. Without further evidence, we have to assume that he tried to arrive at a critical edition using all available early manuscripts at his disposal, and that he chose the best corroborated reading. The same is true for Fan Yingyuan. We know nothing of the origin of his "Old Manuscript(s)," but its relationship to Fu Yi's is so close that one must treat them like Shima Kuniō, as closely related members of a single family of texts. They are even more closely related than the Mawangdui A and B manuscripts. The "Old Manuscripts" of Fu and Fan differ from each other in about 100 places, but their common deviations from other extant texts are substantially higher.

Of extant texts, we have a fair number to consider in reconstructing a new *Wang Bi Laozi*. First, the two Mawangdui manuscripts from the early Han, closely linked, show more deviations from other known texts than against each other. In many cases, the Guodian texts support their reading. Next, Zhuang (Yan) Zun's 莊 (嚴) 遵 *Laozi zhu* 老子注, a work lost since the Tang, is preserved only in quotations. Zhuang (Yan) Zun, who lived at the end of the Former Han, also wrote a *Laozi zhigui* 老子指歸, which, except for the first six chapters, is preserved in the Zhengtong Daozang under the title *Daode zhenjing zhigui* 道德眞經指歸.[38] This text has been little studied and often has been regarded as a fake, however, Shima Kuniō shows convincingly that many of the readings of the *Laozi* inserted in the *Laozi zhigui* are matched by other early evidence. In fact, he took the readings from *Laozi zhigui* for the second part of the *Laozi* as the basis of his own critical edition against which he defines the deviations of the other manuscripts.[39] Third is the *Xiang Er Commentary* 想爾注 to the *Laozi*, a Dunhuang manuscript, first mentioned by Lu Deming, who says that one tradition claims that it was written by Zhang Lu 張魯 (d. 216) of the Celestial Master school. In this regard, the *Maoshan zhi* 茅山誌, by Liu Dabin 劉大彬 of the Tang dynasty, preserves a lengthy quote from Tao Hongjing's 陶宏景 (456–535) *Dengzhen yinjue* 登眞隱訣:

> The Hermit says: "As for the *Daodejing* by Laozi there is the old manuscript of Zhang Zhennan 張鎭南 handcopied by the Master of the Dark, the Immortal Yang 楊. "Zhennan" refers to [Zhang Lu 張陸], the third generation descendant of the Han-dynasty Heavenly Master [Zhang] Lu [張] 魯. [Zhang Lu 張陸] was appointed General of Zhennan by Wudi of the Wei dynasty [i.e., Cao Cao 曹操]. That this, the so-called "5,000 text," *wuqian wen* 五千文, has 5,000 characters, is based on counting the internally [transmitted] classic, *neijing* 內經, of the Master by Inheritance [i.e., Zhang Lu] with its 4,999 characters. The one [character] missing is in the formular "30 spokes . . ." 三十輻 that should be written [with one character less as] 卅輻. One should follow the abbreviated form, not the standard form. The adherents [of the Celestial Master school] do not preserve this authentic form [of the *Laozi*]; today [they] transmit a text in 5,000 characters as the standard text. It has a first and a second *pian*, and no divisions into *zhang*.[40]

The Xiang Er manuscript does write the 三十 in *Laozi* 11 in the form 卅, but it certainly had more than 5,000 characters in its *Laozi* text. The hand-copied manuscript by Yang Xi 楊羲 (active between 326 and 335 on Maoshan) seems to be the antecedent of the version in 5,000 characters commonly associated with Ge Xuan 葛玄. Finally, there is the Heshang gong *Commentary* with its own *Laozi* text or texts. Quotations from the Heshang gong recension indicate that this, too, was a textual family with a variety of readings. Shima Kuniō cites two new pieces of evidence to prove that the Heshang gong *Commentary* must have been written in the fifth century. First, he finds the first verbatim quote in Tao Hongjing's 陶弘景 (452–536) writings. Second, its readings of the characters *che* 轍 and *hui* 恢, written in most *Laozi* manuscripts as *che* 徹 and *tan* 惔, respectively, link the text to the *Laozi jiangshu* 老子講述 by King Wu 武 (464–549) of the Liang.[41] Since he also has discovered loans in the Heshang gong *Commentary* from the *Commentary* of Gu Huan 顧歡 (fl. late fifth century), he concludes that it was written "late in the Six Dynasties period," which would coincide with the dating implied in Fu Yi's narrative.[42] "This," he writes, "is proof that the Heshang gong manuscript is not an old manuscript."[43]

However, in his *Rōshi kōsei* 老子校正 Shima Kuniō seems unaware of the Suo Dan manuscript, published in 1955. As noted by Rao Zongyi, this dated manuscript supports many of the singular readings of the Heshang gong recension.[44] Furthermore, Shima Kuniō does not mention an indirect quotation (albeit of a passage not found in the extant Heshang gong *Commentary*) in Gao You's 高誘 (late second century) *Commentary to the Huainanzi*.[45] He also fails to mention a quotation that occurs in Xie Zong's 謝宗 (d. C.E. 243) *Commentary* to Zhang Heng's 張衡 *Dongjing fu* 東京賦, included in the *Wenxuan*.[46] It must be added, however, that the reliability of this commentary is open to question, since it contains a quotation from Guo Pu's 郭璞 (276–324) *Commentary on the Erya* 爾雅, a text written about sixty years after Xie Zong's death.[47] Whatever the final verdict on the Heshang gong *Laozi*, its prominent role during the Tang makes it a candidate for the text or group of texts that gradually superseded the *Wang Bi Laozi*.

Based on the certified elements of the *Wang Bi Laozi* on the one hand, and the authenticated old versions of the *Laozi*, on the other hand, we shall look for complete texts to replace the *Wang Bi Laozi Receptus* as a basis for the *Wang Bi Laozi*. As shown in Appendix B, the *Wang Bi Laozi* in the hands of Fan Yingyuan closely resembled his own "Old Manuscript," coinciding in forty-four out of the forty-seven places where he provides information. The "Old Manuscript" of Fan Yingyuan also is closely linked to Fu Yi's "Old Manuscript." Given the ongoing hunt for old manuscripts, there is no reason to believe that the texts used by these two were younger than the Mawangdui manuscripts. The Peking editors of the Mawangdui manuscripts recognized the strong affinity between them and Fu Yi's "Old Manuscript," and they provided a synoptic version, juxtaposing Mawangdui A, Mawangdui B and Fu Yi's "Old MS," but not the much more popular *Wang Bi Laozi Receptus*.[48] Strangely enough, Gao Ming's 高明 otherwise very careful reedition of the Mawangdui manuscripts does not follow this practice but goes back to an uncritically accepted *Wang Bi Laozi Receptus* as a reference text to compare the Mawangdui manuscripts.[49]

Together, the two "Old Manuscripts" differ from the *Wang Bi Laozi Receptus* in about 300 places, but they differ from the Heshang gong tradition even more. Therefore, I think that we can assume that the two "Old Manuscripts" together represent a text much closer than the *Receptus* to the *Wang Bi Laozi*. Of the approximately 100 deviations between the two "Old Manuscripts," internal evidence indicates the preferable reading in about sixty places, about half for each side. The three or four cases where the *Wang Bi Laozi* deviates from both "Old Manuscripts" are listed by Lu Deming and Fan Yingyuan.

The *Wang Bi Laozi* is approximately "in the middle" of the two "Old Manuscripts," the three forming a very close textual family. They share a number of deviations against the Guodian and the Mawangdui manuscripts; however, these were written at a time when the connection between written characters and words was still highly unstable. A comparison even between these two sets of texts shows an increasing stability of this word/character relationship.[50] Both texts, therefore, show only moderate interest in the accuracy of the written word. They operate on the assumption that reading largely means identifying spoken words from the graphs. As long as they achieve this goal, all graphs are legitimate, whether operating through a phonetic loan such as 又 for 有, or a graphic variant. Writing stabilized only during the following generations, and the number of written characters with such stabilized connections to words grew dramatically. Some of the thrill coming with this "new medium" can be seen in the plethora of new written characters paraded through the *fu*-poetry of the Han. Due to this instability of the written word, the number of deviations between the "Old MSS" edited (and standardized) by Fu Yi and Fan Yingyuan against the Guodian and Mawangdui manuscripts is extremely high; once these phonetic and graphic variants are eliminated, the common elements dominate. The "Old MSS" and the two Mawang-dui manuscripts have many fewer deviations from each other than jointly from the Heshang gong tradition.

Shima Kuniō has not made explicit the principles that he followed in reconstructing his *Wang Bi Laozi*. He constructs a textual family for the *Wang Bi Laozi* based on the text over the *Daozang* Wang Bi edition and other core pieces of the *textus receptus*. As I have shown, the substantial changes wrought on this *Laozi* version make it a weak candidate for the base text of the *Wang Bi Laozi*. In fact, the textual family to which the *Wang Bi Laozi* belongs has two close members, the "Old MSS" of Fu Yi and Fan Yingyuan, and two more distant members, the Mawangdui manuscripts, with the Guodian manuscripts being further relatives. In his editing work, however, Shima Kuniō pays less attention to the textual family than to the specific evidence at hand: he uses (1) internal evidence from Wang Bi's commentary (in which his contribution is greatest), and (2) external evidence from what he variously calls a "Later Han text" or a "Han Wei text." This second "text" is reconstructed on the basis of quotations from other texts of the period as well as from other *Laozi* versions that he believes circulated at the time. While his references to Zhuang (Yan) Zun, in particular, lend some substance to this reconstruction, two points seem to contradict it. First, the various schools and traditions disputed the authenticity of each other's *Laozi*. These schools often formed fairly cohesive and exclusive intellectual communities; it is probable that at any given time different *Laozi* texts existed in different schools and regions without crossings paths or influencing each other. Second, neither the Zhuang (Yan) Zun nor the Xiang Er and Suo Dan manuscripts (nor, for that matter, the Heshang gong version) are supported by the internal evidence of Wang Bi's commentary as serious candidates for the original *Wang Bi Laozi*. On the other hand, the "critical editions" by Fu and Fan on the basis of "Old Texts" fulfill this requirement, even though put together much later. By constructing a textual family for the *Wang Bi Laozi* that does not qualify for this role, Shima Kuniō deprived himself of the fruits of his own labor, because he allowed himself to change this *receptus* only in those places where he had clear and particular proof and never questioned the *receptus* as a whole.

SUPERIMPOSITION

Having established a high degree of internal cohesion within the group of texts made up by the *Wang Bi Laozi*, the two "Old Manuscripts" and, less closely, the Mawangdui manuscripts, we shall deal now with the direction in which the *Wang Bi Laozi* was altered. Of the twenty-five places where the original text available to Fan Yingyuan is definitely superior to the *Wang Bi Laozi Receptus*, no fewer than twenty-two were changed in favor of the Heshang gong version.[51] Some examples may be cited.

PARTICLES

Laozi 19.1

Wang Bi Laozi Receptus:	此三者	以爲文	不足	
Heshang gong:	" " "	" "	" "	
Wang Bi *Comm.*:	" " "	" "	"而未足	
Old MSS (Fu):	" " "	" " "	" " "也	
Old MSS (Fan):	" " "	" " "	不 " "	
Guodian A:	"言 "	"叀	不 "	
Mawangdui A:	此 " "也 "	"文	未 "	
Mawangdui B:	" " " "	" "	" "	
Xiang Er:	" " "	" "	" "	
Pei Wei 裴頠 (267–300):		" " "	" "52	

From this it is clear that Wang Bi's *Laozi* must have read 此三者以爲文而未足, coinciding with Fu Yi's "Old Manuscript" as well as in the 未 with the Mawangdui manuscripts. The received text was apparently changed in favor of the Heshang gong text.

Laozi 48.1

Wang Bi Laozi Receptus:	爲學	日益
Heshang gong:	" "	" "
Zhuang (Yan) Zun:	" "	" "
Wang Bi quote in *Comm.* on *Laozi* 20.1:	" "者 "	"
Old MSS (Fu and Fan):	" " "	" "
Mawangdui B:	" " "	" "
Guodian B:	" " "	" "

The *Wang Bi Laozi* must have read 爲學者日益, coinciding with the two "Old MSS" and the two Mawangdui manuscripts as opposed to the texts of Heshang gong and Zhuang (Yan) Zun (as well as manuscripts from the Xiang Er tradition not cited here).

TERMS

Laozi 1.2

Wang Bi Laozi Receptus:	無名	天地之始
Heshang gong:	〃　〃	〃　〃　〃　〃
Xiang Er:	〃　〃	〃　〃　　〃
Old MSS (Fu and Fan):	〃　〃	〃　〃　〃　〃
Wang Bi *Comm*.:	未形無名之時則爲萬物之始	
Mawangdui A and B:	無名	萬物之始也
Shiji 史記 127.3220:	無名者	萬物之始也

The *Wang Bi Laozi* must have read 無名萬物之始, supported by the *Commentary*, Mawangdui A and B, and the *Shiji* quotation. The *Wang Bi Laozi Receptus* derives from the Heshang gong version, which here is matched by the Suo Dan version and even the two "Old MSS."

Laozi 2.4

Wang Bi Laozi Receptus:	萬物作焉而不辭
Heshang gong:	〃　〃　〃　〃　〃　〃　〃
Wang Bi quotation on 17.1:	〃　〃　〃　〃　〃　〃爲始
Old MSS (Fan):	〃　〃　〃　〃　〃　〃　〃　〃
Old MSS (Fu):	〃　〃　〃　　〃　〃　〃　〃
Guodian A:	〃　〃　〃　　〃弗　　〃
Mawangdui B:	〃　〃昔　〃　　〃　　〃

The *Wang Bi Laozi* must have read 萬物作焉而不爲始, which involves a substantial change in meaning from that given in the received text. Against the entire family, Wang Bi's *Laozi* has, however, the 焉.

Laozi 20.1

Wang Bi Laozi Receptus:	善之與惡	相去若何
Heshang gong:	〃　〃　〃　〃	〃　〃何若
Wang Bi *Comm*.:	美	〃　〃　〃　〃　〃
Old MSS (Fu):	〃　〃　〃　〃	〃　〃　〃　〃
Old MSS (Fan):	善　〃　〃　〃	〃　〃　〃　〃
Xiang Er:	美　〃　〃　〃	〃　〃　〃　〃
Mawangdui A and B:	〃　　〃　〃其	〃　〃　〃　〃
Guodian B:	〃　　〃　〃　〃	〃　〃　〃　〃

The *Wang Bi Laozi* must have read 美之與惡相去何若, supported in the *mei*, 美, for *shan*, 善, and the 何若 for 若何 by Fu Yi's "Old MSS," the

Guodian B, and the two Mawangdui manuscripts. His commentary predicates the choice between Fu Yi's and Fan Yingyuan's "Old Manuscript."

Laozi 35.3

Wang Bi Laozi Receptus:	道之出口	淡乎其無味
Heshang gong:	" " " "	"兮 " " "
Wang Bi quotation on 23.1:	" " "言	" " " " "也
Old MSS (Fu and Fan):	" " " "	" " " " "
Guodian C:	故 "口口口	"呵 " " " "
Mawangdui A and B:	故 "之出言也曰	" " " " " "
Xiang Er:	" " " "	" "
Suo Dan:	" " " "	" "

The *Wang Bi Laozi* read 道之出言淡兮其無味也, supported in the word 言 *yan* not only by the Wang Bi quotation, the Guodian C, the two "Old MSS," and the two Mawangdui manuscripts, but also by the Xiang Er tradition. The *Wang Bi Laozi Receptus* version is derived entirely from the Heshang gong version.

Laozi 69.2

Wang Bi Laozi Receptus:		
	禍莫大於輕敵輕敵	幾喪吾寶
Heshang gong:	" " " " " " " "	" " " "
Suo Dan:	" " " " " " " "	" " " "
Wang Bi *Comm.*:		
	欲以取強無敵於天下也..	故曰幾亡吾寶
Old MSS (Fu):	禍莫大於無敵無敵	則幾亡吾寶
Old MSS (Fan):	" " " "輕 "輕 "	" " " "
Mawangdui A:	旤 "於 "無適無適	斤 " "葆矣
Mawangdui B:	禍 "大 " "敵 "敵	近 " "琛矣

The *Wang Bi Laozi* read 禍莫大於無敵無敵則幾亡吾寶, supported in the characters 無敵, and 亡, by Wang Bi's *Commentary*, by Fu Yi's "Old Manuscript," and by both Mawangdui manuscripts (discounting the writing of 適 for 敵 in the A Manuscript). The change is dramatic in terms of content.

Phrase Sequence

Laozi 13.6 and 13.7

Wang Bi Laozi Receptus:

	若可	寄	天下	..	若可	託	天下
Heshang gong:	"以	"於	"	"..	"以	"於	" "
Wenzi:	"以	"	"	"..	所以托		" "⁵³
Wang Bi *Comm*.:	"以託	"	"..		可以寄		" "
Old MSS (Fu and Fan):							
	則	" " "	"	"矣..	則 " " "		" "矣
Guodian B:	若	" "厇	"	" "..	若 " "迖		" "
Mawangdui A:	若	" "迬	"	" "..	女 " "寄		" "
Mawangdui B:	若	" "橐	"	"口..	" " " "		" " "
Zhuangzi 26/11/14f:	則	" "託	"	"..	則 " " "		" "
Huainanzi 12/109/18:							
	焉	" " "	"	"..	焉 " " "		" "

The *Wang Bi Laozi* read 則可以託天下 . . . 則可以寄天下. The sequence of the phrases in the *Wang Bi Laozi Receptus* is that of the Heshang gong version, while the commentary has been left in its original order. The *ke yi*, 可以, in the commentary could be an explanatory elaboration of *ke* 可, but the *yi* 以 is supported by such a wealth of early readings that *ke yi* must be accepted as the reading of the *Wang Bi Laozi*. As for the *ze* 則, Wang Bi's commentary reads in full: 如此乃可以 . . . , so that the *nai* 乃 has to be read as an explanation of logical sequence, forcing us to accept the *ze*, well supported in some early versions.

Laozi 69.1

Wang Bi Laozi Receptus:	扔	無	敵	執	無	兵
Heshang gong:	仍	"	"	"	"	"
Suo Dan:	"	"	"	"	"	"
Wang Bi *Comm*.:	執	"兵	扔	"敵		
Zhuang (Yan) Zun:	"	"	"仍	"	"	
Old MSS (Fu):	"	"	"	"	"	"
Mawangdui A and B:	"	"	"乃	"	"	
Lu Deming:	扔					

The *Wang Bi Laozi* read 執無兵扔無敵, which has been replaced in the received text by the Heshang gong version, unique among all other early manuscripts with the single exception of Fan Yingyuan.

ELIMINATION OF WORDS INVOLVING
SUBSTANTIAL CHANGES IN MEANING

Laozi 20.15

Wang Bi Laozi Receptus:	我	獨		異	於	人
Heshang gong:	〃	〃		〃	〃	〃
Wang Bi *Comm.*:	〃	"欲	〃	〃	〃	
Xiang Er:	〃		〃	〃	〃	〃
Old MSS (Fu and Fan):	吾	〃	〃	〃	〃	〃
Mawangdui A and B:	"欲	獨	〃	〃	〃	

The *Wang Bi Laozi* read 我獨欲異於人, again replaced in the received text by the Heshang gong version. The elimination of *yu* 欲 implies a substantial change in the status of "Laozi" (i.e., the person saying "I" in the text). The 我 has to be maintained against the 吾 in the rest of the family, as it is so quoted in Wang's commentary.

Laozi 34.3

Wang Bi Laozi Receptus:												
	萬物歸焉而不爲主							可名爲大				
Heshang gong:												
	〃 〃 〃 〃 〃 〃 〃						故	〃 〃 〃 〃矣				
Wang Bi *Comm.*:												
	〃 〃 〃之以生而力使不知其所由.. 〃							〃於 〃矣				
Xiang Er:	〃 〃 〃 〃		不爲主					〃 〃 〃 〃				
Old MSS (Fu):												
	〃 〃 〃 〃而 〃知 〃							〃 〃 〃 〃 〃				
Old MSS (Fan):												
	〃 〃 〃 〃 〃 〃 〃							〃爲 〃 〃				
Mawangdui A:												
	〃 〃 "焉口口 〃 〃							〃 〃於 〃				
Mawangdui B:												
	〃 〃 "焉 〃弗爲 〃							"命於 〃				

The *Wang Bi Laozi* read 萬物歸之而不知主可名於大矣, the received text being mainly that of the Heshang gong version. The replacement of *zhi* 知 with *wei* 爲 is a fundamental philosophical change and also alters the subject of the phrase. In the Heshang gong version, "he" is not lording it over them (*bu wei zhu*, 不爲主); in Wang Bi's version, the 10,000 kinds of entities remain the subject, and they all render themselves unto him but do not perceive who or what is their lord. This phrase became a cornerstone for Wang Bi's interpretation of *xuan* 玄 (dark), the aspect of Being that it is the base of all entities, which they are unable to perceive and name.

Laozi 39.2

Wang Bi Laozi Receptus:	其致之	
Heshang gong:	" " "	
Wang Bi *Comm*.:	各以其一致此清寧靈盈貞	
Zhuang (Yan) Zun:	其致之	
Old MSS (Fu and Fan):	" " " 一也	
Mawangdui A:	"至 " "	
Mawangdui B:	" " "	

The *Wang Bi Laozi* read 其致之一也, his commentary corresponding to the version contained only in the two "Old MSS."

Laozi 47.1

Wang Bi Laozi Receptus:

	不出　戶　　知天下不闚　牖　　見天道				
Heshang gong:	" "　" 以 " " " " "　" 以 " " "				
Wang Bi *Comm*.:					
	雖處於今可以知古始故不出戶窺牖而可知				
Hanfeizi:	不出於戶可以知天下不窺於牖可以知天道				
Huainanzi:	" "　" 　" " " " " " 　" "見 " "				
Zhuang (Yan) Zun:					
	" "　"　　" " " " "　"　　" " "				
Old MSS (Fu):	" "　" " " " " " " "　" " "知 " "				
Old MSS (Fan):	" "　" " " " " " " "　" " "見 " "				
Mawangdui A and B:					
	" " " "　" " " "規 " "　"知 " "				
Lu Deming:	窺				

The *Wang Bi Laozi* read 不出戶可以知天下不窺牖可以知天道, the received text using the Heshang gong version. However, *jian* 見 in the Heshang gong and Zhuang [Yan] Zun versions seems to be supported as an old variant by a *Huainanzi* quotation and Fan Yingyuan.

These examples show the superimposition of elements of the Heshang gong version over the original *Wang Bi Laozi* to form the *Wang Bi Laozi Receptus*. The *Wang Bi Laozi* is very close to the two "Old Manuscripts," supported in many cases by the Mawangdui manuscripts or by early quotations, and sometimes by the Xiang Er *Commentary*. I propose to abandon the *Wang Bi Laozi Receptus* altogether as a textual base for the reconstruction of the *Wang Bi Laozi* and to replace it with a conflated version of the two "Old Manuscripts" as the core and the two Mawangdui manuscripts as more distant relatives. The differences between the two "Old MSS" are handled on the basis of available internal or, failing this, external evidence. Preference in the latter case should be given to the Mawangdui manuscripts. Only where there is clear proof that the *Wang Bi Laozi* disagreed with all other members of the same textual family is it necessary to deviate from this rule. An example may be adduced from Laozi 21. *LZWZLL* refers to Wang Bi's *Laozi weizhi lüeli* 老子微指略例 that is edited and translated in this volume.

Laozi 21.6

Wang Bi Laozi Receptus:	自古及今其名不去
Heshang gong:	" " " " " " " "
Wang Bi *Comm.*:	" " " " " " " " " 54
Wang Bi in *LZWZLL*:	" " " " " " " "
Xiang Er:	" " " " " " " "
Old MSS (Fu and Fan):	"今 "古 " " " "
Mawangdui A and B:	" " " " " " " "

Despite the readings of the "Old Manuscripts" and the Mawangdui manuscripts, the *Wang Bi Laozi* must have read 自古及今其名不去, as confirmed by his own quotations. Unaware of the supporting Wang Bi quotation elsewhere, Shima Kuniō opted for the version of the textual family. There is an occasional later adaptation of Wang Bi's commentary to the changed main text:

Laozi 70.2

Wang Bi Laozi Receptus:	言有宗事有君
Heshang gong:	" " " " " "
Suo Dan:	" " " " " "
Zhuang (Yan) Zun:	" " " " " "
Mawangdui B:	"又 " "又 "
Mawangdui A:	"有君 "有宗
Wang Bi *Comm.*:	宗萬物之宗君萬物之主
Old MSS (Fu and Fan):	言有宗事有主

The initial *jun* 君 of the second clause of Wang Bi's commentary ought to be changed to *zhu* 主, so that the phrase 君萬物之主 parallels the structure of the preceding phrase 宗萬物之宗, where the term *zong* 宗 is repeated twice. That his text had *zhu* instead of *jun* is not only supported by the two "Old Manuscripts" but also by a statement in Wang Bi's *LZWZLL* which paraphrases the present passage: 言不遠宗 事不失主.[55]

One passage often quoted to determine what "school" the *Laozi* belongs to shows some of the problems in reconstructing the *Wang Bi Laozi*.

Laozi 57.3, 4

Wang Bi Laozi Receptus:	人多伎巧	奇物滋起法令滋彰
Heshang gong:	" " " "	" " " "物" "
Huainanzi 12/106/5:		"令" "
Shiji 62.3131:		" " " "
Zhuang (Yan) Zun:	" " " "	" " " " " " " "
Wenzi 1/5/15:	民 "智能	" " " " " " "章
Old MSS (Fu and Fan):	民 "智慧而衺事	" " " " " "
Guodian A:	人 " "	天敧勿慈记 "勿慈 "
Mawangdui A:	人 "知	而何物茲□□□□□
Mawangdui B:	□□□□□	□□□□□物茲章
Wang Bi *Comm.*:	民 "智	"則巧偽生巧偽生則邪事起
Wang Bi in *LZWZLL*:	息淫在乎去華不在滋章	

The reading *fa ling* 法令, shared by the versions given in the *Huainanzi*, *Shiji*, *Wenzi*, and Zhuang Zun directly attacks the Legalists. The Mawang-dui manuscripts come from a Legalist milieu and thus do not transmit this version, but the Guodian A also has the reading 法勿 [物]. Wang Bi attacked the legalism of the Wei court. If, however, Wang Bi's text had the 法令, why should he have missed out on the occasion to attack the concept of running the state by laws? He did not, however, comment on this term at all. The statement in the *LZWZLL* is further evidence that he had a text that had to do with *hua* 華, luxury, and the "beautiful objects," *fawu* 法物, clearly fit this better. Accordingly, Wang's text followed the GuodianA/Mawangdui reading and had 民多智慧而邪事滋起法物滋章.

THE DIVISION INTO *ZHANG* AND *PIAN*

Wang Bi read the *Laozi* as divided into *zhang* 章. There are three passages where he refers to a "later" or "earlier" *zhang*.[56] In two of these, the *zhang* referred to is found within the same *pian* 篇 of the current editions, while in the third case the reference is to a *zhang* in the other *pian*.[57] The division into *zhang* also is evident in the Guodian and Mawangdui manu-scripts, where it is not only indicated on occasion by dots,[58] but where the *zhang* are ordered in a sequence different from the received texts but remain intact as units. For the Mawangdui manuscripts this is true for *zhang* 38 (marked by its being the beginning), 39, 41, 40, 42, 66, 80, 81, 67, 79, 1, 21, 24, 22, 23, and 25 (in the sequence in which they appear in the Mawangdui manuscripts). A similar situation prevails in the Guodian manuscripts, however, there are neither numbers nor titles to mark the borders between *zhang*. Their beginnings and endings are marked by stylistic and argumentative features with occasional punctuation. The Tang dynasty stone engraving of the *Laozi* shows this same feature. In his short history of the transmission of the *Laozi*, Xie Shouhao writes:

> The manuscripts which are put together today are based on textual links (*wenlian* 文連). [Some] copyists have also given separate headings to each of the 81 *zhang*. But, as with the stanzas of the *Old Poems* where each stanza is separated from the next through its literary cohesion, one can determine the [*Laozi*'s] subsections without the need for a separate heading for each *zhang*.[59]

Thus Wang Bi saw the text as consisting of many *zhang*, but it is not clear whether the *zhang* were separated in his edition by any means similar to those employed in the Guodian and Mawangdui manuscripts. It seems that the earlier habit of marking *zhang* and occasionally even phrase limits with dots which we see in the Guodian manuscripts, was gradually discontinued, considered unnecessary for an increasingly "literate"—that is, writing-oriented—elite. Already in the Mawangdui manuscripts there is much less and much more irregular interpunctuation. We might assume that Wang Bi's text looked more like the Xiang Er *Commentary*, which has no formal separations between the *zhang* or even between the *Laozi* text and the commentary. In the *LZWZLL*, Wang Bi describes each *zhang* (without using the term) as an argumentative unit. This also is evident in his *Commentary*, where he rarely explains the conclusion contained in the last phrase of a *zhang*, since it is deemed to be self-evident.[60]

For the separation of the text into two or more *pian*, the evidence is more complex. Assuming that the internal references to other *zhang* have survived unscathed in Wang Bi's *Commentary*, his original text evidently did not follow the *de/dao* sequence of the two Mawangdui manuscripts. The received Wang Bi editions come in two *pian* (the four-*pian* arrangement in the *Zhengtong Daozang* is based on the print arrangement of this edition); there is substantial evidence from the early Han on that a textual division into two *pian* was quite common. This could, however, have substantial philosophic and interpretive implications, as the titles given for the two sections already in the Mawangdui B manuscript indicate; that is, one of the *pian* deals with *dao* 道, the other with *de* 德. Wang Bi does use the term *pian* with regard to the macrostructure of the *Laozi*. In his commentary to *Laozi* 20, he quotes a passage from *Laozi* 48, with the indication that this could be found "in a, or in the, *xia pian* 下篇. In his *LZWZLL* he introduces two quotations from the *Laozi* by saying, "in the *pian* he says"[61] (there is a variant writing for *pian*, namely, *jing* 經, but this would be the only time that Wang Bi referred to the *Laozi* as a *jing*); evidently *pian* here is a plural and refers neither to a first nor second *pian* but rather is used interchangeably with *zhang*. This is confirmed by the fact already mentioned, that one quotation from "a later *zhang*" crosses the traditional *pian* division, the quotation being in *zhang* 28 and the reference to *zhang* 40.

In his *Fushi ji* 鄜畤記 , a work written in 1111, Chao Yuezhi 晁說之 says: "If we can rely on Fu Yi, Wang Bi wrote at the top of his book [the *Laozi*]: 'The *Daodejing* is not divided into *Dao* and *De* chapters.'"[62] It was on the basis of this note that Dong Sijing 董思靖 (1059–1129) wrote that Wang Bi did not divide the text in this manner,[63] and in the *LZWZLL*, Wang Bi refers to his text simply as *Laozi*, never as "*Daodejing*," or some similar title. This accords well with his polemical rejection of other *Laozi* interpretations current during his life.

CONCLUSION

The above evidence suggests the following:

1. The *Laozi* text transmitted over Wang Bi's commentary is not Wang Bi's text but rather a text gradually superseded by elements of the Heshang gong text.
2. The *Wang Bi Laozi Receptus* has to be abandoned as a base text for a critical edition of the *Wang Bi Laozi*.
3. Internal textual evidence suggests that the two "Old Manuscripts" of Fu Yi and Fan Yingyuan should be considered most closely affiliated with Wang Bi's original text, the Mawangdui manuscripts being more distant members of the same textual family and the Guodian manuscripts even more distantly related.
4. A conflated version of the two "Old Manuscripts," supplemented by the two Mawangdui manuscripts, forms the basic core for a reconstruction of Wang Bi's recension of the *Laozi*, the *Wang Bi Laozi*.

5. The *Wang Bi Laozi* recension was subdivided into *zhang*, probably without formal markers. It was not divided into a *Daojing* and a *Dejing*, but it might have had two *pian*.

My edition of the *Wang Bi Laozi* will try to do what has been suggested under point 4. The question of the transmission and present state of the Wang Bi commentary is treated separately in the next chapter.

APPENDIX A

DIFFERENCES BETWEEN *Wang Bi Laozi Receptus* AND
Laozi TEXT USED IN WANG BI *Commentary*

Abbreviations used:

MWD/A and B:	Mawangdui *Laozi* A and B manuscripts
GD/A/B/C:	Guodian *Laozi* sets A, B, and C
FY:	Fu Yi
FYY:	Fan Yingyuan
HNZ:	*Huainanzi*
ZZ:	Zhuang (Yan) Zun
XE:	Xiang Er
SD:	Suo Dan
I:	indirect evidence

Laozi Phrase	*Wang Bi* Laozi Receptus	*Wang Bi* Commentary	Corroborating Texts
1.2	天地	萬物	MWD/A, B
1.5	此兩者	兩者	MWD/A, B; I
2.2	處	居	MWD/A, B; GD/A
2.4	辭	爲始 (17.1)	MWD/B; GD/A (both only 始); I
2.5	弗[居]	不[居]	FY; FYY
2.4	弗[居]	不[居]	FY; FYY
4.1	或	又	HNZ; MWD/B (有); *Wenzi*; I
4.1	知誰	知其誰	MWD/B; FYY
6.1	地根	地之根	MWD/A, B; FY
9.1	如	若	MWD/B; GD/A; *Guanzi*
9.2	梲	銳	HNZ; FYY; ZZ
10.2	能嬰	能若嬰	FY and FYY: 能如嬰
10.4	無知	無以知	MWD/B; FY, FYY
10.6	無爲	無以爲	MWD/B: 無以知; FY, FYY
13.5, 6	寄..託	託..寄	MWD/A, B; GD/B; FY; FYY; XE; SD

Laozi Phrase	Wang Bi Laozi Receptus	Wang Bi Commentary	Corroborating Texts
14.1	夷	微	MWD/A, B
14.4	以	可以	FY
16.3	**觀**復	**觀**其復	MWD/A, B; FY; FYY
17.6	貴言	貴言也	MWD/A, B; GD/C
19.1	文不足	文而不足	FY (未足)
20.1	善	美	MWD/A, B; GD/B; FY; XE
20.4	獨	廓	Lu Deming
20.12	無止	無所止	MWD/A, B; XE
20.14	似	且	FY
20.15	異	欲異	MWD/A, B; XE; SD; FYY
23.4	德	得	FY (two times)
28.7	不割	無割	MWD/A, B; HNZ; FY; FYY; ZZ
29.4	故	凡	FY
30.1	強天下	強於天下	MWD/B; MWD/A: 強□天下; GD/A
30.4	不敢以取	不以取	MWD/A, B; GD/A; XE; SD
34.2	主常	主故常	FY; FYY
34.3	爲	知	FY; FYY
34.3	爲	於	MWD/A, B; FY; XE; SD
35.3	口	言	MWD/A, B; FY; FYY; XE; SD
37.5	不	無	XE; SD
38.2	無以爲	無不爲	FY; FYY; ZZ; I;
38.2	有以爲	無以爲	FY; FYY; I
38.2	始	首	MWD/A, B; *Hanfeizi*
40.1	動	動也	MWD/A, B; GD/A
40.3	天下萬物	天下之物	MWD/B; GD/A; FY; FYY
41.1	勤而行	董能行	MWD/B; GD/B
41.15	且成	且善成	MWD/B; FYY
42.2	教之	教人	MWD/A; FY; FYY
47.1	戶知	戶以知	MWD/A, B; HNZ; *Wenzi*
48.1	學	學者	MWD/B; GD/B; FY; FYY
48.2	道	道者	MWB/B; GD/B; FY; FYY
48.3	爲而無	爲則無	FY; FYY
48.4	取	其取	———
48.4	天下	天下者	FY; FYY; ZZ
48.6	不	又不	MWD/B (lacuna two spaces); FY
48.6	天下	天下矣	MWD/B（天□□); FY
49.4	歙歙	歙歙焉	MWD/A, B; FY; FYY
49.4	渾其心	渾心	MWD/A; FY; FYY
49.4	心	心焉	FY; FYY
50.2	有三人之生	有三而民之生	FY; FYY (om. 而) ZZ
52.1	以爲	可以爲	FY
54.4	修之於身	修之身	MWD/B; GD/B; FY; FYY; SD (3)
54.4	乃餘	乃有餘	*Wenzi*
55.1	厚	厚者	MWD/B; MWD/A 厚□; GD/A; FY; FYY
55.8	氣日強	氣則強	FY
56.4	分	紛	MWD/A, B; GD/A; FY; FYY; HNZ; I

Laozi Phrase	Wang Bi Laozi Receptus	Wang Bi Commentary	Corroborating Texts
57.3	人多伎巧	民多智慧	FY; FYY; I
58.6	迷	迷也	MWD/B; FY
59.2	服	復	Lu Deming
61.4	以靜爲下	以其靜故爲下也	FYY; FY (竫 for 靜); MWD/B; (爲其靜也故宜爲下也)
61.9	欲大	欲則大	MWD/B
62.4	加人	加於人	FY; FYY
64.8	學復	學以復	FY
65.2	智多	多智	FY (多知)
65.4	常知	能知	FY
67.4	能成	能爲成	MWD/A, B; FYY
67.6	戰	陳	FY; FYY
69.1	扔無敵執無兵	執無兵扔無敵	MWD/A, B (乃 for 扔); ZZ; FY (仍 for 扔)
69.2	輕敵	無敵	MWD/A, B; FY
70.1	莫能	莫之能	MWD/A, B; FY; FYY
70.4	我者貴	我貴矣	MWD/A, B; FY; FYY
77.2	唯有道者	其唯道者乎	FY (惟)
78.1	其 (Daozang)	以其	MWD/A, B; FY; I
81.4	不	無	MWD/A, B; FY; FYY; ZZ

APPENDIX B

Differences between *Wang Bi Laozi Receptus* and Places Where Fan Yingyuan's *Laozi Daode jing guben jizhu* Comments That Wang Bi's Manuscript Coincided with the "Old Manuscript[s]"

The notes are coded as follows:

a: Fan Yingyuan's reading is correct, as evidenced by Wang Bi's commentary
b: Fan Yingyuan's reading is correct, as evidenced by indirect evidence
c: *Wang Bi Laozi Receptus* is correct
d: both readings are incorrect
e: evidence not conclusive

Laozi Phrase	Wang Bi Laozi Receptus	Fan Yingyuan's "Old Manuscript"	Code
2.4	萬物作焉而不辭	萬物作焉而不爲始	a
9.3	金玉滿堂	金玉滿室	b
10.4	愛民治國能無知呼	愛民治國能無以知乎	a
14.1	視之不見名曰夷	視之不見名曰幾	d
15.4	孰能濁以靜之徐清	孰能濁以凈之而徐清	b
18.3	六親不和有孝慈國家昏亂有忠臣	六親不和有孝慈焉國家昏亂有貞臣焉	b
19.1	三者以爲文不足	三者以爲文不足也	d
20.5	儽儽兮若無所歸	儽儽兮其若不足, 似無所歸	c
20.9	俗人昭昭我獨昏昏	俗人皆昭昭我獨若昏	c
21.3	惚兮恍兮其中有象恍兮惚兮其中有物	芴兮芒兮中有象兮芒兮芴兮中有物兮	d
21.6	自古及今	自今及古	c
22.2	枉則直	枉則正	b
25.2	寂兮	宋兮	b
25.5	字之曰道	故強字之曰道	b
26.3	燕處	宴處	b
28.7	不割	無割	a
34.2	衣養	衣被	e
34.3	萬物歸焉而不爲主	萬物歸之而不知主	a
34.4	以其終不自爲大	是以聖人以其終不自爲大	d
35.3	道之出口	道之出言	a
38.1	上德無爲而無以爲	上德無爲而無不爲	a
38.1	下德爲之而有以爲	下德爲之而無以爲	a
39.4	是以侯王自謂孤寡不穀此非以賤爲本邪, 非乎	是以王侯自稱孤不穀是其以賤爲本也, 非歟	b
41.2	故建言有之	故建言有之曰	b
41.15	夫唯道善貸且成	夫惟道善貸且善成	a
42.2	人之所教我亦教之	人之所以教我而亦我之所以教人	d
45.2	大盈若沖	大滿若盅	c
47.2	其知之彌少	其知彌趫	b
48.3	損之又損, 以至於無爲無爲而無不爲	損之又損之, 以至於無爲無爲則無不爲	a
49.4	聖人在天下歙歙爲天下渾其心	聖人之在天下歙歙焉爲天下渾心焉	a
51.3	故道生之德畜之	故道生之畜之	a
57.3	人多伎巧奇物滋起	民多智慧而衰邪事滋起	a
59.2	是謂早服	是以早復	a
64.2	其脆易泮	其脃易判	e
65.4	知此兩者亦稽式常知稽式	知此兩者亦稽式也知此稽式	d
67.2	我有三寶持而保之	我有三寶持而寶之	b
73.8	繟然	坦然	b

Chapter 2

Patronage and the Transmission of the Wang Bi *Commentary*: Foundations for a Critical Edition

THE PROBLEM

Having outlined in the first chapter the evidence on which a new critical edition of the Wang Bi *Laozi* is to be based, we now look at the reliability of the current editions of the Wang Bi *Commentary* in order to determine whether a new edition is needed, and if so on what material it might be based. It is my contention that all current editions of the *Commentary*, with the exception of the edition included in Shima Kuniō's *Rōshi kōsei*, are based on the text printed in the *Daozang* around 1445 and taken up by Zhang Zhixiang during the Wanli (1573–1620) period; that a sizably better text can be extracted from the collections of excerpts from *Laozi* commentaries compiled during the eleventh through thirteenth centuries, but that, as no single complete early text of high quality is available to replace the current edition, a critical edition of the Wang Bi *Commentary* will have to select the best readings for each item as a base text, critically edit it, and note the deviant readings of the other relevant textual traditions. This work will be done in the critical edition of both the Wang Bi *Laozi* and the Wang Bi *Commentary* in this book.

This chapter will present the evidence through a reasoned history of the transmission of the Wang Bi *Commentary*. In the process I hope to provide what may be called the social history of a text focusing on the particular type of interest that the *Commentary* evoked and the patronage it received as a consequence; both were instrumental in preventing the text from disappearing with the disintegration or destruction of the materials on which it was written at any given time.

In 1927, Wang Zhongmin 王重民 compiled many of the relevant references in earlier book catalogues and works by bibliophiles to Wang Bi's *Commentary on the Laozi*.[1] Later scholars down to Hatano Tarō 波多野太郎 and Shima Kuniō 島邦男 have added references.[2]

We still lack, however, a reasoned history of the text integrating the various types of information. Such histories have been written for independent texts such as the *Wenzi*, the *Huainanzi*, or the *Taiping jing*,[3] but perhaps due to the low esteem in which commentaries have been held, not for the philosophical contributions that took the commentary form.

Opinions have ranged from the uncritical assumption that the *Laozi* inscribed over the transmitted Wang Bi *Commentary* is indeed the "Wang Bi *Laozi*" and that the current Wang Bi *Commentary* editions are indeed the best to be had to the radical suggestion by Hong Yixuan 洪頤煊 (1765–1833), who concluded in 1821 from a discrepancy between a Wang Bi quotation in Fa Lin's 法琳 early-seventh-century *Bianzheng lun* 辯正論 and the Wang Bi *Commentary* in his hand that "today's manuscripts of the Wang Bi *Commentary* all have come to light only during the Ming dynasty and have perhaps been put together by later people."[4] In this he was echoing Qian Zeng 錢曾 (1629–1701), who had said: "Sadly enough, [Wang] Fusi's [= Bi's] *Commentary* is not transmitted or sparsely transmitted. The days of this book are already over, alas."[5] In fact, Wang Bi's *Commentary on the Laozi* struggled to survive the Confucian suspicion that its ideological influence had contributed to the demise of the Jin 晉 dynasty and the breakup of China. It competed with the commentaries preferred by the Daoist religious communities and with commentaries written by emperors who had the means to make their reading dominant. The text thus could not rely on the main Chinese patronage lines to secure its own transmission and could not even promise the copyist merit points in the karma register.

The difficulty in writing the history of this *Commentary* is from the outset one of method. Most modern scholars dealing with the history of this text have linked the history of the Wang Bi *Laozi* to the Wang Bi *Commentary*, thus they have looked for the earliest monograph editions in which only these two appear, and together. This has led to the adoption of the texts of this type preserved in the *Daozang* and in the *Siku quanshu* and their derivatives as the standard base texts, down to the 1980 edition by Lou Yulie.[6] As the previous chapter has shown, however, the *Laozi* text over the Wang Bi *Commentary* had a history all its own. It was gradually adapted to the Heshang gong version of the *Laozi*, while the *Laozi* quotations in the Wang Bi *Commentary* remained largely unchanged. We are thus forced in a second step to study the transmission of the *Commentary* independently of the *Laozi* text under which it was transmitted. Shima

Kuniō has again pioneered such an approach in his *Rōshi kōsei*. Instead of following the Ming editions as everyone else had done, he looked for the earliest available texts of the *Commentary* and found them in the various editions of "collected commentaries" to the *Laozi* that had been put together between the eleventh and the thirteenth centuries. His focus though was on the different lineages of the text of the *Laozi*, not on the commentaries. So while quoting what he thought were the best commentary texts, he did not establish a critical text for the commentaries included in his work, including the Wang Bi *Commentary*. The Wang Bi *Commentary* quotations in these collections in turn might have been, and were, attached to *Laozi* texts from lineages other than that to which the Wang Bi *Laozi* belonged.

A HISTORY OF WANG BI'S COMMENTARY ON THE *LAOZI*: THE EVIDENCE

He Shao 何劭 (236–ca. 300), whose dates overlap Wang Bi's, writes in his "Biography of Wang Bi" that Wang "commented on the *Laozi*."[7] Anecdotes collected by Liu Yiqing 劉義慶 (403–444) in his *Shishuo xinyu* (*SSXY*) 世說新語, as well as by Liu Xiaobiao 劉孝標 (462–521) in his *Commentary* on that text, also refer to Wang Bi's *Commentary*.[8] Most of these anecdotes are from earlier collections. According to one, Wang Bi's mentor, He Yan 何晏 (ca. 190–249), rewrote his own commentary on the *Laozi* into two philosophical essays after hearing Wang Bi's interpretation and acknowledging its superiority over his own analysis.[9] This first report on Wang Bi's *Commentary* best defines the reason for its survival. It could not claim a lobby of Confucian scholars, the court, Buddhists, or Daoists. It could rely only on Wang Bi's analytical skill in handling the *Laozi* and on his philosophic depth. Time and again those who took it upon themselves to track down a copy and to spread it to the world were attracted by these qualities. Wang Bi's fame and notoriety among his contemporaries and later generations rested on his two commentaries on the *Laozi* and the *Zhouyi*, and on his two treatises outlining their basic structure. Thus we have direct and indirect contemporary evidence that Wang Bi wrote a *Commentary on the Laozi*, and that it reached instant fame.

The first three explicit verbatim quotations from this *Commentary* are in Zhang Zhan's 張湛 (fl. 320) *Commentary on the Liezi* 列子注. (We leave aside implicit quotations.) Zhang Zhan was related to Wang Bi, and (parts of?) the *Liezi* that he put together came from the library of Cai Rong 蔡邕 (133–192) that had come to the Wang family.[10] Like the *Zhuangzi*

Example 1 from Wang Bi on *Laozi* 6:

1. *Zhang Zhan*[11] [谷神不死是謂玄牝]
2. *Jizhu*[12]
3. *Jiyi*[13]
4. *Daozang*[14]
5. *Siku*[15]

無形無影無逆無違處卑不動

谷神谷中央無谷也

天地之根綿綿

1. 守靜不衰谷以之成而不見其形此至物也處卑而不可得名故謂之玄牝
2. 〃
3. 〃
4. 〃
5. 〃　　　　　　　　　　　　　　　　　　　　　　　　　　　　　"緜緜

1. 若存用之不勤
2. 〃
3. 〃
4. 〃
5. 〃

天地之根綿綿若存用之不勤]玄牝之門玄牝之所由也本其所

1. 由與太極同體故謂　天地之根也欲言存邪　不見其形欲言亡邪萬物以　生故綿
　　　　　　　　　　之　　　　　　　　　　　　　　　　　則　　　　　　　　　　之
　[玄牝之門是謂天地之根]
2. 〃〃〃〃〃〃〃之〃〃〃〃〃〃〃〃〃〃〃〃〃〃〃則〃〃〃〃〃〃〃〃〃〃〃〃之〃
3. 〃
4. 〃
5. 〃　　　　　　　　　　　　　　　　　　　　　　　　　　　　　　　"緜緜

1. 綿綿若存　無物不成　而不勞也故曰　不勤
　　　　　　　　　　　　　　　　　　　　用　　　　　　　　　　　用而
2. 〃〃〃〃〃也〃〃〃〃〃〃〃〃用〃〃〃用而〃〃
3. 〃
4. 〃
5. 緜　　　　　　　　　　　　　　　　　　　　　　　"緜

commentaries by Xiang Xiu and Guo Xiang, Zhang's *Commentary* is in the tradition of Wang Bi's *Commentary on the Laozi*. It is thus probable for both domestic and scholarly reasons that Zhang Zhan was in possession of a good copy of Wang Bi's *Commentary*. Where the *Liezi* and the *Laozi* overlap, Zhang Zhan sometimes quotes Wang Bi's *Commentary*.

Such quotations enclosed in another text often preserve parts of texts otherwise lost or an older reading of available texts. If the separate editions of the text were changed, these quotations very often were not adjusted. The first two quotations in Zhang Zhan's *Commentary* are from Wang Bi's commentary on *Laozi* 6. The editions used for comparison are the oldest available Song and Ming texts. The text in square brackets is the *Liezi/Laozi* text in Zhang Zhan's edition that quotes it, however, as being from the *Book of the Yellow Emperor, Huangdi shu*.

Example 1 (facing page) is from Wang Bi on *Laozi* 6.

Example 2 is a quotation from Wang Bi on *Laozi* 73 not transmitted in any of the Song dynasty commentary collections:

1. Zhang Zhan[16]　孰誰也言誰能知天　　　意　耶其唯聖人也
2. Daozang[17]　　" " " " " " " "下之所惡 "故邪 " " " "
3. Siku[18]　　　" " " " " " " " " " " " " " " " "

In both cases Zhang Zhan's reading in the two major deviations—故謂之玄牝 versus 故謂[之]天地之根綿綿若存用之不勤 and 誰能知天意耶 versus 誰能知天下之所惡意故邪—is superior to all surviving texts, a unanimous opinion among modern editors. The surviving editions, however, share a homogeneous if corrupt reading, suggesting that they all go back to a single edition with a substantial number of misreadings. The same feature is shared by the *Laozi* text printed over Wang Bi's *Commentary* in the surviving editions that feature only Wang's *Commentary*. They rather uniformly disagree with the provable original readings in Wang Bi's *Laozi* text. The comparative study of different surviving Ming and later editions, as undertaken by Hatano Tarō and others, while necessary and useful, does not provide enough textual diversity to allow for the elimination of even the major corruptions.

One element is not visible in the first comparison above. All variants of the *textus receptus* append the whole commentary to this *zhang* to the end of the *Laozi* text. Zhang Zhan in fact quotes two commentary passages. The first ends with 玄牝, then the *Laozi* text 玄牝之門, followed by the rest of the commentary. On the basis of the *textus receptus* of Wang's *Commentary*, it is hard to judge which organization should be preferred. There are many instances where a commentary is attached to each phrase, and sometimes to a section of a phrase, but others, such as the commentary to *Laozi* 38, have a coherent long essay as commentary. Given the date and overall quality of Zhang Zhan's quotations, including the fact that the wording of the *Liezi* text in which he quotes Wang Bi definitely represents with 天地之根 the wording of Wang Bi's *Laozi* text instead of the 天地根 in the Wang Bi *textus receptus*, Zhang Zhan's arrangement seems preferable.

From these two examples we formulate three hypotheses:

1. Since all three quotations reappear in their entirety in the editions surviving to the present, the survival rate of individual passages from Wang Bi's *Commentary* is high.

2. No manuscript find during the last 400 years has enabled scholars to directly base a text of the *Commentary* on an "old" Tang or pre-Tang manuscript. The high degree of coincidence between the quotations and the extant texts suggests a fairly uninterrupted textual transmission down to the first printed editions in our hands.

3. The Wang Bi *Commentary* had a high textual status since the time when the base text for the surviving editions was fixed, so that it was substantially transmitted without further unnoted emendations. This hypothesis by and large also applies to the *Laozi* quotations within the *Commentary*. We shall try to test these hypotheses and add others.

Liu Xiaobiao 劉孝標 (462–521), the commentator of the *Shishuo xinyu*, quotes Wang Bi's *Commentary* once.

Example 3 (facing page) from Wang Bi on *Laozi* 39.

It is evident that Liu Xiaobiao quotes excerpts from two different *Commentary* sections. Both are extant in the transmitted texts. The first is uniformly corrupt in the various prints of the *textus receptus* in the formula 一物之生. The fifth-century Buddhist Huida 惠達 quotes the same passage in his *Zhao lun shu* 肇論疏 in the same wording as Liu Xiaobiao, confirming the assumption that it is the older (and better) reading.[23]

Liu Xiaobiao never refers to the Heshang gong commentary on the *Laozi*. This gives us a glimpse at the circles in which the Wang Bi *Commentary* enjoyed prestige. The *Shishuo xinyu* records and glorifies the intellectual achievements of the scions of the aristocratic families and their friends between the second and fourth centuries. The intellectual tradition recorded here is clearly that of Wang Bi. The *Laozi* quotations in Liu

Example 3 from Wang Bi on *Laozi* 39:

1. Liu Xiaobiao[19]
2. Jizhu[20]
3. Daozang[21]
4. Siku[22]

1. 一者數之始　物之極也各是一物　所以為主也　各得此一以成既成而
2. 〃〃〃〃而〃〃〃〃〃〃〃〃之生〃〃〃〃〃〃〃〃〃〃物　皆〃〃〃〃〃〃〃
3. 〃〃〃〃〃〃〃〃〃〃〃〃〃〃〃〃〃〃〃〃〃〃〃〃〃皆〃〃〃〃〃〃〃
4. 〃〃〃〃〃〃〃〃〃〃〃〃〃〃〃〃〃〃〃〃〃〃〃〃皆〃〃〃〃〃〃〃

1. 各以其一致此清寧 "靈 "盈生 貞
2. 舍一以居成居成則失其母．．．"〃〃〃〃〃〃〃〃〃〃〃貞
3. 〃〃〃〃〃〃〃．．．．〃〃〃〃〃〃〃〃〃〃〃"〃〃
4. 〃〃〃〃〃〃〃．．．

Xiaobiao's *Commentary* accordingly are most probably from Wang Bi's *Laozi* text. Huida, in his turn, wrote a commentary to Seng Zhao's 僧肇 (384–414) *Zhao lun* 肇論, the most important set of Buddhist treatises written in fifth-century China. Like his teacher, Kumārajīva (d. 412?), Seng Zhao is credited with a commentary on the *Laozi*,[24] and both moved within an intellectual framework set by third-century philosophers such as Wang Bi. Liu Xiaobao also provides us with the text's title at the time, *Laozi zhu* 老子注.

The growth of Daoist influence throughout the fifth and sixth centuries, often with strong imperial patronage, gradually led to the ascendance of the Heshang gong commentary and the *Laozi* text transmitted over it. During the same period, the Later Han transformation of Laozi into a high, even supreme, god had been fleshed out with a plethora of stories, including the claim that Laozi had gone West to convert the barbarians, who now came back as Buddhists. Wei Zheng's 魏徵 (580–643) handbook of memorable sayings and principles for the education of the crown prince, the *Qunshu zhiyao* 群書治要, ended up using only the Heshang gong version.[25]

Wang Bi's *Commentary*, however, continued to be copied and is listed in the book catalogue of the *Sui shu* under the title *Laozi Daode jing* in 2 juan with a *Commentary* by Wang Bi. It was further appreciated by scholars active in the revival of classical studies at the time, most prominently Fu Yi 傅奕 (555–629), who collected and analyzed a number of "Old Manuscripts" of the *Laozi*. His interest was in the *Laozi* itself. Since the Later Han, these manuscripts mostly also carried commentaries, so that he often defined them by the commentary with which they came. Among those he found were two "Wang Bi texts," that is, *Laozi* texts with Wang Bi's *Commentary*, one having 5,683, and the other having 5,610 characters. Fu Yi did not express a preference for either the Heshang gong or the Wang Bi commentary or text; his own (surviving) conflated edition of a *Guben Laozi* 古本老子, however, clearly rejects the Heshang gong version of the *Laozi* and might even have been circulated as an antidote against it.[26]

Among the scholars reacting against a style of commenting that was more associative than analytical, we also find Lu Deming 陸德明 (556–627), who decided to base his phonetic notes on the *Laozi*, the *Laozi Daodejing yinyi* 老子道德經音義 (which also contains information on textual variants in the editions over different commentaries), on Wang Bi's text. While not doubting the authenticity of the Heshang gong commentary, he eventually comes out in favor of the Wang Bi *Commentary*, saying:

> [This, Heshang gong's commentary] talks about the essentials
> of bringing order to one's body and to the state. There was

none among the later intellectuals who would not hold his words about the Dark in high esteem. Only Wang Fusi [= Bi] had a finer grasp on the pointers towards the empty and negativity.[27]

In the *Laozi Daodejing yinyi* we have phonetic glosses on terms of Wang Bi's *Commentary* to no less than 56 of the 81 *zhang* of the *Laozi*. There are no phonetic glosses for other commentators. He took Wang Bi as the "standard" commentary in the same manner in which he took the *Lunyu Commentary* compiled by He Yan and his associates as his "standard" for the *Lunyu*. With one single exception, all his notations from Wang Bi's *Commentary* can be found in the extant text. The exception is a missing piece in *zhang* 27.[28] The *Laozi Daodejing yinyi*, in our hands, however, had been tampered with even before the twelfth century, so that it is not as reliable a guide to the Wang Bi text as it might originally have been. In his phonetic notes on the *Xiaojing* 孝經, Lu Deming gives the titles and numbers of the section headings. He does not do so in his *Laozi Daodejing yinyi*.

From this we extract a fourth hypothesis. The *zhang* of the *Laozi* were neither numbered nor titled in the Wang Bi *Laozi zhu* manuscript in Lu Deming's hand. This might reflect the original Wang Bi arrangement. The only dated third-century fragment of a manuscript of a *Laozi* is the Suo Dan of 270, found in Dunhuang. In this manuscript, the *zhang* are not numbered, have no titles, and are separated by beginning a new *zhang* with a new line.[29] The undated but also early Xiang Er 想爾 manuscript from Dunhuang, S 6825,[30] also has no titles. It does not even begin a new *zhang* with a new line, and it does not visibly separate text and commentary. The transformation of texts from an amorphous endless line of Chinese characters to a visibly structured textual body with a title, table of contents, separation of chapters and sections, and text and commentary was a slow process, the history of which is still to be written.[31]

While not giving headings for the *zhang*, Lu Deming gives the titles *dao jing* 道經 and *de jing* 德經 to the two chapters in the manner of the Heshang gong 河上公 commentary. While this tradition can be traced as far back as the Mawangdui B manuscript, it seems not to have been a feature of the original form of Wang Bi's *Commentary on the Laozi*.

Lu Deming's preface and his use of the Wang Bi *Laozi* are important evidence for the esteem in which Wang Bi's *Commentary* was again held, as well as of efforts to make it more widely available. Wang Bi's *Zhouyi zhu* 周易注, *Commentary to the Zhouyi*, at about the same time became the official commentary to this text for the Tang dynasty and had been provided with a subcommentary by Kong Yingda 孔穎達 (574–648). It had achieved this prominence only after years of bitter struggles between the proponents of three different *Zhouyi* commentaries, those of Zheng Xuan 鄭玄 (127–200), Wang Su 王肅 (195–256), and Wang Bi.[32] The analytical method applied by Wang Bi to this text is similar to that applied to the *Laozi*, quite apart from the fact that Wang read both works as approaches to a similar philosophic dilemma.

Another famous scholar from that generation, Yan Shigu 顏師古 (581–645), who wrote the most important commentary to Ban Gu's *Hanshu*, found an "old [Liu] Song-dynasty manuscript," of Wang Bi's *Commentary*, that is, from a time between 420 and 479. There should have been numerous copies of Wang Bi's *Commentary* in the south in the libraries of the northern elite fleeing there, quite apart from the fact that the Liu Song established *xuanxue* 玄學 as the most important of the fields of scholarship, ahead of *ru* 儒, "Confucianism," *wenxue* 文學, "literature," and *shi* 史, "the histories."[33] Although Yan Shigu's own *Xuanyan xinji ming Lao bu* 玄言新記明老部, of which a fragment survives among Pelliot's Dunhuang manuscripts, generally follows Heshang gong's reading and reproduces in the introduction the Heshang gong lore, Yan also was interested in what Wang Bi had to say. He writes in a slightly confusing passage:

> Wang Bi, *zi* Fusi, from Shanyang, managed in his official career to become a *shangshu lang*. [He died] in the 10th year of the zhengshi era [249] in his 24th year. [I, Yan Shigu] checked a [Liu] Song manuscript which said: "Wang Fusi was famous among later [generations] for his *Commentary on the Daode [jing]* in two *pian*; he linked the symbols [for heaven and earth], the highest yang number being the 9, he set the limit at nine times nine. That is why there are 81 *zhang* [in his *Laozi*]."[34]

To my knowledge, no other source makes the claim that it was Wang Bi who established the division in 81 *zhang*. This often is attributed to Liu Xiang.[35] It is plausible, however, that this number should have been fixed since his time. Obviously the Wang Bi *Commentary* in Yan Shigu's hands had this number; the confirmation of this number by the "old" Liu Song text was necessary, since different divisions of the *Laozi*, such as the one by Zhuang Zun, existed and continued to be produced. The second important piece of information is that copies of Wang Bi's *Commentary* were already hard to get. Third, the text seems to have circulated now under the title *Daode jing zhu* 道德經注. We formulate a fifth hypothesis: although not formally divided by number and title, Wang Bi's *Laozi zhu* had eighty-one *zhang*, as confirmed for the fifth and sixth centuries.

The coexistence of the Wang Bi and Heshang gong commentaries in Lu Deming and Yan Shigu also can be observed in Li Shan's 李善 (d. 689) *Commentary to the Wenxuan*, which makes use of both commentaries. Li Shan quotes Wang Bi's *Commentary* twenty-seven times in his own *Commentary to the Wenxuan*.[36] As a rule, he quotes the title as *Laozi zhu*. All but two quotations can be located in the extant texts.[37] The number of quotations with some textual deviation is twenty.[38] Of these twenty readings, internal and external evidence prompted me to accept fourteen, fully or in part, as genuine.[39]

Example 4: Li Shan quotes Wang Bi on *Laozi* 1.5:

1. Li Shan[40] 玄 冥 黑 無有也
2. Jizhu[41] "者 "也默然 " " "
3. Jiyi[42] " " " " "
4. Daozang[43] " " " " "
5. Siku[44] " " " " "

Example 5: Li Shan quotes Wang Bi on *Laozi* 10.9:

滌除邪飾至于極覽

1. Li Shan[45] 言能
2. Jizhu " " " " " "
3. Jiyi " " " " " "
4. Daozang " " " " " "
5. Siku " " " " " "

Example 6: Li Shan quotes Wang Bi on *Laozi* 41.15:

1. Li Shan[46] 有形則亦有分有分者不溫則涼 "炎不炎則寒 "而 故象 者形者非大象也
2. Jizhu " " " "
3. Daozang " " " "
4. Siku " " " "

Most differences are in particles, where textual variations usually are largest but meaning is least likely to be influenced. Substantial clarifications in meaning, as found in Zhang Zhan's quotations, are few, namely, those cases where text has been lost. In one case, the interlocking of text and commentary is arranged differently.[47] The text, however, is quoted in excerpts, and there are no good grounds to accept this arrangement. Li Shan's quotations often are excerpts, and the writing is riddled with mistakes. However, from the high coincidence between the quotations from Wang Bi's *Commentary* and Li Shan's *Commentary on the Wenxuan* we can infer that, in quality and quantity, the seventh-century Wang Bi *Commentary* text had survived the conflagrations of the preceding centuries rather well and is part of a fairly unbroken transmission down to the editions that have come to us.

A few decades after Li Shan, in 719, the famous historian, Liu Zhiji 劉 知幾 (661–721), proceeded to challenge the authenticity of the Heshang gong commentary in a memorial to the Ministry of Propriety and another one directly to the throne.

> The *Laozi* most commonly circulating now, 今俗所行老子, is that with the Heshang gong *Commentary*. Its preface says: "Heshang gong is a man living during the reign of Emperor Wen of the Han (r. 176–159 B.C.E.); he made himself a straw hut at Riverbend 河曲 [near the Huanghe], and took his eponym [Heshang gong, the Gentleman Living by the (Yellow) River] from there. He handed the *Laozi* commented by him to Emperor Wen, and thereupon soared into space and went towards Heaven." Evidently these are trite words not worthy of a classic, trivia as they circulate among the vulgar. [Now] to the facts, as the bibliographical section of the *History of the [Former] Han* lists three scholars with commentaries on the *Laozi*, but has never heard of any explanations coming from someone "by the River, 河上," is this not the case of a [later] commentator making up such a tale because he wanted to have this affair appear miraculous? [This *Commentary*'s] language is uncouth and his reasoning distorted. Already those content with [such simple tasks as] differentiating the purple from the red or to separate the wheat from the beans, will scoff at its fallacies, how much more the knowledgeable! How can [Ho-shang-kung] match Wang Bi's brilliant talent and superb insight [with which he, as the *Xici* 繫辭 says of the divinatory capacity of the milfoil stalks and turtle shells] "explores the abscond and brings out the hidden." As, upon examination,

his [Wang Bi's] comments are superior in terms of meaning and purport [旨 for 者][48] the unequivocal rejection of the Heshang gong and promotion of Wang Fusi [Bi] would indeed be most appropriate for those engaged in study.[49]

In Liu Zhiji's argument we find the same rationale for preserving and spreading Wang Bi's *Commentary* that had made He Yan abandon his own project.

The State Council, to whom the matter was referred, had a committee discuss the issue. Its members were luminaries such as Sima Zheng 司馬貞, a professor at the Imperial University, Xi Changtong 郗嘗通, a professor at the First College, and eight others. At the end of May 719, they came up with a compromise supported by Liu Zhiji.

We also received a memorial claiming that Laozi's [elaborations] on *dao* 道 and *de* 德 are truly [實 for 是][50] words concerning the Dark 玄. Though there have been many commentators, few have exhausted their purport. "Heshang gong" is a fictitious appellation, there is no such person in the historical records of the Han. Yet, his *Commentary* has the nurture of spirit as its principal aim and non-interference as its mainstay. His language is easy, and his principles are encompassing. On the small [scale of the individual], it helps in nurturing the self and to clear up one's sincerity, and on the grand [scale of the state] it can be instrumental to pacify men and bring peace to the state. Hence Gu Huan 顧歡 [read 歡 for 歎; himself a *Laozi* commentator] (390–453) said "Though Heshang gong is called a commentary to a book, it in fact is a text [written in order to] establish a teaching [of his own]. Throughout he dwells little on distant matters but brings out things of immediate application." This may be accepted as a well-informed statement.
    Wang Fusi [Bi] [on the other hand] was sophisticated and skilled at speaking about the Dark and probed the essentials of the Way. [Even with regard to such esoteric topics as] bringing to an end the spiritual functions 神用[51] in [what the *Laozi* 5.3 refers to as] the "drum and flute" [of the space between Heaven and Earth] or maintaining calm and silence in [what *Laozi* 6.1 calls] "the dark female animal 玄牝," his reasonings are clear and the pointers [he discovers] subtle. In the realm of the Philosophy of the Dark 玄學, this [read 是 for 謂] definitely is the best. But when it comes to being accessible to people and setting up [clear] arguments, to nurturing the self and spreading

the Way, Heshang gong has the advantage. With regard to these two commentaries by Wang [Bi] and Heshang gong, we now look forward to and apply for it that students are required to act on them both.[52]

Liu Zhiji's memorial seems to have caused quite a controversy at the university. The final imperial edict closing the matter on May 28 refers disapprovingly to "discussive gatherings of our students." Interestingly, the edict referred to imperial attempts to "search for unnoticed texts and neglected fragments far and wide" in order to secure materials to restore the correct texts. This search had prompted Liu Zhiji to submit his memorial in the first place. The edict decided: "Let . . . the Heshang gong commentary . . . remain in force as before. Since few have used the Wang [Bi] commentary, . . . let encouragement be given to its study so that its transmission might not terminate." Also, during the first half of the eighth century, Zhang Junxiang 張君相 came out with a first collection of commentaries to the *Laozi*, the *Sanshi jia zhujie Daode jing* 三十家注解道德經, the *Assorted commentaries by 30 authors on the "Daode jing,"* in which he included Wang Bi as well as other third-century commentators. The text is lost.[53]

Although "few have used" the Wang Bi commentary at this time, and although the Heshang gong version was "most commonly circulating," Wang Bi's *Commentary* attracted very strong and prominent support, and it was probably more widely copied as a consequence of this 719 edict. It is quoted in sources as diverse as the *Chuxue ji* 初學記 by Xu Jian 徐堅 (659–729),[54] Fa Lin's 法琳 (572–640) *Bianzheng lun* 辯正論,[55] and Hui Lin's 慧琳 (737–820) *Yiqie jing yinyi* 一切經音義.[56] This indicates that the text was relatively widely available in philosophic circles.

Eventually, however, the emperor who had signed the above edict had his own revelation, which installed him as the one, and most authoritative, commentator of the *Laozi*. The Tang Imperial Family Li 李 inherited an old claim by many aspirants for power during the Six Dynasties to have descended from Laozi, to whom the family name Li was ascribed in the *Shiji*. The claim implied the religious authority to rule as well as a social ideal as encoded in the text transmitted under the name of Laozi.[57] Since the Six Dynasties, emperors had taken to writing the official commentary to the *Laozi* themselves, a habit sustained from Liang Wudi (r. 502–550) to the founder of the Ming dynasty. Eventually, in 731 Emperor Xuanzong had a dream encounter with Laozi, who confirmed that Laozi was the ancestor of the Imperial Family.[58] This association made the *Laozi* even more important, and it was introduced into the state examinations for a time.

The emperor had been initiated into the Daoist order in 721, and shortly thereafter he set out to produce an imperial *Laozi* commentary, begun in 724 and finished in about 733, two years after his dream.[59] This text is strictly based on the *Laozi* tradition associated with the Zhuang (Yan) Zun and Heshang gong commentaries, and it seems to have practically eclipsed the Wang Bi *Commentary*. The book catalogues in the two Tang histories probably carry Wang Bi's *Commentary* under the title *Xuanyan xinji daode* 玄言新記道德 in 2 j. with Wang Bi's commentary, and *Wang Bi zhu Xinji xuanyan Daode* 王弼注新記玄言道德 in 2 j.[60] As Takeuchi Yoshiō has pointed out, *xuanyan xinji* is a general title for *Laozi* commentaries, confirmed by Yan Shigu's commentary with the title *Xuanyan xinji ming Lao bu* 玄言新記明老部.[61] However, no steles were engraved with Wang Bi's *Commentary*, and no fragments were found in Dunhuang. Only Du Guangting 杜光庭 (850–933) refers to it in his monumental description of *Laozi* studies.[62]

The Song dynasty again saw a revival of interest in Wang Bi. The authority of the Heshang gong commentary as well as Xuanzong's commentary had suffered from the demise of the Tang dynasty. In the preface to his 1229 compilation of commentaries to the *Laozi*, Peng Si 彭耜 adduces various imperial references to the importance of Wang Bi's *Commentary* for the management of the state. Quoting the section on Buddhists and Taoists from the now lost [*San chao*] *guoshi* [三朝] 國史, Peng Si writes:

> In 994, Emperor Zhenzong said to his prime minister: "The *daojing* and the *dejing* [of the *Laozi*] do [in fact] contain the essentials for regulating the times. But although Minghuang's [= Tang Xuanzong's] commentaries are remarkable in their brilliance, the commentaries by Wang Bi are simple in their words, but profound in their meaning. They truly have grasped the purest purport [of the *Laozi*]." As a consequence he ordered [blocks with the Wang Bi *Commentary*] to be cut.[63]

Zhenzong is known for his efforts in building up the Imperial Library, not only with manuscripts and prints but with printing blocks.[64] Various sources suggest that these blocks were not cut for the immediate printing of some larger number of copies but to prevent copying errors and to establish a reproducible official text without going through the cumbersome labor of cutting it into stone. Whenever a copy was needed, it would be printed. Du Guangting already reports this procedure for his magisterial work. Paul Demiéville has found other sources. For example, a copy of the Buddhist canon was printed from the Sichuan blocks for a Japanese visitor in 985.[65] While the emperor's order did not necessarily make the Wang

Bi *Commentary* publicly available, it was an important sign of imperial patronage. Before Huizong's own *Commentary* of 1118, no Song emperor wrote an "imperial commentary" to the *Laozi*. The statement by Zhenzong therefore dethroned the Tang Emperor Xuanzong's *Commentary* as the guiding light for reading this text and temporarily established the Wang Bi *Commentary* in its place. This palace edition of 994 was probably the first monograph edition of Wang Bi's *Commentary* published under the Song. The Wang Bi *Laozi zhu* 老子註 mentioned in the *Songshi* book catalogue might refer to this edition in the Imperial Library. The title in the *Songshi* rejects the more fanciful titles that the *Laozi* had received during the Tang dynasty and restored Wang Bi's *Commentary* to the name it had in pre-Tang and early-Tang texts. The various editions and selections to be published during the next two centuries reflected an important political element, which we will not be able to explore here.

There was at the same time a renewed philological interest not restricted to Shang and Zhou bronzes and other artifacts but including manuscripts of texts whose tradition had been interrupted by the conflagration and turmoil after the rebellion of An Lushan. We know of at least one private copy of Zhang Junxiang's *Sanshi jia zhujie Daode jing* with its sizable amounts of Wang Bi's *Commentary* surviving into the Song, described by Chao Gongwu in the late twelfth century as being in his huge library in Sichuan.[66] Following Zhang's tradition, various compilations were made during the eleventh and twelfth centuries into which old and contemporary commentaries were included whole or in part.

Chen Jingyuan 陳景元 (1025–1094), a Daoist priest in the Nanzong lineage from Nancheng in Jiangxi, who lived on Tiantai shan, took up this tradition, and from his vast collection of commentaries he put together a compendium of what he considered the best comments on the individual passages of the *Laozi*. Chen was famous for his collection and collation of old Daoist manuscripts, and in 1091 Wang Qinchen 王欽臣, director of the Imperial Library, proposed that he be put in charge of collating Daoist books and establishing standard texts for them at the Imperial Library.[67] Chen Jingyuan's *Daode zhen jing zangshi zuanwei pian* 道德眞 經藏室纂微篇 has survived in the *Daozang*.[68] According to the preface by Yang Zhonggeng 楊仲庚, dated 1258, Chen Jingyuan "collected the best of the various commentaries and collated these [excerpts from the commentaries] for the purposes of private transmission from master" [to student]. When Chen was invited to the palace by Emperor Shenzong 神 宗 between 1068 and 1078, he submitted the manuscript to be included in the Daoist canon that was then being compiled. Nearly two centuries later, Yang Zhonggeng himself used this collation to great benefit, and, "because there was no good print around and it had no wide circulation,

[he] took the volumes from [his own] library, corrected them painstakingly, collected subscriptions from gentlemen of fine virtue and [finally] ordered craftsmen to cut the printing blocks so that it would be handed down without falling into oblivion."[69] Accordingly, the book was published or republished by patronage in 1258, but the text itself—aside from emendations—was written between 1068 and 1078. The book catalogue of the *Songshi* does not list this title, but Wang Zhongmin suggests that a book by this title by a Biyun zi 碧雲子 is actually Chen's book. Chen's Daoist name was Bixu zi 碧虛子, and Wang assumes that *yun* 雲 is a misprint for *xu* 虛.[70]

The text carries Chen's own extensive *Commentary*, many quotations from Zhuang (Yan) Zun's *Commentary*, plus smaller amounts from Heshang gong, Xuanzong, and others. Chen frequently refers to an "old manuscript" of the *Laozi* that probably had no commentary, as well as to the readings of Heshang gong or Wang Bi and to Fu Yi's edition, trying to establish an authentic *Laozi* text beyond the commentary traditions. He gives eight passages where his "Wang Bi MS" or "Old Wang MS" differs from the text he established. In each case the reading he gives is preferable to that of the *textus receptus*. He had a very high-quality Wang Bi *Laozi* text. As he quotes from all parts of Wang Bi's *Laozi Commentary*, we may presume that his text was complete. The quality of his Wang Bi *Laozi* supports the assumption that his text of the Wang Bi *Commentary* was equally authentic. Sadly, there are only four quotations from the Wang Bi *Commentary* in this collection, from 10.9, 13.5/6, 43.2, and 55.3, all matched by the surviving editions. They are excerpts and, in the case of 43.2, bolster a reading different from that presented by some other Song dynasty quotations. Chen's text supports the claim that complete Wang Bi *Commentary* manuscripts survived the conflagrations of the ninth and tenth centuries, and that Wang Bi continued to be regarded as an important commentator, although eclipsed by Zhuang (Yan) Zun and even Xuanzong.

Wang Pang's *Daode zhen jing jizhu* 道德眞經集註[71] that survives in the *Daozang* includes commentaries by Emperor Xuanzong, Heshang gong, Wang Bi, and Wang Anshi's son Pang 王雱 himself. The latter's *Commentary* had been completed in 1070 and seems to have been written to attract Wang Anshi's attention.[72] In the preface to his own *Commentary*, which is reprinted in the beginning of this edition, Wang Pang argues that the two main commentaries "circulating in our times" are those by Wang Bi and Zhang Yue 張說 (d. 730), whose "texts each had their strengths and weaknesses, but both had more than one place where they fell short of the meaning." The postface by Liang Jiong 梁迥, dated 1089, argues that "among the explanations of the three [old] scholars [that is, Heshang gong, Wang Bi and Xuanzong] one could not but accept one part but reject another. However, each one of these [explanations] has its strengths but as to their ultimate purport, they all penetrated to the root of the Great Way."[73] The postface then proceeds to describe the "contemporary scholar," namely, Wang Pang. Preferences are expressed in this edition through the sequence in which commentaries are quoted in each section. In practically all cases, the commentaries by Xuanzong and Heshang gong come first. This seems a political oddity, since these were the official commentaries of the preceding dynasty. A Mr. Zhang, who is described as being quite a scholar, although his full name is not given,

> frustrated by the fact that those who held the [*Daode*] *jing* in their hands did not understand about the Way, ordered scholars from [his?] academy to collate these four commentaries, whereupon, without adding or deleting a thing, he had them printed so that they might circulate in the world and spread the teaching of [the *Laozi*].[74]

The postface was written for this edition. It emphasizes the crucial philosophical and analytical importance of these commentaries in view of the shallow understanding of contemporary Daoists. Wang Zhongmin has suggested that an edition by a Wen Ruhai 文如海, *Jizhu Laozi* 集注老子, listed in the book catalogue of the *Song shi* as containing the very same commentaries, might be identical.[75]

This *Jizhu* edition contains a text of the Wang Bi *Commentary* as complete as it was available to the editors, but under a *Laozi* text from a different tradition. A check of the first twenty *zhang* showed that the Wang Bi commentaries to all but one *zhang* were complete. The last two commentaries from *zhang* 15 are missing, and Wang Bi's commentary for 5.1 has been misassigned to Heshang gong. The edition follows the text/commentary sequence as the editors found it in the base editions. In this respect, there is practically no deviation from all other texts that have come to us. No Song print of this edition survives. While it is possible that the copies surviving in the Ming dynasty had deteriorated, there is no reason to assume that this text had been tampered with before finding its way into the *Zhengtong Daozang* of 1445, and thence into our hands.

This text is the oldest available complete edition of Wang Bi's *Commentary* [without a Wang Bi *Laozi* text]. Its quality is good. Though it shares many of the corrupt passages with the other texts, it also preserves commentaries absent elsewhere as well as many better readings, as will be identified in the notes to my edition/translation. For this reason, Shima Kuniō has made it his base text for most of his edition of the Wang Bi *Commentary* beyond *zhang* 11.

It seems, however, that the availability of Wang Bi's *Commentary* remained low even in the capital. Dong Jiong 董逈 (twelfth century) reports in his *Cangshu zhi* 藏書志: "When during the Chongning era (1102–1107) the present dynasty undertook again to edit the Daoist canon, the books by the other authors [i.e., the commentaries included into Zhang Junxiang's *Jizhu daode jing*] were already no longer present in the [Imperial] Collection; only [the commentaries] by Xuanzong, Heshang gong, Yen Zun, and Lu Xisheng as well as Fu Yi's *Guben Daode jing* 古本道德經 remained."[76]

One generation after Chen Jingyuan and the *Jizhu*, Chao Yuezhi 晁說之 (1059–1129), who admired Sima Guang and was in turn admired by Su Shi [as is well documented in the *Song Yuan xue'an* 宋元學案], joined in efforts to reestablish a reliable tradition of *Laozi* interpretation.[77] His preface, written in 1115, suggests that he was the first private Song scholar on record to come out with a separate edition of Wang Bi's *Commentary on the Laozi*. It had the un-Daoist title of *Wang Bi Laozi Daode jing* 王弼老子道德經 in two *juan*. Well in tune with the high appreciation that scholars from the early Song had of Zhuang (Yan) Zun's writings on the *Laozi*, Chao Yuezhi sets Wang Bi in this tradition and joins in the praise for the philosophical and analytical quality of the Wang Bi *Commentary* and its unique understanding of the *Laozi*. Chao, it should be noted, was not a Daoist, and the title for his text, which has been kept in the preface conserved in later Daozang and Siku editions, although they no longer had Chao's text itself, dissociates itself from the Daoist type of title. Chao writes:

> Studies with a true grasp of the *Laozi* are all in the tradition of Yan Junping's [Zhuang Zun's] [*Daode jing*] *zhigui*. How could his [Wang Bi's] statement [in his comment on *Laozi* 38.2] that humaneness, righteousness, and ritual behavior cannot be used on their own but that one has to make use of them relying on the Way, as well [as his words] that Heaven, Earth, and the ten thousand kinds of entities are all grasped in the One, be only of importance for the *Laozi* [they are universally true]! The hundred scholars have absolutely to be made familiar with this [argumentation]. I thus came to the insight that the core of [Wang] Bi ['s philosophy] was his deep [understanding] of the *Laozi* and that [his understanding of the *Zhou*]*yi* was inferior [to this]. From the fact that in his [*Zhou*]*yi* [*Commentary*] he largely copied the *Laozi*'s pointers while he did not take material for [his] *Laozi* [interpretation] from the [*Zhou*]*yi*,[78] the evidence is absolutely clear to see where he excels and where he is deficient. Alas, how difficult is scholarship!

[Wang] Bi knew that [the *Laozi* 31] from the words 佳兵
者不祥之器 to the words 戰勝以喪禮處之 were not Laozi's
words, but indeed he did not know that one finds [the words in
Laozi 27.5 and 27.6] 常善救人故無棄人常善救物故無棄物
only in Heshang gong, but that they do not appear in the old
MSS, which one can verify in Fu Yi ['s edition]. However, Wang
Bi wrote on top of this book [= *Commentary* of his]: "The
Daode jing does not separate the [*Laozi*] into two parts, one
dealing with *dao*, the other with *de*." This [organization of the
Laozi, present in my, Chao's, edition], is much closer to the old
[original form of the text]. It really is a pity that there are many
mistakes in the characters to the point that there are [passages]
one can barely read [= make sense of]. It is always said that the
relationship of [Wang] Bi with Laozi, Zhang Zhan 張湛 with
Liezi 列子, Guo Xiang 郭象 with Zhuangzi 莊子, Du Yu 杜
預 with Mr. Zuo 左氏 [presumed author of the *Zuo zhuan*],
Fan Ning 范寧 with Gu Liang 穀梁 [presumed author of the
Gu Liang zhuan], Mao Chang 毛萇 with the *Shi*[*jing*] 詩, and
Guo Pu 郭璞 with the *Er Ya* 爾雅 altogether forms scholarship
from one and the same school. Although there are some in later
generations who made the effort [to write new commentaries] it
was not easy [for them] to contribute [something new]. I have
thus [simply] copied out Wang Bi's book [without change for
publication], and affixed this preface to it. Dingchou day, 10th
month, *yimo* cyclical year in the Zhenghe era 政和 (= 1115),
Chao Yuezhi from Songshan [in Henan].[79]

There is to my knowledge no manuscript or quotation from the *Laozi* for
which the above description concerning *zhang* 27 holds true. I assume
that the text has to be read differently. The Fu Yi "Old MS" transmitted
in the *Daozang* is not the text referred to by Fan Yingyuan or by Chao
Yuezhi, and in this transmitted text, the entire passage occurs. Wang Bi's
Commentary, however, has no reference to the second part, namely, the
phrase 常善救物故無棄物 in *Laozi* 27.6, and I therefore think that this
was the passage Chao had in mind, while quoting the first part for textual
framework.[80] The texts in the *Daozang*, Siku quanshu, and Guyi congshu,
to which this preface is appended, do not fit the particulars mentioned in
the preface. It is thus the remnant of a lost early monograph edition of
Wang Bi's *Commentary*. The difficulties of acquiring a monograph edition
of Wang Bi's *Commentary on the Laozi* in the early twelfth century are
epitomized by Chao Gongwu's not having such a copy in his huge Sichuan

collection, although he himself came out with an edition of the *Laozi* text in which all variants were listed.[81]

Chao Yuezhi's text is followed by Xiong Ke's 熊克 (ca. 1111–1184), dated 1170, which gives another story of patronage publishing of the *Laozi* during the Song.

> I have read in the *Xianping sheng yu* 咸平聖語, the Holy [Emperor Zhenzong's] Sayings from the Xianping era [993–1004]: "The *Daode jing* by Laozi contains the essentials for regulating the times; although the explanations [on the *Laozi*] by Minghuang [= Tang Xuanzong] are glittering and spectacular, the commentaries by Wang Bi are simple in their words and profound in their meaning, and it is truly he [Wang Bi] who grasps the pure purport of Mr. Lao."[82] Since that time I have spent much effort to find the commentaries Wang [Bi] had made, but nowadays they are a rarity. I finally got them only after a long [search]: I have been in past years a district examiner in Jianning 建寧 [in Hubei] and was always after publications; in this way I also got hold of the edition with the preface by Mr. Chao Yidao [= Yuezhi], which does not separate the [*Laozi*] into two parts, one dealing with *dao*, the other with *de*, and also has no chapter headings. I was elated at how close to the old [form of the textual organization of the *Laozi*] this [edition of his] was and hand-copied it for [my] collection. In 1170 I was assigned to teach in Jinkou [the port of the Grand Canal on the Yangtse]. [There] I had [this text] again cut on [new] printing blocks so that it might be handed down [to further generations]. As to the mistakes in the [Chinese] characters [in this text], my precursor had been unable to correct them, how could I dare to change them at random! That will have to wait for someone with [more] knowledge. [Written] on the 24th day of the 3rd month [of the year 1170], by Xiong Ke, Gentleman for Attendance and Acting as Professor at the Prefectural School of Zhenjiang prefecture.[83]

Although commercial publishing had been rapidly developing under the Southern Song, circulation seems to have been small: the easiest way to get a copy of a printed book was still to copy it by hand.[84] This Xiong Ke did with the print that he must have seen at a scholar's house. The reading public, however, was national in scale, so that published texts were spread over wide geographic areas.

From Xiong Ke's account we gather that, like Chao Yuezhi, he had not endeavored to correct the errors in his manuscript but, true to the philological spirit of the time, printed it in the form that he found it, without the *daojing/dejing* division and headings for the *zhang*, rejecting with both features the organization of the Heshang gong. It is not made explicit whether the "errors" were in the *Laozi* text or Wang Bi's *Commentary*. Given the philological attention, however, lavished at the time on the establishment of a sound *Laozi* text out of the many different versions, it is highly unlikely that the remark referred to the *Laozi* contained in Chao's manuscript. The particular thing about this manuscript was that it contained the Wang Bi *Commentary*; the remarks have to pertain to it.[85]

It is not clear what happened to these two prints. There was continuous warfare with much destruction of books during this period. The last to mention having seen Chao Yuezhi's edition was Chen Zhensun 陳振孫 (fl. 1211–1249), the latest date in whose descriptive catalogue of his library is 1240.[86]

Chen describes the edition in his hand: "The *Laozi* text circulating in our time separates [the *Laozi*] into two parts, a *daojing* and a *dejing*. This edition of the *Daode jing* [in my hand] has no chapter headings whatsoever, it must be [based on an] old manuscript." The two colophons by Chao Yuezhi and Xiong Ke must, however, have survived into the Ming. Chao came from a learned family, and it is quite conceivable that all of his writings were kept in copies. In fact, the colophon is included in his works. The same is not true for Xiong Ke. He most likely printed Chao's colophon in his own reedition, which must have survived the Song. The three surviving editions, which by reprinting the two colophons claim to descend from the Chao/Xiong edition, namely, the Daozang, Siku quanshu, and Guyi congshu, all share some of its features: they do not separate into *daojing* and *dejing* and do not give the *zhang* headings of the standard Heshang gong editions, but with the exception of the *Daozang* edition, the *zhang* are sequentially numbered. These features became the markers of a "Wang Bi *Laozi*." The prefaces by Chao and Xiong were appended, I presume, not because their text was being reprinted but to authenticate these particular features of the Wang Bi *Commentary on the Laozi*.

The text of these editions contains the very sentence said to be missing in the *Laozi* text in Chao's Wang Bi edition and does not carry the Wang Bi statement above *zhang* 31 as quoted there; these editions are not reeditions of the Chao/Xiong text.

Li Lin 李霖 put together a *Daode zhen jing qushan ji* 道德眞經取善集, a "Collection of the best comments on the Daode jing,"[87] arguing in his preface's critical diatribe against contemporary *Laozi* scholars that many had understood parts of it, but no one had grasped it all.[88] Therefore, he was making this selection. Another preface was written by Liu Chongsheng 劉充升, dated 1172, in the Dschurchen dynasty. Liu argues that the *Laozi* was a guide toward taking care of oneself as well as of the state, and that the old charge that the Jin 晉 dynasty had fallen through adherence to this text was unfounded. He approvingly quotes the Sui dynasty scholar Wang Zhongyan 王仲淹, who maintained that "the empty and dark excels, but the demise of the Jin ruling house was not the fault of the *Laozi* and *Zhuangzi*, but of their inappropriate application."[89] Liu Weiyong 劉惟永 (fl. 1300) would later repeat this statement.[90]

In the tradition of patronage for the printing of the *Laozi* as in the *Jizhu* edition, an old friend of Li Lin's, Wang Binnai 王賓迺, undertook to have the work printed.[91] It includes commentaries by nearly fifty writers. Given the Song preference for other Song authors, most of these commentators are from the Song, with Song Huizong being inevitably quoted at the beginning. There also are many quotations from Wang Bi, Heshang gong, and Xuanzong, whose commentaries survive, and from others such as Kumārajīva (d. 409) and Wang Bi's contemporary Zhong Hui 鐘會, now lost as independent texts.[92] This attests both to the current availability of many commentaries now lost and to the eagerness with which *Laozi* devotees were collecting these texts. Li Lin added his own comments.

Li Lin quotes Wang Bi's *Commentary* with thirty-nine passages relating to the *Laozi*—5, 8, 13, 14, 15, 21, 22, 23, 32, 33, 38, 41, 43, 44, 45, 48, 54, 57, 58, 60, 61, 63, 65, 67, 70, 73, 74, 79, and 81, indicating that the entire text was available to him. In thirty-two cases, the text corresponds to one of the variants within the body of Wang Bi *Commentary* texts that have come down to us. In 13.5/6 and 14.4, Li Lin seems to give a summary of Wang Bi's opinion on the point, in the second case strongly deviating from the available text. In two cases he gives an excerpt of Wang Bi's *Commentary* (32.1 and 38.1), and in three cases he offers a piece of text transmitted nowhere else (5.2, 15.3, and 63.3), in the first and last case an acceptable addition. In short, the coincidence of these quotations with the other surviving texts of Wang Bi's *Commentary* (disregarding the *Laozi* text) is exceedingly high.

Also under the Dschurchen, Zhao Bingwen 趙秉文 (1159–1232) came out with a commentary collection, *Daode zhen jing jijie* 道德眞經集解.[93] The work contains three quotations from Wang Bi's *Commentary to Laozi*—1, 4, and 6—the second transmitted nowhere else, but deserving inclusion. From these two editions we infer the continued availability of the Wang Bi *Commentary* in the north after the Jin had taken over.

In 1229, Peng Si 彭耜 published another collection of commentaries to the *Laozi* from the Southern Song, the *Daode zhen jing jizhu* 道德眞經集註, which is preserved in the *Daozang* and designed to supplement

Chen Jingyuan's work.[94] Peng Si's preface, already quoted, lists imperial utterances on the importance of the *Laozi* and begins each commentary selection with the imperial commentary by Song Emperor Huizong. It includes only those commentaries by Wang Bi included in Chen's own *Commentary*, and thus it provides no new material. His *Daode zhen jing jizhu shiwen* 道德眞經集註釋文 cites places where the Heshang gong *Laozi* text differs from the others, an indicator of the deviation from the then-current Wang Bi *Laozi*.[95]

In 1246, Dong Siqing 董思靖 published his *Commentary* to the *Laozi*, the *Daode zhen jing jijie* 道德眞經集解, which includes quotations from Wang Bi.[96] His preface stresses the philosophic importance of the *Laozi* and affirmatively quotes Bai Juyi's polemics against the "Daoists'" reading of this text: "The five thousand words of the Emperor of the Dark [= the Daode jing] neither talk about [immortality] drugs, nor about becoming an immortal, nor about rising to heaven in broad daylight."[97] Concerning *zhang* 31 and 75, of which the first carries no Wang Bi commentary, Dong says: "Wang Bi says: 'This *zhang* has probably not been written by Laozi.'" This might mean that he had access to the Chao/Xiong edition, although their prefaces say nothing about *zhang* 75, which in fact has a Wang Bi commentary. Dong's quotation of Wang Bi's *Commentary* to *Laozi* 43.2 resembles other Song-dynasty quotations.

Meanwhile, other efforts were underway to establish a correct *Laozi* text. Fan Yingyuan 范應元, frustrated over the danger of losing the *Laozi*'s truth through corrupt texts, put together a *Laozi Daode jing guben jizhu* 老子道德經古本集註. As Wang Zhongmin has shown, it quotes a *Commentary* by Zhang Chongying 張仲應, finished in 1253, and the work itself is first mentioned in a book completed in 1270, which fixes its date between these two.[98] Fan used a wide variety of "old manuscripts," including a Jin dynasty one (he did not provide a complete list), and he had an edition of Wang Bi's *Commentary on the Laozi* among his sources; he frequently noted the readings of Wang Bi's *Laozi* text. It is an important source for Wang Bi's original *Laozi* text, but not for the *Commentary*.

The *Daode zhen jing jiyi* 道德眞經集義 was put together by Liu Weiyong 劉惟永 (fl. 1300) and some of his students.[99] One postface by Yang Ge 陽恪 attached to its introduction text, the *Daode zhen jing jiyi dazhi* 道德眞經集義大旨, is dated 1296, a second by Liu Weiyong himself, dated 1300; a third and a fourth one by Su Qiweng 蘇起翁 and Yu Qingzhong 喻清中 dated 1298, and the last one by Zhang Yucai 張與材, dated 1300.[100] Liu's own preface describes the purpose of the book as well as the subscription process through which it was published. Though Liu was a Daoist priest, this preface contains an aside critical of the low intellectual acumen and educational level of his peers.

Generally speaking, the Daoists might fluently recite the main classic [that is the *Laozi* itself] but I am afraid they don't understand its purport. How should anyone be able to deeply penetrate the dark and minute without perusing the commentaries by different scholars?!"[101]

Liu Weiyong had a fine library himself, and he pooled his holdings with those of fellow scholars for this compilation:

However, the costs for cutting the wood blocks were enormous, beyond what one single person could come up with. So, together with my disciples Zhao Yizhuang 趙以莊 and Liu Yijian 劉以鑒, we went all over the place and asked the officials, gentlemen as well as knowledgeable Daoist priests, to subscribe money so that we might complete the good work together. This [collection of money and the cutting of the blocks] has now already gone on for more than ten years, and, even when I ate or slept, it was never off my mind.[102]

The preface by Yu Qingzhong also mentions the travails of getting the huge work published.[103] The *Daode zhen jing jiyi* assembled the full commentaries on the *Laozi* of thirty-six scholars, including Wang Bi's, along with quotations and excerpts from another forty-two. The original length of this ambitious project is said to have been thirty-one chapters and "ten thousand times hundred million words." Only seventeen chapters survive in the *Daozang*, running through eight volumes of the *Daozang* reprint and dealing with the first eleven *zhang* of the *Laozi*.

The text carefully indicates intersections between text and commentary for each of the commentaries. The intersections for Wang Bi correspond to the *Jizhu* and other editions with a rare exception in *Laozi* 3.6. The *Jizhu* and *Jiyi* texts share the passages that had become incomprehensible in earlier times, such as the commentary to 5.3. Both have occasional scribal errors. In the first eleven *zhang*, the *Jizhu* twice miswrites *you* 又 for *bu* 不, but the *Jiyi* does not follow suit. The *Jiyi*, on the other hand, makes a number of scribal and other errors, bringing it closer to the texts from the Ming dynasty, and it fills in some blatant omissions of the *Jizhu*, such as the *ren shi gou* 人食狗 from 5.1. Because it is slightly superior to the *Jizhu*, Shima Kuniō has selected this text as his base text for the first eleven *zhang* of the Wang Bi *Commentary*, excluding the *Laozi* text.

For the first 11 *zhang*, the two texts, *Jizhu* and *Jiyi*, together are close enough with sufficient variants to establish a firm base text and wipe out most scribal errors. They retain, however, several passages that are patently corrupt. For the remaining *zhang*, the only firm base is the *Jizhu*, and we must rely on the earliest Ming editions for corroboration.

Patronage for the Wang Bi *Commentary* during the Song dynasty was based on the assumption that the understanding of the *Laozi* had deteriorated into a crass superstition. The patronage was thus part of an effort to resuscitate the *Laozi* as a philosophic text against a Daoist community using it for other goals. The numerous philological and philosophical *Laozi* commentaries by Song scholars from Wang Anshi to Su Shi reflect that goal, as do the prefaces and postfaces of the bibliophiles chasing, collating, and editing the Wang Bi *Commentary*.

We finally come to the Ming editions. From Ji Yun's introduction to the Siku quanshu edition of Wang Bi's *Commentary*, which is dated 1778, we know that the *Yongle dadian* 永樂大典 contained an edition of the text. A Siku note to the title of *Laozi* 38 says, "From this *zhang* on the *Yongle dadian* does not carry the [Wang Bi] *Commentary*."[104] The Siku edition quotes all variants from the *Yongle dadian*, which has not survived in its entirety as a separate work. Wang Bi's *Commentary on the Laozi* thus made it into the most important Imperial Collection early in the Ming.

The Siku editors note all differences between their base edition (which I shall show is strictly based on the *Daozang* edition) and the *Yongle dadian* in both text and commentary for the first thirty-seven *zhang*.

For the *Laozi* text itself, they note thirty-eight variants (after subtracting eight for *zhang* 31, which has no commentary by Wang Bi). A study of these variants shows that the *Yongle dadian* Wang Bi *Laozi* text has fewer deformations than the *Daozang* text. It offers some valuable material and is not identical to any other *Laozi* text known to me.[105] Otherwise, the *Laozi* text offered by the *Yongle dadian* definitely preceded that of the *Daozang* and generally stays closer to the versions preserved in Fu Yi and Fan Yingyuan. This is particularly true in the case of one *Laozi* phrase at the end of 34.4, which otherwise appears only in Fu Yi's edition.[106] This edition often accepts variants where Fu Yi, Fan Yingyuan, Xuanzong, and the various manuscripts from the Zhuang (Yan) Zun tradition agree against the *textus receptus*.

The Siku notes forty-one *Yongle dadian* differences from what I will describe as the *Zhang/Daozang* text of Wang Bi's *Commentary*. After again subtracting a number of scribal errors and omissions,[107] the remaining twenty-three differences mostly eliminate scribal errors of the *Zhang/Daozang* text in accordance with the text preserved in Song commentary collections, such as the *Jizhu*. The *Yongle dadian* text, in short, agrees with the Song texts but does not contribute anything new. The altogether small number of deviations for both the text and the *Commentary* shows how unified the text had become.

The *Zhengtong Daozang* 正統道藏, printed in 1445, carries the oldest surviving monographic edition of Wang Bi's *Commentary on the Laozi*. Since the catalogues of the earlier *Daozang* editions are lost, we do not know whether this text had already been included there. Entitled *Daode zhen jing zhu* 道德眞經注, certainly not Wang Bi's original title, it comes in a unique arrangement of four *juan*,[108] the same number as in the Song edition of the Heshang gong *Commentary*, though the chapters divide at other points. In fact, the number of *juan*, as Wang Baoxuan has shown, reflects a technical rearrangement of the Ming dynasty *Daozang*, through which all texts incorporated there doubled the number of their *juan*.[109] The edition has neither *daojing* and *dejing* nor chapter headings either in the form of numbers or titles. The separation between the *zhang* is achieved by beginning a new *zhang* with a new line, and between text and commentary by size of character. It is the oldest text to add the postfaces of Chao Yuezhi and Xiong Ke from their edition.

The *Laozi* text in this edition has been superseded by the Heshang gong tradition and is for the most part identical to the text of other Ming editions that have come to us. The Wang Bi *Commentary* text again contains the standard trouble areas of most other texts and is free of many simple scribal errors. However, Wang Baoxuan's suggestion to base an edition on the *Daozang* text seems unwarranted in view of the much better Wang Bi *Commentary* texts from the Song.

Jiao Hong 焦竑 (fl. 1588) put together in his *Laozi yi* 老子翼 a selection of what he considered the best comments to the individual *zhang* of the *Laozi* that he could find,[110] chosen from 67 different commentaries and essays about the *Laozi*, including Wang Bi's *Commentary*. Two friends undertook to edit the work and have it cut, their preface dated in the Wanli reign, 1588. Jiao does not identify the text on which he bases his edition, which interestingly includes what at that time must have looked like an archaic arrangement similar to the *Daozang* edition. The term and title *Daode jing* appears neither in the title nor the preface. The edition is in two *pian* not associated with *dao* and *de*. Individual *zhang* have neither numbers nor titles. The commentaries are physically separated from the *Laozi* text, having two rows of characters per line as opposed to one for the *Laozi*. He evidently tried to establish an authentic *Laozi* text. He refers to Fu Yi's text and Wang Bi's text (*zhang* 41, 2.8a) and claims to follow them. Among the materials on which he based his edition he quotes a Jiaoding guben 較定古本 by Fu Yi, which obviously served as a basis. He gives three short quotations from Wang Bi in his own commentaries, twice refers to the reading of the *Wang Bi Laozi*, and once quotes a long Wang Bi commentary.

The long quotation is a cut version of the commentary to *zhang* 32.

It is from a definitely corrupt section, but Jiao does not provide an option that would permit the restoration of a meaningful text. The quotation of the commentary 3.2 and 3.3 corresponds to the other editions, but has an explanatory addition not confirmed elsewhere. The quotation from 18.3 corresponds to the other editions. The text he offers differs from the various quotations in commentary selections of the Song, Jin, and Yuan, but by his time most of the commentaries he quotes were no longer available in their entirety, only in excerpts in commentary selections. It is possible that he had a copy of the Chao/Xiong edition, but there is no way to ascertain this. His text of the *Laozi* is not closer to the Urtext of the Wang Bi *Laozi* than other Ming dynasty editions.

During the *wanli* era (1573–1620), Zhang Zhixiang 張之象, about whom nothing further seems to be known, published a *San jing Jin zhu* 三經晉注, in which the Wang Bi *Commentary* was included. The three classics obviously were the *Laozi*, the *Liezi*, and the *Zhuangzi*. Who were the commentators? He might have included various Jin dynasty commentators, or have used just Wang Bi for the *Laozi*, Zhang Zhan for the *Liezi*, and Guo Xiang for the *Zhuangzi*, in fact publishing three complete texts with commentaries bound together. The edition does not survive, but the Siku quanshu edition is based on it. Ji Yun 紀昀 (1724–1805), who wrote the preface for this edition, talks about the "present text [of Zhang's]" as "not being divided into a *daojing* and a *dejing*," a feature adopted in the Siku edition. Ji Yun does mention that Zhang's edition had postfaces by Chao Yuezhi and Xiong Ke printed after the Wang Bi text. The *Daozang* edition carried them both, but Ji Yun did not have the Chao/Xiong edition in his hands.

In fact, Zhang's edition survives in the Siku edition. Even for the first thirty-seven *zhang*, where the editors also had the *Yongle dadian* text, Zhang's text formed the basis, and all deviations from it were identified. As the *Yongle dadian* used by the Siku editors did not contain the Wang Bi *Commentary* after *zhang* 38, and as they "did not have any other text," they simply reprinted in the second part what they found in the Zhang Zhixiang edition.

From Ji Yun's statements we can assume that Zhang Zhixiang printed a complete Wang Bi *Commentary on the Laozi*, not a collection of commentaries attached to a text and a textual organization he himself might have preferred. Zhang Zhixiang's text, however, is not based on the Chao/Xiong edition; it lacks the Wang Bi statements quoted in the postface of Chao Yuezhi. In his preface to the Siku quanshu edition, Ji Yun quotes from Qian Zeng's 錢曾 (1629–1701) *Dushu minqiu ji* 讀書敏求記 the words "Wang Bi's *Commentary on the Laozi* is already not transmitted anymore." Ji Yun continues:

[H]owever, during the Wanli period of the Ming, there was in fact a printed copy from the hands of Zhang Zhixiang [which we have]. We compared it character by character to [Lu Deming's] *Jingdian shiwen* as well as the text in the *Yongle dadian*. In the "Tianduan" chapter of the *Liezi*, six sentences [identical with] *Laozi* [*zhang* 6 which begins] "The spirit of the valley does not die" are quoted, and Zhang Zhan quotes Wang Bi's *Commentary* [to this *zhang*] to explain the passage. Although there are a few characters more or less here and there, the text [basically] is not different [from the text in our hands]. From this we knew that we did not have to rely on [Qian] Hui [= Qian Zeng] who just by a chance happened not to have seen a text. Our edition is thus compiled from Zhang Zhixiang's *San jing Jin zhu* 三經晉注. Although there inevitably are lacunae and mistakes, the grand purport is still discernible.[111]

As the Wang Bi commentaries for *Laozi* 38 ff. were missing in the *Yongle dadian*, Ji Yun was left with only the Zhang text, writing "[from here on] we take the text from Zhang Zhixiang. Wang Bi's *Commentary* [text] is in many places full of mistakes, but we have no other manuscript to compare it with, and have therefore kept to the old text [in Zhang's edition]."[112]

A comparison between the Zhang Zhixiang text of Wang Bi's *Commentary* incorporated into the Siku and the *Daozang* text shows that Zhang based himself either on the *Daozang* text or on the text on which the *Daozang* edition was based. For the forty-two *zhang* of the second part (excluding *zhang* 66, for which there is no commentary) in the Siku edition, which reprint Zhang's edition, there is no difference whatever between the Zhang Zhixiang and the *Daozang* editions in twenty-three *zhang*, namely, 39, 40, 42, 43, 44, 47, 48, 53, 54, 55, 57, 61, 62, 63, 64, 68, 69, 71, 75, 76, 77, 78, and 81. There is a character variant in *Laozi* 65, and there are single deviations through simple scribal errors, mostly but not all on the *Daozang* side in another nine *zhang*—41, 45, 46, 58, 59, 67, 70, 72, and 73. In *zhang* 74, the Siku editors explicitly state that in one phrase they follow the Heshang gong text and not Zhang Zhixiang. We are left with the differences in *zhang* 38, 49, 50, 51, 52, 56, 60, and 80.

In the commentary to *zhang* 38.2, the Siku leaves out twenty-four characters on p. 161.b.6; they fit the context, however, and are confirmed by the text in the *Jizhu*. In *Laozi* 49.4, the Siku forgets the phrase 百姓皆 注其耳目, present in all traditions, its necessity confirmed by Wang Bi's commentary. In *Laozi* 50.2, the *Daozang* text leaves out a *yi* 亦, otherwise well attested, the only case where the Siku has a character more than the

Daozang. In the commentary, the Siku transposes the *yi* by mistake and writes 亦十分有三 instead of the better attested 十分亦有三. In *zhang* 51 the Siku omits the last six characters of the last commentary, which are well attested in earlier sources. In *Laozi* 52 the Siku neglects to copy the first commentary, again well attested. In *zhang* 56.5 and 56.6 the Siku writes 無所特顯則物無所偏爭也 and 無所特賤則物無所偏恥也 instead of the 無所特顯則物無偏爭也 and 無所特顯則物無偏恥也 of the *Daozang*, confirmed by the *Jizhu*. In *zhang* 60.4 the Siku fails to copy a *yi* 亦 after *shengren*, and the *fei du* 非獨 after *yun* 云, both confirmed by the *Jizhu*. In 80.2, the Siku fails to copy the 2 characters 之當, which again are confirmed by the *Jizhu*.

A comparison of the *Yongle dadian* variants to the Zhang edition shows the same features. Time and again (8.3, 10.9, 15.1, 16.6, 16.12, 16.12, 16.13, 18.1, 20.1, 22.1, 26.4, 27.4, 34.2) *Zhang*'s text and the *Daozang* text share the same deviations from the strong body of the Song tradition, including the *Yongle dadian* text. They share unique, even bizarre, mistakes, such as the 自物因然 for 因物自然 in 27.4, or the 鷰 for 燕 in 20.1. The only difference seems to be that Zhang added some copying mistakes of his own (such as 知 for 如 in 35.3, or 焉 for 也 at the end of 23.7 and 30.3). Zhang Zhixiang also took from the *Daozang* edition the two postfaces by Chao Yuezhi and Xiong Ke. From there, they were included in the Siku edition. Zhang Zhixiang seems also to be the first to introduce the system to place numbers for the *zhang* of the *Laozi* into a Wang Bi text, following Fu Yi's edition and its Song imitations. Fu Yi had appended these numbers after the *zhang*, while Zhang puts them before. The *Daozang* edition has neither titles nor numbers. Compared to the alternatives of content-oriented titles from the Heshang gong *Commentary*, or titles based on the first characters of the *zhang*, as in the Xuanzong *Commentary*, this seems to be a most prudent and technical solution. It was adopted in the Siku.

In conclusion:

1. The Siku text intersects text and commentary at the same places as the *Daozang* text.

2. The Siku text is based on the Zhang Zhixiang text, which in turn copies the *Daozang* text. It eliminates some of the scribal errors and adds a few of its own. It fails to copy one longer passage and a number of very short passages or single characters. Only in one case does it add a character to the *Daozang* text. This single character might have been inserted by Zhang Zhixiang from the *Jizhu*.

3. It is not clear whether Zhang's edition or the Siku left out the missing words and passages. In any case, the Siku text for the second part is dependent on the *Daozang* text and is inferior to it by omitting a number of passages. It contributes no serious textual alternatives and eliminates few scribal errors.

4. The Siku is thus indirectly based on the *Daozang* edition. Apart from the few acceptable *Yongle dadian* variants, which at best eliminate *Daozang* mistakes on the basis of Song editions available in their entirety, the Siku offers no new textual material. As a derived text, it is no serious candidate for a base text.

Ji Yun states that "it was already in Song times hard to get hold of good copies of this book." He notes the discrepancy between the claim in Chao Yuezhi's preface that Wang Bi did not separate a *daojing* and a *dejing*, and the fact that the *Jingdian shiwen* 經典釋文 in their hands had this separation. Zhang Zhixiang's edition on which they themselves base their text did not have this separation. The Zhejiang shuju 浙江書局 edition of the *Ershier zi*, 二十二子, of 1875, which opens with the Wang Bi *Laozi Commentary*, claims to be based on an "original from Mr. Zhang from Huating" 華亭張氏原本, which seems to point to the Zhang Zhixiang edition.[113] A comparison with the edition in the hands of the Siku editors quickly shows that while some of the particulars of their text are indeed in this new edition, many others are not. We thus have to assume that this print again has been reworked. This very unstable edition has been selected by Lou Yulie as his base text for the Wang Bi *Laozi Commentary* in his *Wang Bi ji jiaoshi* 王弼集校釋, which is the most widely used edition today.

Also during the Wanli era, Sun Kuang 孫鑛 (1542–1613) came out with an edition; its *Laozi* text was based on Zhang Zhixiang with an even stronger impact from the Heshang Gong, whose chapter titles it inserts into a text that otherwise carries only the Wang Bi *Commentary*. Its text for the Wang Bi *Commentary* follows the *Daozang* text. This edition survives in Japan in a manuscript in the Sonkeikaku bunko 尊經閣文庫, from which it has been reproduced in Yan Lingfeng's collection.[114] It was the basis for the first surviving Japanese edition of 1732, the Fukoku Tōin manuscript 阜谷東嚳本,[115] and it has been the base text for a long series of Japanese studies on Wang Bi's *Laozi Commentary*, beginning with Usami Shinsui 宇佐美灊水 (1710–1776), who came out in 1770 with his critical edition of the *Laozi* with Wang Bi's *Commentary*, the *Rōshi dōtoku shinkyō* 老子道德眞經.[116] In his preface he refers to his use of Jiao Hong's 焦竑 *Laozi yi* 老子翼 and Sun Kuang's critical comparison of different *Laozi* manuscripts. As to the Wang Bi *Commentary*, he says that "the manuscripts of today are full of disorder and lacunae, and it is impossible to get hold of a [Song] 'good manuscript' 善本 to correct them." As his own years were already advanced, he continues, and he has other things to do, he has not paid much attention to correcting the mistakes in Wang's *Commentary*, which he leaves for later scholars. The edition in the Guyi congshu 古逸叢書 is in its turn based on Usami Shinsui's version of this edition and has been inaccurately changed in many places by its editor, Li Shuchang 黎庶昌.[117]

The *Daozang Commentary* text and its derivatives thus have become the basis for all other modern editions of the Wang Bi *Commentary* and *Laozi* text. The entire group is closely linked. Their *Laozi* texts share a large number of common deviations from what we know from internal evidence about the Wang Bi *Laozi* text, and a large number of deviations against the earliest available extensive sources for the Wang Bi *Commentary*, namely, the *Jizhu* and Liu Weiyong's *Jiyi*.

The Siku is an attempt to establish something similar to a critical text. The Guyi congshu edition has been amended by its general editor, Li Shuchang. Since then, many Chinese and Japanese scholars have worked at emendations on the basis of these comparatively late editions. Among the most important are Usami Shinsui (1710–1776), Tōjō Itsudō 東條一堂 (1778–1856), Wei Yuan 魏源 (1794–1856), Tao Hongqing 陶鴻慶 (1860–1918), Liu Guojun 劉國鈞 (1899–1980), Hatano Tarō 波多野太郎, Shima Kuniō 島邦男, and Lou Yulie 樓宇烈.[118] They have made important contributions in those areas where all transmitted texts share corruptions, and ample use of these emendations will be made in the following pages. They did not, however, attempt or succeed in making critical editions of the Wang Bi *Commentary* and the Wang Bi *Laozi* text.

For both the Wang Bi *Laozi* and the Wang Bi *Commentary*, Shima Kuniō has offered the most important methodological advances. First, he separated restoring the Wang Bi *Laozi* from restoring the Wang Bi *Commentary*. Second, he tried to establish a textual family from which the construction of the Wang Bi *Laozi* could be undertaken. Third, he pioneered the idea of constituting a Wang Bi *Commentary* from quotations in the Song collected commentaries. For the last two items, I have come to different conclusions in many places, but this was possible only by following his method.

First, Shima Kuniō's textual family for the Wang Bi *Laozi* consists of the *Laozi* text printed over the Wang Bi *Commentary* in the *Daozang* edition, in the Siku edition, and in the Zhejiang shuju edition, all of which are late and dependent on one single base text, the *Daozang* text; given the evidence of its being overlaid by strong elements from the Heshang gong tradition, its qualification as a textual family does not seem very sound. This text deviates in several cases from the quotations in Wang Bi's *Commentary*. As I have shown in the first chapter, internal evidence from the Wang Bi *Commentary* points to a very close relationship to the Fu Yi/Fan Yingyuan family in Shima Kuniō's list of lineages; the two Mawangdui manuscripts that had not been published when Shima Kuniō came out with his work, have to be added. Actually, what Shima Kuniō establishes as the Wang Bi text is more closely related to this group than to the family in which he groups it.

Second, Shima Kuniō did not set out to establish critical texts of the commentaries included in his work. He merely reproduced whatever version of a Wang Bi commentary note he considered best preserved without scrutinizing the details of this text. This often leads to the preservation of nonsensical textual elements. My own work has made systematic use of the still tentative advances of Shima Kuniō.

CONCLUSIONS

- During the *zhengshi* era (240–249), Wang Bi wrote a commentary to the *Laozi* entitled *Laozi zhu*. It did not divide the text into a *daojing* and a *dejing*, and it did not give titles or numbers to the individual *zhang*. Wang Bi assumed that it consisted of short independent sections called by him *zhang* 章 or *pian* 篇.

- From the arrangement of the Xiang Er *Commentary* manuscript we may presume that text and commentary were optically continuous. New *zhang* did not begin with a new line.

- Wang Bi's *Commentary* circulated in Wei and during the Six Dynasties in intellectual circles, continuing the tradition of ontological inquiry. The text's role was probably strongest in the south, but prominent northern intellectuals and Buddhist monks also used and appreciated it. It was gradually eclipsed by the Heshang gong *Commentary*, but it attained equal standing with it early in the Tang dynasty. Its defenders stressed its philosophic and analytic quality.

- The text of the Wang Bi *Commentary* went through a different history than the Wang Bi *Laozi* text. By and large, the Wang Bi *Commentary* survived the changes of the Wang Bi *Laozi* with little damage. It was widely quoted in the seventh and eighth centuries and was included in Zhang Junxiang's collection of thirty commentaries to the *Laozi*. It received critical attention from the early Song onward. Various monograph editions were made, and it was included in whole or in part in various commentary collections of the period. The eleventh-century *Jizhu* contains the earliest extant text of the *Commentary*, albeit under a *Laozi* text from a different tradition.

- The patronage necessary for ensuring the continuity of the text was only rarely based on reasons of state as for the big Confucian, Daoist, and Buddhist collections. It was not based on the principle of merit accumulation, like many "unofficial" Buddhist and Daoist texts, but on the appreciation of the philosophical quality of Wang Bi's *Commentary*, which was thought to provide a critical antidote to a sectarian or a dietetic and alchemical understanding of the *Laozi*, a rare and satisfying case of a text surviving because of the appeal of its intellectual quality. Such prestige caused it to be imperially cut during the early Song and included in the imperially sponsored *Yongle dadian*, the Daozang, and the Siku quanshu during the Ming and Qing.

- The origin and transmission of Wang Bi's *Commentary on the Laozi* are well attested, down to a time of printed editions or re prints of such editions.

- The two oldest monograph editions, the *Daozang* and the Zhang Zhixiang, copied in the *Siku*, are essentially the same. All later editions are based on this Ming-text. Any deviation from it is the result of critical and often sloppy intervention, not of a different textual base. Both editions contain an unacceptably distorted *Laozi* text, as well as a number of errors and lacunae in the Wang Bi *Commentary* beyond those of the Song commentary collections. They do not qualify as a base text for either the Wang *Laozi* Urtext or the Wang Bi *Commentary*.

- The number of quotations from the *Commentary* in other texts that cannot be identified in the surviving text is extremely small, even smaller if those quotations are discounted for which internal evidence makes their attribution questionable. The text thus survives to a very high degree in its entirety. The Wang Bi *Commentary* had a textual authority of its own, independent of the *Laozi* text to which it was attached.

- The differences between quotations transmitted in other texts and the transmitted text are by and large very small. The text thus survives in a wording rather close to the original.

- All surviving texts since Song times share a number of textual corruptions of a highly specific kind. These cannot be ascribed to diverse copying errors but point to a common source. This source is not the "original text" but a copy with substantial corruptions, noted ever since the eleventh century. Thus the basis of all surviving later editions is one single text predating the mid-eleventh century. This tends to confirm the complaints by Ye Mengde 葉夢德 in a 1034 memorial about the detrimental effect of book printing on textual quality—mistakes were being canonized and manuscripts not further collected.[119]

- For Wang Bi's *Commentary* we must look to the earliest complete and best texts of this unified family of *Commentary* texts with their shared illegible passages, namely, the one in the *Jizhu*, supplemented by other quotations and full texts, especially the surviving part of Liu Weiyong's *Jiyi*, as well as scholarly contributions.

- Given the importance of the Wang Bi *Commentary* and the sizable gains in terms of textual quality that can be achieved by going back to the pre-Ming sources, a critical edition of the Wang Bi *Commentary* is both feasible and desirable. It will be included in this book.

Chapter 3

Wang Bi: "The Structure of the *Laozi*'s Subtle Pointers," *Laozi weizhi lüeli*, a Philological Study and Translation Together with the Text

INTRODUCTION

This chapter[1] purports to check the evidence for the attribution of the anonymously transmitted *Laozi weizhi lüeli* to Wang Bi, to present Wang Bi's analysis of the formal structure of the *Laozi*, and to offer, along with a critical edition of the text, an annotated translation. Wang Bi's surviving works are a *Commentary of the Zhouyi* 周易注 and a structural analysis of this text, the *Zhouyi lüeli* 周易略例,[2] fragments of his *Solving the doubtful points in the Lunyu, Lunyu shiyi* 論語釋疑,[3] which challenged the commentary newly compiled under the editorship of He Yan,[4] and, finally, his *Commentary to the Laozi*.[5] Early records show that Wang Bi also wrote a separate treatise on the *Laozi*, matching the pattern set in his work on the *Zhouyi*. This treatise has been considered lost.

THE AUTHENTICITY OF THE *LAOZI WEIZHI LÜELI (LZWZLL)*

In 1951, Professor Wang Weicheng 王維誠 identified the anonymously transmitted *Laozi weizhi lilüe* 老子微指例略, contained in the Daozang as (all or part of) Wang Bi's treatise on the *Laozi*.[6] The bibliographic record for this treatise begins with He Shao 何劭 (236–ca. 300), who said that Wang

69

"Bi wrote a Commentary to the *Laozi* and made a *Zhilüe* 指略 about it" [i.e., the *Laozi*];[7] includes Liu Xie 劉勰 (465–522), who mentions the text in his *Wenxin diaolong* 文心雕龍 as one of the most brilliant examples of the genre *lun* 論,[8] and, in the same century, Wang Sengqian 王僧虔, who chastises his son for rushing through the *Laozi* without consulting Wang Bi's all-important *Zhilüe*;[9] and ends with bibliographers of the Tang and Song mentioning editions in one or two *juan*,[10] one edition in one *juan* being subdivided into eighteen *zhang*.[11] The titles have slight variations; the edition in two *juan* in the Tang is entitled *Laozi zhi lilüe* 老子指例略. A long and again anonymous quotation from the treatise appears in the very first chapter of Zhang Junfang's 張君房 *Yunji qiqian* 雲笈七籤, a "comprehensive encyclopedia of Daoist learning" (Strickmann), presented to the Court in 1019.[12] As in many other instances in this encyclopedia, no author is given, only the title, *Laojun zhigui lüeli* 老君指歸略例, which is similar to Wang Bi's *Zhouyi lüeli*. This quotation has 1,350 characters. With some minor variants, they can be found in full in the *Daozang* text, which has 2,552 characters. I assume that the original text had the title *Laozi weizhi lüeli*. The preference for *lüeli* instead of *lilüe* is based on the *Zhouyi lüeli* parallel as well as Liu Xie's reference to the "two *lüeli*."

Professor Wang also found the only quotation linking the transmitted treatise directly to the name of Wang Bi. The *Liezi* commentator, Zhang Zhan 張湛 (fl. 320), quotes Wang Bi:

王弼曰形必有所分聲必有所屬若溫也則不能涼若宮也則不
能商.

This passage is found in the *Daozang* text with the sequence of the two phrases inverted.[13] There is no other matching passage in Wang Bi's surviving corpus.

As already shown, the *Laozi* text transmitted over the surviving Wang Bi *Commentary* editions is not Wang Bi's original text of the *Laozi*; information about his *Laozi* version can be gathered from the quotations in Wang's *Commentary*, which often deviate from the *Laozi* text printed in the extant editions of Wang's *Commentary*. Wang Bi's *Laozi* belongs to the textual family made up by the two "old MSS" collated by Fu Yi and Fan Yingyuan, with the two Mawangdui manuscripts as close relatives.[14] If it could be proved that the *Laozi* text used for the *LZWZLL* corresponds to the specific traits of Wang Bi's *Laozi* within this family of texts, we would have further evidence of the *LZWZLL*'s authenticity.

There is a fair amount of direct quotations from the *Laozi* in the *LZWZLL*, mostly uncontroversial in the different textual families. We will focus on the few that are controversial.

- The *LZWZLL*, in the beginning of *zhang* 6, characterizes "the book of the *Laozi*" with the words 言不遠宗事不失主, an obvious reference to *Laozi* 70.2. The decisive point is 主. In his comments on *Laozi* 49.5, Wang Bi comes back to the second part of this phrase when he says 物有其宗事有其主. From these two statements it would seem that both the *LZWZLL* and the *Laozi Commentary* were based on a *Laozi* text linking 事 and 主. In fact, only two "Old MS," namely, Fu Yi and Fan Yingyuan, write 事有主 instead of the 事有君 in the Heshang gong and other traditions, including Mawangdui B; Mawangdui A simply inverts the 君 and 宗. We conclude that Wang Bi's *Laozi* shared the particular reading of this phrase in Fu Yi and Fan Yingyuan, and that the *LZWZLL* did the same.

- The *LZWZLL* writes 息淫在乎去華不在茲(=滋)章. This refers to *Laozi* 57.4. The decisive point is 章. The textual family of Wang Bi's *Laozi* all write 茲/滋章 against the unanimous 滋彰 in the other textual families. Again, the *LZWZLL* shares a special feature with the *Laozi* text used by Wang Bi's *Laozi Commentary*.

- The *LZWZLL* writes 執古可以御今. This refers to *Laozi* 14.4. The crucial element is 可, transmitted only by Fu Yi's "Old MS"; Fu Yi is generally closest to the text used for Wang Bi's *Laozi Commentary*. Wang Bi's commentary on *Laozi* 14.5 takes up this topic and writes 故可執古之道以御今之有. In his comments on *Laozi* 47.1, Wang Bi writes again with a reference to this passage of the *Laozi*: 執古之道可以御今. From these passages it seems probable that Wang Bi's *Laozi* read 執古之道可以御今之有, and that the *LZWZLL* shared this exceptional textual feature. A counterargument may be made. The *Laozi* phrase quoted is followed by the phrase 以知古始. Wang Bi's comment on this phrase also includes a 可: 故雖在今可以知古始, repeated in Wang Bi on *Laozi* 47.1. In the *LZWZLL* he also says 可以知古始. The Fu Yi "Old MS" does not help in this case, because, like Fan Yingyuan, it writes 能知古始, while the two Mawangdui manuscripts write 以知古始, supported by Zhuang (Yan) Zun. There are three options. First, Wang Bi's *Laozi* also read 可以 here; to this date, there is no textual evidence that this was an actual textual option. Second, as Wang Bi often "translates" 以 into 可以 (see textual commentary on *Laozi* 14.5 for references), he had 以 in both cases, and he translated them both in this manner, which would eliminate the relevance of this passage for the point under consideration. Third, Wang Bi's *Laozi* had 可以 for the first instance and 以 for the second and Wang Bi "parallelized" the two in his treatment. Given Wang Bi's routine in such parallelizations, I consider the third option most likely.

- Two *LZWZLL* passages present a conflict. The *LZWZLL* writes 所謂自古及今其名不去者也, referring to *Laozi* 21.6. The decisive point is the conflict between two textual traditions, one reading 自古及今, the other 自今及古. Wang Bi's commentary to *Laozi* 21.6 is transmitted with both versions, the (older) *Jizhu* 集註 gives 自今及古, the *Yongle dadian* 永樂大典 gives 自古及今. According to both editions, Wang Bi writes directly before quoting the *Laozi* text 自古及今無不由此而成. These words indicate that his text actually ran 自古及今, and that the *Yongle dadian* version of the commentary is preferable here, supporting a Wang Bi *Laozi* text that read 自古及今. This is the reading referred to by the *LZWZLL*.

- The second passage concerns the sequence of 王侯 or 侯王. The *LZWZLL* writes that Laozi 明侯王孤寡之義. This might refer to either *Laozi* 39.4 or *Laozi* 42.1; in both, the *Laozi* takes up the notion that the dukes and kings call themselves "orphaned" and "lonely." As Wang Bi refers to 王侯 in his commentary on 42.1, there is strong support for a reading of 王侯 instead of the 侯王 suggested by the *LZWZLL*. On the other hand, both variants appear in different places in Wang Bi's *Laozi*, and, even in the passages in question, there are different textual traditions within the same textual family. For this reason I believe that this deviation is of less weight that the supporting arguments.

- A final point: the *LZWZLL* and Wang Bi's *Commentary* refer to the same *Xici* passage and share one particular writing. The *LZWZLL* writes: 夫途雖殊必同其歸, Wang Bi's commentary on *Laozi* 47.1, 途雖殊而其歸同. The standard editions of the *Xici* write 塗 instead of 途. The *Laozi* references in the *Commentary* and the *LZWZLL* coincide.

Wang Bi created a specific type of analysis for the *Laozi* for which he also fixed a new terminology. The *LZWZLL* uses this terminology systematically. Thus *quyu* 取於 or 取乎, with the meaning "X is taken for (describing this or that specific aspect of) Y" is specific to Wang Bi, and it appears in the commentary on *Laozi* 1.5 and 25.5, and in the *LZWZLL*.[15] Similarly the highly specific differentiation between *ming* 名 as a definition and *cheng* 稱 as an inferred designation occurs in both texts as well as in the *Lunyu shiyi*.[16] The close parallelism between the interpretation of the *LZWZLL* and the *Commentary* is documented in the notes and has been cited by both Wang Weicheng and Yan Lingfeng.

The *LZWZLL* shares with the *Commentary* a set of classics to draw on for statements of hidden truth. Foremost among these are the *Xici* (and *Wenyan*), the *Lunyu*, and the *Laozi* itself. Furthermore, the *LZWZLL* is written in Wang Bi's characteristic style, Interlocking Parallel Style (IPS). It is one of the longest cohesive pieces written in IPS that survives to this day.[17]

Finally, as documented in the notes to the translation, the overlap between the *LZWZLL* and the *Commentary* is overwhelming. Some passages are identical, and many others are closely related. The general orientation of the analysis in both is the same. I see nothing that has to be "explained away" if Wang Bi's authorship is assumed. Only one scholar expressed reservations about the authenticity, but he did not elaborate.[18] We can, I think, safely agree with Wang Weicheng's identification of the text. He has marked all variants. My edition of the text by and large follows his.

WANG BI'S *LZWZLL*
AND THE TRANSMITTED TEXT

Is the transmitted *LZWZLL* all or a part of Wang Bi's original text? The long quotation from Zhang Junfang's encyclopedia appears in full in the *Daozang* text. There is no known quotation that does not appear there. The *Daozang* edition formally separates the text into two sections by ending one line before the low end is reached. Professor Wang infers from this that the *Daozang* text is the edition in two *juan*. A Song source quoted above mentions that the text is subdivided into eighteen *zhang* 章, a number of which would then together form a *juan* 卷; Wang Bi's study of the *Zhouyi*, the *Zhouyi lüeli* 周易略例, is subdivided into *zhang*; so is the *Laozi*, according to Wang Bi. No dots of the kind seen in the Guodian and Mawangdui manuscripts of the *Laozi* and the Former Han manuscript of the *Xici* survive.[19] The *Zhouyi lüeli* might provide a precedent for the *LZWZLL*. The *zhang* there average 400 characters, each *zhang* carrying its own title. To find out whether and where such subdivisions into *zhang* might have been, the structure of IPS might be of help, because it marks the ends of a segment or pericope by a transition to a different a/b pair, the breaking point often indicated by a general statement of principle marked by the particle *fu* 夫.

The first such break occurs in phrase 1.51, giving 393 characters to the pericope. The second deals with epistemological questions and polemics; it is not based on a single a/b pair and ends in phrase 2.69 with 634 characters. There is a probable insert in elements 2.33 through 42. The *you* 又 after phrase 2.69 does not mean "furthermore" in the sense of an additional argument but marks the beginning of a further quotation from the same original text, a common practice. The pericope seems to end in phrase 3.10, leaving it with 162 characters. The first pericope of the second section after the optical divide ends with 282 characters after phrase 4.26, based on the same a/b pair as the very first pericope. The fifth has 162 characters and repeats the parallelism by echoing the second in dealing with name/designation. The sixth and last has 943 characters, including an enclosed essay. It mostly deals with the analysis of the first phrases of *Laozi* 19. Its polemic thrust is directed against a reductive reading of the *Laozi* as advocating the abandonment of all cultural values, a reading present with direct reference to *Laozi* 19 in Ban Gu's introduction to the *Daojia* in his *Hanshu*.[20]

A number of themes treated extensively in the *Laozi Commentary* receive much less attention in the *LZWZLL*, especially the more strictly philosophical exploration of the relationship between entities and negativity. A check of the *Laozi* quotations in the surviving elements of the *LZWZLL*, however, remained inconclusive. The *LZWZLL* quotes twenty-eight of the *Laozi*'s *zhang* or alludes to them directly. Only a few passages are analyzed in great depth. The *LZWZLL* rests on the assumption of the simultaneous presence of the entire *Laozi* in its readers' minds; it draws freely on material argued in all parts of the *Laozi* and inserts it into its own argumentative and structural grid. Even allowing for a wide margin of error, we have to assume that the present text with six *zhang* or sections thereof is substantially shorter than the edition in eighteen *zhang*, and the *Daozang* text is best read as a series of well-wrought pericopes and fragments thereof; the further selection and reduction made in the *Yunji qiqian* compared to the *Daozang* edition show that the sequence of argument is usually maintained in such excerpting. The beginning of the *LZWZLL*, as it has been transmitted, looks like the actual beginning of the original text. The last segment quoted also looks like a good candidate for a concluding *zhang* with its summary statements of the ultimate purport of the *Laozi*. If these two assumptions were true, the overall structure of the *LZWZLL* would be different from the *Zhouyi lüeli*. The later *zhang* of the *Zhouyi lüeli* are devoted to particular problems of *Zhouyi* analysis and do not pretend to operate on the same level of high abstraction as the beginning *zhang*. Consequently, we cannot expect a summary statement at the end of the *Zhouyi lüeli*.

The transmission of the *LZWZLL* in Daoist collections might account for the absence of polemics against the Daojia in the text. The quality of transmission is very high. The two excerpts in our hand have few deviations from each other and require practically no editorial intervention.

THE GENRE OF THE *LZWZLL*

The elements *li* 例, *lüe* 略, and *zhi* 指 appeared in the titles of literary works since the Later Han and the Sanguo period; they purported to elucidate both the structure and meaning of classical texts systematically. The Tang writer Xing Shou 邢璹 explains the meaning of *lüeli* 略例 in his *Commentary* to Wang Bi's *Zhouyi lüeli*:

> *Lüeli* is a term comprehensively explaining the structure (*gang-mu* 綱目) and a designation of systematically illuminating the literary organization (*wenli* 文理) of a work. . . . [Wang Bi] wrote the *[Zhouyi] lüeli* in order to refute the errors of the different schools and to give a systematical exposition of the entire organization [of the *Zhouyi*].[21]

He Shao assigns similar functions to the *LZWZLL*, saying that Wang Bi "wrote the *Commentary* to the *Laozi* and made a *Zhilüe* about it which manages to arrive at a systematic exposition 致有理統."[22] The many polemics in the actual text also confirm the third feature mentioned by Xing Shou.

The element *zhi* 指, "to point," is taken by Wang Bi in a more verbatim sense than by some of his predecessors.[23] However, Dong Zhongshu 董仲舒 (179–104 B.C.E.) uses it in an analysis of the indirect language of the *Chunqiu* 春秋. Dong argues that the *Chunqiu* does not explicitly condemn war but through various descriptive techniques arrives at a sophisticated and more realistic assessment of the different types of war. To understand this, it does not make sense to stare at the words, *ci* 辭, of the *Chunqiu*. He writes, "the words are not able to achieve this [to communicate this complex thought], all is in what [the *Chunqiu*] is pointing at 辭不能及皆在於指." In this sense "he who sees what [the *Chunqiu*'s expressions] are pointing at, will not put the weight on the [particular] words, and only if he does not put the weight on its [particular] words, will it be possible to go along with it [the *Chunqiu*] on the Way 見其指者不任其辭不任其辭然後可與適道矣."[24]

The intrinsic structure of the recondite object of the *Laozi*'s reflection does not permit definition, thus it can only be "pointed at," and the *zhang* of the *Laozi* are such pointers toward an undefinable center. "He, however, who imposes a discursive analysis upon the textual patterns of the *Laozi* will miss what he points at (*zhi*) 然則老子之文欲辯而詰者則失其旨也," Wang Bi says.[25]

His structural analysis thus rebuts commentaries of the *zhangju* 章 句 kind, laying bare the structure of the *Laozi* as part of an answer to the problem ontology has with language. Within Liu Xie's categories in his *Wenxin diaolong*, the *LZWZLL* is a subgenre of the *lun* 論. Liu defines the genre *lun* at the beginning of the chapter devoted to it: "The patterns and regulations of the Sage's time are called *jing* 經, while explanations of the classics' structure (*xuli* 敘理) are called *lun* 論."[26]

The *LZWZLL* forms that subgenre of *lun* that emphasizes *wen* 文, "literary refinement." Liu calls the *LZWZLL* and other *lun* by He Yan 何 晏, Xiahou Xuan 夏侯玄 , Xi Kang 嵇康, Wang Can 王粲, and Fu Jia 傅 假 the "heroes among the *lun*, containing the individual insights of these masters' hearts, the epitome of subtle secrets." With an image borrowed from Wang Bi, he describes the *lun* as the "weir and trap of the hundred thoughts, the weigh and beam for the ten thousand affairs. Thus, as far as meaning goes, [the *lun*] cherish the well-rounded and communicable, and as for formulation, they shun branching off as well as scattered fragments. One must achieve harmony between thought and [literary] structure and arrange it so that no one can see any cracks. When the formulations cohere and the thoughts are dense, the opponents do not know on what to base [an objection]—these are the essentials" [of the genre *lun*].[27]

The *lun* has thus acquired its own philosophic and literary stringency, and the *LZWZLL* is said to excel in this respect. The *LZWZLL* is of twofold importance, as the earliest and most important analysis of the "Structure of the *Laozi*'s Pointers," and as a philosophic treatise in its own right. In my opinion, the *LZWZLL* is the most important surviving Chinese philosophic treatise of the third century.

Wang Bi is not the first to assign a specific purpose and function to the overall structure of a text. The "wings" attached to the *Zhouyi*, especially the *Xici* and *Shuogua*, have pioneered this approach with an analysis of the philosophical implications of the structure of the hexagrams and of their sequence.[28] During the Han dynasty, the *Xici*, with their quotations from "the master," were regarded as works by Confucius with a concomitant rise in the status of this text and of this type of endeavor. The *Great Preface* to the *Shijing* interprets the grouping of the songs into various categories by Confucius as a signal that they belonged to different times and circumstances and reacted to them in terms of their subject matter, their attitude, and their literary devices. They would be songs of praise when the ruler was a Sage and the Dao was prevailing, and they would get more critical with a ruler who failed to live up to the high standard of the Sage, which they kept as their measuring rod, but they also would be forced to use oblique, indirect language in their criticism, because this type of ruler was likely to react harshly to their remonstrance. With a hopelessly

wayless ruler, they would just sigh sadly. For each type of song a different reading strategy was required.[29] Zhuang Zun seems to have been the
first to apply a reading strategy based on the *Xici* model to the *Laozi*; his
own renown and that of his *Laozi* commentary and *Laozi zhigui* 老子指
歸 remained strong throughout the second and third centuries. Wang Bi's
reading often followed the basic track of Zhuang Zun without in any way
going along with his philosophic analysis.[30] With his *Laozi zhigui*, we have
a direct precursor of Wang Bi's *LZWZLL* in terms of genre and subject
matter.

Zhuang Zun wrote a short but highly specific analysis of the structure
of the *Laozi* that is transmitted as a sort of preface to his *Laozi zhigui* under
the title *[Yan] Junping on the Structure of the Two Classical [Chapters of
the Laozi], Junping shuo erjing mu* 君平說二經目.[31] We have to assume
that Zhuang Zun was familiar with the instability of the number of *zhang*
into which the *Laozi* was divided, as well as of the sequence of the *zhang*;
although he himself proposed a number of *zhang*, namely, seventy-two, that
differed from the number contained in the Mawangdui manuscripts and
from the eighty-one *zhang* into which Liu Xiang is supposed to have divided
the *Laozi*, he still was willing to claim for his own number and division
into two *pian* that this was *Laozi*'s original design, and that furthermore
it had a profound meaning. Zhuang Zun opened his analysis with the
statement: "In former times Laozi's work took *Dao* and *De* as the mother
that was causing the transformations, and he took Heaven and Earth as
the image in the imitation of which he was establishing the arrangement
of [his] classic" [i.e., the two chapters of his work] 昔者老子之作也變化
所由道德爲母效經列首天地爲象. As a consequence he linked the forty
zhang of his "upper classic," which would correspond to *zhang* 38–81 in
the current editions, to the numbers associated with Heaven and *Yang*,
and the "lower classic," which would correspond to *zhang* 1–37 in the
current editions, to the number associated with the Earth and *Yin*. From
this he deduced that the "upper classic" was dealing with the "future,"
lai 來, the "lower classic" with the past, *wang* 往. Understanding the
structure of the *Laozi* would establish for "the knowledgeable," *zhizhe* 智
者, a metatext enabling them to "understand the functions of Heaven and
Earth, the line-up of Yin and Yang, the matching of husband and wife, the
close relationship between father and son, as well as the proper behavior
for ruler and minister; [in short, the totality] of the ten thousand kinds
of entities is being laid out" [in this text][32] 通天地之數陰陽之紀父婦之
配父子之親君臣之儀萬物敷矣. Zhuang Zun had announced through
the parallel construction of the first phrase of this preface that the *Laozi*
contained two levels of information, namely, the analysis of the changes
and transformations of the world with the instrument of the explicit verbal

categories of *Dao* and *De*, and the more global analysis contained in the silent patterns of the structure. The parallelism of the two statements is a formal indication that they operate on the same level. Within this totalistic—and in terms of social values quite conservative—reading, the explicit analysis and implicit structure of the *Laozi* become the complete source for the understanding of the structures governing both the universe ("Heaven and Earth") and society.

The title of Wang Bi's "The Structure of the *Laozi*'s Subtle Pointers" seems to engage and directly challenge Zhuang Zun. Yes, there is a structure; yes, it has meaning; but the pointers are "subtle" and not to be subjected to a crude binary Yin/Yang analysis for which the text itself does not offer any support. The *Laozi*'s "subtle pointers" have one single focus; using a variety of structures within the realm of entities, they all point to a common center that structurally defies verbalization and can be approached only through pointers anchored in the realm of entities. There is no difference between the two sections of the *Laozi*, and there is no difference between the ultimate purport of each one of the *zhang*. In terms of method, Zhuang Zun's approach leads astray as it focuses the reader on the surface text as well as the presumed yin/yang structures of the "upper" and "lower" classic. Instead, the proper handling of the *Laozi* is not to stare at the surface text and structure but to deal with its *zhang* as one deals with a pointer, namely, to look into the direction to which it points.

THE *LAOZI*'S STRUCTURE
ACCORDING TO THE *LZWZLL*

The *LZWZLL* extracts from the *Laozi* itself the adequate strategy of reading this text. The *Laozi* warns the reader with a plethora of markers about the unreliability and tentativeness of its language. Quite apart from the well-known reflections on the inability to name the *Dao*, the text constantly repeats formulae such as "I call this" 是謂 . . . , which injects a tentative, unreliable quality. The great variety of topics in the *Laozi* all focus on the same issue. Accordingly, the individual passages must be read in the context of other attempts to express the same thought and must be read from the point they are pointing at, not according to their surface verbiage. This justifies an implosive as opposed to an extensive reading strategy. As I have tried to show in my study of Wang Bi's technique of commenting, the *LZWZLL* establishes the theoretical fundament for the *Commentary*.[33] Going beyond the description of the *Laozi*'s writing strategy, Wang Bi then proceeds to develop explicitly in his own language what he sees as the core notions of the *Laozi* and to spell out in an inserted essay, 6.2 ff., how these core notions would translate into a philosophically guided political practice of a ruler bent on curbing dissonance and conflict in All Under Heaven.

Wang Bi was writing in an intellectual environment where the status of the *Laozi* was matched only by the *Zhouyi*. Among the Wei intelligentsia, the *Laozi* was not a Daoist schoolbook but part of the common philosophical heritage, a challenge to every thinker, whatever his or her particular leanings. The *LZWZLL* accordingly enters into a lively polemic with other readings, which it denounces not because of their creeds but because of their misguided methodology in reading the *Laozi*. They cling to the surface text, attach themselves to individual statements or even terms, and instead of discerning the philosophical core of the entire text, reduce it to the advocacy of a particular school's teaching. "Hence, he who imposes discursive analysis upon the [particular] textual patterns of the *Laozi* will miss what he points at; and he who wishes to put the weight on the [particular] term [under consideration] will deviate from [the *Laozi*'s overall] meaning," the *LZWZLL* 2.43 writes before defining the "core" of the *Laozi* and then proceeding to show in 2.45 ff. in what methodically misguided manner the "schools" have mauled the text. Going far beyond the *Laozi*'s own statements, Wang Bi then proceeds to articulate in explicit philosophic language the implications of the *Laozi*'s practice in terms of a philosophy of language (2.20ff. and 5.14 ff.).

A third point emerges from the *LZWZLL*. Wang Bi's own philosophical architecture with its basic binary grid articulates itself as the systematization of the *Laozi*'s implications. Laozi thus appears as a thinker with a well-ordered system of categories in his head, but since they are not the focus of his philosophical attention, they are not always fully spelled out. While in many cases Wang Bi can base himself on a binary construct in the *Laozi* itself, there are other cases where, in terms of explicit statements, only half of what he would need is provided by the *Laozi*. Wang Bi here simply supplies the missing part in strict IPS analogy. Again, in many cases, this does not seem a heavy imposition; the general binary framework eliminates the problems in passages such as that of the very first phrase in *Laozi* 1, with the loss of an important, possibly fertile anomaly in the text that might have had some better use. In this proceeding, Wang Bi operates with complete control over the text and the ramifications of the individual passages as explained in his *Commentary*. Not a single passage is read differently in the *LZWZLL* from the reading in the *Commentary*.

The *LZWZLL* thus integrates three different analytic approaches. It is philological in developing a reading strategy based on the indications in the text itself. It is philosophical in inserting itself into a philosophical enterprise, the *Laozi*, but it develops out of the careful reading of its insights its own systematized philosophic arguments. And it is political in developing from the first two approaches a philosophically guided political science, which explores the dialectics of social and political behavior in a strongly hierarchical society.

THE BASIS FOR THE EDITION OF THE TEXT

The text in the edition included here is based on

- *Laozi weizhi lilüe* 老子微旨例略 in 2,552 characters contained in the *Zhengtong Daozang*;

- the excerpts from the *Laojun zhigui lüeli* 老君指歸略例 in 1,350 characters contained in Zhang Junfang's *Yunji qiqian* (they overlap with *zhang* 1–5 of the separate edition);

- critical notes on the text contained in the following works:

  a. Wang Weicheng, "Wei Wang Bi zhuan *Laozi zhilüe* yiwen zhi fa-xian"

  b. Yan Lingfeng, "Laozi weizhi lilüe jiaozi," in Yan Lingfeng, *Laozi weizhi lilüe*, as well as his notes on this text in his *Lao Zhuang yanjiu* (1959) postface, 413, and *Lao Zhuang yanjiu* (1966), 636

  c. Zhongguo kexueyuan zhexue yanjiusuo, Zhongguo zhexueshi Beijing daxue zhexueshi jiaoyanshi, eds., *Zhongguo lidai zhexue wenxuan, liang Han Sui Tang bian*, 308 ff.

  d. Lou Yulie, ed., *Wang Bi ji jiaoshi*, 195–210 (this work is largely based on *a* and *c*)

TRANSLATION OF THE *LZWZLL*

The translation is based on my study on IPS.[34] The standard form is:

(1) a   (2) b

(3) a   (4) b

(5) c

The numbers give the sequential order of the phrases, the letters *a* and *b* the two chains, respectively, and the letter *c*, in the middle, contains argumentative elements without parallelism referring to both chains. Phrases written on the same level are parallel.

There are three standard variants to this basic form. The first is the sequence *ab ba c* instead of *ababc*:

(1) a	(2) b
(4) a	(3) b

(5) c

The second is the parallel "staircase" of the form

a

    b

        c

            d . . .

a

    b

        c

            d . . .

The IPS comes in an open and a closed form. In the former, the phrases belonging to one chain (e.g., *a*) explicitly refer to each other by using the same vocabulary. In the closed form, no such explicit reference exists; the link is by implication. Given the possibility of the variant *ab ba*, this often leads to problems of attribution of individual phrases to one of the two chains.

Chang Chung-yue has included a translation of the *LZWZLL* into his unpublished dissertation in 1979. It is very unsatisfactory. My own translation was published in 1986, and Richard Lynn produced another translation in 1999.[35] Although Lynn was aware of the earlier translations, he decided to go his own way and has not engaged in a critical and detailed discussion with his predecessors. The result is a translation that instead of correcting the mistakes and weaknesses in the earlier attempts makes full use of the privilege to impose its own readings, and repeat the mistakes of Lou Yulie's edition. We thus have *zhang* split right down the middle (5 and 6) to the point that a *zhang* starts with "however," a disregard for rhetorical conventions of Wang Bi's such as 是以 and 是故 being read as logical links addressed to the reader instead of references to a known passage in the *Laozi* with the meaning "this is the reason" [why

Laozi says] and otherwise a disregard for the stringent rules of IPS. The translation is informed by the same unproved, and my view unfounded, assumption that the text is engaging the reader in a personal and didactic communication and time and again suffers from a lack of familiarity with the philosophic debates of the time. I confess to be saddened by the fact that such parallel worlds continue to exist, and that our field is still immature enough to treat such translations as personal exercises without the need for critical engagement.

WANG BI: THE STRUCTURE OF THE *LAOZI*'S POINTERS

Note: The quotations from the *Laozi* are taken from the critical edition of Wang Bi's *Laozi* inserted before the translations of the *zhang*. The *Laozi* quotations are taken from my translation.

王弼　老子微指略例 (Base text 老子微旨例略)

[第一章] PART A *Zhang* 1[1]

夫[a]物之所以生，功之所以成，必生乎無形，[b]由乎無名。無形無名者，萬物之宗也。不溫不涼，不宮不商。聽之不可得而聞，視之不可得而彰，體之不可得而知，味之不可得而嘗。故其爲物也則混成，爲象也則無形，爲音也則希聲，爲味也則無呈。故能爲品物之宗主，包通天地，[c]靡使不經也。若溫也則不能涼矣，宮也則不能商矣。形必有所分，聲必有所屬。故象而形者，非大象也，音而聲者，非大音也。然則，四象不形，則大象無以暢；五音不聲，則大音無以至。四象形而物無所主焉，則大象暢矣；五音聲而心無所適焉，則大音至矣。故執大象則天下往，用大音則風俗移也。[d]無形暢，天下雖往，往而不能釋也；希聲至，風俗雖移，移而不能辯也。是故天生五物，無物爲用。聖行五教，不言爲化。是以道可道，非常道；名可名，非常名也。五物之母，不炎不寒，不柔不

---

[a] 夫 for 天: 雲笈七籤.　　　　　　[b] Var.: 形形 for 形: 雲笈七籤.

[c] 包通天地 for 苞通: 雲笈七籤. Support for 包: Wang Bi on *Laozi* 16.6: 乃能包通萬物. Wang Bi on *Laozi* 35.1: 故能包通萬物. 天地 and 萬物 are used interchangeably, so that the two quotations from Wang Bi's *Commentary* support the 雲笈七籤 version, although one would rather have expected a 包通萬物.

[d] Var.: 移 for 移也: 雲笈七籤.

剛：五教之母，不皦不昧，不恩不傷。雖古今不同，時移俗易，此
不變也；所謂自古及今，其名不去者也。天不以此，則物不生；治
不以此，則功不成。故古今通，終始同；執古可以御今，證ᶜ今可
以知古始；此所謂常者也。無皦昧之狀，溫涼之象，故知常曰明
也。物生功成，莫不由乎此，故以閲眾甫也。

(1) It is generally true with regard to[2]

(2) that by which things are created—

(3) that by which achievements are brought about—

(4) that [things] are necessarily created out of the "featureless";

(5) that [achievements] are [necessarily] based on the "nameless."[3]

(6) The featureless and nameless is [what the *Laozi* calls] the "ancestor of the ten thousand kinds of entities."[4]

(7) [Being featureless,] it neither warms nor cools.[5]

(8) [Being nameless,] it neither [lets sound forth the notes] *gong* or *shang*.[6]

(9) [Even when] "listening for it," one is [still] unable to "hear it."

(10) [Even when] "looking for it," one is [still] unable to perceive it.

(11) [Even when] groping for it, one is [still] unable to identify it.

(12) [Even when] going after its taste, one is [still] unable to get its flavor.[7]

(13) That is why [the *Laozi* says about the Dao]

(14) "as a thing" it "completes out of the diffuse,"[8] as an "image" it is "without form";[9]

(15) as a "sound" it "has an inaudible tone,"[10]as a "taste" it is without flavor.[11]

(16) That is why it is able to be

the "principle" and

the "master"[12]

ᶜ 證 for 御: 雲笈七籤.

of all [different] categories of
entities,[13] to cover and
permeate Heaven and Earth[14]
so that there is nothing that
it does not thread through.[15]

(17 [For the fact is,] would it be
warming, then it would not be
able to cool.[16]

(18) [For the fact is,] would it
[be tied to letting sound forth
the note] *gong*, then it would
not be able to [let sound forth
the note] *shang*.[17]

[This is so because]

(19) A form necessarily has
something that specifies it.

(20) A note necessarily has [a
place in the scale] to which it
belongs.[18]

(21) That is why [according
to the *Laozi*]

(22) an image that has taken on
form is not the "Great Image."[19]

(23) a sound that has taken on a
note is not the "Great Sound."[20]

(24) If, however,

(25) the Four Images[21] did not
take on form, then the "Great
Image" would have nothing
in which to shine forth;

(26) the Five Sounds did not
take on notes, then the "Great
Sound" would have nothing
in which to come about.[22]

[Thus]

(27) when the Four Images take
on form and beings have nothing
[else] by which they are
dominated, then the Great Image
shines forth.

(28) when the Five Sounds take
on notes and the minds have
nothing [else] which interferes
with them, then the Great
Sound comes about.[23]

(29) That is why [the *Laozi* says]:

(30) "If [the ruler were to] hold on
to the Great Image," [then] "All
Under Heaven [would] come
[to him]!"[24]

(31) if [a ruler were to] make
use of the Great Sound, then
the customs and habits would
change for the better.[25]

(32) As it is the formless that is [would
be] shining forth, although All Under
Heaven is coming to him, this coming
"to" they [the people] are [would]
not [be] able to explain.

(33) As it is the toneless that is
[would be] coming about,
although the customs and habits
do change for the better, this
change [the people] are [would]

(34) Thus:

not [be] able to analyze.[26]

(35) Heaven creates the Five Things,[27] but it is a no-thing[28] that brings about their usefulness.[29]

(36) the Sage [Confucius] spreads the Five Teachings, but it is "no-words" that bring about the improvement.[30]

(37) That is why [the *Laozi* says]:

(38) "A way that can be spoken of is not the eternal Way.

(39) A name that can be named is not the eternal name."[31]

(40) The mother of the Five Things is neither hot nor cold, neither soft nor hard.

(41) The mother of the Five teachings is neither "bright" nor "dark," neither compassionate nor harsh.[32]

(42) Although old and new are not the same, the times have changed and the habits differ, she has not changed. This is what [the *Laozi*] calls "from antiquity to the present her name has not disappeared."[33]

(43) If Heaven would not rely on her, then beings would not be created.

(44) If government would not rely on her, then achievements would not be brought about.[34]

(45) Therefore, that as antiquity and present are connected, and as end and beginning have the same [structure] "it is possible [for a Sage Ruler] holding [today] on to . . . antiquity to regulate [occurrences of] the present,"[35] and, taking the present as evidence "[he] has something by which to cognize the oldest beginning,"[36] is what [the *Laozi*] styles "the Eternal."[37] As it has neither

(46) a "bright" nor a "dark" appearance,

(47) a warming nor a cooling feature,

(48) that is why [the *Laozi*
says]: "Having knowledge
of [this] Eternal means
being enlightened!"[38]

(49) In the creation of beings,

(50) In the completion of
achievements,

(51) there is nothing that
is not based on this
[Eternal]. That is why
[the *Laozi* says]: "By means
of it one discerns the
beginning of the many."[39]

[第二章] *Zhang 2*

夫奔電之疾猶不足以一時周，御風之行猶不足以一息期。善速在
不疾，善至在不行。故可道之盛，未足以官天地；有形之極，未足
以府萬物。是故歎之者不能盡乎斯美，[a] 詠之者不能暢乎斯弘。名
之不能當，稱之不能既。名必有所分，稱必有所由。有分則有不
兼，有由則有不盡；不兼則大殊其眞，不盡則不可以名，此可演而
明也。夫道也者，取乎萬物之所由也；玄也者，取乎幽冥之所出
也；深也者，取乎探賾而不可究也；大也者，取乎彌綸而不可極
也；遠也者，取乎綿[b]邈而不可及也；微也者，取乎幽微而不可覩
也。然則道，玄，深，大，微，[c]遠之言，各有其義，未盡其極者
也。然彌綸無極，不可名細；微妙無形，不可名大。是以篇[d]云：
字之曰道，謂之曰玄，而不名也。然則，言之者失其常，名之者離
其眞，爲之者[e]則敗[f]其性，執之者[g]則失其原矣。是以聖人不以言爲
主，則不違其常；不以名爲常，則不離其眞；不以爲爲事，則不敗
其性；不以執爲制，則不失其原矣。然則，老子[h]之文，欲辯而
詰[i]者，則失其旨也；欲名而責者，則違其義也。故其大歸也，論
太始之原以明自然之性，演幽冥之極以定惑罔之迷。因而不爲，

---

[a] 美 for 羨: 雲笈七籤.
[b] Var.: 緬 for 綿: 雲笈七籤.
[c] Var.: 妙 for 微: 雲笈七籤.
[d] Var.: 經 for 篇: 雲笈七籤.
[e] Var.: 者 om.: 雲笈七籤.
[f] Var.: 窒 for 敗: 雲笈七籤.
[g] Var.: 者 om.: 雲笈七籤.
[h] Var.: 君 for 子: 雲笈七籤.
[i] Var.: 誥 for 詰: 雲笈七籤.

順[i]而不施；崇本以息末，守母以存子；賤夫巧術，爲在未有；無
責於人，必求諸己；此其大要也。而法者尙乎齊同，而刑[k]以檢
之。名者尙乎定眞，而名[l]以正之。儒者尙乎全愛，而譽以進之。
墨者尙乎儉嗇，而矯[m]以立之。雜者尙乎衆美，而總以行之。夫刑
以檢物，巧僞必生；名以正[n]物，理恕必失；譽以進物，爭尙必
起；矯以立物，乖違必作；雜以行物，穢亂必興。斯皆用其子而棄
其母。物失所載，未足守也。然致同而[o]塗異，至合而[p]趣[q]乖，而
學者惑其所致，迷其所趣[r]。觀其齊同，則謂之法；覩其定眞，則
謂之名；察其純愛，則謂之儒；鑒其儉嗇，則謂之墨；見其不係，
則謂之雜。隨其所鑒而正名焉，順其所好而執意焉。故使有紛紜
憒[s]錯之論，殊趣辯析[t]之爭，蓋由斯矣。

(1) It is a fact that [even]

(2) the speed of racing lightning is still insufficient to go full round in one single moment,	(3) advancing by riding on the wind is still insufficient to arrive in one single breath.[1]

[As the *Xici* says about the spirit]

(4) to be good at "being fast" lies in "not speeding."	(5) to be good at "arriving" lies in "not going."[2]

(6) Thus

(7) the bloom of [what Laozi calls] "that which can be spoken of"[3] is still insufficient to [in the *Zhuangzi*'s words] "administer Heaven and Earth."	(8) the maximum of that which has shape[4] is still insufficient [in the *Zhuangzi*'s words] to "store the ten thousand kinds of entities."[5]

---

[i] 順 for 損: 樓宇烈 on the basis of parallel to Wang Bi on *Laozi* 29.4: 故因而不爲順
而不施.

[k] Var.: 形 for 刑: 雲笈七籤.　　　[l] Var.: 言 for 名: 雲笈七籤.

[m] Var.: 智 for 矯: 雲笈七籤.

[n] 正 for 定: Wagner based on analogy. For all other schools, the term in the second
phrase is taken, namely, 檢, 進, 立 and 行; only for the Mingjia 名者 the term from the first
half—定—is taken instead of 正.

[o] 同而 for 同: 雲笈七籤. Support for 而: indirect quotation from 繫辭: 天下同歸而殊
塗一致而百慮.

[p] 合而 for 合: 雲笈七籤. Support for 而: see previous note.

[q] Var.: 趨 for 趣: 雲笈七籤.　　　[r] Var.: 趨 for 趣: 雲笈七籤.

[s] Var.: 憒 for 憒: 雲笈七籤.　　　[t] 析 for 拚: 雲笈七籤.

(9) That is why [even]

(10) he who sighs in admiration for it is unable indeed to fully account for such a beauty.

(11) he who sings in praise of it is unable indeed to expound such a width.

(12) Giving it a name is unable to match it.

(13) Giving it a designation is unable to fully grasp it.

(14) A name necessarily has something that makes it specific.

(15) A designation necessarily has something on which it is based.

(16) Having a specification, there will, as a consequence, be something that is not included.

(17) Having a base, there will, as a consequence, be something that is not exhausted.

(18) There being something not included, [the name], as a consequence, greatly deviates from its true [essence].

(19) There being something not exhausted, [the designation], as a consequence, cannot be taken as a name.[6]

(20) This can be further clarified. (Enclosed Essay: Names and Designations)

(21) It is a fact that

(22) "Dao" is taken for[7] [its aspect] of being that on which the ten thousand kinds of entities are based.[8]

(23) "Dark" is taken for [its aspect] of being that which lets the Recondite emanate.[9]

(24) "Deep" is taken for [its aspect] that, [even] when "delving into the abstruse" [in which according to the *Xici* the yarrow stalks and tortoise shells excel] it is impossible to get to [the] bottom of it.[10]

(25) "Great" is taken for [its] aspect that, [even if] one "fills it in and rounds it out [ever more]," [as the *Xici* says that the *Yi* 易 does concerning the Way of Heaven and Earth], it is [still] impossible to get to the ultimate point.[11]

(26) "Distant" is taken for [its aspect] that it is so wide and remote that it is impossible to reach it.[12]

(27) "Fine" is taken for [its aspect] that it is so recondite and fine that it is impossible to perceive it.[13]

(28) Thus of the words

"Way,"	"Dark,"
	"deep,"
"great,"	"fine," and
"distant"	

each has its meaning, but they
do not exhaust its totality.

(29) Thus

(30) it is impossible to give to that
which one "fills in and rounds out
[ever more]" without getting to the
ultimate point the name "minute."

(31) it is impossible to give to
that which is fine and subtle
and without form the name
"great."[14]

(32) That is why the
[*Laozi*] chapters say:

"I give it the style 'Way',"[15]   and   "[I] designate [it] the 'Dark',"[16]

but no name is given.

(33) Thus

(34) he who talks about it, misses its [All Under Heaven's] Eternal;

(35) he who gives a name to it, becomes separated from its [All Under Heaven's] true [nature];

(36) "he who interferes with it, destroys" its [All Under Heaven's] nature;

(37) "he who holds on to it, loses" its [All Under Heaven's] source.[17]

(38) That is why the Sage

(39) does not take words as the master so that he does not deviate from its [All Under Heaven's] Eternal;

(40) does not take a name for the Eternal so that he does not become separated from its [All Under Heaven's] true [nature];

(41) does not take actions for his business so that the does not destroy its [All Under Heaven's] nature;

(42) does not take holding onto for control, and thus does not lose its [All Under Heaven's] source.[18]

(43) Hence, he who imposes discursive analysis upon the [particular] textual patterns of the *Laozi* will

miss what he points at; and he
who wishes to put the weight
on the [particular] term [under
consideration] will [deviate from
the *Laozi*'s overall] meaning.[19]

(44) Thus it is the [*Laozi* text's]
great purport to expound the source
of the Great Beginning[20] in order
to elucidate the nature of That-
which-is-of-itself-what-it-is, and to
hold forth on the ultimate of the
Recondite in order to settle the
delusions of doubt and deception.[21]
To respond to, and not to act upon;
to adapt and not to initiate;[22]
to emulate the root by way of bringing
to rest its [the root's] outgrowth;[23]
to keep to the mother by way of
maintaining [her] offspring;[24]
to hold lightly indeed skill and arts
[of government as a means to
control the people];
"act [ondangers to one's life and
position as a ruler]" while "they
have not now come about;"[25]
not to "make demands on others" but
necessarily to make all [demands] on
oneself [as the lord][26]—these are his
[that is, Laozi's] key points.

(45) But

(46) the Legalists promote equality and egality, and then apply punishment
to supervise them [the people];

(47) the Name school promotes the fixation of the true, and then uses
terms to rectify them [the people];

(48) the Ru school promotes complete love, and then uses praise
to drive them [the people] on;

(49) the Mohists promote parsimony and simplicity, and
then use constraint to fixate them [the people] on this;

(50) the Eclectics promote all sorts of treats and use a
variety [of means] to let [the people] act accordingly.

(51) It is a fact that, when

(52) punishments are applied to supervise beings, craft and deceit will inevitably arise;[27]

(53) names are used to make beings orthodox, order and consideration will inevitably be lost;[28]

(54) praise is used to drive beings on, competition will inevitably arise;[29]

(55) enforced reform is used to settle beings, heresy and rebellion will inevitably ensue;

(56) mixed [treats] are used to make beings act, defilement and chaos will inevitably ensue.

57) All these schools make use of the offspring but discard its mother beings lose what so that supports them and cannot be guarded.[30]

(58) However, [to paraphrase the *Xici*, in the *Laozi*]

(59) the destination [of the various arguments] is the same, though the ways thither differ,[31]

(60) [the various arguments'] meanings coincide, but the approaches vary,

(61) but the scholars [from the different schools]

(62) are bewildered as to their [the arguments' common] destination.

(63) are befuddled as to their [the arguments' common] amount.

(64) When they observe them [some of the arguments in the *Laozi* advocating] equalizing, they style him [*Laozi*] Legalist;

(65) when they perceive them [some of the arguments in the *Laozi* advocating] delineating the true, they style him [*Laozi*] a member of the Name school;

(66) when they observe them [some of the *Laozi*'s arguments advocating] pure love, they style him [*Laozi*] a Ruist.

(67) when they perceive them [some of the arguments in the *Laozi* advocating] parsimony and simplicity, they style him a Mohist;

(68) when they see them [some of the arguments in the *Laozi* advocating] unsystematic [tenets], they style him an Eclecticist.

(69) According to what their eyes happen to perceive, they assign the

name; depending on what
they like, they cling to that
meaning. That there are
confused and faulty exegeses
and struggles between
different tendencies and
interpretations is caused
by this [faulty methodology
of other scholars].[32]

[第三章] *Zhang* 3

又：其爲文也，舉終以證始，本始ª以盡終；開而弗達，導而弗
牽。ᵇ尋而後既其義，推而後盡其理。善發事始以首其論，明夫會
歸以終其文。故使同趣而感發於事者，ᶜ莫不美其興言之始，因而演
焉；異旨而獨構ᵈ者，莫不說其會歸之徵，以爲證焉。夫途雖殊，
必同其歸；慮雖百，必均其致，而舉夫歸致以明至理，故使觸類而
思者，莫不欣其思之所應，以爲得其義焉。

(1) Furthermore [Wang Bi's treatise
says]: As for [the *Laozi*'s] literary
form, [its individual arguments] take
up the end by way of giving evidence
of the beginning, and root [them-
selves] in the beginning by way of
fully exhausting the end. [As the
Gentleman does according to the
Liji 禮記 in his teaching which
proceeds through metaphor 喻],
"they open up but do not go all the
way," "they show the way but do
not lead forward."[1]
[Thus,] it is only after careful
searching that one fully realizes
his meaning, and only after
making inferences does one
fully understand the principle
he [is pointing at].[2]

ª 本始 for 不述始: 雲笈七籤.   ᵇ 牽 for 率: 雲笈七籤.
ᶜ 感發於事者 for 感發者: 雲笈七籤.
ᵈ 構 for 搆: 雲笈七籤.

(2) Fine indeed his exposition of a theme's beginning with which he starts his exegesis!

(3) Brilliant truly his conclusion with which he ends his texts![3]

(4) Therefore,

(5) of those who are motivated by the same tendency [as *Laozi*,] there is none who does not relish his beginnings in which he makes the exposition, and they will proceed from there to elaborate.

(6) of those with a different orientation who compose writings on their own, there is none who does not enjoy the proofs with which he concludes, and they will take them as evidence.

(7) It is generally true [for the *Laozi*] that [as the *Xici* say]

(8) "the approaches" may "differ," but by necessity they will be "the same" in their "purport,"

(9) "the deliberations" may be a "hundredfold," but by necessity they are equal in their "destination,"[4]

(10) and he [*Laozi*] takes up indeed their

purport and destination

in order to elucidate the highest ordering principle.[5] Therefore, of those thinking about kindred things, there is none who does not delight in the correspondence [of the *Laozi*] with his [own] thoughts, surmising that he grasps the meaning thereof.

[第四章] PART B *Zhang* 4

凡物之所以存，乃反其形；功之所以尅，乃反其名。夫存者不以
存爲存，以其不忘亡也；安者不以安爲安，以其不忘危也。故保
其存者亡，不忘亡者存；安其位者危，不忘危者安。善力舉秋毫，
善聽聞雷霆，此道之與形反也。安者實安，而曰非安之所安；存者
實存，而曰非存之所存；侯王實尊，而曰非尊之所爲；[a] 天地實
大，而曰非大之所能；聖功實存，而曰絕聖之所立；仁德實著，而
曰棄仁之所存。故使見形而不及道者，莫不忿其言焉。夫欲定物
之本者，則雖近而必自遠以證其始。欲[b]明物之所由者，則雖顯而
必自幽以敘其本。故取天地之外，以明形骸之內；明侯王孤寡之

---

[a] Var.: 尊 for 爲: 雲笈七籤. 　　　　[b] Var.: 夫欲 for 欲: 雲笈七籤.

義，而從道一以宣其始。故使察近而不及流統之原者，莫不誕其言
以爲虛焉。是以云云者，各申其說，人美其亂。或迂其言，或譏其
論，若曉而昧，若分而亂，斯之由矣。

(1) Generally [speaking,][1]

(2) that by which beings persist is the negative opposite indeed to their form.

(3) that by which achievements are performed is the negative opposite indeed to their name.[2]

(4) It is a fact that

(5) he who persists does not take persistence for [the cause] of his persisting, but [his persisting is due] to his not forgetting about [the danger of] perishing!

(6) he who is secure does not take security for [the cause] of his being secure, but [his security is due] to his not forgetting about perils!

(7) That is why [to paraphrase the Sage, Confucius, in the *Xici*,]

(8) "he who guards his persistence" "perishes," while he who [like the Gentleman] "does not forget about [the danger of] perishing" "persists"!

(9) "he who secures his position" "is in peril," while he who [like the Gentleman] "does not forget about peril" "is secure"![3]

(10) [That] he who is [truly] good at strength [restricts himself to] lifting an autumn down,[4]

(11) [That] he who is [truly] good at hearing [restricts himself to] listening to the thunderclap,

(12) this is the negative opposition between Dao and form.[5]

(13) He who is secure is secure indeed, but [the *Laozi*] says he is secure through his refusal of [treating] security [as a given].[6]

(14) He who persists persists indeed, but [the *Laozi*] says he persists through his refusal of [treating] persistence [as a given].[7]

(15) Dukes and kings are elevated indeed, but [the *Laozi* says] this [their status] is brought about by [their] rejecting elevation.[8]

(16) Heaven and Earth are great indeed, but [it is] said that it [their greatness] is achieved through [their] rejection [of acting] great.[9]

(17) Achievements of [a ruler's] wisdom persist indeed, but [the *Laozi*] says they are established by [his] "discarding wisdom."[10]

(18) The capacity for benevolence is manifest indeed, but [the *Laozi*] says it persists through "discarding benevolence."[11]

(19) Therefore, among those who see the form but do not reach as far as the Dao, there is no one who does not loathe his [*Laozi*'s] words.

(20) It is a fact that

(21) he who wants to define the root of entities must, though they [the entities] be near, from afar give evidence of their beginning.

(22) he who wants to elucidate the basis of entities must, though these [entities] be evident, start from the recondite in order to point out their root.

(23) That is why [the *Laozi*]

(24) takes things external like Heaven and Earth in order to elucidate that which is inside the shape and bones [that is, the body].[12]

(25) elucidating the meaning of [the fact that] "dukes and kings" [style themselves] "orphaned and lonely," starts the deduction from the Dao and the One [in *Laozi* 42.1] in order to display the origin of this.[13]

(26) Therefore, among those researching that which is close at hand but not reaching to the source controlling the currents, there is none who does not dismiss his words as empty talk. Thus the babblers each proclaim their own theory while others enjoy their confusion. They either water down [the *Laozi*'s] words or ridicule [the *Laozi*'s] arguments. When the clear becomes obscure and the separate commingled—here is the reason!

[第五章] *Zhang 5*

名也者，定彼者也；稱也者，從謂者也。名生乎彼，稱出乎我。故
涉之乎無物而不由，則稱之曰道，求之乎無妙而不出，則謂之曰
玄。妙出乎玄，眾出乎道。故生之畜之，不禁[a]不塞，通物之性，
道之謂也。 生而不有，為而不恃，長而不宰，有德而無主，玄之

---

[a] 禁 for 壅: Wagner based on Wang Bi on *Laozi* 10.7 and 10.8 不塞其原也不禁其性
也, repeated with 禁 in Wang Bi on *Laozi* 10.9. The term 壅 does not occur in the surviving oeuvre of Wang Bi.

德也。玄，謂之深者也；道，稱之大者也。[1] 名號生乎形狀，稱謂
出乎涉求。名號不虛生，稱謂不虛出。故名號則大失其旨，稱謂則
未盡其極。是以謂玄則玄之又玄，稱道則域中有四大也。[2]

(1) A "name" is that which defines an object.

(2) A "designation" is an inferred style.[1]

(3) The name is born from the object.

(4) The designation comes from the subject.

(5) That is why[2]

(6) when concerned with it as that for which there is no entity which is not based on it, he [Laozi] designates it as "Dao."[3]

(7) when searching for it as that for which there is no subtlety which is not emanating from it, he [Laozi] styles it "the Dark."[4]

As

(8) the subtle emanates from the Dark,[5]

(9) the many are based on the Dao,[6]

(10) [the *Laozi*'s statement] that "it generates them and rears them"[7] [that is,] that it does not block [their source] and does not hem in [their nature] but permeates the nature of entities, refers to the Dao,

(11) [while the *Laozi*'s subsequent statement] [that,] "while they come alive, it has no [specific effort on its side] and, while they act, it does not make them dependent, [that, in short,] while they grow there would be no lording it over [their growth on its side]"—that they have a receipt [from it] but that there is no dominance [from it]—this is the "Receipt [coming from] That-which-is-Dark.[8]

(12) The Dark is the most profound of styles.[9]

(13) The Dao is the greatest of designations.[10]

(14) Names and marks are born from the forms and appearances.

(15) Designations and styles come out of the "being concerned with" and the searching.

(16) Names and marks are no hollow products.

(17) Designations and styles are no hollow emanations.

(18) That is why

(19) with names and marks one greatly misses its significance.

(20) with designations and styles one does not exhaust its absoluteness.

(21) For this reason,

(22) when styling it "Dark" [the *Laozi* says] "Dark and Dark again."[11]

(23) When designating it as "Dao" [the *Laozi* says] "in the Beyond there are four Great Ones."[12]

[第六章] *Zhang 6*

老子之書，其幾乎可一言而蔽之。噫！崇本息末而已矣。觀其所由，尋其所歸，言不遠宗，事不失主。文雖五千，貫之者一；義雖廣瞻，眾則同類。解其一言而蔽之，則無幽而不識；每事各為意，則雖辯而愈惑。嘗試論之曰：夫邪之興也，豈邪者之所為乎？淫之所起也，豈淫者之所造乎？故閑邪在乎存誠，不在善察；息淫在乎去華，不在滋ª章；絕盜在乎去欲，不在嚴刑；止訟存乎不尚，不在善聽。故不攻其為也，使其無心於為也；不害其欲也，使其無心於欲也。謀之於未兆，為之於未始，如斯而已矣。故竭聖智以治巧偽，未若見質素以靜民欲；興仁義以敦薄俗，未若抱樸以全篤實；多巧利以興事用，未若寡私欲以息華競。故絕司察，潛聰明，去勸進，翦華譽，棄巧用，賤寶貨，唯在使民愛欲不生，不在攻其為邪也。故見素樸以絕聖智，寡私欲以棄巧利，皆崇本以息末之謂也。夫素樸之道不著，而好欲之美不隱，雖極聰明ᵇ以察之，竭智慮以攻之，巧愈思精，偽愈多變，攻之彌深，避之彌勤，則乃智愚相欺，六親相疑，樸散眞離，事有其姦。蓋捨本而攻末，雖極聖智，愈致斯災，況術之下此者乎！夫鎮之以素樸，則無為而自正；攻之以聖智，則民窮而巧殷。故素樸可抱，而聖智可棄。夫察司之簡，

ª 滋 for 茲：嚴靈峯.

ᵇ 聰明 for 聖明：Wagner based on Wang Bi's use of 聰明 in comm. on *Laozi* 49.5 勞一身之聰明以察百姓之情.

則避之亦簡；竭其聰明，則逃之亦察。簡則害樸寡，察^c則巧偽深
矣。夫能爲至察探幽之術者，匪唯聖智哉？其爲害也，豈可既^d
乎！故百倍之利未渠多也。夫不能辯名，則不可與言理；不能定
名，則不可與論實也。凡名^e生於形，未有形生於名^f者也。故有此
名必有此形，有此形必有其分。仁不得謂之聖，智不得謂之仁，則
各有其實矣。夫察見至微者，明之極也；探射隱伏者，慮之極也。
能盡極明，匪唯聖乎？能盡極慮，匪唯智乎？校實定名，以觀絕
聖，可無惑矣。夫敦樸之德不著，而名行之美顯尚，則脩其所尚而
望其譽，脩其所顯^g而冀其利。望譽冀利以勤其行，名彌美而誠愈
外，利彌重而心愈競。父子兄弟，懷情失直，孝不任誠，慈不任
實，蓋顯名行之所招也。患俗薄而興名行崇仁義，^h愈致斯僞，況
術之賤此者乎？故絕仁棄義以復孝慈，未渠弘也。夫城高則衝生，
利興則求深。苟存無欲，則雖賞而不竊；私欲苟行，則巧利愈昏。
故絕巧棄利，代以寡欲，盜賊ⁱ無有，未足美也。夫聖智，才之傑
也；仁義，行之大者也；巧利，用之善也。本苟不存，而興此三
美，害猶如之，況術之有利斯以忽素樸乎！故古人有歎曰：甚矣，
何物之難悟也！既知不聖爲不聖，未知聖之爲不聖也；^j既知不仁
爲不仁，未知仁之爲不仁也。故絕聖而後聖功全，棄仁而後仁德
厚。夫惡強非欲不強也，爲強則失強也；絕仁非欲不仁也，爲仁則
僞成也。有其治而乃亂，保其安而乃危。後其身而身先，身先非先
身之所能也；外其身而身存，身存非存身之所爲也。功不可取，美
不可用，故必取其爲功之母而已矣。篇云：既知其子，而必復守其
母。尋斯理也，何往而不暢哉！

(1) The book of Laozi can almost
[as Confucius said about the
Shijing] "be summed up in one
phrase," ah:[1] Emulating the root
[by way] of bringing to rest the
stem and branches [growing from
it]—that is all![2]

---

^c 察 for 密: Wagner based on parallel 簡–察 in parallel phrases.

^d 既 for 記: 嚴靈峯 based on *Laozi* 35.3 用之不可既 and Wang Bi's commentary there
用之不可窮極也.

^e 名 for 民: 王維誠.   ^f 名 for 民: 王維誠.

^g 顯 for 道: Wagner. In a parallel to the previous phrase that takes up the 尚 of the 名
行之美顯尚, this phrase takes up the 顯.

^h 興名行崇仁義 for 名興行崇仁義: 樓宇烈 based on *LZWZLL* above 顯名行.

ⁱ 賊 for 則: 王維誠.

In observing on what [the ten
thousand kinds of entities] are
based, and in investigating whereto
[they] return, [Laozi's] "words"
do not depart from "the principle,"
and [his] activities do not lose
[sight] of "the ruler" [as Laozi
says about himself].³
Although the [*Laozi*] text has
five thousand characters, what
"threads through them" is the
"One" [as is the case for the
Dao of Confucius].⁴ Although
[its] ideas are broad and far-flung,
in their multitude they are of the
same kind. Once it is understood
that it can be "summed up in one
phrase," there is nothing recondite
that is not discerned; but when
each theme is [interpreted] as
having a [separate] meaning, then,
analytic skill notwithstanding,
the delusions will only increase.

[Enclosed essay on the rise of depravity and debauchery and the ways
against them]

(2) [I will] venture to analyze
this:

(3) The rise of depravity—how could   (4) The development of
it be the work of the depraved?   debauchery—how could it be
                                               operated by the debauched?

(5) [It cannot.] That is why

(6) [as Confucius says] "warding off   (7) bringing debauchery to rest
depravity" lies in "holding on to   lies in keeping [oneself as a
sincerity [as a ruler],"⁵ not in the   ruler] aloof from embellish-
improvement of surveillance.   ments, and not in displaying
                                               more beautiful objects.⁶

(8) Stopping robbery lies in keeping   (9) Stopping litigation lies in not
aloof of desires [oneself as the ruler,]   honoring [worthies oneself], not
not in making punishments harsher.⁷   in listening better [to charges].⁸

(10) That is why [a Sage
Ruler]

(11) does not attack their [the people's] desires, but brings it about that they do not have any inclination towards desires.

(12) does not thwart their [the people's] actions, but brings it about that they have no inclination to act.

(13) [According to the *Laozi*] "to take precautions" "as long as there are still no signs [of a danger to his life]" and "to act on [dangers] while they have not yet" begun—that is all!⁹

[End of Enclosed Essay]

(14) Therefore,

(15) to exert wisdom and intelligence in order to regulate tricks and pretensions does not compare to "manifesting" simplicity and "plainness" in order to calm down people's desires;

(16) to promote benevolence and justice in order to destroy the shallow and vulgar does not compare to "embracing the unadorned" in order to complete the sound and real;

(17) to multiply skill and profit interests in order to raise the utility of affairs does not compare to the "diminishing" of "egotism" and "desires" [in oneself] in order to bring the competition for adornments to rest.¹⁰

(18) Therefore, [the *Laozi*'s advocating the]

(19) cutting off of surveillance and the submerging of one's intelligence,

(20) elimination of encouragement and promotion, and the cutting off of adornments and eulogies,

(21) and the dismissal of skills and utility as well as the despising of precious goods

(22) all have only the purpose of preventing the people's craving [for fame] and desires [for goods] from being born, but they do not emphasize attacks on their being depraved. Therefore, manifesting simplicity and being unadorned for the benefit of cutting off wisdom and intelligence, reducing egotism and desires for the benefit of dis-

carding skill and profit interests—
these are all but styles for "emulating the root by way of bringing
to rest the stem and branches"
[growing from it].

(23) It is a fact that if the Dao
of the plain and unadorned
does not shine forth while the
amenities of predilections and
desires are not hidden, [the
ruler] might

(24) go to extremes with his wisdom
and enlightenment in the attempt to
keep them [the people] under
surveillance,

(25) exhaust [his] intelligence
and wit in the attempt to
attack them [the people],

(26) but

(27) the more refined [his] skills are,
the more variegated their [the
people's] pretensions will become,

28) the more intensely his
attacks on them
proceed, the more efforts they
will make to evade him,[11]

(29) and then, indeed, the dull-
witted and the intelligent will get
the better of each other, the [rela-
tives in] the six relationships
will distrust each other, the "unadorned disperses" [*Laozi* 28.6],
and they become separated from
the[ir] true [nature], and there is
debauchery in [all] affairs. Once
the root is abandoned and [its]
outgrowth is attacked, wisdom
and intelligence might be applied
to the maximum; there will only
be more sure disasters—and how
much greater [will they be] when
[a ruler's] art is inferior to this
[maximum wisdom and intelligence]!
If [, on the other hand,] one [as does
the Sage according to *Laozi* 37.3,]
"would quiet them down by means
of [one's own]" plainness and "being
unadorned",[12] then they would

"without [one's] interfering with
them" "rectify themselves."[13]

(30) If [, however,] one attacks
them with wisdom and knowledge,
the people will become exhausted
and tricks will proliferate.
Therefore, one might [as well]
"embrace" plainness and "being
unadorned", and "discard"
"wisdom and intelligence."[14]

(31) It is generally true that,

(32) when surveillance [by
the ruler] is simple, then [the
people's] evasion of it will be
simple as well.

(33) when [the ruler] exerts his intelligence, then [the people's] eluding him
will become more perspicacious.

(34) [Their evasion] being
simple, damage to [people's]
unadorned [nature] will be
small.

(35) [Their evasion] being perspicacious, tricks and pretensions will
become deeper.

(36) But who masters the art of
supreme surveillance and of
ferreting out the hidden if not [a
ruler who has] wisdom and
intelligence? How [consequently,]
could the damage be fully mea-
sured that he inflicts? That is why
[the *Laozi* 19.1 statement about]
"hundredfold gain" [if wisdom
and intelligence are discarded]
is certainly not exaggerated.

(37) It is a fact that, if [someone]
is unable to differentiate between
[different] names, it is impossible
to talk with him about principles;
and, if [someone] is unable to
define names, it is impossible to

discuss reality with him.
Generally spoken, names are born
out of forms and it does not occur
that forms are born out of names.
That is why, if there is this [specific]
name, there must be this [specific]
form, and if there is this [specific]
form, there must be its [specific] lot.

(38) As benevolence can by no means
be styled wisdom,

(39) As intelligence can by no
means be styled benevolence,

(40) each one of them has its own reality.

(41) It is a fact that

(42) he who searches out the most
subtle is at the epitome of
enlightenment.

(43) he who investigates and
goes after the hidden and
crouching is at the epitome of
heedfulness.

(44) What if not wisdom is able to
completely attain the epitome of
enlightenment?

(45) What if not intelligence is
able to completely attain the
epitome of heedfulness?

(46) [Thus, only] by checking
reality and defining the names in
the intention to find out about
[the *Laozi*'s statement concerning]
the "discarding of wisdom" is it
possible to be without error.[15]

(47) It is a fact that, if the capacity
of the "genuine" and "simple"[16]
does not shine forth while the
amenities of the

(48) fame   and   (49) deeds

                    are   (50) praised   and

(51) exalted,   then

(52) [people will] strive for that
which is being exalted and they
hope for the fame.

(53) [people will] strive for that
which is being praised and they
will long for the profit.

                    If

(54) hoping for fame   and   (55) longing for profit

(56) motivates their activity,
then

(57) the more beautiful the name becomes, the more alienated will one be from sincerity.

(58) the weightier the profits become, the more competitive the mind will be.[17]

(59) That between father and son, elder and younger brother the affection they harbor lacks straightforwardness [so that] filial piety will not be displayed with sincerity and compassion will not be displayed with honesty is provoked by the [ruler's] praising of

(60) names   and   (61) deeds.

(62) When, out of disgust for the vulgar and shallow fame and deeds are brought to florish and benevolence and righteousness are being emulated, this will only bring more of those pretensions, and how much more will this be the case when the art [applied] is even inferior to these [two, namely, benevolence and righteousness]. That is why [the *Laozi* 19.1 statement concerning] the [ruler's] "discarding of benevolence and the rejecting righteousness" for the purpose of "[making the people] return to filial piety and parental love" is not exaggerated.[18]

(63) It is a fact that, when the city walls rise, war chariots make their appearance. When profits go up, greed [among those not benefiting] deepens. [But, adapting a statement by Confucius to Ji Kangzi, the ruler of Lu], "If only" [the ruler] "would" keep to "desireless"ness, there "would be no stealing even if a premium were set on it."[19] If [,on the other hand, the ruler] acts out [his] egotism and desires, then craftiness and lust for profit [among the people] will become

ever more dismal. That is why there is
nothing better than [, as *Laozi* 19.1 says,]
to "discard craftiness and reject [the lust
for] profit," and instead to "reduce one's
desires," [with the result that] "there
would be no robbers and thieves."

(64) It is a fact that

(65) Wisdom and intelligence are the heroes among the talents.

(66) Benevolence and righteousness are the greatest among the forms
of conduct.

(67) Trickery and [lust for] profit are the best in usefulness.[20]

(68) If, when [the ruler] does
not keep to the root, but lets
these amenities flourish, the
damage [to the people] is
already such [as described], how
much worse [will the damage be]
if the arts [applied] go even
further than these [which have
been mentioned] in disregarding
plainness and simplicity![21] That
is why people of old sighed:
"Indeed! Why are things so
difficult to understand!"

(69) Having already understood that
non-wisdom is non-wisdom, one still
fails to understand that wisdom
[itself] is non-wisdom.

(70) Having already understood
that non-benevolence is non-
benevolence, one still fails to
understand that benevolence
[itself] is non-benevolence.[22]

(71) That is why [only]

(72) once wisdom is cut off, the
achievements of wisdom will be
completed.[23]

(73) once benevolence is discarded, the capacity of
benevolence will be ample.[24]

(74) To despise strength does
not mean that one does desire
not to be strong, but he who acts
strong loses his strength.[25] To
discard benevolence does not
mean that one desires to be non-
benevolent, but in acting out

benevolence pretensions [among its objects] are brought about. By clinging to order, chaos indeed is brought about. By protecting one's security, peril indeed is brought about.

(75) [In the *Laozi*'s statement that the Sage] "puts his own person in the background and [achieves it in this way] that his own person comes to be to the fore,"[26] that [his] person comes to be to the fore is not brought about by [his] putting [his] person to the fore. [In the *Laozi* statement that the Sage] "disregards his own person and [achieves in this way] that his own person will last,"[27] the lasting of [his] person is not achieved by making [his] person last.

(76) As achievements cannot be grabbed and as amenities cannot be made use of, one must take hold of the mother that brings about the achievements, and that is all.[28]

(77) The chapter [of the *Laozi*] says, once "having understood its [the mother's] offspring [= All Under Heaven]," [the ruler] has to "in turn keep to its [All Under Heaven's] mother."[29] Having come to an understanding of this principle, where could one arrive without being in the clear.

Chapter 4

A Reconstruction and Critical Edition
of the *Laozi* Text Used by Wang Bi;
a Reconstruction and Critical Edition of
Wang Bi's *Commentary on the Laozi*;
an Extrapolative Translation of the
Laozi through Wang Bi's *Commentary*;
and a Translation of Wang Bi's
Commentary on the Laozi

A NOTE ON THE EDITION

The *Laozi* text printed over the Wang Bi *Commentary* in all available pre-modern editions is not the text used by Wang Bi himself.[1] The *Wang Bi Laozi Receptus* has to be abandoned in its entirety. The reconstruction of the Wang Bi *Laozi* attempted here is based on the identification of the textual family to which Wang Bi's *Laozi* belonged. For this purpose *Laozi* quotations in Wang's *Commentary* were compared to extant textual traditions. The result was a textual family consisting of the following four texts:

1. Fu Yi 傅奕. 道德經古本. Contained in the Zhengtong Daozang, Schipper 665. Quoted as 傅奕古本.

2. Fan Yingyuan 范應元. 老子道德經古本集注. Contained in the 續古逸叢書. Quoted as 范應元本.

3. Mawangdui 馬王堆 *Laozi* manuscript A. Contained in 馬王堆漢墓帛書整理小組 (ed.), 馬王堆漢墓帛書 1 (Beijing: Wenwu Press, 1974), vol. 1. Quoted as 馬王堆 A.

4. Mawangdui 馬王堆 *Laozi* manuscript B. Contained in ibid., vol. 2. Quoted as 馬王堆 B.

In this reconstruction of the Wang Bi *Laozi*, the Wang Bi *Commentary* forms the basis because its *Laozi* quotations in this *Commentary* survived most changes of its original *Laozi* text and because many other textual features can be extrapolated from the Commentary. In areas where there is no direct guidance from Wang Bi, the occasional notes in Lu Deming's 陸德明 *Jingdian shiwen* 經典釋文, as well as the common reading within the textual family, have been followed, with Fu Yi and Fan Yingyuan being most important. All deviations within the family are listed. The Mawangdui deviations very often are based on phonetic or graphic similarities at a time when writing was still a fairly unstable form of communication with a small number of standardized characters. The readings of the three Guodian *Laozi* batches from Chu from a tomb dated around 300 B.C.E. support a fair number of the Mawangdui readings, especially in the realm of particles, but offer in many other aspects readings so different from all known traditions that they would require an altogether separate treatment. I have noted their readings where they supported the plausibility of an otherwise weakly documented reading that seemed to impose itself on the basis of the Wang Bi commentary, but I have not given all deviations from my Wang Bi *Laozi*.

My work has most profited from the approach pioneered in Shima Kuniō's 島邦男 *Rōshi kōsei* 老子校正. He grouped the available *Laozi* texts into families and tried to establish a critical text for each family. His Wang Bi *Laozi* is based on the readings of the Wang Bi *Commentary* and members of a textual family based on the Daozang monograph edition of the *Laozi* with Wang Bi's *Commentary*. To this he adds occasional references to textual traditions such as Zhuang Zun 莊遵 and Xiang Er 想爾, which he considered close to Wang Bi because of their proximity in time. Based on the approach he had pioneered, I arrived at different results. The texts he groups together as the Wang Bi textual family are all Ming texts, and he is often forced to go against their common reading in his critical edition of the Wang Bi *Laozi*, the changes in most cases in the direction of the Fu Yi and Fan Yingyuan Old Texts. A close study of these links showed that, in fact, these two, along with—at some distance—the Mawangdui texts (published only after Shima Kuniō's work had come out), were part of Wang Bi's textual family. I have therefore abandoned the transmitted

Wang Bi *Laozi* texts altogether. For each Wang Bi *Laozi* phrase, I have looked in the quotations and the textual family for the best available text ("base text"), and I have taken this as the basis for the edition with all deviations from this text given in the notes as variation ("Var.:") with "om." meaning "omitted." Those elements in the base text which had to be changed are changed as "x for y:aaa本," which means that, instead of the y in the base text, the reading x of the aaa本 is preferable. Where necessary, I have given a short explanation.

The Wang Bi *Commentary* editions circulating today are based on fifteenth- and sixteenth-century editions. As shown elsewhere, they provide only the second best base for a critical edition compared to the Wang Bi texts in Song and Yuan commentary collections. By and large, these latter texts represent not only a distinctly earlier but also a distinctly better state of textual preservation. Hatano Tarō 波多野太郎 has assembled the variant readings of the Wang Bi *Commentary* not only in the various Chinese editions but also the critical commentary by Chinese and Japanese scholars in his monumental *Rōshi Ō chū kōsei*, however, he did not proceed to make a critical edition of the Wang Bi *Commentary*.

Again, Shima Kuniō must be credited with pioneering a new approach. For each segment of the Wang Bi *Commentary* he chose among the available Song- and Yuan-dynasty collections of commentaries the text that seemed to represent the best textual quality. While this approach opened the way for a reconstruction of a much better version of Wang Bi's *Commentary*, Shima Kuniō's focus was on the *Laozi* text, so that he did not proceed to establish a critical edition of the Wang Bi *Commentary* but left the pieces as he found them. The edition in the following pages tries to fill this lacuna. It abandons the texts hitherto used as the basis for Wang Bi's *Commentary* and bases itself on the earliest available texts of his *Commentary*. Although the printed editions of these texts also date from the Ming—most of them are in the Zhengtong Daozang—their cumulative nature, with many commentaries assembled in one single text, made it much less likely that one of the commentaries selected there would be changed later to accord with some separate monograph edition. For each commentary item, my edition selects what seems to be the best available textual base and proceeds, much as with the Wang Bi *Laozi*, to establish a critical text on this basis. The variants in this early core group are given in the notes. In particular, the following texts are used as the basis:

1. Liu Weiyong 劉惟永. *Daode zhen jing jiyi* 道德眞經集義. In Zhengtong Daozang of 1445, Schipper 724. Printed in 1299, this huge compilation of commentaries and critical comments on the *Laozi* survives only in its first part dealing with *Laozi zhang* 1–11.

It contains full texts of Wang Bi's *Commentary* for these *zhang* and, as a rule, preserves the best textual basis. That is why Shima Kuniō has used it as his base text for these *zhang*. Quoted as 劉惟永集義本.

2. Wang Pang 王雱. *Daode zhen jing jizhu* 道德眞經集註. In Zhengtong Daozang of 1445, Schipper 706. Completed in 1070, this collection of commentaries carries the entire commentary texts of the Tang Emperor Xuanzong 玄宗 (明皇), Heshang gong 河上公, Wang Bi, and the editor Wang Pang 王雱 himself, who is Wang Anshi's son. The quality of the Wang Bi text here is not as good as in Liu Weiyong's edition but distinctly superior to the Ming editions. Wang Pang's text is the main base text for the Wang Bi *Commentary* for *zhang* 12–81. Quoted as 集註.

3. Li Lin 李霖. *Daode zhen jing qushan ji* 道德眞經取善集. In Zhengtong Daozang of 1445, Schipper 718. With a preface dated 1172 under the Jin, this text sets out to select for each *Laozi* phrase what it considers the "best" 善 commentaries. This sometimes includes Wang Bi commentaries. Quoted as 取善集.

4. Dong Siqing 董思靖. *Daode zhen jing jijie* 道德眞經集解. In Zhengtong Daozang of 1445, Schipper 705. This collection of commentaries to the *Laozi*, originally published in 1246, includes some quotations from Wang Bi. Quoted as 董思靖.

5. Yongle dadian edition 永樂大典本. A text of Wang Bi's *Commentary* was included in the *Yongle dadian* 永樂大典, compiled between 1403 and 1425. The section is not extant, but the editors of the Siku quanshu *Laozi*, a text referred to here as the Siku 四庫 edition, had a copy of *Laozi* 1–37 in their hands. They noted all of the differences between their own edition, based on the Zheng Zhixiang edition 張之象本, and the *Yongle dadian* edition for these *zhang*. Given the high editorial standards of the Siku edition, we may presume that this gives us the entire *Yongle dadian* edition for *Laozi* 1–37, on the assumption that those passages for which no deviation from the *Yongle dadian* edition is mentioned actually were identical to the text printed in the Siku edition. Quoted as 永樂大典本.

6. *Daode zhen jing zhu* 道德眞經註. In Zhengtong Daozang of 1445, Schipper 690. This separate edition of the Wang Bi *Com-*

mentary is in four *juan*. While this might look like an influence of
the arrangement of the Heshang gong *Commentary*, it is in fact
conditioned by the editorial routine of the Daozang, which led
to a duplication of all *juan* numbers. The text given there is very
close to the Zhang Zhixiang edition 張之象本. Referred to as 道
藏本.

7. Zhang Zhixiang edition 張之象本. This printed text that the Siku
editors consider to be from the *Wanli* period (1573–1620) goes
back to the Daozang text and adds little of interest. The editors of
the Siku text used it as the base for their entire text of the Wang
Bi *Commentary*. As they state in an editorial note to *zhang* 38,
for *Laozi* 1–37 they used the *Yongle dadian* text as a check, but
as the second half of the *Yongle dadian* edition of the *Laozi* "had
no [Wang Bi] commentary," they simply reproduced the Zhang
Zhixiang edition for *Laozi* 38–81. They stated that "the Wang
[Bi] *Commentary* carried in the Zhang Zhixiang edition has lacunae and is faulty in many places, but as we have today no other
edition [to check this text against] we simply reproduce this original." [2] This in fact gives us the entire Zhang Zhixiang edition.
Referred to as 張之象本.

A sizable scholarly literature has dealt with the Wang Bi *Laozi Commentary*. The greatest part has been painstakingly assembled by Hatano
Tarō. Checks have shown that his quotations are accurate, and I have
therefore refrained from giving the original source for each item quoted.
They will be found, if not otherwise noted, with the notes to the respective
phrase of Wang Bi's *Commentary* in his *Rōshi Ō chu kōsei*. The strategies
of the commentators have varied. Some, such as Wei Yuan 魏源[3] (1797–
1857), have handled the text rather liberally and have freely supplemented
what they felt Wang Bi might or should have written. Others, such as Tao
Hongqing 陶鴻慶[4] (1859–1918), Tōjō Itsudō[5] (1778–1857) and Usami
Shinsui 宇佐美灊水[6] (1710–1776), have stayed closer to the text and made
important suggestions. For a critical edition as I propose to present it here,
these suggestions are most valuable, because it is evident that the text needs
emendations in quite a few places. The comparison of different editions of
the same text—and this not only before and after the writing reform took
hold, but also in later times—shows to what degree graphic or phonetic
similarities could prompt a scribe or copyist to involuntarily alter a text.
I have remained fairly conservative in terms of the changes outside of the
options present in the earliest available record, because it also turns out
that emendations quite often have been made because a text has not been

understood. The best example is *Laozi* 1.5, where a misunderstanding of the text has led to a fair number of emendations, all unnecessary.

A NOTE ON EXTRAPOLATIVE TRANSLATION

In *The Craft of a Chinese Commentator*, I have tried to outline Wang Bi's commentarial strategies and have confronted them with other constructions of the same texts. The purpose of this note on my translation of Wang Bi's works on the *Laozi* is to provide some grounding for my own strategies of reading and translating these works.

A text such as the *Laozi* is never read for the first time. Any historical reader has been exposed to this text on various levels, whether through the most general and vague information about its presumed author, through hearsay or reading about "Taoism," through sayings from the text that have become part of the proverbial lore, or, finally, through reading the text with a commentary or in a translation. The modern construction of an "Urtext" with its primordial meaning notoriously trivialized and misunderstood by "later" readers and commentators and gloriously resuscitated by the latest commentator has a long Chinese pedigree. Wang Bi will engage in a pointed polemics against the misconstructions of the text by various schools to fit their own agenda, and he will claim to rediscover the philosophical essence contained and hidden in this text. While we might not wish to commit ourselves to believe his claim, we might be well advised to abandon the concept of some sort of a "Urmeaning" of such a text as a largely useless, inapplicable heuristic assumption. Even if through some magical device the author or authors of the *Laozi* could be brought back to life and were able to tell us their thoughts, they would most certainly be unaware of many elements flowing into their text from the general cultural and philosophical background; their explanations would most probably not help a bit in understanding this text as a cultural focus that redefines and reactivates itself through different readers and commentators at different times and under different circumstances; and, at worst, these explanations might show that their meaning and intentions were light years away from anything a reader, commentator, or translator ever actualized.

A commentator will, as a rule, see his or her work as being in the service of the text; accordingly, he or she will signal that the text belongs to a higher textual register than his or her commentary to the point of perhaps being a canonical text left behind by the sages of antiquity. This hierarchy, however, does not accurately describe the relationship between the *Laozi* and the commentators. True, the *Laozi* text stays by and large the same, while the commentators come and go. Each commentator though makes an effort to fix the meaning of the text, to the point of excluding other possible and already realized meanings. In this fixing of the meaning the commentary attempts a merger with the text. The purpose of a traditional commentator is to provide a unified explanation for the entire text. In this unified explanation the commentator will try, as has been well explained by Mengzi, to grasp what the author "intended" to say, his or her "meaning" will test the meaning so attained against the available evidence, and, if enough supporting textual material comes forth, will subject the entire text to this unifying procedure. On this level, the commentator, and especially a commentator as "meaning-" oriented as Wang Bi, will reconstruct the entire textual material in light of this core "meaning." We thus see the commentator taking over the text's making sense and in this way achieve more than a parity with the text itself. The level of acceptance of a commentator's interpretive claims by a reading community marks the level of the fusion, and we have many cases—such as Wang Yi's *Commentary on the Chuci*—where a commentator achieved a hegemony over the meaning of a given text that remained beyond challenge for millennium.

At the same time the commentary remains subjectively and objectively separate from the text, and it might be discarded, if only after a millennium. Subjectively, because the commentator is aware that he is only one among many who have faced this ultimate challenge of achieving a unified understanding and remains aware of the painful distance between his construction and the textual material that time and again forces him into ever more creative, sophisticated, or simply clumsy efforts to mediate between textual passages that refuse integration and the overall meaning of the text. This might at moments lead him to reject a segment as not fitting this unified body and thus marking itself off as a fake. Objectively, because the reader, after having allowed the commentator to guide him through his reading of the text, might find that the commentary makes use of too many supplementary constructs, and that the gap between the overall meaning that guides the commentator and the surface of the text remains too wide to stomach. In this case the reader will drop the commentator, but not the text; he might in fact want to read another commentary explaining to him the text's meaning.

In the *Laozi*, the commentators are confronted with readers who know the text by and large by heart and have learned to understand it through other commentaries. The new commentator's communication with the reader is not innocent. He does not only have to convince him or her of his own explanations but has to demolish the credibility of the most widely held alternative explanations in the process.

A translator of such a commentary is thus in a bind. Any translation of the Chinese text into a modern language, whether Chinese, Japanese, or a Western language, will have to dramatically reduce the leeway of meaning that the text has acquired in its long history of being understood. This leeway of meaning does not only concern the meaning of certain terms such as *dao* or *xuan*, it concerns grammar, rhetoric, implied subjects and objects, and, of course, the overall purport that never can be fully expressed in one given phrase but might imbue the entire text. In the *Laozi* and many other texts with a canonical status, this historical leeway of meaning can be extraordinarily wide, as the extrapolative translations of a few *zhang* of the *Laozi* in the above-mentioned book have shown. In a first step, the translator of a commentary will thus have to let himself be guided by the commentator and translate the text as he wanted it to be read. This means that for the reader of this translation, the viability of all other commentarial readings will disappear; if Wang Bi reads "grass and dogs," a commentary about the ritual uses and metaphorical meaning of "straw dogs" is perfectly off the mark. This reduction of meaning space through translation also has a sorry victim: the commentator. His analytical contribution, the thrill evoked by his commentary among historical readers, is gone, because it can only be gauged against the then-available readings and the fit between the then-available assumptions of the text's overall meaning and the commentary analyses of the individual statements of the text.

In this manner the translator cannot but deliver a homogeneous text/commentary continuum that articulates the ways in which the commentator proposed to read a given phrase or passage in the context of his construction of the overall meaning. This is what the translation that follows will do. While the result might look easy, to produce such a translation is an excruciatingly difficult process. The commentator in most cases does not give a "translation" of the main text into the fully spelled out meaning, but only implies a certain reading. This reading of the main text has to be extrapolated from these implications of the commentary. Again, no translator of the *Laozi* has the innocence of a first reading. A certain modern routine of translating and understanding the *Laozi* has settled in during the last 200 or so years. In many cases, these translations even claim to follow what they assumed to be "the Wang Bi text," but the general disrespect for commentators as secondhand scholasticists has prevented them from carefully extrapolating from Wang Bi's commentary his construction of the *Laozi*, although I would not know of any text with a greater impact on Chinese thinking about the meaning of the *Laozi* and certain philosophical questions. For a translator to overcome the fairly unified hum of the available translations and to proceed on the slippery road of "reinventing" the *Laozi* through the indications of a Chinese commentator is an exercise that requires the mobilization of a high degree of creativity as well as the imposition of an equally high degree of control. From going time and again over the translation and time and again discovering some reading required by the commentary that I had failed to discover previously and that looked in hindsight perfectly obvious, I am painfully aware that this three-way negotiation between Wang Bi, the *Laozi*, and myself might not have and might never come fully to an end. I still believe that a contribution is made here in helping the reader of the translation understand the principle of the historicity of meaning, to get at one given historical meaning of the *Laozi*, and to get access to the wherewithal to compare different meanings of the *Laozi* as brought out by different commentators whose readings hopefully will be made available in the future.

The unavoidable result of this strategy of translating the text through the commentary will be ideally that the commentary looks self-evident, and that means superfluous. A translation that will highlight the philosophical and analytical achievements of the commentator is, in my opinion and experience, impossible, because the complex interaction between a probing commentator and the particular fluidity of meaning of a text cannot be reproduced. There is no way out of this quandary. The only way to keep the reader aware of the actual efforts and contributions of the commentator is to translate the main text in a manner that makes a reading of the kind proposed by the commentator *possible* but still reminds the reader of the distance between his or her own spontaneous understanding and the meaning of text being bridged by the commentator. Needless to say, this is but little solace.

If the translation of the text follows the directions given in the commentary, it will in the same process by implication translate the commentary's rejection of other options and suggestion of a very particular way of constructing a given passage. As the translation has no way of keeping these other options visible, and as in the case of Wang Bi most other commentaries with which he was engaged in a running battle were lost, it is very hard to locate and mark the construct in our hands in its character of not just being a unified construct but at the same time being a burial ground of rejected options. An ideal translation would start with an endless bracket before each phrase lining up existing alternative readings and pointing out their weaknesses and strengths, and only then would the translation of the new construct be proffered. No reader would willingly enter this hermeneutic torture chamber.

This translation, then, offers two things: a particular historical construction of the *Laozi* that had enormous impact on all later commentators of whatever philosophical or religious bent, and, in the same process, the philosophical exploration of, and elaboration on, the perceived meaning of the *Laozi* by a young genius of the third century C.E.

A NOTE ON
PREVIOUS TRANSLATIONS

This translation is not the first. The three earlier efforts, Paul Lin's (1977),[7] Ariane Rump's (1979),[8] and Richard Lynn's (1999),[9] have all based their translations of the common modern editions of Wang Bi's *Laozi* text and his *Commentary.* Lynn has taken notice of some of the problems with this text but has basically remained within the confines of Hatano Tarō's collection of notes and Lou Yulie's rather weak edition. None of the translators has taken cognizance of the seminal work of Shima Kuniō. This marks an important difference with the work presented here. And as no critical edition was attempted, no or little references is made to the manuscript record.

The first two translations have proceeded from a notion that there is a *Laozi* with an intrinsic meaning to which Wang Bi offers a commentary. They have therefore felt free to stick to existing translations of the *Laozi*, in the case of Rump, the one presented by Wing-tsit Chan quite independently of the Wang Bi commentary, and they have attached their translation of Wang Bi's commentary. No effort at an extrapolative reading of the *Laozi* text through Wang Bi's commentary has been made. This methodological flaw has had very unsatisfactory results, because the commentary seems more often than not quite random and out of tune with the "meaning" of the text. Lynn has made significant headway in this area. His translation moves in the direction of an extrapolative effort, and in quite a few cases, successfully so. He has not made his translation strategy explicit, so we have to go by his actual procedure. This leaves a mixed message of extrapolative translation, adhesion to time-honored, if nonsensical, readings, and personal beliefs and preferences.

He will translate the first phrase of *Laozi* 5 as "Heaven and Earth are not benevolent and treat the myriad things as straw dogs" in the way hundreds of translators have done before him and will then translate Wang Bi's commentary to this phrase: "Heaven and Earth do not make the grass grow for the sake of beasts, yet beasts eat the grass. They do not produce dogs for the sake of men, yet men eat dogs." Evidently, Wang Bi did not read "straw dogs" but read "grass and dogs." As the reader is kept in the dark about this, he or she will have to wonder why Wang Bi should write such a stupid commentary. In general, the translation seems to lack an understanding of the historicity of the meaning of a text.

Lynn firmly believes that the *Laozi* is a text that gives advice to anyone reading it about how to behave. While this might or might not be the case, it definitely was not the way in which Wang Bi read it. If there is an implied reader in Wang Bi's commentary, it is the ruler. The reflections on the philosophical bases of stable rule that Wang Bi extracts from the *Laozi* make sense to no one else. In fact, in Wang Bi's reading, there is not a single prescriptive phrase in the entire *Laozi*. Lynn's translation supplies the prescriptive language out of a reading tradition that he does not seem to have reflected critically. In Wang Bi's commentary on *Laozi* 5, for example, he translates after the passage quoted above, "Heaven and Earth make no conscious effort with respect to the myriad things, yet because each of the myriad things has what is appropriate for its use, not one thing is denied support. As long as you use kindness derived from a personal perspective, it indicates a lack of capacity to leave things to themselves." While this gives homely advice, it can do so only by introducing a new subject, "you," which Wang Bi fails to provide. The second phrase simply continues with the subject of the previous phrase, namely, Heaven and Earth, and reads, to use here the language proposed by Lynn's translation: "Should they [Heaven and Earth] confer kindness on their own [initiative], they would be unable to leave things to themselves." I will come back to the end of this passage. The opinion that the *Laozi* provides a catechism of wise behavior to anyone picking up the book is so firm with this translator that he is, on occasion, willing to drop the text altogether and write his own. Wang Bi's last comment to *Laozi* 8 may serve as an example. The text of this chapter has given a long list specifying the first phrase that sets up the similarity between the Most Excellent, which Wang Bi reads as another name for Dao, and water. The comment runs: 言水皆應於此道也, which translates as, "This means that water corresponds in all these [features] to this Way." Lynn's translation reads, "This states how, like water, one should always be in resonance thus with the Dao." Gracefully, in this case he warns the reader in a footnote that he might have gone a bit far. Sadly, the translation time and again suffers from this kind of unfounded but firm belief in the didactic nature of Wang Bi's *Laozi*.

The three translators have followed tradition by disregarding the rhetorical features that I have tried to analyze in my study on IPS.[10] While it certainly is the good right of Lynn, whose bibliography lists the earlier published version of this study, to consider this stylistic feature a quirky child of my own fantasy, the evidence amassed from within the *Laozi* itself and from the interlocking style features in writings by Wang Bi and many of his contemporaries and later admirers might have warranted a rebuttal. Even in cases such as *Laozi* 22, where Wang Bi goes out of his way to show the IPS features of this chapter, this translator chooses to disregard them. This has led to a substantial loss in precision in this translation, as the connections between phrases within a chapter all too often remain in their traditional muddle.

Translation and scholarly analysis are not necessarily linked, and many scholars excel in one rather than the other field. With a philosophical text of the kind presented by Wang Bi, in which a new philosophical language is being created, the separation of translation and analysis might not go that smoothly. To my knowledge, neither of the three translators has had a long involvement with the study of third-century philosophy, and Xuanxue in particular. The introductions remain much on a general level, the footnotes show little familiarity with Xuanxue discussions, and the bibliographies surprise by their lack of familiarity with even the finest book-length studies in the field, not to mention the numerous articles on particular problems. This is especially sad in the case of the last mentioned translation as there has been an outpouring of very stimulating and highly specific research by scholars from Mainland China during the last fifteen or twenty years. This seeming lack of deeper familiarity with Xuanxue thinking comes with a price. The translators read Wang Bi's philosophical arguments in the context of what they consider shared notions in "philosophical Taoism." While this sometimes is helpful, it more often ends up obscuring the very clear markers identifying Wang Bi's thinking and setting it off against "Taoist" concepts, if it is meaningful to use this term at all. All three translations end up providing a text that is only marginally helpful in understanding a Xuanxue philosophical reading of the *Laozi*, and thus they fail to do what they set out to do—to provide one historically specific and contextualized reading of the *Laozi* as opposed to the general as-you-like-it translations available that claim to render the "original" thought of the *Daodejing*.

I have tried to pursue another course here; it includes a critical reconstruction and edition of the texts involved, a translation that attempts to enrich and specify the understanding through insertion into the philosophical context of Wang Bi himself and his contemporaries, while remaining falsifiable by reducing "openness" of meaning to a minimum; an analysis of the particular technical and analytical strategies pursued in Wang's commentary; and, finally, a philosophical analysis of what I consider the core questions addressed in this work. My criticism of the translations that came out earlier should not be seen as a discouragement to read them. The opposite is the case. I would greatly encourage the reader to do a critical comparison of these translations with my own work. Whatever the final judgment might be, such a comparison will certainly contribute to a deeper understanding of the problems involved with such translations, and the degrees of their reliability, especially for an analysis that will have to live with such translations and cannot hold them against the text.

WANG BI,
COMMENTARY ON THE LAOZI

Zhang 1

1.1 道可道非常道名可名非常名[a] (Base text: 傅奕古本)

> 可道之道可名之名指事造形非其常也其[b]不可道不可名也 (Base text: 道藏本)

1.2 無名萬物[c]之始[d]有名萬物之母[e] (Base text: 馬王堆 A, B)

> 凡有皆始於無故未形無名之時則爲萬物之始及其有形有名之時則長之育之亭之毒之爲其母也言道以無形無名始成萬物[f]萬物以始以成而不知其所以然[g]玄之又玄也 (Base text: 劉惟永集義本)

1.3 故常無欲[h]以觀其妙[i] (Base text: 傅奕古本)

> 妙者微之極也萬物始於微而後成始於無而後生故常無欲空虛其懷[j]可以觀其始物之妙 (Base text: 劉惟永集義本=集註本)

---

[a] Var.: 道可道也非恒道也名可名也非恒名也 for 道可道非常道名可名非常名: 馬王堆 A.

[b] Var.: 故 for 其: 劉惟永集義, 永樂大典本.

[c] Var.: 天地 for 萬物: 傅奕古本; 范應元本. Support for 萬物: Wang Bi commentary 爲萬物之始; Wang Bi, comm. on *Laozi* 21.7 以無名說萬物始; 史記, 日者列傳; Ma Xulun.

[d] 始 for 始也: 傅奕古本; 范應元本.　[e] 母 for 母也: 傅奕古本; 范應元本.

[f] 萬物 add.: Tao Hongqing based on Wang Bi on *Laozi* 21.3 萬物以始以成而不知其所以然.

[g] 所以然 for 所以: Tao Hongqing based on Wang Bi on *Laozi* 21.3, as quoted in previous note.

[h] Var.: 垣 (馬王堆 B: 恒) 无欲也 for 常無欲: 馬王堆 A; 馬王堆 B.

[i] Var.: 眇 for 妙: 馬王堆 A; 馬王堆 B.

[j] Var.: 空虛 for 空虛其懷: 永樂大典本; 道藏本.

1.4 常有欲[k]以觀其徼[l] (Base text: 傅奕古本)

徼歸終也凡有之爲利必以無爲用欲之所本適道而後濟故常有欲可以觀其終物之徼也 (Base text: 劉惟永集義本=集註本)

1.5 兩[m]者同出而[n]異名同謂[o]之玄玄之又玄[p]眾妙[q]之門 (Base text: 傅奕古本=范應元本)

兩者始與[r]母[s]也同出者[t]同出於玄也異名所施不同[u]也在首則謂之始在終則謂之母玄者冥也默然無有也[v]始母[w]之所出也不可得而名故不可言同名曰玄而言謂之玄者[x]取於不可得而謂之然也謂之然則不可以定乎一玄若定乎一玄而已[y]則[z]是[aa]名則失之遠矣故曰玄之又玄也眾妙皆從同[ab]而出故曰眾妙之門也 (Base text: 集註本)

1.1 A way that can be spoken[1] of is not the eternal Way.	A name that can be named is not the eternal name.

---

[k] Var.: 恆有 (馬王堆 B: 又) 欲也 for 常有欲: 馬王堆 A ; 馬王堆 B.

[l] Var.: 噭 for 徼: 馬王堆 A; 馬王堆 B.

[m] 兩者 for 此兩者: 馬王堆 A; 馬王堆 B. Support for 兩者: Wang Bi comm.: 兩者始與母也.

[n] Var.: 同出異名 for 同出而異名: 馬王堆 A; 馬王堆 B.

[o] Var.: 胃 for 謂: 馬王堆 A; 馬王堆 B.

[p] Var.: 同胃玄之有 [馬王堆 B: 又] 玄 for 同謂之玄玄之又玄: 馬王堆 A; 馬王堆 B.

[q] Var.: 眇 for 妙: 馬王堆 A; 馬王堆 B.

[r] Var.: 於 for 與: 劉惟永集義本.

[s] 母 for 毋: 劉惟永集義本; 永樂大典本; 道藏本.

[t] 同出者 for 出者: 劉惟永集義本; 永樂大典本; 道藏本.

[u] 不同 for 不可同: Wang Bi quotation of the passage in 文選孫興公遊天台山賦李善注 11.12b1; Tōjō Itsudō.

[v] Var.: 元 [= 玄] 冥嘿無有也: 文選孫興公遊天台山賦李善注 11.12b1.

[w] 母 for 毋: 劉惟永集義本; 永樂大典本; 道藏本.

[x] Var.: 玄 for 玄者: 劉惟永集義本.

[y] Var.: 定乎一玄而已 for 若定乎一玄而已: 劉惟永集義本; 永樂大典本; 道藏本.

[z] Var.: 謂 for 則: 劉惟永集義本.

[aa] 是名 for 是其名: 劉惟永集義本; 永樂大典本, 道藏本.

[ab] 同 for 門: 劉惟永集義本; 永樂大典本; 道藏本.

A way that can be spoken about   *A name that can be named*
                 is a
demonstrable process   *created shape,*[2]
                 but not their [the way's
                 and the name's] Eternal.
                 This is because [their Eternal]
cannot be spoken about   and   *cannot be named.*

[A new pair begins here]

1.2   When there are not [now] names,   When there [already] are names,
        it [the Way] is the beginning of the   it [the Way] is the mother of the
        ten thousand kinds of entities.[3]   ten thousand kinds of entities.

                 Generally speaking, Entity all
                 begins in negativity.[4] *That is why*
                 it [the Way] will be

at a time when there are neither   *when it comes to a time when*
shapes nor names, the beginning   *there are shapes and names, that*
of the ten thousand kinds of   *which [according to* Laozi *51.3]*
entities.   *"lets [the ten thousand kinds*
                                          of entities] grow, and nurtures
                                          them, specifies them, and com-
                                          pletes them";[5] *[in short,] it will*
                                          be their mother.

                 This means the Way
begins   *and   completes*
                 the ten thousand kinds of entities
                 by means of [its] featurelessness
                 and namelessness. That the ten
                 thousand kinds of entities are
begun by it [the Way] and   *completed by it [the Way],*
                 but that they do not know that
                 through which these [two, their
                 beginning and completion] come
                 to be as they are is [its aspect of
                 being] Dark-and-Dark-Again.

1.3   Therefore,   1.4
while they [the ten thousand kinds   while they [the ten thousand
of entities][6] are [still] constantly   kinds of entities] are constantly
without desire, one has something   with desires, one has something
by means of which to perceive   by means of which to perceive
its [the ultimate principle's] subtlety.[7] its [the ultimate principle's]
                                          limiting.

*"Subtlety" means the ultimate of
minuteness. The ten thousand
entities begin in the minute and
then only become complete, they
begin in negativity, and then only
come to life. Therefore, while they
are permanently without desires
and their concerns are being
emptied, it is possible, "by means
of this to perceive the subtlety [out
of which]" it initiates entities.*

*"Limit" means the final point
to which [entities] return/relate
back. Generally speaking, for
entities to be beneficial, they
have to get their usefulness
from negativity;*[8] *that on which
desires are based will only be
satisfied as a consequence of
adapting to the Way. That is
why, "while they are constantly
with desires," it is possible "by
means of this to perceive the
limiting" [in which] it finalizes
entities.*

1.5   Both emerge from a common [origin]
but they have different names. Their
common [origin] [I] designate as the
Dark, the Dark-and-Dark-Again. It
is the door [from which]
                              the many and
the subtle [emerge].

*"Both" refers to the "beginning" and
the "mother." That they "emerge
from a common [origin]" means
that they equally emerge from the
Dark. That they have "different
names" means that what they bring
about is different.*

*[In its function] at the top, [Laozi]
designates it as "the beginning."*

*[In its function] at the end,
[Laozi] designates it as "the
mother."*

*As to the "Dark," it is obscure,
is silent without [any] entities,
is that which lets the "beginning" and the "mother" emerge.
It is impossible to give a definition [for this Dark]; therefore
[Laozi] cannot say "their
common [source] is defined as
'the Dark,'" but [only] says "[I]
designate as . . . [the Dark]."
The [term] "Dark" is taken for
that*[9] *[aspect of the ultimate*

principle] that it cannot be designated as being thus [and nothing else]. Should one designate it as being thus [and nothing else] it would definitely not be permitted to define it as one [specific] Dark. If one were to define it as being one [specific] Dark and nothing else, this would be a definition, and that would be far off the mark.[10] *That is why [Laozi] says "Dark- and Dark-Again." As the*

the "subtle"   *"many" and both emerge from a common [origin], that is why [Laozi] says: "It is the door from which   the many and*

the subtle [emerge]"!

THE STRUCTURE OF *LAOZI* 1

Laozi 1 has the accoutrements of closed IPS. It begins with two parallel elements, followed by two pairs of parallel elements with no explicit links to each other and one explicitly summarizing non-parallel element. The topics of the first two elements, however, are not taken up in the subsequent binary structure, while the implicit link between pairs two and three is more easily visible. This could be described in two ways—either that the first two phrases are a pair of c phrases giving a general statement, or that everything following consists of binary c phrases. As the first statement is treated as a general statement and its constituent elements 道 and 名 do not form the building blocks for other binary sets in Wang Bi's *Laozi* construction, I have opted for the first reading. Accordingly, the structure of *Laozi* 1 is:

$$
\begin{array}{ccc}
 & c & (1.1) \\
(c1) & (c2) & \\
a & b & (1.2) \\
a & b & (1.3, 1.4) \\
 & c & (1.5)
\end{array}
$$

Zhang 2

2.1 天下皆知美之爲美斯惡巳皆知[a]善之爲善斯不善巳[b]故[c]有無之相生[d]難易之相成[e]長短之相較[f]高下之相盈[g,1]音聲之相和[h]前後之相隨[i] (Base text: 傅奕古本)

美者人心之所進樂也惡者人心之所惡疾也美惡猶喜怒也善不善猶是非也喜怒同根是非同門故不可得而[j]偏擧[k]也此六者皆陳自然[l]不可偏擧之明數也 (Base text: 集註本)

2.2 是以聖人居[m]無爲之事 (Base text: 馬王堆 A = 馬王堆 B= 郭店 A).

自然已足[n]爲則敗也 (Base text: 劉惟永集義本=集註本)

2.3 行不言之教[o] (Base text: 馬王堆 B= 郭店 A= 傅奕古本).

智慧自備爲[p]則僞也 (Base text: 劉惟永集義本)

---

[a] Var.: 天下皆知 for 皆知: 范應元本.

[b] Var.: 天下皆知美之 (馬王堆 A om.: 之) 爲美 (也 add.: 郭店 A) 惡巳皆知善斯 (馬王堆 A:訾; 郭店 A: 此) (其 add.: 郭店 A) 不善矣 (=巳: 郭店 A) for 天下皆知美之爲美斯惡巳皆知善之爲善 斯不善巳: 郭店 A; 馬王堆 A; 馬王堆 B.

[c] Var.: 故 om.: 郭店 A; 馬王堆 A; 馬王堆 B (by number of lacunae). 故 confirmed by Wang Bi comm. 故不可得而偏擧也.

[d] Var.: 生也 for 生: 郭店 A; 馬王堆 A; 馬王堆 B.

[e] Var.: 成也 for 成: 郭店 A; 馬王堆 A; 馬王堆 B.

[f] 較 for 形: 陸德明 based on Wang Bi manuscript. Var.: 刑也 for 刑 (形)/較: 郭店 A; 馬王堆 A; 馬王堆 B.

[g] 盈 for 傾: 馬王堆 A; 馬王堆 B. Var.: 盈也 for 盈: 馬王堆 A; 馬王堆 B.

[h] Var.: 意 for 音: 馬王堆 A. Var.: 和也 for 和: 郭店 A; 馬王堆 A; 馬王堆 B.

[i] Var.: 先後之相隋 [郭店 A:墮] 恒 [恒 om. 郭店 A] 也 for 前後之相隨: 郭店 A; 馬王堆 A; 馬王堆 B.

[j] 不可得而 for 不可: 永樂大典本. Var.: 不可得 for 不可: 道藏本. Support: Wang Bi's standard use of 不可得而 in *LZWZLL* 1.9–12 聽之不可得而聞, 視之不可得而彰, 體之不可得而知, 味之不可得而嘗; comm. on *Laozi* 5.3 不可得而窮, comm. on 14.3 不可得而定也 et al.

[k] Var.: 偏廢 for 偏擧: 劉惟永集義本.　[l] Var.: 自然不 for 自然而不: 劉惟永集義本.

[m] Var.: 處 for 居: 傅奕古本; 范應元本. Support for 居: Wang Bi comm. on *Laozi* 17.1: 居 無爲之事.

[n] Var.: 定 for 足: 永樂大典本.

[o] Wang Bi's comment 智慧自備爲則僞也 relates only to this *Laozi* phrase. I therefore have moved the subsequent *Laozi* phrases 萬物作焉而不爲始生而不有爲而不恃 to join the next phrase in this zhang, 功成而不居. The wrong arrangement is already present in 劉惟永集義本.

[p] Var.: 言 for 爲: 桃井白鹿.

2.4 萬物作焉而^q不爲始^{r,2}生而不有^s爲而不恃^t功成而不居^u(Base text: 范應元本)

　　因物而用^v功自彼成故不居也 (Base text: 劉惟永集義本)

2.5 夫唯^w不^x居是以不^y去^z (Base text: 馬王堆 B; 郭店 A).

　　使功在己則功不可久也 (Base text: 劉惟永集義本=集註本)

2.1　　　　　　　　　Everyone under Heaven knows
　　　　　　　　　　that it is nothing but the
　　　　　　　　　　abhorrent that makes the
　　　　　　　　　　agreeable agreeable; and they
　　　　　　　　　　all know that it is nothing but
　　　　　　　　　　the unacceptable that makes
　　　　　　　　　　the acceptable acceptable.
　　　　　　　　　　That is the reason for the
　　　　　　　　　　having and the not-having
　　　　　　　　　　creating each other, the difficult
　　　　　　　　　　and the easy forming each
　　　　　　　　　　other, the excellent and the
　　　　　　　　　　deficient comparing with each
　　　　　　　　　　other, the high and the low
　　　　　　　　　　supplementing each other, the
　　　　　　　　　　upper and lower tones

---

^q Var.: 作而 for 作焉而: 傅奕古本, 郭店 A. 焉 confirmed by quotation of this passage in Wang Bi comm. on *Laozi* 17.1.

^r Var.: 昔而弗始 for 作焉而不爲始: 馬王堆 B. Cf. note 1. Var.: [始] 也 for 始: 郭店 A; 馬王堆 A.

^s Var.: 生而不有 om.: 郭店 A; 馬王堆 A; 馬王堆 B. Wang Bi has no direct commentary on this phrase. His textual family is split. Wang Bi's commentary reads the phrase 功成而 不居 as a separate unit resulting from something said previously. The phrase is not strictly parallel to the previous phrase, but in the base text the phrases 生而不有 and 爲而不恃 are. I therefore assume for rhetorical reasons of parallel style that his commentary refers to a text having this phrase.

^t Var.: 志也 for 恃: 郭店 A; 馬王堆 A. Var.: 侍也 for 恃: 馬王堆 B.

^u 不居 for 不處: Wang Bi comm.; cf. 馬王堆 A, 馬王堆B: 弗居. Var.: 成功而弗居也 for 功成而不居: 馬王堆 A, 馬王堆B. Var.: 功成不居 for 功成而不居: 永樂大典本. Var.: 功成不處 for 功成而不居: 傅奕古本. Var.: 功 om.: 郭店 A.

^v Var.: 而明 for 而用: 集註本.　　　　　^w Var.: 惟 for 唯: 傅奕古本; 范應元本.

^x 不 for 弗: cf. Wang Bi's previous commentary 不居; 傅奕古本; 范應元本; 永樂大典 本. Var.: 不/弗 om.: 馬王堆 A.

^y 不 for 弗: 傅奕古本; 范應元本; 永樂大典本.

^z Var.: 去也 for 去: 郭店 A.

harmonizing with each other,
and for that which is ahead
and that which is behind
following each other.

The "agreeable" is what people's
hearts promote and appreciate.
The "abhorrent" is what
people's hearts abhor and hate.
"Agreeable" and "abhorrent"
are like enjoying and getting
angry at. "Acceptable" and
"unacceptable" are like agreeing
with and rejecting. Enjoying
and getting angry [thus] have
the same root, agreeing and
rejecting [thus] come out of the
same door; therefore it is not
possible to take up [only one of
them] unilaterally. These six [pairs
following the initial statement]
all proffer clear evidence that
nothing in That-which-is-of-itself-
what-it-is can be taken up
unilaterally.

2.2   This is why the Sage   2.3
takes residence in management   practices teaching without
without interference,   words,

[The other entities'] that-which-   *[The other entities'] intelligence*
is-of-itself-what-it-is already is   *is complete in itself; interfering*
sufficient [in itself]; interfering   *with it would lead [them] to*
with it would destroy it.   *falsehood.*[1]

2.4   [with the result] that the ten
                           thousand entities come about
                           without [his] initiating [them].

[He] creates but does not take   [He] acts [upon them], but does
possession [of them]   not presume[2]

                           [so that the particular] achieve-
                           ments come about without [his]
                           installing [himself in them].

                           Acting in accordance with the
                           entities, [the Sage] brings them
                           [the entities] to use. The
                           [particular] achievements

*[thus] come about through
them [the entities them-
selves]. That is why [the
text says] "he does not
install [himself in them]."*

2.5   It is exactly because he does
not install [himself in these
particular achievements] that
they do not disappear.

*Were the[se particular] achieve-
ments [all] dependent on him
[the Sage], they would be unable to persist over a long time.*

THE STRUCTURE OF *LAOZI* 2

Laozi 2 has an insert in closed IPS after a long general statement. Its structure is:

	c	(2.1)
a	b	(2.2, 2.3)
	c	(2.4)
a	b	(2.4, 2.4)
	c	(2.4)
	c	(2.5)

Zhang 3

3.1 不尙^a賢使民不爭不貴難得之貨使民不爲盜不見可欲使民心^b不亂 (Base text: 傅奕古本)

賢猶能也尙者嘉之名也貴者隆之稱也唯^c能是任尙也曷爲唯^d用是施
貴之曷^e爲尙賢顯名榮過其任下奔而競效^f能相射¹貴貨過用貪者競趣

ª Var.: 上 for 尙: 馬王堆 A; 馬王堆 B.

ᵇ Var.: 民 for 民心: 馬王堆 A; 馬王堆 B. 心 confirmed by Wang Bi comm. 心無所亂也.

ᶜ 唯能 for 惟能: 集註本; cf. infra 唯用是施 in 劉惟永集義本.

ᵈ Var.: 而唯 for 唯: 集註本.

ᵉ 曷爲 for 何爲: 集註本. 也曷 in supra 唯能是任尙也曷爲 confirmed by 陸德明釋文.

ᶠ Var.: 競效 for 競效: 集註本. Var.: 爲而常校 for 下奔而競效: 永樂大典本. 爲而常校 also in 陸德明釋文.

穿窬探篋[g]沒命而盜故可欲不見則心無所亂也 (Base text: 劉惟永集義本)

3.2 是以聖人之治也虛其心實其腹 (Base text: 馬王堆 B)

心懷智而腹懷食虛有智而實無知也 (Base text: 劉惟永集義本 = 集註本)

3.3 弱其志強其骨 (Base text: 馬王堆 B)

骨無志[h]以幹志生事以亂[2] (Base text: 劉惟永集義本 = 集註本)

3.4 常[i]使民無知無欲[j] (Base text: 傅奕古本)

守其眞也 (Base text: 劉惟永集義本=集註本)

3.5 使夫知者[k]不敢爲[l, m] (Base text: 傅奕古本)

知者謂知爲也 (Base text: 劉惟永集義本)

3.6 爲無爲則無不治矣[n, 3] (Base text: 傅奕古本)

3.1   [As a ruler]

not to shower worthies with honors induces the people not to struggle.	not to overly appreciate goods that are hard to get induces the people not to become robbers.

[In short, as a ruler] not to
display [things] that might be

---

[g] Var.: 睹齋篋 for 探篋: 集註本.

[h] 志 for 知: Wagner; cf. note 2 and note on the structure of *Laozi* 3 in the translation of this *zhang*.

[i] Var.: 恒 for 常: 馬王堆 A; 馬王堆 B.

[j] Var.: 欲也 for 欲: 馬王堆 A; 馬王堆 B.

[k] Var.: 知 for 知者: 馬王堆 B.　　　　　[l] Var.: 不敢弗爲 for 不敢爲: 馬王堆 B.

[m] Var.: 爲而己 for 爲: 馬王堆 B. Var.: 爲也 for 爲: 范應元本.

[n] Var.: 治 for 爲: 馬王堆 B. Var.: 爲無爲 om.: 馬王堆 B.

craved for induces the hearts
of the people not to become
prone to chaos.[1]

"Worthy" is like "capable." "To
shower with honors" is a term for
"to emulate."

"To overly appreciate" is an
expression for "to exalt."

What is the purpose of showering
[someone] with honors who is only
capable of handling this [particular]
assignment [and no others]?

Why should [something] be
overly appreciated which is
useful only in this [particular]
application [and in no others]?

If, in granting honors to worthies
and glorifying the famous, the
emulation exceeds their assign-
ment, those below will rush
forward to compete, compare
their [own] capabilities [to those
of those honored], and outdo
each other.

If the appreciation of goods
exceeds their use, the greedy
will compete to rush for them,
they will [as Kongzi says, Lunyu
17.10, *comparing "small men"*
to robbers who] "break through
walls and search in chests," and
will commit robbery without
regard for their [own] life.

That is why [the text says] that,
if [things] that might be craved
for are not displayed [by those
above], the hearts [of the
people] have nothing to disturb
them!

3.2

That is why the governing [tech-
nique] of the Sage consists in
emptying their [the people's]
hearts and filling their bellies,

The heart contains knowledge,
and the belly food. He empties
[that which] has knowledge [the
heart] and fills [that which] has
no knowledge [the belly].

3.3

weakening their [the people's]
ambitions and strengthening
their bones.

Bones are without ambition and
therefore strong. Ambitions
create incidents and therefore
lead to chaos.

3.4   [In this manner] he permanently
                              prompts the people to be
                              without
         knowledge   and   desires.

                              *[That means] he preserves
                              their true [essence].*[2]

3.5   Those, on the other hand, who
                              have knowledge, he prompts
                              into not daring to act.

                              *"Those who have knowledge"
                              refers to those who have knowl-
                              edge about [how to] act.*

3.6   If [they] engage in non-
                              interference there will be
                              nothing that is not well-
                              ordered.
                              [Ditto for those who have
                              desires]

THE STRUCTURE OF *LAOZI* 3

Laozi 3 has the formal trappings of IPS. Wang Bi marks the third phrase
of 3.1 in his commentary as a summary of the two preceding ones, creating a basic pattern of

a   b

c

However, allocating the subsequent pairs of phrases to this pattern is
not easy, because we do not have open interlocking patterns, and second
because, perhaps due to some textual corruption, Wang Bi's commentary
gives mixed messages. The core notions upon which he finally fastens the
a/b pattern are "knowledge" and "desire" from *Laozi* 3.4. However, in
his comments to both 3.2 and 3.3 of the transmitted text, Wang Bi uses
the term "knowledge." While there always is a risk in imposing preset
categories on a text, the pattern of interlocking style is well enough documented in the *Laozi* and in Wang Bi's construction of it that an occasional
emendation, as in this case, seems justified. I have replaced 知 with 志. The
LZWZLL 6.8 makes a clear case associating "robbery" with "desires,"
which establishes quite a stable link between "robbery" of "goods that
are hard to come by," "ambitions," and "desires," on the one hand, and
"struggle" for honors, the "heart," and "knowledge," on the other hand.
The problems do not end here. The text continues in a series of non-parallel

phrases focusing on one of the two core notions here, that is, knowledge. These must accordingly be read as *pars pro toto* constructions of the kind familiar from other parts of the *Laozi*. This creates a shadow text about those "with desires" to match those with "knowledge." I have indicated this in the bracket. The structure of *Laozi* 3 is:

a	b	(3.1, 3.1)
	c	(3.1)
	c	(3.2)
a	b	(3.2, 3.3)
a	b	(3.4, 3.4)
	c	(3.5, 3.6)

Zhang 4

4.1 道沖ᵃ而用之又不ᵇ盈ᶜ淵兮似ᵈ萬物之宗挫其ᵉ銳ᶠ解其紛ᵍ和其光同其塵湛兮似ʰ或存吾不知其ⁱ誰之子ʲ象帝之先 (Base text: 范應元本)

夫ᵏ執一家之量者不能全家執一國之量者不能成國窮力舉重不能爲
用故人雖知萬物治也治而不以二儀之道則不能贍也地雖形魄不法于
天則不能全其寧天雖精象不法ˡ于道則不能保其精冲而用之用乃不
能窮滿以造ᵐ實實來則溢故沖而用之又復不盈其爲無窮亦已極ⁿ矣形
雖大不能累其體事雖殷ᵒ不能充其量萬物舍ᵖ此而求其主ᑫ主其安在

ᵃ Var.: 盅 for 沖: 傅奕古本.　　　　ᵇ Var.: 有弗 for 又不: 馬王堆 B.

ᶜ Var.: 滿 for 盈: 傅奕古本. Support for 盈: Wang Bi comm.: 故沖而用之又復不盈. Var.: 盈也 for 盈: 馬王堆 A. 馬王堆 B.

ᵈ Var.: 瀟 for 淵: 馬王堆 A. Var.: 呵佁 (始: 馬王堆 A) for 兮似: 馬王堆 A; 馬王堆 B.

ᵉ Var.: 銼其 for 挫其銳: 馬王堆 A; 馬王堆 B.

ᶠ Var.: 兌 for 銳: 馬王堆 B. Var.: 銳 om.: 馬王堆 A.

ᵍ Var.: 芬 for 紛: 馬王堆 B.　　　　ʰ Var.: 呵佁 for 兮似: 馬王堆 B.

ⁱ Var.: 其 om.: 馬王堆 A. 傅奕古本. Support for 其: Wang Bi quotation in comm. on *Laozi* 25.1: 不知其誰之子; 馬王堆 B.

ʲ Var.: 子也 for 子: 馬王堆 A; 馬王堆 B.

ᵏ Var.: 執 for 夫執: 集註本.　　　ˡ Var.: 能 for 法: 集註本.

ᵐ Var.: 追 for 造: 集註本.　　　ⁿ Var.: 抑 for 極: 集註本.

ᵒ Var.: 繁 for 殷: 集註本.　　　ᵖ 舍 for 捨: 陸德明釋文; 集註本.

ᑫ Var.: 其生 for 其主: 永樂大典本.

乎不亦淵兮似萬物之宗乎銳挫而無損紛解而不勞和光而不汙其體同
塵而不渝其眞^r不亦湛兮似或存乎^s存而不有沒而不無有無莫測故曰
似存^t地守其形德不能過其載天慊^u其象德不能過其覆天地莫能及之
不亦似帝之先乎帝天帝也 (Base text: 劉惟永集義本)

4.1   The Way is made use of by pouring out and is also not filled up—deep
it is, [but still] resembling the ancestor of the ten thousand kinds of
entities. It numbs their [the ten thousand entities'] sharpness, dissolves
their distractions, mixes with their luster, and joins in the same dust
with them—immersed it is, [but still] it is as if persisting [on its own]. I
do not know whose son it is. It is like the precursor of the lord.

*He who holds on to the measure of one single family will not be able
to make [his] family complete.[1] He who holds on to the measure of
one single state, will not be able to make [this] state complete. [In
short,] he who exhausts [his] strength to lift up something heavy will
not be able to make use [of things]. That is why even a human being [= ruler] who is knowledgeable about the establishment of order
among the ten thousand kinds of entities, but does not proceed in
his ordering by means of the way of the two principles [Heaven and
Earth],[2] will not be able to fully provide [the ten thousand kinds of
entities with order]; why even Earth, its materiality notwithstanding,
is not able to complete its repose if it does not "take" "Heaven" "as
model" [as Laozi says in 25.12]; and why even Heaven, its ethereal
nature notwithstanding, is not able to preserve its ethereal [nature] if it
does not "take" "the Way" "as model" [as Laozi says in 25.12].*

*If [the Way] is "made use of by pouring out," this "use indeed will
not" be able to "exhaust it" [as Laozi says in 45.2]. If, however, it
were filled up to create fullness, it would overflow once fullness has
been achieved. Thus that "[the Way] is made use of by pouring out"
and is "also not filled up" is due to [the fact that] its [the Way's] being inexhaustible is already absolute. A shape, even though it be huge,
cannot contain its [the Way's] substance. A process, even though it be
all-encompassing, cannot fill its measure. If the ten thousand kinds of
entities reject "this" [the specific entities at hand] and search for [their]
lord, where could this lord be found [as no particular entity is able to*

---

^r Var.: 渝其冥 for 渝其眞: 集註本.

^s Var.: 其然乎似或存乎 for 不亦湛兮似或存乎: 集註本.

^t 存而不有沒而不無有無莫測故曰似存 added from 趙學士集解 1.8b. Cf. Translation
note 4. Hatano Tarō, p. 63 and Lou Yulie, p. 13 n.19, do not accept this piece.

^u Var.: 天僞 for 天慊: 集註本.

contain it]? Is that not [as the Laozi *says] "deep it is [but still] resembling the ancestor of the ten thousand kinds of entities?"*

[The ten thousand entities'] "sharpness" is "numbed" without this being of detriment [for the Way]; [their] "distractions" are "dissolved" without any labor spent [by the Way]; it "mixes" with [their] "luster" without its substance's being sullied, and "joins in the same dust" [with them] without its true [nature] being polluted[3]—is this not also [as the text claims] "immersed [in them] it is, [but still] as if persisting [on its own]"?! It persists but is not an entity; it is not there but is not nothing, whether it is or not is hard to make out; that is why [Laozi] says: "It is as if persisting." [4]

The Earth is preserving its [material] shape, [but] its capacity is unable to go beyond its carrying [the ten thousand kinds of entities]. Heaven rests in its images 懔其象, *[but] its capacity is unable to go beyond its covering [the ten thousand kinds of entities].*[5]

[But as already] Heaven and Earth are unattainable by anyone—is it [the Way] not [in this sense] also [as the text says] "like the precursor of the lord?"[6] *"The lord" refers to the lord of Heaven.*

Zhang 5

5.1 天地不仁以萬物爲芻狗 (Base text: 傅奕古本)

天地任ª自然無爲無造萬物自相治理故不仁也仁者必造立施化ᵇ有
恩ᶜ有爲造立施化則物失其眞有恩ᵈ有爲則物不具存物不具存則不足
以備哉ᵉˑᶠ天地ᵍ不爲獸生芻而獸食芻不爲人生狗而人食狗ʰ無爲於ⁱ萬
物而萬物各適其所用則莫不贍矣若惠ʲ由己樹ᵏ未足任也 (Base text:
集註本ˡ)

ª Var.: 在 for 任: 劉惟永集義本.   ᵇ 施化 for 無施: 劉惟永集義本.

ᶜ Var.: 有思 for 有恩: 劉惟永集義本. Support for 恩: Wang Bi on *Laozi* 17.3 以恩仁
令物.

ᵈ Var.: 有思 for 有恩: 劉惟永集義本.

ᵉ Var.: 備載 for 備哉: 劉惟永集義本.

ᶠ Lacuna beginning with 物失其眞: Wagner.

ᵍ Var.: 矣地 for 天地: 劉惟永集義本.

ʰ 而人食狗 omitted in 集註本, suppl. from 劉惟永集義本.

ⁱ 於 for 然: 劉惟永集義本.   ʲ 惠 for 慧: 劉惟永集義本. Hatano Tarō.

ᵏ 樹 for 猶: 劉惟永集義本.

5.2 聖人不仁以百姓[1]爲芻狗 (Base text: 傅奕古本)

　　聖人與天地合其德以百姓比[m]芻狗也 (Base text: 集註本)

5.3 天地之間其猶[n]橐籥乎[o]虛而不掘[p]動[q]而愈[r]出 (Base text: 傅奕古本)

　　橐排橐也[s]籥樂籥也[t]橐籥之中空洞無情無爲故虛而不得[u]窮屈動而不可竭盡也天地之中蕩然任自然故不可得而窮猶若橐籥也 (Base text: 集註本)

5.4 多言[v]數窮不如守中[w] (Base text: 傅奕古本)

　　愈爲之則愈失之矣物避其慧[x]事錯其言其慧不齊[y]其言[z]不理必窮之數也[z]橐籥而守中[aa]則無窮盡棄己任物則莫不理若橐籥有意於爲聲也則不足以供[ab]吹者之求也 (Base text: 劉惟永集義本)[3]

5.1　　　　　　　　　　　Heaven and Earth are not
　　　　　　　　　　　　　kindly. For them, the ten

---

[1] Var.: 省 for 姓: 馬王堆 A.　　　　　[m] Var.: 化 for 比: 永樂大典本.

[n] Var.: 猷 for 猶: 郭店 A; 馬王堆 B.

[o] Var.: 與 for 乎: 郭店 A; 馬王堆 A; 馬王堆 B.

[p] 掘 for 詘: 陸德明釋文. Var.: 屈 for 掘: 郭店 A; 范應元本. Var.: 滒 for 掘: 馬王堆 A; 馬王堆 B.

[q] Var.: 蹱 for 動: 馬王堆 A. Var.: 勭 for 動: 馬王堆 B.

for 詘: 陸德明釋文. Var.: 屈: 范應元本; 郭店 A. Var.: 滒: 馬王堆 A; 馬王堆 B.

[r] 愈 for 俞 (as given in 馬王堆 A; 馬王堆 B; 范應元本): 陸德明釋文; 郭店 A.

[s] Var.: 橐囊也 for 橐排橐也: 慧琳, 一切經音義 676a sub 排籥; cf. ibid. 672c 橐橐囊也. 橐排橐也 supp. by 陸德明釋文.

[t] Var.: 籥樂器 for 籥樂籥: 文選文賦李善注 17.6b3. Var.: 橐排橐也籥樂籥也 omitted in 劉惟永集義本 and in 取善集.

[u] Var.: 能 for 得: 取善集.　　　　　[v] Var.: 聞 for 言: 馬王堆 A; 馬王堆 B; 文子.

[w] Var.: 不若守於中 for 不如守中: 馬王堆 A; 馬王堆 B.

[x] 物避其慧 for 物樹其惡: Wagner based on Wang Bi on *Laozi* 17.4 不能法以正齊民而以智治國下知避之其令不從故曰侮之也, Wang Bi on *Laozi* 10.4 能無以智乎則民不辟而國治之也, and Wang Bi on *Laozi* 18.2 行術用明以察姦僞趣覩形現物知避之. 智慧 is a common binomial, Wang Bi on *Laozi* 17.4 and 18.2.

[y] 其慧不齊 for 不齊: Wagner based on parallel with next phrase 其言不理.

[z] 其言 for 不言: Hatano Tarō based on 事錯其言.

[aa] 守中 for 守數中: Wagner.　　　　　[ab] Var.: 共 for 供: 陸德明釋文.

thousand kinds of entities
are like grass and dogs.

Heaven and Earth let That-
which-is-of-itself-what-it-is [of
the ten thousand kinds of enti-
ties] come into effect. They are

without interference   *without creation*

[with the result that] the
ten thousand kinds of entities
spontaneously order and regulate
each other.[1] *This is why [the*
Laozi *says] "[Heaven and Earth*
are] not kindly!" Someone who
is kindly will by necessity

create and generate,

have pity and interfere.

Would they [Heaven and Earth,
however,] create and generate,
the entities would lose their true
[nature because of the outside
imposition].

Would they [Heaven and Earth,
however,] have pity and interfer-
ence, the entities would not persist
in their entirety [because this pity
and interference would be partial
and prefer some over others]. If
the entities would not persist in
their entirety, then [Heaven and
Earth] would fail to completely
take care of [all of the entities].[2]

[Lacuna beginning with "If the
entities would lose their true
[nature]"]

Heaven and Earth do not
produce grass for the benefit
of cattle, but the cattle [still]
eat grass. They do not produce
dogs for the benefit of men,
but men [still] eat dogs.[3] *As*
they are without interference

*concerning the ten thousand
kinds of entities, each of the
ten thousand kinds of entities
fits into its use so that there
is none that is not provided
for. Would they [Heaven and
Earth] confer kindness on their
own [initiative], they would be
unable to let [the entities' That-
which-is-of-itself-what-it-is]
come into effect.*[4]

5.2   The Sage is not kindly. For him,
the Hundred Families are like
grass and dogs.

*The Sage, "harmonizing [as the
Wenyan of the Zhouyi says of the
"Great Man"][5] his capacity/receipt
德 with [that of] Heaven and Earth,"
likens the Hundred Families to grass
and dogs.*

5.3   [The space] between Heaven
and Earth is like a

drum   or   flute!
             [That is,]   hollow it is, but inexhaustible
                                 [in the variety of sounds it can
                                 produce].

[the more] it is beaten, the more
[sound] comes out of it.

"Drum" is a drum to be beaten.   *"Flute" is a musical flute.*
             Inside,
drum   *and*   *flute are*
empty   *and*   *hollow.*
                                 *[The flute] has no feelings [of its
                                 own to prefer one sound over
                                 the other].*

*[The drum] has no activity [of its
own to create this resonance rather
than another].*

That is why [as the text claims]

                                 *[the flute] "is hollow" but it is
                                 impossible to exhaust it;*

[the drum] all the "beating" not-
withstanding, is inexhaustible.

> In the [space] between
> Heaven and Earth That-
> which-is-of-itself-what-it-is
> [of all entities] is put grandly
> into effect. That is why [the
> space between Heaven and
> Earth] is inexhaustible "like
> a flute and a drum."

5.4　　　　　　　　　　　By multiplying the words, the
reasoning will [only] come to
naught. This does not compare
to keeping to the middle.

> The more [a ruler] interferes
> with them [the entities], the
> more he makes them lose
> [their true nature]. As

the other beings dodge his intelli-　　　the government affairs confuse
gence, his intelligence brings no　　　his words, his words bring no
peace [and]　　　　　　　　　　　　order

> this [kind of] reasoning
> [with many words and
> intelligence] will necessarily
> come to naught.

Drum　　　　　　　　and　　　　　　　flute

> [on the other hand] "keep to
> the middle" [without being
> specified in either way] so
> that they are inexhaustible
> to the maximum. They
> discard their selves and put
> themselves at the service of
> other entities so that there is
> none that is not well ordered. If

the drum　　　　　　　or　　　　　　　the flute

> were bent on making [a specific]
> sound, they would be unable
> to satisfy the requirements of
> flutists [and drummers].[6]

THE STRUCTURE OF *LAOZI* 5

The general structure of *Laozi* 5 with its parallelism between Heaven and Earth in 5.1 and the Sage in 5.2 is clear. Texts 3 and 4 explain positively and negatively the principle on which the capacity of Heaven and Earth, as well as of the Sage, rests, namely to deal with all of the entities simultaneously; the metaphor of flute and drum deals with Heaven and Earth, while the statement in text 4 refers to human affairs. These two statements, however, are not structurally parallel. The statement about the drum and flute is binary; the statement about multiplying words is not. No interlocking can be established here. It should be noted that the statement about the drum and the flute without the succeeding statement in 5.4 forms a separate *zhang* in the Guodian Laozi A on strip 23,[7] marked off by separating dots both at the beginning and in the end.

However, Wang Bi treats the straight statements in 5.1 about Heaven, as well as in 5.4 about multiplying words, as something like summary statements for implied binary propositions, and then he proceeds to link these implied propositions to each other in the fashion of IPS. The rationale for this is obviously the assumption that these statements are structured and that, if the structure is not visible, it must be made explicit. The transition, and even the link, between the two parallel statements about drum and the flute in 5.3 and the nonbinary statement about the words is not at all immediately clear. By unfolding the single statement about the words into a binary proposition, Wang Bi tries to make sense out of a text that starts off with a very clear and parallel structure of statements about Heaven/Earth and the Sage. That is why I have opted for structural writing. This, however, is based on Wang Bi's explosion of what he reads as a compressed text, not on the available text itself.

Wang Bi's commentary for *Laozi* 5.3 and 5.4 is somewhat corrupt, so that only tentative statements can be made. The surviving elements, however, seem to be structured enough to permit the establishment of rules for the editing of the corrupted passages. The basic divide in Wang's commentary is that between interference, *wei* 爲, and creation, *zao* 造. The pair is loosely linked to the statements concerning the flute and the drum. The drum is associated with *wei* 爲, but the corresponding *zao* 造 is missing for the flute. The link with text 4 is even more tentative. Wang Bi seems to duplicate a simple statement in the text to arrive at binary statements involving *yan* 言, "words," and *hui* 慧, "intelligence," respectively. From his other texts it would seem mandatory for this pair to link up with the established binary grouping, but with the surviving text giving no further clues, the linkage indicated in my structural writing is tentative.

Zhang 6

6.1 谷ᵃ神不死是謂玄牝玄牝之門是謂天地之ᵇ根綿綿若存ᶜ用之不勤ᵈ (Base text: 傅奕古本)

谷神谷中央無谷¹也無形無影無逆無違處卑不動守靜不衰谷以之ᵉ成而不見其形此至物也處卑而不可得名故謂之ᶠ玄牝ᵍ門玄牝之所由也本其所由與太極ʰ同體故謂之天地之根也欲言存邪則不見其形欲言亡邪萬物以之生故曰ⁱ綿綿若存也無物不成用而不勞也ʲ故曰用之ᵏ不勤ˡ (Base text: 劉惟永集義本)

6.1　The spirit of the valley does not die. [I] call it "Dark Female." The door [from] which the Dark Female [comes] [I] call the root of Heaven and Earth. Intangible it is, but still it exists. Its being used does not exert it.

"Spirit of the valley" is the non-valley in the middle of the valley. It [this spirit] is without form and contour,[1] without contrariness and deviation; it resides in a lowly position [namely, the valley] and does not move, it keeps the calm and does not deteriorate. The valley is constituted by it, but it does not show its form. This is the highest entity.[2] Its lowly position [notwithstanding], there is no way to define it. That is why [Laozi only] "calls it" Dark Female [but does not "define" it as such]. "Door" is that on which the Dark Female is based.[3] Basically what it is based on has the same substance as the Taiji 太極, the Great Ultimate [of the Xici 11 *of the* Zhouyi *which "creates the two formations (Yin and Yang)"]. That is why [this door] is spoken of [by*

ᵃ Var.: 浴 for 谷: 馬王堆 A; 馬王堆 B.

ᵇ Var.: 之 om.: 范應元本.

ᶜ Var.: 緜緜呵 (馬王堆 B add.: 其) 若存 for 綿綿若存: 馬王堆 A; 馬王堆 B.

ᵈ Var.: 堇 for 勤: 馬王堆 A; 馬王堆 B.

ᵉ Var.: 以成 for 以之成: 集註本.　　ᶠ 謂之 for 謂: 集註本.

ᵍ 玄牝 for 天地之根綿綿若存用之不勤: 張湛列子天端注, p. 4.

ʰ 太極 for 極: 張湛列子天端注, p. 4.

ⁱ 故曰 for 故: 張湛列子天端注, p. 4.

ʲ Var.: 無物不成而不勞也 for 無物不成用而不勞也: 張湛列子天端注. Rejected because this variant breaks the 4-character phrase pattern.

ᵏ Var.: 用而 for 用之: 集註本.　　ˡ Var.: 勤也 for 勤.: 集註本.

*Laozi] as "the root of Heaven and Earth"! If one wished to state that
it exists, [the objection would be that] it does not show its form. If one
wished to state that it does not exist, [it still remains true that] the ten
thousand kinds of entities are generated by means of it. That is why
[the text says]: "Intangible it is but still it exists!" There is no entity
not completed [through it], but, while being used [in this extensive
manner], it does not labor [to have them completed]. That is why [the
text] says: "Its being used does not exert it"!*[4]

Zhang 7

7.1 天長地久天地所以能長且久者以其不自生[a] (Base text: 傅奕古本)

　　自生則與物爭不自生則物歸也 (Base text: 劉惟永集義本)

7.2 故能長久[b]是以聖人後其身[c]而身先外其身而身存[d]不[e]以其無私邪[f]故能成其
私 (Base text: 傅奕古本)

　　無私者無爲於身也身先身存故曰能成其私也 (Base text: 劉惟永集義
本)

7.1	Heaven excels.		Earth persists.
		That by which	
	Heaven	and	Earth

---

[a] Var.: 自生也 for 自生: 馬王堆 A; 馬王堆 B.

[b] 久 for 生: Shima Kuniō. All transmitted texts of the *Laozi* over Wang Bi's *Commentary*
read 故能長生 "therefore they are able to exist for a long time." Wang Bi's *Commentary* does
not take up this formula at all, either here or in other places. In terms of content, it clearly
fits the interpretive line of the Heshang gong *Commentary*, while even the manuscripts of
the Xiang Er family all write (with the exception of the Li Rong manuscript in the Daozang)
長久. In terms of analytical symmetry, the statements about the Sage in the second part take
up the two separate features of Heaven and Earth. The Sage emulates Heaven's excelling in
the way he manages to "be to the fore" and Earth's persisting in the way the Sage manages
to keep himself intact. I therefore follow Shima Kuniō's emendation.

[c] Var.: 芮 [= 退] 其身 for 後其身: 馬王堆 A. Var.: 退其身 for 後其身: 馬王堆 B.

[d] Var.: 外其身而身先外其身而身存 for 外其身而身存: 馬王堆 B.

[e] Var.: 非 for 不: 范應元本.

[f] Var.:輿 [= 與] for 邪: 馬王堆 A; 馬王堆 B.

	are able to	
excel	and	persist
	is that they do not live for	
	their own interests.	

*Should they live for their own
interests, they would struggle
with [other] entities. As they
do not live for their own
interests, the [other] entities
relate back to them.*

7.2 That [indeed] is the reason why
they are able to

| excel | and | persist. |

This [pattern of Heaven and Earth]
is the reason why the Sage [as is
well known]

puts his own person in the back-	disregards his own person and
ground and [achieves in this way]	[achieves in this way] that his
that his own person comes to be	own person will last.[1]
to the fore.	

Indeed, is it not because of his
being without private interests
that he is able to accomplish his
private interests?

*"Being without private interests"
means that he does not act with
regard to his own person. It is
because [in this manner]*

| *his person will excel and* | *his person will last* |

*that [the text] says, "He is able to
accomplish his private interests"!*[2]

THE STRUCTURE OF *LAOZI* 7

Laozi 7 is a fine example of the argumentation in many *zhang* of the *Laozi*. First, it establishes a pattern among the "great" entities of Heaven and Earth to explain a pattern in the behavior of the Sage that is known to the reader but not understood in its logic. Second, it is written in closed IPS, linking the two features of the Sage, his high standing and his capacity to survive to his imitation of Heaven's excellence and Earth's persistence. The structure of the *zhang* is:

	I	a		b	(7.1)
		a		b	(7.1)
			c		(7.1)
			c		(7.2)
	II	a		b	(7.2)
			c		(7.2)

Zhang 8

8.1 上善若ª水水善利萬物而不爭ᵇ處ᶜ眾人ᵈ之所惡ᵉ (Base text: 傅奕古本)

人惡卑也 (Base text: 劉惟永集義本)

8.2 故幾於道矣ᶠ (Base text: 傅奕古本)

道無水有故日幾也ᵍ (Base text: 劉惟永集義本)

8.3 居善地心善淵ʰ與善仁ⁱ言善信ʲ政ᵏ善治ˡ事善能動ˡ善時夫唯ᵐ不爭ⁿ故無尤矣ᵒ
(Base text: 傅奕古本)

言水皆應於此道也 (Base text: 劉惟永集義本)

ª Var.: 治 [= 似] for 若: 馬王堆 A. 如 for 若: 馬王堆 B.

ᵇ Var.: 有靜 for 不爭: 馬王堆 A. Var.: 有爭 for 不爭: 馬王堆 B.

ᶜ 處 for 居: 陸德明釋文.   ᵈ Var.: 眾 for 眾人: 馬王堆 A.

ᵉ Var.: 亞 for 惡: 馬王堆 B.   ᶠ Var.: 道 for 道矣: 范應元本.

ᵍ Var.: 幾 for 幾也: 集註本.   ʰ Var.: 瀟 for 淵: 馬王堆 A.

ⁱ Var.: 仁 for 人; 范應元本. Var.: 予善信 for 與善仁言善信: 馬王堆 A. Var.: 予善天
for 與善仁: 馬王堆 B.

ʲ Var.: 言善信 omitted by 馬王堆 A.

ᵏ Var.: 正善治 for 政善治: 馬王堆 A; 馬王堆 B.

ˡ Var.: 蹱 for 動: 馬王堆 A.   ᵐ 唯 for 惟: 馬王堆 A; 馬王堆 B.

ⁿ Var.: 靜 for 爭: 馬王堆 A.

ᵒ Var.: 尤 for 尤矣: 馬王堆 A; 馬王堆 B; 范應元本. Support for 尤矣: Zhuang Zun
also read 尤矣.

8.1 The most excellent is comparable to water. Water excels in being of use to the ten thousand entities while not struggling [with them], dwelling [as it does] in a place abhorred by the men of the crowd.

> *The others abhor low [positions].*

8.2 That is why [water] is close to the Way [i.e., to the utmost excellent].

> *The Way is negativity. Water[,however,] is an entity. Therefore [the text says that water is only] "close to" [the Way, and not identical with it].*[1]

8.3 [Water's]
—excellence with regard to [its] station is [its lowly] place.
—excellence with regard to [its] heart is [its] depth.
—excellence with regard to giving is its being kindly.
—excellence with regard to words is its sincerity.
—excellence with regard to government is its [achievement of] well-regulatedness.[2]
—excellence with regard to [the handling of] affairs is its capability.
—excellence with regard to action is its timeliness.

Generally speaking, it is only because it is not struggling [with other entities] that there is no resentment [against it].

> *This means that water corresponds in all these [qualities] to this Way.*

Zhang 9

9.1 持ªª而盈之不若ᵇ其已 (Base text: 傅奕古本)

持謂不失德也既不失其德又盈之勢必傾危故不若ᶜ其已也不若其已者ᵈ謂乃更不如無德無功者也 (Base text: 劉惟永集義本)

ª Var.: 揰 for 持: 馬王堆 A; 馬王堆 B.

ᵇ 不若 for 不如: Wang Bi on *Laozi* 9.3 不若其已, supported by 馬王堆 B. Shima Kuniō.

ᶜ 若 for 如: Wagner based on reconstructed main text and Wang Bi comm. on *Laozi* 9.3. This seems to be one of the few instances where a commentary passage has been changed to fit a changed main text.

ᵈ 故不若其已也不若其已者 for 不若其已者: Wagner based on Hatano Tarō's conjecture to supplement 也不如其已 because of the parallel to Wang Bi on *Laozi* 9.2 不可長保也. 故 in Wang Bi's *Laozi* commentary means "that is why" [the text says]. Without the supplement this would be a singular case of a 故 introducing a phrase such as "therefore [the text passage AAA] means. . . ."

9.2 揣^e而銳^f之不可長保^g (Base text: 范應元本)

　　既揣末令尖又銳之令利勢必摧衄故不可長保也 (Base text: 劉惟永集
　　義本)

9.3 金玉滿室^h莫之能守ⁱ (Base text: 傅奕古本)

　　不若其已 (Base text: 劉惟永集義本)

9.4 富貴而驕自遺其咎^j (Base text: 傅奕古本)

　　不可長保也 (Base text: 劉惟永集義本)

9.5 功遂^k身退^l天之道^m (Base text: 馬王堆 B)

　　四時更運功成則移 (Base text: 劉惟永集義本)

| 9.1 | By maintaining [it] and then even adding to it, [a ruler] is not as well off as if he had nothing. | By polishing [it] and then [furthermore] grinding it, [a ruler] will be unable to protect [himself] for long. | 9.2 |

---

　　^e Var.: 敁 for 揣: 傅奕古本. Var.: 掬 for 揣: 馬王堆 B. Var.: 湍 for 揣: 郭店 A.

　　^f Var.: 梲 for 銳: 傅奕古本; 陸德明釋文. Var.: 兊 for 銳: 馬王堆 A; 馬王堆 B. Support for 銳 against Lu Deming, who gives 銳 as the pronunciation for 梲: Wang Bi comm. 又銳之; 淮南子; 文子; 莊 (嚴) 遵. 紀均 claims in a note to the 四庫 ed. that "all old MS read 銳, only Lu Deming gives 梲." Shima Kuniō.

　　^g Var.: 不可長葆也 (馬王堆 A: 葆之): 馬王堆 A; 馬王堆 B.

　　^h Var.: 盈 for 滿: 馬王堆 A; 郭店 A (涅 = 盈). Var.: 堂 for 室: 陸德明釋文. Support for 室: one manuscript quoted by 陸德明釋文; 范應元 states explicitly that his Wang Bi manuscript as well as that with the text by Zhuang Zun read 室. 馬王堆 A; 馬王堆 B. 郭店 A; Hatano Tarō; Shima Kuniō.

　　ⁱ Var.: 莫之能 (馬王堆 A om. 能) 守也 for 莫之能守: 馬王堆 A; 馬王堆 B. Var.: 莫能獸 [= 守] 也: 郭店 A.

　　^j Var.: 自遺咎也 for 自遺其咎: 郭店 A; 馬王堆 A; 馬王堆 B.

　　^k Var.: 功成名遂 for 功遂: 范應元本. Var.: 成名功遂 for 功成: 傅奕古本. I agree with Gao Ming, Boshu 262, that Wang Bi's 功成 is a translation of 功遂, not a quotation from his text. Support for 功遂 against the reading proposed by 馬敍倫 and followed by Hatano Tarō and Shima Kuniō: 郭店 A; 馬王堆 A (both 述 for 遂); 馬王堆 B; 陸德明釋文; (文子); 漢書.

　　^l Var.: 功述身芮 [= 退] for 功遂身退: 馬王堆 A.

　　^m Var.: 道也 for 道: 郭店 A; 馬王堆 B.

"To maintain" refers to [what in Laozi 38.2 is called] "not to let go of the receipt/capacity." If [he] already does not let go of his capacity, but still adds on to it, [this results in] a situation where there is an unavoidable danger of being toppled. That is why [as the text says] "he is not as well off as if he had nothing." "He is not as well off as if he had nothing" means it is not even as good as having neither capacity nor achievements.

If one has already polished the tip [of a sword] so that it becomes pointed, and grinds it in addition so that it becomes sharp, a situation [arises] where it is unavoidable that one will suffer a defeat. That is why [as the text says] "he will be unable to protect [himself] for long!"

9.3

[Accordingly,]

9.4

no one who fills [his already sumptuous] palace [furthermore] with gold and jades will be able to preserve [them].

someone who is [already] wealthy and honored but [in addition turns] arrogant brings calamity upon himself.

[Having these riches] one "is not as well off as if one [had] nothing" [as Laozi had stated in the parallel phrase above].

He "will be unable to protect himself for long" (as Laozi had stated in the parallel phrase above].

9.5

To withdraw [as a ruler] with one's person once the task is achieved—that is the Way of Heaven!

The four seasons alternate, when the task [of one of them] is completed, there is a change [to the next one].[1]

THE STRUCTURE OF *LAOZI* 9

Laozi 9 has nearly all of the formal markers of IPS. Texts 1 and 2 are parallel in the number of characters and structure. Texts 3 and 4 are parallel in the number of characters, and both divide into two blocks of four, but the grammar in the two segments is not parallel. Text 5 is not parallel to any other phrase, and with its grand "that is the way of Heaven" announces itself as a general conclusion for both strains of argument. However, the link between the first and the second pair of texts, between texts 1 and 2 and 3 and 4 is hard to decipher, as the links are "closed" and not explicit, as in other *zhang*. Wang Bi solves the riddle with a simple technique by quoting a segment of text 1 under text 3, and a segment of text 2 under text 4, thus linking two symmetrical pairs and prescribing a strategy for reading that I have tried to make explicit in my translation. This construction of Wang Bi's is supported by the reading of the Guodian Laozi A, which repeats the term 盈 from the first line in the third with the formula 盈室, so that at least the link between lines one and three is explicit. The structure of the *zhang* is thus according to Wang Bi:

$$
\begin{array}{lll}
\text{a} & \text{b} & (9.1, 9.2) \\
\text{a} & \text{b} & (9.3, 9.4) \\
& \text{c} & (9.5)
\end{array}
$$

D. C. Lau has suggested (*Tao Te Ching*, 13) that the terms of text 1 refer to the "ch'ih ying" vessel, which stands in position when empty but overturns when full. His translation strategy has been to cut the text into proverbial segments without much interest for any potentially cohesive argument. Wang Bi's reading strategy has been the opposite.

Zhang 10

10.1 載營魄[a]抱[b]一能無[c]離乎 (Base text: 范應元本)

　　載猶處也營魄人之常居處也一人之眞也言人能處常居之宅抱一清神
　　能常無離乎則萬物自賓也 (Base text: 劉惟永集義本)

10.2 專[d]氣[e]致[f]柔能若嬰兒乎[g] (Base text: 傅奕古本)

　　專任也致極也言任自然之氣致至柔之和能若嬰兒之無所欲乎則物全
　　而性得矣 (Base text: 劉惟永集義本)

10.3 滌[h]除玄覽[i]能無[j]疵乎 (Base text: 傅奕古本)

---

[a] Var.: 袙 for 魄: 馬王堆 B.　　　[b] Var.: 裹 for 抱: 傅奕古本.

[c] Var.: 毋 for 無: 馬王堆 B.　　　[d] Var.: 榑 for 專: 馬王堆 B.

[e] Var.: 炁 for 氣: 范應元本.　　　[f] Var.: 至 for 致: 馬王堆 B.

[g] 能若嬰兒乎 for 能如嬰兒乎 (also in 范應元本): Wang Bi comm.: 能若嬰兒; Shima Kuniō. Var.: 能嬰兒乎 for 能若嬰兒乎: 馬王堆 A; 馬王堆 B.

[h] Var.: 脩 for 滌: 馬王堆 A; 馬王堆 B.

[i] Var.: 藍 for 覽: 馬王堆 A. Var.: 監 for 覽: 馬王堆 B.

[j] Var.: 毋 for 無: 馬王堆 A. Var.: 毋有 for 無: 馬王堆 B.

玄物之極也言能滌除邪飾至於極覽能不以物介其明疵[k]其神乎則終與玄同也 (Base text: 劉惟永集義本)

10.4 愛民治[l]國能無[m]以知[l]乎 (Base text: 傅奕古本)

任術以求成運數以求匿者智也玄覽無疵猶絕聖也治國無以智猶棄智也能無以智乎則民不辟而國治之[n]也 (Base text: 劉惟永集義本)

10.5 天門開[o]闔能爲雌乎 (Base text: 傅奕古本)

天門謂天下之所由從也開闔治亂之際也或開或闔經通於天下故曰天門開闔也雌應而不唱[p]因而不爲言天門開闔能爲雌乎則物自賓而處自安矣 (Base text: 劉惟永集義本)

10.6 明白四達能無以爲[q]乎 (Base text: 傅奕古本)

言至明四達無迷無惑[r]能無以爲乎則物化矣所謂道常無爲侯王若能守則萬物自化[s] (Base text: 集註本)

10.7 生之 (Base text: 傅奕古本)

不塞其原也 (Base text: 劉惟永集義本)

10.8 畜之 (Base text: 傅奕古本)

不禁其性也 (Base text: 劉惟永集義本)

---

[k] Var.: 疵之其神乎 for 疵其神乎: 集註本. Support for 劉惟永集義本 reading is parallelism between 介其明 and 疵其神. Tōjō Itsudō. 易順鼎.

[l] Var.: 栝 (= 活) for 治: 馬王堆 B. [m] Var.: 毋 for 無: 馬王堆 B.

[n] Var.: 民又僻而國治 for 民不辟而國治之: 集註本.

[o] Var.: 啓 for 開: 馬王堆 B.

[p] Var.: 昌 for 唱: 陸德明釋文. Support for 唱 is Wang Bi on *Laozi* 68.2 應而不唱.

[q] Var.: 無 (馬王堆 B:毋) 以知 for 無以爲: 馬王堆 B; 陸德明釋文. Support for 能無以爲乎 is Wang Bi comm.: 能無以爲乎.

[r] 無迷無惑 for 無迷無迷無惑: 劉惟永集義本.

[s] Var.: 萬物自賓也 for 萬物自化: 劉惟永集義本. Support for 萬物自化 is *Laozi* 37.3: 侯王若能守萬物將自化.

10.9 生而不ᵗ有爲而不恃ᵘ長而不ᵛ宰是謂ʷ玄德 (Base text: 傅奕古本)

不塞其原則物自生何功之有不禁其性則物自濟何爲之恃ˣ物自長足
不吾宰成有德無主非玄而何ʸ凡言玄德者ᶻ皆有德而ᵃᵃ不ᵃᵇ知其主ᵃᶜ出
乎ᵃᵈ幽冥者也ᵃᵉ (Base text: 劉惟永集義本)

10.1 [For a ruler] to keep to the camp, to hold on to the[ir] One,[1] and be able not to be separated from it—ah!	[For a ruler] to focus on 10.2 the breath, *qi* 氣, to bring about softness, and [in this] be able to be like a baby—ah!

"To keep to" is like "to stay in." "Camp" is the abode of eternal sojourn of human beings. The "One" is the true [nature] of [the other] human beings. [The sentence] means: If a human being would be able to stay in [his] abode of eternal sojourn, "hold on to the One" and purify [his] spirit [so that] he would be able to be permanently "not separated" from [the abode and the One]—ah, then [indeed] "the ten thousand kinds of entities [would] submit [to him] of their own accord as guests" [as the Laozi *32.1 says].*

"To focus on" means "to put to use." "To bring about" means "to achieve the epitome of." [The sentence] means: If [a ruler] would put the breath of That-which-is-of-itself-what-it-is [of the other entities] to use, achieve the harmony of the utmost softness [in them], and would [himself] be able to be without desires [in this] like a baby—ah, then [indeed] the [other] entities would [remain] intact and fulfill [their]nature.

10.3 [For a ruler] to clean and wipe the perception of That-which-is-Dark and to be able to [keep	[For a ruler] to love the 10.4 people and bring order to the state, and to be able to

---

ᵗ Var.: 弗 for 不: 馬王堆 A; 馬王堆 B.

ᵘ Var.: 爲而不恃 om.: 馬王堆 B; (馬王堆 A as seen from size of lacuna).

ᵛ Var.: 弗 for 不: 馬王堆 B.   ʷ Var.: 胃 for 謂: 馬王堆 B.

ˣ Var.: 情 for 恃: 集註本.   ʸ Var.: 如 for 而: 集註本.

ᶻ 玄德者 for 玄德 (also in 集註本): 文選東京賦李善注 3.17b6.

ᵃᵃ Var.: 而 om.: 文選東京賦李善注 3.17b6.

ᵃᵇ Var.: 又 for 不: 集註本.

ᵃᶜ Var.: 至 for 主: 文選東京賦李善注 3.17b6.

ᵃᵈ Var.: 于 for 乎: 文選東京賦李善注 3.17b6.

ᵃᵉ 幽冥者也 for 幽冥: 文選東京賦李善注 3.17b6; 陳景元纂微.

it] without blemish—ah!

(1) *That-which-is-Dark is the ulti-mate of the entities. [The sentence] means: If [a ruler] would be able to clean and wipe off [all that is] evil and trumped up, and arrive at the perception of the ultimate, and if he would be able to [make sure] that his brightness would not be sullied by other entities nor his spirit be dirtied [by them]—ah, then [indeed] would he eventually become "identical with That-which-is-Dark" [as the* Laozi *56.7 says]*
(3) *[To have] a "perception of That-which-is-Dark" "without blemish" is like [what the* Laozi *19.1 calls] "rejecting wisdom."*

[proceed in this] without using knowledge —ah!

(2) *To apply [as a ruler] artifices to strive for results, to use devices to seek out [the] secrets [of the lower orders]—this is called "knowledge."*

(4) *To "bring order to the state" "without using knowledge" is like [what the* Laozi *19.1 calls] "rejecting intelligence" [the result of which rejection is a "hundredfold increase in the benefits of the people"]. If [a ruler] is "able to [proceed in this] without using intelli-gence—ah," then [indeed] the people will not evade*[2] *him and the state will be regulated.*

10.5   [For a ruler to be, during] the opening as well as the closing of the doors of Heaven, able to be a hen—ah!

[For a ruler] to understand   10.6 [all things going on in] the four directions and be able to [do so] without having a personal interest—ah!

"The doors of Heaven" refers to that from which All Under Heaven comes forth.[3] *The "opening and the closing" are the phases of order and chaos. [The doors'] being opened or closed has pervasive effects on All Under Heaven. That is why [the text] says: "[During] the opening as well as the closing of the doors of Heaven!" A hen responds but does not take the lead in singing,*[4]

[This passage] means: If he succeeds in understanding [all things going on in] the four directions without being deceived or deluded and is able to [do so] without having a personal interest—ah, then [indeed] the [other] entities will change for the better. This is what [the Laozi *37.1–3] means by "The Eternal of the Way is without interference. [. . .] If*

is responsive [to others] but does not [actively] interfere. [The text] means: If [during] the opening as well as the closing of the doors of Heaven, [a ruler] would be able to be a hen—ah, then [indeed] "the [other] entities [would] of their own accord [submit to him] as [his] guests" [as the Laozi *32.1 says] and his abode would be peaceful of its own accord.*

dukes and kings were only able to hold on to [the Eternal of the Way], the ten thousand kinds of entities would change [for the better] of their own acord."

10.7   That it [the Dao] generates them [the entities]

That it [the Dao] rears   10.8
them [the entities]

That is, that it does not block their source.

That is, that it does not hem in their nature.

10.9   [and that,]
while they come alive, it has no [specific effort on its side],

while they act, it does not make them dependent,

[that, in short], while they grow, there would be no lording it over [their growth on its side]—this is called "the Receipt [coming from] That-which- is-Dark" *xuan de* 玄德 [5]

As it does not block their source, the entities create themselves, and what achievement [from its side] should it "have"?

As it does not hem in their nature, the entities regulate themselves, and on what activity [on its side] should they "depend"?

If the entities [in this manner] grow on their own and are sufficient themselves without some "I" lording it over [their] completion, [that is] if they have receipts but no lord [to specifically direct them] how could this come about if not through That-which- is-Dark? Generally this is to say that "Receipt [coming from] That-which-is-Dark" means that all [entities] have Receipts, but that they do not know its

> master [on the basis of whom
> they attain it] [because] indeed
> it [the Receipt] comes forth out
> of the Dark and abstruse.

THE STRUCTURE OF *LAOZI* 10

Laozi 10 does not have a subject. In the commentary on 10.1, *ren* 人, the human being, is inserted as the subject of "to be able." In the commentary on 10.6, however, the "dukes and kings" are quoted as the subjects of "to be able," while the first phrase here about being without deception and delusion recurs in Wang Bi on *Laozi* 29.3. with the Sage as the subject. Finally, in Wang's commentary on *Laozi* 10.9, a *wu* 吾, "I," appears as the implied subject of the preceding sentences.

Generally speaking, Wang Bi reads the *zhang* as a description of the person ideally suited for bringing order to the ten thousand entities. His six abilities are all negative and elusive. They ensure that none of the beneficiaries of his action will be able to have any knowledge of him. This point is made in texts 7–9, which define the paradox of the unknowability of that by which the ten thousand entities are with the term *xuan de* 玄 德, the Receipt coming from That-which-is-Dark. This latter part of the *Laozi* text recurs verbatim in *Laozi* 51.3 ff., where the subject that "creates them" and "rears them" is the Way. The implication will be that the Sage Ruler imitates the Way and shares in his unknowability.

The second problem concerns the structure of *Laozi* 10. Evidently, it comes in two parts. The first six phrases are parallel in grammatical structure, are divided above the same term, *neng* 能, and, with the exception of the first phrase, have the same number of characters.

The rest is one long sentence. I shall deal with this first. It begins with two parallel phrases of two characters each (texts 10.7 and 10.8), followed by a set of three parallel phrases. Wang Bi comments on the first two of these three phrases in sentences that again are parallel, and he links them explicitly to the two preceding sentences by taking up both the vocabulary of 10.7 and 10.8 and his own commentary to them. This gives an easy interlocked sequence ab ab. The commentary on the third parallel phrase ("[that in short] while they grow there would be no lording it over [their growth on its side]") is not parallel to that about the two others. This indicates that this phrase actually is a c phrase relating to both preceding groups. This reading of a third parallel phrase in the *Laozi* as belonging to the c category is standard with Wang Bi and is often supported by slight deviations in the structure of the third phrase, as in the first three phrases of *Laozi* 44. Wang Bi's indications thus give a clear structure for the second part, namely,

a		(10.7)
	b	(10.8)
a		(10.9)
	b	(10.9)
	c	(10.9)

For the first part, things are more difficult. The standard for the first six phrases would be to fall into three pairs of two each in a sequence ab ab ab, or into two groups with the common structure abc. Wang Bi's commentary on 10.1 about the entities "gathering of their own accord as guests" and about the peace in one's abode recurs at the end of his commentary on 10.5, linking these two. The phrase in Wang Bi on 10.1 about "purifying the spirit" is taken up in his commentary on 10.3, where he interprets the "cleaning and wiping the perception of That-which-is-Dark" as the capacity to "not have the spirit dirtied." This establishes a first chain 1/3/5. The remaining three phrases deal, according to Wang's commentary, with the ordering of the state without a personally motivated (government) interference in terms of action or investigation. The *wu suo yu* 無所欲, "without desires," in 10.2 is taken up in the *wu yi wei* 無以爲, "without having personal interest," in 10.6; the topic of the ordering of the state in 10.4 is continued in 10.6 with the quotation from *Laozi* 37 about the kings and dukes. We would thus have a sequence

a		(10.1)
	b	(10.2)
a		(10.3)
	b	(10.4)
a		(10.5)
	b	(10.6)

However, the hints provided by Wang Bi are sparse, and this interpretation remains tenuous.

The third problem is the link between the two parts of the *zhang*. Wang Bi provides the link between the a and b chains already established for the first part and those of the second by identifying the "rearing" of the ten thousand entities with their nature's not being blocked, and this again with their "establishing order on their own," which links to the 10.2/4/6 chain above. This forces us to link the *sheng zhi* 生之 in 10.7 to the chain 10.1/3/5, although the link also seems tenuous.

This leaves us with an overall structure of

a	b	(10.1, 10.2)
a	b	(10.3, 10.4)
a	b	(10.5, 10.6)
a	b	(10.7, 10.8)
a	b	(10.9, 10.9)
	c	(10.9)

The fourth problem is the logical link between the two parts of the *zhang*, also linked in the MWD manuscripts. According to Wang Bi, the common element of the first six phrases in their description of the ideal ruler is his absence of positive, assertive features. He will reach the goal of social order and personal security through the nonexertion of all of the powers and devices at his command and through the elimination of all personal desires, the fulfillment of which would again be seen as his natural prerogative.

The second section is an original, if shortened, quotation from *Laozi* 51. The purport of this section is to describe the *xuan de* 玄德 coming from the Dao. The Dao creates and rears the ten thousand entities without any active, assertive, and necessarily partial interference.

The consequence is that the ten thousand entities enjoy the benefits without any possible knowledge of the ultimate cause of their existence and order. The ideal ruler is to operate by reproducing in his own relations with All Under Heaven the relationship of the Dao with the ten thousand entities. The link between both sections is thus *xuan de*. The identity of the formulations in *zhang* 10 and *zhang* 51 reflects the suggested identity of the dynamics of the interaction between the one and the many in nature and society. For Wang Bi, the *Laozi* gives philosophical advice to a ruler. I think therefore, that the second section has to be read as a rationale for why the negative features of the first section are necessary.

Zhang 11

11.1 三十輻共[a]一轂當其無有車之用[b] (Base text: 傅奕古本)

---

[a] Var.: 同 for 共: 馬王堆 B.

[b] Var.: 用也 for 用: 馬王堆 B. (馬王堆 A has the space).

轂所以能統三十輻者無也以其無能受物之故故能以寡統衆[c]也 (Base text: 劉惟永集義本)

11.2 挺[d]埴以爲器[e]當其無有器[f]之用[g]鑿戶牖以爲室[h]當其無有室之用[i]故有之以爲利無之以爲用 (Base text: 范應元本)

木埴壁所以成三者而皆以無爲用也[j]言[k]有之所以爲利皆賴無以爲用也 (Base text: 劉惟永集義本)

11.1   Thirty spokes share one hub. But it is the [latter's] negativity [vis-à-vis the specificity of the spokes] that is [the basis] for the usability of the existing carriage.

That by which a [= one] hub is capable of holding together thirty [different] spokes is its negativity [vis-à-vis their specific features]. Because of this negativity, [the hub] is capable of taking in the points of origin of [many different] entities. That is why [the hub] is capable, being itself the minimum, to control the many [spokes]![1]

11.2   One kneads clay in order to make a vessel. But its negativity [i. e., the fact that inside the vessel there is no clay so that many different things can be put into it] secures the usability of the existing vessel. One cuts out doors and windows to make a room. But it is their [the doors' and windows'] negativity [vis-à-vis the wall] which secures the usability of the existing room. Therefore that [they are specific] entities secures [their] being beneficial, while negativity secures [their] usability.[2]

The three [wheel, vessel, room] are made from wood, clay, and mortar, respectively, but all [depend] on negativity for their usability. This [Laozi statement] means: Entities in order to be beneficial all depend on negativity for their usability.

---

[c] 以寡統衆 for 以實統衆: 陶鴻慶 based on the opening statement in Wang Bi's 周易略例: 夫衆不能治衆, 治衆者, 至寡者也.

[d] Var.: 埏 for 挺: 傅奕古本. Var.: 然 for 挺: 馬王堆 A. Var.: 燃 for 挺: 馬王堆 B. Support for 挺: 陸德明釋文.

[e] Var.: 爲器 for 以爲器: 馬王堆 A. Var.: 而爲器 for 以爲器: 馬王堆 B.

[f] Var.: 埴器 for 器: 馬王堆 A; 馬王堆 B.

[g] Var.: 用也 for 用: 馬王堆 B.   [h] Var.: 以爲室 om.: 馬王堆 B.

[i] Var.: 用也 for 用: 馬王堆 A; 馬王堆 B.

[j] Var.: 用 for 用也: 永樂大典本.

[k] 言有之所以爲利 for 言無者有之所以爲利: Hatano Tarō without supporting evidence. Supported by Wang Bi on *Laozi* 1.4 凡有之爲利必以無爲用, and Wang Bi on *Laozi* 40.1 有以無爲用.

THE STRUCTURE OF *LAOZI* 11

Three examples are given, all of them parallel. The conclusion in the last phrase establishes a general principle. There is no interlocking structure. For a comparative analysis of different commentaries to this *zhang*, compare my *Craft of a Chinese Commentator*, pages 231–49.

Zhang 12

12.1 五色令^a人目盲^b五音令人耳聾五味令人口爽^c馳騁田獵^d令^e人心發狂 (Base text: 傅奕古本)

爽差失也失口之用故謂之爽夫^f耳目心口皆順其性也不以順性命反以傷自然故曰盲聾爽狂也 (Base text: 集註本)

12.2 難得之貨^g令人行妨^h (Base text: 傅奕古本)

難得之貨塞人正路故令人行妨也 (Base text: 集註本)

12.3 是以聖人ⁱ爲腹不爲目故去彼取此^j (Base text: 傅奕古本)

爲腹者以物養己爲目者以目^l役己故聖人不爲目也 (Base text: 集註本)

12.1 The five colors let man's eyes go blind. The five sounds let man's ears go deaf. The five tastes let man's mouth go numb. Riding and hunting let man's heart go wild.

---

^a Var.: 使 for 令: 馬王堆 A; 馬王堆 B.

^b Var.: 明 for 盲: 馬王堆 A.

^c Var.: 五味使人之口唑五音使人之耳聾 for 五音令人耳聾五味令人口爽 transposed to the end of 12.2: 馬王堆 A. Var.: 五味使人之口爽五音使人之耳口 for 五音令人耳聾五味令人口爽 transposed to the end of 12.2: 馬王堆 B. Sequence for Wang Bi confirmed by commentary sequence of 盲聾爽狂.

^d Var.: 臘 for 獵: 馬王堆 A; 馬王堆 B.

^e Var.: 使 for 令: 馬王堆 A; 馬王堆 B.

^f 夫 for 失: 永樂大典本; 道藏本.　　^g Var.: 價 for 貨: 馬王堆 A.

^h Var.: 使人之行方(馬王堆 B:仿) for 令人行妨: 馬王堆 A; 馬王堆 B.

ⁱ Var.: 聖人之治也 for 聖人: 馬王堆 A; 馬王堆 B.

^j Var.: 罷耳 for 彼取: 馬王堆 A. Var.: 去彼而取此 for 去彼取此: 馬王堆 B.

"Go numb" means "to become deficient and lose." They lose the use of their mouth, therefore [the text] calls it "go numb." It is a fact that ears, eyes, mouth, and heart all are in accordance with [man's specific] nature. If [,as in the above cases, man] is not [acting] by way of "following the true nature" [as the Shuogua *of the* Zhouyi *calls it],[1] he will to the contrary [act] by way of hurting [his] That-which-is-of-itself-what-it-is. That is why [the text] says [they will let a man go] "blind," "deaf," "numb," "wild!"*

12.2   [In short,] goods that are hard to get block man's actions.

Goods that are hard to get block man's correct path. In that sense they "block man's actions."

12.3   That is why the Sage is for [man's] belly and not for [his] eye; therefore he discards the latter and favors the former.

"He who is for the belly" feeds his own person with other things. "He who is for the eye" puts himself into service [of other things] with his eye. Therefore the Sage is not for the eye.

THE STRUCTURE OF *LAOZI* 12

Laozi 12 begins with five parallel phrases. Wang Bi cuts the fifth phrase off by inserting a separate commentary. This phrase thus must refer to the four preceding phrases and must sum them up under the general heading of luxuries hard to come by that destroy men's true nature. The expression "goods that are hard to get" recurs various times in both text and commentary, *Laozi* 3.1 and 64.7. There the Sage does not cherish such goods so as not to encourage the people to go after them. From this we have to infer a strategy for the translation of the last part that deals with the Sage. He is not dealing with himself, but with the people. He takes care of their bellies and not their eyes, prompts them to nourish their own person with other things and to not become dependent on other things as the eye is on objects. The eye here stands for the entire group of pleasures summed up in phrase 2. In *Laozi* 3.2, the Sage is "emptying [the people's] hearts and filling their bellies." The "that is why" in text 3 indicates that the contents of the last phrase are familiar to the reader, and that the text, through the preceding phrases, provides a reason for this familiar adage.

Zhang 13

13.1 寵^a辱若驚貴大患^b若身何謂^c寵^d辱若驚^e寵爲下^f得之若驚失之若驚是謂^g寵^h辱若驚 (Base text: 傅奕古本)¹

寵必有辱榮必有患寵ⁱ辱等榮患同也爲下得寵辱榮患若驚則不足以亂天下也 (Base text: 集註本)

13.2 何謂^j貴大患若身 (Base text: 傅奕古本)

夫貴^k榮寵之屬也生之厚必入死之地故謂之大患也人迷之於榮寵返之於身故曰大患若身也 (Base text: 集註本)

13.3 吾所以有大患者爲吾有身^l (Base text: 傅奕古本)

由有其身也 (Base text: 集註本)

13.4 苟^m吾無身 (Base text: 傅奕古本)

歸之自然也 (Base text: 集註本)

---

^a Var.: 寵 for 寵: 馬王堆 A. Var.: 弄 for 寵: 馬王堆 B.

^b Var.: 梡 for 患: 馬王堆 A. passim.

^c Var.: 苟胃 for 何謂: 馬王堆 A. Var.: 胃 for 謂: 馬王堆 B.

^d Var.: 寵 for 寵: 馬王堆 A. Var.: 弄 for 寵: 馬王堆 B.

^e Var.: 若驚 om.: 范應元本.

^f Var.: 寵(馬王堆 B.: 弄)之爲下 for 寵爲下: 馬王堆 A; 馬王堆 B. Var.: 下也 for 下: 郭店 B; 馬王堆 B.

^g Var.: 胃 for 謂: 馬王堆 A; 馬王堆 B.

^h Var.: 寵 for 寵: 馬王堆 A. Var.: 弄 for 寵: 馬王堆 B.

ⁱ 寵 for 驚: 陶鴻慶 based on statement further down in this commentary section 寵辱榮患若驚.

^j Var.: 胃 for 謂: 馬王堆 A; 馬王堆 B.

^k 夫貴 for 大患: Wagner. The 之 in 故謂之大患也 presupposes that the 貴 should have been mentioned before. In the existing text, this is not the case.

^l Var.: 身也 for 身: 馬王堆 A; 馬王堆 B.

^m Var.: 及 for 苟: 馬王堆 A; 馬王堆 B; 郭店 B (返). There is no hard evidence for preferring the 苟 here.

13.5 吾ⁿ有何患^o故貴以^p身爲^q天下者則^r可以託^s天下矣 (Base text: 范應元本)

無物可以^t易其身故曰貴也如此^u乃可以託天下也^v (Base text: 集註本)

13.6 愛以身爲天下者則^w可以寄天下矣^x (Base text: 傅奕古本)

無物可以^y損其身故曰愛也如此乃可以寄^z天下也不以寵辱榮患損易其身然後乃可以天下付^{aa}之也 (Base text: 集註本)

13.1	[I as a ruler] bestow favor and disgrace as [equally] startling.	Being in a high position is a great disaster if [=as long as] [I] have a personality of [my] own.
	What does "I bestow favor and disgrace as equally startling" mean? [It means that] as to [my] bestowing favors [to them][1]—if those below get them like something startling and lose them like something startling— this is called "bestowing favor and disgrace as equally startling."	

ⁿ Var.: 吾 om.: 馬王堆 A; 馬王堆 B; 郭店 B.

^o Var.: 患乎 for 患: 傅奕古本.   ^p Var.: 爲 for 以: 馬王堆 A; 馬王堆 B.

^q Var.: 於爲 for 爲: 馬王堆 A; 馬王堆 B.

^r Var.: 若 for 者則: 馬王堆 A; 馬王堆 B; 郭店 B. Support for 者則 instead of 若: 此乃 in Wang Bi's *Commentary* translates 者則 rather than 若. Cf. *Laozi* 16.8–11 where *Laozi* 乃 is rendered 則乃 in Wang Bi's *Commentary* and *Laozi* 54.4 where 則 is rendered in Wang's *Commentary* as 乃.

^s Var.: 迊 for 託: 馬王堆 A. Var.: 囊 for 託: 馬王堆 B.

^t 可以 for 以: Tōjō Itsudō based on parallelism with Wang Bi on 13.7 無物可以損其身, Wang Bi on *Laozi* 17.6 無物可以易其言, and Wang Bi on *Laozi* 78.1 無物可以易之也.

^u 如此 for 此: 永樂大典本. Support: parallel in Wang Bi on *Laozi* 13.7 如此乃可以寄天下也.

^v Var.: 如此乃可以託天下也 om.:取善集.

^w Var.: 女 for 者則: 馬王堆 A; 馬王堆 B.

^x Var.: 矣 om.: 馬王堆 A.   ^y Var.: 以 for 可以: 取善集.

^z Var.: 寄託 for 寄: 取善集.

^{aa} 付 for 傅: 取善集. Support: the term is to take up the *Laozi* expressions 寄 and 託, which 付 does better than 傅.

Where there is favor there necessarily is disgrace.
Favor and disgrace are equal.

Where there is splendor, there necessarily is disaster.
Splendor and disaster amount to the same.

If those below receive
favor and disgrace,

splendor and disaster as

[equally] startling, then they will not be in a position to bring chaos to the empire.

13.2

What does "being in a high position is a great disaster if [= as long as] as [I] have a personality of [my] own" mean?

"Being in a high position" be-
longs to the [same] category as
favor and splendor. "Making
too much of life" [spoken of in
Laozi 50.2], will necessarily lead
into the realm of death. That is
why [being in a high position]
is called a "great disaster."
[Other] people mistake [this
high position] for being [the
same as receiving] favors and
[living in] splendor and turn [in
envy] against [my] own person.
Therefore [the text] says: "It is a
great disaster [as long] as [I]
have a personality of [my] own."

13.3

[It means that] that which causes me to suffer a great disaster is [the fact] that I [still] have a personality [of my own].

That is, because he [still] holds
on to his [own] personality.

13.4   —

Would it come about that I would be without a personality,

That is, would [I] relate it back
to That-which-is-of-itself-what-
it-is.

13.5

what disaster would there be for me?

Therefore, he who is respected for taking [his] personality [impartially] as [identical with] All Under Heaven can as a consequence be entrusted with All Under Heaven.

"There is no other" entity by which his personality could be "altered" [if he makes use of the characteristics of soft water in overcoming the hard as the Laozi 78.1 *says], that is why [the text] says "being respected." Once he has come to this point, then indeed he can be entrusted with All Under Heaven.*

13.6

He who is cherished for taking his personality as being [identical with] All Under Heaven can as a consequence be put in charge of All Under Heaven.

There is no other entity capable of diminishing his personality, therefore [the text] says "being cherished." If he has come to this point then indeed he can be put in charge of All Under Heaven. If his personality can be altered or diminished neither because of favor or disgrace nor because of splendor or disaster, then indeed All Under Heaven can be handed over to him.

THE STRUCTURE OF *LAOZI* 13

The beginning of *Laozi* 13 is written in open IPS. The first two statements are explicitly taken up with the explicative formulae "what does it mean," creating a clearly visible ab ab structure. The end following the "therefore" in 13.5 only takes up the b chain about the "personality," *shen*

身, of the first part. As these statements are not matched by corresponding ones about the a chain concerning "favors," and as Wang Bi makes no effort to assign the two concluding phrases about "entrusting" All Under Heaven and about "putting [someone] in charge of All Under Heaven" separately to these two chains, they assume the function of general *pars pro toto* c statements. The overall structure of *Laozi* 13 is thus:

	b	(13.1)
a		(13.1)
	b	(13.2, 3, 4, 5)
c		
c		(10.9)

Zhang 14

14.1 視之ᵃ不ᵇ見名ᶜ曰微ᵈ聽之不ᵉ聞ᶠ名ᵍ曰希搏ʰ之不ⁱ得名ʲ曰夷ᵏ此ˡ三者不可致詰ᵐ故混ⁿ而爲一 (Base text: 馬王堆 A)

ᵃ 視之 for 視之而: 傅奕古本; 范應元本. Support against 而 Wang Bi comm. on *Laozi* 23.1 quoting this *zhang* 聽之不聞名曰希.

ᵇ 不 for 弗: Wang Bi 14.2 不見其形. 傅奕古本; 范應元本.

ᶜ 名 for 名之: 傅奕古本; 范應元本. Support for 名: Wang Bi comm. on *Laozi* 23.1 quoting this *zhang* 聽之不聞名曰希. See, however, 李善, 文選頭陀寺碑文注 59.16a8, which has 名之.

ᵈ 微 for 礬: 馬王堆 B. Var.: 夷 for 微: 傅奕古本; 莊(嚴)遵; 陸德明釋文. Var.: 幾 for 微: 范應元本. Support for 微: 馬王堆 B; Wang Bi definition of 微 in *LZWZLL* 2.27: 微也者, 取乎幽微而不可覩也. It stresses the invisibility that is appropriate here. Wang Bi's definition of 夷 is 平, "smooth": *Laozi* 53.2: 大道甚夷而民好徑, Wang Bi comm.: 言大道蕩然正平. Cf. *Laozi* 41.4.

ᵉ 不 for 弗: Wang Bi 14.2 (不見 analogy). 傅奕古本; 范應元本.

ᶠ 聽之不聞 for 聽之而不聞: 傅奕古本; 范應元本. Support against 而 Wang Bi comm. on *Laozi* 23.1 quoting this *zhang* 聽之不聞名曰希.

ᵍ Cf. note c. Var.: 命 for 名: 馬王堆 B.

ʰ 搏 for 揩 (in both 馬王堆 A and 馬王堆 B): 傅奕古本; 范應元本; 陸德明釋文.

ⁱ 不 for 弗: Wang Bi 14.2 (不見 analogy). ʲ Cf. note g.

ᵏ Var.: 微 for 夷: 傅奕古本; 范應元本; 陸德明釋文. Support: cf. note d. In his own writings, Wang Bi here used a different vocabulary for touch and taste; cf. *LZWZLL* 1.11–12 體之不可得而知, 味之不可得而嘗.

ˡ 此三者 for 三者: 傅奕古本; 范應元本; manuscripts. All available traditions outside the two 馬王堆 manuscripts have 此.

ᵐ 致詰 for 至計 (in both 馬王堆 A and 馬王堆 B): Wang Bi, comm.: 不可致詰. 傅奕古本; 范應元本; 陸德明釋文.

ⁿ 混 for 囷 (馬王堆 B: 緒): 傅奕古本; 范應元本; 陸德明釋文.

無狀無象無聲無響故能無所不通無所不往不可得而知[o]更以我耳目體不知爲名故不可致詰混而爲一也 (Base text: 集註本)

14.2 一者其上[p]不皦[q]其下不昧[r]繩繩兮[s]不可名[t]復歸於無物是謂[u]無狀之狀無物之象 (Base text: 傅奕古本)

欲言無邪而物由以成欲言有邪而不見其形故曰無狀之狀無物之象也 (Base text: 集註本)

14.3 是謂惚怳[v] (Base text: 孫盛老子疑問反訊)

不可得而定也 (Base text: 集註本)

14.4 迎之不見其首隨之不見其後[w]執古[x]之道可以[y]御今之有 (Base text: 傅奕古本)

古今雖異其道常存執之者方能御物[z] (Base text: 取善集) 有有其事 (Base text: 集註本)

14.5 以知[aa]古始是謂道紀 (Base text: 馬王堆 B)

---

[o] 不可得而知 for 不得知: Hatano Tarō. Support: Wang Bi pattern 不可得而; cf. Wang Bi on *Laozi* 1.5. 永樂大典本: 不得而知.

[p] 其上 for 其上之: 馬王堆 A; 馬王堆 B.

[q] Var.: 攸 for 皦: 馬王堆 A. Var.: 謬 for 皦: 馬王堆 B.

[r] 其下 for 其下之: 馬王堆 A; 馬王堆 B. Var.: 忽 for 昧: 馬王堆 A; 馬王堆 B.

[s] Var.: 尋尋呵 for 繩繩兮: 馬王堆 A; 馬王堆 B.

[t] Var.: 名也 for 名: 馬王堆 A. Var.: 命也 for 名: 馬王堆 B.

[u] Var.: 胃 for 謂: 馬王堆 A; 馬王堆 B.

[v] Var.: 芴芒 for 惚怳: 傅奕古本; 范應元本. Var.:沕望 for 惚怳: 馬王堆 B. Support for 怳: 陸德明釋文.

[w] Var.: 隨而不見其後迎而不見其首 for 迎之不見其首隨之不見其後: 馬王堆 B.

[x] Var.: 今 for 古: 馬王堆 A; 馬王堆 B.

[y] Var.: 以 for 可以: 范應元本; 馬王堆 A; 馬王堆 B. Support for 可以: Wang Bi on *Laozi* 47.1 執古之道可以御今. Cf. 故可執古之道以御今之有 in Wang Bi on *Laozi* 14.5; *LZWZLL* 1.45: 執古可以御今.

[z] Var.: 古今雖異其道常存執之者方能御物 om. 道藏本, 永樂大典本. Support for authenticity of the passage: Wang Bi on *Laozi* 47.1 道有大常理有大致執古之道可以御今 雖處於今可以知古始. The 取善集 does not contain the passage 有有其事.

[aa] Var.: 能知 for 以知: 傅奕古本；范應元本. Support for 以: Wang Bi comm.: 可以知古

無形無名者萬物之宗也雖今古不同時移俗易故莫不由乎此以成其治
者也故可執古之道以御今之有上古雖遠其道存焉故雖在今可以知古
始也 (Base text: 集註本)

14.1   That which [I] do not see if [I] look at it [I] call "fine."
       That which [I] do not hear when listening for it [I] call "inaudible."
       That which [I] cannot grasp when reaching for it [I] call "smooth."
       For these three [the senses of sight, hearing, and touch] it is impossible to
       come to a definition [of this], and thus, diffuse it is, [being] the One.

       *It is without shape or image, without sound or echo. That is why it is able
       to leave nothing unpenetrated and nothing unreached. It is not knowable
       and, even with my ear, eye, and touch, I do not know to make a name
       [for it]. That is why [the text says for these three senses] it is "impossible
       to come to a definition [of this]" [and thus] "diffuse it is, being the One!"*

14.2   This One
       —its upper side is not bright;
       —its lower side is not dark.
       Dim it is and impossible to name.
       It returns and relates [the entities] back to the no-thing. This [I] call the
       shape of the shapeless, the appearance of the no-thing.

       *One wishes to say that it does not exist? [The fact still remains] that the
       entities are based on it for their completion. One wants to say it exists?
       [The fact still remains] that it does not show its form. That is why [the
       text] says: "shape of the shapeless, appearance of the no-thing."*

14.3   This [I] call undifferentiated and vague.

       That is, impossible to define.

14.4   Following it upward, [I] do not see its beginning.
       Following it downward, [I] do not see what comes after it.
       That holding [today] on to the Way of antiquity it is possible [for a Sage
       Ruler] to regulate occurrences of the present,

       *Although antiquity and the present are different, their Way persists eter-
       nally. Only he who holds on to it is able to regulate the entities. "Occur-
       rences" means governmental business occurring.*

14.5   and that [from these occurrences of the present] one [the Sage Ruler] has
       something by which to cognize the oldest beginning, this [I] call the conti-
       nuity of the Way.

始也; in Wang's *Commentary* 可以 regularly translates a 以 in the *Laozi*; cf. *Laozi* 42.3 吾
將以爲教父, Wang Bi comm. 故得其違教之徒適可以爲教父也.

The featureless and nameless is the ancestor of the ten thousand kinds of entities. Although the present and antiquity are not the same, although times have changed and customs have changed, there definitely is no one [Sage Ruler] who has not based himself on this [featureless and nameless] by way of completing their regulated order.[1] That is why it "is possible" [for him] to "hold on to the Way of antiquity by way of regulating occurrences of the present"! Although high antiquity is far away, its Way still persists. That is why, although one is existing today, it is possible "by means of this [present-day reality] to cognize the oldest beginning."[2]

Zhang 15

15.1 古之善爲道ᵃ者微妙ᵇ玄通ᶜ深不可識ᵈ夫唯ᵉ不可識ᶠ故強爲之容曰ᵍ豫兮其若ʰ冬涉川ⁱ (Base text: 傅奕古本)

多之涉川豫然若欲度若不欲度其情不可得見之貌也 (Base text: 集註本)

15.2 猶兮其若ʲ畏四鄰ᵏ (Base text: 傅奕古本)

ᵃ Var.: 士 for 道: 范應元本; 郭店 A. Support for 道: Wang Bi defines the person involved in the commentary to 15.2 as 上德之人, who in the commentary to *Laozi* 38 is defined through the formula 唯道是用.

ᵇ Var.: 眇 for 妙: 馬王堆 B.   ᶜ Var.: 達 for 通: 馬王堆 B; 郭店 A.

ᵈ Var.: 志 for 識: 馬王堆 A; 馬王堆 B; 郭店 A.

ᵉ 唯 for 惟: 馬王堆 A; 馬王堆 B.

ᶠ Var.: 志 for 識: 馬王堆 A; 馬王堆 B.

ᵍ Var.: 曰 om.: 范應元本.

ʰ 其若 for 若: 馬王堆 A; 馬王堆 B; 文子. For the entire series of this description early variants exist, including a 其, the most extensive being in 馬王堆 A as far as the text survives, and in 馬王堆 B, as well as the 文子 with a 其 in each item. The 傅奕古本 eliminates all 其 for the first four items and includes them for the remaining three after 敦. Fan Yingyuan has no 其 for the first two items, has one for the item beginning with 儼, none for the subsequent one, and then has them for the rest. 郭店 A has them for all but the first item. Wang Bi does not quote or translate one of the items into his commentary. The evidence from his textual family is not united. I will follow the Mawangdui pattern. Var.: 與呵 for 豫兮: 馬王堆 A; 馬王堆 B.

ⁱ Var.: 水 for 川: 馬王堆 B.

ʲ 其若 for 若: 馬王堆 B; 文子; (郭店 A: 其奴). Var.: 猷呵 for 猶兮: 馬王堆 B.

ᵏ Var.: 哭 for 鄰: 馬王堆 B.

四鄰合攻中央之主猶然不知所趣向[1]也上德之人其端兆不可覩意趣[m]
不可見亦猶此也 (Base text: 集註本)

15.3 儼兮其若客[n]渙兮其若冰[o]之將釋[p]敦兮[q]其若樸[r]曠兮其若谷混[s]兮其若濁[t,1]
(Base text: 范應元本)

凡此諸若皆言其容象不可得而形名也 (Base text: 集註本)

15.4 孰能濁以靜[u]之而徐清[v]孰能安以動[w]之而徐生[x] (Base text: 范應元本)

夫晦以理物則得明濁以靜物則得清安以動物則得生此自然之道也孰
能者言其難也徐者詳愼也 (Base text: 集註本)

15.5 保此道者[y]不欲盈 (Base text: 傅奕古本)

盈必溢也[2] (Base text: 永樂大典本)

---

[1] Var.: 趣向者 for 趣向: 永樂大典本.

[m] 意趣 for 德趣: 陶鴻慶 based on parallel with Wang Bi on *Laozi* 17.6 猶然其端兆
不可得而見也 其意趣不可得而覩也.

[n] 客 for 容: 傅奕古本; 馬王堆 A; 馬王堆 B; 莊遵; 郭店 A. Var.: 儼若客 for 儼兮其
若客: 傅奕古本.Var.: 嚴呵 for 儼兮: 馬王堆 B.

[o] 其若 for 若: 馬王堆 A; 馬王堆 B; 文子; (郭店 A:其奴). 冰 for 氷: 傅奕古本. Support: 莊遵; Shima Kuniō.

[p] Var.: 冰將 for 冰之將: 傅奕古本. Var.: 渙呵其若淩澤 for 渙兮其若冰之將釋: 馬王
堆 A; 馬王堆 B.

[q] Var.: 沌呵 for 敦兮: 馬王堆 B.

[r] Var.: 楃 for 樸: 馬王堆 A.

[s] 混 for 渾: 陸德明釋文; 傅奕古本.

[t] Var.: 湷呵其若濁湉呵其若浴 for 曠兮其若谷混兮其若濁: 馬王堆 B; (馬王堆 A:
湷□□□□□□□若浴). Support for the sequence 曠 . . . 混 . . . : 陸德明釋文. The 郭店
A does not have the item 曠兮其若谷.

[u] 靜 for 靖: Wang Bi comm.: 靜物. 馬王堆 B. Var.: 澄靖 for 靜: 傅奕古本.

[v] Var.: 濁而情 (馬王堆 B: 靜) 之余 (馬王堆 B: 徐) 清 for 孰能濁以靜之而徐清: 馬
王堆 A; 馬王堆 B.

[w] 動之 for 久動之: Wang Bi comm.:安以動物; 永樂大典本. 馬王堆 A; 馬王堆 B.

[x] Var.: 女以重之余 (馬王堆 B.:徐) 生 for 孰能安以動之而徐生: 馬王堆 A; 馬王
堆 B.

[y] Var.: 葆此道 for 保此道者: 馬王堆 A; 馬王堆 B.

15.6 夫唯^z不盈^{aa}是以^{ab}能蔽^{ac}而不成^{ad} (Base text: 傅奕古本)

蔽覆蓋也³ (Base text: 永樂大典本)

15.1   Those in antiquity who were well versed in the Way were recondite and abstruse, so deep that they could not be discerned. As they were unknowable, [I] say, when forced to give a sketch of them: Hesitant they were—as if crossing a [frozen] river in winter.

Someone crossing a [frozen] river in winter is hesitant about whether he should cross or not, and has an expression that makes it impossible to read his feelings.

15.2   Undecided they were—as if fearing four neighbors.

If four neighbors join to attack the lord in the middle, he will be undecided, and one does not not know which way he will turn. That in a person of "highest receipt/capacity" [spoken of in Laozi *38.1] it is impossible to perceive any clues [in]*[1] *his [expression] and it is impossible to make out [his] intentions, is also like this.*

15.3   Formal they were—like a guest;
brittle they were—like ice that is about to melt;
genuine they were—like an uncarved block;
vast they were—like a valley;
murky they were—like turbid water.

Generally speaking, these "they are like" all mean that one is incapable of [assigning a specific] shape and name to their countenance.

15.4   Who [but they] could be capable—being turbid [themselves]—of composedly bringing transparency [to other entities] by calming them down? Who [but they] could be capable—being calm [themselves]—of composedly bringing [the other entities to life] by making them move?

Generally speaking, that, if [something that is in itself] dark is used to regulate entities, they attain clarity; if [something that is in itself] turbid is used to calm down entities, they attain transparency; and if [something that is in itself calm] is used to move entities, they will attain life—this is the Way of That-which-is-of-itself-what-it-is.[2] *[The expression] "Who [but they] could be capable" denotes how difficult this is. "Composedly" means "with circumspection."*

---

^z 唯 for 惟: 馬王堆 A.

^{aa} Var.: 不欲口 for 不盈: 馬王堆 A. Var.: 夫唯不 (欲) 盈 om.: 馬王堆 B.

^{ab} Var.: 故 for 是以: 范應元本.

^{ac} 蔽 for 敝: Wang Bi comm.: 蔽覆蓋也. 陸德明釋文. Var.: 獘 for 蔽: 馬王堆 B.

^{ad} Var.: 新成 for 成: 范應元本.

15.5   He who preserves this Way does not desire to fill [it] up.

Filling up necessarily leads to overflowing.[3]

15.6   Exactly because of his not filling [it] up will he be capable of covering [all the other entities] but not complete [any specific achievements].

"Covering" means "covering over."[4]

THE STRUCTURE OF *LAOZI* 15

While *Laozi* 15 is accessible in its meaning, its rhetorical structure has successfully resisted my efforts at elucidation. It has many of the formal features of a chapter written in IPS. There are six more or less parallel similes for those in antiquity who were well versed in the Way, but although a connection could be seen linking the first with the fourth and the second with the third, the remaining two sections do not seem to be linked. Wang Bi's "these 'are like' all mean . . . " in the third commentary indicates that he saw them as a series. The transition to the next pair of sentences again seems to hold some promise as the term *zhuo* 濁, "turbid water," is taken up. But the same is not true for the term *an* 安, "to rest." The consequence is that the link between the similes and the following pair of sentences is not clear. This influences the translation strategy. From Wang Bi's commentary, it seems evident that the *shu neng* 孰能—with the rhetorical *shu* indicating that the answer is clear—refers to those knowledgeable in the Way who are mentioned in the first phrase.

Zhang 16

16.1 致[a]虛極也[b]守靜[c]篤也[d] (Base text: 范應元本)

言致虛物之極也[e]守靜物之眞正也 (Base text: 集註本)

16.2 萬物并[f]作 (Base text: 傅奕古本)

---

[a] Var.: 至 for 致: 馬王堆 A; 馬王堆 B; 郭店 A. Support for 致: Wang Bi commentary.

[b] 極也 for 極: 馬王堆 A; 馬王堆 B; 文子. Var.: 亙也: 郭店 A.

[c] Var.: 靖 for 靜: 傅奕古本. Var.: 中 for 靜: 郭店 A. Var.: 情 for 靜: 馬王堆 A.

[d] 篤也 for 篤: 馬王堆 B (督也); 郭店 A, 文子. Var.: 至虛極也守情表也 for 致虛極守靜篤: 馬王堆 A. Var.: 至虛極也守靜督也 for 致虛極守靜篤: 馬王堆 B.

[e] 極也 for 極篤: 李善, 文選應吉甫晉武帝華林園集詩注 20.30b7. Var.: 至虛之 for 致虛物之: 文選, *loc. cit.* Cf. note 2 in the translation.

[f] Var.: 旁 for 並: 馬王堆 A; 馬王堆 B; (郭店 A: 方).

動作生長也[g] (Base text: 集註本)

16.3 吾以觀其復[h] (Base text: 傅奕古本)

以虛靜觀其反復凡有起於虛動起於靜故萬物雖并動作卒復歸於虛靜是物之極篤也 (Base text: 集註本)

16.4 凡[i,1]物芸芸[j]各復歸於其[k]根 (Base text: 馬王堆 A)

根始也[l]各反其所始也[2] (Base text: 集註本)

16.5 歸根曰靜[m]靜[n]曰復命復命曰常[o](Base text: 范應元本)

歸根則靜[3]故曰靜靜則復命故曰復命也復命則得性命之常故曰常也 (Base text 集註本)

16.6 知常曰明也[p]不知常則[q]妄作凶[r] (Base text: Wang Bi comm.)

---

[g] 生長也 for 生長: 李善, 文選時興詩注. Var.: 作生長也 for 動作生長也: 李善, 文選時興詩注 30.1b9. Support for 動作: Wang Bi on *Laozi* 16.3: 萬物雖并動作. 動作 in Wang Bi's *Commentary* suggests a 動作 in his *Laozi* text, but there is no tradition supporting such a possibility.

[h] Var.: 復也 for 復: 馬王堆 A. 馬王堆 B. Var.: 居以須違也: 郭店 A.

[i] 凡 for 天 (馬王堆 B: 天): 陸德明釋文; 傅奕古本; 范應元本. Var.: 天道圜圜: 郭店 A.

[j] 芸芸 for 雲雲. Var.: 秐秐 for 芸芸: 馬王堆 B. Var.: 駈駈 for 芸芸: 傅奕古本; 范應元本. Support for 芸芸: 李善, 文選雜體詩注 31.30b.

[k] Var.: 各歸其根 for 各復歸於其根: 傅奕古本; 范應元本. Support for 復歸於其根: Wang Bi comm. on *Laozi* 16.3 卒復歸於虛靜. For 根 there is a lacuna in 馬王堆 A.

[l] 根始也 add.: Wagner on the basis of 慧琳, 一切經音義, T.2128 Taishō vol. 54:351a sub 根株; cf. note 2.

[m] Var.: 曰靜 for 歸根曰靜: 馬王堆 B.

[n] Var.: 靖靖 for 靜靜: 傅奕古本.

[o] Var.: 靜是胃復命復命常也 for 靜曰復命復命曰常: 馬王堆 A; 馬王堆 B. Support for 靜曰復命: Wang Bi comm.: parallelism between 歸根則靜故曰靜, where the *Laozi* text has a 曰, and 靜則復命故曰復命也, which therefore also presupposes a 曰. 馬叙倫.

[p] Var.: 明 for 明也: 傅奕古本; 范應元本.

[q] Var.: 則 om.: 馬王堆 A; 馬王堆 B; 傅奕古本; 范應元本. Given the consistency and reliability of Wang Bi's quotations from the main text, I believe the 則 will have to be accepted as part of his *Laozi*.

[r] Var.: 帝帝 for 妄: 馬王堆 A. Var.: 芒芒作兇for 妄作凶: 馬王堆 B.

常之爲物不偏不彰無皦昧之狀溫涼之象故曰知常曰明也知[s]此復乃[t]
能包通萬物無所不容失此以往則邪入乎分則物離其分[u]故曰不知常
則妄作凶也 (Base text 集註本)

16.7 知常容 (Base text: 傅奕古本)

無所不包通也 (Base text: 集註本)

16.8 容乃公(Base text: 傅奕古本)

無所不包通則乃至于[v]蕩然公平也 (Base text: 集註本)

16.9 公乃王 (Base text: 傅奕古本)

蕩然公平則乃至於無所不周普也 (Base text: 集註本)

16.10 王乃天 (Base text: 傅奕古本)

無所不周普則乃至于[w]同乎天也[x] (Base text: 集註本)

16.11 天乃道 (Base text: 傅奕古本)

與天合德體道大通則乃至于[y]窮極[z]虛無也 (Base text: 集註本)

16.12 道乃久[aa] (Base text: 傅奕古本)

---

[s] 知 for 唯: Wagner. The segment 唯此復乃能 . . . is parallel to the segment further down in this commentary 失此以往則 . . . *Shi* 失 is a verb and *wei* 唯 is not. The next *Laozi* text, 16.7, reads 知常容 "Having knowledge of the Eternal [means being] all-encompassing." Wang Bi comments on this: 無所不包通也 "that is, there is nothing he does not cover and penetrate." From this it is clear that the subject of the "covering and penetrating the ten thousand entities" in the commentary on *Laozi* 16.6 is he who has knowledge about the Eternal, not the Eternal itself. This has prompted me to suggest the replacement of 唯 with 知.

[t] Var.: 復 for 復乃: 永樂大典本.　　[u] 其分 for 分: 陸德明釋文.
[v] Var.: 於 for 于: 永樂大典本.　　[w] Var.: 於 for 于: 永樂大典本.
[x] Var.: 均 for 也: 永樂大典本.　　[y] Var.: 於 for 于: 永樂大典本.
[z] 窮極 for 極: 陶鴻慶 based on Wang Bi on *Laozi* 16.12 窮極虛無.
[aa] Var.: 久 om.: 馬王堆 B.

窮極虛無得物之常則乃至於不可^{ab}窮極也 (Base text: 永樂大典本)

16.13 沒^{ac}身不殆 (Base text: 傅奕古本)

無之爲物水火不能害金石不能殘用之於心則虎兕無所投其爪角兵戈
無所容其鋒刃何危殆之有乎 (Base text: 集註本)

16.1   [As the entities']
achieving emptiness is their   holding on to stillness is [their]
Ultimate,   core,[1]

                        This is to say:

To achieve emptiness is the   *To hold on to stillness is the true*
ultimate for entities.   *regulative for entities.*[2]

16.2   [even while] the ten thousand
                                kinds of entities all act at
                                once,

        "Act" means be born and grow.

16.3   I [as opposed to others] by
                                way of this [emptiness and
                                stillness] perceive that to which
                                they return.

                                It is by way of [their]
        emptiness   *and   stillness*
                                that [I] perceive their return.
                                Generally speaking:

Entity arises out of emptiness.   *Movement arises out of stillness.*
                                Therefore, even while the
                                ten thousand kinds of entities
                                all act at once, their return
                                in the end to
        emptiness   *and   stillness*
                                is
the ultimate and   *the core*
                                of entities.

---

    ^{ab} 不可 for 不: Wagner based on parallels in Wang Bi on *Laozi* 35.3 (道 . . . 用之不可
既): 用之不可窮極; and Wang Bi on *Laozi* 40.2 (弱者道之用): 柔弱同道不可窮極: Var.:
不 om.: 集註本. In both cases, the subject is the Dao.
    ^{ac} Var.: 沕 for 沒: 馬王堆 A. Var.: 歾 for 沒: 范應元本.

16.4   Generally speaking, while the entities are of unending diversity, each one of them returns to its [common] root.[3]

The *"root" is the beginning. That is, each one of them relates back to that which began it.*

16.5   [Their] reverting to [their] roots means stillness. Stillness means return to life endowment. Return to life endowment means the Eternal.

Once they revert to [their] roots, then[4] they [reach] stillness. That is why [the text] says "stillness"!

Once they [have reached] stillness, then they return to [their original] life endowment. That is why [the text] says "return to life endowment!" Once they have returned to [their original] life endowment, then they are getting hold of the Eternal [essence] of their innate nature and life endowment. That is why [the text] says "the Eternal"!

16.6   Having knowledge of [this] Eternal means being enlightened.[5] [But] if he [a ruler] does not know the Eternal, then acting recklessly he brings about a nefarious [outcome].

The Eternal [essence of the entities] as such is neither [inwardly] partial nor manifest [in its preferences]; it has an appearance without either brightness or darkness, and features without either warming or cooling. That is why [the text] says: "Having knowledge of [this] Eternal means being enlightened"! Knowing[6] this [Eternal], he [the ruler] is able indeed to embrace and penetrate the ten thousand kinds of entities without there being anything that is not encompassed. Once he has lost this [knowledge of the Eternal], evil penetrates into the allotted role [of entities which forms their life endowment],[7] and as a consequence entities diverge from [their assigned] stations [with chaos ensuing]. That is why [the text] says: "[But] if he [a ruler] does not know the Eternal, then, acting recklessly, he brings about a nefarious [outcome]"!

16.7   Having knowledge of the Eternal [means being] all-encompassing.

That is, there is nothing he does not cover and penetrate.

16.8   Encompassing [everything] implies being impartial.

If there is nothing he does not cover and penetrate, then indeed he becomes immeasurably[8] impartial and balanced.

16.9   Impartiality implies kingly [stature].[9]

Once one is immeasurably impartial and balanced, then indeed one gets to the point that there is nothing one is not comprehensively concerned with.

16.10   Kingly [stature] implies heavenly [stature].

Once there is nothing one is not comprehensively concerned with, one indeed gets to the point of being equal to Heaven.

16.11   Heavenly [stature] implies [having] the Way.

Once he "brings [his] capacity in line with Heaven's [as the Wenyan *of the* Zhouyi *says about the Great Man]"*[10] *and embodies the great pervasiveness of the Way,*[11] *then indeed he gets to the point of utterly maximizing*[12] *emptiness and negativity.*

16.12   [Having] the Way implies long duration.

Once he fully penetrates to the ultimate emptiness and negativity and attains the Eternal of entities,[13] *then indeed he will get to the ultimate of not being exhaustible.*[14]

16.13   [As a consequence] in all his life there will be no danger.

Negativity as such cannot be hurt by water or fire, and cannot be shattered by metal or stone. If use of it is made in one's heart, "tigers" and "rhinoceroses" "will not find a place [on him] to thrust" "their claws" and "horns," "soldiers" and lances "will not find a place [on him] to insert" their point and "blade" [as the Laozi *50.2 says of those who are good at maintaining their lives]. What danger could there possibly be [for such a person]?*

Zhang 17

17.1 大ᵃ上下知有之 (Base text: 馬王堆 A)

大ᵇ上謂大人也大人在上故曰大ᶜ上大人在上居無爲之事行不言之教萬物作焉而不爲始故下知有之而已ᵈ (Base text: 集註本)

17.2 其次親而譽ᵉ之 (Base text: 馬王堆 A)

ᵃ Var.: 太 for 大: 傅奕古本; 范應元本. Support for 大: 陸德明釋文. Cf. Anm. 1 of the translation.

ᵇ 大 for 太: Wagner. Cf. note 1 of the translation. 陸德明釋文 quotes Wang Bi's *Commentary* with 太.

ᶜ 大 for 太: Wagner. Cf. note 1 of the translation.

ᵈ Var.: 而已言從上也 for 而已: 永樂大典本. Cf. Wang Bi on *Laozi* 17.5 for the surplus of 言從上也.

ᵉ 親而譽 for 親譽: Wang Bi comm.: 親而譽之. Hatano Tarō. Var.: 親之其此譽 for 親而譽: 傅奕古本. Var.: 親之譽 for 親而譽: 范應元本.

不能以無爲居事不言爲教立善施化^f使下得親而譽之也 (Base text: 集
註本)

17.3 其次畏之 (Base text: 傅奕古本)

不能復^g以恩仁令物而賴威權也 (Base text: 集註本)

17.4 其次^h侮之^i (Base text: 傅奕古本)

不能法以正齊民而以智治國下知避之其令不從故曰侮之也 (Base text:
集註本)

17.5 信^j不足焉^k有不信^l (Base text: 馬王堆 A)

言從上也夫^m御體失性則疾病生輔物失眞則疵釁作信不足焉則有不
信此自然之道也己處不足非智之所濟^n也 (Base text: 集註本)

17.6 猶兮^o其貴言也^p功成事遂^q而百姓^r皆曰^s我自然 (Base text: 傅奕古本)

猶然^t其端兆不可得而見也其意趣不可得而覩也無物可以易其言言

---

^f Var.: 行施 for 施化: 陸德明釋文; 永樂大典本. Support for 施化: Wang Bi on *Laozi*
5.1 仁者必造立施化.

^g Var.: 復能 for 能復: 永樂大典本. Support for 能復: Wang Bi on *Laozi* 72.1 威不能
復制民.

^h Var.: 其次 om.: 范應元本.

^i Var.: 其下母之 for 其次侮之: 馬王堆 A; 馬王堆 B.

^j Var.: 故信 for 信: 傅奕古本; 范應元本.

^k 焉 for 案: Wang Bi comm.: 信不足焉; 傅奕古本; 范應元本. Var.: 安 for 焉: 馬王堆
B. 郭店 C.

^l Var.: 信焉 for 信: 范應元本.   ^m Var.: 夫 om.: 陳景元纂微.

^n Var.: 齊 for 濟: 永樂大典本.

^o Var.: 猷呵 for 猶兮: 馬王堆 B. Var.: 悠 for 猶: 陸德明釋文.

^p 也 for 哉 (范應元本: 哉): Wang Bi comm.: 其貴言也; 馬王堆 A; 馬王堆 B; 郭店 C.

^q Var.: 成功遂事 for 功成事遂: 馬王堆 A; 馬王堆 B. Var.: 成事遂功 for 功成事遂:
郭店 C.

^r 而百姓 for 百姓: Wang Bi comm.: 功成事遂而百姓; 馬王堆 A; 馬王堆 B.

^s Var.: 胃 for 曰: 馬王堆 A; 馬王堆 B. Support for 曰: 郭店 C; 莊(嚴)遵.

^t 猶然 for 自然: 桃井白鹿 based on Wang Bi on *Laozi* 15.2 (猶兮其若畏四鄰): 猶然
不知所趣向也上德之人其端兆不可覩意趣不可見.

必有應故曰猶兮其貴言也居無爲之事行不言之教不以形ᵘ立物故功
成事遂而百姓不知其所以然也 (Base text: 集註本)

17.1   If the Great is at the top, those below know [only] that he exists.

*[The "Great" in] "if the Great is at the top" refers to the Great Man [as
mentioned in the Zhouyi.¹] The Great Man rests in the topmost [position,
namely, that of the ruler], that is why [Laozi says: "[if] the Great is at
the top." If the Great Man is at the top "he takes residence in management without interference and practices teaching without words [with
the result] that the ten thousand kinds of entities come about without his
initiating [them]" [as Laozi 2.2 ff. says of the Sage]. That is why [the text
says] "those below know only that he exists" [but cannot define him]!*

17.2   If one second to him [the Great Man] is [at the top], [those below] will be
         close to him and praise him.

*He [the second best] is unable to reside in [his] affairs by means of non-
interference and to make the unspoken his teaching. He establishes the
good² and spreads moral education, thus prompting those below to get
"close to him and praise him."*

17.3   If one second to him [who is second to the Great Man] is [at the top],
         [those below] will fear him.

*He is not anymore capable of getting other beings to do something by
means of [his] kindness and humaneness, but relies on might and power.³*

17.4   If one second to him [who is second to him who is second to the Great
         Man] is [at the top], [those below] do not take him seriously.

*As he is unable to set the law to treat the people equitably by means of
a correct standard,⁴ but "rules the state by means of intelligence [which
Laozi 65.3 describes as being "the plague of the state],"⁵ those below
know how to circumvent him so that his orders are not being followed.
That is why [the text says "they do not take [him] seriously"]!*

17.5   [In short,] as credibility [of those at the top who are of lower caliber than
         the Great Man] is lacking, there is [as a consequence] absence of credibility
         [among those below].

*This means: they [those below] follow those above.⁶ If one is reining in
the body but misses [its original] nature, virulent diseases will spring up.
If one is supporting entities but misses [their] true [essence] then transgressions will occur [committed by them]. It is the Way of That-which-is-*

ᵘ Var.: 刑 for 形: 永樂大典本.

of-itself-what-it-is that if credibility [of those above] is not sufficient, there will be a lack of credibility [among those below]. That which in one's [a ruler's] own position is insufficient[ly regulated] cannot be regulated through intelligence.

17.6   Undecided he is [the Great Man at the top]! And they [those below] watch [his] words. [If in this manner the Hundred Families'] achievements are completed and affairs are followed through, the Hundred Families all say "we are like this [i.e., have this bountiful life] spontaneously."[7]

"Being undecided" means that it is impossible to make out any clues in [his expression] and impossible to make out his intentions [as Wang Bi had already said about the man with superior capacity in his commentary on Laozi 15.2].[8] As there is no other entity that can alter his words,[9] [his] words by necessity are being followed. That is why [the text] says: "Undecided he is! [But] his words are being respected [by those below]." "Taking residence [as Laozi 2.2 says of the Sage] in management without interference and practicing teaching without words," he does not set up the other entities by means of a [definite] shape. That is why "achievements are completed and affairs are followed through" [as the text says], but the Hundred Families do not know how these [two kinds of results] come about![10]

Zhang 18

18.1 大道ᵃ廢焉ᵇ有仁義ᶜ (Base text: 傅奕古本)

失無爲之事更以施慧立善道進物也 (Base text: 集註本)

18.2 智慧ᵈ出焉ᵉ有大僞ᶠ (Base text: 傅奕古本)

ᵃ Var.: 故大道 for 大道: 郭店 C; 馬王堆 A; 馬王堆 B. *Zhang* 17 and 18 of the Wang Bi text were read as one unit in the Guodian C and Mawangdui A and B texts. There, they are linked by a 故 and not separated by formal markers, such as dots in the manuscripts.

ᵇ Var.: 案 for 焉: 馬王堆 A. Var.: 安 for 焉: 馬王堆 B; 郭店 C.

ᶜ Var.: 廢有仁義焉 for 廢焉有仁義: 范應元本.

ᵈ Var.: 惠 for 慧: 范應元本. Var.: 知快 for 智慧: 馬王堆 A. Var.: 知慧 for 智慧: 馬王堆 B.

ᵉ Var.: 案 for 焉: 馬王堆 A. Var.: 安 for 焉: 馬王堆 B.

ᶠ Var.: 智慧出有大僞焉 for 智慧出焉有大僞: 范應元本. 18.2 is altogether missing in 郭店 C.

行術用明以察姦偽趣覩形見物知避之故智慧[g]出 則大偽生也[h] (Base text: 集註本)

18.3 六親不和有孝慈[i]國家昏亂有[j]貞[k]臣[l] (Base text: 傅奕古本)

甚美之名生於大惡所謂美惡同門[m]六親父子兄弟夫婦也若六親自和國家自治則孝慈貞[n]臣不知其所在矣魚相忘[o]於江湖之道失[p]則相濡之德生也 (Base text 集註本)

18.1　　Once [a ruler] has abandoned the Great Way, there will be humaneness and justice [guiding his actions].

Once he has lost "management without interference" [in which, according to Laozi *2.2, "the Sage takes residence"] he will in turn by means of the way of applying insight and establishing good [deeds] promote the other beings.*[1]

18.2　　Once knowledge and insight have appeared [in the ruler's actions], there will be the great deceit [among his subjects].

If he practices tricks and applies his intelligence to spy out cunning and deceit [among the people], his interests become apparent and his shape becomes visible [and, as a consequence,] the others will know how to

---

[g] 慧 for 惠: 陸德明釋文.　　[h] Var.: 生也 om.: 永樂大典本.

[i] Var.: 和案有畜茲 for 和有孝慈: 馬王堆 A. Var.: 和安又孝茲 for 和有孝慈: 馬王堆 B.Var.: 慈焉 for 慈: 范應元本.

[j] Var.: 邦家 (馬王堆 B: 國家) 閍 (郭店 C: 緍) 亂安 (馬王堆 A: 案) 有 for 國家昏亂有: 郭店 C; 馬王堆 A; 馬王堆 B.

[k] 貞 also in 馬王堆 A; 馬王堆 B; 莊遵; 范應元本; Wang Bi comm. : 忠臣 is probably taboo writing for 貞臣, as suggested by Fan Yingyuan, 1.35b. 忠臣, however, is attested as early as 淮南子.

[l] Var.: 臣焉 for 臣: 范應元本.　　[m] 同門 for 內門: 永樂大典本.

[n] 貞 for 忠: Wagner based on Fan Yingyuan's argument that the change to 忠 is due to taboo on 貞.

[o] 魚相忘 for 魚忘: 永樂大典本.

[p] 道失 for 道: Wagner. All scholars agree that the text is not readable in the present form. 陶鴻慶 proposes to amend the original 魚(相)忘於江湖之道則相濡之德生也 to 魚(相)忘於江湖 相濡之道失則相濡之德生也. This emendation seems uneconomical; the insertion of a simple 失 after 道 would result in much of the same reading and offer less interference in the text. Guo Xiang 郭象 comments on the phrase from the 莊子天運篇 (*Zhuangzi yinde* 38/14/59–60): 泉涸魚相與處於陸 相呴以濕相濡以沫不若相忘於江湖 with the words: 失於江湖乃思濡沫, "Only once they have lost the rivers and lakes, do they begin thinking about moistening [each other] with spittle." Cf. *Nanhua zhenjing zhu* 5.26a1.

evade him.[2] *That is why, [the text says] once knowledge and insight have appeared [in the ruler's actions], great deceit [among the subjects] will arise!*

18.3 Once [he does] not [keep] the six relationships in harmony, there will be filial piety and paternal love. Once [his] state is in chaos, there will be loyal ministers.

The concept of the truly beautiful [like filial piety and paternal love, or uprightness] arises out of the greatest ugliness. This is what is referred to as "beautiful and ugly come out of the same door."[3] *The six relationships are [those between] father and son, older and younger brother, husband and wife. If the six relationships were harmonious by themselves and the state were regulated by itself, then [one] would not know where to find filial piety and paternal love as well as upright ministers! [Only] when the way of the "fishes to forget about each other in the rivers and lakes" is lost, is [their] [particular] capacity of "moisturizing each other" [with their mouths while lying on the dry shore] born [of which the* Zhuangzi *speaks].*[4]

Zhang 19

19.1 絕聖棄智ᵃ民ᵇ,¹利百倍ᶜ絕仁棄義ᵈ民復孝慈ᵉ絕巧棄利盜賊無有此三者ᶠ以爲文而ᵍ未足ʰ故令之有所屬ⁱ見素抱ʲ樸少私寡欲ᵏ (Base text: 傅奕古本)

ᵃ Var.: 知 for 智: 馬王堆 A; 馬王堆 B; 范應元本. Support for 智: Wang Bi comm.: 聖智才之善也. Wang Bi comm. on *Laozi* 10.4 治國無以智猶棄智也.

ᵇ Var.: 而民 for 民: 馬王堆 B.

ᶜ Var.: 負 for 倍: 馬王堆 A.

ᵈ Var.: 義而 for 義: 馬王堆 B.

ᵉ Var.: 畜茲 for 孝慈: 馬王堆 A. Var.: 孝茲 for 孝慈: 馬王堆 B.

ᶠ Var.: 三者 for 此三者: 范應元本. Var.: 此三言也 for 此三者: 馬王堆 A; 馬王堆 B. Var.: 三言 for 此三者: 郭店 A.

ᵍ Var.: 以爲文 for 以爲文而: 馬王堆 A; 馬王堆 B. 范應元本. 而 supported by Wang Bi commentary.

ʰ 足 for 足也: Wang Bi comm.: 文而未足; 馬王堆 A; 馬王堆 B. Var.: 不足 for 未足: 范應元本.

ⁱ 令之 for 令: 馬王堆 A; 馬王堆 B. Wang Bi comm.: 令人有所屬 is a translation of 令之有所屬, the reading offered by 馬王堆 A and B. See footnote p.

ʲ Var.: 抱 for 裹: 馬王堆; 馬王堆 B.

ᵏ Var.: 而寡欲 for 寡欲: 馬王堆 A; 馬王堆 B; 莊子山木. The option without 而 is present at an early time in 郭店 A.

聖智^l才之傑^m也仁義行之大也ⁿ巧利用之善也而直云云^o絕文甚不足
不令之有所屬^p無以見其指故曰此三者以爲文而未足故令人有所屬
屬之於素樸寡欲 (Base text: 集註本)

19.1　　If [the ruler] were to discard wisdom and to reject intelligence, the benefit for the people would be a hundredfold.

　　　　If [the ruler] were to discard benevolence and to reject righteousness, the people would return to filial piety and parental love.

　　　　If [the ruler] were to discard craftiness and to reject [lust for] profit, there would be no robbers and thieves.

　　　　These three [pairs of values whose rejection by the ruler is advocated] are as statements still not sufficient.
　　　　Therefore to let [his subjects] have something to go by, [he would]

manifest simplicity,

　　embrace the unadorned, and

　　　　by way of minimizing [his] private interests reduce [his] desires.[1]

Wisdom and intelligence are best among the talents.

　Humaneness and justice are best among the ways of action.

　　Craftiness and [lust for] profit are best in application.

　　　So to bluntly say "discard" is utterly insufficient as far as statements go. It does not let them [the subjects] have some-thing to go by, and there is nothing by which to show the purpose [of this rejection]. That is why [the text] says: "These three are as statements still not sufficient"! Therefore, so that the [other] people would have something to go by, he links them [the three rejections] to

simplicity,

---

^l Var.: 聖人智 for 聖智: 永樂大典本.

^m 才之傑 for 才之善: Wang Bi *LZWZLL* 6.65: 聖智, 才之傑也. Support for 傑: 陸德明釋文: 一本作傑.

ⁿ 仁義行之大也 for 仁義人之善也: Wang Bi *LZWZLL* 6.66: 仁義, 行之大者也. Support for 行: 陸德明釋文.

^o Var.: 云 for 云云: 永樂大典本.

^p 不令之有所屬 for 不令有所屬: 永樂大典本. Support for 之: Wang Bi further down in this commentary 故令人有所屬.

the uncouth, and

the reduction of desires.

THE STRUCTURE OF *LAOZI* 19

The structure of *Laozi* 19 seems troubled by the odd ending.[2] After having given the list of the three discardings, the last phrase 見素抱樸少私寡欲 seems to promise in the first two items to take up, via the opposite, the language of the three discardings, but it ends in an unparallel piece of four characters. In *LZWZLL* 4.17 ff., Wang Bi takes up this passage; he explicitly links the discarding of wisdom and rejection of intelligence to manifesting simplicity, the discarding of humaneness and rejection of justice to embracing the unadorned, and the discarding of craftiness and rejection of profit to subduing private interests and desires. In the text, the last item, the subduing of private interests and reduction of desires comes with two Chinese characters each. As the manifestation of simplicity and embracing of the unadorned also come with two characters each, this last item would in fact consist of two items, breaking the parallel of two sequences with three items each. Already in his commentary here, Wang reduces the phrase 少私寡欲 to the last two characters to arrive at a smoother series of three items, 素樸寡欲. In the *LZWZLL*, he assimilates the three items to a nearly equal length and enhances the other two items to three characters each, with 見質素 as the opposite of 竭聖智, 抱樸 as the opposite of 興仁義, and 寡私欲 as the opposite of 多巧利. From this it is clear that the last item in the *Laozi* text here is read as one single item with a specific reference to the ruler's rejection of "craftiness and profit." The structure of the *zhang* thus consists of two interlocked parallel series with three segments each, separated by a phrase pertaining to all three ("These three [pairs of values whose rejection by the ruler is advocated] are as statements still not sufficient. Therefore to let [his subjects] have something to go by . . . "), called x in the following illustration:

a

b

c

x

a

b

c

Zhang 20

20.1 絕學無憂[a]唯之與阿相去幾何[b]美[c]之與惡相[d]去何若人之所畏不可不畏[e] (Base text: 傅奕古本)

下篇云爲學者日益爲道者日損然則學者[f]求益所能而進其智者也若將無欲而足何求於益不知而中何求於進夫燕雀有匹鳩鴿有仇寒鄉之民必知氊[g]裘自然已足益之則憂故續鳧之足何異截鶴[h]之脛畏譽而進何異畏[i]刑唯阿美惡相去何若故人之所畏吾亦畏焉未敢恃之以爲用也 (Base text: 集註本)

20.2 荒兮[i]其未央哉[k] (Base text: 范應元本)

歎與俗相返之遠也[l] (Base text: 集註本)

---

   [a] There have been suggestions since the Tang dynasty that this phrase should be the last phrase of *zhang* 19. Content, parallel grammar, and rhyme seemed to provide a solid link. Modern scholars such as Ma Xulun, Gao Heng, and Gao Ming have accepted this reasoning and added arguments to support it (Gao Ming, *Boshu*, 315ff.). The 郭店 B contains the first part of *zhang* 20. It does not follow *zhang* 19 of the received sequence, so that a mix-up is not possible. It begins the *zhang* with this very phrase. This brings the argument to rest and might serve as a reminder of the consistency and quality of textual transmission in China and of the frailty of modern critical scholarship. It should be kept in mind that efforts have been made in this century to completely dismantle the *Laozi* into short, disconnected bites, as well as to reassemble the text in a new order. The very early date and the high cohesiveness of the Guodian texts have, in my opinion, soundly disproved these efforts.

   [b] Var.: 唯與訶(馬王堆 B: 呵) 其相 for 唯之與阿相: 馬王堆 A; 馬王堆 B. 郭店 B has 唯與可相去 . . . and 美與惡相去. While Wang Bi's commentary excludes the 其, it does not directly support the 之. It is possible that Wang Bi's text, like the Guodian and Mawangdui manuscripts, did not have the 之.

   [c] Var.: 善 for 美: 范應元本.

   [d] Var.: 美與惡其相 for 美之與惡相: 馬王堆 A; 馬王堆 B.

   [e] Var.: 亦不可以不畏(馬王堆 B add.:人) for 不可不畏: 郭店 B; 馬王堆 B (馬王堆 A: 亦不□□□□).

   [f] Var.: 學 for 學者: 永樂大典本.　　　　[g] 氊 for 旃: 陸德明釋文.
   [h] 鵠 for 鶴: 陸德明釋文.　　　　[i] 畏 for 異: 永樂大典本.
   [j] Var.: 望呵 for 荒兮: 馬王堆 B.

   [k] Var.: 未央 for 未央哉: 傅奕古本. Support for 哉: 未央才 in 馬王堆 B. Var.: 才 for 哉: 馬王堆 B.

   [l] Var.: 歎與俗相返之遠也 om.: 永樂大典本.

20.3 眾人熙熙^m若ⁿ享^o太^p牢如^q春登臺^r (Base text: 傅奕古本)

眾人迷於美進惑於榮利欲進心競故熙熙若^s享太牢如春登臺也 (Base text: 集註本)

20.4 我^t廓兮^u其未兆^v如^w嬰兒未^x咳¹ (Base text: 傅奕古本)

言我廓然無形之可名無兆之可舉如嬰兒未^y能咳^z也 (Base text: 集註本)

20.5 儽儽兮^{aa}若^{ab}無所歸^{ac} (Base text: 馬王堆 B)

若無所宅 (Base text: 集註本)

---

^m Var.: 熙熙 for 熙熙: 馬王堆 A; 馬王堆 B.

ⁿ Var.: 如 for 若: 范應元本. Support for 若: 陸德明釋文; 馬王堆 A; 馬王堆 B.

^o Var.: 亨 for 享: 陸德明釋文. Support for 享: 范應元本. Var.: 鄉 for 享: 馬王堆 A; 馬王堆 B.

^p Var.: 於大牢 for 太牢: 馬王堆 A; 馬王堆 B.

^q 如 for 若: Wang Bi comm.: 太牢如春登臺也. Var.: 而 for 若: 馬王堆 A; 馬王堆 B.

^r Var.: 登春臺 for 春登臺: 范應元本.

^s Var.: 如 for 若: 永樂大典本.

^t 我 for 我獨: Wang Bi comm. does not mention the 獨. Support for leaving out 獨: 馬王堆 A; 馬王堆 B; 永樂大典本; Shima Kuniō; Hatano Tarō.

^u 廓兮 for 魄兮: Wang Bi comm.: 我廓然無形之可名; 陸德明釋文. Var.: 怕兮 for 廓兮: 范應元本. Var.: 泊焉 for 廓兮: 馬王堆 A. Var.: 博焉 for 廓兮: 馬王堆 B.

^v Var.: 未佻 for 其未兆: 馬王堆 A. Var.: 未垗 for 其未兆: 馬王堆 B.

^w 如 for 若 (also in 馬王堆 A; 馬王堆 B): 范應元本. Support for 如: Wang Bi comm.: 如嬰兒.

^x 嬰兒未 for 嬰兒之未: Wang Bi comm.: 嬰兒未能; 馬王堆 B; (馬王堆 A: □□□).

^y Var.: 嬰兒之未 for 嬰兒未: 永樂大典本.

^z 咳 for 孩 (in both 集註本 and 永樂大典本): Cf. note 1.

^{aa} 儽儽兮 for 纍呵 (also in 馬王堆 A): 陸德明釋文; 傅奕古本; 范應元本.

^{ab} 若 for 似: Wang Bi, comm.: 若無所宅; 范應元本. Var.: 如 for 若: 馬王堆 A. Var.: 若 om.: 傅奕古本.

^{ac} Var.: 儽儽兮其不足以無所歸 for 儽儽兮若無所歸: 傅奕古本. Var.: 儽儽兮其若不足似無所歸 for 儽儽兮若無所歸: 范應元本. Fan Yingyuan says Wang Bi followed the text given by him here.

20.6 眾人皆有餘我^{ad}獨若^{ae}遺^{af} (Base text: 傅奕古本)

眾人無不有懷有志盈溢貪心故曰皆有餘也我獨廓然無爲無欲若遺失
之也 (Base text: 集註本)

20.7 我^{ag}愚^{ah}人之心也哉^{ai} (Base text: 傅奕古本)

絕愚之人心無所別析意無所好欲猶然其情不可覩我頹然若此也(Base
text: 集註本)

20.8 沌沌兮^{aj} (Base text: 傅奕古本)

無所別析不可爲名^{ak} (Base text: 集註本)

20.9 俗^{al}人^{am}昭昭 (Base text: 陸德明釋文)

耀其光也 (Base text: 集註本)

20.10 我獨昏昏^{an}俗^{ao}人察察^{ap} (Base text: 范應元本)

[ad] Var.: 而我 for 我: 范應元本. Support against 而: Wang Bi comm. does not repeat it in 皆有餘也我獨廓然.

[ae] Var.: 若 om.: 馬王堆 A.   [af] Var.: 我獨若遺 om.: 馬王堆 B.

[ag] Var.: 我獨 for 我: 范應元本.   [ah] Var.: 禺 for 愚: 馬王堆 A.

[ai] Var.: 心也 for 心也哉: 馬王堆 A; 馬王堆 B.

[aj] Var.: 蠢蠢 for 沌沌兮: 馬王堆 A. Var.: 湷湷呵 for 沌沌兮: 馬王堆 B.

[ak] Var.: 明 for 名: 永樂大典本.   [al] Var.: 鬻 for 俗: 馬王堆 A; 馬王堆 B.

[am] Var.: 俗人皆 for 俗人: 傅奕古本; 范應元本. Support for omission of 皆 against claim by 范應元 that Wang Bi's *Laozi* had 皆: 馬王堆 A; 馬王堆 B.

[an] 昏昏 for 若昏 (in both 傅奕古本 and 范應元本): Wang Bi comm. on *Laozi* 20.14: 悶悶昏昏若無所識. This is a unique case where a reading suggested by Wang Bi's commentary, which is not marked by Lu Deming, goes against the entire textual family but is preserved in one relatively late manuscript. The 永樂大典本 transmits a text 我獨昏昏. The credibility of this tradition is enhanced by the fact that this reading deviates from the Heshang gong reading, which is 若昏 or 如昏, while normally these traditions present texts strongly contaminated by the Heshang gong tradition. I therefore accept the reading 昏昏 suggested by Bi Yuan 畢沅 and followed by Hatano Tarō and Shima Kuniō. Var.: 闓呵 for 昏昏: 馬王堆 A; Var.: 若閩呵 for 昏昏: 馬王堆 B.

[ao] Var.: 鬻 for 俗: 馬王堆 A; 馬王堆 B.

[ap] 察察 for 皆察察: Support for omission of 皆, which is present in both the 傅奕古本 and the 范應元本: analogy to Wang Bi's *Laozi* 20.9 俗人昭昭 (against 俗人皆昭昭 in

分別別析也 (Base text: 集註本)

20.11 我獨悶悶^{aq}澹兮^{ar}其^{as}若海 (Base text: 陸德明釋文)

情不可覩 (Base text: 集註本)

20.12 飂兮^{at}若^{au}無所止 (Base text: 馬王堆 B)

無所繫縶^{av} (Base text: 永樂大典本)

20.13 眾人皆有以 (Base text: 傅奕古本)

以用也皆欲有所施用也 (Base text: 集註本)

20.14 我獨頑^{aw}且^{ax}鄙^{ay} (Base text: 傅奕古本)

無所欲為悶悶昏昏若無所識故曰頑且鄙也 (Base text: 集註本)

20.15 我獨欲^{az}異於人而貴食母^{ba} (Base text: 馬王堆 A)

傅奕古本 and 范應元本); 馬王堆 A; 馬王堆 B. Var.: 皆詧詧 for 察察: 傅奕古本. Var.: 蔡蔡 for 察察: 馬王堆 A.

^{aq} Var.: 閔閔 for 悶悶: 傅奕古本; 范應元本. Support for 悶悶, Wang Bi comm. on *Laozi* 20.14 悶悶. Var.: 閲閲呵 for 悶悶: 馬王堆 A. Var.: 閩閩呵 for 悶悶: 馬王堆 B.

^{ar} Var.: 淡兮 for 澹兮: 傅奕古本. Var.: 忽呵 for 澹兮: 馬王堆 A. Var.: 沕呵 for 澹兮: 馬王堆 B.

^{as} Var.:若 for 其若: 范應元本.

^{at} 飂兮 for 望呵: 陸德明釋文 (with 呵 being the standard writing for 兮 in both 馬王堆 A and 馬王堆 B). Var.: 朢呵 for 飂兮: 馬王堆 A; 馬王堆 B. Var.: 飄兮 for 飂兮: 傅奕古本; 范應元本.

^{au} Var.: 似 for 若: 傅奕古本; 范應元本.

^{av} Var.: 繫繫 for 繫縶: 集註本. Support for 繫縶: 陸德明釋文.

^{aw} Var.: 閔 for 頑: 馬王堆 B, reading of 高明.

^{ax} Var.: 似 for 且: 范應元本. Var.: 以 for 且: 馬王堆 A, 馬王堆 B (the character 以 stands for 似).

^{ay} 鄙 for 圖: Wang Bi comm.: 頑且鄙. Var.: 悝 for 鄙: 馬王堆 A.

^{az} 獨欲 for 欲獨 (in both 馬王堆 A and 馬王堆 B): Wang Bi comm.: 我獨欲; 傅奕古本; 范應元本.

^{ba} Var.: 貴食 for 貴食母: 傅奕古本. Var.: 貴求食於母 for 貴食母: 范應元本. Support for 食母: Wang Bi comm.: 食母生之本也.

食母生之本也人者皆棄生民之本貴末^{bb}飾之華故曰我獨欲異於人
(Base text: 永樂大典本)

20.1   [Laozi says:]¹ To break off studying brings no harm. How much difference
         is there [after all] between "at your orders" and "definitely not"?² How do
         the beautiful and the ugly differ [after all]? What other people fear [I] can-
         not but also fear.

In the second chapter [of the Laozi, *that is, in 48.1] it says: "[A ruler]
who is in favor of study every day has more. [A ruler] who is in favor
of the Way every day reduces more." Consequently, someone studying
is someone who strives to add to what he is capable of doing and to enhance his knowledge. If [I] were satisfied without having [any further]
desires, why should [I] strive for adding [to my studies]; if I were hitting
the mark without knowledge, why should [I] strive for an enhancement
[of my knowledge]?*

*It is a fact that swallows and sparrows mate, pigeons and doves have
hatred for each other, and that people in cold districts inevitably know
about furs and wool. [The entities'] that-which-is-of-itself-what-it-is
already is sufficient [in itself].³ If one adds to it, harm will come. In this
sense, where is the difference between stretching a duck's foot and shortening a crane's neck⁴ [as both mean interference into the self-sufficient
order of That-which-is-of-itself-what-it-is]? In what way does fear of being praised and promoted [after all] differ from fear of suffering corporal
punishment? How do "at your orders" and "definitely not," the beautiful
and the ugly differ? Therefore I also fear what other people fear, and I do
not dare to rely on them [i.e., the things they fear] for [my own] use.*

20.2   Deserted [I am], endlessly!

He is sighing about the distance separating him from the vulgar.

20.3   The vulgar scholars⁵ are excited as if performing the Tailao sacrifice, as if
         going up a terrace in spring.

*The vulgar scholars are beguiled by beauty and promotion, bedazzled by
glory and profits. Their desires press ahead, their hearts are in competition;⁶ that is why [as the text says] they "are excited as if performing the
Tailao sacrifice, as if going up a terrace in spring."*

20.4   I am vacant, without clues [for others to recognize me], like a baby that has
         not yet started to smile.

*This means: I am vacant without a shape that could be named, without a
clue that could be taken up, like a baby that is not yet capable of smiling.*

---

^{bb} Var.: 未 for 末: 集註本.

20.5   Aimless [I am], alas, as if without a place to return to.

As if without a place to live in.

20.6   The vulgar scholars all have too much, I alone am as though I had lost [all].

There is none among the vulgar scholars who does not have concerns and ambitions. These fill [their] breasts and hearts to overflowing. That is why [the text] says: "[They] all have too much." I alone am vacant, without interference and without desires "as though I had lost" them.

20.7   Me—[I have] the heart of a dimwit!

The heart of a complete idiot has nothing to differentiate and analyze, his mind has nothing to prefer or desire. Undecided he is[7] [so that] his feelings cannot be made out. [The text means to say] I am indifferent to such a degree.

20.8   Turbid [is my heart], alas!

There is nothing with which to differentiate and analyze [it and consequently] it is impossible ot make a name [for it].

20.9   The vulgar men are shedding light, shedding light.

That is, they let their lights shine forth [to find out the people's secret hideouts as opposed to the Sage who, according to Laozi *58.10, "enlightens but does not investigate"* 光而不耀].

20.10   I alone am darkened. Vulgar men investigate and investigate.

That is, they separate and differentiate.

20.11   I alone am sealed, turbulent, alas, like the sea,

[My] feelings are impossible to make out.

20.12   stormy as if there is nothing to stop [me].

There is nothing to bind and fetter [me].

20.13   The vulgar scholars all have purposes.

Purpose means application. They all desire to have something to handle and apply.

20.14   I alone am stolid and furthermore stupid.

There is nothing that [I] desire and nothing with which I interfere. [I] am sealed and darkened as if there were nothing I understood. That is why [the text] says: "Stolid and furthermore stupid!"

20.15   I alone desire to be different from the others in that I honor the nourishing mother.

The nourishing mother is the root of life. The others all discard the root that is providing life for the people and honor the dazzle of worldly accoutrements. That is why [the text] says: "I alone desire to be different from the others!"

Zhang 21

21.1 孔德之容唯[a]道是從 (Base text: 范應元本)

孔空也唯[b]以空爲德然後乃能動作從道 (Base text: 集註本)

21.2 道之爲物[c]惟恍惟惚[d] (Base text: 李善, 文選頭陀寺碑文注 59.5.b8)

恍[e]惚無形不繫之貌[f] (Base text: 李善, 文選頭陀寺碑文注 59.5.b8)

21.3 恍[g]兮惚兮其中有物惚兮恍[h]兮其中有象[i] (Base text: 王弼注)[l]

以無形始物不繫成物萬物以始以成而不知其所以然故曰恍[j]兮惚兮
其中有物[k]惚兮恍[l]兮其中有象也 (Base text: 集註本)

---

[a] Var.: 惟 for 唯: 傅奕古本.　　　　　[b] Var.: 惟 for 唯: 永樂大典本.

[c] Var.: 物 for 爲物: 馬王堆 A; 馬王堆 B.

[d] Var.: 惟芒惟芴 for 惟恍惟惚: 傅奕古本; 范應元本. Var.: 唯朢唯忽 for 惟恍惟惚: 馬王堆 A (高明). Var.: 唯朢唯沕 for 惟恍惟惚: 馬王堆 B. Support for 恍: 陸德明釋文. Support for 惚: Wang Bi comm. in 永樂大典本.

[e] Var.: 恍 for 恍: 永樂大典本.

[f] Var.: 歎 for 貌: 永樂大典本. Possible counterevidence: Wang Bi on *Laozi* 21.4 窈兮 冥兮: 窈冥深遠之歎. Var.: from 恍 to 貌: 集註本 om.

[g] 恍 for 恍 (in 傅奕古本 and 范應元本): 文選王簡棲頭陀寺碑文李善注, 59.5b; 陸 德明釋文. cf. *Laozi* 21.2.

[h] 恍 for 恍 (in 傅奕古本 and 范應元本): 李善; 陸德明釋文. Cf. *Laozi* 21.2.

[i] Var.: 芴兮芒兮其(范應元本 om. 其)中有象芒兮芴兮其(范應元本 om. 其)中有物 for 恍兮惚兮其中有物惚兮恍兮其中有象: 傅奕古本; 范應元本. Var.:口口口呵中有象 呵朢呵忽呵中有物呵 for 恍兮惚兮其中有物惚兮恍兮其中有象:馬王堆 A. Var.: 沕呵朢 呵中又象呵朢呵沕呵中有物呵 for 恍兮惚兮其中有物惚兮恍兮其中有象:馬王堆 B.

[j] 恍 for 恍: 李善; 陸德明釋文. Cf. *Laozi* 21.2.

[k] 其中有物 add. 俞樾.

[l] 恍 for 恍: 李善; 陸德明釋文. Cf. *Laozi* 21.2.

21.4 窈[m]兮冥兮[n]其中[o]有精[p] (Base text: 王弼注)

> 窈冥深遠之歎[q]深遠不可得而見然而萬物由之其可[r]得見以定其眞故
> 曰窈兮冥兮其中有精也 (Base text: 永樂大典本)

21.5 其精[s]甚眞其中有信 (Base text: 王弼注)

> 信信驗也物反窈冥則眞精之極得萬物之性定故曰其精甚眞其中有信
> (Base text 集註本)

21.6 自古及今[t]其名不去 (Base text: 王弼注)

> 至眞之極不可得名無名則是其名也自古及今無不由此而成故曰自古
> 及今[u]其名不去也 (Base text: 永樂大典本)

21.7 以閱衆甫[v] (Base text: 傅奕古本)

> 衆甫物之始也以無名閱[w]萬物始也 (Base text: 取善集)

---

[m] Var.: 幽 for 窈: 傅奕古本; 范應元本.

[n] Var.: 淨呵鳴呵 for 窈兮冥兮: 馬王堆 A. Var.: 幼呵冥呵 for 窈兮冥兮: 馬王堆 B.

[o] Var.: 中 for 其中: 范應元本; 馬王堆 A.

[p] Var.: 精兮 for 精: 范應元本. Var.: 請 for 精: 馬王堆 A; Var.: 請呵 for 精: 馬王堆 B.

[q] Var.: 貌 for 之歎: 李善, 文選沈約鐘山詩注 22.28b5. Var.: 欺 for 歎: 集註本.

[r] Var.: 不可 for 其可: 李善, 文選沈約鐘山詩注 22.28b5. Cf. translation note 5.

[s] Var.: 請 for 精: 馬王堆 A; 馬王堆 B.

[t] Var.: 自今及古 for 自古及今: 馬王堆 A; 馬王堆 B; 傅奕古本; 范應元本. Support for 自古及今: Wang Bi in *LZWZLL* 1.43: 自古及今其名不去. Note that Wang Bi's reading here deviates from the entire textual family (although Fan Yingyuan, 1:45.a, refers to a manuscript with the 自古及今 reading). Otherwise it would have to be argued that the quotation in the *LZWZLL* has been adapted to another *Laozi* text. Within the two versions of the commentary, the 永樂大典本 version seems more plausible, not only because it agrees with the *LZWZLL* quotation but also because the immediately preceding phrase, 自古及 今無不由此而成, has in both versions the formula 自古及今, which then is taken up with the 故曰自古及今其名不去也.

[u] Var.: 自今及古 for 自古及今: 集註本.

[v] Var.: 以順衆仪 (馬王堆 B:父) for 以閱衆甫: 馬王堆 A; 馬王堆 B.

[w] Var.: 說 for 閱: 集註本; 永樂大典本.

21.8 吾何以知眾甫^x之狀哉^y以此 (Base text: 馬王堆 A)

此上之所云也言吾何以知萬物之始皆始^z於無哉以此知之也 (Base text: 集註本)

21.1   An attitude [corresponding to] the capacity of the hollow is the only means to follow the Way.

Hollow means empty. Only having taken being empty as [one's] capacity will one then be able to act in accordance with the Way.

21.2   The Way as a thing is vague, ah, diffuse, ah.[1]

[The terms] "vague," and "diffuse" are figurative expressions for [the Way's being] without shape and unfettered.[2]

21.3   Vague, ah, diffuse, ah, [is the Way], [still,] in them there is an entity. Diffuse, ah, vague, ah, [is the Way], [still,] in them there is an image.

By means of being shapeless [the Way] initiates the entities; by means of being unfettered [the Way] completes the entities. The ten thousand kinds of entities are [thus] initiated through it and completed through it, but they do not know that through which this came about.[3] That is why [the text] says: "Vague, ah, diffuse, ah, [is the Way], [still,] in them [the ten thousand kinds of entities] there is an entity [the Way]. Diffuse, ah, vague, ah, [is the Way], [still,] in them [the entities] there is an image [of the Way]"!

21.4   Secluded, ah [is the Way], distant, ah, [still,] in them there is an essence.

[The terms] "secluded" and "distant" are sighs about its depth and abstruseness.[4] The deep and abstruse it is impossible to perceive; however, the ten thousand kinds of entities are based on it; and these it is possible to perceive[5] by way of determining their true nature [which is the Way so that the Way becomes indirectly discernible through them]. That is why [the text] says: "Secluded, ah, [is the Way], distant, ah, [still,] in them [the ten thousand kinds of entities] there is an essence"!

21.5   [If] their essence is verily truthful, there is credible [evidence] in them.

"Credible" means credible evidence. Once entities relate back to the "secluded" and "distant," the ultimate of their true essence is grasped, and the nature of the ten thousand kinds of entities determined. That is

---

^x 甫 for 伀: Wang Bi comm. on 21.7 眾甫. Var.: 父 for 甫:馬王堆 B.

^y 狀哉 for 然: 陸德明釋文. Var.: 然也 for 狀哉: 馬王堆 B. Var.: 然哉 for 狀哉: 傅奕古本; 范應元本.

^z Var.: 萬物之始 for 萬物之始皆始: 永樂大典本.

why [the text] says: "[If] their essence is verily truthful, there is credible [evidence] in them."

21.6   From antiquity to the present its [the truthful essence's] name has not disappeared.

The ultimate of the absolutely true cannot be [determined by means of a] name. "Namelessness" thus is its name. From antiquity to the present there is nothing that did not come about based on this [Namelessness].⁶ That is why [the text] says: "From antiquity to the present, its [the truthful essence's] name [i.e., "Namelessness"] has not disappeared."⁷

21.7   By means of it [the truthful essence] one discerns the beginning of the many.⁸

The "beginning of the many" is the beginning of the entities. [The entire phrase thus reads rephrased:] By means of [truthful essence, that is,] Namelessness, one discerns the beginning of the ten thousand kinds of entities.

21.8   How does it happen that I know the features of the beginning of the many? From this!

"This" refers to the things said above. [The phrase] means: How does it happen that I know that the beginnings of the ten thousand kinds of entities all begin in negativity?⁹ From this [the above] I know it.

Zhang 22

22.1 曲則全ᵃ (Base text: 傅奕古本)

不自見其明則全也ᵇ (Base text: 集註本)

22.2 枉則正ᶜ (Base text: 傅奕古本)

不自是則其是彰也 (Base text: 集註本)

22.3 窪ᵈ則盈 (Base text: 傅奕古本)

不自伐則其功有也 (Base text: 集註本)

ᵃ Var.: 金 for 全: 馬王堆 A.   ᵇ Var.: 全 for 全也: 取善集.
ᶜ Var.: 枉則定 for 枉則正: 馬王堆 A. Var.: 汪則正 for 枉則正: 馬王堆B.
ᵈ Var.: 洼 for 窪: 馬王堆 A: 馬王堆 B.

22.4 蔽^e則新 (Base text: 傅奕古本)

不自矜則其德長也^f (Base text: 集註本)

22.5 少則得多則惑 (Base text: 傅奕古本)

自然之道亦猶樹也轉多轉遠其根轉少轉得其本多則遠其眞故曰惑也少則得其本故曰得也^g (Base text: 集註本)

22.6 是以^h聖人抱ⁱ一爲^j天下式^k (Base text: 范應元本)

一少之極式猶則之也 (Base text: 集註本)

22.7 不自見故明不自是故彰^l不自伐故有功不自矜故長^m夫唯ⁿ不爭故天下^o莫能與之爭古之所謂曲則全^p者豈虛言哉^q誠全^r而^s歸之 (Base text: 傅奕古本)

22.1 Hiding results in completeness.

[*Therefore, as* Laozi 22.7 *says, the Sage*] "*does not show himself*" *with the result that [his]* "*enlightenment*" *becomes complete.*

22.2 Bending results in correctness.

[*Therefore the Sage, as* Laozi 22.7 *says*], "*is not self-righteous*" *with the result that his being right* "*shines forth.*"

---

^e 蔽 for 敝 (also in 馬王堆 A and 范應元本): 陸德明釋文.

^f Var.: 長 for 長也: 取善集.

^g The 永樂大典本 has included this passage in the commentary to the next phrase.

^h Var.: 是以 om: 傅奕古本.

ⁱ Var.: 執 for 抱: 馬王堆 A; 馬王堆 B. Var.: 裒 for 抱: 傅奕古本.

^j Var.: 以爲 for 爲: 傅奕古本; 馬王堆 A; 馬王堆 B. Support for 爲: Wang Bi comm. defines 式 as transitive verb by writing 式猶則之也. Therefore, 爲 must be read in the sense of 使, which excludes the 以爲 option.

^k Var.: 牧 for 式: 馬王堆 A; 馬王堆 B.

^l Var.: 不口視故明不自見故章 for 不自見故明不自是故彰: 馬王堆 A. Var.: 不自視故章 不自見也故明 for 不自見故明不自是故彰: 馬王堆 B.

^m Var.: 弗矜故能長 for 不自矜故長: 馬王堆 A; 馬王堆 B.

^m 唯 for 惟: Wang Bi on *Laozi* 73.5.　　^o Var.: 天下 om.: 馬王堆 A; 馬王堆 B.

^p Var.: 胃曲全 for 謂曲則全: 馬王堆 B.

^q Var.: 言哉 for 言也哉: 范應元本. Var.: 幾(馬王堆 A: 口)語才 for 豈虛言哉: 馬王堆 B.

^r Var.: 金 for 全: 馬王堆 A.　　^s Var.: 而 om.: 馬王堆 A; 馬王堆 B.

22.3   Being a pothole results in getting full.

[Therefore the Sage, as Laozi *22.7 says], "does not brag" with the result that his "achievements" "are" uncontestedly his.*

22.4   Being worn out results in getting new [things].

[Therefore the Sage, as Laozi *22.7 says], "does not praise himself" with the result that his capacity "grows."*

22.5   [In short]

reduction results in attaining,   increase results in delusion.

The Way of That-which-is-of-itself-what-it-is resembles a tree.

The more there is [of the tree], the farther away it is from its root.

The less there is [of the tree], the [better] it attains its root.

By increasing, one gets further away from its true [nature], that is why [the text] says "delusion."

By reducing one attains its root, that is why [the text] says "attaining."

22.6   This [last general principle] is why the Sage holds on to the One, and makes the empire [take it as] a model.

The "One" is the absolute of reduction. "Model" is [a verb and has to be read] as "take as a model."

22.7   [The Sage follows the first maxim; that is why] he does not show himself, and therefore [his] enlightenment [becomes complete].

[The Sage follows the second maxim; that is why] he is not self-righteous, and therefore [his being right] shines forth.

[The Sage follows the third maxim; that is why] he does not brag, and therefore he has [his] achievements [uncontestedly].

[The Sage follows the fourth maxim; that is why] he does not praise himself, and therefore [his capacity] grows.

[Generally spoken] it is a fact that only because he does not

struggle no one in All Under
Heaven is able to struggle with
him.[1] How could empty chatter
be what the people of old called
"hiding results in completeness"
[and so forth]? To him who has
in truth [achieved] completeness,
[All Under Heaven] will render
itself.[2]

THE STRUCTURE OF *LAOZI* 22

The coherence of this *zhang* has puzzled many commentators. Wang Bi presents a strikingly simple and coherent reading by applying a standard form of IPS as an analytic tool. The number of paradoxes given in the beginning is four. The two following ones in 22.5 are easily recognizable as a separate pair by their antithetical structure and thus can be understood to sum up the first series. They will be named x and y here. There is a statement in 22.6 about the Sage applying the general maxim of 22.5. It will be called z here. It is not parallel to the next four specific applications and thus again constitutes a separate general statement. Then come the four phrases in 22.7, formally matching the first four phrases 22.1–22.4, to be followed again by a general statement called z, which furthermore identifies the first sentences as sayings by people of old, the enactment of which explains why the Sage behaves in a certain way. The very last statement in 22.7 deals with the general message of the *zhang* by taking up the relationship between the two parts, I and II, of general principles and the Sage's application of them. I will therefore call it III. The structure of the *zhang* in formalized writing reads:

I	a				(22.1)
	b				(22.2)
		c			(22.3)
			d		(22.4)
				x y	(22.5)
				z	(22.6)
II	a				(22.7)
	b				(22.7)
		c			(22.7)
			d		(22.7)
III				z	(22.7)

Zhang 24 operates with all four phrases from Part II here in *Laozi* 22 but states the same case negatively. Wang Bi uses basically the same commenting method.

Zhang 23

23.1 希^a言自然 (Base text: 范應元本)

> 聽之不聞名曰希下章言道之出言淡兮其無味也視之不足見聽之不足聞然則無味不足聽之言乃是自然之至言也 (Base text: 集註本)

23.2 故^b飄^c風不終^d朝驟^e雨不終^f日孰爲此者天地^g天地尚不^h能久而況ⁱ於人乎 (Base text: 王弼注 on *Laozi* 30.7 for first two phrases, 范應元本 for the rest)

> 言暴疾美興不長也 (Base text: 集註本)

23.3 故從事於道者道者同^j於道 (Base text: 傅奕古本)¹

> 從事謂舉動從事於道者也道以無形無爲成濟萬物故^k從事於道者以無爲爲居^l不言爲教綿綿^m若存而物得其眞行道則與道同體ⁿ故曰同於道 (Base text: 集註本)²

---

^a Var. 稀 for 希: 傅奕古本.　　　^b Var.: 故 om.: 馬王堆 A; 馬王堆 B.

^c Var.: 劋 for 飄: 馬王堆 B.

^d Var.: 崇 for 終: 傅奕古本; 范應元本. Var.: 冬 for 終: 馬王堆 A; 馬王堆 B.

^e Var.: 暴 for 驟: 馬王堆 A; 馬王堆 B; 范應元本.

^f Var.: 崇 for 終: 傅奕古本; 范應元本. Var.: 冬 for 終: 馬王堆 A; 馬王堆 B.

^g Var.: 天地也 for 天地: 傅奕古本.

^h Var.: 孰爲此天地而弗 for 孰爲此者天地天地尚不: 馬王堆 B (孰爲此天地口口: 馬王堆 A).

ⁱ Var.: 有兄 for 而況: 馬王堆 B.

^j Var.: 而道者同 for 於道者道者同: 馬王堆 A; 馬王堆 B.

^k Var.: 故 om.: 取善集.

^l 居 for 君 (in both 集註本 and 永樂大典本): Wagner based on *Laozi* 2.2 聖人居無爲之事.

^m 綿綿 for 緜緜 (in both 集註本 and 永樂大典本): Wagner based on Wang Bi text of *Laozi* 6.1. The 集註本 is inconsistent here, writing in its quotation of Wang's commentary on *Laozi* 6.1 綿綿.

ⁿ 行道則與道同體 for 與道同體: Wagner based on parallel with Wang Bi comm. on *Laozi* 23.4 行得則與得同體 and 23.5 行失則於失同體.

23.4 得[o]者同於得[p] (Base text: 范應元本)

得少也少則得[q]故曰得也行得則與得同體故曰同於得也 (Base text: 永樂大典本)

23.5 失[r]者同於失 (Base text: 范應元本)

失累多也累多則失故曰失也行失則與失[s]同體故曰同於失也 (Base text: 永樂大典本)

23.6 同[t]於道者道亦得之[u]同[v]於得[w]者得亦得之[x]同[y]於失者失亦得之[z] (Base text: 范應元本)

言隨其所行[aa]故同而應之 (Base text: 永樂大典本)

23.7 信不足焉[ab]有不信[ac] (Base text: 傅奕古本)

忠信不足於上[ad]焉有不信也 (Base text: 永樂大典本)

23.1 [Only] inaudible [words] speak about That-which-is-of-itself-what-it-is.

---

[o] 得 for 德 (also in 馬王堆 A; 馬王堆 B): Wagner based on Wang Bi comm.: 得少也; 傅奕古本. Var.: 從事於得者 for 得者: 傅奕古本.

[p] 得 for 德 (also in 馬王堆 A; 馬王堆 B): Wagner based on Wang Bi comm.: 得少也; 傅奕古本.

[q] Var.: 德 for 得: 集註本.

[r] Var.: 從事於失者 for 失者: 傅奕古本. Var.: 者 for 失: 馬王堆 A.

[s] Var.: 則失與失 for 則與失: 集註本. [t] Var.: 同 om.: 傅奕古本.

[u] Var.: 同於道者道亦得之 om.: 馬王堆 A; 馬王堆 B.

[v] Var.: 同 om.: 傅奕古本.

[w] 得 for 德: (also in 馬王堆 A; 馬王堆 B): Wagner based on Wang Bi comm. on 23.4; 傅奕古本.

[x] 得亦得之 for 德亦得之: 傅奕古本. Var.: 道亦德之 for 得亦得之: 馬王堆 A; 馬王堆 B.

[y] Var.: 同 om.: 傅奕古本.

[z] Var.: 道亦失之 for 失亦得之: 馬王堆 A; 馬王堆 B.

[aa] 隨其所行 for 隨行其所: 陶鴻慶.

[ab] Var.: 焉 om.: 范應元本. Support for 焉: Wang Bi comm.: 足於上焉.

[ac] Var.: 信不足焉有不信 om.: 馬王堆 A; 馬王堆 B. Cf. *Laozi* 17.5.

[ad] 上 for 下: Wagner; cf. translation notes 7 and 8.

[As the Laozi 14.1 *says,] "That which [I] do not hear when listening for it, [I] call 'inaudible'." In a later zhang [, namely,* zhang 35.3, *the* Laozi*] says: "Words uttered about the Way, indeed, are stale; they are without taste! Looking for it [the Way] one cannot manage to see it; listening for it [the Way] one cannot manage to hear it." Consequently, it is the words without taste and which one cannot manage to hear that are the ultimate words about That-which-is-of-itself-what-it-is.*

23.2   That is why a cyclone does not outlast a morning, and a cloudburst does not outlast a day.[1] And who after all is it who lets them happen? Heaven and Earth! If even Heaven and Earth cannot keep these [violent outbreaks] up forever, how much less [is] man [able to maintain an interfering government for long]!

This means: A violent outbreak is good at rising but does not last long.

23.3   That is why if [a Sage] manages [all] affairs in [accordance with] the Way,

he will make those who [practice] the Way identical with the Way,[2]

"Manages affairs" means that in [his] comings and goings [he] "manages [all] affairs in accordance with the Way."[3] The Way completes and regulates the ten thousand kinds of entities by means of its being shapeless and without interference. That is why [the Sage] "who manages [all] affairs in [accordance with] the Way" is, by way of making [as the Laozi 2.2 *and 2.3 write about the Sage] "non-interference" his "residence" and the "unspoken" his "teaching," [like the "root of Heaven and Earth" in* Laozi 6.1] *"intangible but still existent" so that the other entities [all] attain their true [nature].*

If they practice the Way, [the Sage's rule] will make them to be of the same substance as the Way. That is why [the Laozi] *says: "He will make [them] identical with the Way."*

23.4   he will make those who [practice] attaining [the Way] identical with attaining,

"Attaining [the Way]" means reducing [according to Laozi 22.5, *which says] "reduction results in attaining" [which Wang Bi there comments: "By reducing one attains its root"]. That is why [the text] says "attaining"! If they practice attaining [the Way], [the Sage's rule] will make them to be of the same substance as [this] attaining.[4] That is why [the text] says: "He will make [them] identical with attaining."*

23.5   and he will make those who [practice] losing [the Way] identical with losing.

"Losing [the Way]" means an increase in attachments. If the attachments increase, one loses [the Way].[5] That is why [the text] says "losing." If they practice losing [the Way], [the Sage's rule]

*will make them to be of the same substance as losing. That is why
[the text] says: "He will make [them] identical with losing."*

23.6   Those whom he has made identical with the Way will also attain the Way;

those whom he has made identical with attaining, will also attain the
attainment;

those whom he has made identical with losing, will also attain
the loss.

> *This means: He adapts to their
> practice. That is why he makes
> [them] identical with [the Way,
> attainment, or loss] by way of
> corresponding to them.*[6]

23.7   If credibility is not sufficient [however, in him who rules the state], there
will be lack of credibility [among his subjects].[7]

*If honesty and credibility are not sufficient at the top, there will be lack of
credibility [below].*[8]

THE STRUCTURE OF *LAOZI* 23

The first part of the *zhang*, 23.1 and 23.2, establishes a rationale of
ruling by the unspoken and by noninterference instead of ruling with
violent measures, which cannot hold for long. Wang Bi shows how he
read the reference to the cyclones and cloudbursts by quoting them in his
commentary on *Laozi* 30 as illustrations for rule by violence. The second
part deals with rule under a Sage who rules in accordance with the Way.
The consequence of this is that all [social] entities follow their true nature.
The structure of this section is an open parallel staircase framed by two
general and connected statements, called *z* here.

	z			(23.1)
	z			(23.2)
	z			(23.3)
a				(23.3)
	b			(23.4)
		c		(23.5)
a				(23.6)
	b			(23.6)
		c		(23.6)
	z			(23.7)

Zhang 24

24.1 企^a者不立 (Base text: 王弼注)

> 物尙進則失安故曰企者不立 (Base text: 集註本)

24.2 跨者不行^b自見者不明自是者不彰^c自伐者無功自矜者不長其於^d道也^e曰餘^f食贅行 (Base text: 傅奕古本)

> 其唯於道而論之若郄^g至之行盛饌之餘也本雖美更可蔵也本雖有功而自伐之故更爲疣^h贅者ⁱ也 (Base text: 集註本)

24.3 物或惡^j之故有道者不處^k (Base text: 范應元本)

24.1 [A ruler][1] who takes a high stand will not stand [firmly].

> *The other entities [his subjects][2] will [,as a consequence of his example,] think much of [their own] advancement and consequently make [him] lose [his] security. That is why [the text] says: "[A ruler] who takes a high stand will not stand [firmly]."*

24.2 [A ruler] who makes great strides will not make headway. [A ruler] who shows himself does not become enlightened. [A ruler] who is self-righteous will not have [his being right] shine forth. [A ruler] who brags will not have [his] achievements [uncontestedly]. [A ruler] who praises himself will not have [his capacity] grow.[3] With regard to the Way I call these [attitudes]

"left-over food"   and   "superfluous actions."

---

^a Var.: 跂 for 企: 范應元本. Var.: 炊 for 企: 馬王堆 A; 馬王堆 B.

^b Var.: 跨者不行 om.: 馬王堆 A; 馬王堆 B.

^c Var.: 自視者(馬王堆 A om. 者)不章自(馬王堆 A: □) 見者不明 for 自見者不明自是者不彰: 馬王堆 A; 馬王堆 B.

^d 於 for 在 (also in 馬王堆 A; 馬王堆 B): Wang Bi comm.: 其唯於道而論之; 范應元本.

^e Var.: 也 om. 馬王堆 A.

^f Var.: 粽 for 餘: 馬王堆 A; 馬王堆 B.

^g Var.: 卻 for 郄: 永樂大典本.

^h Var.: 肬 for 疣: 陸德明釋文; 永樂大典本.

ⁱ Var.: 者 om.: 文選奏彈王源李善注 40.14b6.

^j Var.: 亞 for 惡: 馬王堆 B.

^k Var.: 故有欲者弗(馬王堆 A:□)居 for 故有道者不處: 馬王堆 A; 馬王堆 B. Var.: 處也 for 處: 傅奕古本.

> Judged with regard to the
> Way, [these attitudes] are like
>   the actions of Xi Zhi,[4]

a leftover of rich food.
Although the [food] basically   Although [Xi Zhi] basically had
is delicious, [the leftovers]   merits, he bragged about them
might be rotten.   himself and that was excessive
                                       and "superfluous" [and brought
                                       about his death].[5]

24.3   [The mechanism through which the above negative results come about is
that] other entities might loathe him. That is why one who has the Way
will not opt [for these courses of action].

Zhang 25

25.1 有物ᵃ混ᵇ成先天地生 (Base text: 傅奕古本)

混然不可得而知而萬物由之以成故曰混成也不知其誰之子故先天地
生 (Base text 集註本)

25.2 宋兮寞兮ᶜ獨立而不改ᵈ (Base text: 傅奕古本)

宋寞ᵉ無形體也無物之匹故曰獨立也返化終始不失其常故曰不改也
(Base text 永樂大典本)

25.3 周行而不殆ᶠ可以爲天地ᵍ母 (Base text: 范應元本)

周行無所不至而免殆ʰ能生全大形也故可以爲天地ⁱ母也 (Base text:
集註本)

ᵃ Var.: 楯 for 物: 郭店 A.   ᵇ Var.: 昆 for 混: 馬王堆 A; 馬王堆 B.

ᶜ Var.: 繡呵繆呵 for 宋兮寞兮: 馬王堆 A. Var.: 蕭呵漻呵 for 宋兮寞兮: 馬王堆 B.

ᵈ Var.: 不亥 for 而不改: 郭店 A; this shows that a text without the 而, such as we find
it in the 想爾, is an old variant. Var.: 玹 for 改: 馬王堆 B.

ᵉ 宋寞 for 寂寞: 陸德明釋文 for Wang Bi's *Laozi* text. Var.: 寂寥 for 宋寞: 集註本.

ᶠ Var.: 周行而不殆 om.: 馬王堆 A; 馬王堆 B; 郭店 A.

ᵍ Var.: 天下 for 天地: 傅奕古本; 郭店 A.

ʰ Var.: 危 for 殆: 永樂大典本.

ⁱ Var.: 天下 for 天地: 永樂大典本.

25.4 吾不^j知其名^k (Base text: 范應元本)

名以定形混成無形不可得而定故曰不知其名也 (Base text: 集註本)

25.5 字之^l曰道 (Base text: 王弼老子微指略例)

夫名以定形字以稱可言道取於無物而不由也是混成之中可言之稱最
大也 (Base text: 集註本)

25.6 強^m爲之名曰大 (Base text: 王弼注)

吾所以字之曰道者取其可言之稱最大也責其字定之所由則繫於大大
有繫則必有分有分則失其極矣故曰強爲之名曰大 (Base text: 集註本)

25.7 大曰逝ⁿ (Base text: 范應元本)

逝行也不守一大體而已周行無所不至故曰逝也 (Base text: 集註本)

25.8 逝^o曰遠遠曰返^p (Base text: 傅奕古本)

遠極也周無所不窮極不偏於一逝^q故曰遠也不隨於所適其體^r獨立故
曰返^s也 (Base text: 永樂大典本)

25.9 道^t大天大地大王^u亦大 (Base text: 傅奕古本)

---

^j Var.: 未 for 不: 馬王堆 A; 馬王堆 B; 郭店 A.

^k Var.: 名也 for 名: 馬王堆 B.

^l Var.: 故強字 for 字: 傅奕古本; 范應元本. Support for 強: 韓非子. The 故強 is missing in 馬王堆 A; 馬王堆 B; 郭店 A.

^m Var.: 吾強 for 強: 郭店 A; 馬王堆 A; 馬王堆 B.

ⁿ Var.: 筮 for 逝: 馬王堆 A; 馬王堆 B. ^o Var.: 筮 for 逝: 馬王堆 A; 馬王堆 B.

^p Var.: 反 for 返: 郭店 A; 馬王堆 B; 范應元本.

^q Var.: 所 for 逝: 集註本.

^r Var.: 志 for 體: 集註本.

^s 返 for 反: 集註本.

^t Var.: 故道 for 道: 范應元本.

^u 王 for 人 Wang Bi comm.: 王亦大也. Support for 王: 郭店 A; 馬王堆 A; 馬王堆 B. Var.: 天大地大道大王亦大 for 道大天大地大王亦大: 郭店 A.

天地之性人爲貴而王是人之主也雖不職大亦復爲大與三匹故曰王亦
大也 (Base text: 集註本)

25.10 域^v中有四大 (Base text: 王弼注)

四大道天地王也凡物有稱有名則非其極也言道則有所由有所由然後
謂之爲道然則是道稱中之大也不若無稱^w之大也無稱不可得而名曰
域也^x道天地王皆在乎無稱之內故曰域中有四大者也 (Base text: 永樂
大典本)

25.11 而王處其一^y焉^z (Base text: 傅奕古本)

處人主之大也 (Base text: 集註本)

25.12 人法地地法天天法道道法自然 (Base text: 傅奕古本)

法謂法則也人不違地乃得全安法地也地不違天乃得全載法天也天不
違道乃得^{aa}全覆法道也道不違自然方乃^{ab}得其性法自然也^{ac}法自然者
在方而法方圓而法圓於自然無所違也自然者無稱之言^{ad}窮極之辭
也¹用智不及無知而形魄不及精象精象不及無形有儀不及^{ae}無儀故

---

^v Var.: 國 for 域: 郭店 A; 馬王堆 A; 馬王堆 B.

^w Var.: 自 for 稱: 集註本.

^x Var.: 凡物名有稱無非其極也言道無有一有所由所由然後謂之爲道然則道是稱之
大不若無稱之大也無名不可得而稱謂之域:惠達肇論疏, 續藏經 vol. 155, p. 414.a.b2ff.
The transmission of this text is notoriously bad, visible here in the twofold miswriting of
無 for 則 and the incomprehensibility of the overall text. Still, it is recognizable that a text
very close to the transmitted versions must have been in the hands of Huida.

^y Var.: 居其一 for 處其一: 范應元本. Var.: 居一 for 處其一: 郭店 A; 馬王堆 A; 馬
王堆 B. Support for 處: Wang Bi comm.: 處人主之大也.

^z 焉 for 尊: 郭店 A; 馬王堆 A; 馬王堆 B; 范應元本.

^{aa} Var.: 能 for 得: 集註本.

^{ab} 方乃 for 乃: 集註本. There is a qualitative difference between this last step and the
previous ones that is also announced by the grammatical change from the 得全 to the 得
其. I therefore suggest keeping 方, even though the closeness of the phrases about 方 and
圓 makes a textual mix-up a possibility.

^{ac} 法自然也 add.: 陶鴻慶.

^{ad} Var.: 自然者無義之言 for 自然者無稱之言: 李善, 文選游天台山賦注 11.3b8f.
Support for 無稱: Wang Bi on *Laozi* 25.10: 然則是道稱中之大也不若無稱之大也 無稱
不可得而名曰域也道天地王皆在乎無稱之內.

^{ae} Var.: 如 for 及: 集註本.

轉^{af}相法也道順^{ag}自然天故資焉天法於道地故則焉地法於天人故象
焉所以爲主其一之^{ah}者主也 (Base text 永樂大典本)

25.1　　There is a thing that completes out of the diffuse. It is born before
Heaven and Earth.

*Diffuse it is and [thus] indiscernible, but the ten thousand kinds of
entities base themselves on it for their completion. That is why [the
text] says: "Completes out of the diffuse!" "I do not know whose
son it is" [as the Laozi says of the Way in 4.1]. That is why [the text
says] "It is born before Heaven and Earth [in analogy to the statement
in Laozi 4.1, according to which the Way is "like the precursor of the
lord" whom Wang Bi defines as the "Lord of Heaven"]."*

25.2　　Vacant it is, alas, still.[1] It stands alone and does not change.

*"Vacant" and "still" mean without form and substance. It is no other
entity's mate. That is why [the text] says: "It stands alone!" Aloof from
change, from beginning to end it never loses its eternal [essence].[2] That is
why [the text] says: "It does not change"!*

25.3　　It travels all around but is not in danger.

　　　　One might take it for the mother of Heaven and Earth.

*"It travels all around"—[i.e.,] there is no place to which it does not get—
but evades danger—[i.e.,] it is able to keep intact [its] grand[3] shape. That
is why [the text says] "One might take it for the mother of Heaven and
Earth"!*

25.4　　I [Laozi] do not know its name.

*A name is something to define the shape [of an object]. That which "com-
pletes out of the diffuse" and is "without form" [as the Laozi says in
41.14 about the Great Image] is impossible to define.[4] That is why [the
text] says: "[I] do not know its name"!*

25.5　　I give it the style "Way."

*It is a fact that a name is something to define the shape [of an object],
while a style is something to designate what is sayable.[5] The Way is
taken[6] for [the aspect of that by which all entities are] that there is no
entity which is not based on it.[7] This is the greatest among the sayable
designations concerning "that which completes out of the diffuse."*

---

^{af} Var.: 道 for 轉: 集註本.

^{ag} Var.: 法 for 順: 集註本. Support for 順自然: Wang Bi on *Laozi* 27.1, 37.1, and
65.1.

^{ah} Var.: 其一者主也 for 其一之者主也: 集註本.

25.6   [Only] if forced to make up a name for it, I would say
              "[it is] great."

> *The reason why I gave it the style "Way" was taken from this*
> *being the greatest of sayable designations about it. If one puts too*
> *much weight onto the reason for which this style was determined,*
> *one would tie [the Way] down to being great. If a greatness has*
> *ties, it necessarily has particularity, and once it has particularity,*
> *its absoluteness is lost. That is why [the text] says: "[Only] if*
> *forced to make up a name for it, I would say '[it is] great'"!*

25.7   [That] "[it is] great" means "it passes through."

> *To pass through" means "to travel." It does not keep to one single*
> *great substance and stops there, but "travels all around" [as the* Laozi
> *says in 25.3] and there is no place to which it does not get. That is*
> *why [the text] says: "It passes through"!*

25.8   [That] "it passes through" means "it gets far."

              [That] "it gets far" means "it returns [to its own eternal nature]."

> *"Getting far" means "reaching the very end." It "travels all around" [as*
> *the* Laozi *says in 25.3] and there is no place where it does not reach the*
> *absolute end, it is not one-sidedly [restricted] to one single "passing*
> *through." That is why [the text] says: "It gets far." It does not follow*
> *what it chances upon; its substance "stands alone" [as the* Laozi *says in*
> *25.2]. That is why [the text] says: "It stands aloof [from change]!"*

25.9   The Way is great,

              Heaven is great,

              Earth is great.

              The king, too, is great.[8]

> *[As Confucius says in the* Classic of Filial Piety, Xiaojing, *answering the*
> *question of Zengzi: "May I ask whether among the virtues of the Sage*
> *there is none superior to filial piety?"] "Among the natures [bequeathed*
> *to the ten thousand entities] by Heaven and Earth, the human being is the*
> *most exalted,"[9] but the king is the lord of the human beings. Although*
> *[the king] is not positionally great [by just having this office] he, "too,"*
> *is great [if] matching the other three [Great Ones]. That is why [the text]*
> *says "the king, too, is great!"*

25.10   In the Beyond there are four Great Ones,

              The four Great Ones are

the Way,

Heaven,

 Earth, and

  the king.

Generally speaking, that of entities which has a name and has a designation is not their ultimate. Saying "the Way" presupposes that there is a basis for [this expression]. Only as a consequence of there being a basis for [this expression] will one talk about it as being "the Way." Accordingly, "Way" is [only] the greatest among [aspects that can be assigned] designations, but that is nothing compared to greatness of the designationless. The designationless which it is impossible to name is called [here] "the Beyond." The Way, Heaven, Earth, and the king all are indeed located within the [realm] of the designationless. That is why [the text] says: "In the Beyond there are four Great Ones!" [10]

25.11 and the king has a place as one of them!

He has the place of the great one which is there for the lord of men.

25.12   The human being [qualified to be the lord of men] takes the Earth as model.

    Earth takes Heaven as model.

    Heaven takes the Way as model.

The Way takes That-which-is-of-itself-what-it-is as model.

    "To take as a model" means "to pattern oneself after."

    A human being [qualified to be the lord of men] not deviating from the Earth and consequently managing it to completely maintain [his] security [in his position]—this is what "he takes the Earth as model" means.

    The Earth not deviating from Heaven and consequently managing it to completely carry [the ten thousand kinds of entities]—this is what "she takes Heaven as model" means.

    Heaven not deviating from the Way and consequently managing it to completely cover [the ten thousand entities]—this is what "it takes the Way as model" means. [11]

The Way not deviating from That-which-is-of-itself-what-it-is and consequently achieving their [the ten thousand entities'] nature—this is what "it takes That-which-is-of-itself-what-it-is as model" means. Taking That-which-is-of-itself-what-it-is as model means taking squareness as a model when among the squares, and roundness when among round ones, and thus nothing deviating in nothing from That-which-is-of-itself-what-it-is.

"That-which-is-of-itself-what-it-is" is a word for the designationless, an expression for getting to the Ultimate.[12]

> *Making use of knowledge [as kings are wont to do] does not come close to being without knowledge.*

That which has a physical shape [the Earth] does not come close to the ethereal image [Heaven].

The ethereal image [Heaven] does not come close to the [altogether] shapeless [the Way].

That which has the [two] principles [Yin and Yang, that is, the Way] does not come close to that which is without them [That-which-is-of-itself-what-it-is].

That is why they in turn take each other as model.

The Way goes along with That-which-is-of-itself-what-it-is,[13]

> *that is why Heaven takes it as material [to go by.]*
> *Heaven takes the Way as model,*

>> *that is why Earth takes [it] as a rule [to adhere to].*
>> *Earth takes Heaven as model,*

>>> *that is why the human being [qualified to be a king] takes it as an image [of how to behave].*

[As to] how [someone] becomes the lord [over all human beings]—he who unifies[14] *them is the lord!*

THE STRUCTURE OF *LAOZI* 25

Wang Bi reads the phrases beginning with 25.2 as a series that is taken up in inverse order by phrase 25.6 and those that follow. The link is made explicit by the commentaries under the second series, 25.6 ff., which directly quote the corresponding passages in the first series. The link is generally convincing, but one imbalance remains: the "passing through" and "getting far" together only have one corresponding phrase in the first series. This serialization imposes on 25.1, 25.4 and 25.5, the category of general statement, which they fit rather well. For part I, this gives a sequence formalized as:

I	c		(25.1)
	1		(25.2)
		2	(25.3)
			3	(25.3)
		c		(25.4, 25.5)

3			(25.6)
2			(25.7, 25.8)
1			(25.8)

The serialization of Way, Heaven, Earth, and king subsequent to 25.9 is quite explicit, evident, and not related to the first inverted parallel staircase. It also has the form of an inverted parallel staircase:

II	1				(25.9)
	2				(25.9)
		3			(25.9)
			4		(25.9)
		c	("In the Beyond . . .)		(25.10)
			4		(25.11)
		3			(25.12)
	2				(25.12)
1					(25.12)

The commentary adds a new layer with an implicit series reiterating the sequence of this latter staircase, beginning with "making use of knowledge." The commentary on 25.12 therefore has the form:

	c		
		4	
	3		
2			
1			
		4	
	3		
2			
1			
	c	"That is why they in turn . . .)	
1			
2			
	3		
		4	
	c	("As to how someone . . .)	

Zhang 26

26.1 重爲輕ᵃ根靜ᵇ爲躁ᶜ君 (Base text: 范應元本)

　　凡物輕不能載重小不能鎮大不行者使行不動者制動是以重必爲輕根
　　靜必爲躁君也 (Base text: 集註本)

26.2 是以君子終ᵈ日行不離ᵉ輜ᶠ重 (Base text: 范應元本)

　　以重爲本故ᵍ不離 (Base text: 永樂大典本)

26.3 雖ʰ有榮觀ⁱ宴處ʲ超然ᵏ (Base text: 范應元本)

　　不以經心ˡ也ᵐ (Base text: 集註本)

26.4 如之何ⁿ萬乘之主而以身輕於天下ᵒ輕ᵖ則失本躁ۤ則失君 (Base text: 范應元
本)

　　輕不鎮ʳ重也失本爲喪身也失君謂失君位也 (Base text: 永樂大典本.)

ᵃ Var.: 巠 for 輕: 馬王堆 A.

ᵇ Var.: 清 for 靜: 馬王堆 A. Var.: 靖 for 靜: 傅奕古本.

ᶜ Var.: 趮 for 躁: 馬王堆 A; 馬王堆 B.

ᵈ Var.: 衆 for 終: 馬王堆 A. Var.: 冬 for 終: 馬王堆 B.

ᵉ Var.: 不離 (馬王堆 B:遠) 其 for 不離: 馬王堆 A; 馬王堆 B; 傅奕古本. Support for
omission of 其: 陸德明釋文.

ᶠ Var.: 䌛 for 輜: 馬王堆 A; 馬王堆 B.

ᵍ Var.: 故 om.: 集註本.　　　　　　　ʰ Var.: 唯 for 雖: 馬王堆 A.

ⁱ Var.: 環官 for 榮觀: 馬王堆 A; 馬王堆 B. Support for 榮觀: 陸德明釋文.

ʲ Var.: 燕處 for 宴處: 馬王堆 A; 馬王堆 B. Support for 宴處: 陸德明釋文.

ᵏ Var.: 則昭若 (馬王堆 A:□□若) for 超然: 馬王堆 A; 馬王堆 B.

ˡ 經心 for 經心之: 張之象本.　　　　ᵐ Var.: 不以經心也 om.: 永樂大典本.

ⁿ Var.: 若何 for 如之何: 馬王堆 A; 馬王堆 B.

ᵒ 輕(馬王堆 A: 䌛)於天下 for 輕天下: 馬王堆 A; 馬王堆 B. Support for 於: The 輕 is
read as a comparative "take/be lighter as" so that a commentary 輕不鎮重也 can follow. A
comparative use suggests a 於. Shima Kuniō argued for the 於 without being aware of the
馬王堆 A and 馬王堆 B readings.

ᵖ Var.: 䌛 for 輕: 馬王堆 A.　　　　ۤ Var.: 趮 for 躁: 馬王堆 A; 馬王堆 B.

ʳ Var.: 眞 for 鎮: 集註本.

26.1   The heavy is the basis of the light.   The calm is the lord of the   26.2
                                                  impetuous.

Generally speaking with
regard to entities,

the light cannot support the heavy,   *that which [itself] does not act*
the small cannot press down the   *makes [others] act, that which*
great.   *[itself] does not move controls*
                                        the movement [of others].

That is why

the "heavy" must by necessity be   the "calm" must by necessity be
the "basis of the light."   the "lord of the impetuous."[1]

26.3   That is why the gentleman
does not leave the heavy carts   remains calm and aloof   26.4
[of the army where the weapons   even when there are [enemy]
and provisions are carried even if]   camps with watch towers
the march continues through the   [where he marches with his
whole day.   army].

That is, he considers the heavy the   *That is, he does not let himself*
basis, therefore he does not leave   *be distracted by them [the*
[the heavy carts].   *enemy camps].*

26.5   What will happen if someone
                  [is] lord over ten thousand war
                  chariots but is with his own person
                  light [and impetuous] towards All
                  Under Heaven?

Being light [towards it], he will   Being impetuous [towards it], he
lose the basis!   will lose his princely [position]!

The light [and impetuous]
cannot press down the heavy
[and calm].[2]

"He will lose the basis" means he   He will lose his princely [posi-
will harm his own person.   tion]" means he will lose his
                                        position as the prince.

THE STRUCTURE OF *LAOZI* 26

Laozi 26 is a nearly classical piece of mostly open IPS; for a detailed analysis, see the chapter "Interlocking Parallel Style" in my *The Craft of a Chinese Commentator. Zhong* 重 in phrase 3 (26.2) takes up the same term in the first phrase, and *chaoran* 超然 in phrase 4 indirectly relates to *jing* 靜 in the second phrase. The two last phrases return to the terms *qing*

輕 and *zao* 躁 in the first two phrases. There is one single irregularity; it occurs in the first phrase of 26.5. In this phrase the term *light, qing* 輕, seems to relate to the same term in the left series. The phrase, however, stands without parallel and thus is a general phrase relating to both chains. *Qing* 輕 accordingly is a *pars pro toto* for both *qing* 輕 and *zao* 躁. The *zhang* comes in three segments, segment I presenting the universal rule, II its application by the gentleman/Sage, and III the consequence of the ruler's inability to enact the universal law of the first pair of phrases. The overall structure of *Laozi* 26 is:

I	a	b	(26.1, 26.2)
II		c	(26.3) (That is why the gentleman . . .)
	a	b	(26.3, 26.4)
III		c	(26.5)
	a	b	(26.5, 26.5)

Zhang 27

27.1 善行者無徹迹ᵃ (Base text: 傅奕古本)

順自然而行不造不始故物得至而無徹ᵇ迹也 (Base text: 集註本)

27.2 善言者無瑕讁ᶜ (Base text: 傅奕古本)

順物之性不別不析ᵈ故無瑕ᵉ讁各得其所也ᶠ (Base text: 永樂大典本)

ᵃ Var.: 䗂 for 徹: 馬王堆 A. Var.: 達 for 徹: 馬王堆 B. Var.: 轍 for 徹: 范應元本. Var.: 跡 for 迹: 陸德明釋文.

ᵇ 徹 for 轍: 陸德明釋文 concerning the *Laozi* 27.1.

ᶜ Var.: 適 for 讁: 馬王堆 A; 馬王堆 B.

ᵈ Var.: 折 for 析: 集註本.

ᵉ Var.: 取 for 瑕: 集註本.

ᶠ 各得其所也 for 可得其門也: Wagner. All commentators agree that this passage is flawed. 桃井白鹿 has suggested writing 所 for 門. From the parallel with Wang Bi on *Laozi* 27.2, this goes in the right direction. The Wang Bi passages using 所 in this context of the proper place of entities write 各得其所也; Wang Bi on *Laozi* 34.2, 36.2, or 61.8. Other options used by Wang Bi instead of 門, which does not occur elsewhere in such a construction, are 性, 德, 本, 眞, or 極.

27.3 善數者不用^g籌策^h (Base text: 馬王堆 B)

因物之ⁱ數不假形也 (Base text: 永樂大典本)

27.4 善閉者^j無關楗^k而不可開^l善結者^m無繩ⁿ約而不可解^o (Base text: 傅奕古本)

因物自然不設不施故不用關楗^p繩約而不可開解也此五者皆言不造
不施因物之性不以形制物也 (Base text: 集註本)

27.5 是以聖人常^q善救^r人而^s無棄人 (Base text: 馬王堆 B)

聖人不立形名以檢於物不造進尙^t以殊棄不肖輔萬物之自然而不爲始
故曰無棄人也不尙賢能則民不爭不貴難得之貨則民不爲盜不見可欲
則民心不亂常使民心無欲無惑則無棄人矣^u (Base text: 永樂大典本)

27.6 ^l是謂襲明^v故善人^w不善人之師^x (Base text: 范應元本)

舉善以師不善故謂之師矣 (Base text: 集註本)

---

^g Var.: 無 for 不用: 傅奕古本; 范應元本. Var.: 不以 for 不用: 馬王堆 A. Support for 不用: 不假 in Wang Bi comm.

^h 籌策 for 檮筭: 陸德明釋文. Var.: 檮筭 for 籌策: 馬王堆 A.

ⁱ Var.: 是乎 for 物之: 集註本.　　　^j Var.: 者 om.: 范應元本.

^k 關楗 for 關鍵: 陸德明釋文. Var.: 闌籥 for 關楗: 馬王堆 A. Var.: 關籥 for 關楗: 馬王堆 B.

^l Var.: 而不可開 om.: 范應元本. Var.: 啓也 for 開: 馬王堆 A; 馬王堆 B.

^m Var.: 者 om.: 范應元本.　　　ⁿ Var.: 纆 for 繩: 馬王堆 B.

^o Var.: 而不可解 om.: 范應元本. Var.: 解也 for 解: 馬王堆 A; 馬王堆 B.

^p Var.: 揵 for 楗: 集註本.

^q 常 for 恒: 陸德明釋文 passim; 傅奕古本; 范應元本.

^r 救 for 怵 (in both 馬王堆 A and 馬王堆 B): 傅奕古本; 范應元本.

^s Var.: 故人 for 而: 傅奕古本; 范應元本. Support against 人: Wang Bi comm.: 故曰無棄人也. Support for 而: Wang Bi comm.: 聖人 … 輔萬物之自然而不爲始故曰無棄人也.

^t 尙 for 向: 樓宇烈. The 尙 refers to the high estimation for worthies 尙賢. While this connection is well supported by the immediate textual environment, one would rather expect 貴 referring to the "goods that are hard to come by" than 進.

^u Var.: 心 for 矣: 集註本.

^v Var.: 是胃愧明 for 是謂襲明: 馬王堆 A. Var.: 是胃曳明 for 是謂襲明: 馬王堆 B.

^w Var.: 善人者 for 善人: 傅奕古本.　　　^x Var.: 善人之師 for 不善人之師: 馬王堆 B.

27.7 不善人^y善人之資^z (Base text: 范應元本)

資取也善人以善齊不善以善棄不善也故不善人善人之所取也 (Base text: 集註本)

27.8 不貴其師不愛其資^{aa}雖智^{ab}大迷^{ac} (Base text: 傅奕古本)

雖有其智自任其智不因物於其道必失故曰雖智大迷² (Base text: 集註本)

27.9 是^{ad}謂要妙^{ae} (Base text: 范應元本)

27.1   He who is good at making [other entities] act [provides] no [guiding] tracks [for them to follow].

He makes them act in accordance with [their] That-which-is-of-itself-what-it-is, and neither creates nor initiates. That is why the other entities attain achievement, but there are "no [guiding] tracks" [from him to follow].

27.2   He who is good at speaking [about other entities does so] without [pointing out] blemishes [in them to be avoided].

He adapts to the nature of other entities and neither differentiates nor analyzes [them].[1] Therefore, as he is "without blemishes" [that have been pointed out in other entities], each attains its place.

27.3   He who is good at calculating [other entities] does not use counting rods.

He goes by the number of the entities [to be counted] and does not borrow some [outer] shape [like counting rods to count them].

27.4   He who is good at locking [doors] will [do this] without the catch of a lock, and still [the door] cannot be opened. He who is good at tying [strings] will [do this] without a knot, and still [the tie] cannot be opened.

---

^y Var.: 人者 for 人: 傅奕古本. Support against 者: No 者 in Wang Bi comm.: 不善人善人之所取也.

^z Var.: 資也 for 資: 馬王堆 B. Var.: 齎也 for 資: 馬王堆 A.

^{aa} Var.: 齎 for 資: 馬王堆 A.

^{ab} 智 for 知 (also in 馬王堆 A; 馬王堆 B; 范應元本): Wang Bi comm.: 雖智大迷. Var.: 唯 (馬王堆 B:雖) 知乎 for 雖智: 馬王堆 A; 馬王堆 B.

^{ac} Var.: 眯 for 迷: 馬王堆 A.   ^{ad} Var.: 此 for 是: 傅奕古本.

^{ae} Var.:胃眇要 for 謂要妙: 馬王堆 A; 馬王堆 B.

He goes by the other entities' That-which-is-of-itself-what-it-is, and neither sets [them] up nor makes [them] do [something]. Therefore he does not use the catch of a lock or a knot, and still [the door and the tie] cannot be opened. These five [statements] all say that he does not create [other entities] or makes them do [something]. He goes by the nature of other entities and does not control other entities by means of [specific] shapes.[2]

27.5   That is why the Sage is constantly good at saving other people, and for this reason there is no rejecting other people [by him].[3]

The Sage does not establish shapes and names in order to impose restrictions on other entities. He does not create promotions and honors in order to separate and reject the incapable. He "boosts the ten thousand kinds of entities' That-which-is-of-itself-what-it-is," [as the Laozi says in 64.9] but "does not initiate" [as the Laozi says about the Sage in 2.4]. That is why [the text] says: "There is no rejecting other people [by him]!" [As the Sage according to Laozi 3.1] "does not shower worthies" and capable persons "with honors," the people, as a consequence, "do not struggle"; [and as he] does not "overly appreciate goods that are hard to get, the people," as a consequence, "will not become robbers"; [as he] "does not [, in short,] display [things] that might be craved for, the hearts of the people," as a consequence, "will not become prone to chaos." "He permanently prompts the people to be without" "desires" and without delusions [as the Laozi says in 3.4] so that "there is no rejecting other people [by him]."

27.6   This I call "Being in accor-
                             dance with enlightenment."
                             That is why [the Sage]

[makes] the good ones into the
teachers of the not good ones,

*He elevates the good ones to be
the teachers of the not good ones.
Therefore [the text] speaks of
them as "teachers,"*

27.7   and   [makes] the not good ones into
                                              the material of the good ones,[4]

                                              *"Material" means "take into
                                              one's hand."*[5] *The good ones
                                              keep order among the not good
                                              ones by means of their [own]
                                              goodness and reject the not good
                                              ones by means of their [own]
                                              goodness.*[6] *That is why the not*

good ones are that which the
good ones take in hand;

27.8   [but he does]

neither honor their [the not   nor does he love their [the good
good ones'] teachers;   ones'] material.[7]

Even [for someone with] knowledge, it would be a great error
[to do this].

Even if someone had his [own]
knowledge, but would personally
make use of his knowledge and
not go by the entities' [own nature
in regulating them], he would nec-
essarily be failing on his way . That
is why [the text] says: "Even [for
someone with] knowledge, it would
be a great error" [to do this]!

27.9   This is called the essential mystery.

THE STRUCTURE OF *LAOZI* 27

Laozi 27 comes with all of the accoutrements of IPS—two parallel
sentences followed by a third that has no parallel, two more parallel
sentences, followed by the *shiyi shengren*, 是以聖人 . . . "that is why the
Sage . . . ," introduction to a new section. The general principle is stated
first together with the definition in text 6, to be followed by two sets of
parallel phrases explicitly interlocked through their terminology. While
the question of IPS is no problem for text 6 and those that follow, because
the connections are explicit, I have not been successful with regard to the
entire first part. There is nothing that I can see in Wang Bi's commentary to
prompt linkages between the two pairs in texts 1 and 2, and 4, respectively.
Wang Bi, in fact, lumps these five statements together into a general "These
five [statements] all say . . . " We can only presume that even Wang Bi was
unable to find a link. Beginning with 27.6, the structure has this form:

	c		(27.6)
a		b	(27.6, 27.7)
a		b	(27.8, 27.8)
	c		(27.8)
	c		(27.9)

Zhang 28

28.1 知其雄守其雌爲天下谿ᵃ爲天下谿ᵇ常ᶜ德不離ᵈ復歸於ᵉ嬰兒 (Base text: 傅奕古本)

雄先之屬雌後之屬也知爲天下之先者ᶠ必後也是以聖人後其身而身先也谿不求物而物自歸之嬰兒不用智而合自然之智 (Base text: 集註本)

28.2 知其白守其黑ᵍ爲天下式 (Base text: 傅奕古本)

式模ʰ則也 (Base text: 集註本)

28.3 爲天下式常ⁱ德不忒ʲ (Base text: 傅奕古本)

忒差也 (Base text: 集註本)

28.4 復歸於無極 (Base text: 傅奕古本)

不可窮也 (Base text: 集註本)

28.5 知其榮ᵏ守其辱爲天下谷ˡ爲天下谷ᵐ常德乃足ⁿ復歸於樸ᵒ (Base text: 傅奕古本)

ᵃ Var.: 溪 for 谿: 馬王堆 A. Var.: 雞 for 谿: 馬王堆 B.

ᵇ Var.: 溪 for 谿: 馬王堆 A. Var.: 雞 for 谿: 馬王堆 B.

ᶜ Var.: 恆 for 常: 馬王堆 A; 馬王堆 B.

ᵈ Var.: 恆德不雞恆德不雞 for 常德不離: 馬王堆 A. Var.: 恆德不离恆德不离 for 常德不離: 馬王堆 B.

ᵉ Var.: 於 om.: 馬王堆 A.　　　ᶠ Var.: 也 for 者: 永樂大典本.

ᵍ Var.: See note o.　　　ʰ Var.: 摸 for 模: 陸德明釋文.

ⁱ Var.: 恒 for 常: 馬王堆 A; 馬王堆 B.

ʲ Var.: 貸 for 忒: 馬王堆 A; 馬王堆 B. Var.: 恒德不貸恒(馬王堆 A om.)德不貸 for 常德不忒: 馬王堆 A; 馬王堆 B.

ᵏ Var.: 曰 for 榮: 馬王堆 A (高明).

ˡ Var.: 浴 for 谷: 馬王堆 A; 馬王堆 B.　　ᵐ Var.: 浴 for 谷: 馬王堆 A; 馬王堆 B.

ⁿ Var.: 恒德乃足(馬王堆 A:□) 恒德乃足(馬王堆 A:□) for 常德乃足: 馬王堆 A; 馬王堆 B.

ᵒ Var.: The phrases 28.2–4 are given in the inverted sequence in 馬王堆 A; 馬王堆 B: 知其日 (白) 守其辱爲天下浴爲天下浴恒德乃足恒德乃足復歸於樸知其白 [日 om.: 馬王

此三者言常反終後乃德全其所處也下章云[p]反者道之動也功不可取
常處其母也 (Base text: 永樂大典本)

28.6 樸[q]散則爲器聖人用之[r]則爲官長 (Base text: 傅奕古本)

樸眞也[s]眞散則百行出殊類生若器也聖人因其分散故爲之立官長以
善爲師不善爲資移風易俗復歸[t]於一也 (Base text: 集註本)

28.7 大[u]制無割[1] (Base text: 傅奕古本)

大制者以天下之心爲心故無割也 (Base text: 集註本)

28.1   He who knows that as its [All Under Heaven's] cock he [has to] keep [be-
        ing] its hen, will be All Under Heaven's valley.[1] Being All Under Heaven's
        valley, he will continuously achieve it[2] not to be separated [from the One so
        that the other entities come to him of their own accord], and he has them
        [the other entities] return again to being babies.

        A cock belongs to the category of those standing at the fore, a hen to the
        category of those standing in the background. He who knows how to be
        [the person] standing at the fore [in All Under Heaven] will by necessity
        keep in the background. That is why the Sage [as the Laozi *says in 7.2]*
        "puts his own person in the background and [achieves in this way] that
        his own person comes to be to the fore." A "valley" does not yearn for
        other entities; the other entities render themselves to it on their own. "Ba-
        bies" make no use of knowledge, but are in accord with the knowledge of
        That-which-is-of-itself-what-it-is.[3]

28.2   [He who] who knows that as its [All Under Heaven's] whiteness he [has to]
        keep to [being] its blackness will be the rule for All Under Heaven.[4]

        "Rule" means "model."[5]

堆 A] 守其黑爲天下式爲天下式恒德不貸恒德不貸復歸於無極 for 知其白守其黑爲天下
式爲天下式常德不忒復歸於無極知其榮守其辱爲天下谷爲天下谷常德乃足復歸於樸.

   [p] Var.: 云 om.: 集註本.

   [q] Var. 楃 for 樸: 馬王堆 A. Var.: 璞 for 樸: 一切經音義 353a sub 金璞 quoting Wang
Bi.

   [r] Var.: 之 om.: 馬王堆 A; 馬王堆 B.

   [s] Var.: 璞眞也 for 樸眞也: 一切經音義 353a sub 金璞. See, however, id. 386c sub 魯
樸, where Huilin is quoting Wang Bi with 樸眞也.

   [t] Var.: 復使歸 for 復歸: 永樂大典本.

   [u] Var.: 夫大 for 大: 馬王堆 A; 馬王堆 B. Var.: 故大 for 大: 范應元本.

28.3 Being the rule of All Under Heaven, he continuously achieves it not to deviate [from the One],

"Deviate" means "differ."

28.4 and [he] has them [the other entities] return again to the unlimited.

[That is, to] that which is inexhaustible.

28.5 [He who] knows that as its [All Under Heaven's most] glorified [person] he [has to] keep being its [most] disgraced [person], will be the gorge of All Under Heaven. Being the gorge of All Under Heaven, he continuously achieves it to have enough,[6] and has them [the other entities] return again to the Unadorned.

These three [statements about being the cock, whiteness, and the most glorified person] mean that [the Sage] after [the process] of relating back to [the negative] has been completed, will achieve it to completely fill his position [that is, after having utterly kept to being the "hen" of All Under Heaven as the negative opposite of the cock, he will be able to completely fill the position of being its cock and leader, and so forth]. In a later zhang, [namely, 40.1, the Laozi] says: "He who acts by way of the negative opposite [i.e., the Sage] is the one who moves [in accordance with] the Way." It is impossible to get hold of [the Sage's specific] merits [with regard to the other entities] as he continuously resides with their [the merits'] mother.[7]

28.6 Once the Unadorned has dispersed, they [the entities] become instruments. Making use of them, the Sage makes officials and elders for [them].[8]

The Unadorned is the True. Once the True has dispersed, the hundred styles of action emerge, and the different categories[9] are born. These are like "[specialized] instruments." Responsive to [the fact] that their [the people in All Under Heaven's] allotments have dispersed,[10] the Sage [does not cut and trim them but] purposely sets up officials and elders for them. "Making the good ones into teachers . . . " and "the not good ones into [their] material . . . ," [as the Laozi 27.6 and 27.7 says] and changing [in this manner] the[ir] habits and altering the[ir] customs is [his way] of "returning [them] again to the" One [as the Laozi said in 28.5].

28.7 The Great Regulator [i.e., the Sage, regulates] without [any] cutting off.

The Great Regulator takes the heart of All Under Heaven for [his own] heart. That is why he is [, as the text says,] "without [any] cutting off."[11]

Zhang 29

29.1 將欲取天下而爲之者^a (Base text: 傅奕古本)

爲造爲也 (Base text: 集註本)[1]

29.2 吾見其不得已夫天下神器也^b (Base text: 傅奕古本)

神無形無方也器合成也無形以合故謂之神器也 (Base text: 集註本)

29.3 不^c可爲^d也爲之^e者敗之執之^f者失之 (Base text: 傅奕古本)

萬物以自然爲性故可因而不可爲也可通而不可執也物有常性而造爲
之故必敗也物有往來而執之故必失矣 (Base text: 集註本)

29.4 凡物^g或行或隨^h或歔ⁱ或吹^j或強或羸^k或挫^l或隳^m是以聖ⁿ人去甚去奢^o去泰^p

---

^a Var.: 爲之 for 爲之者: 馬王堆 A.

^b 神器也 for 神器 (in both 傅奕古本 and 范應元本): 馬王堆 A; 馬王堆 B. Support
for 也: Wang Bi comm. treats 天下神器 as a complete sentence.

^c Var.: 非 for 不: 馬王堆 A; 馬王堆 B.   ^d Var.: 爲者 for 爲: 馬王堆 A; 馬王堆 B.

^e 爲之 for 爲: 馬王堆 B. Support for 爲之者: *LZWZLL* 2.37: 爲之者則敗其性. Note
the reading without 者 in the 雲笈七籤 quotation there.

^f 執之 for 執: 馬王堆 B. Support for 執之者: *LZWZLL* 2.37: 執之者則失其原矣.
Note the reading without 者 in the 雲笈七籤 quotation there.

^g Var.: 物 for 凡物: 馬王堆 A; 馬王堆 B. Var.: 故物 for 凡物: 范應元本. Support for
凡: Wang Bi comm.: 凡此諸或言.

^h Var.: 隋 for 隨: 馬王堆 B.

ⁱ 歔 for 嘘: 陸德明釋文. Var.: 炅 for 歔: 馬王堆 A. Var.: 熱 for 歔: 馬王堆 B. Var.: 或
行或隨 om: 陸德明釋文.

^j Var.: 𩑼 for 吹: 馬王堆 B.

^k 羸 for 剉 (in both 傅奕古本 and 范應元本): 陸德明釋文. Var.: 或強或羸 om.: 馬
王堆 B.

^l 挫 for 培 (in both 傅奕古本 and 范應元本): 陸德明釋文. Var.: 坏 for 挫: 馬王堆 A.
Var.: 陪 for 挫: 馬王堆 B.

^m 隳 for 墮 (in both 傅奕古本 and 范應元本): 陸德明釋文. Var.: 撆 for 隳: 馬王
堆 A.

ⁿ Var.: 聲 for 聖: 馬王堆 A.   ^o Var.: 大 for 奢: 馬王堆 A; 馬王堆 B.

^p Var.: 楮 for 泰: 馬王堆 A. Var.: 諸 for 泰: 馬王堆 B. Both MSS invert the sequence
奢/楮–泰/大.

(Base text: 傅奕古本)

凡此諸或言物事逆順反覆不施爲執割也聖人達自然之性[q]暢萬物之
情故因而不爲順而不施除其所以迷去其所以惑故心不亂而物性自得
之也 (Base text: 集註本)

29.1   As to someone who desires
to get hold of All Under Heaven
                 and   to interfere with it,

                     "Interfere" means act upon.

29.2   I [Laozi] see that he will not
be able to manage. It is a fact
that All Under Heaven is a vessel
of something spiritual.

*[Things] spiritual are "without
form" [as the* Laozi *says of the
Great Image in 41.14, and Wang
Bi repeats of the "spirit" in his
commentary on Zhouyi 2.11.a.5]
and "without corners" [as the* Xici
*says of the spirit in Zhouyi 7.3.b.2].
"Vessel" is something completed
through combination [with something
else which fills it]. As [in the case of
All Under Heaven], it is combined
with something shapeless, [the text]
calls it [=All Under Heaven] "a vessel
of something spiritual."*

29.3   It is impossible to interfere with it
[All Under Heaven] [and still hold on
to it]![1]

                     He who interferes with it,
                       destroys it!

He who holds on to it, loses it!

*The ten thousand kinds of
entities have That-which-is-of-
itself-what-it-is as their nature.
That is why*

---

[q] 性 for 至: 嚴靈峰, 老子微旨例略後敘 p. 8, based on 老子微旨例略: 故其大歸也,
論太始之原以明自然之性, 演幽冥之極以定惑罔之迷. 因而不爲, 順而不施.

*it is possible to be responsive to
them but impossible to act upon
them.*

*it is possible to penetrate them
but impossible to hold on to
them.*

*The [other] entities have an
eternal nature but acting upon
them will definitely lead to their
unavoidable destruction.*

*The [other] entities have their
comings and goings, but holding
on to them will definitely lead to
their unavoidable loss.*

29.4   Generally speaking, entities
either go ahead or they follow;
they either sniffle or they blow;
they are either strong, or they
are weak; they either suppress
or are beaten down [according
to their own nature]. That is
why the Sage [only] does away
with excesses, does away with
exaggeration, and does away
with extremes.

*Generally speaking, all these
"either/ors" mean: entities and
processes deviate and follow,
go this way or the other without
being
                initiated and interfered with,
held on to or cut into shape.*

*The Sage understands the
nature of [the entities'] That-
which-is-of-itself-what-it-is,
and is clear about the feelings
of the ten thousand kinds of
entities. Therefore he is
responsive [to them], but does
not interfere, he adapts [to
them], but does not initiate. He
[only] wipes out what might
cause them to be deluded, and
does away with what might
make them confused.*[2]

Consequently, [under his
guidance their] "hearts do not
become prone to chaos" [as the
Laozi 3.1 *says of "the people"*
under the guidance of a Sage Ruler],
and the nature of the entities is
automatically fulfilled.

THE STRUCTURE OF *LAOZI* 29

Laozi 29 has a weak element of open IPS grouped around the terms
of *wei* 爲 and *zhi/qu* 執/取 in an ab cc ba c sequence. This gives the following overall structure:

a	b		(29.1, 29.1)
		c	(29.2)
		c	(29.2)
	b		(29.3)
a			(29.3)
		c	(29.4)

Zhang 30

30.1 以道佐人主ª不以ᵇ兵強於ᶜ天下¹ (Base text: 馬王堆 B)

以道佐人主尙不可以兵強於天下況人主躬於道者乎 (Base text: 集註
本)

30.2 其事好還 (Base text: 傅奕古本)

爲治ᵈ者務欲立功生事而有道者務欲還反無爲故云其事好還也 (Base
text: 集註本)

ª Var.: 主者 for 主: 傅奕古本; 范應元本; 郭店 A. Support against 者: Wang Bi comm.:
以道佐人主尙不可以 does not repeat the 者.

ᵇ Var.: 不谷以 for 不以: 郭店 A.

ᶜ Var.: 強天下 for 強於天下: 傅奕古本; 范應元本. Support for 於: Wang Bi comm.:
強於天下. Wang Bi on *Laozi* 30.4 不以兵力取強於天下也 and Wang Bi on *Laozi* 30.7 喻
以兵強於天下者也.

ᵈ Var.: 始 for 治: 永樂大典本. Support for 治: 陸德明釋文.

30.3 師之所處^e荆棘^f生焉^{g,h} (Base text: 傅奕古本)²

言師凶害之物也無有所濟必有所傷賊害人民殘荒田畝故曰荊棘生也
(Base text 集註本)

30.4 故善ⁱ者果而已矣^j不^k以取強矣^l (Base text: 馬王堆 A)

果猶濟也言善用師者趣以濟難而已矣不以兵力取強於天下矣 (Base text: 集註本)

30.5 果而勿矜果而勿伐果而勿驕^m (Base text: 傅奕古本)

吾不以師道爲尙不得已而用何矜驕之有也ⁿ (Base text: 集註本)

30.6 果而不^o得已果而勿強^p (Base text: 傅奕古本)

言用兵雖趣功果濟難然時故不得已當復用者但當以除暴亂不遂用果
以爲強也 (Base text: 集註本)

---

e Var.: 居 for 處: 馬王堆 A.　　　　　f Var.: 楚杓 for 荊棘: 馬王堆 A.

g Var.: 生之 for 生焉: 馬王堆 A; 馬王堆 B.

h 師之所處荊棘生焉 for 師之所處荊棘生焉大軍之後必有凶年: 馬王堆 A: 口口居
楚杓生之 (= om. 大軍之後必有凶年); 馬王堆 B: 口口口口棘生之 for 師之所處荊棘
生焉大軍之後必有凶年 ((= om. 大軍之後必有凶年). Support for omission of 大軍之後必
有凶年: Wang Bi does not comment on the phrase. Shima Kuniō. For the textual history of
this passage, cf. Xu Huijun 徐慧君 and Li Dingsheng 李定生, *Wenzi yaoquan* 文子要詮,
6ff. 郭店 A omits both passages under discussion here. 陸德明釋文 had the 大軍 . . . 凶年
text in his edition.

i 故善 for 善: 傅奕古本; 范應元本. Support for 故: Wang Bi comm. links 善 with the
師 of *Laozi* 30.1 ff.

j Var.: 而已 for 而已矣: 范應元本; 郭店 A.

k 不 for 毋: Wang Bi comm.: 不以兵力取強於天下也; 傅奕古本; 范應元本; 郭店 A.

l 矣 for 焉 (also in 傅奕古本): Wang Bi comm. Var.: 強 for 強矣: 范應元本; 郭店 A.

m Var.: 果而毋驕(馬王堆 A: 驕)果而毋矜果而毋口口伐 (馬王堆 A:果而口口; 馬王堆
B:果口口伐) for 果而勿矜果而勿伐果而勿驕: 馬王堆 A; 馬王堆 B. Support for sequence
with 矜 at the beginning: Wang Bi comm.: 何矜驕之有也. Var: 伐 (伐)–喬 (驕)–矜 (矜)
sequence: 郭店 A.

n 陶鴻慶 has suggested a radical revision of this commentary: 吾本以道爲尙不得已
而用師何矜驕之有也.

o Var.: 毋 for 不: 馬王堆 A; 馬王堆 B.

p Var.: 已居是胃果 (馬王堆 A:口) 而不(馬王堆 B om.不) for 已果而勿強: 馬王堆
A; 馬王堆 B.

30.7 物壯則^q老是謂^r不道不道^s早^t已 (Base text: 范應元本)

壯武力暴興^u喻以兵強於天下者也飄風不終朝驟雨不終日故暴興必不道早已也^v (Base text: 永樂大典本)

30.1　　[Even] someone who [only] supports the lord of men by means of the Way will not impose violent [rule] in All-under-Heaven by means of soldiers.

If it is already impossible for someone who [only] supports the lord of men by means of the Way to impose violent [rule] in All Under Heaven by means of soldiers, how much less [will this be possible] for a lord of men who personally [makes use] of the Way!

30.2　　In his dealings, he will [rather] emulate returning.

Someone who actively brings about order[1] will make efforts and desires to establish achievements and get things done, while "someone who has the Way" [,as mentioned in Laozi 31,] will make efforts and desires [to make All Under Heaven] return and relate back [to the One] and [to himself practice] non-interference.[2] That is why [the text] says: "In his dealings, he will [rather] emulate returning"!

30.3　　Where troops are stationed, [only] brambles will grow![3]

This means: troops are nefarious and harmful. There is nothing to which they can bring order, but necessarily something to which they inflict harm. They loot and harm the people, and they lay the fields to waste. That is why [the text] says: "Brambles will grow"!

30.4　　That is why someone who is good at it [using troops] will just get [things] done and that is all. He will not by means of [troops] impose violent [rule]!

"Get [things] done" is like "bring order." [The above phrase] means: someone who is good at using troops will just set his mind on bringing order to troubles and that is it, but he will not by means of military force impose violent [rule] in All Under Heaven.

30.5　　[Thus,] having got [things] done [by military means], he does not brag; having got [things] done [by military means], he does not show off; having got [things] done [by military means], he does not boast.

---

^q Var.: 而 for 則: 馬王堆 A; 馬王堆 B.

^r Var.: 胃之 for 謂: 馬王堆 A. Var.: 胃之 for 是謂: 馬王堆 B.

^s Var.: 非道非道 for 不道不道: 傅奕古本.

^t Var.: 蚤 for 早: 馬王堆 A; 馬王堆 B.

^u Var.: 興也 for 興: 集註本.

^v In 集註本 this entire commentary page is ascribed to 王雱.

Once the subject[4] [the ruler] does not emulate the way of the military, but [, as the Laozi 31 *says,] "makes use [of the troops] only because he cannot help it," what is there to brag and boast about?*

30.6 [In short,] he gets [things] done [by means of the military], but [only because he] cannot help [but make use of troops temporarily]. This means getting [things] done [by means of soldiers], but not imposing violent [rule].

This means although in making use of soldiers he sets his mind on good results in getting [things] done and bringing order to troubles, still it is only appropriate again to make use [of the soldiers] when, due to circumstances, he cannot help it. But this [use of troops] is appropriate only to wipe out riots, and he will not as a consequence of getting things done [through] the use [of the military] by this means impose violent [rule].

30.7 If an entity grows mighty, it will age [quickly]. This I call "not on the Way." What is not on the Way is quickly finished.

"Growing mighty" means a rapid surge of military might. [The expression] is a metaphor for imposing violent [rule] in All Under Heaven by means of soldiers. [As the Laozi 23.2 *says], "A cyclone does not outlast a morning, and a cloudburst does not outlast a day." That is why [the text says that such a] rapid surge [in military might] is by necessity "not on the Way" and "quickly finished!"*

Zhang 31

31 夫佳兵者不祥之器物或惡之故有道者不處是以君子居則貴左用兵則貴右兵
者不祥之器非君子之器不得已而用之恬澹為上勝而不美也若美必樂之樂之者
是樂殺人也夫樂殺人者不可以得志於天下矣故吉事尚左凶事尚右是以偏將
軍處左上將軍處右言居上勢則以喪禮處之殺人眾多則以悲哀泣之戰勝者則
以喪禮處之

No commentary by Wang Bi is extant for this *zhang*. It is, however, quoted in Wang's commentary on *Laozi* 30.5 and other sections of his commentary to the *Laozi*. The *Jizhu* quotes Wang Bi with the words under this *zhang*: "I have doubts whether this has been written by *Laozi*," a statement also quoted by Dong Siqing in his *Daodejing jijie*. Chao Yuezhi 晁說之 writes in 1115 in his *Fuzhi ji*, 鄜畤記, "Wang Bi knew that the text from 佳兵者不祥之器 to 戰勝以喪禮處之 was not words by *Laozi*." This statement is included in a preface appended to the Siku edition of Wang Bi's *Laozi Commentary*, p. 185. Hatano Tarō has assembled the various statements. The suggestion made by Ma Xulun in his *Laozi jiaogu*, that the chapter in fact consists of a melange of the original text plus Wang Bi's commentary, a suggestion that has led to some attempts at reconstruction, has been disproved by the Mawangdui manuscripts, both of which have the text in a form as difficult to understand as ever. As there is no commentary by Wang Bi, I shall not translate this *zhang* but just give a text for reference. There is, however, besides the passage in Wang Bi on *Laozi* 30, already mentioned, one other possible quotation from this text in Wang's *Commentary*, namely, the term *tian dan* 恬淡 in Wang Bi on *Laozi* 63.1, which in terms of content, however, seems more closely related to *Laozi* 35.3 and the commentary there. Wang Bi might have considered *zhang* 31 corrupt and only partially usable.

Zhang 32

32.1 道常ᵃ無名樸ᵇ雖ᶜ小天下莫能臣也ᵈ 侯王ᵉ若能守ᶠ萬物將自賓 (Base text: 傅奕古本)

> 道無形不繫常不可名ᵍ以無名爲常故曰道常無名也ʰ,¹樸之爲物以無
> 爲心也亦無名故將得道莫若守樸夫智者可以能臣也勇者可以武使ⁱ
> 也巧者可以事役也力者可以重任也樸之爲物憒然不偏近於無有故曰
> 莫能臣也抱樸無爲不以物累其眞不以欲害其神則物自賓而道自得
> 矣ʲ (Base text: 集註本)

32.2 天地相合以降甘露ᵏ民ˡ莫之令而自均焉ᵐ (Base text: 傅奕古本)

> 言ⁿ天地相合則甘露不求而自降我守其眞性無爲則民不令而自均也
> (Base text: 集註本)

ᵃ Var.: 恆 for 常: 馬王堆 A; 馬王堆 B.

ᵇ Var.: 楃 for 樸: 馬王堆 A.　　　　ᶜ Var.: 唯 for 雖: 馬王堆 A; 馬王堆 B.

ᵈ 臣也 for 臣: 陸德明釋文. Var.: 而天下弗敢臣 for 天下莫能臣: 馬王堆 B. Lacuna in 馬王堆 A has the same length. Var.: 天地弗敢 for 天下莫能: 郭店 A.

ᵉ 侯王 for 王侯: 陸德明釋文; 郭店 A; 馬王堆 A (□王); 馬王堆 B.

ᶠ Var.:守之 for 守: 郭店 A; 馬王堆 A; 馬王堆 B; 范應元本. Support against the 之: Wang Bi comm. on *Laozi* 10.6 所謂道常無爲 侯王若能守則萬物自化, which quotes *Laozi* 37.3.

ᵍ Var.: 道無形 故不可名 for 道無形不繫 常不可名: 取善集.

ʰ Var.: 名 for 名也: 取善集.　　　ⁱ Var.: 使 for 君: 永樂大典本.

ʲ Var.: 也 for 矣: 永樂大典本.

ᵏ Var.: 以兪 (郭店 A: 逾) 甘洛 for 以降甘露: 郭店 A; 馬王堆 A; 馬王堆 B.

ˡ Var.: 人 for 民: 范應元本.　　　　ᵐ Var.: 均 for 均焉: 范應元本.

ⁿ Var.: 言 om.: 取善集.

32.3 始制有名名亦既有夫亦將知止知止所以不殆 (Base text: 傅奕古本)

始制謂樸散始爲官長之時也始制官長不可不立名分以定尊卑故始制有名也過此以往將爭錐刀之末故曰名亦既有夫亦將知止也遂任名以號物則失治之母也故知止所以不殆也 (Base text: 集註本)

32.4 譬[o]道之在天下[p]猶[q]川谷之與江海也 (Base text: 傅奕古本)

川谷之不[r]求江[s]與海非江海召之不召不求而自歸者也[t]行道於天下者不令而自均不求而自得故曰猶川谷之與江海也[2] (Base text: 集註本)

32.1 The Eternal of the Way is namelessness.[1] Even though the Unadorned may be small, no one in All Under Heaven is able to put [it] to service. If only the dukes and kings were able to keep to it [the Unadorned], the ten thousand kinds of entities would submit [to them] of their own accord as guests.

The Way is without shape and attachment.[2] *[Its] Eternal cannot be named; [thus] namelessness is taken for [its] Eternal. That is why [the* Laozi*] says: "The Eternal of the Way is namelessness!" The Unadorned as such has negativity as its heart. [It], too, is nameless. That is why, if one [i.e, a ruler] intends to achieve the Way, there is nothing better than to keep to the Unadorned. It is a fact that the intelligent can be put to service for [his] ability; the brave can be employed for [his] warlike ser- vice s; the dexterous can be put to use for [his ability to] handle affairs; the strong can be given assignments for [his capacity to handle] heavy loads. The Unadorned as such [, however,] is diffuse and not one-sided [and thus] close to not having [any specific feature at all]. That is why [the* Laozi *says: "No one is able to put [it] to service [for a particular quality]." If [only the dukes and kings] would [, as the* Laozi *says in* 19.1,*] "embrace the Unadorned," be without interference, and would not let their true [nature] become fettered through [particular] entities nor their spirit be hurt by [their] desires, the other "entities" would [as the text says] "submit [to them] of their own accord, as guests" and the Way would automatically be achieved.*

---

[o] Var.: 俾 for 譬: 馬王堆 A. Var.: 卑 for 譬: 馬王堆 B; 郭店 A.

[p] Var.: 天下也 for 天下: 馬王堆 B. Lacuna in 馬王堆 A would leave space for 也; 郭店 A.

[q] Var.: 猷小 (郭店 A: 少) 浴 for 猶川谷: 馬王堆 B; 郭店 A.

[r] Var.: 不 om.: 永樂大典本.

[s] 江 for 水: 永樂大典本.

[t] 也 for 世: 陶鴻慶.

32.2   [In the same manner as] Heaven and Earth being in harmony, will induce sweet dew to fall down, the people, without anyone's order, become regulated automatically [as a consequence of my, the Sage's, preserving the Unadorned].

This means: As a consequence of Heaven and Earth being in harmony, sweet dew falls down automatically without their striving for it. As a consequence of the I's [the Sage's] preserving their [the other entities'] true nature and being without interference [with regard to other entities], the people will automatically become regulated without being given [particular] orders.[3]

32.3   With the beginning of [my social] regulation [I, the Sage will] have names. Once the names are there, [I, the Sage] set out to have an understanding about [how to] put a stop [to the ensuing developments]. [Only] having an understanding about [how to] put a stop [to them] is what gets [me] out of danger.

"The beginning of [the Sage's social] regulation" is the time [referred to in Laozi *28.6] when "the Unadorned has dispersed" and [the Sage as the Great Regulator of* Laozi *28.7] begins "to make officials and elders." With the beginning of [his social] regulation with officials and elders it is impossible [for him] to do without setting up names and classifications by way of determining the honored and the lowly. That is why [the text says], "With the beginning of [my social] regulation, I [,the Sage,] will have names." Going beyond this would [mean the emergence of] [what the* Zuozhuan *refers to as] "struggle [even] for [trifles as minute as] the point of an awl or a knife."*[4] *That is why [the text] says: "Once the names are there, [I, the Sage] will set out to have an understanding about [how to] put a stop [to the ensuing developments]." The subsequent use of names to mark entities, [would] engender a loss of the mother of [social] order. That is why [the text says], "[Only] having an understanding about [how to] put a stop to [these developments] is what gets [me] out of danger [from the resulting social conflicts]."*

32.4   [I] compare the [role] of the Way in All Under Heaven to the [relationship] of rivers and the sea with rivulets and streams.

The rivulets and streams are not striving [to flow into] the rivers and seas, nor is [their running into them] caused by the rivers and the seas calling them; [thus] without either calling [by the latter] or striving [by the former] they render themselves [into the rivers and the seas] on their own. If the Way is practiced in All Under Heaven,[5] *it [All Under Heaven] is regulated automatically without [anyone] giving orders, and [All Under Heaven] achieves [the Way] automatically without striving [for it]. That is why [the text says]: "[I] compare the [role] of the Way in All Under Heaven to the [relationship] of rivers and the sea with rivulets and streams."*[6]

Zhang 33

33.1 知人者智^a也自知者^b明也 (Base text: 傅奕古本)

　　知人者有智^c而已矣 未若^d自知者 超智之上也 (Base text: 集註本)

33.2 勝^e人者有力也自勝^f者強也 (Base text: 傅奕古本)

　　勝人者有力而已矣未若自勝者無物以損其力用其智於人未若用其智
　　於己也用其力於人未若用其力於己也明用於己則物無避焉力用於己
　　則物無巧焉^g (Base text: 集註本)

33.3 知足者富也 (Base text: 傅奕古本)

　　知足者^h自不失 故富也 (Base text: 集註本)

33.4 強行者有志也ⁱ (Base text: 王弼注)

　　勤能行之 其志必獲^j故曰強行者有志矣 (Base text: 永樂大典本)

33.5 不失其所者久也 (Base text: 傅奕古本)

　　以明自察量力而行不失其所必獲久長矣 (Base text: 集註本)

33.6 死而不亡^k者壽也 (Base text: 傅奕古本)

---

　　^a Var.: 知 for 智: 馬王堆 A; 馬王堆 B; 范應元本.

　　^b Var.: 自知 for 自知者: 馬王堆 B.

　　^c 有智 for 自智: Hatano Tarō. Support for 有智: Wang Bi comm. on *Laozi* 33.2 (勝人者有力也): 勝人者有力而已矣 although there text already has 有力. Var.: 智 for 有智: 永樂大典本.

　　^d Var.: 未若 om.: 永樂大典本.　　　^e Var.: 朕 for 勝: 馬王堆 B.

　　^f Var.: 朕 for 勝: 馬王堆 B.

　　^g 巧 for 改: Wagner. 服部南郭 suggests 攻 for 改 Var.: 力用於己 則物無改焉 om.: 永樂大典本.

　　^h Var.: 知足 for 知足者: 永樂大典本.

　　ⁱ 也 for 矣: 馬王堆 A; 馬王堆 B; 傅奕古本; 范應元本.

　　^j Var.: 穫 for 獲: 集註本.　　　^k Var.: 忘 for 亡: 馬王堆 A; 馬王堆 B.

雖死而以爲生之道不亡乃得全其壽身沒而道猶存況身存而道不卒¹乎
(Base text: 取善集)

33.1 He [a ruler] who sees through others has intelligence. He [a ruler] who sees through himself has enlightenment.

He who sees through others merely has intelligence; that is nothing compared to seeing through oneself. [The latter] is superior to having intelligence.

Using one's intelligence on others is nothing compared to using one's intelligence on oneself.

If one's enlightenment is used on oneself, the other entities will be without evasion!

33.3 He [a ruler] who knows how to have enough, will be wealthy.

He who knows how to have enough, will automatically have no loss, that is why [the text says] he will be "wealthy."

He [a ruler] who vanquishes others has strength. He [a 33.2 ruler] who vanquishes himself, powerfully [practices the Way].¹

He who vanquishes others has merely strength; that is nothing compared to vanquishing oneself [as] there is no other entity able to wear down one's strength.

Using one's strength on others is nothing compared to using one's strength on oneself.

If one's strength is used on one-self, the other entities will be without craftiness.

He [a ruler] who powerfully 33.4 practices [the Way], will have his will.

[The *Laozi* 41.1 says, "When a gentleman of highest [caliber] hears of the Way, he will practice it to the utmost of his capacities," on which Wang Bi comments: "That is 'He will have his will' (, as the *Laozi* 33.3 says)."] "Practicing it [the Way] to the utmost of his capacities" [, as the Laozi 41.1 says], he will by necessity have his will satisfied. That is why [the text] says: "He [a ruler] who powerfully prac-tices [the Way], will have his will"!

---

¹ Var.: 存 for 卒: 集註本.

33.5   He who does not go astray
                             from his place, will stay
                             long [in it].

If by means of [his] enlighten-   If he measures his strength and
ment he investigates himself,   acts [accordingly],

                             [and thus] "does not go
                             astray from his place," he by
                             necessity will manage to stay
                             long [in it].[2]

33.6   He who, while mortal [him-
                             self], does not [assume that
                             the Way] perishes, will live
                             a long life.

                             If one, although mortal [one-
                             self], assumes that the Way
                             of Life does not perish, then
                             indeed one will manage it to
                             complete one's years. When the
                             body dies, the Way still persists;
                             all the more does the Way not
                             end while the body is still alive.

THE STRUCTURE OF *LAOZI* 33

Laozi 33 has the formal signals associated with IPS. The two pairs
in texts 1 and 2 are parallel with a minor difference, *you li* 有力 being
two characters but *zhi* 智 only one. Texts 3 and 4 again are parallel
with a similar minor difference. Texts 5 and 6 have the same number of
characters and closely related terms at their ends, *jiu* 久 and *shou* 壽, but
their grammar greatly differs, particularly in Wang Bi's reading. The only
clear indicator linking the first two texts with the second pair is the term
powerful, *qiang* 強, in text 4, which links up with the same term in text
2. However, neither text nor commentary give a clear indication linking
text 1 with text 3. The term *qiang* is not commented upon in the commentary to text 2 and is defined through the quotation from *Laozi* 41 in
the commentary to text 4 as meaning *qin neng* 勤能, "to the utmost of
one's capacities," and provided with a supplement, "to practice the Way."
There are two possible strategies here, either to read the definition in text
4 as fundamentally different from that suggested in text 2 and abandon
the attempts at discovering more than a serial structure, or to transfer the
content of *qiang* from text 4 to text 2. I opt for the second strategy because
of text 5. The commentary to this text directly takes up the terminology of

texts 1 and 2 in a parallel manner, indicating that it is a general statement referring to two previous chains begun by them. Text 6 also comes in as a general statement. Text 5 refers to the stability of position that a Sage Ruler enjoys, and text 6 to his personal survival. The overall structure of *Laozi* 33 thus is:

a	b		(33.1, 33.2)
a	b		(33.3, 33.4)
		c	(33.5)
		c	(33.6)

Zhang 34

34.1 道氾ᵃ兮ᵇ其可左右也ᶜ (Base text: 馬王堆 B)

言道氾ᵈ濫無所不適可左右上下周施而用 則無所不至也 (Base text: 永樂大典本)

34.2 萬物恃之而ᵉ生而不辭ᶠ功成而不居ᵍ衣被萬物而不ʰ爲主 故常ⁱ無欲ʲ可名於ᵏ小矣ˡ (Base text: 傅奕古本)

ᵃ 氾 for 汎: Wang Bi comm.; 陸德明釋文. Var.: 大道 for 道 (also in 馬王堆 A): 傅奕古本; 范應元本. Support against 大: Wang Bi comm.: 道氾; 陸德明釋文 only registers 道氾 without 大. Counterargument: 文選劉孝標 辨命論李善注 54.15b4 quotes this textual passage with 大 over elements from Wang Bi's commentary. Var.: 道氾氾 for 道氾: 范應元本. Var.: 道汎汎 for 道氾: 傅奕古本. Support against duplication: Wang Bi comm. 道氾; 陸德明釋文 only registers 道氾 without duplication; 馬王堆 B writes 渢 for 氾 but does not duplicate.

ᵇ 兮 for 呵: passim; 傅奕古本; 范應元本.

ᶜ Var.: 左右 for 左右也: 傅奕古本; 范應元本.

ᵈ Var.: 汎 for 氾: 集註本.

ᵉ 而 for 以: Wang Bi comm.: 由道而生; 文子.

ᶠ Var.: 萬物恃之而生而不辭 om.: 馬王堆 A; 馬王堆 B.

ᵍ Var.: 不名有 for 而不居: 范應元本. Var.: 成功遂事 (馬王堆 B: 口口) 而弗名有也 for 功成而不居: 馬王堆 A; 馬王堆 B.

ʰ Var.: 萬物歸焉而弗 for 衣被萬物而不: 馬王堆 A; 馬王堆 B.

ⁱ Var.: 則恒 for 故常: 馬王堆 A; 馬王堆 B.

ʲ Var.: 欲也 for 欲: 馬王堆 A; 馬王堆 B.　　ᵏ Var.: 爲 for 於: 范應元本.

ˡ Var.: 小 for 小矣: 馬王堆 A; 馬王堆 B.

萬物皆由^m道而生 既生而不知其所由ⁿ故天下常無欲之時萬物各得
其所 而^o道無施^p於物 故可^q名於小矣 (Base text: 永樂大典本)

34.3 萬物歸之而不知^r主可名^s於^t大矣^u (Base text: 傅奕古本)

萬物皆歸之以生而力使不知其所由此不爲小故復可名於大矣 (Base
text: 永樂大典本)

34.4 是以聖人之^v能成大^w也 以其^x不爲大也^y故能成大^z (Base text: 馬王堆 B)

爲大於其細圖難於其易^{aa} (Base text: 集註本)

34.1　　　The Way overflows! Thus it is possible [to make use of it all around] to the
right as well as to the left.

*This means: The Way overflows to the extent that there is no [place] that
it does not reach. As it is possible to make use [of it] all around, to the
right and to the left, above and below, there is no [place] to which it does
not go.*[1]

34.2　　　The ten thousand kinds of entities depend on it [the Way] for their being

---

^m Var.: 得 for 由: quotation in 文選劉孝標辨命論李善注 54.15b4.

ⁿ 所由 for 由所: 集註本.

^o 而 for 若: Wagner. The subsequent 故 must mean "that is why" in analogy to Wang
Bi on *Laozi* 34.3, therefore the 若 here would be ungrammatical.

^p Var.: 施 om.: 集註本.

^q 故可 for 故: Wagner based on parallel with Wang Bi on *Laozi* 34.3: 故可名於大.

^r Var.: 爲而弗爲 for 之而不知: 馬王堆 A; 馬王堆 B. Support for 知: Wang Bi
comm.

^s Var.: 命 for 名: 馬王堆 B.　　　　^t Var.: 爲 for 於: 范應元本.

^u Var.: 大 for 大矣: 馬王堆 A; 馬王堆 B.

^v Var.: 之 om.: 傅奕古本.　　　　^w Var.: 成其大 for 成大: 傅奕古本.

^x Var.: 聖人以其 for 聖人之能成大也 以其: 范應元本. Var.: 其終 for 其: 傅奕古本;
范應元本; 陸德明釋文.

^y Var.: 不自爲大 for 不爲大: 陸德明釋文; 傅奕古本; 范應元本. Support against 自:
Wang Bi's commentary does not link this passage to the Sage's keeping himself in the background but with his acting while problems are still small, therefore there is no echo of the
自 in the commentary.

^z Var.: 成其大 for 成大: 傅奕古本; 范應元本.

^{aa} Var.: 於易 for 於其易: 陸德明釋文.

born, but it does not give orders. Achievements are completed [through it], but it does not take station [in them]. It dresses the ten thousand kinds of entities but does not become [their] overlord. That is why, [when everything] is constantly without desires, it may be named among the small;

The ten thousand kinds of entities all are generated on the basis of the Way. But, although they are born [on this basis], they do not know that which they are based on.² That is why, insofar as at the time "while" All Under Heaven "is constantly without desire" [as the Laozi *1.3 says] and the ten thousand kinds of entities all manage to be in their [proper] places, the Way does not act on the entities [by being their commander, taking station among them or becoming their overlord], it [, as the text says,] "may be named among the small."³*

34.3 and [insofar as] the ten thousand kinds of entities go back to it but do not know the[ir] master, it [the Way] may be named among the great.

Insofar as each of the ten thousand kinds of entities relates back to it for their generation, but a force causes them not to know that on which they are based, this is not "small." That is why again, [as the text says,] it "may be named among the great!"

34.4 That is why—[as far as] the Sage's capacity to complete big [enterprises is concerned]—by not acting on [things when they are already] big, he is capable of completing big [enterprises].

[As the Laozi *63.3 says of the Sage,] "He acts on [what is eventually] big while it is still minute" and "makes plans against [eventual] difficulties when things are still easy [to resolve]."*

Zhang 35

35.1 執大象者ª天下往 (Base text: 傅奕古本)

大象天象之母也不炎不寒不溫不涼ᵇ故能包通ᶜ萬物無所犯傷主若執之則天下往也 (Base text: 集註本)

ª Var.: 大象 for 大象者: 郭店 C; 馬王堆 B. The size of the lacuna in 馬王堆 A suggests the absence of 者.

ᵇ 不炎不寒不溫不涼 for 不寒不溫不涼: Wagner based on *LZWZLL* 1.17 若溫也則不能涼, which shows that 溫 and 涼 form a pair, and on Wang Bi on *Laozi* 41.14: 不炎則寒, which shows that 炎 and 寒 form a pair. A construction with three elements as in the transmitted text is extremely unlikely.

ᶜ 通 for 統: Wagner based on Wang Bi on *Laozi* 16.7 無所不包通也 and *LZWZLL* 1.16 包通天地.

35.2 往而不害安平泰^d (Base text: 傅奕古本)

> 無形無識不偏不彰故萬物得往而不害妨也 (Base text: 集註本)

35.3 樂與餌過客^e止道^f之出言^g淡兮^h其無味也^{i,1}視之不足見^j聽之不足聞^k用之^l不可既^m (Base text: 傅奕古本)

> 言道之深大人聞道之言乃更不如樂與餌應時感悅ⁿ人心也樂與餌則能令過客止而道之出言淡然無味視之不足見則不足以悅其目聽之不足聞則不足以娛其耳若無所中然乃用之不可窮極也 (Base text: 集註本)

35.1   If [the ruler were to] hold on to the Great Image, [then] All Under Heaven [would] come [to him].[1]

The Great Image is the mother of the heavenly images.[2] It is neither hot nor cold, neither warming nor cooling. That is why it is capable of embracing and penetrating the ten thousand kinds of entities without there being one that is crossed or hurt. If [only] the ruler were able to hold on to it, All Under Heaven would come to him!

35.2   [If All Under Heaven] came to him and [would] not suffer damage, security and peace [would be] optimal.

[He would be] without shape and discernibility, neither [inwardly] partial nor conspicuous [in his preferences].[3] That is why the ten thousand kinds of entities [would] manage to "come" [to him] without suffering damage or obstruction!

35.3   Music and fragrant food cause [even] a passing customer to stop. The

---

   ^d Var.: 大 for 泰: 郭店 C; 馬王堆 A; 馬王堆 B.

   ^e Var.: 格 for 客: 馬王堆 A; 馬王堆 B.

   ^f Var.: 故道 for 道: 郭店 C; 馬王堆 A; 馬王堆 B.

   ^g Var.: 言也曰 for 言: 馬王堆 A; 馬王堆 B.

   ^h Var.: 呵 for 兮: 馬王堆 A; 馬王堆 B.

   ⁱ 味也 for 味: Wang Bi quotation in commentary on *Laozi* 23.1; 郭店 C; 馬王堆 A; 馬王堆 B.

   ^j Var.: 見也 for 見: 馬王堆 A; 馬王堆 B.

   ^k Var.: 聞也 for 聞: 馬王堆 A; 馬王堆 B.   ^l Var.: 而 for 用之: 郭店 C.

   ^m Var.: 既也 for 既: 郭店 C; 馬王堆 A; 馬王堆 B.

   ⁿ Var.: 說 for 悅: 陸德明釋文.

words [however], uttered about the Way indeed are stale; they are without taste! Looking for it [the Way], one cannot manage to see it; listening for it [the Way], one cannot manage to hear it; making use of it [the Way], it is impossible to exhaust it.

This [passage of the text] explains the depth and greatness of the Way. When others hear words about the Way, these indeed are no match for music and fragrant food in moving and pleasing their hearts in accordance with the moment. Music and fragrant food, accordingly, are capable of making a passing customer stop, but the "words uttered about the Way are stale" and "without taste." "Looking for it one cannot see it"—this means it is not able to please [people's] eyes. "Listening for it one cannot hear it"—this means it is not able to tickle [people's] ears. As there is nothing in it, its "use" can "not exhaust it" [,as the Laozi 45.2 says about the Great Filling which is "as if empty"].

Zhang 36

36.1 將欲翕ᵃ之必固ᵇ張之將欲弱之必固ᶜ強之將欲廢ᵈ之必固ᵉ興ᶠ之將欲奪ᵍ之必固ʰ與ⁱ之是謂ʲ微明 (Base text: 傅奕古本)

將欲除強梁去暴亂當以此四者因物之性令其自戮不假刑爲大以除強物也ᵏ故曰微明也足其張令之足而又求其張則衆ˡ所翕ᵐ也翕ⁿ其張之不足而攻ᵒ其求張者愈益而已反危 (Base text: 永樂大典本)ˡ

ᵃ Var.: 僖 for 翕: 陸德明釋文. Var.: 拾 for 翕: 馬王堆 A. Var.: 擒 for 翕: 馬王堆 B. Support for 翕: Wang Bi comm.; 集註本: 所翕也.

ᵇ Var.: 古 for 固: 馬王堆 A; 馬王堆 B.

ᶜ Var.: 古 for 固: 馬王堆 B.

ᵈ Var.: 去 for 廢: 馬王堆 A; 馬王堆 B.

ᵉ Var.: 古 for 固: 馬王堆 A; 馬王堆 B.

ᶠ Var.: 與 for 興: 馬王堆 A; 馬王堆 B.

ᵍ Var.: 取 for 奪: 范應元本.　　　ʰ Var.: 古 for 固: 馬王堆 A; 馬王堆 B.

ⁱ Var.: 予 for 與: 馬王堆 A; 馬王堆 B.

ʲ Var.: 胃 for 謂: 馬王堆 A; 馬王堆 B.

ᵏ 強物 for 將物: Wagner. Var.: 不假刑爲大 以除將物也 om.: 集註本.

ˡ Var.: 象 for 衆: 集註本.

ᵐ 翕 for 歙: 集註本.

ⁿ 翕 for 與: Wagner; cf. note 1 in translation.

ᵒ 攻 for 改: 服部南郭.

36.2 柔之勝剛弱之勝強^p魚不可脫^q於淵國^r之^s利器不可以示^t人 (Base text: 傅奕古本)

利器利國之器也^u唯^v因物之性不假刑^w以理物器不可睹而物各得其所^x則國之利器也示人者任刑也刑以利國則失矣魚脫於淵則必見失矣利國器而立刑^y以示人亦必失也^z (Base text: 永樂大典本)

36.1 Having the intention to make them contract, to definitely expand them; having the intention to weaken them, to definitely strengthen them; having the intention to do away with them, to definitely bring them to flourish; having the intention to take away from them, to definitely add to them: This I call "insight into the minute."

If [a ruler] intends to wipe out the "violent and brutal" [who, according to Laozi 42.3, "will not meet their (natural) death"] and do away with upheavals and riots, he has to proceed according to these four [precepts] and adapt to the nature of entities to have them self-destruct instead of relying on the magnitude of the physical punishment to eliminate violent entities. This is why [the text] calls this "insight into the minute [i.e., the nature of entities]"!

If, the expansion [of the violent] being sufficient, [the ruler with insight into the minute] prods them to crave for further expansion beyond this sufficient [level], they will be made to contract by the multitude [of those being envious of their powers who will cooperate to attack them]. If [,on the other hand, a ruler] contracts what is [already] deficient in their expansion and attacks their craving for expansion [by means of punishments], he will, the more he does this, put himself into danger [because of the growing hostility of the violent].

36.2 [This is] the soft's overcoming the hard, and the weak's overcoming the strong. A fish cannot be taken out of the deep water. [In the same manner,] the state's useful instrument cannot prevail by showing it to people.

"Useful instrument" is an instrument useful to the state. If [the ruler] only adapts to the nature of entities and does not rely on physical punishments

---

^p Var.: 柔弱勝強 for 柔之勝剛弱之勝強: 馬王堆 A. Var.: 柔弱朕強: 馬王堆 B.

^q 脫 for 佷: 陸德明釋文. Var.: 不脫 for 不可脫: 馬王堆 A. Var.: 說 for 脫: 馬王堆 B.

^r 國 for 邦 (also in 馬王堆 A; 范應元本): Wang Bi comm.: 國之利器也. Wang Bi consistently uses the term 國 for 邦.

^s Var.: 之 om.: 馬王堆 A; 馬王堆 B.   ^t Var.: 視 for 示: 馬王堆 A.

^u Var.: 器 for 器也: 集註本.   ^v Var.: 以唯 for 唯: 集註本.

^w Var.: 形 for 刑: 集註本.   ^x Var.: 性 for 所: 集註本.

^y Var.: 形 for 刑: 集註本.   ^z Var.: 矣 for 也: 集註本.

to regulate the other entities so that the instruments [of government] cannot be perceived, but the entities still each attain their place, then [government truly] is "the state's useful instrument." "To show it to people" means applying physical punishment. If physical punishments [are applied] to be useful to the state, it will be a failure. If a fish is taken out of the deep water, it will necessarily be lost. If, [as] an instrument useful to the state, [the ruler] sets up physical punishments to show it to people, this inevitably will also be a failure.

Zhang 37

37.1 道常無爲[a] (Base text: 傅奕古本)

順自然也 (Base text: 集註本)

37.2 而無不爲[b] (Base text: 傅奕古本)

萬物無不由之[c]以始[d]以成[e]也 (Base text: 集註本)[1]

37.3 侯王[f]若能守[g]萬物將自化 化[h]而欲作吾[i]將鎮[j]之以無名之樸[k] (Base text: Wang Bi comm. on *Laozi* 10.6 for 侯王若能守 萬物將自化, Wang Bi comm. 化而欲作, and 吾將鎮之以無名之樸 for the rest)

化而欲作作欲成也吾將鎮之以[l]無名之樸不爲主也[2] (Base text: 集註本)

---

[a] Var.: 恒無名 for 常無爲: 馬王堆 A; 馬王堆 B. Var.: 互亡爲也 for 常無爲: 郭店 A.

[b] Var.: 而無不爲 om.: 郭店 A; 馬王堆 A; 馬王堆 B.

[c] 由之 for 由爲: 陶鴻慶.

[d] 始 for 治: 東條一堂 based on Wang Bi on *Laozi* 1.2 道以無形無名始成萬物 . . . ; Wang Bi on *Laozi* 21.3 萬物以始以成 . . . .

[e] 成 for 成之: 陶鴻慶.

[f] Var.: 王侯 for 侯王: 傅奕古本; 范應元本.

[g] Var.: 若守 for 若能守: 馬王堆 A. Var.: 守之 for 守: 馬王堆 A; 馬王堆 B; 郭店 A; 傅奕古本. Var.: 能守之 for 若能守: 郭店 A.

[h] Var.: 戀戀 for 化化: 馬王堆 A.

[i] Var.: 吾 om.: 郭店 A.

[j] Var.: 闐 for 鎮: 馬王堆 B.　　　　[k] Var.: 楃 for 樸: 馬王堆 A.

[l] Var.: 以 om.: 永樂大典本.

37.4 夫^m亦將無欲ⁿ (Base text: 陸德明釋文)

無欲競也 (Base text: 集註本)

37.5 無欲^o以靜^p天下^q將自正^r (Base text: 范應元本)

37.1   The Eternal of the Way is without interference,

It adapts to [the entities'] That-which-is-of-itself-what-it-is.[1]

37.2   and still leaves nothing undone.

There is none among the ten thousand kinds of entities that does not base itself on it [the Way] to be begun and perfected.

37.3   If dukes and kings were only able to hold on to [the Eternal of the Way], the ten thousand kinds of entities would change [for the better] of their own accord. If, this change notwithstanding, desires should arise [among them], I [the Sage] would quiet them down by means of the simplicity of the Nameless [of myself].

"If, this change notwithstanding, desires should arise" means "if desires form." "I would quiet them down by means of the simplicity of the Nameless" means [in the words of Laozi *34.2 about the Dao] "[I would] not become [their] overlord."*

37.4   and would also make [them] be without desire.

[That is,] to be without desire for competition.

37.5   Being without desire, [they] would therefore be calm and All Under Heaven would go about regulating itself.

---

^m Var.: 無名之樸 ins. before 夫: 馬王堆 A [with 㮶 for 樸]; 馬王堆 B; 范應元本.

ⁿ Var.: 不欲 for 無欲: 傅奕古本; 范應元本. Var.: 夫將不辱 for 夫亦將無欲: 馬王堆 A; 馬王堆 B. Support for 無欲: Wang Bi comm.: 無欲競也. Var.: 知足 for 無欲: 郭店 A.

^o 無欲 for 不欲 (also in 傅奕古本): see previous textual note. Var.: 不辱 for 無欲: 馬王堆 A; 馬王堆 B. Var: 知足 for 無欲: 郭店 A.

^p Var.: 靖 for 靜: 傅奕古本. Var.: 情 for 靜: 馬王堆 A.

^q Var.: 萬物 for 天下: 郭店 A. Var.: 天地 for 天下: 馬王堆 A; 馬王堆 B.

^r Var.: 定 for 正: 郭店 A.

Zhang 38

38.1 上德不德 是以有德 (Base text: 傅奕古本)

有德則遺其失不德則遺其得 (Base text: 范應元本)[1]

38.2 下德不失德是以無德上德無爲而無不[a]爲[b]下德爲之而無以爲[c]上仁爲之而無以爲[d]上義[e]爲之而有以爲[f,2]上禮爲之而莫之應[g]則攘臂而扔[h]故失道而[i]後德失德而後[j]仁失仁而後[k]義失義而後[l]禮夫禮者忠信之薄[m]而亂之首也前識者道之華[n]而愚之首也[o]是以大丈夫處[p]其厚不處其薄[q]處[r]其實不處[s]其華故去彼[t]取此 (Base text: 傅奕古本)

德者得也常得而無喪利而無害故以德爲名焉何以得德由乎道也何以盡德以無爲用以無爲用則莫不載也故物無焉則無物不經有焉則不足以全其生[u,3]是以天地雖廣以無爲心聖王雖大以虛爲主故曰以復而視則天地之心見至日而思之則先王之主[v]覿也故滅其私而無其身則四

---

[a] Var.: 以 for 不: 馬王堆 A; 馬王堆 B. Cf. note 2.

[b] Var.: 爲也 for 爲: 馬王堆 A; 馬王堆 B.

[c] Var.: 下德爲之而無以爲 om.: 馬王堆 A; 馬王堆 B.

[d] Var.: 爲也 for 爲: 馬王堆 A; 馬王堆 B.

[e] Var.: 德 for 義: 馬王堆 B.

[f] Var.: 爲也 for 爲: 馬王堆 A; 馬王堆 B.

[g] Var.: 應也 for 應: 馬王堆 B.

[h] Var.: 仍 for 扔: 傅奕古本. Support for 扔: 陸德明釋文. Wang Bi comm.: 則攘臂而扔之. Var.: 乃 for 扔: 馬王堆 A; 馬王堆 B.

[i] Var.: 故失道 失道矣而 for 故失道而: 馬王堆 A.

[j] Var.: 句 for 后: 馬王堆 B.   [k] Var.: 句 for 后: 馬王堆 B.

[l] Var.: 句 for 后: 馬王堆 B.   [m] Var.: 泊也 for 薄: 馬王堆 B.

[n] Var.: 華也 for 華: 馬王堆 A; 馬王堆 B.

[o] 首也 for 始: Wang Bi comm.: 道之華而愚之首. The 也 is inferred from the parallel with 亂之首也. Support for 首也: 馬王堆 A; 馬王堆 B.

[p] Var.: 居 for 處: 馬王堆 A; 馬王堆 B.

[q] Var.: 其厚而不居其泊 for 其厚 不處其薄: 馬王堆 A. Var.: 口口口居其泊 for 其厚不處其薄: 馬王堆 B.

[r] Var.: 居 for 處: 馬王堆 A; 馬王堆 B.

[s] Var.: 居 for 處: 馬王堆 A; 馬王堆 B.

[t] Var.: 皮 for 彼: 馬王堆 A. Var.: 罷而 for 彼: 馬王堆 B.

[u] 全 for 免: Wagner. Cf. note 3.   [v] Var.: 至 for 主: 張之象本.

海莫不瞻遠近莫不至殊其己而有其心[w]則一體不能自全肌骨不能相
容是以上德之人唯道是用不德其德無執無用故能有德[x]而無不爲不求
而得不爲而成故雖有德而無德名也下德求而得之爲而成之則立善以
治物故德名有焉求而得之必有失焉爲而成之必有敗焉善名生則有不
善應焉故下德爲之而無[y]以爲也無以爲者無所偏爲也[z]凡不能無爲而
爲之者皆下德也仁義禮節是也將明德之上下輒擧下德以對上德至於
無以爲極下德[aa]之量上仁是也是及於無以爲而猶爲之焉爲之而無以
爲故有有爲[ab]之患矣本在無爲母[ac]在無名棄本而適其末舍母[ad]而用其
子[ae]功雖大焉必有不濟名雖美焉僞亦必生不能不爲而成不興而治則
乃爲之故有弘普博施仁愛之者而愛之無所偏私故上仁爲之而無以爲
也愛不能兼則有抑抗[af]正直[ag]義理[ah]之者忿枉祐直助彼攻[ai]此物事而有
以心爲矣故上義爲之而有以爲也直不能篤[aj]則有斿[ak]飾修文而禮敬
之者[al]尙好修敬校責往來則不對之間忿怒生焉故上禮爲之而莫之應

---

[w] 其心 for 心: 張之象本.

[x] Var.: 上德之人唯道是用不德其德無執無用故能有德 quoted as commentary to *Laozi* 38.1 上德不德是以有德 in 取善集.

[y] 無 for 有: 范應元. Cf. note 2. Support for 無: Wang Bi comm. infra 上仁及於無以 爲 with the 上仁 being the highest form of 上德.

[z] Var.: 下德爲之而無以爲者 無所偏爲也 for 故下德爲之而無以爲也 無以爲者 無 所偏爲也: 范應元.

[aa] Var.: 下德下 for 下德: 張之象本.

[ab] 有有爲 for 有爲爲: 中國科學院, 中國歷代哲學文選 2. 301.

[ac] 母 for 毌: 張之象本. Cf. Wang Bi infra: 棄本捨母.

[ad] Var.: 舍本 for 棄本: 陸德明釋文: Support for 棄本: Wang Bi comm. infra 舍 (捨) 其母而用其子棄其本而適其末.

[ae] 棄本而適其末舍母而用其子 for 棄本捨母而適其子: 陶鴻慶: based on Wang Bi comm. infra 捨其母而用其子棄其本而適其末. Without emendation, there would be no statement taking up the 棄本. The terms 舍 and 捨 are interchangeable.

[af] 抑抗 for 折抗: 張之象本. Var.: 亢 for 抗: 陸德明釋文.

[ag] Var.: 眞 for 直: 張之象本.

[ah] 義理 for 而義理: 中國歷代哲學文選 based on parallel with previous phrase 仁 愛.

[ai] 攻 for 功: 張之象本. Support: 攻 is opposite to 助 in phrase 助彼攻此.

[aj] 篤 for 售: 張之象本.

[ak] Var.: 游 for 斿: according to 陸德明釋文 in one manuscript. 張之象本. Lu Deming himself opts for 斿.

[al] 則有斿飾修文而禮敬之者 for 則有斿飾修 又禮敬之者: Wagner based on parallel with 愛不能兼 則有抑抗正直 而義理之者 and 文 for 又 in 張之象本.

則攘臂而扔之[am]夫大之極也其唯道乎自此已往豈足尊哉故雖德盛業大富有[an]萬物猶各有其德[ao]而未能自周也故天不能爲載地不能爲覆人不能爲贍[ap]雖貴[aq]以無爲用不能全[ar]無以爲體也不能全[as]無以爲體則[at]失其爲大矣[4]所謂失道而後德也以無爲用則得[au]其母故能己不勞焉而物無不理下此已往則失用之母不能無爲而貴博施不能博施而貴正直不能正直而貴飾敬所謂失德而後仁失仁而後義失義而後禮也夫禮之[av]所始首於忠信不篤通簡不暢責備於表機微爭制夫仁義發於內爲之猶僞況務外飾而可久乎

故夫[aw]禮者忠信之薄而亂之首也前識者前人而識也即下德之倫也竭其聰明以爲前識役其智力以營庶事雖得其情姦巧彌密雖豐其譽愈喪篤實勞而事昏務而治穢[ax]雖竭聖智而民愈害舍己任物則無爲而泰守夫素樸則不須[ay]典制耽[az]彼所獲棄此所守故曰前識[ba]道之華而愚之首故苟得其爲功之母則萬物作焉而不辭也萬事存焉而不勞也用不以形御不以名故仁義可顯禮敬可彰也夫載之以大道鎮之以無名則物無所尚志無所營各任其眞[bb]事用其誠則仁德厚焉行義正焉禮敬淸焉棄其所載舍其所生用其成形役其聰明仁則僞焉[bc]義則[bd]競焉禮則[be]爭焉故

仁德之厚非用仁之所能也行義之正非用義之所成也禮敬之清非用禮
之所濟也載之以道統之以母故顯之而無所尙彰之而無所營^{bf}用夫無
名故名以篤焉用夫無形故形以成焉守母以存其子崇本以舉其末則形
名俱有而邪不生大美配天而華不作故母不可遠本不可失仁義母之所
生非可以爲母形器匠之所成非可以爲匠也舍^{bg}其母而用其子棄其本
而適其末名則有所分形則有所止雖極其大必有不周雖盛其美必有患
憂功在爲之豈足處也 (Base text: 集註本)

38.1 I.

He with the highest receipt/capacity[1] does not make anything of [his] receipt/capacity. That is why he is in possession of the [highest] receipt/capacity.

Insofar as he "possesses the receipt/capacity," he is beyond letting it go; insofar as "he does not make anything of the receipt/capacity," he is beyond getting it.

He with the inferior receipt/capacity does not let go of the receipt/capacity. That is why he is without receipt/capacity. **38.2**

He with the highest receipt/capacity does not interfere and still nothing remains undone.

He with the inferior receipt/capacity interferes with them [the other entities], but has no ulterior motive.

II. (Parts II and III must be read as describing subdivisions under the "inferior receipt/capacity" category written above on the right side.)

---

^{bf} 營 for 競: Wagner. The terms 顯 and 尙 in the parallel phrase 顯之而無所尙 have been taken from the sentence earlier 故仁義可顯禮敬可彰也夫載之以大道鎭之以無名則物無所尙志無所營. By analogy, the parallel phrase dealing with 事 should use the terms 彰 and 營. The transmitted text reads 彰之而無所競, which means that 競 is a mistake for 營.

^{bg} 舍 for 捨: 陸德明釋文, passim.

He [who possesses] the highest kindliness interferes with them [the other entities] but has no ulterior motive [in this].

He [who possesses] the highest sense of righteousness interferes with them [the other entities] but has ulterior motives [in this].

He [who possesses] the highest [understanding of] ritual interferes with them [the other entities], but, when no one is heeding [his orders], he will roll up [his] sleeves and use violence [to enforce his will].

III.

That is why once the Way has been lost,

[one will] thereafter [resort to using the highest] receipt/capacity;

once [the highest] receipt/capacity is lost, [one will] thereafter [resort to using the highest] kindliness;

once [the highest] kindliness is lost, [one will] thereafter [resort to the highest] sense of righteousness;

once [the highest] sense of righteousness is lost, [one will] thereafter [resort to the highest] understanding of ritual.

IV.

Generally speaking, [however,]

ritual is [the result of the] wearing thin of truthfulness and credibility, and [thus] the beginning of [social] chaos.	foreknowledge is [the result] of the Way's becoming an [external] ornament, and [thus] the beginning of stupidity [violent and counter-productive government].[2]

That is why the Great Man[3]
[the Sage]

resides in their [truthfulness' and credibility's] abundance, and does not take residence where they have worn thin.	resides in its [the Way's] substantialness, and does not take residence where it [has become] an ornament.

Thus he rejects the latter [i.e., the place where truthfulness and credibility have worn thin and the Way has become an ornament] and takes hold of the former [i.e., the place where truthfulness and credibility are abundant and the Way is substantial].

I.

> *He who [has] receipt/capacity,*
> de 德, *receives [it],* de 得.[4] *He*
> *constantly receives [it] and is*
> *without loss; has the advantage*
> *[of it] and [remains] without*
> *damage. That is why* de, *receipt/*
> *capacity, is taken as a name for it.*
> *By means of what does one receive*
> *[one's] receipt/capacity? On the*
> *basis indeed of the Way! By means*
> *of what does one make complete*
> *[use] of [one's] receipt/capacity? By*
> *taking negativity [as the basis of its]*
> *us[ability]. Once negativity is taken*
> *[as the basis of its] usability, there*
> *will be no [entity] that will not be*
> *sustained. That is why, if something*
> *is negative with regard to the [other]*
> *entities, there will be no entity that*
> *it does not thread through; [but] if*
> *it is an existing [= specific, entity*
> *with regard to the other entities] it*
> *will not be able to keep their lives*
> *complete. That is why*

Heaven and Earth, although   *the Sage Rulers, although they*
they are wide, have negativity   *are great, take emptiness as*
as [their] heart.   *[their] principle.*

Thus [the Zhouyi] *says*

[in the tuan *to hexagram* fu 復,   *[in the* xiang *to hexagram* fu 復,
Return] if looking for it in the   *Return] if one considers [the*
"return" [of entities] "the heart   *fact that], on the day of the*
of Heaven and Earth" "becomes   *winter solstice [the "former*
visible."   *kings" "closed the passes so that*
                                        the merchants and traders
                                        (would) not travel and the rulers
                                        (would) not inspect affairs"] the
                                        guiding principle of "the former
                                        kings" becomes evident.[5]

[A new pair of opposites begins here, which is based on the pair dominating *Laozi* 38.1 and the first phrase of 38.2.]

As a consequence, if [a ruler]

annihilates his private interests and negates his person, all [within] the four seas will look up to him and all from far and near will flock to him;

gives prominence to his own self and insists upon his inclinations, he will not [even] be able to keep [his] one body intact, and will not be able to make his sinews and bones accommodate each other.

That is why

the person [ruler] with highest receipt/capacity will make use only of the Way and will not take his capacity to be [any particular] capacity.[6] He does not hold on to anything, and does not make use of anything. That is why he is able to "possess receipt/capacity" and still "nothing remains undone." He does not strive, but still obtains, he does not interfere, but still completes.[7] That is why, although he "possesses receipt/capacity," he does not have the definition of [someone having a particular] receipt/capacity.

As [a ruler who possesses] lower receipt/ capacity obtains [things] by striving [for them] and completes [things] by interfering [with them], he is establishing the good to bring order to the entities. That is why [he] has the definition of [someone having specific] capacity. As he is obtaining [things] by striving [for them], he will necessarily have losses; as he is completing [things] by interfering [with them], he will necessarily have destruction. [In short,] once the notion of the good is born, there will be a not-good to correspond to it. That is why [the text says], "He [who possesses] lower receipt/ capacity [at best][8] interferes with them [the other entities] but has no ulterior motive!" Being "without ulterior motive" means being without one-sided interference.

II.

Generally speaking, all [capacities] unable to interfere [= act on] with them [the entities] without interference [belong to] the lower capacity. [Having] kindliness, [sense of] righteousness, and [understanding of] ritual regulations are [the forms] of this [lower capacity].

In order to make clear [the
basic difference between] the
highest and the lower [forms]
of receipt/capacity, [the text]
directly confronts the lower
capacity with the highest
capacity. It is highest humanity
which reaches [as high] as
"being without ulterior
motives" and [thus] com-
pletely fulfills the highest
potential of lower capacity.
[Someone who possesses
highest kindliness] is capable
of managing to be "without
ulterior motives," but he still
interferes. As he interferes,
but without ulterior motives,
he still has the troubles [that
come] with interfering.

The root lies in non-interference.   The mother lies in the Nameless.

By
discarding the root but going   rejecting[9] the mother but
along with the branches   making use of the offspring of
[growing out of the root]—   [the mother]—
there will by necessity, even if   there will by necessity, beautiful
the achievements be great, some   though the name may be, false-
[things] remain unachieved.   hood be also born.

If [a ruler] is unable to
complete without   to bring about order without
interfering   [violent] exertion,[10]

then he definitely interferes
with them [the other entities].

Thus there will be one who with broadly and generally dispensed kindliness loves them [the other entities], but this love for them includes
nothing partial or self-interested; that is why [the text says], "[He who
possesses] the highest kindliness interferes with them, but has no ulterior
motive [in this]!"

As [this] love is incapable of being all-encompassing, there will be
one who will regulate them [the other entities] with a [sense of] righteousness which is promoting [the one] and demoting [the other],
corrective and straight; loathing the crooked and protecting the
straight, he supports the latter and attacks the former, and with re-

gard to things and affairs he has intentional interference. That is why [the text says], "He [who possesses] the highest sense of righteousness, interferes with them [the other entities], but has ulterior motives [in this]"!

> As [this] straightening [through righteousness] is unable to be generous, there will be one who with richly ornamented and elaborately patterned rituals will have them [the other entities] show respect. He will greatly emphasize cultivating [the art] of obeisance, will deal with the smallest details of [human] intercourse, with the consequence that among [people] who do not respond [to these rules] resentment grows. That is why [the text says], "He [who possesses] the highest [understanding of] ritual interferes with them [the other entities], but when no one is heeding [his orders], he will roll up [his] sleeves and use violence [to enforce his will]!"

III.

It is a fact that the ultimate of greatness is only the Way! What is there from this [the Way] downward that deserves to be honored? [Nothing.] That is why, although [as the Xici 上 5 of the Zhouyi says of the Great Men/Sages], "[Their] capacity" might be "blossoming" and [their] "achievements" "great" [so that] [although] they "richly endow" the ten thousand kinds of entities, still each obtains his [particular] capacity and they are not, by themselves, able to be "all-encompassing," [which, according to Laozi 25.3, is the quality of the Way].

Thus Heaven [which is able to cover all ten thousand kinds of entities] is [by itself] unable to manage carrying [them]; Earth [which is able to carry the ten thousand kinds of entities] is unable [by itself] to manage covering [them]; and the [Sage Lords of] men [who might be able to know all about bringing order to society] are unable [by themselves] to fully provide [the ten thousand kinds of entities].[11] Although they highly esteem taking negativity as [the basis of] usability, they are unable to complete negativity to make it [completely identical with] their [own] substance. As they are unable to complete negativity to make it [completely identical with] their [own] substance, they lose out on their being Great [in the absolute sense in which the Dao is Great].[12]

This is what [the text] talks of as, "once the Way has been lost, one will thereafter [resort to using the highest] receipt/capacity." As [the Great One] makes use of negativity, he obtains its [this use's] mother. Thus he is able to [bring it about] that without his exerting himself there is no entity that is not regulated.

> From here on downwards the mother of [this making] use [of the Way] is lost. [The rulers] are not able to [practice] non-interference, but value the broad effect [of kindliness].

Once unable to broadly affect [other beings by means of kind-
liness] they will value the correctness and straightforwardness
[of righteousness].

Once unable to [practice] the correctness and straightforwardness [of righteousness] they will value elaborate obei-
sances.

This is what [it means when the text] says:

"Once [the highest] capacity is lost, [one will] thereafter [resort to
using the highest] kindliness;

once [the highest] kindliness is lost, [one will] thereafter [resort
to the highest] sense of righteousness;

once [the highest] sense of righteousness is lost, [one will]
thereafter [resort to the highest] understanding of ritual."

IV.

It is a fact that what begins ritual has its start in truthfulness and credibility not being genuine, and the penetrating and simple not being clear
[anymore] [so that] all importance is given to [matters of] external [form],
and struggle breaks out about trifles. Kindliness and righteousness arise
from within, and, as acting on them already [generates] pretense, how
much less durability will attention to external accouterments have! That
is why [the text says], "Ritual [,however,] is [the result of the] wearing
thin of truthfulness and credibility, and [thus] the beginning of chaos"!
[Having] foreknowledge means having knowledge before others [have it]
and thus [belongs to] the category of "lower capacity."[13]

If [a ruler] exhausts his intelligence in order to create foreknowledge,	applies the powers of his knowl- edge in order to manage the manifold affairs,
he will, even if he gets the information, [only bring it about] that cunning- ness and craftiness become even more secretive.	even if he enriches his renown, [only bring it about] that genu- ineness and honesty become even more damaged.
	[The more] he labors, the more abstruse will affairs get.
[The more] efforts he makes, the more will order become entangled.	

Even if he exhausts
wisdom   and   knowledge

[as referred to in Laozi 19*],*
the damage [done to] the
people will [only] become
worse. If [the ruler, however]
"discards [his] own self" [as
Emperor Shun did][14] *and puts*
himself at the disposition of
the [other] entities, there will
be great prosperity without
[his] interfering; and if he
preserves the simple and un-
adorned, he will not need
regulations and statutes. It
is because [foreknowledge]
is obsessed with what the
former [the use of wisdom
and knowledge] might catch
and rejects what the latter
[discarding his own self]
preserves that [the text] says,
"Foreknowledge is [the
result] of the Way's becoming
an [external] ornament,and
[thus] the beginning of
stupid[ly violent government]"!
That is why, if only [the ruler]
would obtain the mother
bringing about the achieve-
ments,[15]

"the ten thousand kinds of entities | *the ten thousand kinds of affairs*
[as the Laozi 2.4 *says,] [would]* | *[would] persist without [his]*
come about without their being | *laboring.*[16]
given orders [by him],"[17] |

In making use [of the entities] he | *In regulating [affairs] he*
[would] not go by [their] shape. | *[would] not go by [their] name.*

Thus [his]
kindliness and [sense of] righteous- | *[understanding of] ritual and*
ness could radiate. | *respects could shine forth.*

If indeed he would
support them by means of the | *[, as the* Laozi 37.3 *says, with*
great Way, | *probable reference to the Sage,]*
 | *"quiet them down by means of*
 | *the Nameless,"*[18]

the [other] entities would have nothing they could value highly.

the ambitions would have nothing they could busy themselves about.

And if [then] each [entity] would bring to bear its true nature,

processes would [all] make use of their true essence,

> *the capacity of kindliness would be abundant,*

> *the practice of righteousness correct, and*

> *rituals and respects pure.*

If [, however,] he discards what supports them [the entities], makes use of their [the entities'] completed shape,

rejects what generates them [the processes], establishes their [the processes'] clarity,[19]

> *kindliness will turn into pretense,*

> *righteousness will turn into competition,*

> *and ritual will turn into struggle.*

That is why

> *the abundance of the capacity of kindliness cannot be brought about by making use of kindliness;*

> *the correctness of the practice of righteousness cannot be achieved by making use of righteousness;*

> *and the purity of rituals and respect cannot be effected by making use of ritual.*

By supporting them [the entities] by means of the Way

controlling them [the processes] by means of the mother

[a ruler would]

let [his kindliness and righteousness] radiate without [the other entities] having anything to value highly;

let [his understanding of ritual and respect] shine forth without [the ambitions] having anything to busy themselves about. Only by making use indeed of the Nameless, names will thereby be made straightforward!

*Only by making use indeed of the
Shapeless, shapes will thereby be
completed!*

If

the mother was kept to as the
means to maintain her [the
mother's] offspring,

the root was emulated as the
means of keeping up its [the
root's] outgrowth,

then the

shapes and names
[of the ten thousand entities]
would persist in their completeness and evil would not arise;

their [achievements'] and their [names'] beauty
greatness

would match Heaven's[20] and
the [transformation of the Way
into an external] "ornament"
[, as mentioned by the Laozi
here,] would not come about.

This is why [a ruler] should
not distance [himself] from
the mother.

not to lose the root.

Kindliness and righteousness
are generated by the mother,
but they should not be taken
as the mother! Shaped vessels
are made by the artisan, but
they should not be taken as
the artisan [i.e., confused with
the artisan].[21]

If [the ruler, however]

rejects their [the processes']
mother and makes use of her
offspring,

discards their [the things'] root
and handles its outgrowth, then indeed, as a name has
something that specifies it,

then indeed, as a shape has some-
thing that limits it, it will, even if it
maximizes its greatness, by necessity
have something that it does not
encompass.

it will, even if it [the name]
makes its beauty abundant, by
necessity have something worri-
some and painful.

[In short] as long as the
achievements depend on
interfering with them [the
entities], how should they
suffice as "residence" [for
the Great One or Sage as
mentioned in the main text]?

THE STRUCTURE OF *LAOZI* 38

Zhang 38 consists of four parts that follow different stylistic patterns. Part I is written in open IPS setting off 上德 and 下德 against each other. It has the form

I	a	b	(38.1, 38.2)
	a	b	(38.2, 38.2)

Parts II and III are made up of two parallel staircases consisting of three segments each. The corresponding segments in each part are openly linked. The key terms of both of these triple series form subsegments of 下德 in descending order. Part III, however, has four such segments, because it starts with the loss of the Dao, which itself is not a part of 下德, but of 上德. These two parts thus have to be read as inscribing themselves as subdivisions under the right segment above (下德), apart from the first sentence in Part IV, which describes the transition from 上德 to 下德

	a	b	(33.1, 33.2)
	a	b	(33.3, 33.4)
		c	(33.5)
		c	(33.6)
II	(a)	(b)	
	2		
3			
4			

III
        1

          2

            3

              4

Part IV returns to the binary structure of Part I, dealing however with those political strategies that are below 下德, namely, ritual and foresight. It defines the realm of political strategies with 德 from below as much as Part I had defined it from above. It is written in open IPS. As it is not based on the same a, b, and c as Part I, I will use x, y, and z. It has the form:

    x   y

       z   (That is why the Great Man . . .)

    x   y

       z

Wang Bi's commentary largely follows the IPS arrangement of the main text. *Zhang* 38 is a good example of the highly complex three-dimensional structural and argumentative arrangement of which IPS was capable.

The *zhang* is read as describing a historical and logical process of political degeneration, not a structure. The use of the staircase is well suited for this purpose. At the same time, the segmentation allows it to mark differences of quality between 上德 and 下德, on the one hand (as in Part I), and 德 and 亂, on the other hand, as in Part IV. Political order descends through three stages from the Dao through the various value-oriented political strategies of Parts II and III to the maintenance of power by social formality and cunning government devices devoid of any values.

Zhang 39

39.1 昔之得^{a}一者 (Base text: 傅奕古本)

　　昔始也一^{b}數之始而^{c}物之極也各是一物所以^{d}爲主也物各得此一以成
　　既成而舍一以居成居成則失其母故皆裂發歇竭蹷^{e}也 (Base text: 集註
　　本)

39.2 天得一以清地得一以寧神得一以靈谷^{f}得一以^{g}盈^{h,1}王侯^{i}得一以爲天下貞^{j}其
　　致之一也^k (Base text: 傅奕古本)

　　各以其一致此清寧靈盈貞^l (Base text: 集註本)

39.3 天^{m}無以^{n}清將恐裂^o (Base text: 傅奕古本)

　　用一以致清耳非用清以清也守一則清不失用清則恐裂也故爲功之母
　　不可舍也是以皆無用其功恐喪其本也 (Base text: 集註本)

---

^{a} Var.: 昔得 for 昔之得: 馬王堆 B.

^{b} Var.: 一者 for 一: 世說新語言語篇劉孝標注 AA20a. Support against the 者: Quotation in 文選遊天台山賦李善注 2.25b7: 一數之始.

^{c} Var.: 而 om.: 世說新語言語篇劉孝標注.

^{d} 物所以 for 物之生所以: 世說新語言語篇劉孝標注, AA20a; 慧達, 肇論疏, 834a.16.

^{e} 蹷 for 礩: 陸德明釋文 on *Laozi* 39.4.

^{f} Var.: 浴 for 谷: 馬王堆 A; 馬王堆 B.　^{g} Var.: 以 om.: 馬王堆 B.

^{h} 萬物得一以生 om.: 馬王堆 A; 馬王堆 B; 莊(嚴)遵, Shima Kuniō. Cf. note 2.

^{i} Var.: 侯王 for 王侯: 馬王堆 A; 馬王堆 B; Support for 王侯: quotation of this phrase in 韓康伯, 周易繫辭下注, in 樓宇烈, 王弼集校釋 II.557.

^{j} Var.: 正 for 貞: 馬王堆 A; 馬王堆 B. Support for 貞: Wang Bi comm. Var.: 而以爲正 for 以爲天下貞: 馬王堆 A

^{k} Var.: 其至也 for 其致之一也: 馬王堆 B. Var.: 其致之也 for 其致之一也: 馬王堆 A. Support for 一: Wang Bi comm.: 各以其一致此 …

^{l} 盈貞 for 貞盈生: Wagner. Cf. note 2, for elimination of 生. The inversion to 盈 [生] 貞 from 貞盈 [生]: 張之象本. Var.: 清寧貞 for 清寧靈盈貞: 世說新語言語篇劉孝標注 AA20a.

^{m} Var.: 胃天 for 天: 馬王堆 A; 馬王堆 B.

^{n} Var.: 毋已 for 無以: 馬王堆 A; 馬王堆 B.

^{o} Var.: 蓮 for 裂: 馬王堆 B.

39.4 地^p無以^q寧將恐發神^r無以^s靈將恐歇谷^t無以^u盈將恐竭^v王侯^w無以^x爲貞而貴高^y將恐蹶^z故^{aa}貴以賤爲本高^{ab}以下爲基是以^{ac}王侯^{ad}自謂^{ae}孤寡不穀^{af}是^{ag}其以賤爲本也非歟^{ah}故致^{ai}數譽^{aj}無譽^{ak}不欲^{al}琭琭^{am}若玉珞珞^{an}若石 (Base text: 傅奕古本)

清不能爲清盈不能爲盈皆有其母以存其形故清不足貴盈不足多貴在其母而母無貴形貴乃以賤爲本高乃以下爲基故致數譽乃無譽也玉石琭琭珞珞^{ao}體盡於形故不欲也 (Base text: 集註本)

39.1   That which [entities] attain as the [most] ancient is the One.

---

^p Var.: 胃地 for 地: 馬王堆 A.

^q Var.: 毋已 for 無以: 馬王堆 A (毋口); 馬王堆 B.

^r Var.: 胃神 for 地: 馬王堆 A.

^s Var.: 毋已 for 無以: 馬王堆 A ; 馬王堆 B (毋口).

^t Var.: 浴 for 谷: 馬王堆 A.   ^u Var.: 毋已 for 無以: 馬王堆 A ; 馬王堆 B.

^v 萬物以生將恐滅 om.: 馬王堆 A ; 馬王堆 B; Shima Kuniō, cf. note 2. Var.: 渴 for 竭: 馬王堆 A ; 馬王堆 B.

^w Var.: 胃侯王 for 王侯: 馬王堆 A. Var.: 侯王 for 王侯: 馬王堆 B.

^x Var.: 毋已 for 無以: 馬王堆 A ; 馬王堆 B.

^y Var.: 貴以高 for 爲貞而貴高: 馬王堆 A (貴口口); 馬王堆 B.

^z 蹶 for 蹷 (also in 范應元本): 陸德明釋文.

^{aa} Var.: 必貴而 for 貴: 馬王堆 A. Var.: 必貴 for 貴: 馬王堆 B.

^{ab} Var.: 必高矣而 for 高: 馬王堆 A ; 馬王堆 B.

^{ac} Var.: 夫是以 for 是以: 馬王堆 A ; 馬王堆 B.

^{ad} Var.: 侯王 for 王侯: 馬王堆 A ; 馬王堆 B.

^{ae} Var.: 胃 for 謂: 馬王堆 A (胃口); 馬王堆 B. Var.: 稱 for 謂: 范應元本.

^{af} Var.: 秦 for 穀: 馬王堆 A; 馬王堆 B.

^{ag} Var.: 此其賤 for 是以賤: 馬王堆 A ; 馬王堆 B.

^{ah} Var.: 賤之本與非也 for 賤爲本也非歟: 馬王堆 B. (馬王堆 A: 賤口口與非口).

^{ai} Var.: 至 for 致: 馬王堆 B.

^{aj} Var.: 與 for 譽: 馬王堆 A. Var.: 輿 for 譽: 馬王堆 B. Support for 譽: 陸德明釋文, Wang Bi comm. on loc. (in 集註本). The editor of the 四庫 claims to have seen another edition of the 陸德明釋文, which gives 輿.

^{ak} Var.: 與 for 譽: 馬王堆 A. Var.: 輿 for 譽: 馬王堆 B. See note aj.

^{al} Var.: 是故不欲 for 不欲: 馬王堆 A ; 馬王堆 B.

^{am} 琭琭 for 碌碌: 陸德明釋文; 范應元本. Var.: 禄禄 for 琭琭: 馬王堆 B.

^{an} 珞珞 for 落落 (also in 范應元本): 陸德明釋文. Var.: 硌硌 for 珞珞: 馬王堆 A ; 馬王堆 B.

^{ao} 珞珞 for 落落: 陸德明釋文; 張之象本.

*The "[most] ancient" is the beginning. The One is the beginning of the
numbers and the ultimate of the entities. In each case it is the One by
which the [great] entities [mentioned below, such as Heaven, Earth, and
the Spirits,] are dominated.*[1] *Each one of these entities attains this One for
its completing, but [if], having once completed, [each] would discard the
One in order to settle in [what is] completed, it [would], having [thus] settled in [its] completion, as a consequence, lose its mother [i.e., the One];
that is why [the text further down speaks of the danger of]*

[Heaven's] "being torn apart"

   [Earth's] "getting into commotion"

      [the spirit's] "becoming exhausted"

         [the valley's] "being drained"

            [and the dukes' and kings'] "being toppled."

39.2   As long as Heaven attains the One, it will be clear through it [the One].

As long as Earth attains the One, it will be calm through it [the One].

As long as the spirits attain the One, they will be efficacious
through it [the One].

As long as the valley attains the One, it will be full through it
[the One].

As long as the kings and dukes attain the One, they
will be the standard for All Under Heaven through it
[the One].

It is the One that brings these [clarity, calmness, and so forth] about.

*Each one of them comes through this One to such
clarity,*

   calmness,

      efficaciousness,

         fullness, and

            being the standard.

39.3   Once Heaven is not clear through [the One], it is in danger of being torn
apart.

*[Heaven] makes use of the One and thus achieves clarity, but does not
make use of [its intrinsic] clarity to achieve clarity. As long as it preserves
the One, [its] clarity will not be lost, but once it makes use of its [intrin-
sic] clarity [to achieve clarity] it "is in danger of being torn apart." That is*

why the mother bringing about these achievements [i.e., of clarity, etc.] is not to be discarded. That is why all [entities] that do not make use of her [the mother's] achievements [but of their own qualities] are in danger of losing their root.

39.4   Once Earth is not calm through [the One], it is in danger of getting into commotion.

Once the spirit is not efficacious through [the One], it is in danger of becoming exhausted.

Once the valley is not full through [the One], it is in danger of being drained.

Once the kings and dukes are not the standard through [the One] and thus esteemed and elevated, they are in danger of being toppled.[2]

Therefore to be esteemed takes [acting as if] being despised as [its] root, and to be elevated takes [acting as if] being lowly as [its] base.[3] If, therefore, the dukes and kings refer to themselves as "I lonely one," "I orphaned one," and "I needy one," is that not their taking being despised as the root?! That is why that which brings about manifold fame is [itself] without fame,[4] and [the dukes and kings] do not wish to be polished like jade and cut like stone.

[Heaven's] clarity is unable to bring about clarity nor can [the valley's] fullness bring about fullness. [The same is true for the achievements of the other entities mentioned]. For all of them [the different entities mentioned] it is their having their mother through which they preserve their [particular] form [e.g., clarity, calmness, etc.]. That is why [Heaven's] clarity [itself] does not qualify for high esteem and [the valley's] fullness does not qualify for being considered abundance. What [qualifies] for high esteem [in Heaven's clarity] is due to the mother, but the mother [herself] is without an estimable form. To "be esteemed" thus [,as the text claims for the dukes and kings,] indeed "takes [acting as if] being despised as its root," and "being elevated" "takes [acting as if] being lowly as the base." That is why [the text says], "That which brings about manifold fame is" indeed "[itself] without fame"! In polished jade and cut stone the substance is fully realized in [their] form. That is why [the text says,] "[The dukes and kings] do not wish [to be polished and cut like them]"!

THE STRUCTURE OF *LAOZI* 39

The chapter is written in open IPS. It has two explicitly parallel staircases at its core, framed by two general statements. These in fact refer to one element in the staircase series, the kings and dukes. Thus it is clear that the general purpose of the chapter lies in this construction in making applicable the c rule in the first line to the kings and dukes. The structure is:

				c		(39.1)
1						(39.2)
	2					(39.2)
		3				(39.2)
			4			(39.2)
				5		(39.2)
			c			(39.2)
1						(39.3)
	2					(39.4)
		3				(39.4)
			4			(39.4)
				5		(39.4)
			c			(39.4)
			c			(39.4)

Zhang 40

40.1 反者道之動ᵃ (Base text: 王弼注)

> 高以下爲基貴以賤爲本有以無爲用此其反也動皆之ᵇ 其所無則物通矣故曰反者道之動也 (Base text: 集註本)

40.2 弱者道之用ᶜ (Base text: 傅奕古本)

> 柔弱同通不可窮極 (Base text: 集註本)

ᵃ Var.: 反 (郭店 A: 返) 也者 (馬王堆 A: □□□) 道之動也 for 反者道之動: 郭店 A; 馬王堆 A; 馬王堆 B.

ᵇ Var.: 知 for 之: 張之象本.

ᶜ Var.: 弱也 (馬王堆 B: □□) 者道之用也 for 弱者道之用: 郭店 A; 馬王堆 A; 馬王堆 B.

40.3 天下之物生於有有生於無 (Base text: 傅奕古本)

天下之物皆以有爲生有之所始以無爲本將欲全有必反於無也 (Base text: 集註本)

40.1   He who acts by way of the negative opposite [i.e., the Sage] is the one who moves [in accordance with] the Way.[1]

That [, as Laozi 39.4 says,] "to be elevated takes [acting as if] being lowly as [its] base" and that [, as he says in the same section,] "to be esteemed takes [acting as if] being despised as [its] root"; [in short] that Entity takes negativity as that which [makes it] usable[2] means "acting by way of" its "negative opposite." Once his [the Sage Ruler's] moves all go towards[3] what is its [his actual status'] negation, the entities will [all] be penetrated [by the Dao]. That is why the text says: "He who acts by way of the negative opposite [i.e., the Sage] is the one who moves [in accordance with] the Way"!

40.2   He who is weak [i.e., the Sage] is the one who makes use of the Way.

Being soft and weak penetrates [the other entities] in likewise manner, without [oneself] being exhaustible.[4]

40.3   The entities of All Under Heaven have [their] life in [the realm of] Entity, but Entity has [its] life in negativity.

The entities of All Under Heaven [all] take [their being in the realm of] Entity as [the basis of their] life, [but] that which begins Entity takes negativity as the root.[5] In order to keep Entity complete, it has to be related back to negativity [as is done by the Sage].

Zhang 41

41.1 上士聞道勤能[a]行之 (Base text: 范應元本)

有志也 (Base text: 集註本)

---

[a] 勤能 for 勤而: Wang Bi comm. on *Laozi* 33.4 (強行者有志也): 勤能行之其志必獲故曰強行者有志矣. Support for 勤能: 郭店 B and 馬王堆 B: 菫能; three manuscripts from the 想爾 textual family (敦煌李榮本, 天寶神沙本, 次解本) also write 勤能. Var.: 菫能 for 勤能: 郭店 B; 馬王堆 B. Var.: 而勤 for 勤能: 傅奕古本.

41.2 中士聞道若存^b若亡下士聞道而^c大笑^d不^e笑不 足以爲道^f 故^g建言有之曰^h
(Base text: 傅奕古本)

　　建猶ⁱ立也 (Base text: 張之象本)

41.3 明道若昧^j (Base text: Wang Bi comm. on *Laozi* 58.10)

　　光而不耀 (Base text: 集註本)

41.4 夷道若^k纇^l (Base text: 傅奕古本)

　　纇坳^m也大夷之道因物之性不執平ⁿ以割物其平不見乃更反若纇坳^o也
(Base text: 集註本)

41.5 進道若^p退^q (Base text: 傅奕古本)

　　後其身而身先外其身而身存 (Base text: 集註本)

41.6 上德若谷^r (Base text: 傅奕古本)

　　不德其德 無所懷也 (Base text: 集註本)

---

^b Var.: 昏 for 若存: 郭店 B.　　　^c Var.: 而 om.: 郭店 B; 馬王堆 B.

^d Var.: 笑之 for 笑: 郭店 B; 馬王堆 B. Based on 莊遵, who also writes 笑之, Shima Kuniō assumes that Wang Bi's *Laozi* had 笑之. The case cannot be decided.

^e Var.: 弗 for 不: 郭店 B; 馬王堆 B.

^f Var.: 道矣 for 道: 郭店 B.　　　^g Var.: 是以 for 故: 郭店 B; 馬王堆 B.

^h Var.: 曰 om.: 郭店 B.　　　ⁱ Var.: 由 for 猶: 集註本.

^j Var.: 女孛 for 若昧: 郭店 B. Var.: 如費 for 若昧: 馬王堆 B.

^k Var.: 如 for 若: 馬王堆 A.　　　^l 纇 for 纇 (also in 馬王堆 B): 陸德明釋文.

^m Var.: 內 for 坳: 陸德明釋文.　　　ⁿ Var.: 平 for 乎: 張之象本.

^o Var.: 內 for 坳: 陸德明釋文, in analogy to previous note.

^p Var.: 如 for 若: 馬王堆 B.

^q Var. 范應元本 and 馬王堆 B invert the sequence of *Laozi* 41.4 and 41.5, writing 進 道若退 夷道若纇. Support for 夷道若纇 進道若退: 郭店 B; presence of this sequence in the 漢書 biography of Zhang Heng 張衡.

^r Var.: 如浴 for 若谷: 郭店 B; 馬王堆 B.

41.7 大白若ˢ黷ᵗ (Base text: 傅奕古本)

　　知其白守其黑大白然後乃得 (Base text: 集註本)

41.8 廣德若ᵘ不足 (Base text: 傅奕古本)

　　廣德不盈 廓ᵛ然無形不可滿也 (Base text: 集註本)

41.9 建德若ʷ偷ˣ (Base text: 傅奕古本)

　　偷匹也建德者因物自然不立不施故若偷匹 (Base text: 集註本)

41.10 質眞若渝ʸ (Base text: 范應元本)

　　質眞者不矜其眞故渝 (Base text: 集註本)

41.11 大方無隅ᶻ (Base text: Wang Bi comm. on *Laozi* 58.7)

　　方而不割故無隅也 (Base text: 集註本)

41.12 大器晚ᵃᵃ成 (Base text: 傅奕古本)

　　大器成天下不持全別故必晚成也 (Base text: 集註本)

　　ˢ Var.: 如 for 若: 郭店 B; 馬王堆 B.

　　ᵗ Var.: 辱 for 黷: 郭店 B; 馬王堆 B. Support for 黷: Wang Bi comm. read 黷 as 黑 in 知其白守其黑.

　　ᵘ Var.: 如 for 若: 郭店 B; 馬王堆 B.

　　ᵛ 廓 for 霩: 張之象本. Support for 廓: in the 集註本 version of Wang Bi on *Laozi* 20.4 我廓然無形之可名, which comments 我廓兮. The text writes 廓.

　　ʷ Var.: 如 for 若: 郭店 B; 馬王堆 B.

　　ˣ 偷 for 媮: Wang Bi comm.: 偷匹也.

　　ʸ Var.: 輸 for 渝: 傅奕古本. Var.: 愉 for 渝: 郭店 B.

　　ᶻ Var.: 禺 for 隅: 郭店 B; 馬王堆 B.

　　ᵃᵃ Var.: 曼成 for 晚成: 郭店 B. Var.: 免 for 晚: 馬王堆 B.

41.13 大音希^{ab}聲 (Base text: 范應元本)

聽之不聞名曰希不可得聞之音也有聲則有分有分則不宮而商矣分則
不能統衆故有聲者非大音也 (Base text: 集註本)

41.14 大^{ac}象無形^{ad} (Base text: 傅奕古本)

有形則亦^{ae}有分 有分者不溫則涼^{af}不炎則寒^{ag}故象而^{ah}形者非大象
(Base text: 集註本)

41.15 道隱^{ai}無名 夫唯^{aj}道善貸^{ak}且善成^{al} (Base text: 范應元本)

凡此諸大^{am}皆是道之所成也在象則爲大象而大象無形在音則爲大音
而大音希聲夫道物^{an}以之成而不見其形^{ao}故隱而無名也貸之非唯供^{ap}
其乏而已一貸之則足以永終其德故曰善貸也成之不加^{aq}機匠之裁無
物而不濟其形故曰善成 (Base text: 集註本)

---

^{ab} Var.: 稀 for 希: 傅奕古本. Support for 希: Wang Bi comm.; Wang Bi in *LZWZLL* 1.15: 爲音也則希聲. Var.: 祇聖 for 希聲: 郭店 B.

^{ac} Var.: 天 for 大: 郭店 B; 馬王堆 B.

^{ad} Var.: 刑 for 形: 馬王堆 B.

^{ae} 則亦 for 則: 文選顏延之應昭讌曲水作詩李善注 20.30a6.

^{af} 涼 for 炎: 文選顏延之應昭讌曲水作詩李善注 20.30a6.

^{ag} Var.: 不炎則寒 om.: 文選顏延之應昭讌曲水作詩李善注 20.30a6.

^{ah} Var.: 者 for 而: 文選顏延之應昭讌曲水作詩李善注 20.30a6.

^{ai} Var.: 襃 for 隱: 馬王堆 B.

^{aj} 唯 for 惟 (also in 傅奕古本): Wang Bi passim; 馬王堆 B.

^{ak} Var.: 始 for 貸: 馬王堆 B.

^{al} Var.: 成 for 善成: 傅奕古本. Support for 善成: Wang Bi comm. : 故曰善成; 馬王堆 B.

^{am} 大 for 善 (also in 張之象本): 東條一堂. Support: Wang Bi context 在象則爲大象而 大象無形在音則爲大音而大音希聲. In similar summing-up statements in Wang Bi's comments on *Laozi* 15.3, 29.4, and 45.6, the core term from the *Laozi* is taken up each time.

^{an} 夫道物 for 物: 文選應詔讌曲水作詩李善注 20.30a7, quoting Wang Bi.

^{ao} Var.: 其成形 for 其形: 張之象本. Support against the 成: quotation from Wang Bi in 文選應詔讌曲水作詩李善注: 不見形; Wang Bi on *Laozi* 14.2 欲言有邪而不見其形 and Wang Bi on *Laozi* 6.1 欲言存邪 則不見其形. Var.: 形 for 其形: 文選應詔讌曲水作 詩李善注.

^{ap} Var.: 恭 for 供: 陸德明釋文. Lu also indicates that one manuscript writes 供.

^{aq} Var.: 如 for 加: 張之象本.

41.1 When a gentleman of highest [caliber, that is, a Sage] hears of the Way, he will practice it to the utmost of his capacities.[1]

That is, "He will [, as Laozi 33.3 says about "him who powerfully practices the Way,"] have his will."

41.2 When a gentleman of mediocre [caliber] hears of the Way, [he is unsure] whether it exists or not. When a gentleman of inferior [caliber] hears of the Way, he greatly ridicules it. Were he not ridiculing it, it would not qualify to be taken for the Way. That is why there are sayings which [I] establish [about the Way] saying:

"[I] establish" is like "[I] set up."

41.3 ["]It is the [Sage's] Way of enlightening to be well-nigh dark.["]

[The Sage, according to Laozi 58.10,] "enlightens but does not investigate [dark and hidden actions of the populace]."

41.4 ["]It is the [Sage's] Way of evening out [the ten thousand kinds of entities] to [leave things] well-nigh uneven.["]

"Uneven" is like "bumpy." The [Sage's] Way of bringing about Great Evenness is to go by the nature of entities[2] and not to hold onto [the ideal of] equalization by way of "cutting off from" the entities [i.e., to regulate them according to the model of the "Great Regulator," in Laozi 28.7, who regulates "without any cutting-off"]. As the equalization by him is not visible, it is inversely [as the text says] "well-nigh uneven."

41.5 ["]It is the [Sage's] Way of advancing to well-nigh retreat.["]

[The Sage, according to Laozi 7.2] "puts his own person in the background and [achieves in this way] that his own person comes to be to the fore; disregards his own person and achieves in this way] that his own person will last."

41.6 ["]It is [the Sage's] highest capacity to be well-nigh a valley.["]

He will not take his capacity to be [any particular] capacity, and has in nothing a personal interest.[3]

41.7 ["]It is [the Sage's achievement of being All Under Heaven's] Great Whiteness to be well-nigh black.["]

[He who] "knows that as its [All Under Heaven's] whiteness he [has to] keep to [being] its blackness" [, as the Laozi says in 28.2,] will as a consequence achieve [being] the "Great Whiteness."[4]

41.8 ["]It is [the Sage's] capacity of broadness to be well-nigh insufficient.["]

[His] capacity for broadness does not fill up. Vacant it is and without shape,⁵ [and thus] it is impossible to fill it up.

41.9   ["]It is [the Sage's] capacity to establish [things] to be well-nigh common.["]

"Common" means "ordinary."⁶ Someone with the capacity to establish [things like the Sage] goes by the entities' That-which-is-of-itself-what-it-is, and neither sets [things] up nor does he initiate them.⁷ That is why [the text says] he is "well-nigh common"!

41.10   ["]It is [the Sage's] true essence of simplicity to be well-nigh dirtied.["]⁸

Someone with the true essence of simplicity [like the Sage] "does not brag" about his true essence.⁹ That is why [the text says] it is "dirtied."

41.11   ["]The Great Squaring is without corners!["]¹⁰

[As the Laozi *58.7 says: "The Sage] makes square but does not trim [others]." That is why [the text says] it "is without corners"!*

41.12   ["][The Great Instrument does complete in the nick of time!["]

In completing All Under Heaven, the Great Instrument does not completely go through all particulars.¹¹ That is why by necessity [,as the text says,] it "completes in the nick of time"!

41.13   ["]The Great Sound has an inaudible tone!["]

[As Laozi *14.1 says,] "That which [I] do not hear when listening for it [I] call 'inaudible.'" It [the Great Sound] thus is a sound one is unable to hear. Once there is a [particular] tone, it will have specifications, and, if it has specifications, it will [let sound forth the note] shang, if it does not [let sound forth the note] gong.¹² Being specific it could [in this case] not encompass the entire multitude [of notes]. That is why that which has taken on a specific tone is not the Great Sound!¹³*

41.14   ["]The Great Image is without form!["]

If something has form, then it will also have specifications. That which has specifications will be cooling if it does not warm, and will be cold if it is not hot. That is why an image that has taken on form is not the Great Image!¹⁴

41.15   [In short, all these "established sayings" mean to say:] The Way is hidden and nameless. In fact [, however,] it is only the Way that is good at providing as well as good at completing.

Generally spoken, all these "great" [things] are made up by the Way. Among the images, [the Way] is the Great Image, but "the Great Image is without form;" among the sounds, it is the Great Sound, but the "Great Sound has an inaudible tone." As to the Way, the entities are completed by it [the Way], but they do not see its form; that is why [the text says the Way] "is hidden" and "nameless"!

When [the Way] is "providing" for them [the entities], he is not just supplementing their deficiencies, but [his] one provision for them is sufficient for the ultimate completion of their capacity. That is why [the text] says [the Way] is "good at providing"! When [the Way] is "completing" them [the entities], it is not [simply] contributing the [particular] trimmings of a craftsman, but there is no entity that does not have its form completed. That is why [the text] says [the Way is] "good at completing"!

THE STRUCTURE OF *LAOZI* 41

Laozi 41 consists of three parts, the introduction up to the "established sayings" in 41.2, the series of these sayings up to 41.14, and an authorial comment summing up these sayings in 41.15. The problem lies in the "established sayings." They are twelve in number. The last four form a formally distinct group. This leaves eight, all of which have the *ruo* 若. It is to be expected that these would form two groups of four in a parallel staircase, and that these two groups would again be taken up in the same sequence by the last group of four that deals with the "great" ones. For the first two groups the evidence for parallelism is good and in my view incontrovertible. The *ming* 明 in 41.3 is linked in the commentary to the investigative activities of the state, frequently attacked as counterproductive by Wang Bi. The parallel in 41.7 with the "Great Whiteness" refers to the same phenomenon. The second pair, 41.4 and 41.8, is loosely linked through the commentary; 41.4 refers to a passage saying that the Sage does "nothing for himself," while the *ying* 盈 in the commentary to 41.8 might refer to the Great Filling, *da ying* 大盈, in *Laozi* 45.2, which according to Wang Bi means that it "gives in adaptation to the entities, and there is none of them that it loves and respects [in particular]." The link, however, is not very solid. The link between 41.5 and 41.9 is again loose, and based on content and position. The last pair, 41.6 and 41.10, again are linked through statements that the Sage is not "taking his capacity to be [any particular] capacity" in the first, and that he "does not brag about his true essence" in the second commentary. The relationship of the two series remains a problem, as they seem more or less to repeat each other. Compared to other *zhang*, Wang Bi gives little information about the structural links between these two groups. He is completely silent about the relationship of these two lots of four sentences with the third lot. The link is not evident from the text, and the commentary gives no help. Structurally, however, all indicators are there that there should be such a link. I have left the puzzle in place and hope that other scholars may come up with a solution. As far as I can ascertain, the structure looks as follows (with the last four phrases nonassigned):

x			(41.1)
	y		(41.2)
		z	(41.2)
	c	("establish sayings")	(41.2)
1			(41.3)
	2		(41.4)
		3	(41.5)
			4	(41.6)
1			(41.7)
	2		(41.8)
		3	(41.9)
			4	(41.10)
	1		(41.11)
	2		(41.12)
	3		(41.13)
	4		(41.14)
	c		(41.15)

Zhang 42

42.1 道生一¹一生二二生三三生萬物萬物負陰而裹陽沖ᵃ氣以爲和人ᵇ之所惡唯ᶜ
孤寡不穀ᵈ而王侯ᵉ,²以自稱ᶠ也故物ᵍ或損ʰ之而益或ⁱ益之而損ʲ (Base text: 傅奕
古本)

> 萬物萬形其歸一也何由致一由於無也由ᵏ無乃一一可謂無已謂之一
> 豈得無言乎有言有一非二如何有一有二遂ˡ生乎三從無之有數盡乎
> 斯過此以往非道之流故萬物之生吾知其主雖有萬ᵐ形沖氣一焉百姓
> 有心異國殊風而王侯得一者主焉ⁿ以一爲主一何可舍愈多愈遠ᵒ損則
> 近之損之至盡乃得其極既謂之一猶乃至三況本不一而道可近乎損之
> 而益豈虛言也 (Base text: 張之象本)

42.2 人之所教亦我教人ᵖ (Base text: 莊遵指歸本)³

> 我之教人�q非強使人從之也而用夫自然舉其至理順之必吉違之必凶

ᵃ Var.: 中 for 沖: 馬王堆 A. Var.: 盅 for 沖: 范應元本.

ᵇ Var.: 天下 for 人: 馬王堆 A.

ᶜ 唯 for 惟: Wang Bi passim.　　　ᵈ Var.: 橐 for 穀: 馬王堆 A; 馬王堆 B.

ᵉ Var.: 王公 for 王侯: 馬王堆 A; 馬王堆 B.

ᶠ Var.: 名 for 稱: 馬王堆 A. Var.: 謂 for 稱: 范應元本.

ᵍ Var.: 勿 for 故物: 馬王堆 A.

ʰ Var.: 敚 for 損: 馬王堆 A. Var.: 云 for 損: 馬王堆 B.

ⁱ Var.: 或 om.: 馬王堆 A (或敚之□□□之而); from the length of the lacuna, 馬王堆
B probably also omitted this 或.

ʲ Var.: 敚 for 損: 馬王堆 A. Var.: inversion of the phrase sequence 或損之而益 或益之
而損 to 或益之而損 [或] 損之而益: 馬王堆 B, because last word in lacuna is 益. Var.: 云
for 損: 馬王堆 B.

ᵏ Var.: 因 for 由: 集註本.　　　ˡ Var.: 子 for 遂: 集註本.

ᵐ Var.: 主 for 萬: 集註本.

ⁿ 而王侯得一者主焉 for 而得一者王侯主焉: 陶鴻慶. Support: Wang Bi comm. on
Laozi 10.6 所謂道常無爲 侯王若能守則萬物自化. The 若能 here supports the statement
that only those among the kings and dukes who attain the One are able to truly be the
lord.

ᵒ Var.: 一何可今先多愈遠 for 一何可舍 愈多愈遠: 集註本.

ᵖ 教人 for 教之: 馬王堆 A; 傅奕古本; 范應元本. Var.: 故人□□□□夕議而教人 for
人之所教亦我教人: 馬王堆 A. Var.: 人之所以教我 (范應元本 adds 而) 亦我之所以教人
for 人之所教亦我教人: 傅奕古本; 范應元本.

�q 我之教人 for 我之: 陶鴻慶.

故人相教違之必自取其凶也亦如我之教人勿違之也 (Base text: 集註本)

42.3 強梁[r]者不得其死吾將以爲教父[s] (Base text: 傅奕古本)

強梁則必不得其死人相教爲強梁則必如我之教人不當爲強梁也舉其強梁不得其死以教耶若云[t]順吾教之必吉也故得其違教之徒適可以爲教父也 (Base text: 張之象本)

42.1   The Way generates the One.[1] The One generates the two. The two generates the three. The three generates the ten thousand entities. The ten thousand entities [might] carry the Yin on their back [or] embrace the Yang,
but they take the ether of emptiness as their harmonizing [factor]. What
people abhor is indeed being orphaned, lonely, and needy, but kings and
dukes refer to themselves with these [terms]. That is why entities are either
increased as a consequence of their being reduced, or reduced as a consequence of their being increased.

*What the ten thousand forms of the ten thousand kinds of entities go
back to is the One. On the basis of what is the One brought about? On
the basis of negativity. As it is on the basis of negativity that there is the
One, is it possible to call the One negativity? As it is already[2] called the
One, how could one manage to remain without a word [namely, the word
One]? As there are both the word and the One, how could they not be
two? Once there is both the One and the two, the three is generated as
a consequence. The existing numbers coming from negativity end at this
point [i.e., with number three]; from the point of going beyond this [all
further entities] do not belong anymore of the realm of the Way.[3] That is
why, with regard to the generation of the ten thousand kinds of entities,
one[4] is able to know their master, [because], although they [the entities]
have ten thousand [different] forms, the[ir] "ether of emptiness" is one.
The Hundred Families hold on to their [variegated] ambitions,[5] different
states have distinct customs, but those of the kings or dukes who attain
the One are [their] lord.[6] As they [the dukes and kings] take the One as
[the entities'] master, how can this One be dismissed [by them]? The more
they have, the further they get away [from the One],[7] while as a consequence of reduction they get closer to it; once reduction has reached the
extreme, then they will attain this Ultimate [of entities mentioned in the
commentary on Laozi 39.1]. As by speaking of it as the One, one already
gets to three, how much less could one get closer to the Way if the root*

---

[r] Var.: 故強良 for 強梁: 馬王堆 A.

[s] 教父 for 學父 (also in 馬王堆 A; 范應元本): Wang Bi comm.: 可以爲教父也.

[t] Var.: 以教即吉云 for 以教耶 若云: 集註本.

*was not the One? How [then] can [the Laozi's statement about the enti-
ties' being] "increased as a consequence of their being reduced, or reduced
as a consequence of their being increased" be empty chatter?*

42.2   What other people teach, I also teach other people.

*My teaching of other people does not consist in forcing them to follow,
but in making use of [their] That-which-is-of-itself-what-it-is. [I] take up
their highest ordering principle [and teach that,] following it, they will
necessarily enjoy luck, [while] deviating from it, they will necessarily suffer misfortune. That is why other people's teaching each other to deviate
from it [with the result] that they necessarily draw their own misfortune
upon themselves, is like my teaching them not to deviate from it [which
will necessarily bring them luck and thus positively teach them the same
lesson others will teach negatively].*[8]

42.3   Those who are violent and brutal will not meet their [natural] death. I
intend to make them teachers.

*Being violent and brutal they will by necessity not meet their [natural]
death. Other people's teaching each other to act violently and brutally
with the consequence that they by necessity will not meet their [natural]
death is like my teaching others not to act violently and brutally [because
what they positively learn from me, they learn negatively from the consequences of the others' teaching]. [My] pointing out how the violent and
brutal do not meet their [natural] death by way of teaching [the others]
is as if [I] said that those following my teaching will necessarily be lucky.
That is why it is possible that these [violent and brutal] fellows who deviate from [my] teaching are appropriately taken [by me] as teachers [by
their negative example].*

Zhang 43

43.1 天下之至柔馳騁於ª天下之至ᵇ堅無有ᶜ入於無閒ᵈ (Base text: 范應元本)

氣無所不入水無所不出ᵉ (Base text: 集註本)

ª Var.: 于 for 於: 馬王堆 A. Var.: 馳騁乎 for 馳騁於: 馬王堆 B. Var.: 馳騁 for 馳騁
於: 傅奕古本.

ᵇ Var.: 致 for 至: 馬王堆 A.

ᶜ 無有 for 出於無有(also in 傅奕古本): Wang Bi comm. on *Laozi* 43.2 treats 無有 as
a noun parallel to 至柔 in 無有不可窮 至柔不可折.

ᵈ Inclusion of 無有入於無閒 in *Laozi* 43.1: Wagner. Support: Wang Bi comm. takes
up the term 入, while Wang Bi comm. on *Laozi* 43.2 does not specifically deal with 無有入
於無閒 but treats it on an equal footing with 至柔.

ᵉ Var.: 出於經 for 出: 張之象本.

43.2 吾ᶠ是以知無爲之有益也ᵍ (Base text: 傅奕古本)

虛無柔弱ʰ無所不通ⁱ無有不可窮 至柔不可折ʲ以此推之故知無爲之有益也ᵏ¹ (Base text: 集註本)

43.3 不言之教無爲之益天下希及ˡ之矣ᵐ (Base text: 傅奕古本)

夫孰能過此哉² (Base text: 集解本)

43.1	The softest of All Under Heaven swiftly gets through the hardest of All Under Heaven.	That which has nothing penetrates into that which has no gap.
		For ether there is nothing that it does not penetrate;
	for water there is nothing that it does not get through.	
43.2		From these [two] I surmise that non-interference brings benefits.
		There is nothing that
		the empty and negative
		as well as the
	soft and weak	
		do not penetrate.
		That which is without entity is inexhaustible;
	the softest cannot be broken.	
		He is extrapolating from these [two]; that is why [the Laozi says] [I] "surmise"

ᶠ Var.: 五 for 吾: 馬王堆 A.　　ᵍ Var.: 益 for 益也: 范應元本.

ʰ Var.: 柔弱虛無 for 虛無柔弱: 取善集.

ⁱ Var.: 虛無柔弱 無所不通 om.: 集解本.

ʲ Var.: 至柔不可折 無有不可窮 for 無有不可窮 至柔不可折: 集解本.

ᵏ Var.: 知無爲之道 有益於物 for 知無爲之有益也: 集解本. Cf. note 1.

ˡ Var.: 能及 for 及: 馬王堆 A.

ᵐ Var.: 及之 for 及之矣: 范應元本.

that "non-interference brings benefits" for [the other entities]!

43.3 As to the teaching without words and the benefits of non-interference, there is little in All Under Heaven to get that far.

[That is,] who could surpass this?

THE STRUCTURE OF *LAOZI* 43

Wang Bi constructs for the first two phrases a parallelism of content not matched by a parallelism in grammar, number of characters, or the like. Accordingly, the chapter is not written in IPS, and the structural writing is designed merely to link related passages optically in the way Wang Bi designed these links.

Zhang 44

44.1 名與身孰親 (Base text: 傅奕古本)

尚名好高其身必疏 (Base text: 集註本)

44.2 身與貨孰多 (Base text: 傅奕古本)

貪貨無厭其身必少 (Base text: 集註本)

44.3 得與亡孰病 (Base text: 傅奕古本)

得名利ª而亡其身何者爲病也 (Base text: 集註本)

44.4 是故ᵇ甚愛必大費多藏必厚亡 (Base text: 傅奕古本)

甚愛不與物通多藏不與物散求之者多攻之者衆爲物所病故大費厚亡也 (Base text: 集註本)

ª 名利 for 多利: 魏源. The 多利 would only refer back to 貨. Given the summary nature of this third phrase, it should refer to both issues, 名 and 貨.

ᵇ Var.: 是故 om.: 郭店 A; 馬王堆 A.

44.5 知ᶜ足不辱知止不殆可以長久 (Base text: 傅奕古本)

44.1   When fame is joined to the person,[1]   When the person is joined by   44.2
        which [of the two] does [in fact]   goods, which [of the two] is [in
        become dearer?   fact] increased?
        [Fame, of course.][2]   [The goods, of course.]

        When fame is esteemed and high   *When goods are craved for*
        position coveted, it will inevitably   *without satiety, it will inevitably*
        be one's person that will be   *be one's person that will be*
        neglected.   *diminished.*

44.3   If [in this manner] getting
                        [more fame and goods] and
                        losing [with regard to one's
                        person] come together, who
                        is it [after all] that causes
                        the affliction [done to one's
                        person? The others in their
                        envy, of course].

                        [This means], if one gets fame
                        and profit, but loses out in one's
                        person, who is it [after all] that
                        causes the affliction?

44.4   That is why

        too much craving [for fame]   too much hoarding [of goods]
        inevitably leads to great expen-   inevitably leads to vast losses.
        diture;

        Too much craving [for fame means]   *Too much hoarding [of goods*
        that one does not have interaction   *means] that one does not*
        with the other entities.   *disperse them among the other*
                                                       entities.

                        As [, however,]

        those who strive after him [who is   *those who attack, him [who has*
        infatuated with fame] are many,   *hoarded the goods] are great in*
                                                       number,

                        it is through the other entities
                        that affliction is brought upon
                        him. That is why [the text speaks
                        of]

──

ᶜ Var.: 故知 for 知: 郭店 A; 馬王堆 A.

"great expenditure" and　　　　　*"vast losses."*

44.5　　　　　　　　　[Consequently, it is he]

who knows how to be satisfied
[with what goods he has] that
will have no loss!

who knows how to halt [the
craving for ever greater fame]
that will be without danger!

[In this way] it is possible

to excel　　　　　and　　　　　last long.

THE STRUCTURE OF *LAOZI* 44

Laozi 44 is written in closed IPS with the regular variant abba. A detailed analysis is given in my *The Craft of a Chinese Commentator*, pp. 82-86. Fan Yingyuan, *Laozi Daode jing guben jizhu*, 2:16a (p. 46a), has spelled out the connections within this *zhang* clearly and explicitly in his commentary. His solutions for this piece of closed IPS have turned out to be exceedingly well founded. The structure of *Laozi* 44 contains one inversion abba. It is:

a	b		(44.1, 44.2)
		c	(44.3)
a	b		(44.4, 44.4)
	b		(44.5)
a			(44.5)
a	b		(44.5, 44.5)

Zhang 45

45.1 大成若缺其用不弊ᵃ (Base text: 傅奕古本)

隨物而成不爲一象故若缺也¹ (Base text: 張之象本)

ᵃ Var.: 幣 for 弊: 郭店 B; 馬王堆 A.

45.2 大盈若沖[b]其用不窮[c] (Base text: Wang Bi comm. 大盈 . . . 若沖; for second half: 傅奕古本)

大盈充足隨物而與無所愛矜故若沖也 (Base text: 集註本)

45.3 大直若[d]屈[e] (Base text: Wang Bi comm. on *Laozi* 58.9)

隨物而直直不在一[f]故若屈也 (Base text: 集註本)

45.4 大巧若[g]拙 (Base text: 傅奕古本)

大巧因自然以成器不造為異端故若拙也 (Base text: 集註本)

45.5 大辯若訥[h] (Base text: 傅奕古本)

大辯因物而言 己[i]無所造 故若訥也 (Base text: 張之象本)

45.6 躁[j]勝[k]寒[l]靜[m]勝熱[n]知清靜[o]為[p]天下正 (Base text: Wang Bi comm.: 躁 . . . 勝寒

[b] Var.: 大滿若盅 for 大盈若沖: 傅奕古本; 范應元本. Support for 大盈: Wang Bi comm.; 馬王堆 A; 馬王堆 B. Var.: 濡 for 沖: 馬王堆 A. Var.: 如沖 for 若沖: 馬王堆 B.

[c] Var.: 窵 for 窮: 馬王堆 A.   [d] Var.: 如 for 若: 馬王堆 A.

[e] 屈 for 詘 (also in 馬王堆 A; 范應元本): Wang Bi comm., 陸德明釋文.

[f] Var.: 在己 for 在一: 取善集. Support for 在一: Parallel with Wang Bi on *Laozi* 45.1 隨物而成不為一象; Wang Bi comm. on *Laozi* 58.9 以直導物令去其僻而不以直激拂於物 也所謂大直若屈也 quotes this *Laozi* passage with 直, referring to some unified standard, not to one's "own" standard. However, 服部南郭 and Hatano Tarō support 在己.

[g] Var.: 如 for 若: 馬王堆 A.

[h] Var.: 大羸如炳 for 大辯若訥: 馬王堆 A. 馬王堆 B has a lacuna of seven characters for this item followed by 紬. This means that it has a further four-character phrase here. Var.: 大成若詘 for 大辯若訥: 郭店 B.

[i] Var.: 已 for 己: 集註本.

[j] Var.: 臭 for 躁: 郭店 B; 馬王堆 B. Var.: 趮 for 躁: 馬王堆 A.

[k] Var.: 朕 for 勝: 馬王堆 B.   [l] Var.: 蒼 for 寒: 郭店 B.

[m] Var.: 靚 for 靜: 馬王堆 A. Var.: 青 for 靜: 郭店 B. Var.: 靖 for 靜: 傅奕古本.

[n] Var.: 炅 for 熱: 馬王堆 A.

[o] 知清 for 清: 傅奕古本; 范應元本. Support for 知: Wang Bi comm.: 以此推之 (則清 靜為天下正也). Cf. Wang Bi comm. on *Laozi* 43.2, where 以此推之故知無為之有益也 comments on a *Laozi* phrase 吾是以知無為之有益也, that is 以此推之, is also linked to a 知 in the text. Var.: 請靚 for 知清靜: 馬王堆 A. Var.: 靖 for 靜: 傅奕古本.

[p] Var.: 可以為 for 為: 馬王堆 A. Var.: 以為 for 為: 傅奕古本; 范應元本.

靜 . . . 勝熱 . . . 清靜 爲天下正 with 傅奕古本 for the 知)

躁罷[q]然後[r]勝寒靜無爲以勝熱以此推之則清靜爲天下正也靜則全物之眞躁則犯物之性故唯[s]清靜乃得如上諸大也 (Base text: 張之象本)

45.1 [It is the mark of] the Great Completion to be as if scattered. Its application does not wear it out.

It completes in adjustment to the entities, and is not one single image. That is why [the text says it is] "as if scattered."

45.2 [It is the mark of] the Great Filling to be as if empty. Its use does not exhaust it.

The Great Filling is utterly sufficient. It gives in adaptation to the entities, and there is none of them that it loves and respects [in particular]. That is why [the text says that it is] "as if empty."

45.3 [It is the mark of] the Great Straightening to be as if crooked.

It straightens in adaptation to the entities, and its straightening does not go by one single [standard]. That is why [the text says it is] "as if crooked."

45.4 [It is the mark of] the Great Skillfulness to be as if clumsy.

The Great Skillfulness adapts to That-which-is-of-itself-what-it-is [of the entities] in order to complete artifacts, and it does not contrive special features. That is why [the text says that it is] "as if clumsy."

45.5 [It is the mark of] the Great Eloquence to be as if blurting out.

The Great Eloquence speaks in adaptation to the entities, and there is nothing it makes up by itself. That is why [the text says it is] "as if blurting out."

45.6 [From the way] in which

bustling activity [ends up] maximizing cold

calmness [ends up] maximizing heat

[I] know that pure calmness is the correct regulator for All Under Heaven.

---

[q] Var.: 罷 om.: 集註本.

[r] Var.: 後能 for 後: 集註本. (This 能 might be a corrupted leftover from the missing 罷.)

[s] 唯 for 惟: 集註本.

*After the end of bustling activity
cold will be at its maximum;*

*being calm and without interfer-
ence is the means to maximize
heat.*

*Extrapolating from this,
I know that [as the text
says] "[Only a ruler's] pure
calmness is the correct
regulator for All Under
Heaven."*

*Being calm keeps intact the true
essence of entities.*

*Bustling activity contra-
venes the nature of entities.*[1]

*That is why only [he who has
achieved] pure calmness*[2] *will
indeed attain the above "Great"
[things and thus become the
correct regulator for All Under
Heaven].*

THE STRUCTURE OF *LAOZI* 45

In his comments on *Laozi* 45.6, Wang Bi unfolds two phrases from the *Laozi* text on "movement" and "calmness" into a commentary structured in IPS. In the *Laozi* text itself, no interlocking elements occur.

Zhang 46

46.1 天下有道却ᵃ走馬以糞ᵇ (Base text: 范應元本)

天下有道知足知止無求於外各修其內而已故却ᶜ走馬以治田糞也ᵈ
(Base text: 集註本)

ᵃ Var.: 郤 for 却: 傅奕古本. Support for 却: 陸德明釋文.

ᵇ Var.: 播 for 糞: 傅奕古本. Support for 糞: 陸德明釋文.

ᶜ Var.: 郤 for 却: 張之象本.

ᵈ Var.: 天下有道 修於內而已故却走馬以糞田 for 天下有道知足知止無求於外各修其內而已故却走馬以治田糞也: 文選張景陽七命李善注 35.21b7.

46.2 天下ᵉ無道戎馬生於郊 (Base text: 傅奕古本)

貪欲無厭不修其內各求於外故戎馬生於郊也 (Base text: 集註本)

46.3 罪莫大於ᶠ可欲ᵍ 禍ʰ莫大於ⁱ不知足咎莫憯於欲得故ʲ知足之足ᵏ常ˡ足矣 (Base text: 傅奕古本)

46.1　　When All Under Heaven has the Way, riding horses are kept back for [transporting] dung.

> *When All Under Heaven has the Way, he [a Sage Ruler, as the* Laozi *44.5 says] "knows how to be satisfied [with what goods he has]" and "knows how to halt [the craving for ever greater fame]," and there is no striving for [things] outside but each and everyone just takes care of his internal matters. That is why [the text says] "riding horses would be kept back for" managing the dung on the fields!*

46.2　　When All Under Heaven is without the Way, war horses are bred at the borders.

> *[When] cravings and desires are without restraint, no one takes care of his internal matters, but each and everyone strives for [things] outside.[1] That is why [the text says] "war horses are bred at the borders"!*

46.3　　There is no greater crime than [as a ruler to show things that] may be desired.[2] [In particular,] there is no greater calamity than [a ruler who does] not to know how to be satisfied [and instead displays his wealth in material goods], and there is no greater disaster than [a ruler's] desire to achieve [renown].[3] That is why the satisfaction of [a ruler] who knows how to be satisfied [provides] eternal satisfaction.

ᵉ Var.: 天下 om.: 馬王堆 B.

ᶠ Var.: 厚乎 for 大於: 郭店 A. Var.: 於 om.: 馬王堆 B.

ᵍ Var.: 罪莫大於可欲 om.: 陸德明釋文. Lu adds that a Heshang gong text had this passage. All other members of Wang Bi's textual family have the passage. Shima Kuniō accepts it. Var.: 甚欲 for 可欲: 郭店 A.

ʰ Var.: 憨 for 禍: 馬王堆 A.　　ⁱ Var.: 虧 for 於: 郭店 A. Passim.

ʲ Var.: 故 om.: 郭店 A.　　ᵏ Var.: 爲足 for 足: 郭店 A.

ˡ Var.: 恒 for 常: 馬王堆 A. Var.: 此亘 for 常: 郭店 A.

Zhang 47

47.1 不出ᵃ戶 以ᵇ知天下不窺ᶜ牖ᵈ以ᵉ知ᶠ天道 (Base text: Wang Bi comm. on *Laozi*
54.7 (所謂)不出戶以知天下(者也), 馬王堆 A for second half)

事有宗而物有主途雖殊而其歸同ᵍ也慮雖百而其致一也道有大常理
有大致執古之道可以御今雖處於今可以知古始故不出戶窺ʰ牖而可
知也 (Base text: 集註本)

47.2 其出彌ⁱ遠ʲ其知彌ᵏ尠ˡ (Base text: 范應元本)

無在於一而求之於眾也道視之不可見聽之不可聞搏之不可得如ᵐ其
知之不須出戶若其不知出愈遠愈迷也 (Base text: 張之象本)

47.3 是以聖人不行而知不見而名 (Base text: 傅奕古本)

得物之致故雖不行而慮可知也識物之宗故雖不見而是非之理可得而
名也 (Base text: 集註本)

47.4 不ⁿ爲而成 (Base text: 傅奕古本)

ᵃ Var.: 出於 for 出: 馬王堆 A; 馬王堆 B. Support against 於: Wang Bi comm.: 不出
戶.

ᵇ Var.: 可以 for 以: 傅奕古本; 范應元本. Support for 以: Wang Bi comm. on *Laozi*
54.7 以知天下.

ᶜ 窺 for 規於(馬王堆 B 親於): Wang Bi comm.: 窺牖; 陸德明釋文. Var.: 闚 for 窺: 范
應元本.

ᵈ Var.: 羑牖 for 牖: 陸德明釋文.

ᵉ Var.: 可以 for 以: 傅奕古本; 范應元本. Support for 以: analogy to 以知天下.

ᶠ Var.: 見 for 知: 范應元本.

ᵍ Var.: 而同歸 for 而其歸同: 張之象本. Support for 而其歸同: analogy to next phrase
而其致一.

ʰ Var.: 闚 for 窺: 張之象本.

ⁱ Var.: 籬 for 彌: 馬王堆 B. Var.: 爾 for 彌: 傅奕古本.

ʲ Var. 遠者 for 遠: 馬王堆 B.

ᵏ Var.: 籬 for 彌: 馬王堆 B. Var.: 爾 for 彌: 傅奕古本.

ˡ Wang Bi's commentary routinely translates 尠 into 少. Support for the reading of 尠
is 傅奕古本.

ᵐ Var.: 去 for 如: 集註本.

ⁿ Var.: 弗 for 不: 馬王堆 A.

明物之性因之而已故雖不爲而使之成矣 (Base text: 集註本)

47.1　[Only when] not going out of
doors [into All Under Heaven
one has something] by means of
which to cognize All Under
Heaven;

[Only when] not peeping out of
the window [to Heavenly phenomena one has something] by
means of which to cognize the
Way of Heaven;[1]

As processes have a principle,

As things have a master,[2]

[as Confucius says in the
Xici: *"What is (everyone) in*
All Under Heaven thinking
about and cogitating about?!
In All Under Heaven"]

although the "roads [of thinking]"
are "manifold," "what they lead
to" is the "same [end]";

although the "thoughts" are
"hundredfold," "what they are
directed to" is "one."[3]

The ways have a Great Eternal.

The ordering principles have a
Great Purport.[4]

[As the Laozi 14.4f *says]*
"Holding [today] on to the
Way of antiquity, it is possible
[for a Sage Ruler] to regulate
occurrences of the present,"
and although one is living in
the present time, "one [the Sage
Ruler] has something by which
to cognize the oldest beginning."
That is why [the text says]

"[Only when] not going out of
doors"

"[Only when] not peeping out
of the window"

one is able to cognize [both
All Under Heaven and the
Way of Heaven]!

47.2　while the further one ventures out, the less one cognizes.

[This is so because] negativity [as the "principle" and "master"] lies in the
One, but would [if one ventures out] be searched for among the many.
The Way is [,according to Laozi 14.1,] *"that which [I] do not see if [I]*
look at it," "that which [I] do not hear when listening for it," and "that
which [I] cannot grasp when reaching for it." If one has cognized this
[Way], there is no need to "go out of doors"; if one has not cognized this
[Way], the further one ventures out, the more confused one gets.

47.3   That is why the Sage

cognizes without going to   gives [the correct] name to [the
[the objects].   objects] without looking at
                                             [them].

He gets the end point of entities;   *He understands the principle of*
that is why even without "going   *entities; that is why, even "with-*
to" [them] it is possible for him   *out looking at [them]," it is*
"to cognize" [their] concerns.   *possible for him to give the*
                                             [correct] "name" to the ordering
                                             principle of right and wrong.

47.4   [In short,] without his acting [on
                              them], he gets [them] completed.[5]

                              As he is clear about the nature of
                              the entities, he just goes by that
                              [nature] and nothing more. That is
                              why [, as the text says,] even "with-
                              out his acting [on them,]" he has them
                              become "complete" [themselves]!

THE STRUCTURE OF *LAOZI* 47

Laozi 47 is written in closed IPS. An analysis of the structure of this *zhang* is hampered by the fact that the terminology used in the two chains is not consistent. The terms *zhu* 主 and *zong* 宗 appear in opposite places in Wang Bi on *Laozi* 49.5, which indicates that they are interchangeable. Thus the recurrence of *zong* in the commentary on *Laozi* 47.3 does not mean that this passage has to share the same references ["processes"] as the one above. In fact, I have grouped the second passage on the other side because of the term *li* 理, "ordering principle." This, however, leads to the next quandary. It is not clear whether the term *da zhi* 大致 "Great Purport," which appears on the right along with *li,* 理 "ordering principle" in the commentary to 47.1, is the same as the simple *zhi* 致 in the commentary on 47.3, where it has to go to the left. I have been forced to read it in 47.3 as a general term, exchangeable with the *gui* 歸 of the *Xici* quoted in the commentary on *Laozi* 47.1. My [tentative] reading of the structure of *Laozi* 47 is:

                    a   b   (47.1, 47.1)

                              c   (47.2)

                    a   b   (47.3, 47.3)

                              c   (47.4)

Zhang 48

48.1 爲^a學者日益 (Base text: Wang Bi on *Laozi* 20.1)

務欲進其所能益其所習 (Base text: 集註本)

48.2 爲^b道者日損^c (Base text: Wang Bi on *Laozi* 20.1)

務欲反虛無也 (Base text: 集註本)

48.3 損之又^d損之^e以至於^f無爲^g無爲則^h無不爲 (Base text: 傅奕古本)

有爲則有所失故無爲乃無所不爲也ⁱ (Base text: 集註本)

48.4 其^j取^k天下者^l常以^m無事 (Base text: Wang Bi on *Laozi* 57.1)

動常因也 (Base text: 集註本)

48.5 及其有事ⁿ(Base text: Wang Bi on *Laozi* 57.1)

自己造也 (Base text: 集註本)

48.6 又^{1,o}不足以取天下矣^p (Base text: Wang Bi on *Laozi* 57.1)

失統本也 (Base text: 集註本)

48.1   [A ruler] who is in favor of study everyday has more.

He makes efforts and desires to enhance his capabilities and increase his learning.

48.2   [A ruler] who is in favor of the Way everyday reduces more.

He makes efforts and desires to revert to emptiness and negativity.

48.3   He reduces and reduces again until he gets to non-interference. [Only when] non-interference [is achieved], then nothing will remain undone.

As long as there is interference, there will be some things that are missed. That is why the text says "[only when] non-interference [is achieved]," then indeed will there be "nothing" that is "not done."

48.4   His getting hold of All Under Heaven is due to [his] eternally not engaging in [government] activity.

[That is,] in his activities he eternally goes by [the nature of entities].[1]

48.5   Once it would come to his engaging in [government] affairs,

That is, once he himself would create [such government action].

48.6   he would also not qualify for getting hold of All Under Heaven.

That is, he would have lost the root that holds [everything] together.

Zhang 49

49.1 聖人無常[a]心以百姓[b]心[c]爲心 (Base text: 傅奕古本)

動常因也 (Base text: 集註本)

49.2 善者吾[d]善之不善者吾[e]亦善之 (Base text: 傅奕古本)

各因其用則善不失也 (Base text: 集註本)

---

[a] Var.: 恆 for 常: 馬王堆 B.

[b] Var.: 省 for 姓: 馬王堆 B.

[c] Var.: 之心 for 心: 馬王堆 A: 馬王堆 B; 范應元本. Support against 之: Wang Bi on *Laozi* 54.6 以天下百姓心 觀天下之道也.

[d] Var.: 吾 om.: 馬王堆 A.

[e] Var.: 吾 om.: 馬王堆 A.

49.3 德^f善矣^g (Base text: 范應元本)

無棄人也 (Base text: 集註本)

49.4 信者吾^h信之不信者吾ⁱ亦信之德^j信矣^k聖人之在天下^l歙歙^m焉爲爲天下渾ⁿ心焉^o百姓皆注^p其耳目焉^q (Base text: 范應元本)

各用聰明 (Base text: 集註本)

49.5 聖人皆孩之^r (Base text: 范應元本)

皆使和而無欲如嬰兒也夫天地設位聖人成能人謀鬼謀百姓與能^s能者與之資者取之能大則大資貴則貴物有其宗事有其主如此則可冕旒充^t目而不懼於欺黈纊塞耳而無戚於慢又何爲勞一身之聰明以察百姓之情哉夫以明察物物亦競以其明應之以不信察物物亦競以其^u不信應之夫天下之心不必同其所應不敢異則莫肯用其情矣甚矣害之大也莫大於用其明矣夫在智則人與之訟在力則人與之爭智不出於人而立乎訟地則窮矣力不出於人而立乎爭地則危矣未^v有能使人無用其智力乎^w己者也如此則已以一敵人而人以千萬敵己也若乃多其法網煩其刑罰塞其徑路攻其幽宅則萬物失其自然百姓喪其手足鳥亂於上魚亂於下是以聖人之於天下歙歙焉心無所主也爲天下渾心焉意無所

<hr>

^f Var.: 得 for 德: 傅奕古本. Support for 德: Although both 馬王堆 have a lacuna here, 馬王堆 B has the subsequent passage about 信, and there writes 德信.

^g Var.: 也 for 矣: 馬王堆 B.　　　　^h Var.: 吾 om.: 馬王堆 B.

ⁱ Var.: 吾 om.: 馬王堆 B.　　　　　　^j Var.: 得 for 德: 傅奕古本.

^k Var.: 也 for 矣: 馬王堆 A. 馬王堆 B.

^l Var.: 天下也 for 天下: 馬王堆 B.

^m Var.: 惏惏 for 歙歙: 馬王堆 A. Var.: 欿欿 for 歙歙: 馬王堆 B.

ⁿ Var.: 渾渾 for 渾: 傅奕古本.

^o Var.: 焉 om.: 馬王堆 A. 焉 confirmed by Wang Bi on *Laozi* 49.5.

^p Var.: 屬 for 注其: 馬王堆 A.

^q 耳目焉 for 耳目 (also in 傅奕古本): Wang Bi comm.: 百姓各皆注其耳目焉; 馬王堆 A.

^r 孩之 for 咳之 (also in 傅奕古本 and 陸德明釋文): Wang Bi comm.: 吾皆孩之而已. Support for 孩之: 陸德明釋文 mentions one manuscript that read 孩之.

^s 能 for 能者: 集註本.　　　　　　^t Var.: 垂 for 充: 集註本.

^u Var.: 其 om.: 集註本.

^v Var.: 未有能使人無用智者未 for 未: 集註本. Cf. translation note 9.

^w Var.: 於 for 乎: 集註本.

適莫也無所察焉百姓何避無所求焉百姓何應無避無應則莫不用其情矣人無爲舍其所能而爲其所不^x能舍其所長而爲其所短如此則言者言其所知行者行其所能百姓各皆注其耳目焉吾皆孩之而已 (Base text: 張之象本)

49.1　　　　　　　　　　　As a Sage [I am] without a permanent heart [of my own]. The hearts of the Hundred Families [I] take as [my] heart.

[That is,] in [my] activities [I] eternally go by [the nature of entities].[1]

49.2　Of the good ones I make good [use], and of the not good ones I also make good [use].

[That is,] with each I proceed in accordance with its usefulness so that good [elements] are not lost.

49.3　[Thus] [I] attain [the best use] of goodness.

[According to Laozi *27.5, "the Sage is constantly good at saving other people and for this reason] there is no rejecting other people [by him]."*[2]

49.4　　　　　　　　　　　Those who are trustworthy, I trust. Those who are not trustworthy I also trust. [Thus I] attain [maximum] trustworthiness.

[As a] Sage, [I am] in [my existence] in All Under Heaven sometimes this, sometimes the other way. [I am] All Under Heaven's diffuse heart. [As a consequence,] the Hundred Families all make the best of their ears and eyes,

---

^x Var.: 否 for 不: 集註本.

*[This means] everyone makes
use of his intelligence.*

49.5   [while I, the] Sage, make all
of them into infants.

*[That is to say I] get them all
to be in harmony and without
desires like infants.³ As it is a fact
[, according to the* Xici *8.9.b3ff.]
that "Heaven and Earth establish
the positions [of entities], and
[that I,] the Sage, complete the[ir]
capabilities [so that each gets its
place]; that other people [I] consult, the spirits [I] consult [in any
endeavor], to the Hundred Families
[I] give [their] capabilities";⁴ to
those who are capable, [I] give
[their capabilities]; those qualified,
I will take [for officials]. If the
capabilities [of the former] are
great, they will be great [but I will
not honor or flatter them]. If the
qualifications [of the latter] are
eminent, they will be eminent [but
I will not emulate and prefer them].
[Thus] things will have their principle,
and affairs will have their master
[without anything being distorted].⁵
Once that is the case, it is possible
for [me, the Sage Ruler,]*

*to let the pearl strings of [my] mian
hat obscure [my] eyes without fear
of being deceived;*

*to let the yellow pillows stuff
[my] ears without concern about
slanderous comments.⁶*

*Furthermore, what is the purpose of
[the ruler's] exerting the intelligence
of his single body to spy out the
sentiments of the Hundred Families?
It is a fact that, if*

*I were to spy out other entities by
means of [my] insight, the other
entities would compete with me
by reacting to this with their own
insight.*

*I were to spy out other entities
by means of [my] distrust [of
them], the other entities would
compete with me by repro-
cating with their own distrust
[of me].*

It is a fact that the minds of
[people in] All Under Heaven
are not necessarily [all] in
agreement [with the ruler].
But if in their reactions [to me]
they do not dare to differ [from
me because of the pervasiveness
of my security network], this
would mean that no one would
be willing to make use of his
[own natural] feelings. Truly
indeed! Among the things causing
great damage, none is greater
than [a ruler's] making use of his
intelligence! It is a fact [, as the
Huainanzi 14.138.9 *ff. says,]*
that, "if [I] were to

rely on [my] knowledge, the	*rely on [my] physical strength,*
others would litigate against	*the others would fight against*
[me]."	*[me]."*[7]
As [my own] knowledge does	*As [my own] physical strength*
not surpass that of [the multitude	*does not surpass that of [the*
of] others, I am lost once I take a	*multitude] of others, I am in*
stand in litigation [with them].[8]	*danger once I take a stand on*
	the battlefield [against them].

[Under these conditions] it
is not possible anymore [for
me] to prevent others from
using their

knowledge	*and*	*physical strength*
	on me.[9]	

Things being thus, [I] myself
am alone in confronting the
others as enemies, but the others
confront me in their millions as
an enemy. Were [I] indeed

to multiply the mesh of laws	*to make the punishments for*
for them,	*them more vexatious,*
to block their byways and	*to attack their hideouts,*

the ten thousand kinds of
entities would lose their

That-which-is-of-itself-what-it-
is, and the Hundred Families
would lose their hands and feet
[through physical punishment]; [in
short, as the Zhuangzi, 25/10/35ff.
says of the consequences of the ruler's
cherishing knowledge,] "the birds
would be in turmoil above," and "the
fishes would be in turmoil" below.[10]
That is why [the text says "as a]
Sage [I am] in [my existence] in All
Under Heaven sometimes this, some-
times the other way," [that is, my]
heart has no [constant] master; and
"[I am] All Under Heaven's diffuse
heart," [i.e., my] intentions have
nothing they "prefer" or "disdain"
[, as Confucius says in Lunyu 4.10
about the attitude of the Gentleman
towards All Under Heaven].[11]

As there definitely is nothing that
[I] spy out [with my insight], what
should the Hundred Families
evade?

As there definitely is nothing [I]
go after [with distrust], against
what should the Hundred
Families reciprocate?[12]

As [the Hundred Families]

do not evade [me by using their
own insight],

do not reciprocate [against me
by means of their own distrust],

there will be none among them
who does not make use of his
[natural] feelings. Not one will
discard what he is capable of and
do what he is not capable of, dis-
card what he excels in and do what
he cannot handle. When things
are this way, those who speak
will speak about [things] they
know, and those who act will do
[things] they are capable of, [in
short,] each one in the "Hundred
Families will make the best of
his ears and eyes" while I [, the
Sage,] will "make all of them
into infants," and that is all.

THE STRUCTURE OF *LAOZI* 49

Laozi 49 is written with the formal elements of closed IPS; the links between the treatment of the good ones and the trustworthy ones, on the one hand, and the Sage's role in the world, on the other hand, are not immediately visible. The parallel structure, however, mandates that there should be such links, and Wang Bi's commentary brings them out. The structure of the *zhang* is:

c		(49.1)
a	b	(49.2, 49.3, 49.4)
a	b	(49.4, 49.4)
c		(49.4)
c		(49.5)

Zhang 50

50.1 出生入死 (Base text: 傅奕古本)

　　出生地入死地 (Base text: 集註本)

50.2 生之徒十有三死之徒十有ª三而ᵇ民之ᶜ生生而ᵈ動ᵉ皆ᶠ之死地亦ᵍ十有三夫何故ʰ 以其生生之厚ⁱ也ʲ 蓋聞善攝ᵏ生者陸ˡ行不遇ᵐ兕ⁿ虎入軍不被甲兵ᵒ兕無

ª Var.: 又 for 有: 馬王堆 B.

ᵇ Var.: 而 om.: 范應元本. Support for 而: Wang Bi comm.: 十分有三耳 而民生生 . . .

ᶜ Var.: 之 om.: 馬王堆 A; 馬王堆 B.

ᵈ Var.: 而 om.: 馬王堆 A; 馬王堆 B.

ᵉ 動 for 動動: 范應元本; 馬王堆 A and 馬王堆 B both have single verbs here. Var.: 勭 for 動: 馬王堆 A. Var.: 僮 for 動: 馬王堆 B.

ᶠ Var.: 皆 om.: 范應元本.　　　　ᵍ Var.: 之 for 亦: 馬王堆 A; 馬王堆 B.

ʰ Var.: 故也 for 故: 馬王堆 A; 馬王堆 B. Var.: 哉 for 故: 范應元本.

ⁱ Var.: 之厚 om.: 馬王堆 A; 馬王堆 B.

ʲ Var.: 也 om.: 馬王堆 B.　　　　ᵏ Var.: 執 for 攝: 馬王堆 A; 馬王堆 B.

ˡ Var.: 陵 for 陸: 馬王堆 A; 馬王堆 B.

ᵐ Var.: 辟 for 遇: 馬王堆 B.

ⁿ Var.: 矢 for 兕: 馬王堆 A. Var.: 㺇 for 兕: 馬王堆 B. Passim.

ᵒ Var.: 兵革 for 甲兵: 馬王堆 B.

所投[p]其角虎無所錯[q]其瓜[r]兵無所容其刃夫何故也[s]以其無死地焉[t] (Base text: 傅奕古本)

十有三猶云十分有三分取其生道全生之極十分有三耳取死之道全死之極十分亦[u]有三耳而民生生之厚更之無生之地焉善攝生者無以生爲生故無死地也器之害者莫甚乎戈兵獸之害者莫甚乎兕虎而令兵戈無所容其鋒刃虎兕無所投[v]其瓜角斯誠不以欲累其身者也何[w]死地之有乎夫蚖蟺[x]以淵爲淺而鑿[y]穴其中鷹鸇以山爲埤[z]而增巢其上矰繳不能及綱罟不能到可謂處於無死地矣然而卒以甘餌乃入於無生之地豈非[aa]生生之厚乎故物苟不以求離其本不以欲渝其眞雖入軍而不可害[ab]陸行而不可犯也赤子之可則而貴信矣 (Base text: 集註本)

(Pair of opposites 1: Life vs. Death)

50.1		[They]	
	come forth into life	[but]	enter into death.
		[This means, they]	
	come forth into the realm of life but		*enter into the realm of death.*
50.2		[It is a fact that]	
	three out of ten are followers of life	and	three out of ten are followers of death.[1]
		But why is it that the people who make much of life but nonetheless in all their actions go to	

[p] Var.: 椯 for 投: 馬王堆 A.

[q] 錯 for 措: 陸德明釋文; 范應元本. Var.: 昔 for 錯: 馬王堆 A.

[r] Var.: 蚤 for 瓜: 馬王堆 A; 馬王堆 B.

[s] Var.: 哉 for 故也: 范應元本. [t] Var.: 焉 om.: 范應元本.

[u] Var.: 亦十分 for 十分亦: 張之象本.

[v] 投 for 措 (also in 張之象本): Wang Bi on *Laozi* 16.13 虎兕無所投其爪角兵戈無所容其鋒刃. The 措 seems to have come from a textual tradition of the *Laozi* text reading 虎無所措其瓜; according to Lu Deming, however, Wang Bi's *Laozi* read 錯.

[w] 何 for 向: 張之象本.

[x] Var.: 黿蚖蟺 for 蚖蟺: 陸德明釋文. Support for 蚖蟺: parallelism with 鷹鸇.

[y] Var.: 襲 for 鑿: 陸德明釋文. [z] 埤 for 卑: 陸德明釋文.

[aa] 非 for 弗: 張之象本.

[ab] 可害 for 害: Wagner based on parallel with 不可犯.

the realm of death also number
three out of ten?[2] Because they
make too much of life!

[Pair of opposites 2: Noxious animals vs. harmful arms]

One hears it [said] that he who
is good at holding on to life

will neither hit upon rhinoceros   will not suffer from [enemy]
nor tiger when traveling over   weapons when going into
land,   battle,

[because]

a rhinoceros would not find a
place [on him] to thrust its horn,
and a tiger would not find a place
[on him] to set its claws;   a weapon would not find a place
                                         [on him] to insert its blade.

Why is this so? Because such
a one is [in] a realm without death.

[Pair of opposites 1]

"Three out of ten" is as if
[the text] said "there are
three parts out of ten parts."

Of those who seize the way   *Of those who seize the way of*
of their being alive, [that is]   *death, [that is] utterly complete*
utterly complete the ultimate   *the ultimate of death, there also*
of life, there are three out of ten; *are three out of ten;*

but "people's" "making too
much of life" instead prompts
them [to] go to the realm where
there is no life.

[Pair of opposites 2]

"He who is good at holding
on to life" [as mentioned in
the text] does not take life for
[that which keeps up] life, and
that is why [,as the text says,]
he "is in a realm without death."

                                       Among the instruments inflicting
                                       harm, there are none worse than
                                       swords and lances.

*Among the wild animals
inflicting harm, there are none
worse than rhinoceroses and
tigers*

> *so that he who [is able] to
> make*

>> *the swords and lances "find no
>> place [on him] to insert their"
>> points and "blades,"*

*the rhinoceroses and tigers find
"no place [on him] to thrust"
their horns and claws*

> *is truly the one who does
> not bind his person through
> desires. What realm of death
> could there be for him? It is a
> fact that*

*for a sea turtle and an eel [even]
a deep abyss is shallow, and they
dig their nests there.*

*for an eagle and a hawk [even] a
mountain is low, and they perch
their nests on top of it.
[As] the stringed arrows cannot
reach [the eagle and the hawk
up there]*

*[As] the nets and fishtraps
cannot get [to the sea turtle
and eel down there]*

> *one may say that they dwell in
> a "realm without death."³ But
> isn't it due to their making too
> much of life if suddenly through
> sweet bait they enter into the
> realm where there is no life?*

> *That is why [only] entities*

*which do not become separated
from their root through cravings*

*which do not pollute their true
essence through desires
cannot be hurt even when
"going into battle."*

*cannot run into adversity even
when "traveling over land."*

> *[Then only] it is possible for them
> to imitate the infant [who in* Laozi

*55.1 is the model for "him who
carries the fullness of capacity in
himself" and who "will not be
stung by wasps and vipers, nor
attacked by wild beasts and birds
of prey" because, as Wang Bi
explains in the commentary, "it is
without cravings and without
desires and [thus] will not offend
the multitude of other entities"] and
hold credibility in high regard.*[4]

THE STRUCTURE OF *LAOZI* 50

Laozi 50 consists of two sections, both written in open IPS. The first section has the structure:

a	b	(50.1)
a	b	(50.2, 50.2)
	c	(50.2)

The second has the structure:

	c	(50.2)
a	b	(50.2, 50.2)
a	b	(50.2, 50.2)
	c	(50.2)

Both operate with independent pairs of opposites.

Zhang 51

51.1 道生之ᵃ德畜之物形之ᵇ勢ᶜ成之 (Base text: 傅奕古本)

物生而後畜畜而後形形而後成何由而生道也何得而畜德也何因ᵈ而
形物也何使而成勢也唯因也故能無物而不形唯使ᵉ也故能無物而不

ᵃ Var.: 之而 for 之: 馬王堆 A.   ᵇ Var.: 之而 for 之: 馬王堆 A; 馬王堆 B.

ᶜ Var.: 器 for 勢: 馬王堆 A; 馬王堆 B.

ᵈ 因 for 由: 陶鴻慶 on the basis of Wang Bi's next phrase 唯因也故能無物而不形.

ᵉ 使 for 勢: Wagner on the basis of parallel with 唯因也.

成凡物之所以生功之以成皆有所由有所由焉^f則莫不由乎道也故推
而極之亦至^g道也隨其所因故各有稱^h焉 (Base text: 張之象本)

51.2 是以萬物莫不ⁱ尊道而貴德 (Base text: 傅奕古本)

道者物之所由也德者物之^j所得也由之乃得故^k不得不尊失之則害故
不得不貴也^l (Base text: 張之象本)

51.3 道之尊^m德之貴ⁿ夫莫之爵^o而常^p自然^{q,1}故^r道生之畜^s之^t長之育^u之亭之毒之
蓋之覆之^v (Base text: 范應元本)

....亭謂品其形毒謂^w成其質^x....各得其庇蔭^y不傷其體矣² (Base
text: 初學記 the for first half, 集註本 for the second)

---

^f Var.: 有所由焉 om.: 集註本. ^g Var.: 志 for 至: 集註本.

^h Var.: 道 for 稱: 集註本; support for 稱: 陸德明釋文.

ⁱ Var.: 莫不 om.: 馬王堆 A; 馬王堆 B.

^j Var.: 之 om.: 集註本.

^k 故 for 故曰: 集註本. Support against 曰: in Wang Bi, the formula 故曰 always introduces a verbatim quotation from the *Laozi*. What follows is no quotation.

^l 由之乃得 故不得不尊 失之則害 故不得不貴也 for 由之乃得 故不得不失 尊之則害不得不貴也 (also in 集註本): 陶鴻慶.

^m Var.: 尊也 for 尊: 馬王堆 B. ⁿ Var.: 貴也 for 貴: 馬王堆 A; 馬王堆 B.

^o Var.: 財 for 爵: 馬王堆 A. Var.: 爵也 for 爵: 馬王堆 B.

^p Var.: 恒 for 常: 馬王堆 A; 馬王堆 B.

^q Var.: 自然也 for 自然: 馬王堆 A; 馬王堆 B.

^r Var.: 故 om.: 馬王堆 A; 馬王堆 B.

^s 畜 for 蓄: 馬王堆 A; 馬王堆 B; 傅奕古本.

^t Var.: 德畜之 for 畜之: 傅奕古本. Support for omission of 德: 馬王堆 A; 馬王堆 B; argumentation in Wang Bi on *Laozi* 1.2, where both parts of the ontogenetic process are ascribed to the Dao, and no mention is made of 德: 凡有皆始於無故未形無名之時則爲萬物之始及其有形有名之時則長之育之亭之毒之爲其母也 言道以無形無名 始成萬物.

^u Var.: 遂 for 育: 馬王堆 A.

^v Var.: 養之復之 for 蓋之覆之: 馬王堆 B. Support for 蓋: quotation in Xu Jian, *Chuxue ji* 9.206 (亭之毒之蓋之覆之) with Wang Bi commentary. From this, it is evident that early Tang texts had 蓋 in the Wang Bi *Laozi* edition.

^w ...亭謂品其形 毒謂 for 謂(in both 集註本 and 張之象本): Quotation of Wang Bi commentary in Xu Jian, *Chuxue ji* 9.206, and 文選劉孝標辨命論李善注 54.16a4.

^x Var.: 實 for 質: 張之象本. Support for 質: quotation in Xu Jian, *Chuxue ji* 9.206, and 文選劉孝標辨命論李善注 54.16a4.

^y Var.: 廕 for 蔭: 陸德明釋文.

51.4 生而不^z有爲而不恃^{aa} (Base text: 傅奕古本)

爲而不有 (Base text: 集註本)

51.5 長而不^{ab}宰是^{ac}謂^{ad}玄德 (Base text: 傅奕古本)

有德而不知其主也出乎幽冥^{ae}故謂之玄德也^{af} (Base text: 集註本)

51.1 | The Way generates them.

What they get is that it nourishes them:

As entities it [the Way] lets them assume form.

As situations it has them fully develop.[1]

Once entities are created, they are nourished.
Once they are nourished, they assume form.

Once they have assumed form, they fully develop.

On the basis of what are they created? [On the basis of] the Way.

What is it that attains to be nourished? [Their] Capacity.

Going by what does it [the Way] let them assume form? [Going by their nature as] entities.
It is because it [the Way] only goes by [the nature of the entities and does not impose itself] that it is able [to manage] that there is no entity that does not assume form.

What does it [the Way] cause to fully develop? Situations.
It is because it [the Way] only causes [situations] to fully develop, [but does not do the developing itself] that there is no entity that does not fully develop.

---

^z Var.: 弗有也 for 不有: 馬王堆 A.   ^{aa} Var.: 弗寺也 for 不恃: 馬王堆 A.

^{ab} Var.: 勿宰也 for 不宰: 馬王堆 A. Var.: 弗宰也 for 不宰: 馬王堆 B.

^{ac} Var.: 此之 for 是: 馬王堆 A.   ^{ad} Var.: 胃 for 謂: 馬王堆 B.

^{ae} Var.: 寈 for 冥: 張之象本.   ^{af} Var.: 故謂之玄德也 om.: 張之象本.

Generally speaking,

that by which enti-	*that by which*
ties are generated	*achievements are*
	brought about

*have something that is
the base [for them]. As
they have something that
is the base for them, there
is none of them that is not
based on the Way. That is
why, if one carries the extra-
polation from them [the
entities and the situations]
to the extreme, one also will
arrive at the Way. Depending
on what [in particular] it
[the Way] is [seen as] being
the basis for, there will
[accordingly] be different
designations [for that by
which the ten thousand
kinds of entities are.]*[2]

51.2   That is why there is none
among the ten thousand
kinds of entities that does not

honor the Way and	value the receipt/capacity.
The Way is that which is the basis for the [ten thousand kinds of] entities.[3]	*Receipt/capacity is that which the [ten thousand kinds of] entities receive[from the Way].*[4]
It is on the basis of the [former that they] indeed receive [the latter];[5] *that is why they cannot but "honor" [the Way].*	*Losing [their receipt/capacity] will hurt them; that is why they cannot but "value" [the Capacity they receive].*

51.3   The honoring of the   and   the valuing of the capacity,
Way

continuously [comes out] of [the
entities'] That-which-is-of-itself-
what-it-is, without anyone's order.
That is why the Way

generates them [the ten thousand
entities] and   nourishes them:

it lets them grow and nurtures
them, specifies them and completes them, protects and covers
them;[6]

... *"specifies them" means it
groups their shapes; "completes
them" means it perfects their
substance. .... Each [one of the
entities] attains its [the Way's]
protection without its doing
damage to their substance.*

51.4   [But if], while they [the entities]   [and if], while they [the entities]
       come alive, it [the Way] has no   act, it [the Way] does not make
       [specific effort on its side]   [the entities] dependent,[7]

*[That is] if while they proceed, it [the Way] has no [specific effort on its
side].*[8]

51.5   [if, in short,] while they grow [it]
                                   does not lord it over them, this
                                   is called the Capacity [coming
                                   from] That-which-is-Dark."

                                   *That [the entities] have [their]
                                   receipt/capacity but do not know
                                   its master [on the basis of whom
                                   they attain it] is [because] it
                                   [their receipt/capacity] comes
                                   forth out of the Recondite.
                                   That is why [the text] speaks
                                   of it as of the Capacity's [coming
                                   from] That-which-is-Dark."*[9]

THE STRUCTURE OF *LAOZI* 51

Laozi 51 is written mostly in open IPS. In 51.4, the link is made by
recourse to parallel formulae elsewhere where the links are explicit. The
zhang has the following structure:

a		b	(51.1, 51.1)
	b1		(51.1)
		b2	(51.1)
	c		(51.2)
a		b	(51.2, 51.2)

a		b		(51.3, 51.3)
	c			(51.3)
a		b		(51.3, 51.3)
a		b		(51.4)
	c			(51.5)

Zhang 52

52.1 天下有始可ᵃ以爲天下母 (Base text: 傅奕古本)

　　善始之則善養畜之矣故天下有始則可以爲天下母矣ᵇ (Base text: 集註本)

52.2 既ᶜ得其母以知其子既知其子ᵈ復守其母沒ᵉ身不殆ᶠ (Base text: 傅奕古本)

　　母本也子末也得本以知末不舍本以逐末也 (Base text: 集註本)

52.3 塞其兌ᵍ閉其門ʰ (Base text: 傅奕古本)

　　兌事欲之所由生門事欲之所由從也 (Base text: 集註本)

52.4 終ⁱ身不勤ʲ (Base text: Wang Bi, comm.)

　　無事永逸故終身不勤 (Base text: 集註本)

ᵃ Var.: 可 om.: 馬王堆 A; 馬王堆 B; 范應元本. Support for 可: Wang Bi comm.: 則可以爲天下母.

ᵇ Var.: The entire comment is omitted in the 張之象本.

ᶜ Var.: 惡 for 既: 馬王堆 A.

ᵈ Var.: 既知其子 om.: 馬王堆 A.

ᵉ Var.: 歿 for 沒: 范應元本.

ᶠ Var.: 佁 for 殆: 馬王堆 B.

ᵍ Var.: 閲 for 兌: 馬王堆 A. Var.: 垬 for 兌: 馬王堆 B.

ʰ Var.: 閉其門 賽其兌 for 塞其兌 閉其門: 郭店 B.

ⁱ Var.: 冬 for 終: 馬王堆 B.

ʲ Var.: 堇 for 勤: 馬王堆 A; 馬王堆 B.

52.5 開^k其兌^l濟^m其事終身不救ⁿ (Base text: 傅奕古本)

    不閉其原而濟其事故雖終身不救 (Base text: 集註本)

52.6 見小曰明守柔曰強 (Base text: 傅奕古本)

    爲治之功不在大見大不明見小乃明守強不強守柔乃強也 (Base text: 集註本)

52.7 用其光 (Base text: 傅奕古本)

    顯道以去民迷^o (Base text: 張之象本)

52.8 復歸其明 (Base text: 傅奕古本)

    不以明^p察也 (Base text: 集註本)

52.9 無^q遺身殃^r是謂襲常 (Base text: 傅奕古本)

    道之常也 (Base text: 集註本)

52.1   As All Under Heaven has a beginning, this may [also] be taken for All Under Heaven's mother.

    Being good at beginning it [All Under Heaven], it will consequently [also] be good at maintaining and nourishing it. That is why [the text says] "As All Under Heaven has a beginning, this [beginning]," as a consequence, "may [also] be taken for All Under Heaven's mother." [1]

52.2   Once [a ruler] has gotten hold of its [All Under Heaven's] mother by way of understanding its [the mother's] offspring [= All Under Heaven], and if,

---

   [k] Var.: 啓 for 開: 馬王堆 A; 馬王堆 B; 郭店 B.

   [l] Var.: 悶 for 兌: 馬王堆 A. Var.: 堄 for 兌: 馬王堆 B.

   [m] Var.: 齊 for 濟: 馬王堆 B. Var.: 賽 for 濟: 郭店 B.

   [n] Var.: 棘 for 救: 馬王堆 B.   [o] Var.: 迷 om.: 集註本.

   [p] 以明 for 明: Wagner. The phrase here, 不以明察也, takes up a formula which Wang Bi mentions several times; cf. 以明察物 in Wang Bi on *Laozi* 49.5 or 行術用明以察姦僞 in Wang Bi on *Laozi* 18.2. These parallels prompt the insertion of the 以.

   [q] Var.: 毋 for 無: 馬王堆 A.   [r] Var.: 央 for 殃: 馬王堆 A; 馬王堆 B.

once having understood its [the mother's] offspring, he in turn will keep to its [All Under Heaven's] mother, he will not be in danger all his life.

"Mother" is [the same as] "root." The "offspring" are the stem and branches.[2] *He gets hold of the root by way of understanding the stem and branches [springing from it], and does not [then] discard the root in order to go after the stem and branches.*

52.3   If he stuffs its [All Under Heaven's] openings and blocks its doors,

"Openings" are the basis from which desires for action arise. "Doors" are the basis on which desires for action are pursued.[3]

52.4   he will [even] to the end of his life not [have to] toil.

There will be no actions [to take care of,] and he [can] be eternally withdrawn. That is why [the text says,] "he will to the end his life not [have to] toil"!

52.5   If he [the ruler] opens its [All Under Heaven's] openings and manages its [All Under Heaven's] actions, he will [even] to the end of his life never be saved [from toil and danger].

If he does not block its [All Under Heaven's] source [of desire for action], but manages its [All Under Heaven's] actions, that is why [,as the text says,] even "to the end of his life he will never be saved"!

52.6   [For a ruler] to manifest smallness means being enlightened.[4]
[For a ruler] to hold on to [his] being weak means being overpowering.

[A ruler's] achievements of acting and ordering do not consist in [acting] great. Showing off being great is not being enlightened, "to manifest smallness is," in fact, "being enlightened." [For a ruler] to hold on to being overpowering is not being overpowering, "to hold on to [his] being weak is," in fact, "being overpowering."

52.7   If he [the ruler] makes use of his enlightenment

[That is, if he] makes shine forth the Way in order to dispel the errors of the people

52.8   and withdraws his intelligence,

[That is, if he] does not use [his] intelligence to spy [on other entities],[5]

52.9   he does not attract disaster to himself. This I call 'being in agreement with the Eternal.'

[That is, with] the Eternal of the Way [mentioned in Laozi *32.1].*

Zhang 53

53.1 使我介然^a有知^b行於大道唯^c施^d是畏 (Base text: 范應元本)

言若使我可介然有知行大道於天下唯施爲^e是畏也 (Base text: 集註本)

53.2 大道甚夷而^f民^g好徑^h (Base text: Wang Bi comm.)

言大道蕩然正平而民猶尙舍之而不由好從邪徑況復施爲以塞大道之中乎故曰大道甚夷而民好徑 (Base text: 集註本)

53.3 朝甚除 (Base text: Wang Bi comm. on *Laozi* 53.4)

朝宮室也 除 潔好也 (Base text: 集註本)

53.4 田甚蕪倉甚虛 (Base text: Wang Bi comm.)

朝甚除則田甚蕪倉甚虛矣ⁱ設一而衆害生也 (Base text: 集註本)

53.5 服文采帶利劍厭^j飮^k食 貨^l財有餘是謂盜夸^m盜夸ⁿ非道也哉 (Base text: 集註本)

---

^a Var.: 潔 for 介然: 馬王堆 A. Var.: 然 om. 馬王堆 B.

^b Var.: 知也 for 知: 馬王堆 A.

^c Var.: 惟 for 唯: 傅奕古本.   ^d Var.: 他 for 施: 馬王堆 B.

^e Var.: 爲之 for 爲: 張之象本.

^f Var.: 佚 for 夷而: 范應元本.

^g Var.: 民甚 for 民: 馬王堆 A; 馬王堆 B; 范應元本.

^h Var.: 解 for 徑: 馬王堆 A. Var.: 僻 for 徑: 馬王堆 B. Support for 徑: 陸德明釋文.

ⁱ Var.: 矣 om.: 張之象本.

^j 厭 for 猒: 陸德明釋文.

^k Var.: 飮 om.: 馬王堆 B.   ^l Var.: 而齎 for 貨: 馬王堆 B.

^m Var.: A character with a 木 radical to the left for 夸: 馬王堆 B.

ⁿ Var.: 盜夸 om.: 范應元本. Support for the repetition of 盜夸: 陸德明釋文; the size of the lacuna in both 馬王堆 A and 馬王堆 B suggests that both also repeated 盜夸, although again Gao Ming sees the lacuna as smaller than the Mawangdui Hanmu boshu zhengli xiaozu.

凡物不以其道得之則皆邪也邪則盜也貴而不以其道得之竊位也竊則
夸也°故舉非道以明非道則皆盜夸ᴾ也 (Base text: 集註本)

53.1   If I [as a Sage Ruler] were [able] to reduce to insignificance [All Under
        Heaven's] having knowledge, and have [it] march on the Great Way, [the]
        only [thing I] would [then] be worried about would be that [I] might [still]
        interfere [with it].[1]

        This means: Assuming it would be possible for me to curb [All Under
        Heaven's] having knowledge and to make the Great Way prevalent in All
        Under Heaven, [the] only [thing I] would [then] be worried about would
        be that [I] might [still] interfere with it [All Under Heaven] and act on it.

53.2   [I say this in view of the fact that] the Great Way [,true,] is very smooth,
        but the people [still] love the bypaths.[2]

        This means: The Great Way is vast in its correctness and smoothness, but
        the people nonetheless reject it and do not abide by it. They rather follow
        the heterodox bypaths, and how much more [would they do this] were
        [I] in turn to interfere [with them] and to act on [them], thereby blocking
        the midst of the Great Way! That is why [the text] says: "The Great Way
        [,true,] is very smooth, but the people [still] love the bypaths"!

53.3   If the court is very much tidied up,

        The "court" is the [ruler's] palace. "Tidied up" means well cleaned,   ·

53.4   the fields will be full of weeds, and the granaries will be utterly empty.

        As the consequence of the court's being very much tidied up, the fields
        will be full of weeds, and the granaries will be utterly empty. [I] take care
        of one [thing, that is, having my court much tidied up], and the multitude
        of damaging effects ensues.

°邪則盜也貴而不以其道得之竊位也竊則夸也 for 夸而不以其道得之盜夸也貴而不
以其道得之竊位也: Wagner. Var.: 盜夸也貴而不以其道得之 om.: 張之象本. All scholars
agree that the transmitted text needs emendation. The only significant variant is in the 集
註 text, which reads 邪則盜也夸而不以其道得之竊夸也貴而不以其道得之竊位也. Lou
Yulie suggests the following emendation 邪則盜也 夸而不以其道得之竊也 貴而不以
其道得之 竊位也. The evident weakness of this is that it operates with three sentences not
grounded in the terminology and structure of the main text, and that, by leaving the 夸 in
the first position, it eliminates the parallelism of the patterned dress and sharp sword as a
sign of high rank, and of drink, food, and wealth as a sign of material wealth in the text,
there directly linked to two terms, not three, namely, "robbery" and "bragging" 盜 and
夸. I have made use of the 集註 tradition by using the *gui* 貴 as a parallel to the *wu* 物 in
the first phrase here, and I have supplemented the equivalent of 邪則盜也 in the end of the
second sentence as 竊則夸也.

ᴾ 夸 for 誇: 張之象本. Support for 夸: 陸德明釋文.

53.5   If [people] will [, as a
                                     consequence,]

wear patterned and embroidered   gorge themselves with drink and
dresses, and carry sharp swords at   food, and have goods and
their sides,   wealth in excess,

                        these are called

                                     robbery and

[empty] bragging.

                        These truly are at variance
                        with the Way!³

                        Generally speaking,
                                if things are not gotten [by the
                                people] by means of the Way,
                                they [have] all [been gotten]
                                [through] heterodox [means]. If
                                they [have been gotten through]
                                heterodox [means,] then that is
                                robbery.

If [people are] in an honored
[position], but have not gotten it by
means of the Way, [they] have
usurped the position. If [they] have
usurped the position, [their being
in it] is [empty] bragging.

                        That is why [the text] stresses
                        "at variance with the Way"
                        to make clear that everything
                        that is at variance with the
                        Way is [merely]
                                        robbery and
[empty] bragging.

THE STRUCTURE OF *LAOZI* 53
The text is written in sequential order until the end, where a short
passage in IPS based on the terms *robbery* and *bragging* occurs. The overall
structure is thus:

	c	(53.1)
	c	(53.2)
	c	(53.3, 53.4)

c		(53.5)
a	b	(53.5, 53.5)
	b	(53.5)
a		(53.5)
	c	(53.5)

Zhang 54

54.1 善建者不拔 (Base text: 傅奕古本)

固其根而後營其末故不拔也 (Base text: 集註本)

54.2 善抱^a者不脫^b (Base text: 傅奕古本)

不貪於多齊其所能故不脫也 (Base text: 集註本)

54.3 子孫以^c祭祀不輟^d (Base text: 馬王堆 B)

子孫傳此道以祭祀則不輟也 (Base text: 集註本)

54.4 修^e之身其德乃眞修之家其德乃有餘^f (Base text: 馬王堆 B)

以身及人也修之身則眞修之家則有餘修之不廢所施博^g大 (Base text: 集註本)

---

   ^a 抱 for 褒: 范應元本. Support for 抱: Wang Bi *LZWZLL* 6.30 writes 抱樸.

   ^b Var.: 挩 for 脫: 范應元本. Support for 脫: Wang Bi comm. Var.: 兌 for 脫: 郭店 B.

   ^c Var.: 以 om.: 傅奕古本; 范應元本. Support for 以 Wang Bi comm.: 傳此道以祭祀. Var.: 以其 for 以: 郭店 B.

   ^d 輟 for 絕: Wang Bi comm.: 則不輟也; 陸德明釋文; 傅奕古本; 范應元本. Var.: 屯 for 輟: 郭店 B.

   ^e 修 for 脩 (also in 范應元本): Wang Bi comm.; 傅奕古本. Passim.

   ^f 乃有餘 for 有餘: Wang Bi comm. : 則有餘 (則 translates 乃). Support for 乃有餘: 文子. Var.: 乃餘 for 乃有餘: 傅奕古本; 范應元本. Var. 又舍 for 乃有餘: 郭店 B.

   ^g Var.: 轉 for 博: 取善集; 張之象本. Support for 博: Wang Bi on *Laozi* 38.2: 不能無爲而貴博施 . . . .

54.5 修之鄉其德乃長修之國^h其德乃豐ⁱ修之天下其德乃博^j故以身^k觀身以家觀家
以鄉觀鄉以國觀國 (Base text: 馬王堆 B with 傅奕古本 for the lacuna)

　　彼皆然也 (Base text: 集註本)

54.6 以天下觀天下 (Base text: 馬王堆 B)

　　以天下百姓心觀天下之道也天下之道逆順吉凶亦皆如人之道也 (Base
　　text: 集註本)

54.7 吾何^l以知天下之然哉^m以此 (Base text: 馬王堆 B with 傅奕古本 for the
lacunae)

　　此上之所云也言吾何以得知天下乎察己以知之不求於外也所謂不出
　　戶以知天下者也 (Base text: 集註本)

54.1　　He who is good at anchoring will not be uprooted.

　　　　*He consolidates his root and then only he takes care of his stem and
　　　　branches.*[1] *That is why [the text says] "he will not be uprooted"!*

54.2　　He who is good at holding on to [the One] will not be stripped [of any-
　　　　thing].

　　　　He has no craving for having more and manages what he is capable of.[2]
　　　　That is why [the text says] "will not be stripped [of anything]"!

54.3　　If sons and grandsons proceed by way of examining themselves, then [this]
　　　　will not be interrupted.

　　　　*If sons and grandsons transmit this Way [of "anchoring" that is, con-
　　　　solidating the root, and "holding on to the One"] by way of examining
　　　　themselves, then this Way "will not be interrupted."*[3]

54.4　　If [I] strive after this [Way] as far as [my] person is concerned, [my] receipt/
　　　　capacity from it [the Way] is the true [essence]. If [I] strive after this [Way]

---

^h Var.: 邦 for 國: 郭店 B; 馬王堆 A; 傅奕古本; 范應元本. Passim.

ⁱ 豐 for 夆: 傅奕古本; 范應元本.

^j Var.: 溥 for 博: 傅奕古本. Var.: 普 for 博: 范應元本.

^k 故以身 for 以身: 傅奕古本; 范應元本. Var.: 故 om.: 馬王堆 A.

^l Var.: 奚 for 何: 傅奕古本; 范應元本. Support for 何: Wang Bi comm.: 吾何以得知
天下乎

^m 哉 for 茲: 傅奕古本; 范應元本.

as far as [my] family is concerned, [my family's] receipt/capacity from it [the Way] is abundance.

[The text] proceeds from one's own person to the others. As a consequence of one's cultivating it [this Way] with regard to one's person, it [the person] will [realize its] true [nature]. As a consequence of one's cultivating it [this Way] with regard to one's family, it [the family] will have abundance. As long as one's cultivating it does not deteriorate, what one effects [through the cultivation of this Way] becomes ever broader and greater.

54.5   If [I] cultivate it [this Way] with regard to [my] district, the receipt/capacity from it [the Way] will indeed be to excel. If [I] cultivate it [this Way] with regard to [my] state, the receipt/capacity from it [the Way] will indeed be to be rich. If [I] cultivate it [this Way] with regard to All Under Heaven, the receipt/capacity from it [the Way] will indeed be to be all-encompassing. Therefore from [striving for this Way in one's own] person one understands [what it is in all] persons. From [striving for this Way in one's own] family one understands [what it is in all] families. From [striving for this Way in one's own] district one understands [what it is in all] districts. From [striving for this way in one's own] state one understands [what it is in all] states.

The others [persons, families, districts, states] all are in the same way [as one's own].

54.6   From [striving for this Way in the people of] All Under Heaven one [even] understands All Under Heaven.

On the basis of the intentions of the Hundred Families of All Under Heaven one understands the Way of All Under Heaven. The Way of All Under Heaven is, with regard to deviation and conformity, auspiciousness and inauspiciousness, altogether like the Way of men.[4]

54.7   What is it through which I know that All Under Heaven is this way [and no other]? Through this [the above].

"This" refers to the [things] said above [in this zhang *after the "therefore" in text 5]. This means: What is it through which I manage to cognize All Under Heaven? I examine myself by way of cognizing it [All Under Heaven], and I do not strive [for this cognition] on the outside. This is what [in* Laozi *47.1] is called "[Only when] not going out of doors [into All Under Heaven one has something] by means of which to cognize All Under Heaven."*

Zhang 55

55.1 含德之厚者比^a於赤子也^b蜂蠆虺蛇^c不^d螫^e猛獸^f攫鳥^g不^h搏ⁱ (Base text: 傅奕 古本)

赤子無求無欲不犯眾物故毒螫^j之物無犯之^k人也含德之厚者不犯於 物故無物以損其全也 (Base text: 集註本)

55.2 骨弱筋柔^l而握固 (Base text: 傅奕古本)

以柔弱之故故握能堅^m固 (Base text: 集註本)

55.3 未知牝牡之合ⁿ而全作^o (Base text: 傅奕古本)

作長也無物以損其身故能全長也言含德之厚者無物可以損其德渝其 眞柔弱不爭而不摧折皆若此也 (Base text: 集註本)

55.4 精之至也 終^p日號而不嗌^q (Base text: 馬王堆 B)

無爭欲之心故終日出聲而不嗌^r也 (Base text: 集註本)

---

^a 比 for 比之: 馬王堆 A; 馬王堆 B; 郭店 A; 范應元本.

^b Var.: 也 om.: 郭店 A; 馬王堆 A; 馬王堆 B.

^c 蜂蠆 虺蛇 for 蜂蠆: 陸德明釋文; 范應元本. Var.: 逢俐螟地 for 蜂蠆虺蛇: 馬王堆 A. Var.:蟲癘虫蛇 for 蜂蠆虺蛇: 馬王堆 B.

^d Var.: 弗 for 不: 馬王堆 A; 馬王堆 B.

^e Var.: 赫 for 螫: 馬王堆 B.   ^f 不據 om.: 馬王堆 A; 馬王堆 B; 范應元本.

^g Var.: 攫(馬王堆 B: 據)鳥猛獸 for 猛獸 攫鳥: 郭店 A; 馬王堆 A; 馬王堆 B.

^h Var.: 弗 for 不: 馬王堆 A; 馬王堆 B.

ⁱ Var.: 捕 for 搏: 馬王堆 B. Var.:扣 for 搏: 郭店 A.

^j Var.: 蟲 for 螫: 張之象本.   ^k 之 for 於: 張之象本.

^l 骨筋弱柔 for 骨弱筋柔: 馬王堆 B.

^m Var.: 周 for 堅: 張之象本.   ⁿ Var.: 會 for 合: 馬王堆 B.

^o 全作 for 朘作 (also in 范應元本 and 朘 also in 馬王堆 B.): Wang Bi comm.: 作長 也 ... 故能全長也; 陸德明釋文. Var.: 朘怒 for 全作: 郭店 A; 馬王堆 B.

^p 終 for 冬: Wang Bi comm. 陸德明釋文; 馬王堆 A; 傅奕古本; 范應元本.

^q 嗌 for 嗄: Wang Bi comm.: 而不嗌也; commentary in the 集註本: "[Wang] Bi's [*Laozi*] text writes 嗌 for 嗄." Var.: 嗄 for 嗌: 陸德明釋文; 范應元本. Var.: 发 for 嗌: 馬王堆 A. Var.: 嗌不數 for 不嗌: 傅奕古本. Var.: 嗌 for 不: 范應元本.

^r Var.: 嗄 for 嗌: 張之象本.

55.5 和之至也知ˢ和曰常 (Base text: 傅奕古本)

　　物以和爲常故知和則得常也 (Base text: 集註本)

55.6 知常ᵗ曰明 (Base text: 傅奕古本)

　　不皦不昧不溫不涼此常也無形不可得而見故曰知常曰明ᵘ (Base text: 集註本)

55.7 益生曰祥 (Base text: 傅奕古本)

　　生不可益益之則妖ᵛ也 (Base text: 集註本)

55.8 心使氣則ʷ強 (Base text: 傅奕古本)

　　心宜無有使氣則強 (Base text: 集註本)

55.9 物壯則ˣ老 謂ʸ之不道 不道早ᶻ已ᵃᵃ (Base text: 傅奕古本)

55.1　[A ruler] who has the fullness of capacity in himself is like an infant: wasps, scorpions, and vipers do not sting him; wild beasts and birds of prey do not seize him.[1]

An infant is without cravings and without desires, and [thus] does not offend the multitude of [other] beings. That is why it is a human being which [in turn] beings like poisonous insects will not offend. [The ruler] who has the fullness of capacity in himself will not offend the multitude of other entities. That is why there will be no other entity detrimental to his intactness.

55.2　That [its] bones are weak and [its] sinews soft, but its grip is firm,

---

ˢ Var.: 知 om.: 郭店 A; 馬王堆 A.　　　ᵗ Var.: 和 for 常: 郭店 A; 馬王堆 A.

ᵘ 不可得而見 故曰知常曰明 for 不可得而見曰明: 宇佐美灊水 based on Wang Bi on *Laozi* 16.6.

ᵛ Var.: 夭 for 妖: 張之象本; 陸德明釋文.

ʷ Var.: 曰 for 則: 郭店 A; 馬王堆 A; 馬王堆 B; 范應元本. Support for 則: Wang Bi comm.: 使氣則強.

ˣ Var.: 即 for 則: 馬王堆 A.　　　ʸ Var.: 胃 for 謂: 馬王堆 A; 馬王堆 B.

ᶻ Var.: 蚤 for 早: 馬王堆 B.　　　ᵃᵃ Var.: 不道早已 om.: 郭店 A.

It is because of this weakness and softness that its grip is capable of holding firm,

55.3   that it is ignorant about the union of female and male but makes it intact,

"Makes it" means grows up. As there is no entity to be detrimental to its body, it is capable of growing up intact. This means: For him who has the fullness of capacity in himself there is no other entity to be detrimental to his capacity and to pollute his true [essence].[2] [An infant's] being weak [in the sinews] and soft [in the bones] and not struggling [with other entities] but [still] not having anything broken is altogether like him.

55.4   this is the culmination of the [true] essence.[3] That all day long it mutters but still does not become hoarse,

It has no mind for struggle and desire; that is why, although it emits sounds all day long, it does not become hoarse.

55.5   this is the culmination of harmony. Having knowledge of harmony means [having] the Eternal.

Entities take harmony as the Eternal. That is why, as a consequence of one's having knowledge of harmony, one attains the Eternal.

55.6   Having knowledge of [this] Eternal means being enlightened.

What is neither bright nor dark, neither warming nor cooling, that is the Eternal.[4] It is formless and it is impossible to see it. That is why [the text] says: "Having knowledge of [this] Eternal means being enlightened"![5]

55.7   [But for a ruler] having life in excess means distress;

One should not let life become excessive. If one goes into excess, then one will die young.

55.8   having the heart engage the vital breath means becoming violent.[6]

The heart should be without having [particular ambitions]. If it engages the vital breath, then one will become violent.[7]

55.9   If an entity grows mighty, it will age [quickly]. This I call "not on [= according to] the Way." What is not on the Way is quickly finished.[8]

Zhang 56

56.1 知者[a]不言也[b] (Base text: 傅奕古本)

因自然也 (Base text: 集註本)

56.2 言者[c]不知也[d] (Base text: 傅奕古本)

造事端也 (Base text: 集註本)

56.3 塞其兌[e]閉其門[f] (Base text: 傅奕古本)

含守質也 (Base text: 集註本)

56.4 挫[g]其銳[h,1]解其紛 (Base text: 傅奕古本)

除爭原也 (Base text: 集註本)

56.5 和其光 (Base text: 傅奕古本)

無所特顯則物物無偏爭也[i] (Base text: 集註本)

56.6 同其塵[j,2] (Base text: 傅奕古本)

無所特賤則物物無偏耻[k,3] (Base text: 傅奕古本)

---

[a] Var.: 智之者 for 知者: 郭店 A.

[b] Var.: 弗言 for 不言也: 郭店 A; 馬王堆 A; 馬王堆 B.

[c] Var.: 言之者 for 言者: 郭店 A.

[d] Var.: 弗知 (郭店 A: 智) for 不知也: 郭店 A; 馬王堆 A; 馬王堆 B.

[e] Var.: 悶 for 兌: 馬王堆 A. Var.: 堄 for 兌: 馬王堆 B.

[f] Var.: 閟其逆賽其門 for 塞其兌 閉其門: 郭店 A.

[g] Var.: 坐 for 挫: 馬王堆 A. Var.: 銼 for 挫: 馬王堆 B. Support for 挫: 陸德明釋文.

[h] Var.: 閱 for 銳: 馬王堆 A. Var.: 兌 for 銳: 馬王堆 B. Var.: 剢其龠 for 挫其銳: 郭店 A.

[i] Var.: 物無所偏爭也 for 物物無偏爭也: 張之象本. Cf. textual note 3 here.

[j] Var.: 鬏 for 塵: 馬王堆 A.

[k] Var.: 物無所偏恥 for 物物無偏耻: 張之象本. Cf. textual note 3 here.

56.7 是謂[l]玄同不[m]可得而親亦不可得而踈[n] (Base text: 傅奕古本)

　　可得而親則可得而踈[o]也 (Base text: 集註本)

56.8 不可得而利亦不可得而害 (Base text: 傅奕古本)

　　可得而利則可得而害也 (Base text: 集註本)

56.9 不可得而貴亦不可得而賤[p] (Base text: 傅奕古本)

　　可得而貴則可得而賤也 (Base text: 集註本)

56.10 故爲天下貴 (Base text: 傅奕古本)

　　無物可以加之者[q] (Base text: 集註本)

56.1　　　[A ruler] who knows, does not speak.[1]

　　　　　He goes by [the entities'] That-which-is-of-itself-what-it-is.

56.2　　　[A ruler] who speaks, does not know.

　　　　　He contrives particular government action.

56.3　　If [a ruler] stuffs their [the other entities'] openings, and blocks their doors,

　　　　[So that they] have in themselves and conserve the[ir] unadorned [true nature].[2]

56.4　　　blunts their sharpness, dissolves their distractions,

　　　　　[that is,] eliminates the sources for struggle.

56.5　　　mixes with their luster,[3]

　　　　　If he has nothing which [he considers] particularly illustrious, then none of the entities has anything in particular for which to struggle.

---

[l] Var.: 胃 for 謂: 郭店 A; 馬王堆 A; 馬王堆 B.

[m] Var.: 故不 for 不: 郭店 A; 馬王堆 A; 馬王堆 B.

[n] 踈 for 疏: Wang Bi comm.; 范應元本.

[o] Var.: 疎 for 踈: 張之象本.

[p] Var.: 淺 for 賤: 馬王堆 A.　　　　[q] Var.: 也 for 者: 張之象本.

56.6   and joins in the same dust with them,

If he has nothing which [he considers] particularly lowly, then none of the entities has anything to be particularly ashamed of.

56.7   this I call "being identical with That-which-is-Dark."

That is why [the other entities] are unable to come close [to him] and unable to get distant [from him as their openings are stuffed and their doors closed],

If they were able to come close [to him], then they would be able to get distant [from him].

56.8   unable to benefit [him] and unable to hurt [him], [because he has blunted their sharpness and dissolved their distractions],

If they were able to benefit [him], then they would be able to hurt [him].

56.9   and unable to honor [him] and unable to degrade him [because he has mixed with their luster and joined in the same dust with them].

If they were able to honor [him] then they would be able to put him down lowly.

56.10   That is why he is the [most] honored one in All Under Heaven.

There is no entity that could add anything to him.

THE STRUCTURE OF *LAOZI* 56

After the first two antonymic phrases, three pairs of grammatically parallel short phrases with three characters each follow. They are summarized by a nonparallel phrase referring to all of them in the beginning of text 7. "That is why" in text 7 is followed by three more pairs of sentences in strict parallel, which are again concluded by a nonparallel summarizing statement in text 10. We have thus the formal indicators of closed IPS in the form of parallel staircases. Wang Bi explicitly links the two groups only in one instance, namely, through the use of the same term *jian* 賤 in his commentaries to the last pair in the first and the last pair in the second group. However, once the parallel is indicated, it is not too difficult to see the same link between the first and second pairs of each group. I have indicated this by repeating the statement from the first group in the respective parts of the second group in brackets. The formal structure of the *zhang* is:

c	(56.1)
c	(56.2)
x	(56.3)
y	(56.4)
z	(56.5 and 56.6)
c	(56.7, first half)
x	(56.7, second half)
y	(56.8)
z	(56.9)
c	(56.10)

Zhang 57

57.1 以正^{a}治^{b}國^{c}以奇^{d}用兵以無事取天下 (Base text: 范應元本)

以道治國則國平以正治國則奇兵^{e}起也以無事則能取天下也上章云
其取天下者常以無事及其有事又不^{f}足以取天下也故以正治國則不
足以取天下而以奇用兵也夫以道治國崇本以息末以正治國立辟以攻
末本不立而末淺民無所及故必至於奇用兵也 (Base text: 集註本)

57.2 吾何^{g}以知^{h}其然哉^{i}以此^{j}夫天下多忌諱而民彌^{k}貧^{l}民多利器而^{m}國家^{n}滋^{o}昏
(Base text: 范應元本)

利器凡所以利己之器也^{p}民強則國家弱 (Base text: 集註本)

---

^{a} Var.: 政 for 正: 傅奕古本.

^{b} Var.: 之 for 治: 郭店 A; 馬王堆 A; 馬王堆 B.

^{c} Var.: 邦 for 國: 郭店 A; 馬王堆 A.　　^{d} Var.: 畸 for 奇: 馬王堆 A; 馬王堆 B.

^{e} Var.: 正 for 兵: 張之象本.　　　　^{f} 又不 for 不: 張之象本. Cf. 48.6, note 1.

^{g} 何 for 奚 (also in 傅奕古本): 馬王堆 A; 馬王堆 B. Cf. 54.7.

^{h} 天下 after 知 (also in 傅奕古本.) om.: 郭店 A; 馬王堆 A; 馬王堆 B.

^{i} Var.: 也 for 哉: 郭店 A. Var.: 也哉 (馬王堆 B:才) for 哉: 馬王堆 A; 馬王堆 B.

^{j} Var.: 以此 om.: 郭店 A; 馬王堆 A; 馬王堆 B.

^{k} Var.: 爾 for 彌: 傅奕古本.　　　　^{l} Var.: 畔 for 貧: 郭店 A.

^{m} Var.: 而 om.: 傅奕古本.

^{n} Var.: 邦家 for 國家: 馬王堆 A. Var.: 邦 for 國家: 郭店 A.

^{o} Var.: 茲 for 滋: 馬王堆 A. Var.: 慈 for 滋: 郭店 A.

^{p} Var.: 也 om.: 取善集.

57.3 民^q多智慧^r而邪^s事滋^t起 (Base text: 傅奕古本)

民多智慧則巧僞生巧僞生則邪事起 (Base text: 集註本)

57.4 法物滋章^u而^v盜賊多有 (Base text: 范應元本)

立正欲以息邪而奇兵用多忌諱欲以止貧者也^{w,1}而民彌貧多利器^x欲以強國者也而國愈昏^y皆^z舍本以治末故以致此也 (Base text: 集註本)

57.5 故^{aa}聖人之言云^{ab}我無爲^{ac}而民自化我好靜^{ad}而民自正我無事而民自富我欲無欲^{ae}而民自樸^{af,2} (Base text: 馬王堆 B)

上之所欲民從之速也我之所欲唯無欲而民亦無欲而自樸也此四者崇本以息末也 (Base text: 集註本)

---

^q Var.: 人 for 民: 郭店 A; 馬王堆 A.

^r 智 for 知: Wang Bi comm.; 范應元本. Var.: 知 (郭店 A: 智) for 智慧: 馬王堆 A; 郭店 A.

^s 邪 for 衰 (also in 范應元本): Wang Bi comm.

^u 口(郭店 A:法)物茲(郭店 A:勿慈) for 法令滋章: 郭店 A; 馬王堆 B. Further support for 章: Wang Bi *LZWZLL* 6.7 indirect quotation of this passage 息淫在乎去華, 不在茲(滋)章. The 去華 here suggests that Wang Bi read 法物. I am greatful to Mr. Peng Hao for suggesting this.

^v Var.: 而 om.: 郭店 A; 傅奕古本.

^w 止貧者也 for 耻貧: Wagner taking up the replacement of 耻 with 止 suggested by 藤澤東畡, and adding 者也 in analogy to 強國者也. Cf. note 1.

^x 多利器 for 利器: Wagner, cf. text note 1.

^y 昏 for 昏多: Wagner, cf. text note 1.

^z 皆 for 多皆: Hatano Tarō. The suggestion by 陶鴻慶 to read the 多 as 弱 (國愈昏弱) has some support from Wang Bi's commenting on the *Laozi* 57.2 國家滋昏 as 國家弱.

^{aa} 故 for 是以: 傅奕古本; 范應元本. Var.: 是以 for 故: 郭店A.

^{ab} 云 for 曰: 莊遵; 傅奕古本; 范應元本. Var.: 之言 om.: 傅奕古本; 范應元本. Cf. note 2.

^{ac} Var.: 無爲也 for 無爲: 馬王堆 A.

^{ad} Var.: 靖 for 静: 傅奕古本.

^{ae} 我欲無欲 for 我欲不欲: Wang Bi comm.: 我之所欲唯無欲. 無欲 also in 傅奕古本; 范應元本. Cf. note 2. Var.: 我無欲 for 我欲無欲: 傅奕古本; 范應元本.

^{af} Var.: 我無事 . . . 我亡爲 . . . 我好靜 for 我無爲 . . . 我好靜 . . . 我無事: 郭店 A.

57.1   [A ruler] who rules the state by means of standards will with cunning make use of the military.

[Only a ruler who rules the state] by means not of busying himself [with government] activity will get hold of All Under Heaven.

If a state is ruled by means of the Way, the state will be at peace.

"*If a state is ruled by means of standards,*" the cunning use of the military will arise.

[If the state is ruled] "by means of not busying [with government] activity," [the ruler] will be able to "get hold of All Under Heaven."

In an earlier zhang *[namely,* 48.4–6, Laozi*] says:*

"*His getting hold of All Under Heaven is due to [his] eternally not engaging in [government] activity.*

Once it would come to his engaging in [government] affairs, he would also not qualify for getting hold of All Under Heaven."

That is why

if [a ruler] "rules the state by means of standards" he does not qualify for "getting hold of All Under Heaven," but "will with cunning make use of the military"!

It is a fact that

[a ruler] who rules the state by means of the Way will emulate the root as a means of bringing to rest the stem and branches [growing from it].

[a ruler] who "rules the state by means of standards" will establish punishments as the means to take on the stem and branches [without

further care for their "root"]. If the
root is not well established and [as a
consequence] the stem and branches
are shallow [in their fixture], the people
will have nothing to attach themselves
to. That is why [under these conditions]
there will necessarily come about the
"cunning use of the military."

57.2   How do I know that this [that
                        the ruler ruling by means of
                        standards will make use of the
                        military, while a ruler who does
                        not busy himself with govern-
                        ment activity will control All
                        Under Heaven] is so? From the
                        following:

It is a fact that

—the more taboos there are in All
Under Heaven [as established by the
ruler], the poorer people will get;

—the more profitable instruments the
people have [due to the ruler's promo-
tion], the paler the state will get;

"Profitable instruments" are generally
instruments by means of which to
profit oneself. If the people get strong,
the state weakens.

57.3   —the more [due to the ruler's policies]
         the people increase [their] knowledge,
         the more depraved activities will arise.

Once [, due to the ruler's policies,] "the
people increase [their] knowledge,"
craftiness and deceit will come about.
Once craftiness and deceit come about,
"depraved activities" will "arise."

57.4   [In short,] the more beautiful objects
         are displayed [by the ruler], the more
         robbers and thieves there will be.

[That is,] he [the ruler] establishes
standards with the purpose of bringing

to rest depravity, but [ends up with]
the "cunning use of the military."
The "increase in taboos" has the
purpose of putting a stop to poverty,
but [ends up with] the people's being
even poorer. That he "increases the
beneficial instruments" has the
purpose of strengthening the state,
but [ends up] with the state's get-
ting "paler." [All of] these [efforts]
discard the root by way of regulating
the stem and branches. That is why
it comes to this [rise of evil, increase
in beautiful objects, multiplication
of robbers, and use of the military
against them].

That is why the words   57.5
of the Sage are:

—I [as a ruler would] not interfere, and the people would on
their own transform themselves
[for the better];

—I [would] emulate stillness,
and the people would on their
own rectify themselves;

—I [would] not engage in [gov-
ernment] activity, and the people
would on their own become rich.

[In short,] I [would] desire to
have no desire, and the people
would on their own become
unadorned.

What the ruler desires will be
quickly followed by the
people['s own ambitions]. What
I [the Sage as a ruler] desire is
only to be without desires, and
thus the people will also be
without desires and on their
own become unadorned. These
four [statements] are [specifica-

tions of the general strategy] to
emulate the root as a means to
bring the stem and branches to
rest.

THE STRUCTURE OF *LAOZI* 57

Laozi 57 has a fairly clear macro-structure. Two alternatives are set out in phrase 1 and 2, to be followed by a general question, "How do I know that this is so?" Then follow three parallel sentences and a fourth, text 4, which is nearly but not quite parallel, the difference being that it lacks the beneficiary [All Under Heaven, people] in the beginning that the other three sentences have. These four, or three plus one, phrases specify the general rule why the ruler who rules by means of a standard will end up using force to enforce it. The statement "that is why the Sage says" begins another set of four sentences, detailing the correct way of government, indicated in the beginning with the statement about the ruler who rules "by means of not busying himself [with government] activity" and thus "will get hold of All Under Heaven." The first three of these four sentences again are strictly parallel. The fourth again is transmitted in a rigidly parallel structure but has to be changed on the basis of Wang Bi's commentary in accordance with a reading transmitted in MWD B and in *Laozi* 64.7. Thus again we have three sentences plus one. The last sentences in both series must then be summarizing statements, which I will define as X and Y, respectively. Up until this point, we thus have the following structure:

a	b	(57.1, 57.1)
	c	(57.2)
a		
1,		(57.2)
	2,	(57.2)
	3	(57.3)
	X	(57.4)
	b	
1,		(57.5)
	2,	(57.5)
	3	(57.5)
	Y	(57.5)

The problem starts here. In other *zhang*, it has been possible on the basis of Wang Bi's commentary to link the corresponding pieces in both series, resulting in a rigid parallelism of specific content, not only one in numbers and general content. Wang Bi's commentary in this *zhang* is, it seems to me, not well transmitted. The first commentary is repetitive and badly argued, very uncharacteristic of Wang Bi. The same is true for the commentary to text 4, which takes up in a haphazard way various elements from the preceding texts and leaves others uncommented on, such as the very phrase to which the commentary is attached. There is one single indicator in the main text that suggests a link, namely, the contrast between "the people will get poorer" in the first series and "the people would on their own become rich" in the second. Their positions in their series, however, are different, the first being in the first position, the second in the third. For the remaining two I have been unable to extract either from this *zhang* or from other *zhang* in which the same terms occur clear criteria for grouping them together. We thus are left with a structure that is as rigid in its numerical parallelisms and macro-order as it is loose in the details of interlocking.

Zhang 58

58.1 其政ᵃ悶悶ᵇ其民惇惇ᶜ'¹ (Base text: Wang Bi comm.)

言善治政者無形無名無事無正ᵈ可舉悶悶然卒至於大治故曰其政悶悶也其民無所爭競寬大惇惇ᵉ故曰其民惇惇ᶠ也 (Base text: 集註本)

58.2 其政ᵍ察察ʰ其民ⁱ缺缺ʲ (Base text: for first two characters 傅奕古本 and for rest Wang Bi comm.)

ᵃ Var.: 正 for 政: 馬王堆 B.

ᵇ Var.: 闌闌 for 悶悶: 馬王堆 B. Var.: 閔閔 for 悶悶: 傅奕古本; 范應元本.

ᶜ 惇惇 for 淳淳: 纂微 with regard to Wang Bi text. Cf. note 1. Var.: 屯屯 for 惇惇: 馬王堆 B. Var.: 偆偆 for 惇惇: 傅奕古本; 范應元本.

ᵈ Var.: 政 for 正: 張之象本.

ᵉ 惇惇 for 淳淳: Wagner, based on 纂微. Cf. note 1.

ᶠ 惇惇 for 淳淳: Wagner, based on 纂微. Cf. note 1.

ᵍ Var.: 正 for 政: 馬王堆 A; 馬王堆 B.

ʰ Var.: 詧詧 for 察察: 傅奕古本; 范應元本.

ⁱ Var.: 邦 for 民: 馬王堆 A.   ʲ Var.: 夬夬 for 缺缺: 馬王堆 A.

立刑名明賞罰以檢姦僞故曰其政察察[k]也殊類分析民懷爭競故曰其民缺缺 (Base text: 集註本)

58.3 禍兮[l]福之所倚[m]福兮[n]禍之所伏孰知其極其無正也[o] (Base text: 傅奕古本)

言誰知善治之極乎唯無正可舉無形[p]可名[q]悶悶然而天下大化是其極也 (Base text: 集註本)

58.4 正復爲奇 (Base text: Wang Bi comm.)

以正治國則便復以奇用兵矣故曰正復爲奇 (Base text: 集註本)

58.5 善復爲妖[r] (Base text: 傅奕古本)

立善以和物[s]則便復有妖佞之患也[t] (Base text: 集註本)

58.6 民[u]之迷[v]也[w]其日固已[x]久矣 (Base text: Wang Bi comm. on 周易 Hex. 明夷九三 4.7a4)

言民[y]之迷惑失道固久矣不可便正善治以責 (Base text: 集註本)

---

[k] 其政察察 for 察察: 宇佐美灊水 based on parallel with 其政悶悶 in Wang Bi on *Laozi* 58.1.

[l] Var.: 虪 for 禍兮: 馬王堆 A. 馬王堆 B has no place in a lacuna for 兮.

[m] Var.: 禍兮福之所倚 om.: 馬王堆 B.

[n] Var.: 兮 om.: 馬王堆 A. 馬王堆 B.

[o] 也 for 㝈: 馬王堆 B. Var.: 邪 for 也: 范應元本; Note in 集註本 about a Wang Bi *Laozi* writing 邪.

[p] 形 for 刑: 張之象本.

[q] Var.: 唯無可正舉 無可形名 for 唯無正可舉無形可名: 張之象本.

[r] 妖 for 袄 (also in 范應元本): Wang Bi comm.:妖佞之患.

[s] Var.: 萬物 for 物: 張之象本.

[t] 則便復有妖佞之患也 for 則便復有妖妖佞之患也: Hatano Tarō. Var.: 則便復有妖之患也 for 則便復有妖佞之患也: 張之象本.

[u] Var.: 人 for 民: 傅奕古本.   [v] Var.: 悉 for 迷: 馬王堆 B.

[w] Var.: 也 om.: 范應元本.   [x] Var.: 已 om.: 馬王堆 B; 傅奕古本.

[y] 民 for 人: Wagner, based on Wang Bi quotation of text. Both the *Laozi* above the 集註本 and that above the 張之象本 write 人. I assume the commentary was later adjusted to this reading.

58.7 是以聖人^z方而不割 (Base text: 傅奕古本)

以方導物 令^{aa}去其邪不以方割物所謂大方無隅 (Base text: 集註本)

58.8 廉而不劌^{ab} (Base text: 傅奕古本)

廉清廉也劌傷也以清廉清民令去其污^{ac}不以清廉劌傷於物也 (Base text: 集註本)

58.9 直而不肆^{ad} (Base text: 傅奕古本)

以直導物令去其僻而不以直激拂^{ae}於物也所謂大直若屈也 (Base text: 取善集)

58.10 光而不燿^{af} (Base text: Wang Bi comm. on 41.3, 傅奕古本)

以光鑑其所以迷不以光照求其隱匿^{ag}也所謂明道若昧也此皆崇本以息末不攻而使復之也 (Base text: 集註本)

58.1 He [a ruler] whose government is hidden [from view] will have his people be generous.

This means: [A ruler] who is good at regulating government will have neither shape nor name, neither [government] activity nor standard that could be pointed out. [His government] is "hidden [from view]" [but] eventually will bring about the Great Order. That is why [the text] says: "He [a ruler] whose government is hidden [from view]." His people will have nothing to struggle about and compete for, wide and grand [they are in their] generosity; that is why [the text] says: "will have his people be generous."

58.2 He [a ruler] whose government is bent on surveillance will see his people divided.

---

^z Var.: 聖人 om.: 馬王堆 B.   ^{aa} 令 for 舍: 陸德明釋文.

^{ab} Var.: 兼而不刺 for 廉而不劌: 馬王堆 B.

^{ac} Var.: 令去其邪 令去其污 for 令去其污: 取善集; 張之象 本. The phrase 令去其邪 duplicates the same phrase from Wang Bi on 58.7.

^{ad} Var.: 紲 for 肆: 馬王堆 B.

^{ae} Var.: 沸 for 拂 for: 集註本; 張之象本. Support for 拂: 陸德明釋文.

^{af} Var.: 燿 for 燿: 陸德明釋文.

^{ag} Var.: 慝 for 匿: 張之象本. Support for 匿: 陸德明釋文.

He establishes punishments and names [corresponding to social ranks]
and publishes rewards and punishments in order to bring the cunning
and deceiving under control. That is why [the text] says "He [a ruler]
whose government is bent on surveillance . . . " The different categories
[of people] are allocated and split [so that] the people are concerned with
struggle and competition. That is why [the text] says: "will see his people
divided"!

58.3   If [, in this manner,] it is disaster indeed on which luck rests, and luck
       under which disaster crouches—who is to know what the epitome [of being
       good at regulating government] is? [Hardly anyone]. It is in being without
       standards!

This [last phrase] means who [possibly] knows what the epitome of being
good at regulating [government] is? Only that there is no standard by
which one could to point it out and no shape that could be named, but
just being "hidden" [from view] while All Under Heaven greatly changes
[for the better]—this is its epitome!

58.4   A standard [by which a ruler rules] will in turn lead to [military] cunning.

[As the Laozi 57.1 says,] "[A ruler] who rules the state by means of stan-
dards will" in turn "with cunning make use of the military." That is why
[the text] says " A standard [by which a ruler rules] will in turn lead to
[military] cunning."

58.5   Goodness [as a governing instrument of a ruler] will in turn lead to evil.

[If a ruler] establishes the good in order to harmonize the ten thousand
kinds of entities, then in turn he will experience the distress of evil.[1]

58.6   [On the other hand, it is true that] the delusion of the people has definitely
       already been around for a long time.

This means: The delusion of the people and [their] loss of the Way defi-
nitely has lasted for a long time already. It will not do [simply] to hold
ruling [by means of] a standard and goodness responsible for it.[2]

58.7   This is why the Sage makes square but does not trim [others].

By means of squareness he guides the other entities and has them do
away with their evil, but he does not trim the other entities by means of
squareness . This is what is said [in Laozi 41.11]: "The Great Squaring is
without corners."

58.8   He makes clean but does not injure [others].

"Clean" means pure cleanness. "To injure" means to wound. By means
of pure cleanness he makes the people pure and has them do away with
the pollution [of their true nature], but does not injure and wound the
other entities by means of pure cleanness.

58.9   He straightens but not does not bully.

With straightness he guides the other entities and has them do away with their depravities, but he does not shock and suppress the other entities with straightness. This is what is said [in Laozi 45.3*]: "[It is the mark of] the Great Straightening to be as if crooked."*

58.10   He enlightens but does not investigate.

By means of enlightenment he clears up what has deluded them [the people] but does not by means of [his] enlightenment shed light on and search out their [the people's] secret hideouts. This is what is said [in Laozi 41.3*]: "It is the [Sage's] Way of enlightening to be well-nigh dark." All these [proceedings of the Sage] are [specifications of the general strategy] to emulate the root as a means to bring the stem and branches to rest but not to attack [the other entities] in order to get them to relate back [to the root].*

Zhang 59

59.1 治人事天莫如ᵃ嗇 (Base text: 傅奕古本)

莫如ᵇ猶莫過也嗇農也ᶜ夫農人之治田務去其殊類歸於齊一也ˡ全其自然不急其荒病除其所以荒病上承ᵈ天命下綏百姓莫過於此 (Base text: 集註本)

59.2 夫唯ᵉ嗇是以早ᶠ復ᵍ (Base text: 馬王堆 B)

復ʰ常也 (Base text: 集註本)

59.3 早復ⁱ謂之ʲ重積德 (Base text: Wang Bi comm.)

ᵃ 如 for 若: Wang Bi comm.: 莫如猶莫過也; 陸德明釋文.

ᵇ Var.: 若 for 如: 張之象本.   ᶜ 農也 for 農: Wagner.

ᵈ Var.: 於 om. 張之象本.   ᵉ Var.: 惟 for 唯: 傅奕古本; 范應元本.

ᶠ 早 for 蚤: Wang Bi comm.; 陸德明釋文; 傅奕古本; 范應元本.

ᵍ 復 for 服 (also in 郭店 B; 馬王堆 A; 傅奕古本; 范應元本): Comment by Fan Yingyuan about his Wang Bi manuscript, which read 復, 2.42b; Wang Bi comm.; 陸德明釋文. Wang Bi's *Laozi* is the only known old text reading 復 here. Many Song editions and commentators such as the 集註 adopted this reading.

ʰ Var.: 早服 for 復: 張之象本.

ⁱ Var.: 服 for 復: 郭店 B; 馬王堆 B; 傅奕古本; 范應元本.

ʲ Var.: 是胃 for 謂之: 郭店 B; 馬王堆 B.

唯重積德不欲銳速然後乃能使早復^k其常故曰早復^l謂之重積德者也 (Base text: 集註本)

59.4 重積德則無不克無不克則莫知其極 (Base text: 傅奕古本)

道無窮也 (Base text: 集註本)

59.5 莫知其極可以^m有國 (Base text: 傅奕古本)

以有窮而涖國非能有國也 (Base text: 集註本)

59.6 有國之母可以長久 (Base text: 傅奕古本)

國之所以安謂之母重積德是唯圖其根然後營末乃得其終也 (Base text: 集註本)

59.7 是謂ⁿ深根^o固柢^p長生久視之道^q (Base text: 傅奕古本)

59.1 In managing men and serving Heaven nothing compares to be reductive.

"Nothing compares" means nothing surpasses. "Being reductive" [refers to] farming. It is a fact that the field management of the farmers takes care to eliminate the different varieties [of plants] from them [the fields] and reduce [the plants] to one [and the same variety]. They completely maintain [the fields'] That-which-is-of-itself-what-it-is by not fretting about their going wild, but by eliminating that by which they [might] go wild. [For a ruler] who from above receives the Mandate of Heaven and below comforts the Hundred Families nothing surpasses this [reductionism of the farmer].

59.2 It is a fact that only by being reductive will [a ruler] have them [the Hundred Families] return soon.

[That is,] return to the Eternal.[1]

59.3 [A ruler's] having them return soon is described as [his] putting emphasis [only] on the accumulation of receipt/capacity [and not on speeding up this return].

Only by putting emphasis on accumulating receipt/capacity without desiring perked-up acceleration will he eventually be capable of having [the Hundred Families] return early to their Eternal.

59.4   If he is putting emphasis [only] on accumulating receipt/capacity, then there will be nothing that he does not bring under control. If there is nothing that he does not bring under control, then there will be no one [among the Hundred Families] who will know his [the ruler's] perfection.

[That no one will be able to know his perfection is due to the fact that his] Way is inexhaustible.

59.5   Once there is no one [among the Hundred Families] who knows his perfection, it is possible for him to possess the state.

Were he to manage the state by means of an exhaustible [way], he would not be capable of possessing the state.

59.6   Being in possession of the mother of the state, it is possible for him to persist long.[2]

That by which peace is brought to the state is called [its] mother. Putting emphasis on accumulating receipt/capacity means focusing only on its [All Under Heaven's] root, and only then managing the stem and branches. [Doing so] he [the ruler who follows this way] will indeed manage to reach his [natural] end.

59.7   This I call the Way of deeply [implanting] the root, consolidating the base, prolonging life, and extending the perspective.

Zhang 60

60.1 以治大國ª若烹ᵇ小鮮ᶜ (Base text: 傅奕古本)

不擾也躁則多害靜則全眞故其國彌大而其主彌靜然後乃能廣感ᵈ衆心矣 (Base text: 集註本)

60.2 以道莅ᵉ天下ᶠ其鬼不神 (Base text: 范應元本)

ª Var.: 國者 for 國: 范應元本.

ᵇ Var.: 亨 for 烹: 馬王堆 B; 范應元本. Support for 烹: 陸德明釋文. Wang Bi comm. on *Laozi* 60.2 若烹小鮮.

ᶜ Var.: 鱗 for 鮮: 范應元本. Support for 鮮: 陸德明釋文.

ᵈ Var.: 得 for 感 (also in 取善集): 張之象本.

ᵉ Var.: 立 for 莅: 馬王堆 B. Var.: 涖 for 莅: 傅奕古本.

ᶠ Var.: 天下者 for 天下: 傅奕古本.

治大國則若烹小鮮以道蒞天下則其鬼不神也 (Base text: 集註本)

60.3 非其鬼不神^g其神不傷人^h (Base text: 傅奕古本)

神不害自然也物守自然則神無所加神無所加ⁱ則不知神之爲神也
(Base text: 集註本)

60.4 非其神^j不傷人^k聖人亦不傷人^l (Base text: 傅奕古本)

道洽則神不傷人神不傷人則不知神之爲神道洽則聖人亦不傷人聖人
不傷人則亦不知聖人之爲聖也猶云非獨^m不知神之爲神亦不知聖人
之爲聖也夫恃威網以使物者治之衰也使不知神聖之爲神聖道之極也
(Base text: 集註本)

60.5 夫ⁿ兩不相傷故^o德交歸焉 (Base text: 傅奕古本)

神不傷人聖人亦不傷人聖人不傷人神亦不傷人故曰兩不相傷也神聖
合道交歸之也 (Base text: 集註本)

60.1 [In] managing a big state [the Sage Ruler acts] as if he were frying small
fish.

*[That is,] he does not worry. Bustling activity [as in stirring the fish] will
cause much damage [to the small fishes], [but] if he is calm, then he will
keep their true [essence] intact.[1] That is why the bigger the state but the
calmer its lord the broader, as a consequence, will he be able to influence
the hearts of the many.*

60.2 [But] if by means of the Way he governs All Under Heaven [and not just a
big state], its ghosts do not [manifest themselves as active] spirits.

[This means] "If he manages a big state," then "[he acts] as if he were fry-

---

^g Var.: 神也 for 神: 馬王堆 A; 馬王堆 B.

^h Var.: 人也 for 人: 馬王堆 A; 馬王堆 B. Var.: 民 for 人: 范應元本.

ⁱ 神無所加 for 神無加: 張之象本.

^j Var.: 申 for 神: 馬王堆 A.

^k Var.: 人也 for 人: 馬王堆 A; 馬王堆 B. Var.: 民 for 人: 范應元本.

^l Var.: 弗傷也(馬王堆 A: 弗傷口) for 不傷人: 馬王堆 A; 馬王堆 B. Var.: 民 for 人:
范應元本.

^m Var.: 非獨 om.: 張之象本.   ⁿ Var.: 夫 om.: 范應元本.

^o Var.: 則 for 故: 范應元本.

*ing small fish, [but] if by means of the Way he governs All Under Heaven,"
then "its ghosts do not [manifest themselves as active] spirits.*[2]

60.3   Not [only] do its ghosts not [manifest themselves as active] spirits, its spirits [also] do not harm people.

*The spirits do not harm That-which-is-of-itself-what-it-is. Because [as a
consequence] the entities keep [their] That-which-is-of-itself-what-it-is,
there is nothing that the spirits add to [them]. If there is nothing that
the spirits have to add to [them], then [the people] do not know that the
spirits are spirits.*

60.4   And not [only] do its spirits not harm people, the Sage [himself] also does
not harm people.

*If [All Under Heaven is governed] in accordance with the Way, the
"spirits will not harm people," and, if the spirits do not harm people,
then [people] do not know the spirits to be spirits. If [All Under Heaven
is governed] in accordance with the Way, the "Sage also does not harm
people," and if the Sage does not harm people, then [they] also do not
know the Sage to be sagely. It is as if [the Laozi] said: Not alone do [they]
not know the spirits to be spirits, [they] also do not know the Sage to be
a Sage. It is a fact that to prod entities on through reliance on a network
of authority is the demise of the management [of a state], but to bring it
about that [they] do not know the spirits and the Sage to be spirits and
the Sage is the ultimate [achievement] of [governing by means of] the
Way.*

60.5   It is a fact that both [the spirits and the Sage] together do not harm [peo-
ple]. That is why what they [the spirits and the Sage] achieve[3] is to interact
in returning [the people to the root].

*As the spirits do not harm people, the Sage also does not harm people. As
the Sage does not harm people, the spirits also do not harm people. That
is why [the text] says "both together do not harm [people]." As spirits
and the Sage are in accordance with the Way, they "interact in returning"
them [the people to the root].*

Zhang 61

61.1 大國ᵃ下流ᵇ也ᶜ (Base text: Wang Bi comm.)

江海居大而處下則百川流之大國居大而處下則天下流ᵈ之故曰大國
下流也 (Base text: 集註本)

61.2 天下之所ᵉ交ᶠ也ᵍ (Base text: 范應元本)

天下之ʰ所歸會也 (Base text: 集註本)

61.3 天下之牝ⁱ也ⁱ·¹ (Base text: 傅奕古本)

靜而不求物自歸之ᵏ (Base text: 集註本)

61.4 牝常ˡ以靜ᵐ勝ⁿ牡以其靜故爲下也ᵒ (Base text: 范應元本)

以其靜故能爲下也牝雌也雄躁動貪欲雌常以靜故能勝雄也以其靜復
能爲下故物歸之也 (Base text: 集註本)

ᵃ Var.: 邦者 for 國: 馬王堆 A. Var.: 國者 for 國: 傅奕 古本; 范應元本.

ᵇ Var.: 天下之下流 for 下 流: 傅奕古本; 范應元本.

ᶜ Var.: 也 om.: 傅奕古本; 范應元本.

ᵈ Var.: 歸 for 流: 取善集.

ᵉ Var.: 所 om.: 馬王堆 A; 馬王堆 B; 傅奕古本. Support for 所: Wang Bi comm.

ᶠ Var.: 郊 for 交: 馬王堆 A.

ᵍ Var.: 也 om.: 傅奕古本.

ʰ Var.: 之 om.: 取善集; 張之象本.

ⁱ Var.: 牲 for 牝: 范應元本. Support for 牝: 陸德明釋文.

ʲ 牝也 for 牝 (also in 馬王堆 A; 也 also absent in 范應元本): 馬王堆 B. Support for
也: parallelism to *Laozi* 61.2.

ᵏ Var.: 之也 for 之: 張之象本.

ˡ Var.: 恒 for 常: 馬王堆 A; 馬王堆 B.

ᵐ Var.: 靚 for 靜: 馬王堆 A. Var.: 靖 for 靜: 傅奕古本.

ⁿ Var.: 朕 for 勝: 馬王堆 B.

ᵒ Var.: 爲其靜 (馬王堆 A: 靚) 也故宜爲下也 (馬王堆 A om. 也) for 以其靜故爲下
也: 馬王堆 A; 馬王堆 B.

61.5 故[P]大國[q]以下小國 (Base text: 馬王堆 B with 傅奕古本 for the lacuna 以下□國)

　　　大國以下猶云以大國下小國 (Base text: 集註本)

61.6 則取[r]小國 (Base text: 馬王堆 B)

　　　小國則附之 (Base text: 集註本)

61.7 小國以下大國則取於[s]大國 (Base text: 馬王堆 B)

　　　大國納之也 (Base text: 集註本)

61.8 故[t]或下以取或下而取 (Base text: 馬王堆 A)

　　　言唯脩[u]卑下然後乃各得其所 (Base text: 集註本)

61.9 大[v]國[w]不過欲兼[x]畜人小國[y]不過欲入事人兩者各得[z]其所[aa]欲則[ab]大者宜爲下 (Base text: 傅奕古本 until 各, from then Wang Bi comm.)

　　　小國脩[ac]下自全而已不能令天下歸之大國脩下則天下歸之故曰各得其所欲則大者宜爲下也 (Base text: 集註本)

61.1　　　　　　　　　　　　If a state [, although] big,
　　　　　　　　　　　　　　lowers itself, [all others] will
　　　　　　　　　　　　　　flow [towards it].

[P] Var.: 故 om.: 馬王堆 A.

[q] Var.: 邦 for 國: 馬王堆 A. Passim in this *zhang*.

[r] Var.: 取於 for 取: 傅奕古本.　　　　[s] Var.: 於 om.: 范應元本.

[t] Var.: 故 om.: 傅奕古本.　　　　[u] Var.: 修 for 脩: 張之象本.

[v] Var.: 故大 for 大: 馬王堆 B. 馬王堆 A has a lacuna that would leave space for the 故.

[w] Var.: 邦者 for 國: 馬王堆 A. Var.: 國者 for 國: 馬王堆 B.

[x] Var.: 并 for 兼: 馬王堆 B.　　　　[y] Var.: 邦者 for 國: 馬王堆 A.

[z] Var.: 夫皆得 for 兩者各得: 馬王堆 A (馬王堆 B: 夫□□).

[aa] Var.: 所 om.: 馬王堆 A; 馬王堆 B.

[ab] Var.: 故大者 for 則大者: 傅奕古本. Var.: 故大國者 for 則大者: 范應元本.

[ac] Var.: 修 for 脩: 張之象本.

Rivers and seas, [although]
covering a big [area], take
their place in low[er reaches];
as a consequence, the hundred
streams flow towards them. If
a big state, [although] covering
a big [area], takes a lowly place,
All Under Heaven will flow
towards it.[1] *That is why [the*
text] says: "If a state, [, although]
big, lowers itself, [all others] will
flow [towards it]"!

61.2   It [will be the] point where All
Under Heaven converges.

It [will be the point] where All
Under Heaven renders itself
and comes together.

61.3   It [will be] the female of All
Under Heaven.

Being [like the female] calm and
without cravings, the other entities
will render themselves to it of
their own accord.[2]

61.4   The female constantly overcomes
the male through its calmness.
Because of its calmness it adopts
the lowly [position].

Because of its calmness it is capable
of adopting a lowly [position].
"Female" means "hen." The cock
is agitated and full of sexual desire.
The hen is constant through [its]
calmness; that is why it is capable
of overcoming the cock. If [the big
state] because of its calmness again
is able to adopt a lowly [position],
the other entities will therefore
render themselves to it.

61.5   This is why,

if the big state proceeds by way
of lowering itself below the small states,

*"If the big state proceeds by
way of lowering itself" is as
if the text said "if with a big
state one [takes a position]
below the small states."*

61.6   then it will get hold of the
         small states.

*The small states will as a
consequence [of the big
state's lowering itself]
associate themselves with it.*

if the small states proceed by   61.7
way of lowering themselves
under the big state, they will be
gotten hold of by the big state.

*The big state will accommodate
them.*

61.8   That is why
one [the big state] lowers itself   one [the small state] lowers itself
in order to get hold of;   and is gotten hold of.

*This means: As long as [the
big state] cultivates a humble
and lowly [position], they will
[as the next sentence of the
Laozi says] "each attain their
[proper] place."*

61.9   The big state desires nothing   The small state desires nothing
         more than to unite and bring   more than to join and serve
         together the others.   others.

It is a fact that for the two
[the big state and the small
state] to each get what they
desire, it is mandatory for the
big [state] to adopt a lowly
[position and not for the small
one].

*If a small state cultivates a lowly
[position], it will not achieve
more than to keep intact, but
will not be able to get All Under
Heaven to render itself to it [the
small state].*

*If a big state cultivates a lowly
[position], then All Under
Heaven will render itself to it
[the big state].*

> *That is why [the text] says:
> "For each to get what they
> desire, it is mandatory for
> the big [state] to adopt a
> lowly [position and not
> for the small one]"!*

THE STRUCTURE OF *LAOZI* 61
Laozi 61 has a simple insert in open IPS, giving it the structure:

c		(61.1)
c		(61.2)
c		(61.3)
c		(61.4)
a	b	(61.5/6; 61.7)
a	b	(61.8; 61.8)
a	b	(61.9; 61.9)
c		(61.9)

Zhang 62

62.1 道者萬物之奧ᵃ也ᵇ (Base text: 傅奕古本)

奧猶曖ᶜ也可得庇蔭之辭 (Base text: 張之象本)

62.2 善人之所ᵈ寶ᵉ (Base text: 傅奕古本)

寶以爲用也 (Base text: 集註本)

ᵃ Var.: 注 for 奧: 馬王堆 A; 馬王堆 B.

ᵇ Var.: 也 om.: 范應元本.

ᶜ Var.: 愛 for 曖: 集註本. Support for 曖: 陸德明釋文.

ᵈ Var.: 所 om.: 馬王堆 A; 馬王堆 B. Support for 所: Wang Bi comm. reads with 寶 以爲用也 the term 寶 as a verb that corresponds to a 所 construction.

ᵉ Var.: 瑱也 for 寶: 馬王堆 A; 馬王堆 B.

62.3 不善人之所保[f,l] (Base text: 傅奕古本)

    保以全也 (Base text: 集註本)

62.4 美言可以市[g]尊[h]行[i]可以加於[j]人 (Base text: Wang Bi comm. for 尊行 in second part; Wang Bi comm. in connection with 傅奕古本)

    言道無所不先物無有貴於此也雖有珍寶璧馬無以匹[k]之美言之則可以奪衆貨之賈故曰美言可以市也尊行之則千里之外應之故曰可以加於人也 (Base text: 張之象本)

62.5 人之不善[l]何棄之有[m] (Base text: 傅奕古本)

    不善當保道以免放[n] (Base text: 張之象本)

62.6 故立天子置三公[o] (Base text: 傅奕古本)

    言以尊行道也 (Base text: 集註本)

62.7 雖有拱[p]璧以先駟[q]馬 不如[r]坐而[s]進此道[t] (Base text: 范應元本)

    此道上之所云也言故立天子置三公尊其位重其人所以爲道也物無有貴於此者故雖有拱抱寶璧以先駟馬而進之不如坐而進此道也 (Base text: 集註本)

---

    [f] Var.: 瑧也 for 保: 馬王堆 A. Var.: 保也 for 保: 馬王堆 B.

    [g] Var.: 於市 for 市: 傅奕古本; 范應元本.

    [h] Var.: 奠 for 尊: 馬王堆 B.   [i] Var.: 言 for 行: 傅奕古本.

    [j] Var.: 賀 for 加於: 馬王堆 A; 馬王堆 B.

    [k] Var.: 正 for 匹: 集註本.   [l] Var.: 善也 for 善: 馬王堆 A.

    [m] Var.: 何棄也口有 for 何棄之有: 馬王堆 A.

    [n] Var.: 傲 for 放: 集註本.

    [o] Var.: 卿 for 公: 馬王堆 A. Var.: 鄉 for 公: 馬王堆 B.

    [p] 拱 for 琪: Wang Bi comm.; 陸德明釋文; 傅奕古本. Var.: 共之 for 拱: 馬王堆 A.

    [q] Var.: 四 for 駟: 馬王堆 A. 馬王堆 B.

    [r] Var.: 善 for 如: 馬王堆 A. Var. 若 for 如: 馬王堆 B.

    [s] 坐而 for 坐: Wang Bi comm.: 不如坐而進此道; 馬王堆 A. 馬王堆 B. Var.: 坐而 om: 傅奕古本.

    [t] Var.: 道 om.: 馬王堆 A. 馬王堆 B. Var.: 道也 for 道: 傅奕古本.

62.8 古之所以貴此道^u者何也^v不曰^w以求得^x有罪以免邪^y故爲天下貴 (Base text: 傅奕古本)

以求則得求以免則得免無所而不施故爲天下貴也 (Base text: 集註 本)

62.1

The Way is what covers [all] the ten thousand kinds of entities.

"Cover" is like "spread over." It is an expression that each one of them attains [the Way's] protection.[1]

62.2 It is what is treasured by good men

They treasure it in order to make use of it.

62.3 It is what men who are not good protect.

They protect it means that through it they stay unharmed.

62.4 [If someone good] spoke [of the Way] with appreciation, it would [even] be possible [for him] to [compete] in the market. [If someone in an honored [position] would practice [the Way], it would [even] be possible [for him] to have an impact on others.

This means: There is nothing in which the Way is not the best. None of the entities has anything superior to this [Way]. Even having precious and valuable jade and horses [, as referred to in Laozi 62.7,] is no match for it. If [someone good] says beautiful words about it, it is possible to surpass with it the price of all

62.5 [If things are thus,] how could there be any of the not good ones among men to reject it [this Way]?

The not good ones have to protect the Way in order to escape [punishment].

---

^u Var.: 道 om.: 馬王堆 A.   ^v Var.: 也 om.: 范應元本.

^w Var.: 胃 for 曰: 馬王堆 A. 馬王堆 B.

^x 以求 得 for 求以得 (also in 馬王堆 A (求口得); 馬王堆 B; 范應元本): Wang Bi comm.: 以求則得求.

^y Var.: 輿 for 邪: 馬王堆 A. Var.: 與 for 邪: 馬王堆 B.

the goods [in the market]. That
is why [the text] says: "[If some-
one good] spoke [of the Way] with
appreciation, it would [even] be
possible [for him] to [compete]
in the market." "If someone in an
honored [position] would practice"
it [the Way], then [even people]
further away than a thousand miles
would respond to him. That is why
[the text] says: "It would [even] be
possible [for him] to have an impact
on others"!

62.6

[Thus] when purposefully
enthroning a Son of Heaven
and installing the three [high-
est] ministers,

This means to practice the
Way in an honored position.

62.7

even if there was available a
jade [disk so large that one
needs both arms to] get around
[it] to precede [their] carriage
with [its] four horses, this still
would not compare to [their]
promoting this Way by [just]
sitting [in their official seat].

"This Way" refers to what has
been said above [in Laozi 62.1–3].
This means: When "purposefully
enthroning a Son of Heaven and
installing the three [highest]
ministers" in making honorable
the position of [the former] and
giving importance to the personal-
ities of [the latter], as the Way is
such that none of the entities has
anything superior to it, even if there
was available a precious jade disk
[so large that one needs two arms
to] get around to precede [their]
carriage with [its] four horses so

*as to promote [the Way from this
honored position] this still would
not compare to their "promoting
this Way by [just] sitting [in their
official seat]."*

62.8   What is the reason why the ancients
valued this Way?

Did they not say:

[If the good ones] strive by means
of it [the Way], they will achieve it,   while those [the not good ones]
who have committed crimes
avoid [punishment] by means of
it [the Way]?

That is why it is [most]
valued by All Under Heaven.

*If [the good ones] strive by   If [the not good ones] avoid
means of it, then they achieve   [punishment] by means of it [the
what they strive for.   Way], they manage to avoid it.*

*There is nothing that it [this
Way] does not bring about.
That is why it is [most] valued
in All Under Heaven.*

THE STRUCTURE OF *LAOZI* 62

Laozi 62 contains some formal elements signaling IPS. In 62.2 and 62.3 a pair is set up of "good men" and "men who are not good," and in the reason given for the appreciation of the Way by the ancients in 62.8 this pair seems to return. There is a reference to the "not good ones" in 62.5. It does not qualify for standing alone, because the further argument does not build on it. On the other hand, it is not in a formal parallel to 62.4, although in terms of content it makes sense to associate the statement of 62.4 with the "good ones." I have done this, although there is no question that the formal requirements of IPS are not being followed here. Worse, 62.4 itself consists of a parallel pair for which I see no echo elsewhere in this *zhang*, because Wang Bi's commentary to 62.6 seems to take up only the 尊行 element and not the 美言—if the 言 in this commentary is not a corrupted relic of 美言. My analysis of the structure thus has to remain tentative with the consequence that the translation also is not really satisfactory.

	c		(62.1)
a		b	(62.2, 62.3)
a		b	(62.4, 62.5)
	c		(62.6)
	c		(62.7)
	c		(62.8)
a		b	(62.8, 62.8)
	c		(62.8)

Zhang 63

63.1 爲無爲事無事 味無味[a] (Base text: 傅奕古本)

以無爲爲居以不言爲教以恬淡爲味治之極也 (Base text: 集註本)

63.2 大小[b]多少報怨以德 (Base text: 傅奕古本)

小怨則不足以報大怨則天下之所欲誅順天下之所同者德也 (Base text: 集註本)

63.3 圖難乎於其易爲大乎於[c]其細[d]天下之難事必作[e]於易天下之大事必作[f]於細是以聖人終[g]不爲大故能成其大夫輕諾者必寡信[h]多易者[i]必多難是以聖人猶[j]難之 (Base text: 傅奕古本)

以聖人之才猶尙難於細易 況非聖人之才 而欲忽於此乎 故曰猶難之也 (Base text: 集註本)

---

[a] Var.: 未 for 味: 馬王堆 A.

[b] Var. 少之 for 小: 郭店 A. This text continues further down with 多易 (惕) in 63.3. The scribe seems to have jumped the line from one 多 to the next.

[c] Var.: 於 om.: 馬王堆 B.   [d] Var.: 細也 for 細: 馬王堆 B.

[e] Var.: 難作 for 難事 必作: 馬王堆 A. (Number of spaces in lacuna of 馬王堆 B corresponds to reading of 難作.)

[f] Var.: 大作 for 大事 必作: 馬王堆 A.

[g] Var.: 冬 for 終: 馬王堆 A.

[h] Var.: 輕若口口信 for 輕諾者必寡信: 馬王堆 B.

[i] Var.: 者 om.: 馬王堆 B.   [j] Var.: 猷 for 猶: 馬王堆 A.

63.4 故終無難矣^k (Base text: 傅奕古本)

惟其難於細易故終無難大之事¹ (Base text: 取善集)

63.1 | [A Sage Ruler] practices non-interference, engages in non-activity, and relishes the flavorless!¹

[The Sage Ruler's] "taking" "non-interference" as [his] "residence" [as the Laozi *2.2 says], taking the "wordless" as [his] "teaching" [as the* Laozi *2.3 says], and taking the sub-dued and insipid as relish,² is the epitome of [creating] order!*

63.2 | With regard to big and small, many and few [resentments], [he] reciprocates for the resentment by means of [his] receipt/capacity.

If there is a small resentment it is not worth reciprocating. If it is a big resentment, then it is a case where All Under Heaven desires the execution [of the culprit]. [His] going along with what All Under Heaven agrees on is [meant by his] "receipt/capacity."

63.3 | [He] makes plans against [eventual] difficulties when things are still easy [to resolve]. | He acts on [what is eventually] big while it is still minute.

Because the difficulties in All Under Heaven inevitably grow out of easily [resolvable troubles], | Because the big affairs in All Under Heaven necessarily grow out of minute ones,

[even] the Sage only by not acting upon [things] that have already become big is in the end able to complete their greatness. [Ditto with the difficulties.]³

---

^k Var.: 多於無難 for 終無難矣: 馬王堆 A; lacuna in 馬王堆 B of the same size as text in 馬王堆 A. Var.: 矣 om.: 郭店 A.

It is a fact
that he who makes promises
easily, inevitably finds little
trust.[4]

that he who takes many [things]
lightly will inevitably have many
difficulties.

That is why the Sage treats even
[light problems] as difficulties.
[Ditto with trust.][5]

If even with the gifts of the
Sage he still takes [things] as

difficult   *important and*
and easy [to solve],   *while [they are] still small*

how much less will someone
without the gifts of the Sage wish
to be negligent in this respect!
That is why [the text] says: "[He]
treats even [easy and small
problems] as difficulties"!

63.4   That is why throughout he has
no difficulties.[6]

It is only because he treats
[problems] as difficult while
they [still]

are small and
easy [to solve]

that in the end he has no
difficult and   *big affairs*
[to settle].

THE STRUCTURE OF *LAOZI* 63

Laozi 63 is written in IPS. Among the particularities is its extensive
(triple) use of *pars pro toto* constructions for the general conclusions. The
links between the first four phrases of text 3 are explicit. The link between
the two parallel phrases at the end of text 4 and the two previously established chains is somewhat tenuous. The overall structure is:

	c	(63.1)
	c	(63.2)
a	b	(63.3, 63.3)
a	b	(63.3, 63.3)
	b	(63.3)
a		(63.3)
	c	(63.3)
	c	(63.4)

Zhang 64

64.1 其安ᵃ易持ᵇ其未兆ᶜ易謀ᵈ (Base text: 傅奕古本)

以其安不忘危其存ᵉ不忘亡謀之無功之勢故曰易也¹ (Base text: 張之象本)

64.2 其脆ᶠ易泮ᵍ其微ʰ易散ⁱ (Base text: 陸德明釋文 for first half, 傅奕古本 for second half)

雖失無入有以其微脆之故未足以興大功故易也此四者皆說愼終也不可以無之故而不持不可以微之故而弗散也無而弗持則生有爲微而不散則生大爲故慮終之患如始之禍則無敗事 (Base text: 集註本)

64.3 爲之乎ʲ其未有ᵏ (Base text: 傅奕古本)

謂其安未兆也 (Base text: 集註本)

ᵃ Var: 安也 for 安: 郭店 A; 馬王堆 A.

ᵇ Var.: 持也 for 持: 郭店 A 馬王堆 A.

ᶜ Var.: 洮 for 兆: 范應元本. Var.: 萴也 for 兆: 郭店 A.

ᵈ Var.: 悔也 for 謀: 郭店 A.

ᵉ 其存 for 持之: Hatano Tarō. Support for 其存: Wang Bi *LZWZLL*, 4.6–7 夫存者不以存爲存以其不忘亡也安者不以安爲安以其不忘危也故保其存者亡不忘亡者存安其位者危不忘危者安.

ᶠ Var.: 胞 for 脆: 范應元本. Var.: 靐也 for 脆: 郭店 A.

ᵍ Var.: 判 for 泮: 傅奕古本; 范應元本. Var.: 畔也 for 泮: 郭店 A.

ʰ Var.: 幾也 for 微: 郭店 A.   ⁱ Var.: 後也 for 散: 郭店 A.

ʲ Var.: 於 for 乎: 郭店 A.   ᵏ Var.: 亡又也 for 未有: 郭店 A.

64.4 治之乎[l]其未亂 (Base text: 傅奕古本)

謂[m,2]微脆也 (Base text: 張之象本)

64.5 合抱[n]之木生[o]於毫[p]末九成之臺起[q]於累[r]土千里之行[s]始[t]於足下爲者[u]敗之[3]執者失[v]之 (Base text: 范應元本)

當以愼終除微愼微除亂而以施爲治之形[w]名執之反生事原巧辟滋作故敗失也 (Base text: 張之象本)

64.6 是以聖人無爲[x]故無敗[y]無執[z]故無失[aa]民之從事[ab]常[ac]於其幾成[ad]而敗之[ae] (Base text: 傅奕古本)

不愼終也 (Base text: 集註本)

---

[l] Var.: 於 for 乎: 郭店 A. [m] Var.: 謂閑 for 謂: 集註本.

[n] Var.: 褢 for 抱: 傅奕古本.

[o] Var.: 作 for 生: 馬王堆 B. 高明 reads the 馬王堆 B character as 生.

[p] 毫 for 豪 (also in 傅奕古本): 馬王堆 A; 馬王堆 B. The character 毫 is used by Wang Bi in *LZWZLL* 4.10 善力舉秋毫; the character 豪 is not.

[q] Var.: 作 for 起: 馬王堆 A; 馬王堆 B. Var.: 甲 for 起: 郭店 A.

[r] Var.: 贏 for 累: 馬王堆 A. Var.: 虆 for 累: 馬王堆 B.

[s] Var.: 百仁(馬王堆 B:千)之高 for 千里之行: 馬王堆 A; 馬王堆 B.

[t] Var.: 台 for 始: 馬王堆 A.

[u] Var.: 爲之者 for 爲者: 馬王堆 B; 郭店 A; 郭店 C. Compare *Laozi* 29.3 with its different reading.

[v] Var.: 遠 for 失: 郭店 A.

[w] Var.: 刑 for 形: 集註本. Support for 形: Wang Bi on *Laozi* 25.5 聖人不立形名以檢於物; Wang Bi comm. on *Laozi* 38.1 崇本以舉其末 則形名俱有而邪不生.

[x] Var.: 口(爲)也 for 爲: 馬王堆 A.

[y] Var.: 敗口 for 敗: 馬王堆 A.

[z] Var.: 執也 for 執: 馬王堆 A.

[aa] Var.: 失也 for 失: 馬王堆 A.

[ab] Var.: 事也 for 事: 馬王堆 A; 馬王堆 B.

[ac] Var.: 恒 for 常: 馬王堆 A; 馬王堆 B.

[ad] Var.: 成事 for 幾成: 馬王堆 A. Var.: 幾 om.: 馬王堆 B.

[ae] Var.: 臨事之紀 for 民之從事 常於其幾成而敗之: 郭店 A. Var.: 人之敗也亙於其叡成也敗之 for 民之從事 常於其幾成而敗之 om.: 郭店 C. Phrase transferred to position after 無敗事矣.

64.7 愼終如始^{af}則^{ag}無敗事矣^{ah}是以^{ai}聖人欲不欲不^{aj}貴難得之貨^{ak} (Base text: 傅奕古本)

好欲雖微爭尙爲之興難得之貨雖細貪盜爲之起也 (Base text: 集註本)

64.8 學不學^{al}以^{am}復衆人之所過 (Base text: Wang Bi comm.)

不學而能者自然也喻^{an}於不學者過也故學不學以復衆人之所過 (Base text: 集註本)

64.9 以^{ao}輔萬物之自然而不^{ap}敢^{aq}爲也 (Base text: 傅奕古本)

64.1 [For a Sage Ruler]
as long as [he] is [still] secure
[in his position], [this security]
is [still] easy to maintain. As
long as there are still no signs
[of a danger to his life] it is
[still] easy to take precautions
against [such danger].

Because [the Sage Ruler as the
Xici 8.5.a3ff. *says about the*
Gentleman in a quotation from
Confucius] "while being in security
[in his position]" "does not forget
the [threat of] danger" and [thus]
maintains this [security], and while
still "in existence" "does not
forget [the threat of his physical]

---

^{af} Var.: 故愼終若始 for 愼終如始: 馬王堆 A. Var.: 故曰愼冬若始 for 愼終如始: 馬王堆 B. Var. 若 for 如: 郭店 C.

^{ag} Var.: 此 for 則: 郭店 A.　　　^{ah} Var.: 矣 om.: 范應元本.

^{ai} Var.: 是以 om.: 郭店 A.　　　^{aj} Var.: 而不 for 不: 馬王堆 A; 馬王堆 B.

^{ak} Var.: 臏 for 貨: 馬王堆 A.　　　^{al} Var.: 教不教 for 學不學: 郭店 A.

^{am} Var.: 而 for 以: 馬王堆 A. Var.: 以 om.: 馬王堆 B; 郭店 A; 郭店 C. 范應元本. Support for 以: Wang Bi comm.

^{an} 喻 for 喻: 陶鴻慶.

^{ao} Var.: 能 for 以: 馬王堆 A; 馬王堆 B. Var.: 是以能 for 以: 郭店 C. Var.: 是故聖人能 for 以: 郭店 A.

^{ap} Var.: 弗 for 不: 馬王堆 A; 郭店 A; 郭店 C.

^{aq} Var.: 能 for 敢: 郭店 A.

demise," and [thus] takes pre-
cautions against this [danger and
demise] in a situation where [still]
no effort [is needed], that is why
[the text] says "it is easy [to main-
tain security and to take precautions]!"[1]

64.2

as long as [a threat to his security] is [still] soft, it is [still] easy to break. As long as [a threat to his existence] is [still] minute, it is [still] easy to disperse.

Although [the threats] have
moved from non-existence to
existence, because of their being
"soft" and "minute" they still
do not qualify for prompting a
big effort. That is why [the text
says] "easy."

These four [statements] all
explain [the need] for "a
careful consideration of the
[eventual] outcome" [of
small beginnings as men-
tioned in Laozi 64.7].[2]

It does not avail [for a ruler]
not to maintain [the security
of his position] just because
there is no [present danger] to
it. If, while there is no [present
danger to his position], he does
not maintain [the security of
his position], then [such danger]
will come about.

It does not work [for a ruler]
not to disperse [threats to his
existence] just because they are
minute. If, while [the threat to
a ruler's existence] is minute, he
does not disperse it, [the threat]
will grow large.

That is why, if he considers the
calamity in "the end as" but
[the extreme development of
the small] misfortune of "the
beginning, then there will be
no failure of activity" [as the
Laozi *says in 64.7].*

64.3   He [therefore] acts on them [dangers] while they have not yet come about.

He [therefore] brings to   64.4
order [minute and soft dis-
turbances] while [they] have
not yet [developed into] chaos.

This means while he is [still]
"secure" and "no signs [of
danger]" are there.

This means when [disturbances]
are still minute and soft.

64.5 A tree that can only be
encircled with both arms
grows out of a tiny shoot.
A terrace nine stories high
is begun with a handful of
earth. A march of a thou-
sand *li* begins under the foot
[where one stays]. [However,
for the ruler who has missed
the moment of "easy" intervention when threats are still
non-existent or small and
now tries to use stronger
methods, the rule is:]

He who interferes [when things
have come into existence]
destroys them [the other
entities];

He who holds fast [onto things
that have reached their full
form] loses them [the other
entities].[3]

One should "with a careful
eye on the outcome" [, as the
Laozi *says in 64.7,] eliminate*
[even] minute [threats], and
with a careful eye on the
minute eliminate [threatening]
chaos, but

if they [other entities] are
brought to order by means of
prodding and interference, one
inversely creates causes for
[government] action.

if they [other entities] are held
onto by means of [their] shapes
and names, cunning and perver-
sion will amply sprout.

That is why [the text says]
"destroys [them]" and
"loses [them]."

64.6   That is why the Sage

does not interfere and thus does
not destroy,

does not hold fast, and thus
does not lose,

[while] when people go about
[their] business, they always
destroy them [the other

entities] when they are about
to complete [their business].

That is, they [people] do not
"carefully consider the [eventual]
outcome."

64.7   [Only] if one carefully considers
the eventual outcome as being
just the [extreme development
of a small] beginning will there
be no failure of activity. That is
why the Sage desires [only] to
have no desires and does not
put high value on goods that
are hard to get.

Even when [his] desires and
preferences are [only] minute,
competition and emulation
[among the people] are called
forth by them. Even when goods
[in his hands] that are hard to
get are [only] tiny, greed and
robbery are evoked by them.

64.8   He studies not to study [only] in
order to redress the superfluities
of the men of the crowd

That what one is capable of with-
out studying [comes from] That-
which-is-of-itself-what-it-is, while
going beyond this [capability acquired]
without study is a superfluity. That
is why [the text says the Sage]
"studies not to study [only] in order
to redress the superfluities of the
men of the crowd."

64.9   so as to boost the ten thousand kinds
of entities' That-which-is-of-itself-
what-it-is, but he does not dare to
interfere [with them].

THE STRUCTURE OF *LAOZI* 64
The structure of the first part is made explicit through Wang Bi's
commentary as IPS. The first two units, however, are subdivided into

two subunits that refer to the ruler's social rank and physical existence, respectively. They create a second interlocking grid.

From the middle of text 5 on, beginning with "however," another binary structure begins, centering on the terms *wei* 爲, "to interfere," and *zhi* 執, "to hold fast." They do not fit the pair dominating the first part of the text. The first and second parts, however, form a contrast. The first part describes the "easy" and early action of the Sage Ruler, and the second the clumsy efforts to save matters after they have evolved into disaster. However, there is no visible link between, say, the "interfering" and the period when there still is no threat, or the "holding fast" and the period when things are already "minute" and "soft," so that the two chains in the two parts cannot be linked. I therefore have decided to treat the pair in the second part as a subgroup of c statements. The structure of the *zhang* is:

I	a		b	(64.1, 64.2)
	a		b	(64.3, 64.4)
II		c		(64.5)
	c1	c2		(64.5, 64.5)
	c1	c2		(64.6, 64.6)
		c		(64.6)
		c		(64.7)
		c		(64.7)
		c		(64.8)
		c		(64.9)

Zhang 65

65.1 古之ᵃ善ᵇ爲道者非以明民ᶜ將以愚之ᵈ (Base text: 傅奕古本)

明謂多見巧詐散ᵉ其樸也愚謂無知守眞順自然也 (Base text: 取善集)

ᵃ Var.: 故曰 for 古之: 馬王堆 A.   ᵇ Var.: 善 om.: 馬王堆 A; 馬王堆 B.
ᶜ Var.: 民也 for 民: 馬王堆 A.   ᵈ Var.: 之也 for 之: 馬王堆 A; 馬王堆 B.
ᵉ Var.: 蔽 for 散: 集註本; 張之象本. Support for 散: Wang Bi on *Laozi* 32.3 始制謂樸散始爲官長之時也; Wang Bi *LZWZLL* 6.29 樸散眞離. . . . Both uses go back to *Laozi* 28.6 樸散則爲器. The term 蔽 does not occur with 樸 in Wang Bi's oeuvre.

65.2 民^f之難治^g以其多智^h也 (Base text: Wang Bi comm. on *Laozi* 65.3)

多智巧詐故難治也 (Base text: 集註本)

65.3 故以智治ⁱ國國^j之賊也^k (Base text: Wang Bi comm.)

智猶術^l也^{m,1}民之難治以其多智也當務塞兌閉門令無知無欲而以智
術動民邪心既動復以巧術防民之僞民知其術隨防ⁿ而避之思惟密巧
姦僞益滋故曰以智治國國之賊也 (Base text: 集註本)

65.4 不以智^o治^p國國^q之福也^r常^s知此兩者亦稽式也能^t知^u稽式是^v謂^w玄德玄德深
矣遠矣 (Base text: 傅奕古本 until 式也, from there Wang Bi comm.)

稽^x同也今古之所同則不可廢能知稽^y式是謂玄德玄德深矣遠矣 (Base
text: 張之象本)

65.5 與物反矣^z (Base text: 傅奕古本)

反其眞也 (Base text: 集註本)

65.6 乃復至於^{aa}大順 (Base text: 傅奕古本)

---

^f Var.: 夫民 for 民: 馬王堆 B.　　　^g Var.: 治也 for 治: 馬王堆 B.

^h Var.: 知 for 多智: 馬王堆 B. Var.: 多知 for 多智: 傅奕古本. Var.: 知多 for 多智: 范
應元本.

ⁱ Var.: 知知 for 智治: 馬王堆 A; 馬王堆 B.

^j Var.: 邦 邦 for 國 國: 馬王堆 A.　　　^k Var.: 賊 for 賊也: 范應元本.

^l 術 for 治: Wagner based on 以智術動民 further down.

^m 以智而治國 所以謂之賊者 故謂之智也 del. Wagner, cf. note 1.

ⁿ 隨防 for 防隨: 陶鴻慶.

^o 智 for 知: Wang Bi comm. on *Laozi* 65.3; 文子.

^p Var.: 知知 for 智治: 馬王堆 A; 馬王堆 B.

^q Var.: 邦 邦 for 國 國: 馬王堆 A.　　　^r Var.: 德也 for 福也: 馬王堆 A; 馬王堆 B.

^s Var.: 恒 for 常: 馬王堆 A; 馬王堆 B. Var.: 常 om.: 范應元本.

^t Var.: 恒 for 能: 馬王堆 A; 馬王堆 B. Var.: 能 om.: 范應元本.

^u Var.: 知此 for 知: 范應元本.　　　^v Var.: 此 for 是: 馬王堆 A.

^w Var.: 胃 for 謂: 馬王堆 A; 馬王堆 B. ^x Var.: 楷 for 稽: 集註本.

^y Var.: 楷 for 稽: 集註本.　　　^z Var.: 也 for 矣: 馬王堆 B.

^{aa} Var.: 乃至 for 乃復至於: 馬王堆 B. (Size of lacuna in 馬王堆 A suggests the same
formula as in 馬王堆 B).

65.1   Those in old times who were
                             good at the Way

did not proceed by making
people enlightened,   [but proceeded] by keeping
                                       them stupid.

"Making enlightened" refers to   *"Keeping stupid" refers to [their]*
showing [them] cunning and   *being without intelligence and*
deceit. This will [in the words   *preserving the true [essence].*
of Laozi 28.6] "disperse" their   *[Being thus,] they will go along*
"Unadorned."   *with [their] That-which-is-of-*
                                       itself-what-it-is.

65.2   That people are hard to keep
                             in order is due to their
                             intelligence being increased.

                   With the increase in their
                   intelligence [comes] cunning
                   and deceit, that is why they
                   are "hard to keep in order."

65.3   That is why   65.4

governing the state by means of   governing the state not by
intelligence is the plague of the   means of intelligence is the
state.   bliss of the state.

[Continued text 65.4]
                             One should eternally know
                             that these two [governing
                             methods of "those in old
                             times who were good at the
                             Way," namely, "not to proceed
                             by making people enlightened
                             but by making efforts to keep
                             them stupid"] are also common
                             rules [for all times]. To be able
                             [as a ruler] to know these com-
                             mon rules I call [having] "the
                             capacity coming from That-
                             which-is-Dark." The capacity
                             coming from That-which-is-Dark
                             is deep, is distant.[1]

[Commentary on 65.3]
"Intelligence" is like tricks. [As
the Laozi *said in 65.2,] "That*
people are hard to keep in order,
is due to their intelligence being

increased." [A ruler] has to take
care to "stuff [the people's]
openings, and block [their] doors"
[as the Laozi *says in 52.3 and*
56.3 of All Under Heaven] to get
them to be "without knowledge
and without desires" [, as the
Laozi *says in 3.4 of the people].*
But if [a ruler] gets the people
moving by means of intelligence
and tricks, what is [in fact] being
moved will be their depraved
hearts. If he then again with
cunning and tricks blocks the
deceptions by the people, the
people will know his tricks and
will thereupon thwart and evade
them. The more cunning his [the
ruler's] devices become, the more
exuberantly will falsehood and
deceit sprout [among the people].
That is why [the text says]
"Governing the state by means of
intelligence is the plague of the state"!

[Commentary on 65.4]

"Common" means "identical."
That which is the common
model for old and new times
cannot disappear[2] *[therefore*
one can eternally know these
common "rules" shi 式, *which*
are defined as ze 則, *"model,"*
in Wang Bi on Laozi 22.6 *and*
on Laozi 28.2]. *"To be able [as*
a ruler] to know these common
rules I call [having] 'the capacity
coming from That-which-is-Dark.'"
The capacity coming from That-
which-is-Dark is deep, is distant."[3]

65.5   He will provide the other entities
with a return,

A return to their true [essence].

65.6   and [they] will then arrive at the
Great Adaptation [to the Way].

THE STRUCTURE OF *LAOZI* 65

Laozi 65 is written in IPS. The two antonym parameters are established in the first phrase and taken up again in the two sentences about the "plague" and the "bliss" for the state. The subsequent statements technically only deal with government in the tradition of "those in old times who were good at the Way," but, as they have no parallel counterpart, they present the *pars pro toto* summary of both chains. The structure of the *zhang* is:

		c	(65.1)
a		b	(65.1, 65.1)
		c	(65.2)
a		b	(65.3, 65.4)
		c	(65.4)
		c	(65.5)
		c	(65.6)

Zhang 66

66.1 江海所以能ᵃ爲百谷ᵇ王者 以其善下之ᶜ也ᵈ故ᵉ能爲百谷王是以ᶠ聖人ᵍ欲上民ʰ
必以其言下之欲ⁱ先民ʲ必以其身後之是以聖人處之上ᵏ而ˡ民弗重ᵐ處之前ⁿ而ᵒ

ᵃ Var.: 能 om. :郭店 A.

ᵇ Var.: 浴 for 谷:郭店 A; 馬王堆 A, B. Passim.

ᶜ Var.: 以其能爲百浴下 for 以其善下之也:郭店 A.

ᵈ Var.: 也 om: 郭店 A; 馬王堆 A; 范應元本.

ᵉ Var.: 是以 for 故: 郭店 A; 馬王堆 A; 馬王堆 B.

ᶠ Var.: 是以 om.: 郭店 A.

ᵍ Var.: 聖人之欲 for 聖人欲: 馬王堆 A; 馬王堆 B.

ʰ Var.: 民也 for 民: 馬王堆 A; 馬王堆 B.

ⁱ Var.: 其欲 for 欲: 馬王堆 A; 馬王堆 B.

ʲ Var.: 民也for 民: 馬王堆 A; 馬王堆 B.

ᵏ Var.: 故居上 for 是以聖人處之上:馬王堆 B (馬王堆 A: 故 ... 居上). Var.: 其在民
上: 郭店 A.

ˡ Var.: 而 om.: 郭店 A.

ᵐ Var.: 厚 for 重 : 郭店 A. Var.: 重也 for 重: 馬王堆 A, B.

ⁿ Var.: 居前 for 處之前 :馬王堆 A, B. Var.: 其才民前也 for 處之前: 郭店 A.

ᵒ Var.: 而 om.: 郭店 A.

民弗[p]害也[q,1]是以[r]天下樂推[s]而不[t]厭[u]不[v]以其不爭[w]故天下莫能與之爭[x] (Base text: 傅奕古本)

There is no commentary by Wang Bi, and the text is not quoted in Wang Bi's surviving works, including the commentaries to passages in other *zhang*, such as *Laozi* 28.1 and 32.4, which deal with the same simile. I have located only one quotation from this *zhang* in Han Kangbo's commentary to the *Xici*, of which I gave a translation in note 4 to *zhang* 49 of the *Laozi*. Lu Deming refers to a Wang Bi *Laozi* text of this *zhang* but does not quote elements from the commentary. There is no tradition that Wang Bi regarded this *zhang* as spurious and, in terms of content, it fits all too well into his reading of the *Laozi*. As it does not provide many difficulties, I will offer a minimalist translation for reference, short of leaving it untranslated.

As to that by which the rivers and seas are able to be the lords over the hundred rivulets—that they are good at lowering themselves under them is why they are able to be the lords over the hundred rivulets! This is why the Sage

in his wish to be above the people will by necessity lower himself under them in his verbal utterances.

in his wish to be ahead of them will by necessity put his own person behind them.

This is why while a Sage

---

[p] 弗 for 不: Wagner based on 范應元本, consistency with 弗重 and 郭店 A, 馬王堆 A, B.

[q] Var.: 故居前而民弗害也居上而民弗重也 for 是以聖人處之上而民弗重處之前而民不害也: 馬王堆 A. Var.: 聖人之才民前也以身後之其才民上也以其言下之其才民上也民弗厚也其才民前也民弗害也 for 是以聖人處之上而民弗重處之前而民不害也: 郭店 A.

[r] Var.: 是以 om.: 郭店 A; 馬王堆 A; 馬王堆 B.

[s] Var.: 進 (郭店 A), 隼 (馬王堆 A), 誰 (馬王堆 B) for 推.

[t] Var.: 弗 for 不: 郭店 A, 馬王堆 A; 馬王堆 B.

[u] 厭 for 猒 in 傅奕古本; 馬王堆 A; 范應元本; 陸德明釋文. Var.: 猒也 for 厭: 馬王堆 A; 馬王堆 B.

[v] Var.: 非 for 不: 馬王堆 A. Var.: 不 om.: 郭店 A.

[w] Var.: 無諍與 for 不爭: 馬王堆 A. Var.: 無爭與 for 不爭: 馬王堆 B. Var.: 不靜也 for 不爭: 郭店 A.

[x] Var.: 諍 for 爭: 馬王堆 A. 靜 for 爭: 郭店 A.

takes his place above them, the people will not attach great importance to [his position]!	is ahead of them, the people will not do damage [to his person]!

And this is why All under Heaven rejoices in promoting [him] without harboring any resentment! Is it not because he does not go for a competitive struggle that no one in All Under Heaven is able to get into a competitive struggle with him?

THE STRUCTURE OF *ZHANG* 66

The *zhang* is written in open IPS. It has the structure:

```
              c
              c
         a         b
              c
         a         b
              c
              c
```

The Guodian A as well as the MWD A texts both have abba sequences in the middle.

Zhang 67

67.1 天下皆謂ᵃ我ᵇ大似不肖ᶜ,¹夫唯ᵈ大故似不肖ᵉ若肖久矣其細也夫ᶠ (Base text: 傅奕古本 up to 若, from then Wang Bi comm.)

ᵃ Var.: 胃 for 謂: 馬王堆 B.

ᵇ 我 for 吾 (also in 范應元本): 馬王堆 B. *Laozi* 67.2. The case is not tight, as Wang Bi does not repeat the "I" term in his commentary here. When the Sage refers to himself in other parts of the *Laozi*, Wang Bi's text regularly gives 我.

ᶜ Var.: 大而不宵 for 大似不肖: 馬王堆 B.　　ᵈ 唯 for 惟: 馬王堆 B; 陸德明釋文.

ᵉ Var.: 不宵 for 似不肖: 馬王堆 A. Var.: 夫唯不宵故能大 for 夫唯大故似不肖: 馬王堆 B.

ᶠ Var.: 若宵細久矣 for 若肖久矣其細也夫: 馬王堆 A. Var.: 若宵 for 若肖: 馬王堆 B.

久矣其細猶曰其細久矣肖則失其所以爲大矣故^g曰若肖久矣其細也
夫^h (Base text: 取善集)

67.2 我ⁱ有三寶^j持而寶^k之一曰慈^l二曰儉^m三曰不敢爲天下先夫慈ⁿ故能勇 (Base text: 范應元本)

夫慈以陳則勝以守則固故能勇也 (Base text: 集註本)

67.3 儉^o故^p能廣 (Base text: 傅奕古本)

節儉愛費天下不匱故能廣也 (Base text: 集註本)

67.4 不敢爲天下先故能爲成^q器^r長 (Base text: 范應元本)

唯後外其身爲物所歸然後乃能立成器爲天下利爲物之長也 (Base text: 集註本)

67.5 今舍^s其慈^t且勇 (Base text: 范應元本)

且猶取也 (Base text: 集註本)

---

g Var.: 故夫 for 故: 集註本.

h Var.: 也 for 也夫: 集註本. It seems that the 夫 from the end was erroneously transferred to follow the 故.

i Var.: 我恒 for 我: 馬王堆 A; 馬王堆 B. Var.: 吾 for 我: 傅奕古本.

j Var.: 葆 for 寶: 馬王堆 A. Var.: 琛 for 寶: 馬王堆 B.

k Var.: 持而寶 om.: 馬王堆 A. Var.: 市而琛之 for 持而寶之: 馬王堆 B.

l Var.: 茲 for 慈: 馬王堆 A; 馬王堆 B.

m Var.: 檢 for 儉: 馬王堆 A; 馬王堆 B.

n Var.: 茲 for 慈: 馬王堆 B.　　　　o Var.: 檢 for 儉: 馬王堆 B.

p Var.: 敢 for 故: 馬王堆 B.

q Var.: 成 for 爲成: 傅奕古本. Support for 爲: Wang Bi comm.: 爲天下利; 馬王堆 A; 馬王堆 B.

r Var.: 事 for 器: 馬王堆 A.

s Var.: 捨 for 舍: 傅奕古本. Support for 舍: 陸德明釋文. Passim.

t Var.: 茲 for 慈: 馬王堆 A; 馬王堆 B.

67.6 舍其儉^u且廣^v舍其後且先則死矣^w夫慈^x以陳^y則勝^z (Base text: 馬王堆 B until 矣, thereafter Wang Bi comm. on *Laozi* 67.2)

相憨而不辟^{aa}於難故勝^{ab}也 (Base text: 張之象本)

67.7 以守則固天將救^{ac}之以慈衛之^{ad} (Base text: for first segment Wang Bi comm. on *Laozi* 67.2, for the remaining two 傅奕古本)

67.1　　　　　　　Everyone in All Under Heaven says my [the Sage Ruler's] greatness[1] seems to be [so pitiful as to be] not comparable [to anything others would consider great]. In fact, only because of [its being real] greatness it seems [so pitiful as to be] not comparable. Were it comparable [to anything others consider great], it would already have become minute a long time ago![2]

　　　　　　　　"It would already have become minute a long time ago" is as if [the text] said "its becoming minute would have happened long ago." Were [my greatness] comparable, then it would lose that through which it is great. That is why [the text] says: "Were it comparable [to any-

---

　^u 儉 for 檢: 傅奕古本; 范應元本.　　　^v Var.: 舍其儉且廣 om.: 馬王堆 A.

　^w Var.: 則必死矣 for 則死矣: 馬王堆 A. Var.: 是謂入死門 for 則死矣: 傅奕古本; 范應元本. My choice of 則 is determined by the assumption that Wang Bi would have commented upon a term such as 死門.

　^x Var.: 茲 for 慈: 馬王堆 A; 馬王堆 B.

　^y Var.: 單 for 陳: 馬王堆 B.

　^z Var.: 朕 for 勝: 馬王堆 B. Var.: 正 for 勝: 傅奕古本; 范應元本.

　^{aa} 辟 for 避: 陸德明釋文.

　^{ab} Var.: 正 for 勝: 集註本. This text has adapted the Wang Bi commentary to its own preferred reading of the end of *Laozi* 67.6, which is 則正.

　^{ac} Var.: 建 for 救: 馬王堆 A; 馬王堆 B.

　^{ad} Var.: 如(馬王堆 A: 女)以茲坦之 for 以慈衛之: 馬王堆 A; 馬王堆 B.

thing others consider great], it
would already have become
minute a long time ago"!

67.2   I have three   treasures. To these I keep and [I] treasure them.

The first is called "compassion."
The second is called "frugality."
The third is called "not to dare to come to be to the fore
in All Under Heaven."

It is a fact that

it is due to [my] compassion, that [I am] able to be valiant;

[As the Laozi *says in 67.6 and 67.7] "It is a fact that as to compassion,*
one will win [only] if one abides in [open] battle by it, and one will be
safe [only] if in the defense [of a city] one abides by it." That is why [I
am] "able to be valiant."

67.3   it is due to [my] frugality [I am] able to be generous;

[If I as the ruler] make frugality a rule and cut down wasteful
expenses, All Under Heaven will not be in need. That is why
[I am] "able to be generous."

67.4   it is due to [my] not daring to come to be to the fore in All Under
Heaven that [I am] able complete instruments for [All Under
Heaven] and be the leader.

It is only as a consequence of [the Sage's] "putting his own person
in the background" and "disregarding his own person" [as the
Laozi *says in 7.2] and becoming that to which the other entities*
render themselves, that he is able indeed to "establish and com-
plete instruments for the benefit of All Under Heaven" [as the
Xici *7.9b.8ff. say about the Sage] and to be the leader among the*
entities.[3]

67.5   If nowadays [, however, rulers]

discard their compassion and yet [strive to be] valiant,

"and yet" [strive to be valiant] is like "get hold of" [being valiant].[4]

67.6   discard their frugality and yet [strive to] be generous,
discard their keeping in the background and yet [strive
to] be to the fore,
then they will die.

[This is so because] it is a fact that as to
compassion, one will win [only] if one abides
in [open] battle by it,

> As [if compassion is used, the
> soldiers] care for each other
> and [thus] do not shirk hardships,
> therefore "one will win."

67.7
and one will be safe [only] if in
the defense [of a city] one abides
by it. He whom Heaven intends
to save it will guard by means of
compassion. [The same applies
for frugality and not daring to
come to be to the fore.]

THE STRUCTURE OF *LAOZI* 67

Laozi 67 is written in open IPS. As opposed to the normal binary structure, there are three elements involved, which are repeated three times, each in a parallel staircase. The last statement on compassion beginning at the end of text 6 is a classical *pars pro toto* construction. The argument is made only with regard to one of the three elements but is valid for all three, therefore, it is set in a c position. The resulting shadow text has been indicated in the last bracket. The overall structure of the *zhang* is:

		c			(67.1)
		c			(67.2)
1					(67.2)
	2				(67.2)
		3			(67.2)
1					(67.2)
	2				(67.3)
		3			(67.4)
1					(67.5)
	2				(67.6)
		3			(67.6)
		c			(67.6)
		c			(67.7)
(1					
	2				
		3)			

Zhang 68

68.1 古之^a善爲士者不武^b (Base text: 范應元本)

　　士卒之帥也武尙先陵人也 (Base text: 集註本)

68.2 善戰^c者不怒 (Base text: 范應元本)

　　後而不先應而不唱故不在怒 (Base text: 集註本)

68.3 善勝^d敵者不^e與^f (Base text: 馬王堆 B)

　　不與爭也 (Base text: 集註本)

68.4 善用人者爲之下是謂^g不爭^h之德是謂ⁱ用人之力^j (Base text: 傅奕古本)

　　用人而不爲之下則力不爲用也 (Base text: 集註本)

68.5 是謂^k配^l天古之極也 (Base text: 傅奕古本)

68.1		68.2
Those of old who were good at being officers were not martial.		who were good at fighting did not get angry.
"Officer" is a commander of soldiers. To be "martial" means		*They kept [their own persons] in the background [like the Sage*

---

^a Var.: 古之 om.: 馬王堆 A. Var.: 故 for 古之: 馬王堆 B.

^b Var.: 武也 for 武: 傅奕古本.

^c Var.: 單 for 戰: 馬王堆 B.

^d 勝 for 朕: 馬王堆 A; 傅奕古本; 范應元本.

^e 不 for 弗 (also in 馬王堆 A): Wang Bi comm.: 不與爭也; 傅奕古本; 范應元本.

^f Var.: 爭 for 與: 傅奕古本; 范應元本. Support for 與: Wang Bi comm.

^g Var.: 胃 for 謂: 馬王堆 A; 馬王堆 B.

^h Var.: 靜 for 爭: 馬王堆 A.

ⁱ Var.: 胃 for 謂: 馬王堆 A; 馬王堆 B.

^j Var.: 之力 om.: 馬王堆 A; 馬王堆 B.

^k Var.: 胃 for 謂: 馬王堆 A; 馬王堆 B.

^l Var.: 配 om.: 馬王堆 A. Var.: 肥 for 配: 馬王堆 B.

to appreciate being at the fore
and to suppress others.

according to Laozi 7.2] *and did
not [press to be] at the fore, they
fell in but did not sing the lead
[as, according to Wang Bi on
Laozi 10.5, the hen does whose
attitude the Sage is emulating].
Therefore, it did not depend on
their getting angry [to make
them good at fighting].*

68.3　　　　　　　　　　　　[This is so because]

he who is good at overcoming
enemies does not engage with
them.

*That is, does not engage in
fighting.*

68.4　　he who is good at using others,
lowers himself beneath them.

This [not engaging in fighting] I
call the capacity for not fighting.

That [lowering oneself as an
officer beneath one's men] I
call making use of the strength
of others.

*Were he using others, but not
lowering himself beneath them,
then [their full] strength would
not be used.*[1]

68.5　　　　　　　　　　　These [two abilities] I call
matching Heaven. They are the
ultimate [achievement] of antiquity.

THE STRUCTURE OF *LAOZI* 68

Laozi 68 is written in closed IPS. The relationship between the officer
of the first text and he "who is good at using others" has to be inferred.
There are a number of particular features in this *zhang*.

- The second group of two texts actually gives the reason for the
  logic of the texts in the first group without there being any explicit
  indicator.
- The identical three *shi wei* 是謂, "this I call," in fact refer to three
  different objects and thus have to be translated differently each

time. For a detailed analysis of the structure of this *zhang*, compare my *The Craft of a Chinese Commentator*, pp. 77-82.

- There is an abba sequence.

The structure of the *zhang* is:

a	b	(68.1, 68.2)
	b	(68.3)
a		(68.4)
	b	(68.4)
a		(68.4)
	c	(68.5)

Zhang 69

69.1 用兵^a有^b言曰吾不敢爲主而爲客不敢進寸而退^c尺是謂^d行無行攘無臂執無兵扔^e無敵^{f1} (Base text: 傅奕古本 until 是謂, from then on Wang Bi comm.)

行謂行陳也言以謙退哀慈不敢爲物先用戰猶行無行攘無臂執無兵扔^g無敵也言無^h與之抗也 (Base text: 張之象本)

69.2 禍ⁱ莫大於無ⁱ敵^k無敵則幾亡吾^l寶^m (Base text: 傅奕古本)

言吾哀慈謙退非欲以取強無敵於天下也不得已而卒至於無敵斯乃吾之所以爲大禍也寶三寶也故曰幾亡吾寶 (Base text: 集註本)

---

^a Var.: 兵者 for 兵: 范應元本.   ^b Var.: 又 for 有: 馬王堆 B.

^c Var.: 芮 for 退: 馬王堆 A.   ^d Var.: 胃 for 謂: 馬王堆 A; 馬王堆 B.

^e 扔 for 仍: 陸德明釋文. Var.: 乃 for 扔: 馬王堆 A; 馬王堆 B.

^f Var.: 敵矣 for 敵: 馬王堆 A. Var.: 扔無敵 執無兵 for 執無兵 扔無敵: 范應元本.

^g Var.: 仍 for 扔: 集註本.   ^h 無 for 無有: 集註本.

ⁱ Var.: 䵼 for 禍: 馬王堆 A.

^j Var.: 輕 for 無: 范應元本. Support for 無: Wang Bi comm. : 卒至於無敵 ...

^k Var.: 莫於於無適 for 莫大於無敵: 馬王堆 A.

^l Var.: 無適斤亡吾吾 for 無敵則幾亡吾: 馬王堆 A. Var.: 無敵近 for 無敵則幾: 馬王堆 B.

^m Var.: 葆矣 for 寶: 馬王堆 A. Var.: 琛矣 for 寶: 馬王堆 B.

69.3 故抗[n]兵相若[o]則哀者勝矣[p] (Base text: 傅奕古本)

抗舉也若[q]當也哀者必相惜而不趣利避害故必勝 (Base text: 集註本)

69.1 Those who [truly understand how to] use soldiers have too many sayings that run: "I do not dare act the master, but act the guest; I do not dare advance an inch, but retreat a foot." This [I] call march on a no-march, roll up the sleeves on the no-arm, take hold of the no-weapon, and throw back the no-enemy.

"To march" refers to marching into a battle. This means: If [as a commander] one makes use for warfare of modest reserve, pity, and compassion, as well as [an attitude] of not daring to stand above other entities [, these three being the "three treasures" of the Sage in Laozi 67, *namely, frugality, compassion, and not daring to come to the fore in All Under Heaven], then this is like "marching on a no-march, rolling up the sleeves on the no-arm, taking hold of the no-weapon, and throwing back the no-enemy," which means there is nothing to offer resistance to such a one.*

69.2 [Another one of their sayings is]: "There is no greater misfortune than not having enemies. Not having enemies would be about equal to the demise of my [the sage commander's] treasures."

This means: I practice pity and compassion as well as modest reserve, and I do not desire by "imposing violent [rule]" [as the Laozi *says in* 30.4 *about "someone who is good at it [using troops]" and who "will just get [things] done"]*[1] *[to come to the point that] there is no enemy [of mine] in All Under Heaven. If unintentionally it eventually should come to the point that there is no enemy [left], I would consider this to be a great misfortune. The "treasures" are the "three treasures" [of* Laozi 67.2.*] That is why [the text] says "[Having no enemy] would be about equal to the demise of my [the sage commander's] treasures."*

69.3 That is why, when troops are raised to meet each other, those with pity [for each other] will win.

"Raise" means to "bring forward." "To meet" means "to confront." Those with pity will necessarily take care of each other and will not rush after spoils and shirk hardships. That is why they will necessarily "win"![2]

---

[n] Var.: 稱 for 抗: 馬王堆 A.

[o] Var.: 加 for 若: 范應元本.

[p] Var.: 而依者朕口: for 則哀者勝矣: 馬王堆 B.

[q] Var.: 加 for 若: 張之象本. Support for 若: The 集註本 gives 若, although its own *Laozi* text says 加.

Zhang 70

70.1 吾言甚[a]易知[b]甚[c]易行[d]而人莫之能知[e]莫之能行[f] (Base text: 傅奕古本)

可不出戶窺牖而知故曰甚易知也不爲[g]而成故曰甚易行也惑於躁欲故曰莫之能知也迷於榮利故曰莫之能行也 (Base text: 集註本)

70.2 言有宗事有主[h,1] (Base text: 傅奕古本)

宗萬物之宗也主[i]萬事[j]之主也 (Base text: 集註本)

70.3 夫唯[k]無知[l]是以不我[m]知[n] (Base text: 馬王堆 B)

以其言有宗事有主[o]之故故有知之人不得不知之也 (Base text: 集註本)

70.4 知我[p]者希[q]則我貴矣 (Base text: 范應元本)

唯深也故知之者希也知我益希我亦無匹故曰知我者希則我[r]貴也 (Base text: 集註本)

---

[a] Var.: 甚 om.: 馬王堆 B.

[b] Var.: 知也 for 知: 馬王堆 A; 馬王堆 B.

[c] Var.: 甚 om.: 馬王堆 B.

[d] Var.: 行也 for 行: 馬王堆 A; 馬王堆 B.

[e] Var.: 知也 for 知: 馬王堆 A; 馬王堆 B.

[f] Var.: 行也 for 行: 馬王堆 A; 馬王堆 B.

[g] 不爲 for 無爲: Wagner based on *Laozi* 47.4, of which this is a quotation.

[h] Var.: 言有君事有宗 for 言有宗事有主: 馬王堆 A. Var.:言又宗事又君 for 言有宗事有主: 馬王堆 B. Cf. note 1.

[i] 主 for 君: Wagner based on *LZWZLL* 6.1; cf. note 1.

[j] Var.: 萬物 for 萬事: 張之象本.

[k] Var.: 惟 for 唯: 傅奕古本; 范應元本.

[l] 知 for 知也: 傅奕古本; 范應元本.

[m] Var.: 吾 for 我: 傅奕古本; 范應元本.

[n] Var.: 知也 for 知: 傅奕古本; 范應元本.

[o] 主 for 君(also in 張之象本): Wagner based on Wang Bi *LZWZLL* 6.1, cf. note 1.

[p] Var.: 我 om.: 馬王堆 B. Lacuna in 馬王堆 A would leave space for 我.

[q] Var.: 稀 for 希: 傅奕古本. Support for 希: Wang Bi comm.

[r] Var.: 我者 for 我: 張之象本.

70.5 是以聖人被^s褐而懷^t玉 (Base text: 傅奕古本)

被褐者同其塵懷玉者寶其眞也聖人之所以難知以其同塵而不殊懷玉
而不顯^u故難知而爲貴也 (Base text: 取善集)

70.1 My words [Laozi says, and ditto for my activities]

are very easy to understand and very easy to put into practice.

But [still even] them of the others

no one is able to understand and no one is able to put into practice.

It is possible to understand [his words] "without going out of doors" and [without] "looking out of the window" [as the Laozi says in 47.1 about understanding All Under Heaven]. That is why [the text] says: "[My words] are very easy to understand"!

"Without his acting on them [the other entities] he [the Sage] gets [them] completed" [as the Laozi 47.4 says].[1] That is why [the text] says: "[My activities] are very easy to put into practice"!

[The others] are deluded by excitement and desires; that is why [the text] says: "No one is able to understand [my words]"!

[The others] are led astray by glory and profit; that is why [the text] says: "No one is able to put [my activities] into practice"![2]

70.2 [My] words have the principle. [My] activities have the ruler.

"Principle" is the principle of the ten thousand entities.

"Ruler" is the lord of the ten thousand processes.

70.3 It is [hence] a fact that only those without any understanding will therefore not understand me [and ditto for practice].[3]

This is so because his

---

^s Var.: 披 for 被: 范應元本.

^t Var.: 裹 for 懷: 馬王堆 A; 馬王堆 B.

^u Var.: 渝 for 顯: 集註本; 張之象本.

"words have the   *and*   *his "activities have the ruler."*
principle"

That is why people with
understanding cannot fail
to understand him.

70.4   [Consequently] the fewer there
                            are of those who understand me
                            the more I am honored.

"Insofar as I [he] [pursue(s) to
the very end] the deep" [, as the
Xici 7.8.a9, *says about the Sage,],*[4]
there are few of those who under-
stand me. The fewer there are of
those who understand me, the more
I also shall be without equal. That
is why [the text] says: "The fewer
there are of those who understand
me the more I am honored!"

70.5   This is why the Sage wears coarse
                            cloth but carries a piece of jade in
                            his bosom.

"He wears coarse cloth" is identical
with [what the Laozi *says in 56.6*
about the wise ruler, and in 4.1
about the Way, namely,] "he joins
in the same dust with them [the
other entities]." "He carries a piece
of jade in his bosom" means he is
treasuring his true [nature]. The
reason the Sage is hard to under-
stand is [in fact] that he "joins in
the same dust [with them]" but
does not stand out, that he carries
a piece of jade in his bosom but
does not let it show. That is why
he is hard to understand but
honored!

THE STRUCTURE OF *LAOZI* 70

Laozi 70 is written in open IPS. The *zhi* 知 from text 3 on is a *pars pro toto* construction for both *zhi* 知 and *xing* 行. The *zhang* has the following structure:

a	b	(70.1, 70.1)
a	b	(70.1, 70.1)
a	b	(70.2, 70.2)
	c	(70.3)
	c	(70.4)
	c	(70.5)

Zhang 71

71.1 知不知尙矣不知知ª病矣 (Base text: 傅奕古本)

　　不知知之不足任則病也 (Base text: 集註本)

71.2 夫唯病病是以不病聖人ᵇ之不病ᶜ以其病病ᵈ是以不病¹ (Base text: 傅奕古本)

　　病病者知所以爲病² (Base text: 集註本)

71.1　If [a ruler] knows that [he should] not [make use of] knowledge, he will be esteemed. If [a ruler] does not know about knowledge [not being fit for application], he will be in trouble.

*If [a ruler] does not know that knowledge is not fit for application, then he is in trouble.*¹

71.2　It is a fact that only [a ruler] who recognizes trouble as trouble [caused by the application of knowledge which one should avoid] will therefore not have trouble. The Sage's not having trouble is due to his recognizing trouble as trouble [in this sense]. That is why he does not have trouble.

He who "recognizes trouble as trouble" understands the reason for which trouble comes about [namely, the application of knowledge in government].

ª Var.: 不知不知 for 不知知: 馬王堆 A.

ᵇ Var.: 是以聖人 for 夫唯病病是以不病聖人: 馬王堆 A; 馬王堆 B.

ᶜ Var.: 囗(病)也 for 病: 馬王堆 B.

ᵈ Var.: 病也 for 病: 馬王堆 B.

Zhang 72

72.1 民不畏威[a]則大威[b]將至[c]矣無[d]狎[e]其所居無[f]厭[g]其所生 (Base text: Wang Bi comm.)

清靜[h]無爲謂之居謙後不盈謂之生離[i]其清靜[j]行其躁欲棄其謙後任其威權則物擾而民僻[k]威不能復制民[l]民不能堪其威則上下大潰矣天誅將至故曰民不畏威則大威將至[m]無狎[n]其所居無厭其所生言威力不可任也 (Base text: 張之象本)

72.2 夫唯[o]不[p]厭[q] (Base text: 馬王堆 B)

不自厭也 (Base text: 集註本)

72.3 是以不[r]厭 (Base text: 馬王堆 B)

不自厭是以天下莫之厭 (Base text: 集註本)

---

[a] Var.: 畏畏 for 畏威: 馬王堆 A; 馬王堆 B.

[b] Var.: 畏 for 威: 馬王堆 B.

[c] 將至 for 至: Wang Bi comm.: 天誅將至; 馬王堆 B; lacuna in 馬王堆 A has four spaces between 則 and 矣 and thus could accommodate the 將. The quotation in the Wang Bi commentary has been changed to accommodate the *Laozi* text, given in both 集註本 and 張之象本.

[d] Var.: 毋 for 無: 馬王堆 A; 馬王堆 B.

[e] Var.: 閘 for 狎: 馬王堆 A. Var.: 伻 for 狎: 馬王堆 B.

[f] Var.: 毋 for 無: 馬王堆 A; 馬王堆 B.

[g] 厭 for 猒 (also in 馬王堆 A; 馬王堆 B; 傅奕古本; 范應元本): 陸德明釋文.

[h] 靜 for 淨: 集註本. Support for 清靜: *Laozi* 45.6.

[i] Var.: 雖 for 離: 集註本.

[j] 靜 for 淨: 集註本. Support for 清靜: *Laozi* 45.6.

[k] Var.: 辟 for 僻: 陸德明釋文.

[l] Var.: 良 for 民: 集註本.

[m] Var.: 將至 for 至: Wagner, see note c.

[n] Var.: 狹 for 狎: 集註本.

[o] Var.: 惟 for 唯: 傅奕古本; 范應元本.

[p] 不 for 弗 (also in 馬王堆 A): Wang Bi comm. Var.: 無 for 不: 傅奕古本; 范應元本.

[q] 厭 for 猒 (also in 馬王堆 A; 傅奕古本; 范應元本): 陸德明釋文.

[r] Var.: 無 for 不: 傅奕古本; 范應元本. Support for 不: Wang Bi comm.

72.4 是以聖人自知而不自見也^s (Base text: 馬王堆 B)

不自見其所知以耀光行藏^t也 (Base text: 集註本)

72.5 自愛而不自貴也^u (Base text: 馬王堆 B)

自貴則物狎^v厭居生 (Base text: 張之象本)

72.6 故去彼^w取此 (Base text: 傅奕古本)

72.1
When the people are not in awe of [their ruler's] authority [anymore], then the Great Authority will come.[1] [Only]

being without recklessness is what makes him [the ruler] have rest.	being without repression is what makes him [the ruler] have [= keep] [his] life.
Having "purity" and "calmness" [Laozi 15.4] and [thus] being "without interference," [Laozi 2.2] [Laozi] calls "having rest."	*Being modest[2] and "putting [one's person as a ruler] in the background" [Laozi 7.2 and 67] [and thus] "not filling [it] up" [Laozi 15.6 ff.] [Laozi] calls "having life."[3]*
If [the ruler] leaves his purity and calmness and acts out his excitements and desires,	*abandons his modesty and his "putting himself] in the [background" and applies his authority and power,*
then	*the other entities will make trouble*
and the people will become wicked.	
Once	*[his] authority is not able [anymore] to establish control over the people,*
and [once]	

---

^s Var.: 也 om.: 傅奕古本; 范應元本.   ^t Var.: 威 for 藏: 張之象本.

^u Var.: 也 om.: 傅奕古本; 范應元本.

^v Var.: 狹 for 狎: 集註本.

^w Var.: 被 for 彼: 馬王堆 A. Var.: 罷而 for 彼: 馬王堆 B.

the people are unable to bear
his authority [any longer],

> *then high and low are in great*
> *turmoil: Heaven's death penalty*
> *[for the ruler] will come. That*
> *is why [the text] says: "When*
> *the people are not in awe of*
> *[the ruler's] authority [anymore],*
> *then the Great Authority will*
> *come"! That [only]*

"being without recklessness is
what makes him [the ruler] have
rest"

"being without repression is
what makes him [the ruler] have
[= keep] his life"

> *means that he definitely should*
> *not apply the power of [his]*
> *authority.*

72.2   It is a fact that only as he does
not repress,

> *That is, that he himself does*
> *not repress.*

72.3   he will not be repressed [and
ditto for recklessness.]

> *As he does not repress himself,*
> *there will therefore be no one in*
> *All Under Heaven to repress him.*

72.4   That is why the Sage has knowledge
on his own but does not himself
make a show [of it].

> *He does not himself show what he*
> *knows by way of shedding light on*
> *the behavior in and out of office*
> *[of others].*[4]

72.5   He loves himself but does not exalt
himself.

> *Would he exalt himself, the other*
> *entities would be*

reckless with and

rest

[his]
and

repress

life.

72.6 That is why he rejects the latter
[to make a show and to exalt
himself] and keeps the former
[his own knowledge and the
love for himself].

THE STRUCTURE OF *LAOZI* 72

Laozi 72 has some of the formal elements of IPS. The two parallel phrases with identical grammar in 72.1 are followed by two parallel phrases in texts 4 and 5. However, from Wang Bi's commentary, especially to 72.5, it is quite clear that he read these two phrases as referring to both chains set up in 72.1. According to Wang Bi, we have thus in 72.1 a binary structure that echoes that in a number of other *zhang*, followed by a string of c phrases. Thus although within the *zhang* itself there is no "interlocking," the interlocking here is with the pairs in other *zhang*. This is primarily of importance for the definition of the phrases 72.2 and 72.3. They take up the element 厭 of the b phrase in 72.1. By being inserted into a basic framework of IPS, their lack of a parallel phrase assigns to them the position of a c phrase in a *pars pro toto* construction with an appropriate shadow text, which I have indicated in the bracket. The structure of the *zhang* is:

		c	(72.1)
a		b	(72.1, 72.1)
		c	(72.2, 72.3)
		c	(72.4)
		c	(72.4)

Zhang 73

73.1 勇於敢[a]則殺 (Base text: 傅奕古本)

必不得其死也 (Base text: 集註本)

73.2 勇於不敢[b]則活[c] (Base text: 傅奕古本)

必濟[d]命也 (Base text: 集註本)

---

[a] Var.: 敢者 for 敢: 馬王堆 A.   [b] Var.: 敢者 for 敢: 馬王堆 A.
[c] Var.: 栝 for 活: 馬王堆 A; 馬王堆 B.   [d] Var.: 齊 for 濟: 張之象本.

73.3 此兩者或利或害 (Base text: 傅奕古本)

俱勇而所施者異利害不同 故曰或利或害也 (Base text: 集註本)

73.4 天之所惡[e]孰知其故是以聖人猶難之[f.1] (Base text: 傅奕古本)

孰誰也言誰能知天意邪其唯聖人也[g]夫聖人之明猶難於勇敢況無聖
人之明而欲行之也故曰猶難之也 (Base text: 張湛列子力命篇注 p.
206 until 夫, thereafter 張之象本)[2]

73.5 天之道不爭[h]而善勝[i] (Base text: 傅奕古本)

夫[j]唯不爭故天下莫能與之爭 (Base text: 集註本)

73.6 不言而善應 (Base text: Wang Bi comm.)

順則吉逆則凶不言而善[k]應也 (Base text: 張之象本)

73.7 不[l]召而自來 (Base text: 傅奕古本)

處下則物自歸 (Base text: 集註本)

73.8 坦然[m]而善謀 (Base text: Wang Bi comm.)

垂象而見吉凶先事而設誠[n]安而不忘危未兆[o]而謀之故曰[p]坦[q]然而善

---

[e] Var.: 亞 for 惡: 馬王堆 B.

[f] Var.: 是以聖人猶難之 om.: 馬王堆 B; (lacuna in 馬王堆 A too small to accommodate this phrase).

[g] Var.: 能知天下之所惡意故耶其唯聖人 for 能知天意邪其唯聖人也: 集註本; 張之象本.

[h] Var.: 單 for 爭: 馬王堆 B.   [i] Var.: 朕 for 勝: 馬王堆 B.

[j] Var.: 天 for 夫: 張之象本. Support for 夫: The commentary here is a verbatim quotation of a phrase in *Laozi* 22.7, which has 夫.

[k] Var.: 臨 for 善: 集註本.   [l] Var.: 弗 for 不: 馬王堆 B.

[m] Var.: 默然 for 坦然: 傅奕古本; 范應元本. Var.: 彈 for 坦然: 馬王堆 A. Var.: 單 for 坦然: 馬王堆 B. Support for 坦: comment by Fan Yingyuan that Wang Bi had 坦, 2.68a, and 集註 version of Wang Bi comm., Lu Deming also signals a text with 坦然.

[n] 誠 for 誠: 集註本.

[o] 兆 for 召: 集註本. Support: *Laozi* 64.1 其未兆易謀.

[p] Var.: 曰 for 曰: 集註本.   [q] 坦 for 繹: 集註本.

謀也 (Base text: 張之象本)

73.9 天網ʳ恢恢ˢ踈ᵗ 而不失 (Base text: 傅奕古本)

73.1 If someone is courageous in daring [to do], he will be killed.

By necessity he "will not come to his natural death" [as the Laozi says in 42.3 about "those who are violent and brutal"].

If someone is courageous in **73.2** not daring [to do], he will live.

By necessity he will complete his [allotted] life [span].

73.3 Of these two [kinds of courage,] one is beneficial, the other is harmful.

Both are courage, but what they effect is different. They differ with regard to benefit and harm.

That is why [the text] says: "one is beneficial, the other is harmful"!

73.4 Who is there who would know the reason why Heaven loathes [something]? [Of course only the Sage]. That is why already the Sage considers it difficult [to put into practice what follows from the first two sentences].

"Who is there" is "who."[1] *This means: "Who is able to understand Heaven's intentions? Only the Sage." It is a fact that, if already the insight of the Sage "considers difficult" the "courage" "to dare," how much more [will this be the case] for those lacking the insight of the Sage, but desiring to put*

ʳ Var.: 罔 for 網: 馬王堆 B.   ˢ Var.: 絓絓 for 恢恢: 馬王堆 B.
ᵗ 踈 for 踈: *Laozi* 56.7. Var.: 疏 for 踈: 馬王堆 B.

*into practice [what follows
from] these [two statements
in text 1 and 2]. That is why
[the text] says: "Already [the
Sage] considers it difficult."!*

73.5   It is the Way of Heaven [as
practiced by the Sage] not to
struggle but still to be good at
winning,

[As the Laozi *says about the Sage
in 22.7]* "It is a fact that only because he does not struggle no one
in All Under Heaven is able to
struggle with him."

73.6   not to speak but still to be good
at being followed,

*That following [his teachings]
brings luck, deviating from them,
misfortune [is meant by] "not to
speak but still being good at
being followed."*²

73.7   not to call, but have [the other
entities] come on their own,

*If he positions himself in a lowly
[station], the other entities will
on their own submit themselves
to him.*

73.8   and to be at ease but still be good
at taking precautions.

As [as the Xici *7.10.a1, says, "Heaven]
lets hang down the images and shows
fortune and misfortune" ["and the
Sage imitates them"], he establishes
a warning before something has
happened. [As the* Xici *8.5.a3 says
about the Gentleman]* "While being
in security [in his position] he does
not forget the [threat of] danger" *and
[, as the* Laozi *says about the Sage
Ruler in 64.1,] while* "there are still
no signs [of danger to his life]" *he*

"takes precautions."[3] *That is why
[the text] says "to be at ease but still
be good at taking precautions."*

73.9　　　　The net of Heaven is vast, [its mesh]
is wide, but still nothing gets lost.

THE STRUCTURE OF *LAOZI* 73

Laozi 73 begins with a short section written in closed IPS, and then continues straight on one single line of thought. Its structure is:

a	b	(73.1, 73.2)
	b	(73.3)
a		(73.3)
	c	(73.4)
	c	(73.5)
	c	(73.6)
	c	(73.7)
	c	(73.8)
	c	(73.9)

Zhang 74

74.1 民[a]常[b]不畏死如之何其以死懼之[c]若使[d]民常[e]畏[f]死而[g]爲奇[h]者吾得[i]而殺之孰[j]敢也[k] (Base text: 傅奕古本)

---

[a] Var.: 若民 for 民: 馬王堆 B.　　　　[b] Var.: 恒且? (高明:畏) for 常: 馬王堆 B.

[c] Var.: 奈何以殺愳之也 for 如之何其以死懼之: 馬王堆 A. Var.: 若何以殺曜之也 for 如之何其以死懼之: 馬王堆 B.

[d] Var.: 使 om.: 馬王堆 A; 馬王堆 B.

[e] Var.: 恒且 for 常: 馬王堆 B.

[f] Var.: 是 for 畏: 馬王堆 A. Var.: 而畏 for 常畏: 范應元本.

[g] Var.: 則而 for 而: 馬王堆 A.

[h] Var.: 奇 om.: 馬王堆 A. Var.: 畸 for 奇: 馬王堆 B.

[i] Var.: 將得 for 得: 馬王堆 A. Var.: 得執 for 得: 范應元本.

[j] Var.: 夫孰 for 孰: 馬王堆 A; 馬王堆 B.

[k] Var.: 矣 for 也: 馬王堆 A; 馬王堆 B. Var.: 也 om.: 范應元本.

詭異亂眞^l謂之奇也 (Base text: 取善集)

74.2 常^m有司殺者殺而ⁿ代^o司殺者殺是代大匠斲^p夫代大匠斲者^q希^r不傷^s其手矣^t (Base text: 傅奕古本)¹

爲逆者順者^u之所惡忿也不仁者仁者之^v所疾也故曰常有司殺也 (Base text: 集註本)

74.1 As the people are not afraid of death continuously, how could they be frightened by [the threat] of death? And, even if people could be made continuously afraid of death, and one [, that is, a ruler, personally] would be able to consign those committing outrages to execution, who would there be to dare [to do these executions]? [No one].[1]

Odd and uncommon [acts] to confuse the true [essence] [Laozi] calls "[committing] outrages."

74.2 [No one, because] there are always [people] handling executions who do the executing. It is a fact [, however,] that to replace [the people] handling executions at executing is replacing the Great Carpenter at cutting [wood]. It is a fact that few among those replacing the Great Carpenter at cutting will [get away] with their hands unharmed.

Those committing deviations will be loathed and resented by those going along; those who are not humane will be hated by those who are humane [and these other people will handle the execution of such villains automatically]. That is why [the text] says: "There are always [people] handling executions"![2]

---

^l Var.: 辜 for 眞: 集註本; 張之象本.

^m Var.: 若民□□(馬王堆 B: 恒且)必畏死則恒 for 常: 馬王堆 A; 馬王堆 B.

ⁿ Var.: 夫 for 殺而: 馬王堆 A; 馬王堆 B. Var.: 而 om.: 范應元本.

^o Var.: 伐 for 代: 馬王堆 A. Passim.

^p Var.: 斲也 for 斲: 馬王堆 A.

^q Var.: 者則 for 者: 馬王堆 A; 馬王堆 B.

^r 希 for 稀: 馬王堆 B; 范應元本. Var.: 希有 for 希: 范應元本.

^s 不傷 for 不自傷: 馬王堆A; 馬王堆 B; 范應元本.

^t Var.: 矣 om.: 馬王堆 B.

^u 爲逆者 順者 for 爲逆 順者: 服部南郭.

^v 不仁者 仁者之 for 不仁者 人之: Wagner based on parallel with 爲逆者 順者.

Zhang 75

75.1 民[a]之饑者[b]以其上[c]食稅[d]之多也[e]是以饑民之難治者[f]以其上之[g]有爲[h]也是以難[i]治民之輕[j]死者[k]以其上求[l]生生[m]之厚也是以輕[n]死夫唯[o]無以生爲貴者[p]是賢於[q]貴生也[r] (Base text: 傅奕古本)

言民之所以僻治之所以亂皆由上不由其下也民從上也[1] (Base text: 集註本)

75.1 That people do not gather the harvest[1] is due to their ruler's eating too much tax grain. That is why they do not gather the harvest!

That people are hard to rule is due to their ruler's practicing interference. That is why they are hard to rule!

[In short,] that people take death easily is due to their ruler's striving for the fullness of life. That is why they take death easily! It is a fact that only the absence of appreciation of life

---

[a] Var.: 人 for 民: 馬王堆 A; 馬王堆 B. Support for 民: Wang Bi comm.: 民之所以僻.

[b] Var.: 也 for 者: 馬王堆A; 馬王堆 B.

[c] Var.: 取 for 上: 馬王堆A; 馬王堆 B.

[d] Var.: 逆 for 稅: 馬王堆 A. Var.: 跣 for 稅: 馬王堆 B.

[e] Var.: 也 om.: 馬王堆 B.

[f] Var.: 百姓 (馬王堆 B: 生) 之不治也 for 民之難治者: 馬王堆 A; 馬王堆 B.

[g] Var.: 之 om.: 馬王堆 A.

[h] Var.: 有以爲 for 有爲: 馬王堆A; 馬王堆 B.

[i] Var.: 難 for 不: 馬王堆 A; 馬王堆 B.

[j] Var.: 巠 for 輕: 馬王堆 A.

[k] Var.: 者 om.: 馬王堆 A. Var.: 也 for 者: 馬王堆 B.

[l] Var.: 上 om.: 馬王堆 A; 馬王堆 B. Var.: 上求 om.: 范應元本. Support for 上求: Wang Bi comm.: 民之所以僻治之所以亂皆由上不由其下也 with the 皆 implying that this is the case for all items mentioned.

[m] Var.: 生 for 生生: 馬王堆 A; 馬王堆 B.

[n] Var.: 巠 for 輕: 馬王堆 A.

[o] 唯 for 惟: 馬王堆A; 馬王堆 B.

[p] Var.: 無以生爲者 for 無以生爲貴者: 馬王堆A; 馬王堆 B. 貴 also omitted in 范應元本. Var.: 以爲生 for 以生爲貴: 范應元本.

[q] Var.: 於 om.: 馬王堆A; 馬王堆 B.

[r] Var.: 也 om.: 馬王堆A; 馬王堆 B.

is more worthy than the
appreciation of life.

This means: That by which
people are turned wicked,   and   order is turned into chaos

is all based on the ruler['s behav-
ior] and not on [that of] those
below. The people [only] follow
[the precedent] of the ruler.[2]

THE STRUCTURE OF *LAOZI* 75

Laozi 75 is short of the minimal number of phrases for one full set of IPS. The three parallels, however, are not read by Wang Bi as three equal sentences. He can point to the fact that the fourth, nonparallel phrase ("It is a fact that only . . .") takes up only the vocabulary of the third phrase, thus marking it as a part of the general statement, as opposed to the two first phrases, which deal with the material and social aspects of life, as is frequent. Wang Bi thus comments upon the first two, which by implication groups the third phrase with the fourth. While this might seem a bit pedantic, the relevant point is that the status of the third phrase changes, and with it the reading strategy to be applied to it. This is indicated here by the "in short" in brackets. In Wang Bi's reading, the *zhang* thus has the following structure:

$$a \qquad b \qquad (75.1, 75.1)$$
$$c \qquad (75.1)$$
$$c \qquad (75.1)$$

Zhang 76

76.1 人之生也柔弱其死也堅強ª萬物草木ᵇ之生也柔脆ᶜ其死也枯槁ᵈ故ᵉ堅強者ᶠ死

ª Var.: 楅仞賢強 for 堅強: 馬王堆 A. Var.: 脴信堅強 for 堅強: 馬王堆 B.

ᵇ 萬物草木 for 草木: 馬王堆 A; 馬王堆 B; 范應元本.

ᶜ Var.: 椊 for 脆: 馬王堆 B. Var.: 脃 for 脆: 范應元本.

ᵈ Var.: 㮏橐 for 枯槁: 馬王堆 A. Var.: 㮏槁 for 枯槁: 馬王堆 B.

ᵉ Var.: 故曰 for 故: 馬王堆 A; 馬王堆 B.

ᶠ Var.: 者 om.: 馬王堆 B.

之徒也^g柔弱^h者ⁱ生之徒也^j是以^k兵強者^l則滅^{m,1} (Base text: 傅奕古本)

強兵以暴於天下者物之所惡故必不得終焉ⁿ (Base text: 集註本 until 者, thereafter 張湛列子黃帝篇注)

76.2 木強則折^o (Base text: 張湛列子黃帝篇)

物所加也 (Base text: 集註本)

76.3 故^p強大^q居^r下 (Base text: 馬王堆 B)

木^s之本也 (Base text: 張之象本)

76.4 柔弱居^t上 (Base text: 馬王堆 B)

枝條是也 (Base text: 集註本)

76.1   When people

are alive, they are supple and   are dead, they are hard and of
soft;   violent [rigor].[1]

                                         [In the same way,] when the ten
                                         thousand living beings,[2] the
                                         grasses and trees

live, they are supple and tender;   are dead, they are dry and
                                         withered.

---

[g] Var.: 也 om.: 范應元本.   [h] Var.: 柔弱微細 for 柔弱: 馬王堆 A.

[i] Var.: 者 om.: 馬王堆 A; 馬王堆 B. Var.: 柔弱微細 for 柔弱: 馬王堆 A.

[j] Var.: 也 om.: 范應元本.   [k] Var.: 是以 om.: 馬王堆 A.

[l] Var.: 者 om.: 馬王堆 A; 馬王堆 B; 范應元本. Support for 者: Wang Bi comm.: 強兵
以暴於天下者 . . .

[m] 兵強則滅 for 兵強者則不勝(馬王堆 B:朕): 張湛列子黃帝篇 quoting Wang Bi's
commentary directly afterwards. Support for 滅: 文子, 道原; 淮南子, 原道.

[n] Var.: 惡也 故必不得勝 for 惡 故必不得終焉: 集註本; 張之象本.

[o] Var.: 恒 for 折: 馬王堆 A. Var.: 兢 for 折: 馬王堆 B. Var.: 共 for 則折: 傅奕古本; 范
應元本. Support for 折: 文子, 淮南子.

[p] Var.: 故 om.: 馬王堆 A.   [q] Var.: 堅彊 for 強大: 傅奕古本.

[r] Var.: 處 for 居: 傅奕古本. Var.: 取 for 居: 范應元本.

[s] Var.: 大 for 木: 集註本.   [t] Var.: 處 for 居: 傅奕古本; 范應元本.

| | That is why | hardness and violent rigor are the companions of death. |

suppleness and softness are
the companions of life.

And this is why, if someone
[, that is, a ruler, makes use of]
violent military [action], he
will go under,

*Someone who [makes use] of
violent military [action] to impose
his hegemony in All Under Heaven
will be loathed by the other entities.
That is why he will of necessity not
reach [his natural] end.*

76.2   And if a tree is violently rigid,
                                        it will break.

*This [breaking] will be done to
[the tree] by the other entities.*

76.3   That is why   the hard and violently rigid
                                        takes its place below,

This refers to the root of the tree.

76.4   and the supple and soft takes
            its place above.

*This refers to the twigs and
branches.*

THE STRUCTURE OF *LAOZI* 76

Laozi 76 is written in open IPS. The textual arrangement follows the formal structure, which opposes the structures of the dead to those of the living in the beginning as well as in texts 4 and 5. In this sense, the structure of the *zhang* is:

a	b	(76.1, 76.1)
a	b	(76.1, 76.1)
	b	(76.1)
a		(76.1)
	c	(76.1)
	c	(76.2)
	b	(76.3)
a		(76.4)

There is, however, a second structure that opposes the situation among humans and among trees with regard to life and death. The statements on these two subjects also are parallel in the sense that the same kind of statement is made on both. In terms of content, this structure is dominant. As no three-dimensional arrangements are possible on paper, we have to describe this structure in a separate formula. To make things clearer, the items are numbered, and a list is appended identifying the numbers.

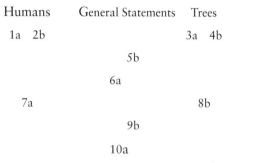

	Humans	General Statements	Trees
	1a 2b		3a 4b
		5b	
		6a	
	7a		8b
		9b	
		10a	

1. "While people are alive." 2. "When [people] are dead." 3. "While the grasses and trees live." 4. "When [the grasses and trees] are dead." 5. "Hardness and violent rigor." 6. Suppleness and softness." 7. "Someone [makes use] of violent military [action]." 8. "A tree is violently rigid." 9. "The hard and violently rigid." 10. "The supple and soft."

Zhang 77

77.1 天之ª道其猶ᵇ張弓者歟ᶜ高者抑ᵈ之下者舉之有餘者損ᵉ之不足者補之天ᶠ之道損ᵍ有餘以ʰ補ⁱ不足ʲ人之道則不然 (Base text: 傅奕古本)

ª Var.: 天下口口 for 天之道: 馬王堆 A.

ᵇ Var.: 酉 for 其猶: 馬王堆 B.

ᶜ Var.: 者也 for 者歟: 馬王堆 A. Var.: 也 for 者歟: 馬王堆 B. Var.: 與 for 歟 : 陸德明釋文.

ᵈ Var.: 印 for 抑: 馬王堆 A; 馬王堆 B.

ᵉ Var.: 歟 for 損: 馬王堆 A; Var.: 云 for 損: 馬王堆 B.

ᶠ Var.: 故天 for 天: 馬王堆 A.

ᵍ Var.: 歟 for 損: 馬王堆 A. Var.: 云 for 損: 馬王堆 B.

ʰ 以 for 而 (also in 馬王堆 B and 范應元本): Wang Bi comm. on *Laozi* 77.2 損有以補無.

ⁱ Var.: 益 for 補: 馬王堆 B.

ʲ Var.: 則不然 om.: 馬王堆 B. 馬王堆 A lacuna ends with 不然 and would have a place for 則 if it otherwise had the same number of characters as 馬王堆 B here.

與天地合德乃能包之如天之道如人之量則各有其身不得相均如唯[k]
無身去[l]私乎自然然後乃能與天地合德 (Base text: 集註本)

77.2 損[m]不足以[n]奉有[o]餘孰[p]能損[q]有[r]餘以[s]奉不足於天下者[t]其唯[u]道者乎[v,1]是以聖
人爲而不恃[w]功成而不[x]居[y]其[z]不欲見賢邪[aa] (Base text: 傅奕古本)

言誰[ab]能處盈而全虛損有以補無和光同塵蕩而均者其唯[ac]道也是以
聖人不欲示其賢以均天下 (Base text: 張之象本)[ad]

77.1   The Way of Heaven—it is truly like
              someone drawing a bow!

What is high up [in a bow] he   What is down below he brings
presses down,   up,

              [in other words]

what has too much he reduces,   what is deficient he supple-
                                 ments.

              While the Way of Heaven [thus]

---

[k] Var.: 惟 for 唯: 張之象本.

[l] 去 for 無 (in both 集註本 and 張之象本): 陸德明釋文.

[m] Var.: 云 for 損: 馬王堆 B.   [n] Var.: 而 for 以: 馬王堆 B.

[o] Var.: 又 for 有: 馬王堆 B.   [p] Var.: 夫孰 for 孰: 馬王堆 B.

[q] Var.: 損 om.: 馬王堆 A; 馬王堆 B. Support for 損: Wang Bi comm.: 言唯能處盈而
全虛 損有以補無.

[r] Var.: 又 for 有: 馬王堆 B.

[s] 以 for 而 (also in 馬王堆 A; 馬王堆 B): Wang Bi comm.: 損有以補無; 范應元本.

[t] Var.: 而有以取奉於天者乎 for 以奉不足於天下者: 馬王堆 A. Var.: 而□□奉於天
者 for 以奉不足於天下者: 馬王堆 B. Var.: 以奉天下 for 以奉不足於天下者: 范應元本.
See note 1.

[u] 唯 for 惟: 馬王堆 B; 范應元本.

[v] Var.: 唯又道者乎 for 其唯道者乎: 馬王堆 B. See note 1.

[w] Var.: 弗又 for 不恃: 馬王堆 B.   [x] Var.: 弗 for 不: 馬王堆 B.

[y] Var.: 居也 for 居: 馬王堆 B. Var.: 處 for 居: 范應元本.

[z] Var.: 若此其 for 其: 馬王堆 B.

[aa] Var.: 也 for 邪: 馬王堆 A; 馬王堆 B.

[ab] 誰 for 唯: 桃井白鹿.   [ac] 其唯 for 唯其: *Laozi* text 其唯道者乎.

[ad] This text is not transmitted in the 集註本.

reduces excess by way of   supplementing deficiency,

this is not true for the way
of men.

Only [a man who is a Sage] who [as the Wenyan *for the first hexagram of the* Zhouyi *says in 1.5.a2 ff. about the Great Man, identified as the Sage,] is "[with his] Capacity in accord with [that of] Heaven and Earth"¹ will be able to "encompass them" [Heaven and Earth] as the Way of Heaven does [in accordance with the* Zhuangzi *(Chuang-tzu yin-te 67/24/70), who says "the Sage encompasses Heaven and Earth"]. If someone has [only] the measure of a man then as each one [of them] has his [individual] person, they in no way can manage to rule each other equitably. Only someone without an [individual] person who has eliminated his private [interests] from [his] That-which-is-of-itself-what-it-is will then indeed be able to "be [with his] Capacity in accord with [that of] Heaven and Earth."*

77.2   [The way of men] reduces
                              what is

[already] deficient by way of   bringing up what [already] has
                                       excess.

                              What is [after all alone]
                              capable of
reducing the excess by way of   bringing up what is deficient

in All Under Heaven? Only [the]
Way! That is why that the Sage
acts, but does not presume [upon
the other entities]; and that [his
particular] achievements come
about without his installing
[himself in them]² is due to his not
wanting to display [his] capabilities.

*This means: What is capable of
residing in the overflowing but
keeping intact [its] emptiness, reducing that which is to supplement
that which is not, "mixes with [the
other entities'] luster" and "joins in
the same dust [with them]" [as the
Laozi writes in 4.1, 56.5, and 56.6
about the Way and the Sage, respec-
tively] and is [undefinably] vast and
rules equitably—only the Way! That*

*is why the Sage does not desire to dis-
play his capabilities, so as to equitably
rule All Under Heaven.*[3]

THE STRUCTURE OF *LAOZI* 77

Laozi 77 is written in open IPS. The structure of the phrase about the Sage in *Laozi* 77.2 suggests with its three parts, two of which are parallel, an abc construction. However, I can find no clues in either the text or the commentary about how to associate the first two statements ("that the Sage acts, but does not presume [upon the other entities] and that [the particular] achievements come about without his installing [himself in them]") with the established a/b chains. I therefore have subsumed these two phrases under the c category. *Laozi* 77 has the following structure:

	c		(77.1)
a		b	(77.1, 77.1)
a		b	(77.1, 77.1)
	c		(77.1)
a		b	(77.1, 77.1)
	c		(77.1)
a		b	(77.2, 77.2)
a		b	(77.2, 77.2)
	c		(77.2)
	c		(77.2)

Zhang 78

78.1 天下莫柔弱於水而攻堅強者莫之能先ᵃ以ᵇ其無以易之也 (Base text: 傅奕古本)

以用也其謂水也言用水之柔弱無物可以易之也 (Base text: 張之象本)[1]

78.2 柔^c之勝^d剛^e弱之勝強^f天下莫不^g知^h莫之能行ⁱ故^j聖人之言云^k受國^l之垢^m是謂ⁿ社稷之主受國^o之^p不祥是謂^q天下之王^r正言若反^s (Base text: 傅奕古本)

78.1　Nothing in All Under Heaven is more supple and soft than water, but for one [a ruler] attacking the firm and violently rigid nothing is capable of surpassing [these features]. [If he acts] by means of it[s characteristics] there will be nothing by which he could be altered.

"By means of" means "making use of." "It" refers to water. This [entire passage] means: If [a ruler] were to make use of the suppleness and softness of water, there would be no other entity that could change him.[1]

78.2　That the supple overcomes the hard and the soft the violently rigid is known to everyone in All Under Heaven, but no one is able to put [this] to practice. That is why in the statements of the Sage, "[Only] he who takes on himself the humiliation of the state I call the lord of the altars of the nation; [only] he who takes upon himself the misfortune of the state I call the king of All Under Heaven" straight words seem paradoxical.

---

　　^c Var.: 水 for 柔: 馬王堆 B.

　　^d Var.: 朕 for 勝: 馬王堆 B.

　　^e Var.: 剛也 for 剛: 馬王堆 B.

　　^f Var.: 強也 for 強: 馬王堆 B.

　　^g Var.: 弗 for 不: 馬王堆 B.

　　^h Var.: 知也而口 (= 莫) for 知莫: 馬王堆 B.

　　ⁱ Var.: 行 (馬王堆 B:口) 也 for 行: 馬王堆 A; 馬王堆 B.

　　^j Var.: 是故 for 故: 馬王堆 B. Var.: 是以 for 故: 范應元本.

　　^k Var.: 云曰 for 云: 馬王堆 A; 馬王堆 B. Var.: 聖人言 for 聖人之言云: 范應元本.

　　^l Var.: 邦 for 國: 馬王堆 A.

　　^m Var.: 詢 for 垢: 馬王堆 A; 馬王堆 B.

　　ⁿ Var.: 胃 for 謂: 馬王堆 A; 馬王堆 B.

　　^o Var.: 邦 for 國: 馬王堆 A.

　　^p Var.: 之 om.: 范應元本.

　　^q Var.: 胃 for 謂: 馬王堆 A; 馬王堆 B.

　　^r 王 for 主: 馬王堆 A; 馬王堆 B; 范應元本. Var.: 王也 for 王: 范應元本.

　　^s 反 for 反也: 馬王堆 A; 馬王堆 B; 范應元本.

Zhang 79

79.1 和ᵃ大怨必有餘怨 (Base text: 傅奕古本)

不明理其契以致大怨已至而德以ᵇ和之其傷不復故必ᶜ有餘怨也 (Base text: 集註本)

79.2 安ᵈ可以爲善是以聖人執左契ᵉ (Base text: 傅奕古本)

左契者ᶠ防怨之所由生也 (Base text: 集註本)

79.3 而不ᵍ責於人故有ʰ德司契ⁱ (Base text: 傅奕古本)

有德之人念思其契不令ʲ怨生而後責於人也 (Base text: 集註本)

79.4 無德司徹ᵏ (Base text: 傅奕古本)

徹司人之過也 (Base text: 集註本)

79.5 天ˡ道無親常ᵐ與善人 (Base text: 傅奕古本)

79.1   [Even after someone] has settled a great resentment, there will necessarily be leftover resentments.

By not being clear in the management of his [own part] of the contract,

---

ᵃ Var.: 禾 for 和: 馬王堆 B.　　ᵇ Var.: 以 om.: 張之象本.

ᶜ Var.: 必 om.: 張之象本.　　ᵈ Var.: 焉 for 安: 馬王堆 A.

ᵉ Var.: 聖右介 for 聖人執左契: 馬王堆 A. Var.: 芥 for 契: 馬王堆 B.

ᶠ Var.: 者 om.: 取善集; 張之象本.

ᵍ Var.: 不以 for 不: 馬王堆 A; 馬王堆 B. Support against 以: Wang Bi on *Zhouyi* hexagram 訟, 1.12a3 有德司契而不責於人.

ʰ Var.: 又 for 有: 馬王堆 B.

ⁱ Var.: 介 for 契: 馬王堆 A. Var.: 芥 for 契: 馬王堆 B.

ʲ Var.: 念 for 令: 張之象本.

ᵏ Var.: 勶 for 徹: 馬王堆 A; 馬王堆 B.

ˡ Var.: 夫天 for 天: 馬王堆 A. From the number of spaces in lacuna 馬王堆 B might not have had 夫.

ᵐ Var.: 恒 for 常: 馬王堆 A.

great resentment will be brought about [by the other party's non-fulfillment of the contract obligations]. [Even if,] once this [resentment] has come, receipt/capacity[1] is used to settle it, the harm already done cannot be undone, that is why [the text says] "there will necessarily be leftover resentments [in oneself]"!

79.2   How can [such a procedure] be considered good? [It cannot]. That is why the Sage holds on to the "left contract" [which establishes the claim against a debtor and is presented for repayment]

[Holding on to] the "left contract" blocks the basis on which resentments arise [by its not being presented for payment].

79.3   and does not claim payment from the other [contract partner]. Thus he who has capacity pays attention to [his part of] the contract,

A man with capacity [the Sage] is concerned [only] with his [part of the] contract. [Thus] he does not let a resentment arise and then claim payment from the other.

79.4   while he who is without capacity pays attention to finding out.

"Finding out" means paying attention to the mistakes of others.[2]

79.5   The Way of Heaven is without partiality. It constantly gives to the good people.[3]

Zhang 80

80.1 小國ᵃ寡民 (Base text: 傅奕古本)

國既小民又寡尚可使反古況國大民衆乎故舉小國而言也 (Base text: 集註本)

80.2 使民有ᵇ什伯ᶜ之器而無用ᵈ (Base text: 傅奕古本)

言使民雖有什伯之器而無所用之當何ᵉ患不足也 (Base text: 集註本)

ᵃ Var.: 邦 for 國: 馬王堆 A.

ᵇ Var.: 民有 om.: 馬王堆 A. Var.: 民 om.: 馬王堆 B.

ᶜ Var.: 十百人 for 什伯: 馬王堆 A. 馬王堆 B. Support for 什伯: Wang Bi comm.: 什伯之器.

ᵈ 無用 for 不用也 (also in 范應元本): Wang Bi comm.: 而無所用; 馬王堆 A and 馬王堆 B: 毋用. Var.: 毋 for 無: 馬王堆 A and 馬王堆 B.

ᵉ Var.: 用何 for 用之 當何: 張之象本.

80.3 使民重死而不^f遠徙 (Base text: 傅奕古本)

使民^g惟身是寶不貪貨賂故各安其居重死而不遠徙也 (Base text: 集註本)

80.4 雖有舟輿^h無所乘之雖ⁱ有甲兵無所陳之使民^j復結繩而用之至治之極民各^{k,1}甘其食美其服樂其俗安其居¹鄰國^m相望ⁿ雞狗^o之聲相聞使^p民至老死^q不相^r往來 (Base text: 傅奕古本)

無所求欲^s (Base text: 集註本)

| 80.1 | If in a small state with few people |
| | |

If, though the state were small and furthermore the people few, it would be possible to bring about a return to [the time in] antiquity [when order was established by "knotted cords"],[1] how much more would this be the case were the state big and the people numerous? That is why [the text] discusses [the return to antiquity] by taking the small state [as the example].

---

^f Var.: 不 om.: 馬王堆 A and 馬王堆 B.

^g 使民 for 使民不用: Wagner. The 不用 is a carryover from the previous commentary.

^h Var.: 有車周 for 雖有舟輿: 馬王堆 A. Var.: 又周車 for 雖有舟輿: 馬王堆 B.

ⁱ Var.: 雖 om.: 馬王堆 A; 馬王堆 B.

^j Var.: 人 for 民: 陸德明釋文. Support for 民: Wang Bi comm. on *Laozi* 80.3 使民: 馬王堆 A.

^k Var.: 至治之極 民各 om.: 馬王堆 A; 馬王堆 B. Cf. note 1.

^l 樂其俗 安其居 for 安其居 樂其業 (also in 范應元本): 馬王堆 A; 馬王堆 B. Support for this sequence and wording: 莊遵.

^m Var.: 鄰邦 for 鄰國: 馬王堆 A. Var.: 叟國 for 鄰國: 馬王堆 B.

ⁿ Var.: 壂 for 望: 馬王堆 A.

^o 狗 for 犬 (also in 馬王堆 B): 馬王堆 A; 范應元本. Support for 狗: 莊遵指歸.

^p Var.: 使 om.: 馬王堆 A; 馬王堆 B.

^q Var.: 死而 for 死: 范應元本.

^r 相 for 相與: 馬王堆 A; 馬王堆 B; 范應元本.

^s Var.: 欲求 for 求欲: 張之象本.

80.2 the people could be induced   the people could be induced   80.3
[, even though they] possessed   to consider death important
[military] devices [to be collec-   and not travel far,
tively used by] ten or a hundred
soldiers, not to use them,

This means: If people could   *[That is,] if the people could be*
already be induced, although   *induced to treasure only their*
they possess [military] devices   *persons and not crave goods,*
[to be collectively used by] ten   *they would then each [as the*
or a hundred soldiers, not to   Laozi *says further down] "be*
make use of them at all, what   *content in their place," "con-*
deficiency would they then [still]   *sider death [i.e., their life]*
be worried about? [None].   *important and not travel far."*

80.4   [that is to say if they
could be induced]

although they had ships and
carriages, absolutely not to
board them,

although they had the armor,
absolutely not to field it,

[in short] if the people could be
induced to return to the knotted
cords [and according to *Xici* 8.3.a7
"in high antiquity knotted cords
[were used] to establish order 上古
結繩而治] and make use of these,
this would be the epitome of the
highest social order![2]
People each would then enjoy

their food and find pleasure in
their clothing,

their [local] customs and be
content in their place,

and, [although] neighboring
states would be in sight of each
other and could hear the sounds
of each others' cocks and dogs,
the people until their old age and
death would never communicate
with each other [through either
trade or warfare].

They would have nothing they
desire or crave.

THE STRUCTURE OF *LAOZI* 80

Laozi 80 is written in closed IPS. The formal elements give a good indication. Texts 2 and 3 are parallel within narrow bounds of deviation. So are the first two sentences of text 4. The third sentence there, dealing with the "knotted cords," stands alone, which marks it as a c phrase. The weapons mentioned in text 2 are taken up in the armor in the second phrase of text 4; the traveling in text 3 is taken up by the ships and carriages in the first phrase of text 5. In the subsequent four short parallel phrases in text 5 after the summary statement, the second pair obviously deals with not traveling, while the first pair must deal with what Wang Bi calls the absence of any worry about "deficiencies" as a consequence of the nonuse of sophisticated weapons. I assume that even the subsequent two sentences could be apportioned, but, there being no commentary, I shall refrain from doing so, since the links are tenuous. The neighboring states would probably deal with the potential warfare side, the closeness of the animal voices with the lure of trading with the neighbors. The structure of the *zhang* is:

	c		(80.1)
a		b	(80.2, 80.3)
		b	(80.4)
a			(80.4)
	c		(80.4)
a		b	(80.4, 80.4)
	c		(80.4)

Zhang 81

81.1 信言不美 (Base text: 傅奕古本)

實在質也 (Base text: 集註本)

81.2 美言不信知者不博 (Base text: for first phrase 傅奕古本, for second 馬王堆 B)

本在樸也 (Base text: 集註本)

81.3 博者不知善者不多^a (Base text: 馬王堆 B)

　　極在一也 (Base text: 集註本)

81.4 多^b者不善^{c,1}是故聖人^d無積 (Base text: 馬王堆 B)

　　無私自有唯善是與任物而已 (Base text: 集註本)

81.5 既以爲人己愈^e有 (Base text: 傅奕古本)

　　物所尊也 (Base text: 集註本)

81.6 既以與^f人^g己愈^h多 (Base text: 傅奕古本)

　　物所歸也 (Base text: 集註本)

81.7 天ⁱ之道利而不害 (Base text: 傅奕古本)

　　動常生成之也 (Base text: 集註本)

81.8 聖^j人之道爲而不^k爭 (Base text: 傅奕古本)

　　順天之利不相傷也 (Base text: 集註本)

81.1　　Credible words are not beautified.

---

[a] Var.: 辯 for 多: 傅奕古本; 范應元本. Cf. note 1.

[b] Var.: 辯 for 多: 傅奕古本; 范應元本. Cf. note 1.

[c] Var.: 善言不辯辯言不善知者不博博者不知 for 知者不博博者不知善者不多多者不善: 傅奕古本; 范應元本. Sequence 知/善 supported by 莊遵.

[d] 是故聖人 for 聖人 (also in 馬王堆 A): 傅奕古本; 范應元本. Support for 是故: 莊遵.

[e] Var.: 俞 for 愈: 馬王堆 B; 范應元本. Support for 愈: 陸德明釋文.

[f] Var.: 予 for 與: 馬王堆 B.

[g] Var.: 人矣 for 人: 馬王堆 B. Var.: 俞 for 愈: 馬王堆 B; 范應元本.

[h] Var.: 俞 for 愈: 馬王堆 B; 范應元本.

[i] Var.: 故天 for 天: 馬王堆 B.　　[j] Var.: 聖 om.: 馬王堆 B.

[k] Var.: 弗 for 不: 馬王堆 B..

*The essential is in the [unadorned]
substance.*

81.2   Beautified words are not
        credible.

Someone [truly] knowledgeable
is not broadly [learned].

The root is in the Unadorned.

81.3

Someone broadly [learned] is
not [truly] knowledgeable.

Someone who does good
does not go in for quantity.

The absolute is in the One.

81.4

Someone who goes in for
quantity does no good. That
is why the Sage is without
accumulation.

*Without having self-interest he
has [things] spontaneously; he
does nothing but give to the good
and just puts himself into the
service of other entities.*

81.5

Thus because of acting for others,
he has more himself.

*That is, he is being honored by
the other entities.*

81.6

Thus by giving to others, there
will be more with him.

*That is, he is the one to whom the
other entities submit themselves.*

81.7

It is the Way of Heaven to be
beneficial and not harmful.

*In its movement it constantly
generates and perfects [and never
harms] them [the entities].*

81.8

It is the Way of the Sage to act
but not to struggle.

*He adapts to Heaven's being
beneficial and will not hurt other
[entities].*

THE STRUCTURE OF *LAOZI* 81

Laozi 81 has a section in the beginning that operates within patterns of IPS. The three parallel double phrases do break down into two that are summarized in a third, but there is no visible interlocking structure with the rest. After the break beginning with "the Sage," we would expect a structure that takes up the statements made before this break and fit into the same IPS pattern. In the present case, however, a link between the two parallel sentences after the break, texts 5 and 6, and the two double phrases in the beginning is not decipherable to me. Wang Bi gives no hint of such a link. In fact, his own commentary to text 4 takes up the two core notions of the two subsequent texts, "giving," *yu* 與, and "working for others," which is *wei ren* 爲人 in the *Laozi* and *ren wu* 任物 in Wang Bi. This indicates that Wang Bi saw the relationship as rather tenuous and read the phrases 5 and 6 between the initial statements and those about the Sage as unfoldings of the "absence of accumulation." I still assume that there is more to the structure of this *zhang* but have not found the clue. The structure, as far as understood, runs:

a/a	(81.1, 81.2)
b/b	(81.2, 81.3)
c	(81.3–81.8)

Notes

CHAPTER 1

1. An earlier version of this chapter appeared in *Early China* 14 (1989), "The Wang Bi Recension of the *Laozi.*" I am grateful to the editor, Professor E. Shaughnessy, who reviewed the manuscript and graciously permitted its use in this book.

2. See the listing in Shima Kuniō, *Rōshi Kōsei*, 25ff. Recently, two editions of the Heshang gong have been published. See Zheng Chenghai, *Laozi Heshang gong zhu jiaoli*, and Wang Qia, ed., *Laozi Daode jing Heshang gong zhangju.*

3. Lu Deming, *Laozi Daodejing yinyi*, in id. *Jindian shiwen* j.25, 1400. Also see Fu Yi, *Daode jing guben pian.*

4. Fan Yingyuan, *Laozi Daode jing guben jizhu.*

5. Rao Zongyi, "Wu jianheng er nian Suo Dan xieben Daode jing canjuan kaozheng (jianlun Heshang gong ben yuanliu (The Su Tan Fragment of the Tao-te-ching (A.D. 270))," *Journal of Oriental Studies* 2:1 (1955):1–28; id., *Laozi Xiang Er zhu jiaojian*; id., "Laozi Xiang Er zhu xulun," in *Fukui hakase shoju kinen Tōyō bunka ronshū*, 1151–71. For the dating of the Xiang Er text to the late second century, see Chen Shixiang "'Xiang Er' Laozi Daojing Dunhuang canjuan lunzheng," *Tsing Hua Journal of Chinese Studies* 1:2 (1957): 41 ff; for the fifth century date, see Mugitani Kuniō, "Rōshi Sōji shū' ni tsuite," *Tōhō gakuhō* 57 (March 1985), 75 ff.

6. Mawangdui Hanmu boshu zhengli xiaozu, "Mawangdui Hanmu chutu Laozi shiwen," *Wenwu* 11 (1974), 8–20. Photostatic reproductions are given in Mawangdui Hanmu boshu zhengli xiaozu, *Mawangdui Hanmu boshu*, 2 vols.

7. See Jingzhou shi Bowuguan, ed., *Guodian Chu mu zhujian*, 3–10, for the photostats and 111–22 for the transcriptions. For the dating, cf. p. 1. It is based on the close similarity of the burial gifts to those in the nearby Baoshan No. 2 tomb, which contains dated manuscripts, and on the assumption that after the Qin attack on Chu in 278 B.C.E., Chu came under strong Qin influence so that later Chu tombs would show cultural influences from Qin that are absent in the Guodian No. 1 tomb. Wang Baoxuan, "Shilun Guodian Chu jian gepian de zhuanzho shidai

jiqi beijing," has objected to the arguments for this dating, saying that there was much cultural resistance in Chu after the invasion. He proposed a date between 278 and 265 B.C.E.

8. See Shima Kuniō, *Rōshi Kōsei*, 33. Yao Nai, *Laozi zhangyi*; Xu Dachun, *Daode jing zhu*.

9. Ma Xulun, *Laozi jiaogu*, 6. Ma argued that certain mistakes from Wang Bi's text had entered the Heshang gong *Laozi* text. This was considered proof that Heshang gong's commentary is later than Wang Bi's. In view of the Mawangdui texts, this judgment does not withstand scrutiny.

10. See, e.g., D. C. Lau, *Chinese Classics, Tao Te Ching*, 155; Chan Wing-tsit, *The Way of Lao-tzu*, 162 ff. Lau used the "Wang Bi" text for his *Laozi* translation. Ariane Rump, with Wing-tsit Chan, trans., *Commentary on the "Lao-Tzu" by Wang Bi*, and Paul J. Lin, *A Translation of Lao Tzu's Tao Te Ching and Wang Bi's Commentary*, both use the "Wang Bi" text of the *Laozi*. William Boltz merges the "Wang Bi" and the Heshang gong text into a conflated "textus receptus"; see William Boltz, "The Religious and Philosophical Significance of the 'Hsiang Erh' *Lao tzu* in the Light of the Ma-Wang-Tui Silk Manuscripts," *Bulletin of the School of Oriental and African Studies* 45 (1982), 107; "The *Lao Tzu* Text That Wang Bi and Ho-shang Kung Never Saw," *Bulletin of the School of Oriental and African Studies* 48:5 (1985), 493–501. R. Lynn, *The Classic of the Way and Virtue. A New Translation of the* Tao-te ching *of Laozi*, again follows this text, with minor changes.

11. Hatano Tarō, *Rōshi Ō chū kōsei*. Lou Yulie, *Wang Bi ji jiaoshi*. Gao Ming's otherwise fine *Boshu Laozi jiaozhu* (1996) also operates with the same "standard text."

12. I am grateful to Terry Kleeman for directing my attention to this valuable work, which also is referred to by William Boltz in his paper "The Religious and Philosophical Significance of the 'Hsiang Erh'," p. 99, n. 14.

13. In the following discussion and examples, *Wang Bi Laozi Receptus* refers specifically and exclusively to the received "Wang Bi version" of the text as available in Lou Yulie's edition. This should be strictly differentiated from what I shall try to reconstruct as the original text known to Wang Bi, which I refer to as *Wang Bi Laozi*.

14. Wang Bi, "Zhouyi zhu," 397.

15. Lu Deming, *Laozi Daodejing yinyi*. See also Hatano Tarō, *Rōshi Ō chū kōsei*, Ser. A-2, 12.

16. In 10.6, *wu yi* 無以 is given for *wu* 無, in 16.4, *fan wu* 凡物 for *fu wu* 夫物, and in 20.4 *kuo*, 廓 for *bo/pa* 泊/怕.

17. Hatano Tarō, *Rōshi Ō chū kōsei*, Ser. A-2, 12.

18. For these and the following variations, see Appendix B.

19. Ban Gu, *Hanshu*, 53.2410.

20. Lu Xisheng, *Daode zhen jing zhuan*; Xie Shouhao, *Hunyuan shengji*, preface.

21. P. Van der Loon, *Taoist Books in the Libraries of the Sung Period*, 108, for the record of this title. Peng Si's reference to Du Guangting as the source is in his *Daode zhen jing jizhu zashuo*, 2.31a.

22. Professor Shima Kuniō punctuates these phrases in such a manner as to leave those he does not need for his own analysis unintelligible; see *Rōshi Kōsei*, 27.

23. The Commentary to Fan Ye's *Hou Han shu* quotes the biography of Anqiu Wang (not Anqiu Wangzhi) from Xi Kang's 嵇康 (223–262) now lost *Sheng xian gaoshi zhuan* 聖賢高士傳. A native of Changling 長陵 with a *zi* Zhongdu 仲都 and a *hao* Anqiu zhangren 安丘丈人, he studied the "classic of Laozi" since his youth and refused to become an official. Emperor Cheng 成 (reigned 32–6 B.C.E.) wanted to meet him, but he refused. He lived as a shaman healer 巫醫 among the common people. See Fan Ye, *Hou Han shu*, 19.703. He had disciples, among them Geng Kuang 耿況, a minor official in charge of "elucidating the classics," *ming jing* 明經, at the end of the Former Han, who along with Wang Mang's 王莽 paternal first cousin, Wang Ji 王伋, studied the *Laozi* with Anqiu Wang. See Comm. to Fan Ye, *Hou Hanshu*, 19.703. In the preface to his *Laozi Daode jing yinyi*, 1.64, Lu Deming refers to a *zhangju* 章句 commentary on the *Laozi* by Wuqiu Wangzhi 毌丘望之, which also is listed in the Liang Dynasty book catalogue, see Wei Zheng, *Suishu* 34.1000. It seems highly probable to me that Wuqiu Wangzhi is the same person as Anqiu Wang, and that the replacement of Anqiu by Wuqiu was due to the fact that, during the Jin at least, a family name 毌丘 did exist, while Anqiu 安丘 basically is a place name. In the chronological sequence implied in Lu Deming's narrative, however, this commentary figures before that by Zhuang Zun and after that by Heshang gong. I have not been able to locate quotations from his commentary. Anqiu Wangzhi had a biography in the *Daoxue zhuan* 道學傳, of which one fragment survives, which in turn seems to have quoted from a section of Ge Hong's *Baipuzi* that is not in the current editions but is quoted in *Taiping yulan*, 666.2b7–12. According to this information, he was greatly esteemed by emperor Cheng. The *Baopuzi* quotation also says that after he had withdrawn from the court contacts, "he proceeded with a *Laozi zhangju* 老子章句, and there was a school of Anqiu." Similar information is in Huang-fu Mi's *Gaoshi zhuan*. See S. Bumbacher, *The Fragments of the Daoxue zhuan*, fragments 59 and 60, pp. 188–90.

24. On Kou Qianzhi, see Richard Mather, "K'ou Ch'ien-chih and the Taoist Theocracy at the Northern Wei Court (425–451)," 103–22.

25. Sima Qian, *Shiji*, 63.2141.

26. Peng Si, *Daode zhen jing jizhu zashuo*, 2.30a f; Xie Shouhao, *Hunyuan shengji*, 3.20a ff. The most important difference between the two texts is in the end of the description of the first group of manuscripts. Peng Si ends the report about Qiu Yue with a clear 仇嶽傳之 "handed down by Qiu Yue." He then

starts a new phrase 三家本有五千七百二十二字. The three previously named manuscripts accordingly all had the same number of characters. Xie Shouhao obviously misquotes this passage by writing 仇嶽傳家之本有五千七百二十二字, which would translate as "the manuscript handed down in the family of Qiu Yue has . . ." and would not give a number for the two other manuscripts mentioned previously, although the introduction specifically states that Fu Yi counted the characters in these old manuscripts. My own previous translation in *Early China* 14 (1989) was based on this faulty text.

27. Cf. Lu Deming, *Laozi Daodejing yinyi*, 1397, on 博 and 豫; 1398 on 德之容 and 窪; 1401 on 夷道若纇; 1402 on 歙歙; 1403 on 其充 and other places. In the introduction to his *Jingdian shiwen*, vol. 1, 62 ff., Lu Deming mentions several commentaries to the *Laozi* at his disposal but no bamboo-strip text. For a description of the transmission of Lu Deming's text and efforts at amending some of the defects on the basis of older transmissions, see Huang Zhuo, *Jingdian shiwen huijiao*.

28. Xia Song, *Guwen sisheng yun*, preface, 1b. References to characters in this manuscript are frequent in the *Guwen sisheng yun*. Xia made use of a second old *Xiaojing* that had been transmitted privately along with another text. As no one was able to read this, it was given to Han Yu, who in turn gave it to a Guigong 歸公, who was an "amateur of antiquity and was able to understand it."

29. Guo Zhongshu, *Hanjian*, 1, has the list of the texts used.

30. Li Ling 李零, postface to Xia Song, *Guwen sisheng yun*, 3.

31. In ibid., 1b, Xia Song gives a short history of the transmission of one *Laozi* in seal script, but there is no indication that he had the Laozi manuscript from the Xiang Yu concubine's tomb. In the work itself, Xia makes use of two *Laozi* texts, one referred to as *Daode jing* and quoted very often, the other as *Gu Laozi* 古老子 and quoted more rarely, for example, on 16a (= 上平 31b).

32. For a detailed study on Li Yangbing, see L. Wagner, "Art As an Instrument for Political Legitimation during the Tang: The Small Script and the Legitimation Seal," *Oriens Extremus* 40 (1997): 2; the transmission of the *Laozi* manuscript is treated there on pp. 175–80.

33. Xia Song, "Preface" to *Guwen sisheng yun*, 1a–b.

34. Lu Deming, *Jingdian shiwen*, 1.64. In the internal chronology of Lu Deming's list, this commentary figures before that by Zhuang [Yan] Zun 莊 [嚴] 遵 and after that by "Heshang gong."

35. Cf. *Shiji*, 20.2436.

36. Cf. *Sui shu*, 34.1000.

37. Ibid.

38. Zhuang (Yan) Zun, *Daode zhenjing zhigui*. For a modern edition and translation into the Chinese vernacular, see Wang Deyou, *Laozi zhigui quanyi*.

39. Shima Kuniō, *Rōshi Kōsei*, 51.

40. Liu Dabin, *Maoshan zhi*, 9.1a.

41. Shima Kuniō, *Rōshi Kōsei*, 33.

42. Ibid., 117.

43. Ibid., 109.

44. Rao, "Wu jianheng er nian Suo Dan . . .," 13 ff.

45. This quotation seems to have been discovered by Li Qiao, *Laozi guzhu* 2.24b. It has been referred to by E. Erkes, *Ho-shang-kung's Commentary on the Lao-tse*, 9, and by Anna Seidel, *La Divinisation du Lao Tseu dans le Taoisme des Han*, 32, n. 4. However, W. Hung, "A Bibliographical Controversy at the T'ang Court," 81, 121, has noted that this quotation is indirect, not verbatim.

46. *Liuchen zhu wenxuan*, 3:79b. See, too, Seidel, *La Divinisation*, 32, n. 4.

47. *Liuchen zhu wenxuan*, 3:66b, 67a, 70b.

48. *Laozi jiaben yiben Fu Yi ben duizhao biao* in Mawangdui Hanmu boshu zhengli xiaozu, ed., *Mawangdui Hanmu boshu Laozi*, 65–94.

49. Gao Ming, *Boshu Laozi jiaozhu*.

50. Cf. my "'Shu bu jin yan'—Xian Qin shiqi duiyu wenzi zhi bukekao de piping yu chutu wenzi zhong suojian de dui wenzi zhi zuoyong de taidu" ('Writing does not fully express the spoken word'—On the criticism of the unreliability of written characters before the Qin and the attitude towards the functions of written characters as visible in the archaeological textual finds) talk given at the Chūgoku shūto shiryō gakkai, Tokyo, March 15, 1999.

51. An exception is 59.2, while 65.4 and 67.2 differ otherwise.

52. Pei Wei, *Chongyou lun* 崇有論, quoted in Fan Xuanling, *Jin shu*, 35.1046.

53. *Wenzi yaoquan*, 178, following the text in *Tongxuan zhenjing zhu*, 10: 2b. The *Wenzi zhuzi suoyin* gives a text 則可以寄天下..乃可以托天下, which follows the *Tongxuan zhenjing zuanyi*, 10:3a.

54. In fact, the two main old sources for this commentary section disagree. The 集註本 writes 自今及古, while the 永樂大典本 gives 自古及今. See my notes to the edition and p. 71 for the importance of this passage for the *LZWZLL*.

55. See my notes to the edition for this *zhang*.

56. The commentary to *Laozi* 23.1 refers to "*zhang*" 35; the commentary to *Laozi* 57.1 refers to "*zhang*" 48, and the commentary to *Laozi* 28.5 refers to "*zhang*" 40.

57. This is the case in the commentary to *Laozi* 28.5, which quotes *Laozi* 40, which is in another *pian*.

58. Robert G. Henricks, "A Note on the Question of Chapter Divisions in the Ma-Wang-Tui Manuscripts of the Lao-tzu," 49–51; see also his "Examining the

Ma-Wang-Tui Silk Texts of the Lao-Tzu, with Special Note of their Differences from the Wang Bi Text," 166–98, and "Examining the Chapter Divisions in the Lao-Tzu," 501–24.

59. Xie Shouhao, *Hunyuan shengji*, 3.18b.

60. See my *The Craft of a Chinese Commentator*, p. 263.

61. Cf. *LZWZLL* 2.32, p. 89.

62. Chao Yuezhi, "Fuzhi ji." Quoted in the appendix of the *Siku quanshu* edition of the *Laozi Daodejing*, vol. 1055, p. 184b ff.

63. Dong Sijing. *Daode zhen jing jijie*, preface.

CHAPTER 2

1. Wang Zhongmin, *Laozi kao*, 78–87.

2. Hatano Tarō, *Rōshi Ō chū kōsei*; Shima Kuniō, *Rōshi Kōsei*, 9 ff.

3. See, among others, B. Kandel, *Wen tzu: Ein Beitrag zur Problematik und zum Verständnis eines taoistischen Textes*; B. Kandel, *Taiping jing: The Origin and Transmission of the "Scripture on General Welfare": The History of an Unofficial Text*; Harold D. Roth, *The Textual History of the Huai-nan tzu*.

4. Hong Yixuan, *Dushu conglu* 讀書叢錄, 12.1.

5. Qian Zeng, *Dushu min qiu ji* 讀書敏求記, 3.80 quoted in Ji Yun, "Laozi Daode jing tiyao," 137.

6. Lou Yulie, *Wang Bi ji jiaoshi*.

7. He Shao 何劭, *Wang Bi biezhuan* 王弼別傳, quoted in Pei Songzhi, *Sanguo zhi zhu*, 759.

8. Liu Yiqing, *Shishuo xinyu*, AB 8b; Richard Mather, trans., Liu I-ch'ing, *Shih-shuo hsin-yu, A New Account of Tales of the World*, 95; *Shishuo xinyu* AB 9b; Mather, *A New Account of Tales*, 97.

9. Cf. my *The Craft of a Chinese Commentator*, 15–16.

10. Zhang Zhan, *Liezi zhu*, 278ff. For the library, see my *The Craft of a Chinese Commentator*, 12–14.

11. Zhang Zhan, *Liezi zhu*, 4–5.

12. *Daode zhenjing jizhu*, 1.24a–b.

13. Liu Weiyong, *Daode zhen jing jiyi*, 11.2b–3a.

14. *Daode zhen jing zhu*, 1.5a.

15. *Laozi Daode jing*, 141b.

16. Zhang Zhan, *Liezi zhu*, 129, line 5.

17. *Daode zhen jing zhu*, 4.8b–9a.

18. *Laozi Daode jing*, 181b.

19. Liu Xiaobiao, *Shishuo xinyu zhu*, 61, line 5.

20. *Daode zhenjing jizhu*, 6.11b, 6.21a.

21. *Daode zhen jing zhu*, 3.4b–5a.

22. *Laozi Daode jing*, 162b.

23. Huida, *Zhaolun shu*, Z. 150.6a16.

24. See my "Exploring the Common Ground: Buddhist Commentaries on the Taoist Classic *Laozi*."

25. Shima Kuniō, *Rōshi Kōsei*, inserts the *Laozi* quotations in the *Qunshu zhiyao* into the Heshang gong textual family.

26. Cf. the excerpts from Fu Yi's report about the different manuscripts quoted on pp. 10–11.

27. Lu Deming, preface to *Laozi Daodejing yinyi*, 1393.

28. The *zhang* from which Lu Deming quoted no Wang Bi *Commentary* piece are: 1, 2, 7, 8, 11, 12, 21, 23, 29, 31, 33, 37, 39, 40, 46, 48, 52, 56, 57, 66, 71, 74, 76, 78, and 81. The quotation from the missing piece(s) in *zhang* 27.4–8 run: 所好; 裕; 長. *Laozi Daodejing yinyi* 4a.

29. Cf. the facsimile reproduction of the Suo Dan manuscript in Rao Zongyi/Jao Tsung-i 饒宗頤, "Wu jianheng er nian Suo Dan xieben Daode jing canjuan kaozheng (jian lun Heshang gong ben yuan liu) 吳建衡二年索統寫本道德經殘卷考證 (兼論河上公本源流). The Su Tan Manuscript Fragment of the Tao-Te Ching (A.D. 270)," n.p.

30. Facsimile reproduction of the Xiang Er manuscript in Rao Zongyi, *Laozi Xiang Er zhu jiaojian*.

31. For the same process in Europe, several excellent studies have appeared. Cf. Ivan Illich, *Im Weinberg der Texte*.

32. Wang Baoxuan, *Zhengshi xuanxue*, 4 ff.

33. Ibid., 2 f.

34. Yan Shigu, *Xuanyan xinji ming Lao bu* P 2462. The manuscript text has been typeset in Yan Lingfeng, ed., *Wuqiubeizhai Laozi jicheng*, where the quotation is on p. 4.

35. This claim is not too credible. The Mawangdui manuscripts, fortified by the more extensive interpunctuation of the *zhang* borders in the Guodian manuscripts, definitely had a different overall number of *zhang*, but they were within the range of 75–80. If Liu Xiang had fixed the number at 81 editing, it is not probable that Zhuang Zun would shortly thereafter have developed a theory in which he provided a higher meaning for the number of 72 *zhang*. This only makes sense if the text in his hand already had this number and he now offered an explanation

for it, but it does not make sense if he himself had fixed this number and then gave it greater meaning as the original intention of Laozi.

36. Li Shan, *Wenxuan Li Shan zhu*. The list of the quotations is: 1. 11.12.a7 (*Laozi* 1.2); 2. 11.12.a8 (*Laozi* 1.5); 3. 11.12.b1 (*Laozi* 1.5); 4. 26.34.b7 (*Laozi* 4.1); 5. 17.12.a5 (*Laozi* 5.3); 6. 3.10.a8 (*Laozi* 10.3); 7. 20. 28.b1 (*Laozi* 10.3); 8. 3.17.b6 (*Laozi* 10.9); 9. 59.16.a8 (*Laozi* 14.1); 10. 20.24.b7 (*Laozi* 16.1); 11. 30.1.b9 (*Laozi* 16.2); 12. 31.31.a2 (*Laozi* 16.3,4,5); 13. 59.5.b8 (*Laozi* 21.2); 14. 22.28.b5 (*Laozi* 21.4); 15. 53.8.b3 (*Laozi* 22.6); 16. 40.14.b6 (*Laozi* 24.4); 17. 3.17.b6 (*Laozi* 25.12); 18. 24.15.a5 (*Laozi* 26.1); 19. 21.21.b3 (*Laozi* 27.4); 20. 54.15.b5 (*Laozi* 34.2); 21. 11.12.a7 (*Laozi* 40.4); 22. 20.30.a5 (*Laozi* 41.14); 23. 20.30. a6 (*Laozi* 41.15); 24. 11.6.a6 (*Laozi* 42.1); 25. 35. 21. b7 (*Laozi* 46.1); 26. 54.16.a4 (*Laozi* 51.4); 27. 50.5.a10 (*Laozi* 55.3).

37. Quotations 24 and 26 of the list in the preceding note present material otherwise lost.

38. These are quotations 2, 3, 5, 8–16, 20, and 22–27 in note 35.

39. Exceptions are 10, 12, 14, 20, and 27 in note 35.

40. *Wenxuan Li Shan zhu*, 11.12.a8.

41. *Daode zhen jing zhu*, 1.5b.

42. Liu Weiyong, *Daode zhen jing jiyi*, 1.8a.

43. *Daode zhen jing zhu*, 1.1b.

44. *Laozi Daode jing*, 139a.

45. *Wenxuan Li Shan zhu*, 20.28.b1.

46. Ibid., 20.30.a6.

47. No. 12 in the list in note 35.

48. Reading according to Wang Pu, *Tang huiyao*, 77:1408.

49. Li Fang, *Wenyuan yinghua*, 766:4033b ff.; most of the passage also is translated in the fine study by W. Hung, "A Bibliographical Controversy at the T'ang Court A.D. 719," *HJAS* 20 (1957):78.

50. This emendation follows the reading in *Wenyuan yinghua*, 766.4034b.

51. The *Tang huiyao* 77.1409 and the *Wenyuan yinghua* 766.4034b both read 神用 against 神明 in the *Cefu yuangui* text, which is the base text here.

52. Wang Qinruo et al., eds., *Cefu yuangui*, 604.7249, Cf. W. Hung, "A Bibliographical Controversy," 81.

53. For Zhang Junxiang's dates, see Wang Zhongmin, *Laozi kao*, 142. Following earlier suggestions by Ruan Yuan, he assumes that Zhang's work is in fact the *Daode zhen jing zhushu* 道德眞經註疏 which is preserved in the *Zhengtong Daozang*, Schipper 710, but ascribed to Gu Huan 顧歡. A postface by Liu Zhenggan to the Jiaye tang congshu edition supports the claim. The list of commentators included, according to Chao Gongwu's (fl. 1144) copy (Chao Gongwu, *Junzhai*

dushu zhi jiaozheng, 464). did not mention Xiang Er, but the text contains a quotation from the Xiang Er commentary to *Laozi* 15.1. Liu Zhenggan claims that the extant edition has "only Wang Bi . . . " left, while other parts have vanished. There are numerous quotations from a "Wang" commentary in the first third of the text, and no other "Wang" apart from Wang Bi is supposed to have been quoted. However, a check of these quotations shows no connection with anything known about the Wang Bi commentary, apart from one passage where a commentary to *Laozi* 14.4 ascribed to "Wang" in the *Daode zhen jing zhushu* 2.10a–b takes up, in inverse order, a comment on *Laozi* 14.2 in the *Jizhu* version of the Wang Bi *Commentary*: *Laozi* text 14.4: 迎之不見其首; *Zhushu*: . . . . 欲言有也不見其形 欲言無也物由之以生成; *Laozi* text 14.2 . . . . 是謂無狀之狀無物之象; *Jizhu*: 欲言無邪而物由以成欲言有邪而不見其形.

54. Xu Jian, *Chuxue ji*, 6.206, 17.548.

55. Fa Lin, *Bianzheng lun*. A part of this text is contained in Shi Daoxuan's *Guang Hongming ji*, where the reference is to *Laozi* 25.12, and is in Taishō, vol. 52:187a.18 ff. The longer version is included into the Taishō Canon as a separate text, T.2110, where the quotation with a less well transmitted text is in Taishō, vol. 52:537a.10ff.

56. Hui Lin, *Yiqie jing yinyi*, T.2128, Taishō vol. 54:351a. sub 根株; :353a sub 金鏷; :386c sub 魯樸; :583b sub 轒轑; :676a sub 排筒; :705a sub 橐籥; :782c sub 橐師; 853c sub 樸素; :913c sub 樸散.

57. A. Seidel, "The Image of the Perfect Ruler in Early Taoist Messianism: Lao Tzu and Li Hung," 216–47.

58. J.J.L. Duyvendak, "The Dreams of the Emperor Hsüan Tsung," 102–108.

59. Cf. Charles Benn, "Taoism As Ideology in the Reign of Emperor Hsüantsung (712–755)," 85.

60. *Jiu Tangshu*, 2026; *Xin Tangshu*, 1514.

61. Takeuchi Yoshiō, *Rōshi genshi*, 71.

62. Du Guangting, *Daode zhen jing guang shengyi*, preface 2b and text 5.20b ff., mentions Wang Bi and his historical position. Du's commentary, however, does not seem to quote Wang Bi.

63. Peng Si, preface to *Daode zhen jing jizhu*, 4a ff.

64. Cf. P. Pelliot, *Les Débuts de l'Imprimerie en Chine*, 75. For the entire complex, see also S. Cherniak, "Book Culture and Textual Transmission in Song China," *HJAS* 54:1 (1994):5–125.

65. P. Pelliot, *Les Débuts*, 83 ff., and P. Demiéville, "Notes additionelles sur les éditions imprimées du Canon Bouddhique," in P. Pelliot, *Les Débuts*, 121 ff. For an overview of the development of printing and book publishing during this period, cf. D. Twitchett, *Printing and Publishing in Medieval China*.

66. Cf. note 61.

67. P. van der Loon, *Taoist Books in the Libraries of the Sung Period*, 10 ff.; J. Boltz, *A Survey of Taoist Literature, Tenth to Seventeenth Century*, 203–05.

68. Chen Jingyuan, *Daode zhen jing zangshi zuanwei pian.*

69. Yang Zhonggeng, preface to Chen Jingyuan, *Daode zhen jing zangshi zuanwei pian*, 9b–10a.

70. Wang Zhongmin, *Laozi kao*, 227ff.

71. *Daode zhen jing jizhu.*

72. Wang Zhongmin, *Laozi kao*, 205, quotes a passage to this effect from Wang Anshi's biography in the *Songshi.*

73. Wang Pang, "Preface" in *Daode zhen jing jizhu*, preface, 5a ff. From the organization of the text, Liang Jiong should have been involved in compiling the *Jizhu*, as he wrote the postface in which the selection of commentators was explained, although the man responsible for the publication was a Mr. Zhang. The life dates of a man of this name, however, as Judith Boltz has pointed out (*A Survey of Taoist Literature*, 332, n. 610), do not fit the date of the postface. They are 928–986. For this text cf. Wang Shiu-hon in E. Balacs, Y. Hervouet, eds., *A Sung Bibliography*, 360 ff.

74. Liang Jiong, "Houxu," in *Daode zhen jing jizhu*, 2a.

75. Wang Zhongmin, *Laozi kao*, 208.

76. Peng Si, *Daode zhen jing jizhu zashuo*, 1.3a.

77. His biography is in Huang Zongxi (*Zengbu*) *Song Yuan xue'an*, j. 22, p. 1 ff.

78. A glance at both Wang Bi's *Laozi Commentary* and the *LZWZLL* will quickly disprove this argument, because in fact the *Xici* references are frequent.

79. Chao Yuezhi 晁說之, "Wang Bi Laozi Daode jing ji 王弼老子道德經記." The earliest reference known to me to this preface includes two long excerpts from it in Peng Si (fl. 1229), *Daode zhen jing jizhu zashuo*, 1.26b–27a. The full text is in *Daode zhen jing zhu*, appendix, in the *Daozang*. The text also is appended to the Siku quanshu edition *Laozi Daode jing*, 184b–185a, and the *Ji Tangzi Laozi Daode jing zhu* 集唐字老子道德經注, Guyi congshu no. 6, as well as included in Chao's collected works: Chao Yuezhi, *Songshan Jingyu sheng ji* 嵩山景迂生集, in Chao Yiduan 晁貽端, ed., *Chao shi congshu* 晁氏叢書, 18.6b ff.

80. Cf. my edition of the text, p. 209, note 1.

81. The edition, listed in the book catalogue of the *Songshi*, is lost. Wang Zhongmin suggests that the long commentary to the *Laozi Daode jing* in the *Junzhai dushu zhi*, 457 ff., is in fact the preface to this edition. See Wang Zhongming, *Laozi kao*, 237.

82. The same text is quoted with slight variants by Peng Si from another source, the *Sanchao guoshi*; cf. note 62.

83. Xiong Ke 熊克, "Postface" to *Laozi Daode jing*, 185a. In other editions, this postface is entitled "Ke fu song 克伏誦."

84. See D. Twitchett, *Printing and Publishing in Medieval China*; Ming-sun Poon, "Books and Publishing in Sung China"; Soren Edgren, "Southern Song Printing at Hangzhou," *Bulletin of the Museum of Far Eastern Antiquities* 61 (1989):1–212; Susan Cherniak, "Book Culture and Textual Transmission in Sung China," *HJAS* 54:1 (1994):5–125.

85. In 1128, Chao Yuezhi published an uncommented *Laozi* manuscript "in a script that was close to the old form," which also was not divided into *daojing* and *dejing*. See his preface, Chao Yuezhi, "Ti xieben *Laozi* hou (postface to a manuscript [print] of the *Laozi*)," *Songshan Jingyu sheng ji*, 18.7b–8a.

86. Chen Zhensun, *Zhizhai shulu jieti*, 285; for Chen, cf. P. Van der Loon, *Taoist Books*, 27 ff.

87. Li Lin, *Daode zhen jing qushan ji*.

88. Li Lin, preface to *Daode zhen jing qushan ji*, 2b–3a. The criticism was based on the assumption that they had misunderstood the *Laozi*. The argument has tradition. Lu Xisheng 陸希聲 (fl. 888–903), for example states in the preface to his *Daode zhen jing zhuan* 道德眞經傳, 上 3a, his criticism of the misunderstandings of the *Laozi*: "Wang [Bi] and He [Yan] missed the Way of Laozi and got lost in emptiness and negativity. These six [Yang Zhu, Zhuang Zhou, Shen Buhai, Hanfeizi, Wang Bi, and He Yan] have committed crimes against Laozi." The counterexamples are Huangdi and Kongzi.

89. Liu Chongsheng, "Daode zhen jing qushan ji xu," in Li Lin, *Daode zhen jing qushan ji*, 1b.

90. Liu Weiyong, *Daode zhen jing jiyi dazhi*, 下 12b.

91. Liu Chongsheng, "Preface," 2a.

92. Li Lin quotes Zhong Hui's *Laozi zhu* 老子注 a total of thirteen times. The quotations are all from the first two thirds, namely, Laozi 11, 12, 16, 18, 19, 22, 23, 25 (2), 27, 28, 36, and 41.

93. Zhao Bingwen, *Daode zhen jing jijie*; cf. the extensive bibliographical note by Qian Peiming 錢培名 to the Xiaowanjuanlou congshu edition printed in Wang Zhongmin, *Laozi kao*, 280 ff.

94. Peng Si, *Daode zhen jing jizhu*.

95. Peng Si, *Daode zhen jing jizhu shiwen*.

96. Dong Siqing, *Daode zhen jing jijie*.

97. Dong Siqing, preface to *Daode zhen jing jijie*, 6b. In the commentary to this passage, which seems to come from Dong's own hands, Su Shi's polemics against contemporary Taoists are quoted. Cf. Takeuchi Yoshiō, *Rōshi no kenkyū*, 484 ff.

98. Wang Zhongmin, *Laozi kao*, 266.

99. Liu Weiyong, *Daode zhen jing jiyi.*

100. Liu Weiyong, *Daode zhen jing jiyi dazhi.*

101. Ibid., 3.23a.

102. Ibid., 3.23b.

103. Ibid., 3.25b f.

104. *Laozi Daode jing,* 160b.

105. There are some freak readings for which not a single confirmation exists in 18.3, 20.11, 21.1, 26.4, 29.1, and 34.2; there are two major blunders in the arrangement of the sentences, directly contradicted by Wang Bi's commentary in 19.1 and 28.1; and there are some readings immediately disproved by Wang Bi's commentary, such as the *ren* 人 for *min* 民 in 32.2.

106. Cf. p. 230 n. x.

107. In *Laozi* 1.5, 2.2, 5.2, 11.2, 16.10, 17.1, 17.5, 17.6, 18.2, 19.1, 20.2, 20.8, 22.5, 25.3, 26.3, 33.2, 34.2, 36.2.

108. *Daode zhen jing zhu.*

109. Wang Baoxuan, *Zhengshi xuanxue,* 169.

110. Jiao Hong, *Laozi yi,* in Yan Lingfeng, ed., *Wuqiubeizhai Laozi jicheng.*

111. Ji Yun, preface to *Laozi Daode jing,* 137 b–138 a.

112. Ji Yun commentary to the chapter numbering for *zhang* 38, *Laozi Daode jing,* 160a.

113. A photomechanical reprint of the 1875 Zhejiang shuju edition of the *Ershier zi* is available from the Shanghai guji Press, 1986. This edition does not mention the original title of Zhang Zhixiang's book, nor his full name. Cf. Hatano Tarō, *Rōshi Ō chū kōsei,* A–2 no. 8, p. 29.

114. Sun Kuang, *Laozi daode jing* 老子道德經, as *Wang Bi zhu Laozi* 王弼注老子 in Yan Lingfeng, ed., *Wuqiubeizhai Laozi jicheng.*

115. *Laozi daode jing* with Wang Bi's commentary, pref. by Fukoku Tōin, in Yan Lingfeng, ed., *Wuqiubeizhai Laozi jicheng.*

116. Usami Shinsui, *Rōshi dōtoku shinkyō—Ōchū Rōshi dōtoku kyō,* orig. 1770, repr. in Yan Lingfeng, ed., *Wuqiubeizhai Laozi jicheng.*

117. Li Shuchang preface to the Guyi congshu as well as the imprint on the first page of the Guyi congshu edition, which says "Edition amended by Mr. Li from Zunyi."

118. These editions include: Usami Shinsui, *Rōshi dōtoku shinkyō—Ō chū Rōshi dōtoku kyō,* originally published in 1770 but now available with a concordance in Kitahara Mineki, ed., *Rōshi—Ō Hitsu chū sakuin;* Tōjō Itsudō (1778–1857), *Rōshi Ō chū hyoshiki,* originally published in 1814; Tao Hongqing (1860–1918), "Laozi Wang Bi zhu kanwu," in Yan Lingfeng, "Tao Hongqing 'Laozi Wang Bi zhu kanwu' buzheng"; Liu Guojun, "Laozi Wang Bi zhu jiaoji,"

Tushuguanxue jikan 8.1 (1934):91–116; Hatano Tarō, *Rōshi Ō chū kōsei*; Lou Yulie, ed., *Wang Bi ji jiaoshi*, 2 vols.

119. Cf. Susan Cherniak, "Book Culture," *HJAS* 54:1 (1994): 48 ff.

CHAPTER 3

1. This chapter is a revised version of my article of the same title, which appeared in *T'oung Pao* LXXII (1986): 92–129. The permission of the editors of *T'oung Pao* to make use of this article is graciously acknowledged.

2. Wang Bi, "Zhouyi zhu"; Wang Bi, "Zhouyi lüeli"; the commonly used but not critically edited text is in Lou Yulie, ed., *Wang Bi ji jiaoshi*. A translation is in R. Lynn, *The Classic of Changes. A New Translation of the I Ching As Interpreted by Wang Bi*.

3. Wang Bi, "Lunyu shiyi." Lou Yulie, ed., *Wang Bi ji jiaoshi*, 621–35.

4. He Yan, ed., *Lunyu jijie*. See my "Die Unhandlichkeit des Konfuzius."

5. Wang Bi, *Laozi zhu*. See my edition in this book.

6. Wang Weicheng, "Wei Wang Bi zhuan *Laozi zhilüe* yiwen zhi fajian," *Guoxue jikan* 7:3 (1951): 367–76. Two later editions are based on his discovery. See Zhongguo Kexueyuan zhexue yanjiusuo, Zhongguo zhexueshi zu and Beijing daxue zheshi jiaoyanshi, eds., *Zhongguo lidai zhexue wenxuan. Liang Han Sui Tang bian*, 308ff., and Lou Yulie, ed., *Wang Bi ji jiaoshi*, 195 ff. Professor Yan Lingfeng repeated the discovery some years later. Cf. Yan Lingfeng, *Laozi weizhi lilüe*; *Lao Zhuang yanjiu*, postface, 413; *Lao Zhuang yanjiu*, 1966 ed., 636. The text is transmitted in the Zhengtong Daozang, Schipper 1255.

7. He Shao, *Wang Bi zhuan*, quoted in Pei Songzhi, *Commentary to the Sanguo zhi*, ch. 28, p. 785, line 3.

8. See infra note 26.

9. Cf. *Nan Qi shu*, ch. 33, p. 598 lines 10 ff.; cf. editor's note on p. 604.

10. Cf. Lu Deming, *Jingdian shiwen*, vol. 1, preface, 32b (1 j. ed.); *Xin Tangshu*, ch. 59, p. 1514a; *Jiu Tangshu*, ch. 47, 2028a (2 j. ed., author not mentioned in second source); Tuo Tuo, *Songshi*, ch. 205, p. 5177a, and *id.*, p. 5206a, lists a *Daode lüegui* 道德略歸 by Wang Bi and an anonymous *Laozi zhi lilüe* 老子旨例略, both in 1 j. Zheng Qiao 鄭樵 (1102–1160), *Tongzhilüe*, mentions a *Laozi lüeli* by Wang Bi and an anonymous *Laozi zhi lüelun*, both in 2 j.; Wang Yinglin, *Yuhai*, ch. 63, p. 12a, mentions Wang Bi's *Laozi lüelun*; Ming and Qing bibliographers simply reproduce earlier listings; cf. Jiao Hong (Ming), *Guoshi jingji zhi*, ch. 4, p. 9a, and Zhou Zhongfu (1768–1831), *Zhengtang dushuji*, ch. 69, p. 1346.

11. Chao Gongwu's 晁公武 (?–1171?) entry in Zhao Xibian (?–after 1250), *Zhaode xiansheng junzhai dushu houzhi*, ch. 2, p. 823; this note is taken up by Ma Duanlin in *Wenxian tongkao*, ch. 211, p. 1730 b ff.

12. Zhang Junfang, *Yunji qiqian*, in Zhengtong Daozang, Schipper 1032, ch.1, p. 2b ff. Cf. M. Strickmann, "The Longest Taoist Scripture," *History of Religions*, 17 (1978):3–4.

13. Zhang Zhan, *Liezi zhu*, p. 9, line 4. The quotation is from phrase 16 through 19 in Part A, *zhang* 1.

14. Cf. ch. 1 of this book.

15. See *LZWZLL* 2.21 ff.

16. Cf. *LZWZLL* 2.12–36 and 5.1 ff.; Wang Bi, *Laozi zhu* 3.1, 25.10; *Lunyu shiyi* on *Lunyu* 7.6, 624.

17. Cf. my *The Craft of a Chinese Commentator*, chapter 3.

18. Cf. Wing Tsit Chan in his preface to the *Commentary on the "Lao-tzu" by Wang Bi*, trans. Ariane Rump, with Wing-tsit Chan, xxix ff.

19. Cf. *Mawangdui Hanmu boshu*; R. Henricks, "A Note on the Question of Chapter Divisions, 49–51; *id.*, "Examining the Chapter Divisions," 501–24; Qu Wanli, *Han shijing Zhouyi canzi jizheng* ch. 1, 25a ff; W. Peterson, "Making Connections: 'Commentary on the Attached Verbalizations' of the Book of Changes," *HJAS* 42:1 (1982):71.

20. Ban Gu, *Hanshu*, 1732.

21. Xing Shou, "Zhouyi lüeli zhu," preface.

22. Cf. note 7.

23. Cf. the notes on this notion in *Mozi* in A. C. Graham, *Later Mohist Logic, Ethics, and Science*, 547–48. See also Christopher Harbsmeier, *Language and Logic*, 192. Sima Tan 司馬談 (–110 B.C.E.), according to his son, "discoursed on the essential purports, *yaozhi* 要指, of the six schools." Sima Qian, *Shiji*, ch. 130, p. 3288; Zhuang (Yan) Zun's *Laozi zhigui guanyi* 老子指歸 (*Daode zhen jing zhigui* 道德眞經指歸 in the Zhengtong Daozang, Schipper 693) and Li Xi's 李洗, *Chunqiu zuozhuan zhigui* 春秋左傳指歸 (referred to in Yao Shixue 姚氏學, *Bu Sanguo yiwenzhi* 補三國藝文志, ch. 1, p. 50a) as well as his (?)*Taixuan zhigui* 太玄指歸, (referred to in Yao Shixue, *Bu Sanguo*, ch. 3, p. 2b) all use *zhi* 指 in titles of interpretive works.

24. Su Yu, ed., *Chunqiu fanlu yizheng*, 50f.

25. See *LZWZLL* 2.43.

26. Zhan Ying ed., *Wenxin diaolong yizheng*, vol. 2, p. 665.

27. Ibid., p. 55.

28. Cf. *Xici shang* V and VI (*Zhouyi yinde* 41 繫上 5 and 6) *Shuogua* I, II (*Zhouyi yinde* 49 説 1 and 2).

29. *Mao shi zhengyi*, 2b–4c.

30. Cf. my *The Craft of a Chinese Commentator*, 176–256.

31. Zhuang (Yan) Zun, "Junping shuo er jing mu."

32. Ibid., 131.

33. See my *The Craft of a Chinese Commentator*, 116–19.

34. Ibid., ch. 3.

35. Chang Chung-yue, "The Metaphysics of Wang Bi,"; R. Wagner, "Wang Bi: 'The Structure of the Laozi's Subtle Pointers' (Laozi weizhi lilüe)"; R. Lynn, *The Classic of the Way and Virtue*, 30–41.

Zhang 1 TRANSLATION NOTES

1. The numbers attached to the *zhang* follow their sequence within the available text. While they cannot claim to be the numbers of the original text, it is probable that *zhang* 1 in fact was part or the whole of the first *zhang*, and it is equally probable that the *zhang* were following each other within the original text, as they do in the surviving excerpts. Thus they might correspond to the original *zhang* 1, 4, 8, 12, 15, and 18, but not 1, 18, 4, 15, 12, and 8. In other words, the surviving excerpts are likely to give an idea about the initial argument as well as what an editor might have considered the main line of argument. The experience with premodern Chinese text excerpts shows that the sequence of the original is, as a rule, kept.

2. The term *fu* 夫 signals a statement of general validity beyond the immediate instance. It often is misunderstood as a simple marker for a paragraph's beginning.

3. The pair "the nameless" and "the featureless" 無名無形 takes up the terminology of the *Laozi*. While "the nameless" or "namelessness" appears as the characterization of the Dao in *Laozi* 32.1 and 41.14, the "formless" or "featureless" does not occur as a noun in the *Laozi*; it occurs only in *Laozi* 41.14 in the phrase "the Great Image is without form." The argumentative rigor entering Wang Bi's text with the juxtaposition of name and form, things (or beings) 物 and achievements 功 or processes, *shi* 事, cannot be found in the *Laozi*. The expressions 無形 and 無名 appear in two successive phrases in *Laozi* 41, but the first is the last in a series of parallel paradoxes, such as "the Great Instrument does complete in the nick of time!" while the second is in what Wang Bi sees as the summary statement about this series. In other words, the status of the two phrases there is different. The transition from a philosophy operating with the paradox and the parallel to a systematic philosophy characteristic of Wang Bi becomes clearly visible in this transformation of the *Laozi* vocabulary and imagery into a systematic, analytic discourse. For parallels in Wang Bi's *Commentary*, cf. Wang Bi on *Laozi* 51.1: "Generally speaking, that by which entities are generated and that by which achievements are brought about have something that is the base [for them]. As they have something that is the base for them, there is none of them that is not based on the Way." Cf. also Wang Bi on *Laozi* 1.2: "Generally speaking, Entity all begins in negativity. . . . This means the Way begins and completes the ten thousand kinds of entities by means of [its] featurelessness and namelessness."

4. *Laozi* 4.1, "The Way is made use of by pouring out and is also not filled up—deep it is, [but still] resembling the ancestor of the ten thousand kinds of entities." Wang Bi on *Laozi* 14.5 has phrase 5 verbatim.

5. Cf. Wang Bi on *Laozi* 35.1: "The Great Image is . . . neither warming nor cooling. That is why it is capable of embracing and penetrating the ten thousand kinds of entities without there being one that is crossed or hurt." Cf. Wang Bi on *Laozi* 41.14: "If something has form, then it will also have specifications. That which has specifications will be cooling if it does not warm and will be cold if it is not hot. That is why an image that has taken on form is not the Great Image." Cf. Wang Bi on *Laozi* 55.6: "What is neither bright nor dark, neither warming nor cooling, that is the Eternal. It is formless, and it is impossible to see it." Note that "featureless" and "formless" mean the same and translate the same Chinese expression.

6. Cf. Wang Bi on *Laozi* 41.13: "It [the Great Sound] thus is a sound one is unable to hear. Once there is a [particular] tone, it will have specifications, and, if it has specifications, it will [let sound forth the note] *shang*, if it does not [let sound forth the note] *gong*. Being specific it could [in this case] not encompass the entire multitude [of notes]. That is why that which has taken on a specific tone is not the Great Sound."

7. Phrases *Laozi* 14.1 and 35.3 are the sources for the first two of these statements and, with a different vocabulary, for the fourth. *Laozi* 14.1 runs: "That which [I] do not see if [I] look at it [I] call 'fine.' That which [I] do not hear when listening for it [I] call 'inaudible.' That which [I] cannot grasp when reaching for it, [I] call 'smooth.' For these three [the senses of sight, hearing, and touch] it is impossible to come to a definition [of this], and, thus diffuse it is, [being] the One." It thus deals with the senses of the ear, the eye, and touch, but it uses a more abstract vocabulary than the *Laozi* for the last. There is no attempt in the *Laozi* to systematize the senses of perception into two groups of two each and to link them to the concepts of name and form. Wang Bi supplements the missing fourth link about taste from the series in *Laozi* 35.3, which again does not fit the rigid argument proffered here: "The words [, however], uttered about the Way indeed are stale; they are without taste! Looking for it [the Way] one cannot manage to see it; listening for it [the Way], one cannot manage to hear it; making use of it [the Way], it is impossible to exhaust it." In this second case, we have sight, ear, and use as well as a general statement outside of this sequence dealing with the insipidness of the Way. The eye, ear, and taste are then systematized into the foursome used by Wang Bi here. *Laozi* 35.3 also is the evidence for the allocation of the phrases dealing with taste and flavor to the chain about sound and hearing, because taste there is associated with the mouth and language. Note the ease with which abba constructions are being used. Both *Laozi* passages have a sequence sight/ear, but Wang Bi inverts this, creating an abba sequence instead of the regular abab.

8. "As an entity" (the terms *entity* and *thing* translate the same term 物) is taken from *Laozi* 21.2: "The Way as a thing is vague, ah, diffuse, ah," while the "completes out of the diffuse" comes from *Laozi* 25.1; "There is a thing that

completes out of the diffuse." Wang Bi comments: "Diffuse it is and [thus] indiscernible, but the ten thousand kinds of entities base themselves on it for their completion."

9. *Laozi* 41.14: "The Great Image is without form."

10. *Laozi* 41.13: "The Great Sound has an inaudible tone."

11. The expression "without flavor" has no counterpart in the *Laozi*. It has been created to match the three other expressions and is based on the "staleness" and "tastelessness" of the Dao mentioned in *Laozi* 35.3.

12. The separate translation of 宗 and 主 is based on Wang Bi on *Laozi* 47.1 "Processes have a principle and things have a master." However, the allocation of the two terms to the two chains is hampered by the fact that Wang Bi uses them interchangeably; cf. Wang Bi on *Laozi* 49.5, where "things will have their principle and affairs will have their master."

13. *Pinwu* 品物 is from the first Hexagram of the *Zhouyi*; cf. *Zhouyi*, 1.14a; "The clouds drift and the rains scatter, and the different categories of beings float and take on shape." There is no comment by Wang Bi, but his subcommentator, Kong Yingda 孔應達, renders *pinwu* as 品類之物, "entities of different categories."

14. The functions of the Dao's "embracing and penetrating" 包通 are repeatedly addressed by Wang Bi in these terms; cf. Wang Bi on *Laozi* 16.6: "knowing this [Eternal], he [the ruler] is able indeed to embrace and penetrate the ten thousand kinds of entities without there being anything that is not encompassed"; and Wang Bi on 35.1: "That is why it [the Great Image] is capable of embracing and penetrating the ten thousand kinds of entities without there being one that is crossed or hurt."

15. Cf. Wang Bi on *Laozi* 38: "That is why, if something is negative with regard to the [other] entities, there will be no entity it does not thread through."

16. This type of hypothetical argument is highly characteristic of Wang Bi's thinking and is regularly used to check the viability of the counterargument. Cf. *Laozi* 41.14: "The Great Image is without form." Wang Bi comments: "If something has form, then it will also have specifications. That which has specifications will be cooling if it does not warm, and will be cold if it is not hot. That is why an image that takes on form is not the Great Image."

17. Cf. Wang Bi on *Laozi* 41.13: "Once there is a [particular] tone, it will have specifications, and if it has specifications it will [let sound forth the note] *shang*, if it does not [let sound forth the note] *gong*. Being specific it could [in this case] not encompass the entire multitude [of notes]. That is why that which has taken on a specific tone is not the Great Sound."

18. These general rules do not occur in the *Laozi*. Wang Bi states them also in his comments on *Laozi* 14.13 and 14.14, as quoted in the two previous notes.

19. Cf. *Laozi* 41.14: "The Great Image is without form." Wang Bi's com-

mentary ends with exactly the same words as the text here: "That is why an image that has taken on form is not the Great Image."

20. Cf. *Laozi* 41.13: "The Great Sound is toneless." Wang Bi's comment there ends with a formula slightly different from the one used here in the *LZWZLL*: "That is why that which has taken on a specific tone is not the Great Sound."

21. This notion does not occur in the *Laozi* and is not used elsewhere in the surviving Wang Bi corpus. The assumption reported by Chung-yue Chang, "The Metaphysics of Wang Bi," 225, on the basis of Wang Huai's 王淮 "Wang Bi zhi Laoxue" 王弼之老學, 192—an unpublished M.A. thesis that I have not been able to consult—that it refers to the four seasons is obviated by Wang Bi's use of *sishi* 四時 for the four seasons; cf. Wang Bi on *Laozi* 9.5 and in *Lunyu shiyi* on *Lunyu* 17.17. The notions of "hot" and "cold" seem to be used as examples for specificity without reference to any single phenomenon; cf. Wang Bi on *Laozi* 41.14 on *Laozi* 16.6 and on *Laozi* 55.6. I assume that the Four Figures here refer to the phrase in the *Xici*, 7.9b3: "The Yi has the Great Ultimate. This generates the two Principles [Yin and Yang]. The two Principles generate the Four Images. The Four Images generate the eight Trigrams." Han Kangbo does not comment on the Four Images, but the subcommentator, Kong Yingda, sees them as referring to the four elements of metal, wood, fire, and water. However, Wang Bi talks about five things in the *LZWZLL* 2.35, which might be the five elements. From the context it is clear that the Four Images must refer to the basic constituents of form as the five sounds refer to those of sound.

22. This argument is crucial for Wang Bi's philosophy. Again, it begins with a hypothetical counterproposition. Its falsification opens the way for the positive argument, which is that the entities still contain the traces of their That-by-which with the consequence that the ten thousand kinds of entities become a source of ontological information and are not just the obstacle for ontological insight. For a detailed analysis of Wang Bi's argument about the "traces" of the That-by-which, see the chapter "Discerning the That-by-which: The Language of the *Laozi* and the *Lunyu*," in my *Language, Ontology, and Political Philosophy: Wang Bi's Scholarly Exploration of the Dark (Xuanxue)*, SUNY Press, 2003.

23. In these two phrases, Wang Bi outlines the conditions under which the Great Image and the Great Sound as metaphors for the Dao will "shine forth" and "come about." These conditions are that the specific entities "relate back" to their That-by-which; the moment they "discard" it, *she* 舍, and become dominated by some entity, their "true nature" will be dissipated, they will enter a different dynamics, and they will in fact block the philosophical access to the Dao. The notion of the *zhu* 主, the dominating principle, was at the heart of third century philosophical discussion. Wang Bi maintained that the real dominating principle was the Dao itself, but a generation later, with Guo Xiang, this thought was abandoned and replaced by the complete self-regulation of entities who were *wu zhu* 無主, without a (or an even utterly negatively defined) dominating principle. The meaning of the expression "nothing else by which they are dominated," *wu suo zhu* 無所主, becomes clear from Wang Bi's description of the way in which

the Sage will, as *Laozi* 37.3 says, "quiet them [the Hundred Families] down by means of the simplicity of the Nameless:" "This means [in the words of *Laozi* 34.2] [I would] not become [their] overlord" 不爲主 in the sense of giving detailed instructions. The expression *shi* 施 goes back to Wang Bi's reading of *Laozi* 53.1: "If I [as a Sage Ruler] were [able] to reduce to insignificance [All Under Heaven's] having knowledge, and to have [it] march on the Great Way, [the] only [thing I] would [then] be worried about would be that [I] might [still] interfere with it." This "interfering," which in other passages in Wang *Commentary* is linked to verbs such as "create" 造立, "generate" 施化 (5.1), and "setting up" 設 (27.4), is identical in meaning to *wei* 爲, "to interfere," with which 施 forms a binominal in Wang Bi on 53.2.

24. Quoted from *Laozi* 35.1. Wang Bi's commentary makes the desperate tone in this reading quite clear: "If [only] the ruler were able to hold on to it, All under Heaven would come to him!"

25. The *Laozi* has no statement about the Great Sound matching that about the Great Image. Wang Bi provides it by analogy and symmetry. The Great Sound refers to the teaching of the Way, and the pair thus refers to the Sage's "taking residence in management without interference" and "practicing teaching without words." (*Laozi* 2.2/3).

26. Statements 30–33 are derived from the *Laozi* in an interesting process. The *Laozi* has a statement about All Under Heaven submitting to a ruler able to "hold on to the Great Image." The Great Image is then read as being identical with the Great Image of *Laozi* 14, which Wang Bi reads as one of the expressions for the Dao. From a parallel phrase, the notion of the Great Sound is introduced, and Wang Bi constructs a second statement about the ruler holding on to the Great Sound to match that about the Great Image. This pair again is, within the *Laozi*, seemingly quite unrelated to the stock phrase about the Sage practicing noninterference and teaching without words. This statement is now paired with the Great Image/Great Sound pair. The Sage "makes use" of the Great Image and Great Sound through his two government strategies. In these strategies it is thus the Dao that is manifesting itself. Wang Bi can rightly point out that the *Laozi* uses the very same language for the description of the unknowability, elusiveness, or "darkness" of the Sage and the Dao. Thus the elements 32 and 33 go back to Wang's reading of the "darkness" of the Dao. Cf. Wang Bi on *Laozi* 1.2: "That the ten thousand kinds of entities are begun by it [the Way] and completed by it [the Way], but that they do not know that through which these [two, their beginning and completion] come to be as they are is [its aspect of being] Dark-and-Dark-Again." Cf. also Wang Bi on 34.2 and on *Lunyu* 8.19. For the elusiveness of the Sage, cf. *Laozi* 17.1 and 17.6 as well as Wang Bi's commentary there.

27. The term *wuwu* 五物 is not clear. The editors of *Zhongguo lidai zhexue wenxuan, liang Han Sui Tang bian* link it to *wucai* 五材 in the *Zuozhuan*, where it says: "Heaven creates the Five Materials and the people all use them" (J. Legge, *The Chinese Classics: Chun Tsew with Tso Chuen*, 531). Commentators identify these as the five elements.

28. The daring term 無物 *no-thing*, is taken from a statement in *Laozi* 14.2 about the One: "This One—its upper side is not bright—its lower side is not dark. Dim it is and impossible to name. It returns and relates [the entities] back to the no-thing."

29. Wang Bi extracts from his reading of *Laozi* 11 this key concept that entities do not receive their function from their interrelationship with other entities but from their *fan* 反, their *Rückbezug* or relationship back with negativity as their Being. "Thirty spokes share one hub. But it is the [latter's] negativity [vis-à-vis the specificity of the spokes] that is [the basis] for the usability of the existing carriage." Wang Bi comments: "That by which a [= one] hub is capable of holding together thirty [different] spokes is its negativity [vis-à-vis their specific features]. Because of this negativity, [the hub] is capable of taking in the points of origin of [many different] entities. That is why [the hub] is capable, being itself the minimum, to control the many" [spokes]. At the end of *Laozi* 11, Wang Bi summarizes: "This means: entities in order to be beneficial all depend on negativity for their usability." See also Wang Bi on *Laozi* 1.4: "Generally speaking, for entities to be beneficial, they have to get their usefulness from negativity."

30. The Five Teachings refer to the virtues guiding the relationship between father and son, ruler and minister, husband and wife, older and younger brother, and among friends. *Locus classicus* is *Mengzi* 3A.4, which does not, however, use the term. There is no internal link between the "no-thing" in *Laozi* 14.2 and the "no-words" in *Laozi* 2.3, "[The Sage] practices the teaching without words," but Wang Bi welds them into a systematic relationship. Confucius verifies this wanting to imitate the way in which Heaven regulates the seasons without giving commands by "wishing to be without words" himself; cf. *Lunyu* 17.17 and Wang Bi's comment, both translated in ch. 1 of my *Language, Ontology, and Political Philosophy*, 9.

31. *Laozi* 1.1.

32. "Mother" is read by Wang Bi as a philosophic metaphor. It appears in *Laozi* 1, 10, 25, 52, and 57. On Wang Bi's merging these different concepts, see my *The Craft of a Chinese Commentator*, 281–98. Cf. Wang Bi on *Laozi* 52.2: "'Mother' is [the same as] 'root.'" In *Laozi* 14.2, the specifications given here for the "mother," that it is neither bright above nor dark below, appear in a description of the One.

33. Cf. *Laozi* 21.6; there it refers to the Dao, showing the interchangeability of these terms for Wang Bi. Wang Bi comments: "The ultimate of the absolutely true cannot be [determined by means of a] name. 'Namelessness' thus is its name. From antiquity to the present there is nothing that did not come about based on this [Namelessness]. That is why [the text] says: 'From antiquity to the present, its [the truthful essence's] name [e.g., 'Namelessness'] has not disappeared'." Cf. Wang Bi on *Laozi* 14.5: "The featureless and nameless is the ancestor of the ten thousand kinds of entities. Although the present and antiquity are not the same, although times have changed and customs have changed, there definitely is no one [Sage Ruler] who has not based himself on this [featureless and nameless] by way

of completing their regulated order. That is why it 'is possible' to 'hold on to the Way of antiquity by way of regulating occurrences of the present'."

34. The pair Heaven, 天, and government, 治, which does not occur in the *Laozi*, conceptualizes the two realms of entities discussed in parallel chains since the first line of this *zhang*. The realm here called "Heaven" is that of the creation of things and beings 物, while that of the human realm, of "government" or "ordering," is that where social achievements 功 are being brought about. The argument in this pair goes back to Wang Bi's reading of *Laozi* 39.2: "As long as Heaven attains the One, it will be clear through it [the One]. As long as Earth attains the One, it will be calm through it. As long as the spirits attain the One, they will be efficacious through it. As long as the valley attains the One, it will be full through it. As long as the kings and dukes attain the One, they will be the standard for All Under Heaven through it. It is it the One that brings these [clarity, calmness, etc.] about."

35. *Laozi* 14.4.

36. *Laozi* 14.5.

37. The phrase from *Laozi* 14.5 that Wang Bi here quotes ends with "this [I] call the continuity of the Way 道紀." This term does not occur elsewhere in the *Laozi*, but the notion of the "Eternal of the Way" 道常 is frequently addressed; cf. *Laozi* 32.1 and 37.1. Wang Bi therefore inserts this notion here. A close parallel to the entire statement is Wang Bi on *Laozi* 47.1.

38. A quotation from *Laozi* 16.6 and 55.6. Wang Bi comments on the first passage: "The Eternal [essence of the entities] as such is neither [inwardly] partial nor manifest [in its preferences]; it has an appearance without either brightness or darkness, and features without either warming or cooling. That is why [the text] says: 'Having knowledge of [this] Eternal means being enlightened!'" Wang Bi comments on *Laozi* 55.6: "What is neither bright nor dark, neither warming nor cooling, that is the Eternal. It is formless and it is impossible to see it."

39. *Laozi* 21.7. This refers to what Wang Bi describes on 21.6 as the "ultimate of the absolutely true 至眞之極," not to the Eternal, but Wang merges the two notions. Wang Bi comments on *Laozi* 21.7: "The 'beginning of the many' is the beginning of the entities. [The entire phrase *Laozi* 21.7 thus reads rephrased:] By means of [truthful essence, that is,] Namelessness one discerns the beginning of the ten thousand kinds of entities."

Zhang 2 TRANSLATION NOTES

1. According to the *Zhuangzi*, Liezi moved in this manner; cf. *Zhuangzi yinde*, 2/2/19.

2. This pair of statements about Thunder and Wind go back to the *Shuo gua* 說卦 of the *Zhouyi* 9.2b3: "As to setting the ten thousand kinds of entities into

motion, there is nothing more speedy than Thunder. As to making the ten thousand kinds of entities bend, there is nothing more speedy than Wind." This statement follows a phrase about the spirit, 神, which, being a "no-thing" 無物 in itself, as Han Kangbo writes in his commentary, is still at the core of the specific entities such as Thunder and Wind, which set the entities into motion. The *Xici* A (*Zhouyi* 7.8b1) argues without reference to Thunder or Wind. that "being spirit [the Sage] is therefore able to be fast without speeding and to arrive without going" 唯神也 故不疾而速不行而至. The terms used in the *Shuogua* for both Wind and Thunder were both "speeding" 疾. By using the terms used here for the spirit, namely, 疾 and 行, in a description of Thunder and Wind, Wang Bi links the two statements. The *Xici* statement simply states a paradox. In a move typical of his intellectual radicalism, Wang Bi transforms this into a proposition by not simply claiming that the spirit is able to be fast without speeding, but that its fastness is a function of its not speeding. The formula used here, "lies in, *zai*" 在, is the same he used in his transformation of the *Zhuangzi*'s statement on the fish trap; cf. the chapter "Discerning the That-by-which: The Language of the *Laozi* and the *Lunyu*," in my *Language, Ontology, and Political Philosophy*, 31. For more details on the history of the use of this *Xici* quotation, see my "Die Fragen Hui-yuans an Kumarajiva," 190 ff.

3. *Laozi* 1.1.

4. There is no parallel in the *Laozi* to the 可道 of *Laozi* 1.1, however, from the present passage, we know that Wang Bi read 可名 as in fact meaning 有形, so that element 8 in fact refers to *Laozi* 1.1. This leads to the ironical situation that the phrases referring to 名 have to be associated with the chain under 可道.

5. The first halves of phrases 7 and 8 take up the argument in the end of Wang Bi on *Laozi* 38 with the segments belonging together written together:

If [the ruler, however,]

rejects their [the processes'] mother and makes use of her offspring, then indeed, as a name has something that specifies it, it will, even if it [the name] makes its beauty abundant, by necessity have something worrisome and painful.	discards their [the things'] root and handles its outgrowth, then indeed, as a shape has something that limits it, it will, even if it maximizes its greatness, by necessity have something that it does not encompass.

The expressions in quotation marks at the end of elements 2.7 and 2.8 are from *Zhuangzi*, 5/13/12.

6. The difference between name and designation is central to Wang Bi, based on statements in the *Laozi*. For example, in *Laozi* 25.4, "I do not know its name," the "its" here is referring to the "thing that completes out of the diffuse" in 25.1. Wang Bi comments: "A name is something to define the shape [of an object]. That which 'completes out of the diffuse' and is 'without form' [as the *Laozi* says

in 41.14 about the Great Image] is impossible to define." The *Laozi* goes on: "I give it the style 'Way.'" Wang Bi: "It is a fact that a name is something to define the shape [of an object], while a style is something to designate what is sayable. The Way is taken for [the aspect of that by which all entities are] that there is no entity which is not based on it. This is the greatest among the sayable designations concerning 'that which completes out of the diffuse.'" The *Laozi* pursues: "[Only] if forced to make up a name for it, I would say '[it is] great.'" Wang Bi comments: "The reason why I gave it the style 'Way' was taken from this being the greatest of sayable designations about it. If one puts too much weight onto the reason for which this style was determined, one would tie [the Way] down to being great. If a greatness has ties, it necessarily has particularity, and, once it has particularity, its absoluteness is lost. That is why [the text] says: "[Only] if forced to make up a name for it, I would say '[it is] great.'" Cf. also *Laozi* 25.10: "In the Beyond there are four Great Ones." Wang Bi: "The four Great Ones are the Way, Heaven, Earth, and the king. Generally speaking, that of entities which has a name and has a designation is not their ultimate. Saying 'the Way' presupposes that there is a basis for [this expression]. Only as a consequence of there being a basis for [this expression] will one talk about it as being 'the Way.' Accordingly, 'Way' is [only] the greatest among [aspects that can be assigned] designations, but that is nothing compared to greatness of the designationless. The designationless, which it is impossible to name, is called [here] 'the Beyond.'" The term *wei* 謂, 'to call,' in the *Laozi* is also read as referring to *cheng* 稱, 'designation.'" The terminology is also present in *Lunyu shiyi* on *Lunyu* 8.19. Only in Wang Bi on *Laozi* 3.1 do both *ming* and *cheng* seem to mean the same.

7. *Quhu* 取乎, "is taken for," is a neologism created by Wang Bi. In the form *quyu*, 取於, it also occurs in Wang Bi's commentary on *Laozi* 1.5 and 25.5.

8. Wang Bi reads the Dao as the generative aspect of the That-by-which of the entities. For this he relies on statements in the *Laozi*, such as *Laozi* 34.2: "The ten thousand entities depend on it [the Way] for their being born. . . . Achievements are completed [through it]"; or, *Laozi* 51.1: "The Way generates them. What they get is that it nourishes them: As entities it [the Way] lets them assume form. As situations it has them fully develop." On this basis, Wang Bi constructs the other references to the Dao or its synonymns; cf. his reading of *Laozi* 21.1–4 and 24.5.

9. The phrase refers to *Laozi* 1.5, where the Dark is described as the "door [from which] the many and the subtle [emerge]." The difficulty lies in the transitive grammatical function of 出 here, which suggests some creative process, while the actual meaning in Wang Bi's context is that that by which the ten thousand entities are remains undiscernable, "dark." The logic and necessity underlying the undiscernability of the That-by-which is one of Wang Bi's most important philosophical discoveries. He develops the notion out of a careful reading of the *Laozi* language concerned with this aspect, such as *xuan* 玄, *yin* 隱, or *wuming* 無名. He merges these concepts into the notion of the Dark. The formal parallelism between these two phrases might hide a difference in grammatical relationships. Beyond *Laozi*

1.5, there are other statements about the Dark, such as Wang Bi on *Laozi* 51.5 and 10.9. Commenting on the *Laozi* expression 玄德, Wang Bi writes on 51.5: "That [the entities] have [their] receipt/capacity 德 but do not know its master [on the basis of whom they attain it] is [because] it [their *de* 德] comes forth out of the Recondite. That is why [the *Laozi*] speaks of it as of 'Capacity [coming from] That-which-is-Dark'" 出乎幽冥故謂之玄德. In his comments on *Laozi* 10.9, Wang uses nearly the same terms. These passages suggest that the phrase 玄也者 取乎幽冥之所出也 in the *LZWZLL* has been deformed by the forced parallelism and in fact should be translated—against the actual grammar, as prompted by the parallel "'*Xuan*' is taken for [its aspect] of being that which lets come forth out of the Recondite." For the phrase about the Dao there is a close parallel in Wang Bi on *Laozi* 25.5: "The Way is taken for [the aspect of that by which all entities are] that there is no entity which is not based on it" 道取於無物而不由. The term 幽冥, *youming*, rendered here as "the Recondite," does not seem to originate in classics such as the *Laozi* or the *Zhouyi*, although there is a loose relationship with the pair 窈兮冥兮 in *Laozi* 21.4, which also characterizes the Dao. The expression *youming*, however, had become part of the philosophical vocabulary in the context of *Laozi* reading, even before the Han dynasty was founded. The *Wenzi* 文子 writes in the section 上德, *Wenzi yaoquan*, 117, with a semi-quotation from *Laozi* 14.1: "The Dao has not-having as [its] substance. As one does not see its form when looking for it, nor hear its sound when listening for it—it is called the Recondite. The [expression the] Recondite is a means to discourse about the Dao, but it is not the Dao." *Locus classicus* for the definition of the Dark is Wang Bi on *Laozi* 1.5: "As to the 'Dark,' it is obscure, is silent without [any] entitities, is that which lets the 'beginning' and the 'mother' emerge. It is impossible to give a definition [for this Dark]; therefore [Laozi] cannot say 'their common [source] is defined as 'the Dark,' but [only] says 'designate as.' The [term] 'Dark' is taken for that [aspect of the ultimate principle] that it cannot be designated as being thus [and nothing else]. Should one designate it as being thus [and nothing else] it would definitely not be permitted to define it as one [specific] Dark. If one were to define it as being one [specific] Dark and nothing else, this would be a definition, and that would be far off the mark." Darkness is thus the necessary undiscernability of that by which the ten thousand kinds of entities are.

10. *Laozi* 65.4: "The capacity coming from That-which-is-dark is deep, is distant." This links "deep" with the Dark. Cf. *Laozi* 15.1: "Those in antiquity who were well versed in the Way were recondite and abstruse, so deep that they could not be discerned." This is indeed the aspect that *xuan* 玄 denotes. The "delving into the abstrusive" comes from *Xici*, 7.9b9. Within a long series of specific entities such as Heaven, Earth, or the ruler, which deal with the multitude of entities and benefit the world, emerges a statement about the yarrow stalks and tortoise shells: "As to delving into the abstrusive and finding out the hidden, probing the deep and getting at the far away by way of determinining auspicious and inauspicious [premonitions] for All-under-Heaven and to bring to fruition the untiring efforts of All Under Heaven, none is greater than yarrow stalks and tortoise shells."

11. The word "great" is assigned to the Way in *Laozi* 25.6. The expression "filling in and rounding out [ever more]," 彌綸, is from the *Xici* 7.3a1: "The *Yi* gives a standard to Heaven and Earth, that is why it is able to fill in and round out the Way of Heaven and Earth." Cf. also Wang Bi on *Laozi* 25.6.

12. *Yuan* 遠, "distant," appears with Dao in *Laozi* 25.8. This forces a rereading of *Laozi* 65.4, in which the *yuan* 遠 is in fact assigned to the generative aspect, there represented by *de* 德.

13. The definition of the "fine" is taken from *Laozi* 14.1: "That which [I] do not see if [I] look at it [I] call 'fine.'"

14. With this argument Wang Bi defines the tentative and heuristic manner of the *Laozi*'s and the *Xici*'s speaking as conditioned by the structure of the object of their inquiry. The tentative, connotative nature of the language they use explains the contradictions and paradoxes in this language and establishes a framework for reading this language.

15. *Laozi* 25.5.

16. *Laozi* 1.5.

17. For elements 34 and 35, there seems to be no source in the *Laozi* or the *Xici*. Elements 36 and 37 contain quotations appearing in *Laozi* 29.3 and *Laozi* 64.5. In the commentary on *Laozi* 29.3, the object "All Under Heaven" or "the other entities" is identified: "The ten thousand kinds of entities have That-which-is-of-itself-what-it-is as their nature. That is why it is possible to be responsive to them but impossible to act upon them, it is possible to penetrate them but impossible to hold on to them. The [other] entities have an eternal nature but acting upon them will definitely lead to their unavoidable destruction. The [other] entities have their comings and goings, but holding on to them will definitely lead to their unavoidable loss."

18. The argumentative pattern of this entire passage is based on *Laozi* 64, while some of the matter is taken from *Laozi* 29 and Wang's commentary there. Wang Bi supplements the two forms of physical action, *wei* 爲 and *zhi* 執, with two forms of verbal action, *yan* 言 and *ming* 名, in tune with *Laozi* 2.2, where the Sage "takes residence in management without interference" and "practices teaching without words," a statement often quoted by Wang Bi; see his comments on *Laozi* 7.1, 23.3, and 63.1. The entire passage from element 33–42, which forms a parallel staircase, does not seem to fit into the context here, dealing as it does with the Sage's behavior and not the *Laozi*'s language. This impression is reinforced by the double *ranze* 然則 just before phrase 33 and in the beginning of phrase 43. I believe the entire passage to be a fragment slipped in here for superficial similarity of context.

19. If indeed the elements 33–42 belong here, *Laozi* would belong to the Sage category. Given the Sage's understanding of the nature of language as a feeble instrument for the communication of insight about the That-by-which, it can be expected that his literary remains are at best hints or pointers, which then inform

the reading strategy proposed by Wang Bi for the *Laozi* itself. For the relative status of *Laozi* in relationship to the Sage, cf. my *The Craft of a Chinese Commentator*, 120–50.

20. The notion of the Great Beginning, *taishi* 太始, has its origin in the term *dashi* 大始 in the *Xici* 7.1b1, which says 乾知大始 "*qian* is in charge of the Great Beginning." In its elevated form as *taishi* it became part of the *Zhouyi* interpretation of the Han dynasty. One of the most important interpretive texts of the period, the *Yi wei qian zuodu* 易緯乾鑿度, says (p. 24): "The Great Beginning is the beginning of forms" 太初形之始也.

21. The discussion of the generative aspect of the Great Beginning refers to the Dao; that of the elusiveness of the That-by-which as the "ultimate of the Recondite" refers to the Dark.

22. A formula coined by Wang Bi. On *Laozi* 29.4, he says: "The Sage understands the ultimate of [the entities'] That-which-is-of-itself-what-it-is, and is clear about the feelings of the ten thousand kinds of entities. Therefore he is responsive [to them], but does not interfere, he adapts [to them], but does not initiate."

23. A formula created by Wang Bi. The *ben/mo* 本/末 pair does not occur in the *Laozi*. The formula is repeated throughout Wang Bi's *Commentary*; cf. Wang Bi on *Laozi* 38.1, 57.1, 57.5, and 58.10.

24. Another formula created by Wang Bi out of material in *Laozi* 52.2 守其母, "keeping to the mother," and the repeated arguments that the Dao maintains the entities. Wang's commentaries on *Laozi* 57 and 58 extensively develop this formula.

25. Another formula created by Wang Bi. *Laozi* 18.2: "Once knowledge and insight have appeared [in the ruler's actions], there will be the great deceit [among his subjects]." Wang Bi: "If he practices tricks and applies his intelligence to spy out cunning and deceit [among the people], his interests become apparent and his shape becomes visible [and, as a consequence,] the others will know how to evade him." Thus "knowledge" in the *Laozi* is read by Wang Bi as the art of government. The combination "skill and arts" appears in Wang Bi on *Laozi* 65.3: "But if [a ruler] gets the people moving by means of intelligence and tricks, what is [in fact] being moved will be their depraved hearts. If he then again with cunning and tricks blocks the deceptions by the people, the people will know his tricks and will thereupon thwart and evade them. The more cunning his [the ruler's] devices become, the more exuberantly will falsehood and deceit sprout" [among the people]. The second part is taken from *Laozi* 64.3, which says about the Sage: "He [therefore] acts on them [dangers] while they have not yet come about."

26. The formula is Wang Bi's, based on *Laozi* 79.3, on which Wang comments: "A man with capacity [the Sage] is concerned [only] with his [part of the] contract. [Thus] he does not let a resentment arise and then claim payment from the other." My translation here, "make demands on others," tries to match the generalization given by Wang Bi to this phrase. The man "without capacity" will in his turn "pay attention to the mistakes of others." Wang takes up the theme in his comments to the *xiang* 象 for hexagram *song* 訟, "litigation," in the *Zhouyi*,

Wang Bi ji jiaoshi, 249, which invokes the authority of Confucius' statement in *Lunyu* 12.13, that one should take care that litigation is altogether stopped. "Stopping litigation depends on 'taking precautions as to the beginning.' . . . The reason why litigation occurs is the overstepping of [one's own part in] the contract. Therefore [as *Laozi* 79.3 says] 'he who has capacity [= the Sage] pays attention to [his part of] the contract' and 'does not claim payment from the other'." This summary of the *Laozi* in four "key points" is reduced into a single phrase further down; cf. 6.77.

27. In his attacks on the Legalism prevailing at the Wei Court, Wang Bi draws on *Laozi* 58.2: "He [a ruler] whose government is bent on surveillance will see his people divided." The disastrous consequences of this policy for the ruling house are depicted in Wang Bi on *Laozi* 49.5. For a detailed analysis, see the chapter "Wang Bi's Political Philosophy," in my *Language, Ontology, and Political Philosophy*. The sequential order of the schools here puts the greatest villain, the Legalists, first. Such sequential series are based on *Laozi* 17 and 38. In *Laozi* 17, the lowest above those who are not even taken seriously by the lower orders is the one they "fear." Wang Bi on *Laozi* 17.3: "He is not anymore capable of getting other beings to do something by means of [his] kindness and humaneness, but relies on might and power."

28. The Name school, Mingjiao, had a strong influence in Wang Bi's times. Liu Shao, the author of the *Renwu zhi* 人物志, who also developed the examination system that was designed to keep the very group to which Wang Bi belonged from government posts, adhered to its tenets. Cf. my "Lebensstil und Drogen im chinesischen Mittelalter," *T'oung Pao* 59 (1973):79–178. With the words "order and consideration," Wang Bi takes up *Lunyu* 4.15: "The Way of the master is loyalty and consideration, and nothing else." He comments: "'Consideration' is going against one's own feelings in order to be at one with other beings. . . . It does not happen that someone is able to perfect his consideration, 全其恕, without penetrating to the absolute of order, 理之極. Being able to penetrate to the absolute of order, there is no being [who] is not included. The absolute cannot be two; therefore, it is spoken of as the One. 'If there is some word' that for attaining the maximum in investigating one's own person, in encompassing other beings, and in penetrating [their] various categories 'can be practiced all life long, it is consideration'" [as *Lunyu* 15.14 says]. *Lunyu shiyi*, in *Wang Bi ji jiaoshi*, 622.

29. According to *Laozi* 17 (which has the inverse order, starting with the best), this refers to a ruler practicing the government doctrine above the Legalists' school—who is described in *Laozi* 17.2—"[those below] will be close to him and praise him." Wang Bi comments: "He [the second best] is unable to reside in [his] affairs by means of non-interference and to make the unspoken his teaching. He establishes the good and spreads moral education, thus prompting those below to get "'close to him and praise him.'" In Wang Bi on *Laozi* 17.3, the representative of this school is said to be still able to command beings by "kindness and humaneness." Wang read this as a characterization of the Ru, but their use of emulation will lead to struggles. *Laozi* 3.1: "[As a ruler] not to shower worthies with honors induces the people not to struggle . . . " Wang Bi: "What is the pur-

pose of showering [someone] with honors who is only capable of handling this [particular] assignment [and no others]? . . . If, in granting honors to worthies and glorifying the famous, the emulation exceeds their assignment, those below will rush forward to compete, compare their [own] capabilities [to those of those honored], and outdo each other."

30. For the mother/son metaphor, see above, 2.44.

31. In *Xici* 8.3b8, the master (Confucius) says: "What about the thoughts and deliberations in the empire? In the empire they have the same purport, but different approaches, one destination, but a hundred deliberations." In his comments on *Laozi* 47.1, Wang Bi refers to the same passage.

32. These polemics against the schools show that Wang Bi was engaged in a lively and broad argument with other interpreters of the *Laozi*. The success of his own work led to the disappearance of practically all of the writings to which he must have been referring. For an analysis of this section, cf. my *The Craft of a Chinese Commentator*, pp.167–68.

Zhang 3 TRANSLATION NOTES

1. This quotation from the *Liji* 18.6/97/16, cf. S. Couvreur, *'Li Ki,' ou Mémoires sur les bienséances et les cérémonies*, vol. 2, p. 37, defines, by implication, the argumentative strategy of the *Laozi* as not being literal but metaphorical. The complete quotation runs (with the inverted order of the two elements): "The instruction by the Gentleman, 君子之教 , is metaphoric; he shows the way, but he does not lead forward . . . he opens up, but he does not go all the way." This has important consequences for understanding Wang Bi's strategy for reading the *Laozi*.

2. Element 1 in this *zhang* has clear markings of being written in IPS, consisting as it does of 3 pairs of parallel phrases. However, the chains do not link up readily, because there is both too much overlapping vocabulary and too little to make a firm case for the establishment of the two chains and their link with the a/b chains further down.

3. Wang Bi's *Commentary* attempts to make the inner logic of a *zhang* transparent, so that the conclusion can be understood without a further comment by Wang Bi; cf. his comments on *zhang* 3, 22, 24, 27, 43–46, 55, 59, 63–68, 71–73, 78, and 79.

4. Cf. *Xici* 8.3b8, where the Master (Confucius) says: "What about the thoughts and deliberations in the empire? In the empire they have the same purport, but different approaches, one destination, but a hundred deliberations."

5. *Li* 理 in Wang Bi means "to regulate, to put to order." For the term, cf. P. Demiéville, "Le vocabulaire philosophique chinois, I; Tchouang-tseu, ch. II," in *id.*, *Choix d'Études Sinologiques (1921–1970)*, 49 ff. The term *zhili* 至理 (here

"highest ordering principle"], also occurs in Wang Bi on *Laozi* 42.2 (*Laozi*: "What other people teach, I also teach other people"]: "My teaching of other people does not consist in forcing them to follow, but in making use of [their] That-which-is-of-itself-what-it-is. [I] take up their highest ordering principle [and teach that,] following it, they will necessarily enjoy luck, [while] deviating from it, they will necessarily suffer misfortune. That is why other people's teaching each other to deviate from it [with the result] that they necessarily draw their own misfortune upon themselves, is like my teaching them not to deviate from it" [which will necessarily bring them luck and thus positively teach them the same lesson others will teach negatively].

Zhang 4 Translation Notes

1. This second part is set off against the first in the only edition we have for this section of the text, the 老子指例略, by leaving some empty space in the text line finishing element 10 of the previous *zhang*. This creates an optical divide. This device is not used for separating the *zhang*.

2. The text now turns from ontogenetics to ontology and, by deduction, to questions of practical politics, ontocontrol. For an analysis of the notion of the negative opposite, cf. chapter 1 in my *Language, Ontology, and Political Philosophy*.

3. Cf. *Xici* 8.5a1ff: "The Master [Confucius] says:

He is in danger who acquiesces in his position [as a ruler].

He goes under who clings to his persistence.

He ends in chaos who holds on to his order.

Therefore the Gentleman

in his security does not forget about [threatening] danger;

in his persistence does not forget about [the danger of his] going under;

in his order does not forget the [threat of] chaos.

Therefore his person is secure and the state can be protected.

The [Zhou]yi says: "There is doom [threatening]! There is doom [threatening]! He stays tied to the mulberry tree!"

The piece is a parallel staircase written in open IPS. There are many echoes of this thought in Wang Bi's *Commentary*; cf. Wang Bi on *Laozi* 39, 64.1, and 73.8.

4. *Qiuhao* 秋毫, here "autumn down," refers to the extremely fine new hair

growing on animals in the fall. It is first used in the *Zhuangzi* for something extremely minute and light.

5. The strategy for translating elements 10–12 is based on Wang Bi's reading of *Laozi* 40.1: "He who acts by way of the negative opposite [i.e., the Sage] is the one who moves [in accordance with] the Way."

6. Based on *Laozi* 64.1: "[For a Sage Ruler] as long as [he] is [still] secure [in his position], [this security] is [still] easy to maintain. As long as there are still no signs [of a danger to his life] it is [still] easy to take precautions against" [such danger]. Wang Bi: "Because [the Sage Ruler, as the *Xici* 8.5.a3ff. says about the Gentleman in a quotation from Confucius] 'while being in security [in his position]' 'does not forget the [threat of] danger' and [thus] maintains this [security], and while still 'in existence,' 'does not forget [the threat of his physical] demise,' and [thus] takes precautions against this [danger and demise] in a situation where [still] no effort [is needed], that is why [the text] says, 'It is easy [to maintain security and to take precautions]!'" Cf. also Wang Bi on *Laozi* 73.8.

7. The translation of 非安 and 非存 as "refusal of [treating] security [as a given]" and "refusal of [treating] persistence [as a given]" is prompted by the parallels with elements 17 and 18, where 絕 and 棄 in "cutting off of sageliness" and "rejection of benevolence" make it quite clear that the terms after 曰 are transitive verbs. This prevents the easy translation "is not security through which security is brought about."

8. Wang Bi here refers to *Laozi* 32.1, where dukes and kings are admonished to keep to the small and simple in order to fill their high office: "Even though the Unadorned may be small, no one under Heaven is able to put [it] to service. If only the dukes and kings were able to keep to it [the Unadorned], the ten thousand kinds of entities would submit [to them] of their own accord as guests." Cf. *Laozi* 39.4: "Once the kings and dukes are not the standard through [the One] and thus esteemed and elevated, they are in danger of being toppled. Therefore to be esteemed takes [acting as if] being despised as [its] root, and to be elevated takes [acting as if] being lowly as [its] base. If, therefore, dukes and kings refer to themselves as 'I lonely one,' 'I orphaned one,' and 'I needy one,' is that not their taking being despised as the root?" Cf. also *Laozi* 42.1.

9. There is no direct source in the *Laozi*, but the thought is present that Heaven and Earth are able to achieve their greatness only by emulating the One or negativity. Cf. *Laozi* 25.10 and 25.12, and *Laozi* 39.2.

10. Cf. *Laozi* 19.1: "If [the ruler] were to discard wisdom and to reject intelligence, the benefit for the people would be a hundredfold." Commenting on *Laozi* 10.3 and 10.4, Wang Bi develops this argument.

11. *Laozi* 19.1: "If [the ruler] were to discard benevolence and to reject righteousness, the people would return to filial piety and parental love." The beneficial effects of the Sage's imitating the absence of benevolence in Heaven and Earth are described in *Laozi* 5: "Heaven and Earth are not kindly. For them, the ten thousand kinds of entities are like grass and dogs." See also Wang Bi's commentary there.

12. This refers to chapters such as *Laozi* 5, 7, and 43, where the Sage imitates Heaven and Earth.

13. *Laozi* 42.1 begins: "The Way generates the One," and then it proceeds to talk about dukes and kings calling themselves "orphaned." It is important to note that Wang Bi here assumes that the only motive for the *Laozi* to talk about the Dao and the One is to elucidate the meaning of these self-references of the rulers in terms of political philosophy. The ontological explorations are thus read as a grounding for pursuits in the field of political philosophy. Wang Weicheng has suggested reading 得一 for 道一 of the transmitted text. This would refer the passage to *Laozi* 39, which again ends with an explanation of the reasons for which the rulers call themselves orphaned. I see no need for this.

Zhang 5 NUMBERED TEXT NOTES

1. The entire passage from 天地實大, 而曰非大之所能 through 道, 稱之大者也 is not contained in the 雲笈七籤 selection but replaced by a single phrase 皆理之大者也.

2. The selection contained in the 雲笈七籤 ends here.

Zhang 5 TRANSLATION NOTES

1. Cf. the analysis of these terms in chapter 1 of my *Language, Ontology, and Political Philosophy*.

2. Elements 5–15 treat a subdivision of designations. In phrase 16, the argument returns to the "name/designation" dichotomy. Another such subdivision occurs in phrases 22–24. This is one of the few places where the usefulness and economy of Wang Bi's IPS reach its limit, because it has to rely on the reader's attention to notice that the text continues in a subgroup of one of the strains.

3. *Laozi* 25.5.

4. *Laozi* 1.5.

5. This refers to *Laozi* 1.5, where the Dark is described as the "door [from which] the many and the subtle" [emerge].

6. This is a reference to *Laozi* 21.7: "By means of it [the truthful essence] one discerns the beginning of the many." On the other hand, *Laozi* 1.5 describes the Dark as the "door" from which both the subtle and the many emerge.

7. *Laozi* 10.7: "It [the Dao] generates them [the entities]." Wang Bi: "That is, it does not block their source." *Laozi* 10.8: "It [the Dao] rears them [the entities]." Wang Bi: "That is, it does not hem in their nature."

8. The quotations are taken from *Laozi* 10.9. The passage here gives an im-

portant clue for the translation of 玄德 by inserting a 之 between the two terms, making it 玄之德. "Receipt" translates *de* 德. Wang Bi reads it as that which entities "receive," *de* 得, from the Dao. In this sense it is also the capacity of entities, and is, in other places, translated in this way.

9. The term *shen* 深 is used with *xuan* 玄 in *Laozi* 15.1 and 65.4.

10. *Laozi* 25.6.

11. *Laozi* 1.5.

12. *Laozi* 25.10. The excerpts of the *LZWZLL* printed in the *Yunji qiqian* end here.

Zhang 6 TRANSLATION NOTES

1. *Lunyu* 2.2: "The master said: 'The *Shi [jing]* has three hundred poems, [but] they be can summed up in one phrase: Do not think anything decadent.'" This reference is more than an educated allusion. It points to a common structure in both the *Laozi* and the *Shijing*. Both contain a wide variety of materials, but the claim is that they all share a common orientation; cf. Liu Baonan, *Lunyu zhengyi*, 21ff.

2. It remains quite amazing that Wang Bi should return to the theme of summing up the *Laozi* after having done so in a longer series of statements in 2.44. Still, from this extreme variant of a summary, it is quite clear that Wang Bi's agenda lay primarily in the realm of political philosophy.

3. In *Laozi* 70.2, Laozi says of himself: "[My] words have the principle. [My] activities have the ruler."

4. *Lunyu* 4.15 reads through Wang's commentary: "The Master said: 'What threads through my Way is [the] One.' Zengzi said: 'Yes.' The Master left."

5. Cf. *Zhouyi* 1.2b8 2.1, hexagram 1, *Wenyan*. This is assumed to be an utterance of Confucius.

6. Applied in *Laozi* 20.15: "I alone desire to be different from the others in that I honor the nourishing mother." Wang Bi: "The nourishing mother is the root of life. The others all discard the root that is providing life for the people and honor the dazzle of wordly accoutrements." Cf. *Laozi* 57.4: "[In short,] the more beautiful objects are displayed [by the ruler], the more robbers and thieves there will be."

7. *Laozi* 64.7: "That is why the Sage desires [only] to have no desires and does not put high value on goods that are hard to get." Wang Bi: "Even when [the ruler's] desires and preferences are [only] minute, competition and emulation [among the people] are called forth by them. Even when goods [in the ruler's hands] that are hard to get are [only] tiny, greed and robbery are evoked by them."

8. Cf. Wang Bi's commentary to the hexagram *song* 訟, Litigation, *Zhouyi*, 249, *xiang*: "The Gentleman will, when the affair [litigation] has come about, take precautions as to the beginning." Wang Bi: "'In entering litigation I am like others. But what is really necessary is that litigation must be made to stop' [altogether] [says Confucius in *Lunyu* 12.13]. Stopping litigation depends on 'making precautions as to the beginning.' 'Taking precautions as to the beginning' depends on setting up controls. The fact that one's [own part of the] contract is not clearly delineated is that which generates litigations. If beings keep to their roles and there is no overlapping in their offices, what basis for litigation should there be? The reason why litigation occurs is the overstepping of [one's own part in] the contract. Therefore [as *Laozi* 79.3 says] 'he who has capacity [= the Sage] pays attention to [his part of] the contract' and 'does not claim payment from the other [contract partner]'."

9. *Laozi* 64.1 and 64.3. Wang Bi replaces 有 in 未有 in the *Laozi* by 始. There is no text supporting this reading, and it is possible that 始 entered here from the *Zhouyi* passage quoted above.

10. Phrases 14–16 and their links to phrases 18–20 refer to *Laozi* 19.1, where Wang Bi offers an exceedingly elegant explanation for the two pairs of three phrases each, namely, a parallel staircase. Thus it reads:

If [the ruler] were to discard wisdom and to reject intelligence, the benefit for the people would be a hundredfold.

If [the ruler] were to discard benevolence and to reject righteousness, the people would return to filial piety and parental love.

If [the ruler] were to discard craftiness and to reject [lust for] profit, there would be no robbers and thieves.

These three [pairs of values whose rejection by the ruler is advocated] are as statements still not sufficient. Therefore to let [his subjects] have something to go by, [he would]

manifest simplicity,

embrace the unadorned, and

by way of minimizing [his] private interests reduce [his] desires.

11. See chapter 3 of my *Language, Ontology, and Political Philosophy*.

12. *Laozi* 37.3: "If dukes and kings were only able to hold on to [the Eternal of the Way], the ten thousand kinds of entities would change [for the better] of their own accord. If, this change notwithstanding, desires should arise [among them], I [the Sage] would quiet them down by means of the simplicity of the Nameless" [of myself].

13. Cf. *Laozi* 57.5: "That is why the words of the Sage are: I [as a ruler would] not interfere, and the people would on their own transform themselves [for the

better]; I [would] emulate stillness, and the people would on their own rectify themselves." Wang Bi combines the "not interfering" of the next-to-last phrase with the "rectifying themselves" of the last.

14. These quotations all go back to *Laozi* 19.1.

15. Elements 23–44 contain a polemics concerning the interpretation of the first phrase of *Laozi* 19.1: "If [the ruler] were to discard wisdom and to reject intelligence, the benefit for the people would be a hundredfold." A formal element to denote and separate this segment from the next is the rigid parallelism in their beginning 夫素樸之道不著而好欲之美不隱 versus 夫敦樸之德不著而名行之美顯尙. The first phrases of *Laozi* 19 have been the preferred quotation in writings by Confucian scholars such as Ban Gu when they set out to prove the *Laozi*'s incompatibility with the teachings of Confucius.

16. These terms are a reference to *Laozi* 15.3, which describes "those in antiquity who were well versed in the Way": "genuine they were—like an uncarved block."

17. Elements 45–56 allude to *Laozi* 44.

18. The overall theme in elements 45–60 is the second phrase in *Laozi* 19.1: "If [the ruler] were to discard benevolence and to reject righteousness, the people would return to filial piety and parental love."

19. *Lunyu* 12.18: "Ji Kangzi was afraid of robbers. He asked Confucius about it. Confucius answered: 'If only you had no desires, you would not be robbed even if a premium were set on it'" 苟子之不欲雖賞之不竊. Wang Bi radicalizes the statement by replacing 不欲 with 無欲.

20. The same statement occurs verbatim in Wang Bi on *Laozi* 19.1.

21. The phrase might be corrupted as it has no parallel in other constructions with 況術. A typical construction of this kind would be 況術之下此者乎 or 況術之賤此者乎. Based on these parallels, however, my reading follows the punctuation suggested by the edition marked (c) in the list given at the beginning of the translation (況術之有利斯以忽素樸乎) and identifies the 斯 in the sense of the 此 of the other examples. Lou Yulie separates 況術之有利, 斯以忽素樸乎, but he suggests a reading similar to mine.

22. The logic of these two phrases is that the outcome of wisdom- and benevolence-guided action of the ruler is in fact harmful to the other entities.

23. Only the dismantling of the state surveillance apparatus will prompt the people to cherish sincerity so that order is established and the ruler is secure.

24. Only the abandonment of particular favors will enable the Sage to be the basis of an order in which all entities find their place in a prestabilized harmony. This pair of phrases mark another example of the systematic turn in Wang Bi's philosophy. While the *Laozi* simply states that the consequence of the ruler's discarding wisdom and intelligence will be a grand benefit for the people, Wang Bi argues the logic of it and comes to the conclusion that, through the very act

of discarding these instruments of governing, their intended result is brought about.

25. *Laozi* 73.1: "If someone is courageous in daring [to do], he will be killed." Wang Bi: "By necessity he 'will not come to his natural death'" [as *Laozi* 42.3 says about '"those who are violent and brutal"]. Cf. *Laozi* 68.

26. *Laozi* 7.2.

27. Ibid.

28. For the expression "the mother that brings about the achievements," which seems to be a Wang Bi neologism, cf. chapter 2 in my *Language, Ontology, and Political Philosophy*.

29. *Laozi* 52.2. The quotation is interpretive and operates with crucial additions such as 必, "has to."

CHAPTER 4

1. The evidence for this argument will be found in ch. 1 of this study.

2. Editorial note to *Laozi* 38.

3. Wei Yuan, *Laozi benyi*.

4. Tao Hongqing, *Du Laozi Zhaji*.

5. Tōjō Itsudō, *Rōshi Ō chū hyōshiki*.

6. Usami Shinsui, *Ō chū Rōshi dōtoku kyō*.

7. Paul J.Lin, *A Translation of Lao Tzu's* Tao Te Ching *and Wang Pi's Commentary*, Michigan Papers in Chinese Studies , No. 30, Ann Arbor: Center for Chinese Studies, The University of Michigan, 1977.

8. Ariane Rump and Wing-tsit Chan, trans. *Commentary on the Lao Tzu by Wang Pi*. Monographs of the Society for Asian and Comparative Philosophy, No. 6. Honululu: University Press of Hawaii, 1979.

9. Richard J.Lynn, *The Classic of the Way and Virtue. A New Translation of the* Tao-te ching *of Laozi as Interpreted by Wang Bi*, New York: Columbia University Press, 1999.

10. See my *The Craft of a Chinese Commentator*, chapter 3.

Zhang 1 Translation Notes

1. Dao 道 with the meaning "speak of" is used by Wang Bi in *LZWZLL* 2.7 in his discussion of this passage. The same reading in He Yan 何晏, "Dao lun 道論 (On Dao)," quoted by Zhang Zhan, *Liezi zhu*, 1.3.14: "If indeed one is speaking

about it [the eternal *dao*], there are no words, and if one is naming it [the eternal name] there are no names." Both follow Zhuang Zun: "Generally spoken, what is written down on bamboo and silk and engraved in metal and stone and thus can be transmitted among men are the ways 'that can be spoken about'" 夫著於竹帛鏤於金石可傳於人者可道之道也. It should be noted that Zhuang read *dao* only as written communication in the sense of "transmit to later generations" *chuan*. Quoted in Li Lin, *Daode zhen jing qushan ji*, 1.1a–b.

2. According to *LZWZLL* 2.7, the xing 形, "shape," points to the term *ming* 名, and by inference, the term *shi* 事 must refer to *dao* 道. Wang Bi writes: "The bloom of [what Laozi calls] 'that which can be spoken about' is still insufficient to 'administer Heaven and Earth.' The maximum of that which has shape is still insufficient to 'store the ten thousand entities'" 故可道之盛, 未足以官天地; 有形之極, 未足以府萬物. In the *LZWZLL*, Wang Bi in fact treats the 有名 in *Laozi* 1.1 as if it were a 有形.

3. The term "ten thousand kinds of entities" is used because it encompasses living beings and material things as well as processes and mental constructs such as "names." In Wang Bi's order of things, it is the general term above *wu* 物 with their fixed forms, *xing* 形, and shi 事 with their names, ming 名. Cf. my *Language, Ontology, and Political Philosophy*, Chapter 2.

4. Cf. *Laozi* 40.3 with Wang's commentary and Wang Bi on *Laozi* 21.8.

5. Cf. *Laozi* 51.4 and Wang Bi comm.

6. The identification of the ten thousand kinds of entities as the subject of "being without desire" rests on the reference to this passage in Wang Bi on *Laozi* 34.2 天下常無欲之時 . . . All Under Heaven is the social counterpart to the ten thousand kinds of entities.

7. According to Wang Bi on *Laozi* 34.2, this is also the time when "the ten thousand kinds of entities all manage to be in their proper places." The term used there for the Dao is "small" 小.

8. This is a paraphrase of the last sentence of *Laozi* 11, 有之以爲利無之以爲用, which is translated by Wang Bi in his commentary there as "entities in order to be beneficial all depend on negativity for their usability." 有之所以爲利皆賴無之以爲用也

9. The term *quyu* 取於 for an aspectual description of something intrinsically undefinable seems to be one of the new terms of Wang Bi. He uses it extensively in the passage of the *LZWZLL* that deals with the various ways of describing aspects of the That-by-which; cf. *LZWZLL* 2.22 ff.

10. Tao Hongqing followed by Lou Yulie considered this passage corrupt and has tried to amend it. Lou Yulie has added punctuation. The text reads: 不可得而名故不可言同名曰玄而言謂之玄者取於不可得而謂之然也謂之然則不可以定乎一玄若定乎一玄而已則是名則失之遠矣. Once the core point is understood that the commentary explains why the term wei 謂, "to speak of," is used instead of ming 名, "to define," no amendment is necessary. Lou Yulie's amendment with punctuation reads: 不可得而名, 故不可言同名曰玄. 而言[同]謂之玄者, 取於

不可得而謂之然也. [不可得而] 謂之然則不可以定乎一玄而已 [若定乎一玄],
則是名則失之遠矣.

Zhang 2 NUMBERED TEXT NOTE

1. The preference for 盈 instead of the 傾 in Fu Yi and Fan Yingyuan is based on the better fit of this term with the others in the series, 相生, 相成, 相較, 相和, and 相隨, none of which involve an antagonistic relationship. I am grateful to Mr. Peng Hao 彭浩 for this suggestion. Wang Bi does not comment on this passage, nor does he quote it elsewhere, so there is no confirmation.

2. 不爲始 instead of the 不辭 of the Heshang gong tradition is confirmed by the long quotation in Wang Bi on *Laozi* 17.1. However, Wang Bi, on *Laozi* 38.1 again seems to quote this passage, this time with the formula 不辭. In this latter case, however, the context differs. Wang Bi in fact uses a phrase from *Laozi* 34.2.

Zhang 2 TRANSLATION NOTES

1. Cf. Wang Bi's commentary to *Laozi* 18.2. In all available editions, this part of the *Commentary*, beginning with "knowledge" and ending with "falsehood," is placed after the next phrases ending with "does not presume" [upon them]. As the above commentary phrase refers to the sentence "practices teaching without words," I have placed this commentary here. Transferring this commentary segment into this position has the consequence that 2.4 is separated from 2.2 and 2.3 and becomes a *c* segment summarizing the two strains of thought followed in the preceding lines.

2. The change in subject from the ten thousand kinds of entities to the Sage is forced by the identical passage in *Laozi* 77.2, where the Sage is the subject of the phrase. In *Laozi* 10.9, these two segments also appear, but there the commentary defines the entities as the subject.

Zhang 3 NUMBERED TEXT NOTES

1. All authors quoted on this passage by Hatano Tarō consider this passage corrupt, because the construction of 尚賢顯名 is not clear and does not find a parallel in the next statement, and because a parallel to 沒命而盜 is missing. The second parallel passage is well attested through a quotation in the *Beitang shuchao* 北堂書鈔. While the first issue can be handled with the existing text—albeit not elegantly—the second issue is more important. A remainder of a phrase paralleling 沒命而盜 might be contained in the phrase 爲而常 before 校能相射 that is transmitted in 陸德明釋文 and 永樂大典本. This could be a

fragment of a phrase such as 作爲而爭 to come at the end here after 校能相射. This, however, is very tentative. I therefore have stayed with the existing earliest versions.

2. After 弱其志, which is misplaced into a position above the first commentary by Wang Bi in this *zhang*, 陸德明釋文 writes: 心虛則志弱也本無爲字. The 四庫 editors have read 心虛則志弱也 as a lost part of Wang Bi's *Commentary* and have included it, followed by Tōjō Itsudō, Hatano Tarō, and others. The passage is very unclear because of the second part, which translates "there is one MS that does not have the character 爲"; in the *Laozi* passage to which this is appended, no such character could possibly be missing. Still, the passage is badly transmitted, primarily because of the repetition of the term 知, which in its form 智 was also used in the previous commentary. This breaks the IPS structure. I have therefore amended 知 to 志. For the rest I have followed the reading of the base text.

3. The 傅奕古本 and 范應元本 have transmitted a reading 使夫知者不敢爲 (也) 爲無爲則無不爲矣. I have opted against the 馬王堆 B and for this reading, because the expression 知者 in both the *Laozi* and Wang Bi's text refers to persons who have understood the Way (*Laozi* 56.1, 81.3), and because Zhuang Zun, to whose analytical line Wang Bi generally is close, clearly had a text with 爲無爲 and 無不治. From this follows that I had to accept the 馬王堆 B reading of 治 for 爲.

Zhang 3 TRANSLATION NOTES

1. *Laozi* 3.1 is quoted in Wang Bi on *Laozi* 27.5 with the Sage as the subject. These phrases are stated in 3.1 as a general principle followed by the Sage; my insertion of the Sage as the subject into the bracket might slightly overexplain things. In 27.5, Wang Bi writes: 不尙賢能則民不爭不貴難得之貨則民不爲盜不見可欲則民心不亂. As *shi* 使 in 3.1 is well attested in all transmissions, we have to read the *ze* 則 in the quotation as an interpretation of 使.

2. Cf. Wang Bi on *Laozi* 65.1: "'Keeping stupid' refers to [their] being without knowledge and preserving the true [essence]. [Being thus,] they will go along with [their] That-which-is-of-itself-what-it-is."

Zhang 4 TRANSLATION NOTES

1. Cf. Wang Bi on *Zhouyi*, hexagram *jiaren* 家人, where he says: "It is the meaning of the hexagram *jiaren* that everyone is only concerned with the way of one single family and therefore is unable to understand the affairs of other people outside this family."

2. This refers to the king's "taking the Earth as model" and the Earth in turn "taking Heaven as model" in *Laozi* 25.

3. The same formula occurs in Wang Bi on *Laozi* 50.2 and 55.3.

4. The 道德眞集解 by Zhao Xueshi 趙學士 (1217) alone transmits the phrase from "It persists" to "as if persisting." It does not fit well, because the commentary section in question has been concluded with the quotation from the *Laozi* text, and now a second explanation seems to begin. It does, however, fit Wang Bi's argument and language. Cf. *Laozi* 56.3–6, as well as the commentary on *Laozi* 70.5 and 77.2. Hatano Tarō, p. 63, and Lou Yulie argue that as no other manuscript evidence supports this passage as being from Wang Bi, it cannot be accepted.

5. This entire argument is repeated in more detail in the commentary to *Laozi* 38, cf. p. 245.

6. The point that the Way is born before Heaven and Earth is also made in *Laozi* 25.1.

Zhang 5 NUMBERED TEXT NOTES

1. The 集註本 erroneously attributes this entire commentary passage to the Heshang gong *Commentary*. The transmission of the original Heshang gong *Commentary* to this section is solid; so is, both in formal terms and in terms of content, the attribution of the above commentary section to Wang Bi. In fact, the 集註本 makes another mistake in the same section by in turn attributing the actual Heshang gong Commentary 天地生萬物. . . . to the Tang Emperor Minghuang 明皇; cf. Hatano Tarō, p. 63.

2. Scholars agree that this passage is corrupt. I have based my emendation on other passages in Wang's *Commentary*. The emendation by Momoi Hakuroku 桃井白鹿, quoted in Hatano Tarō, of the text originally in 劉惟永集義本 and 集註本: 物樹其惡事錯其言不濟 (齊) 不言不理必窮之數也 to become 物樹其惠事錯其言其惠不濟其言不理必窮之數也 requires an unannounced reference change for the 其, which in the first two phrases would refer to the 物 themselves, while in the second pair would refer the second to the 言 of the political leader. This seems highly unsatisfactory.

3. There is agreement that this commentary is not legible in the present form. Cf. the opinions listed by Hatano Tarō, p. 70. Li Lin's 李霖取善集 1.18a alone transmits in its selections of commentaries to *Laozi* 5.4 a text following 王弼曰 that does not at all overlap with the transmitted commentary but runs as follows: 若不法天地之虛靜同彙籥之無心動不從感言不會機動與事乖故曰數窮不如內懷道德抱一不移故曰守中. Shima Kuniō is to my knowledge the only scholar who has accepted this as authentic, while Hatano Tarō, p. 71, argued that its "tone did not fit" Wang Bi's and therefore expressed strong doubts. In fact, it seems to come from a textual environment stressing the internal cultivation of the Dao by the individual. This is an aspect patently absent in Wang Bi's reading. Cf. my translation in note 6 to the translation of this *zhang*.

Zhang 5 Translation Notes

1. A similar formula in *Wenzi* 3.8, where the *Wenzi* quotes a saying: "Do not disturb and do not stir, and the ten thousand kinds of beings will become pure on their own accord. Do not frighten and do not shock, and the ten thousand kinds of beings will be regulated on their own accord. 萬物將自理 This is called the Way of Heaven." The surviving early commentators each read the first phrase "Heaven and Earth are not kindly" as being stated against an implied assumption of the reader. Zhuang Zun comments on this phrase: "Heaven is clear and bright due to its being high, Earth is moist and calm due to its being massive, *hou* 厚. The Yin [of Earth] and the Yang [of Heaven] interact, the Harmony, *he* 和, and the Ether, *qi* 氣, interflow [so that], while they [all] disinterestedly practice non-interference, the ten thousand entities are born on their own account, and there is no particular concern [of Heaven and Earth] which might be taken for kindliness and love." In his reading, the reader's assumption was that Heaven and Earth create all the ten thousand entities, and therefore were extremely "kindly"; against this assumption, the *Laozi* makes the shocking statement that they are not, and that they create the ten thousand entities by letting the natural process take its course. The *Xiang Er Commentary* reads: "Modeling themselves on the Dao, Heaven and Earth are kindly towards all those who are good, and not kindly towards all those who are evil. Thus [their] being not loving [a "translation" of "not kindly," *bu ren* 不仁], means that they exterminate the evil ones among the ten thousand entities, and regard them as worthless as grass and as dogs." This comment thus reads the *Laozi* statement against a reader's assumption that Heaven and Earth establish justice. Although the text is quite clear in its claim that Heaven and Earth are treating all ten thousand entities as grass and dogs, the *Xiang Er* introduces a distinction between good and evil ones. Extrapolating from the commentary, the main text has thus to be read as "Heaven and Earth [in their establishment of justice] are not kindly [towards all the ten thousand entities]. They treat [some of] the ten thousand entities as grass and dogs." The *Heshang gong Commentary* takes still another line. Commenting on the first sentence, it writes: "Heaven's initiating and Earth's generating does not happen by way of kindliness and favor, but by relying on [任 for 性] That-which-is-of-itself-what-it-is" [of the ten thousand entities]. Commenting on the phrase "they treat the ten thousand entities like grass and dogs," this commentary writes: "Heaven and Earth generate the ten thousand entities. [Among them] man is the most precious. That they regard [even man] as grass and dogs means that they do not expect any [gratitude] in return." Extrapolating from this commentary, the *Laozi* text has to be read as "Heaven and Earth [who create the ten thousand entities] are not kindly [towards even the most exalted among them]. They treat [all of] the ten thousand entities alike as [if they were not more exalted] than grass and dogs." For Wang Bi's commentary, the assumption of the *Laozi*'s implied reader concerning Heaven and Earth matches none of the three options described above [leaving aside the question of the *Heshang gong Commentary*'s date]. Here Heaven and Earth manage that "the ten thousand

kinds of entities order and regulate each other," so that, although the entities have many interactive relationships with each other, their order does not come about by interference with their own nature but by living out their own nature. In this way grass is not produced for cattle, but cattle will still eat the grass, and so on. The four commentators thus imply four rather different assumptions about Heaven and Earth in the reader's mind against which the *Laozi* statement has to be read. All of these assumptions were in fact present.

2. The variant 備載 in Liu Weiyong's text would be acceptable only if 備 were changed to 覆, "to cover." *Fu* 覆, "to cover," and *zai* 載, "to carry," describe the functions of Heaven and Earth, respectively (cf. Wang Bi on *Laozi* 4.1).

3. The modern Western translations have routinely translated *chu gou* 芻狗 as "straw dogs." Straw/grass dogs in fact appear in the Tianyun 天運 chapter of the *Zhuangzi* (*Zhuangzi yinde* 37/14/31 and 38/14/33). According to this passage, the grass dogs were made for a sacrifice; they were treated with great deference during the sacrifice and discarded directly afterward. Apart from Zhuang Zun, from whom no statement is known to survive which spells out his reading of this expression, the Xiang Er, Wang Bi, and Heshang gong commentaries all agree to read it as "grass and dogs." For the Xiang Er and Heshang gong commentaries, "grass and dogs" stands for something utterly worthless. Furthermore, the Xiang Er commentary gives quite a different story about the term. In the commentary to the next phrase of the *Laozi* about the Sage's not being kindly and treating the Hundred Families like grass and dogs, it writes: "Taking his model on Heaven and Earth, the Sage is kindly towards the good and not kindly towards the evil. As a king He will control and extirpate the evil ones, and also [like Heaven and Earth] regard them as being [as worthless and despicable] as grass and dogs. Therefore [true] human beings [the term *ren* 人 alone has this meaning in the Xiang Er commentary, who directly confronts it in the commentary on *Laozi* 17.4 with "grass dogs"] should accumulate merits of good [deeds]. Their spirit communicates with Heaven, and, should there be someone who wishes to attack or hurt them, Heaven will come to their rescue. The vulgar people [on the other hand] all belong to the category of grass and dogs. [Their] spirit cannot communicate with Heaven, because their harboring evil is like that of robbers and thieves who dare not meet eye to eye with an official. [In this way their] spirit will quite naturally not be close to Heaven [so that], when [they] come to a critical juncture between life and death, Heaven will not know them [and not come to their help]. The benevolent Sage Huangdi knew the minds of later generations [when mankind deteriorated and not every man was a true human being anymore]. Therefore he bound grass and made it into dogs and attached [the grass dogs] above the doors [of family houses]. [In this manner] he wanted to say that the 'doors' [families] of later generations would all belong to the category of grass and dogs [i.e., would be as worthless as grass and dogs]. People [however] did not understand the subtle intention of Huangdi [which was to warn them against becoming so worthless], and in a meaningless manner imitated him [in placing the grass dogs above their doors] without reforming their evil hearts. This may be called a great evil." In this reading, the grass/dogs are definitely not the sacrificial grass dogs but symbolic contraptions, where out

of worthless material a worthless animal is made as a symbol of utter worthlessness. It is quite unlikely that the above-quoted commentators were unaware of the existence of the statements about "grass dogs" in the *Zhuangzi, Huainanzi,* and elsewhere. In fact, Wang Bi had a copy of the Zhuangzi and quoted him often. The commentators thus opted for the "grass and dog" reading in full knowledge of the option of the ritual "grass dog," unanimously rejecting it. In fact, were one to read the passage as referring to the ritual grass dog, the *Laozi* would read, when translated into plain language, "Heaven and Earth are not kindly, they treat the ten thousand entities first as something very precious, and then discard them as worthless." There is to my knowledge not a single statement in the other parts of the *Laozi* that would confirm that this text assumed that there was such a change in the attitude of Heaven and Earth. The modern Western translators have thus opted for the "straw dog" version against both the inner evidence of the text and the unanimous opinion of the early commentators. Needless to say, Wang Bi also accepted the "grass and dog" reading but interpreted it differently. In his reading, they were entities manifestly related to others [who would consume them], so that these others might be considered beneficiaries of the kindliness of Heaven and Earth. He reads the *Laozi* here as arguing against this assumption.

4. The passage 若惠由己樹 has a variant reading 若慧由己樹. This would have to be read in the context of Wang Bi on *Laozi* 5.4, where the opposite of *shu* 樹, "to establish," is given with *qi* 棄, "to discard," both with *hui* 慧 as the object. The linkage seems contrived, however.

5. *Wenyan* on *Zhouyi* Hex. 1; cf. the same reference in Wang Bi on *Laozi* 77.1, and a reference to the *Zhouyi*'s Great Man in Wang Bi on *Laozi* 17.1. The *Mengzi* is also using the term *daren* 大人. Although in some cases it is just an important personality, he also uses it in a similar way as the *Wenyan*. "As to the Great Man, he is the one who has [all] beings rectified by way of rectifying himself" 大人者 正己而物正者也. Cf. J. Legge, *The Chinese Classics: The Works of Mencius,* Bk. VII.19, p. 458.

6. Li Lin, *Daode zhen jing qushan ji* 1.18a, quotes Wang Bi as continuing this commentary: "If [the Ruler-Sage] does not model himself after the emptiness and calm of Heaven and Earth to match the intentionlessness of the flute and the drum, does not follow [his] feelings when moving, nor adapt to the occasion when speaking, his movements [and words] will diverge from reality. Therefore [the text] says: 'The reasoning will come to naught.' This [above attitude] cannot compare to internally cherishing *dao* and *de* and embracing the One without fretting. Therefore [the text says,] 'Keep to the middle.'"

7. *Guodian Chu mu zhujian,* p. 5.

Zhang 6 Numbered Text Note

1. Because 陸德明釋文 does not quote Wang Bi's 中央無谷 in full, but only 中央無 and then provides an alternative reading for the 無, Yi Shunding 易順鼎 argues that the commentary stopped here. Lu Deming gives a comment under the *Laozi* term 谷, which is 中央無者. Yi suggests that this actually is Wang Bi's commentary. I cannot agree with Yi Shunding's assumption that "the meaning [of 谷神谷中央無谷] is not understandable." Wang Bi has used quite a few daring terms to craft his new thinking, such as 無物.

Zhang 6 Translation Notes

1. Cf. Wang Bi on *Zhouyi* 2.11a.5: "'Spirit [as mentioned in the preceding *Zhouyi* sentence] is that which is formless."

2. This expression *zhiwu* 至物, "highest entity," seems to be a neologism of the middle of the third century; it also occurs in Xi Kang, "Yangsheng lun," 養生論 *Xi Kang ji jiaozhu*, 155: "It is a fact that the highest entity is subtle and recondite; it is possible to discern it by means of the ordering principle [which it supports] but it is hard to know it with one's eyes" 夫至物微妙可以理知難以目識.

3. This certainly looks like an unhappy translation. The natural rendering would be that "door" should be that from which the Dark Female "emerges." The term *you* 由, however, is consistently used in Wang Bi as "condition for the possibility of." The shift is transferring an ontogenetic concept into an ontological one.

4. For a comparative study of the way in which different early commentators read this chapter, see my *The Craft of a Chinese Commentator*, 209–30.

Zhang 7 Translation Notes

1. Wang Bi quotes these two passages in his commentary on *Laozi* 41.4 and the latter passage alone on *Laozi* 28.1.

2. The absence of such personal interests also is extracted from a statement made about Confucius in *Lunyu* 9.4 according to He Yan's reading. Among the four things that the master wholly eschews, the fourth is called *wuwo* 毋我 "he rejects personal [interests]." He Yan comments: "[According to *Lunyu* 7.1 Confucius says of himself that] he 'hands down' antiquity and 'does not make up [things]' himself; he resides amongst the masses and does not make himself stand out; it is only the Way that he follows; that is why he does not hold on to his person" 故不有其身 (Lunyu jijie 9.11a).

Zhang 8 Numbered Text Note

1. Li Lin's 取善集 2.3b here quotes a commentary by Wang Bi not reported elsewhere: 爲政之善無穢無偏如水之治至清至平. The reliability of the 取善集 is undermined by the fact that this is the second in a total of three passages hitherto quoted from Wang Bi, not repeated elsewhere. In terms of content, its general drift would agree with Wang Bi. However, if Wang Bi's overall commentary to this last line in *Laozi* 8 is genuine, the subject would remain the "water." The commentary given by the 取善集, however, presupposes a direct application to a ruler, and thus a reading of 人 in the commentary, which seems quite definitely to be a later change. I therefore agree with Hatano Tarō and do not include this comment in Wang Bi's *Commentary*. For a translation, see note 2 in the translation of this *zhang*.

Zhang 8 Translation Notes

1. The term ji 幾, "close to something ultimate," is used in a similar sense in the *Xici* 下 4. Wang Bi's formula in his commentary on *Laozi* 32.1, that the "uncarved," *pu* 樸, is "close to not having [any specific feature at all]" 近於無有, expresses the same concept.

2. Li Lin. *Daode zhen jing qushan ji* quotes a Wang Bi commentary after this line: "The excellency in handling government consists in being unsullied and without partiality, just as well-regulatedness in water consists in supreme cleanness and perfect evenness." For the argument against accepting this quotation, cf. note 1 in the edition of this *zhang*.

Zhang 9 Translation Note

1. Cf. *Shiji*, 79.2419. "In the sequence of the four seasons, the [season] that has completed its task departs" 四時之序成功者去.

Zhang 10 Numbered Text Note

1. The term 知 is taken up in the commentary in the form 智. This is unusual for Wang Bi. However, only 陸德明釋文 mentions one 河上公 text that writes 智, and there is no textual tradition anywhere writing 智 in a Wang Bi *Laozi* in this *Laozi* passage. I have resigned myself to accept 智 as Wang's interpretation of the 知 of the text, already suggested in 陸德明釋文 with the statement there that

the pronunciation for 知 is 智. Wang Bi's interpretation is based on *Laozi* 65.3 故以智治國國之賊也.

Zhang 10 TRANSLATION NOTES

1. In *Laozi* 22.6, the person to naturally "hold on to the One" is the Sage.

2. Similar formulas in Wang Bi on *Laozi* 5.2, 17.4, 18.2, and 49.5; the text there reads 避 for 辟.

3. The formula 由從 is also used in Wang Bi on *Laozi* 52.3, where the terms 兌 and 門 are being defined: 兌事欲之所由生門事欲之所由從也. From this use, it is clear that the 由 is subordinate to the 從, not parallel.

4. A similar formula in Wang Bi on *Laozi* 68.2.

5. The same formula appears verbatim in *Laozi* 51.4 ff., but there subjects are attached to the verbs in texts 10.7 and 10.8. In *LZWZLL* 5.8 ff., Wang Bi takes up this entire passage as a core piece for the explanation of the Dao/Xuan relationship. Cf. the structural analysis of this *zhang* below.

Zhang 11 TRANSLATION NOTES

1. Zheng Xuan paved the ground for this commentary. In his commentary to the notion of the hub 轂 in the section 輪人 in the *Zhouli* 周禮, he wrote: "A hub has its not having anything [in it] as its usefulness" 轂以無有爲用也. *Zhouli zhushu*, 39.269 (= p. 907c). Kong Yingda links Zheng Xuan's commentary in his subcommentary to *Laozi* 11. The expression *tong zhong* 統衆, "control the many," also occurs in Wang Bi on *Laozi* 41.13.

2. Cf. the passage in Wang Bi on *Laozi* 1.4, where the formula runs: 凡有之爲利 必以無爲用. See also Wang Bi on *Laozi* 40.1 有以無爲用.

Zhang 12 NUMBERED TEXT NOTE

1. Hatano Tarō has suggested reading 爲目者以物役己 instead of the 爲目者以目役己 of the 集註本. In support of this reading, which is shared by the 永樂大典本 and others, the parallel between 以物養己 and 以物役己 can be adduced. A check of the uses of 役 in Wang Bi's writings, however, suggests that this term is regularly used with cognition, as in Wang Bi on *Laozi* 38.1 役其智力以營庶事 and 役其聰明. I therefore accept the 集註本 reading.

Zhang 12 TRANSLATION NOTE

1. In Wang Bi, the term *xing ming* 性命 is identical to the term *xing* 性 and denotes the eternal nature of men and other entities. Cf. Wang Bi on *Laozi* 16.5 and *Zhouyi, Shuogua* 2, 49: "In antiquity, in their composing the *[Zhou]yi*, the Sages went by the ordering principle of following the true nature" [of the entities they were describing]. 昔者聖人之作易也將以順性命之理.

Zhang 13 NUMBERED TEXT NOTES

1. This passage clearly shows the close relationship within the textual family to which Wang Bi's *Laozi* text belongs. Although there are numerous graphic variants, the basic grid is largely the same, and the deviations against other textual traditions such as the 想爾 (寵辱若驚貴大患若身 何謂寵辱爲下得之若驚 . . .), which leaves out the three characters 若驚寵 before 爲下, and the Heshang gong (Dunhuang manuscript: 寵辱若驚貴大患若身何謂寵辱辱爲下得之若驚), which replaces the 若驚寵 with the term 辱, so that the startling thing is reduced to imperial disgrace, are markedly larger. The passage is one of the few points where Shima Kuniō has been disproved. His assumption that the Wang Bi text must have been closer to the Xiang Er and Heshang gong traditions has led him to suggest—against Lu Deming and Fu Yi—to drop the 若驚寵. The Mawangdui manuscripts, however, which had not been discovered when he published his study, have shown that the Fu Yi version in fact represents a solid early tradition, while the Guodian B text has shown that the 寵爲下, with an elimination of the previous 若驚 also is a solid option.

Zhang 13 TRANSLATION NOTE

1. Both Mawangdui manuscripts insert 之 after the phonetic graphs *long* 龍 and *nong* 弄 that they use for the modern text's 寵, "bestowing favor." This 之 brings out the transitive nature of this "bestowing" and sets off the Sage Ruler's "bestowing favor" from "those below" 爲下, who clearly are the subject of the following phrase and not the object of the "bestowing favor." Although I find no textual evidence that Wang Bi also had the 之 in his text, he clearly read the grammar in the same manner as the Mawangdui manuscripts.

Zhang 14 TRANSLATION NOTES

1. Similar statements are found in Wang Bi *LZWZLL* 1.46 and in Wang Bi on *Laozi* 21.6, 47.1, and 65.4.

2. The same argument is made in *LZWZLL* 1.46 and Han Kangbo on *Xici* 下 3.

Zhang 15 Numbered Text Notes

1. The 取善集 alone quotes the following Wang Bi *Commentary* after this last phrase: 王弼曰: 藏精匿炤外不異物波塵故曰若濁. I agree with Hatano Tarō, that neither terminology nor content fit this ascription to Wang Bi.

2. This commentary passage is not quoted in the 集註本. The oldest surviving text after it is the 永樂大典本.

3. This commentary passage is not quoted in the 集註本. The oldest surviving text after it is the 永樂大典本.

Zhang 15 Translation Notes

1. Through the term 兆, Wang Bi links this statement to *Laozi* 20.4 "I am vacant without clues [for others to recognize me], like a baby that has not yet started to smile."

2. My punctuation here deviates from that suggested by Shima Kuniō. He cuts before the 物 in all phrases; this gives 夫晦以理, 物則得明, 濁以靜, 物而得清, and so on. I read the 物 here in the commentary phrases as a specification of the 之 in the *Laozi* phrases, such as 孰能濁以靜之而徐清. Consequently, the break should be after 物.

3. Cf. Wang Bi on *Laozi* 4.1 and 9.1.

4. The term *fu* 覆, used to explain the *bi* 蔽 of the text, seems to be used in the meaning it has in *Laozi* 51.4.

Zhang 16 Numbered Text Notes

1. The Mawangdui/Guodian tradition strongly suggests 天物 here. As Lu Deming explicitly gave 凡 as Wang Bi's reading and there is no evidence from Wang Bi himself, I have followed Lu Deming.

2. Shi Huilin 釋慧琳 (737–820), 一切經音義, T. 2128 j. 8, p. 350a, quotes Wang Bi's *Commentary* with the words 根始也. They are not found in the present texts and might originally be part of this commentary passage. It is not clear where the passage was originally attached. Cf. Hatano Tarō, p. 74.

3. 李善, 文選雜體詩注 31.30b quotes elements from Wang Bi's *Commentary* on *Laozi* 16.3–16.5. Wang Bi's reconstructed text will be set in parenthesis after each passage where it deviates: 凡有起於虛動於靜 (動起於靜) 故萬物離并動作 (萬物雖并動作) 卒復歸於虛靜 (om: 是物之極篤也) 各反其始 (各反其所始) 歸根則靜也 (歸根則靜).

Zhang 16 TRANSLATION NOTES

1. This *zhang* is not written in IPS. The use of the graphic writing here only serves the purpose of optically linking the commentary to the notions of the main text in the first part.

2. In this commentary, Wang Bi indicates with the *yan* 言 that he is rephrasing the *Laozi* formula with more elaborate grammar and vocabulary to reduce ambivalence. We thus have to expect the full content and grammatical structure of Laozi 16.1 in this comment. The *ye* 也 in the end marks at least the second phrase as a defining phrase of the type A B 也. Via parallelism, the same can be assumed for the first phrase. This makes *ji* 極 and *du* 篤 into verbal nouns and leads to my translation as well as to accepting the MWD A, B and *Wenzi* 也 at the end of both phrases as Wang Bi's text (against the different reading of Fu Yi and Fan Yingyuan). Its viability is confirmed by the restating of *Laozi* 16.1–3 in the commentary on 16.3. There the phrasing 卒復歸於虛靜是物之極篤也, their "return in the end to emptiness and stillness is the ultimate and the core of entities," confirms the AB 也 construction with the grammar 復歸 ... 是 ... 極篤也 and evidently replaces with 復歸 the more unwieldy 致 and 守 of the first sentence as verbs preceding 虛 and 篤. The large textual tradition for Wang Bi writing 言致虛物之極篤 is not convincing. The 篤 belongs to the second part of 16.1 and cannot be used to comment on the first part. Li Shan's quotation without 篤, namely 言至虛之極 也, is definitely more convincing in this point although it lacks the necessary 物 and a second word to form a pair matching the 真正 from the second part. While there is no way to supplement this character, Li Shan's reading must be preferred because 極 and 篤 reoccur together in Wang Bi on 16.3 not as a binominal but in a clear reference to their separate use in the text of 16.1. There is authority for linking *jing* 靜 with *zheng* 正 in *Laozi* 45.6 "pure calmness [of the ruler] is the correct regulative for All Under Heaven 清靜爲天下正." The term *zheng* 正 is usually associated in the *Laozi* with interventionist government methods, cf. *Laozi* 58.4, where the consequence of a government by *zheng* is the use of the military. The term in this sense corresponds to its use in *Xunzi*, where it denotes regulations together with *fa* 法. The statement in *Laozi* 45.6 清靜爲天下正 "[But only a ruler's] pure calmness is the correct regulative for All Under Heaven!" is read as a polemic against the conventional notion of *zheng*. In the present commentary passage, the term *zhen zheng* 真正 is used in the sense of *Laozi* 45.3 to which it actually refers.

3. The passage 夫物芸芸, 各歸其根 is parallelled by a passage in the *Zhuangzi* 萬物芸芸, 各復其根, *Zhuangzi yinde* 28/11/55.

4. In his commentary to *zhang* 55.6 and 55.7, Wang Bi also reads *Laozi*'s 曰 as 則; in his commentary to *Laozi* he "translates" it as 乃, which is similar.

5. The same passage occurs in *Laozi* 55.6. See the translation of the commentary there. Wang Bi treats the term *chang* 常, "the eternal," in the *LZWZLL* 1.47 ff. in a passage very close to his commentary here.

6. Should the emendation 唯 to 知 not be accepted, the *ci* 此 would have to be read as a reference to the 知常, not to 常 alone. The translation would then be "only with this [knowledge of the Eternal] is he able indeed..." and "once he fails to have this" [knowledge of the Eternal].

7. Wang Bi inserts a treatise on the origin of evil into his *LZWZLL* 6.2ff.

8. The expression, "immeasurable," is close to the expression Kongzi used to express his admiration for Yao in *Lunyu* 8.19: "Immeasurable he is so that none of the people were able to give a name to him" [= define him] 蕩蕩乎民無能名焉. Wang Bi comments the 蕩蕩: "It is an appellation for [something] without shape and name." *Wang Bi ji jiaoshi*, 626.

9. Strangely, the commentary does not repeat the term *wang* 王 here or in the next commentary but in both cases uses *zhou pu* 周普. This would imply *zhou* 周 instead of *wang* in Wang Bi's *Laozi* text, a suggestion made by Ma Xulun, *Laozi jiaogu*, 201. Hatano Tarō quotes Lao Jian's 勞健 remark that the rhyme between *rong* and *gong* in the preceding sentences and the rhyme between *dao* and *jiu* in the sentences following would require a rhyme also in the sentences in between, but the *wang* and the *tian* do not rhyme. He therefore suggests *quan* 全 instead of *wang*, because it rhymes with *tian*; cf. Hatano Tarō, *Rōshi Ō chu kōsei*, 117. The second explanation cannot stand because, again, the new term suggested does not appear in the commentary; the first explanation, although with merit, is not supported by a single transmitted text, and Wang Bi does not explicitly claim that *zhou* appeared in the main text. In his commentary to the *Zhouyi* hexagram *song* 訟, Wang Bi links the notion of the king, *wang*, and public-mindedness, *gong*, *Wang Bi ji jiaoshi* I.251, in a comment on a lord occupying the fifth position. I therefore retained the *textus receptus*.

10. Cf. Wang Bi on *Laozi* 5.2: "The Sage [as the Wenyan to the unbroken line in the fifth position of the first hexagram of the *Zhouyi* says of the Great Man] 'harmonizing his capacity/receipt with [that of] Heaven and Earth . . .'" The formula here 與天合德 is somewhat pared down from the 與天地合其德 in the Wenyan.

11. For the expression *tidao* 體道, "to embody the Way," cf. my *The Craft of a Chinese Commentator*, pp. 129–30.

12. Cf. note 12 to the translation of *zhang* 25 for a study of the meaning of the term 窮極. It also appears in Wang Bi on *Laozi* 25.8 and 40.2, in both cases denoting "reaching to the end" or "penetrating to the utmost." But in the expression "its [the Dao's] being used cannot exhaust it" in Wang Bi on *Laozi* 35.3, the meaning emerges that I have preferred here.

13. A case can be made for a reading of 道 for the 物 here, which would give "Eternal of the Way." This reading is given by the 張之象本. In the last sentence of *Laozi* 52, the text says: "If he [the ruler] makes use of his enlightenment and withdraws his intelligence, he does not attract disaster to himself. This I call 'being in agreement with the Eternal.'" Wang Bi comments on this last segment: "[That is with] the Eternal of the Way." Thus the evasion of danger and misfortune for the

Sage's person is linked to his being in unison with the Eternal of the Way, which is the context we have here in *Laozi* 16.

14. The text is not satisfactory here, because the repetition of the expression 窮極 does not sound plausible. Obviously what is to be explained is the expression 久. Under this assumption, the 張之象本 gives a reading 至於不有極, "will get to the point of not having an ultimate point." While more satisfying than the earlier texts, I consider it an emendation, which also is unsatisfactory because no link between 久 and 不有極 is visible elsewhere in Wang Bi.

Zhang 17 TRANSLATION NOTES

1. *Zhouyi*, Hex. 1, nine in the fifth position:

Aflight the dragon rests in the Heavens. [They] have the benefit of seeing the Great Man. 飛龍在天利見大人

Wang Bi comments: "As [the dragon] neither acts [in the manner he does in the third position], nor wavers [in the manner he does in the fourth position because both are only transitional on his way to the supreme fifth position], but [simply] 'rests in' the Heavens 在天, how else should he do this but by 'being aflight?' That is why [the text] says: 'Aflight the dragon [rests in Heaven].' As the dragon has achieved being in the Heavens, the road of the Great Man has reached [the goal]. Generally speaking, the position [in this highest rank] is brought to flourish by [his] capacity, *de* 德, and [his] capacity is brought to fruition by [his] position. It is by means of supreme capacity, *zhi de* 至德, that he occupies the grandest position. Is it not appropriate that the ten thousand entities go to 'look' [at him as the *Wenyan* to this line claims]?" (*Wang Bi ji jiaoshi* I.212). Lou Yulie, followed by Lynn, misreads the 之 as meaning 往, "to go to."

The *Wenyan* commentary to this line reads: "'Aflight the dragon rests in the Heavens. [They] have the benefit of seeing the Great Man' [says the *Zhouyi*]—what does this mean? The Master answered: 'Sounds of the same kind correspond to each other; ethers of the same kind seek each other out. Water flows to what is wet; fire turns to what is dry. Clouds follow the dragon; wind follows the tiger. Once the Sage is going about [in the highly visible position of the ruler being as high in the fifth position as if he were 'in the Heavens'], the ten thousand kinds of entities perceive [him with the consequence that] those rooted in Heaven will associate with things above, those rooted in Earth, will associate with things below so that each follows its own kind'" (*Wang Bi ji jiaoshi* I.215).

The *Wenyan* thus defines the Great Man in the fifth position as the Sage. The Wilhelm/Baynes translation of *li jian daren* 利見大人, "it furthers one to see the great man," is inappropriately prescriptive. The Wenyan sentence "the ten thousand kinds of entities perceive him" in fact interprets and translates the *li jian* 利見 and thus forces the translation: "[They] have the benefit of seeing the Great Man." This identification of the Great Man with the Sage in turn justifies the quotation from *Laozi* 2.2, the subject of which is the Sage. Wang Bi reads the hierarchy descending from the Great Man in *Laozi* 17.1 to the ruler in 17.4 who is not taken seriously by his subjects as parallel to the hierarchy in *Laozi* 38. There a qualitative difference is marked between the rulers of "supreme capacity" 上德 and those of "lower capacity" 下德. Wang Bi's commentary to the fifth line of the first hexagram refers to this type of ruler with the variant expression "supreme capacity" 至德 in the sentence: "It is by means of supreme capacity that he [the Great Man] occupies the grandest position." In this manner it also becomes clear that Wang Bi identified the Great [Man] 大 of *Laozi* 17.1 with the man of "supreme capacity," *shang de* 上德, of *Laozi* 38, who in this very chapter is himself referred to as the Great Man 大丈夫 and described in the commentary through a quotation from the *Zhouyi*, which there pertains to the Sage. Another quotation pertaining to the Great Man in the first hexagram of the *Zhouyi* is used to comment on the Sage in Wang Bi on *Laozi* 5.2 and *Laozi* 77.1, confirming the merging of the Great Man and the Sage.

2. Wang Bi reads the descending hierarchy of *Laozi* 17.2–17.4 as similar to the one established in *Laozi* 38. The expression "establishing the good," *li shan* 立善, is there linked to the highest rank within those of "lower capacity," *xia de* 下德, that is, those who make use of "kindliness," *ren* 仁. Cf. p. 243. This identification is confirmed by the commentary on *Laozi* 17.3, which says that the protagonist of the present phrase acts "by means of kindness and humaneness."

3. The expression "might and power" does not occur in the text or commentary of *Laozi* 38, with which Wang Bi links the hierarchy presented here. In the next commentary, this government technique is described as "regulating the people by means of laws and regulations," which corresponds well with what is said in the commentary on *Laozi* 38 on ruling by *yi* 義 and *li* 禮. Cf. p. 244–245.

4. The terms *fa* 法 and *zheng* 正 appear together in Wang Bi's polemics against the Legalists in the *LZWZLL* 2, as well as in some of the commentaries. The option to invert the awkward 法以正 into 以法正 might take up this use of 法正 in *Xunzi* 23 (cf. Wang Xianqian, *Xunzi jijie*, 2.440: "Because the Sages of old saw man's nature as evil, . . . they established for them the power of rulers in order to be close to them, made clear ritual and justice in order to transform them, set up laws and regulations in order to regulate them" 起法正以治之 . . .), but does not fit the parallel in the second half of the phrase 以智治國, which requires a single noun after 以, not two.

5. In the commentary on *Laozi* 38, Wang Bi identifies the ruler who rules by "foresight," as someone who "exhausts his intelligence" and "applies the powers of his knowledge" 役其智力. The people then are said to learn to be cunning to evade him. This is the very argument made here in Wang Bi on *Laozi* 17.4. Cf. *Lunyu* 2.2.

6. This reading is reinforced by the implicit reference to *Lunyu* 13.4, where Confucius gives a series of three statements showing that the people will echo the attitude of their rulers. "If the man at the top loves ritual, none among the people will dare to be disrespectful. If the man at the top loves righteousness, none among the people will dare to be disobedient. If the man at the top loves credibility, none among the people will dare not to make use of his honest feelings." The *Laozi*

statement argues similarly but stresses the negative effects of a lack of credibility in the ruler upon the people.

7. A parallel passage to this last phrase is in *Guanyin zi* 關尹子, chapter *San ji* 三極, page 6b. "The Sage does not bring order to All Under Heaven by means of his own self; he brings order to All Under Heaven by means of All under Heaven. All Under Heaven attributes this achievement to the Sage, but the Sage transfers this achievement to All under Heaven. That is why when Yao, Shun, Yu, and Tang brought order to All Under Heaven, [people] in All Under Heaven all said '[this is so] as something which is of itself what it is.'"

8. The formula "It is impossible to perceive any clues [in] his [expression], and it is impossible to make out [his] intentions" has been used by Wang Bi on *Laozi* 15.2 to describe the inscrutability of "man with supreme capacity" 上德之人 for the four neighbors intent on attacking him. The term of the "clues" 兆 is taken from the description of the baby in *Laozi* 20.4. The expression 上德 is taken from *Laozi* 38, and the person endowed with this supreme capacity is there identified by Wang Bi as identical to the Sage. The first section of the commentary here in 17.6 ends with the repetition of the formula: "That is why [the text] says 'Undecided he is! [But] his words are being respected [by those below].'" This means that this first part of the comment only explains this first phrase of the *Laozi* text but not the subsequent phrases. The term *ziran* 自然, however, which all surviving editions place at the beginning of this commentary instead of the 猶兮 suggested by me, only occurs at the end of these subsequent phrases and is explained in the end of this commentary. It is therefore out of place here. The commentary here in fact explains the expression *you xi* 猶兮.

9. This interprets the term *gui* 貴 in the main text; in a similar fashion, the expression *gui shen* 貴身 is interpreted in Wang Bi on *Laozi* 13.5.

10. For this last thought, cf. Chapter 2 in my *Language, Ontology, and Political Philosophy*.

Zhang 18 Translation Notes

1. In the descending scale of philosophical values used by a ruler in his ordering of society, this formula always comes after the Dao is lost; cf. Wang Bi on *Laozi* 5.1 and 17.2.

2. The relationship between a ruler's surveillance apparatus and the subsequent development of evasiveness among the subjects is treated more in detail in Wang Bi's treatise on the origin of evil in *LZWZLL* 6.2ff. See also chapter 3 in my *Language, Ontology, and Political Philosophy*.

3. Cf. Wang Bi on *Laozi* 2.1.

4. See Textual Notes p.

Zhang 19 Numbered Text Note

1. Wang Bi identifies the object of 令 in 令有所屬 as 人, saying 令人有所屬. Within the *Laozi*, the object of 令 is what Wang Bi's textual family describes as 民. Wang Bi's use of 人 instead of 民 suggests the possibility that his text read 人利百倍 and 人復孝慈 instead of 民利百倍 and 民復孝慈. This option is present in two manuscripts of the 想爾 tradition, namely, the 次解本 and the Li Rong's 李榮 edition in the *Daozang*. Because none of the texts in Wang Bi's textual family presents this option, and it is not marked as a special feature of Wang Bi's text by Lu Deming or Fan Yingyuan, I have left the 民 in the text.

Zhang 19 Translation Notes

1. For the argument assigning this third item to "craftiness and profit," see the note on the structure of this *zhang*.

2. For an analysis of this *zhang* and its rhetoric, see my "The Impact of Conceptions of Rhetoric and Style upon the Formation of the Early *Laozi* Editions: Evidence from Guodian, Mawangdui and the Wang Bi *Laozi*," pp. 50–55.

Zhang 20 Numbered Text Note

1. The 集註本 as well as the 永樂大典本 give 孩 in Wang Bi's *Commentary* here. 陸德明釋文, the 傅奕古本, the 范應元本 as well as 馬王堆 A and 馬王堆 B all read 咳 for the *Laozi* text here, although 陸德明釋文 mentions one text with 孩. The modern *Laozi* texts transmitted over the Wang Bi commentary, however, all read 孩. I therefore assume that the original 咳 in Wang's commentary has been adapted to the changed 孩 in the *Laozi*.

Zhang 20 Translation Notes

1. The *zhang* has a distinct speaker who uses "I" to talk about himself. As Wang Bi assumed the text to be written by a historical person, Laozi, it would be natural to assume that in his eyes the "I" would refer to Laozi if not otherwise specified. In the present case, it is interesting to see that the "I," while claiming to be unrecognizable, also notes a certain deficiency when saying in the last phrase "I desire to be different from the others," which might imply that this desire has not now been fully realized. For the entire question of the speaker and the related question of the implied subject, cf. my *The Craft of a Chinese Commentator*, pp. 120–150.

2. The meaning of the pair 唯/阿 is still under discussion. From the presence of the 善/惡 pair, one would expect a harsh contrast. Mawangdui A writes 訶, which is defined in the *Shuowen* as "shouting angrily 大言而怒也." Wang Bi does not give guidance. I assume he followed a contrastive reading.

3. The same phrase in Wang Bi on *Laozi* 2.2.

4. Cf. *Zhuangzi yinde* 21/8/9. "What is long, has no surplus; what is short, is not lacking [anything]. That is the reason why, although a duck's foot is short, stretching it would cause grief and, although a crane's neck is long, shortening it would cause suffering." See also Wang Bi's commentary on hexagram *sun* 損: "It is the essence of That-which-is-of-itself-what-it-is to fix for each its allotment 分. What [has an allotment to] be short cannot be taken as lacking [in something]; what [has an allotment to] be long cannot be taken as having a surplus; what accordingly will reducing [the latter] and adding [to the former] contribute?" [Nothing] (*Wang Bi ji jiaoshi*, 422).

5. For the translation of the term *zhongren* 衆人, see the analysis in my *The Craft of a Chinese Commentator*, pp. 128–29.

6. The two sections in this commentary seem to refer to the two elements addressed in the text, the Tailao sacrifice and going up a terrace in spring. However, I lack indicators to link the corresponding sections.

7. Cf. the use of the term 猶然 in *Laozi* 17.6 and Wang Bi's commentary there.

Zhang 21 Numbered Text Note

1. The members of Wang Bi's textual family all have these two phrases in the inverted order with 象 in the first, and 物 in the second half. The two surviving early Wang Bi commentaries are identical, but both seem corrupted, reading 恍兮惚兮惚兮恍兮其中有象也. Independent of the reading of 恍, which Li Shan quotes as 怳, it is clear that this fragment presupposes a sequence of 物 and 象. Yu Yue 俞樾 first suggested supplementing 其中有物 in Wang's commentary after the 恍兮惚兮. This has been accepted by Hatano Tarō and Shima Kuniō. In fact, there is a textual tradition with the sequence 物–象/像; the *Xiang Er* manuscript gives this sequence as does the *Daozang* manuscript of the *Heshang gong*. I have therefore accepted the very unusual dissociation of the Wang Bi *Laozi* from its own tradition in this case.

Zhang 21 Translation Notes

1. The formula X 之爲物 is well attested elsewhere with the meaning "X as such" to be followed by a definition. Wang Bi also uses it in this manner in his

comments on *Laozi* 16.6 for *chang* 常, 16.13 for *wu* 無, and in 32.1 for *pu* 樸. In the present case, there is a problem in the light of Wang Bi on *Laozi* 21.3. There Wang says that the Way initiates and completes entities 始物, 成物 by means of its being without shape and unfettered. For this "initiating" and "completing" of "entities," there is no direct textual basis in this chapter, so I have toyed with the violent idea of translating the 道之爲物 as "the Dao's acting on entities." However, in Wang Bi's definition, Dao is only an appellation for this very "initiating and completing," therefore, this information is already contained in the term. The formula 爲物 is furthermore used for the Dao in the beginning of the *LZWZLL* in a series 爲物, 爲象, 爲音, 爲味, where the *wei* 爲 clearly means "as a . . . "

2. The same expression is in Wang Bi on *Laozi* 32.1.

3. The same two-step genesis appears in Wang Bi on *Laozi* 1.2.

4. Li Shan on *Wenxuan* 22.28.b5 quotes this passage replacing the 歎, "sigh," with a 貌, "figurative expression" that has been accepted by Lou Yulie, who is inconsistent, however, by not suggesting the same change for the commentaries on 21.2 and 20.2. In the *LZWZLL* 2.10 ff., Wang Bi himself speaks about "those who sigh about it" 歎 in their helpless attempt to express the beauty of the Dao. This has prompted me to reject Lou's suggestion. The two terms *shen* 深 and *yuan* 遠 are taken from *Laozi* 65.4, where the phrase runs 玄德深矣遠矣, "the capacity coming from That-which-is-Dark is deep, is distant." As predicates of aspects of the "That-by-which," they appear in *LZWZLL* 2.24 and 2.26.

5. The Li Shan quotation mentioned in the previous note here contains an important variant 不可 for 其可. If accepted, this would prompt a translation: "it is not possible to perceive it [the deep and abstruse] by way of determining its true" [nature]. I do not think that this was Wang Bi's text. Pragmatically, the statement would only repeat what has been said directly before, namely, that it is impossible to perceive the deep and distant. This would be very atypical for Wang Bi. In terms of Wang Bi's philosophy, the reading preferred by me here links up with many other statements by Wang Bi about the fact that the "That-by-which" of the entities is shining forth in and through them as the condition of their possibility; cf. my *Language, Ontology, and Political Philosophy*, Chapter 2. The main purpose of the *Laozi* phrase in Wang Bi's construction was to make sure that, although the Dao is not perceivable, it is discernable indirectly in some of its aspects from the "essence" or "semen" present in the ten thousand kinds of entities.

6. In slightly varying forms, this expression recurs often in Wang Bi's writings; cf. Wang Bi on *Laozi* 14.5, 34.2, 37.2, 51.1 and 51.2, *LZWZLL* passim.

7. The translation of *wu ming* 無名 here not as "the nameless" but as "namelessness" rests on two grounds. First, Wang Bi uses *wu ming* as a noun related to the Way. In the commentary on 1.2, for example, he says 道以無形無名始成 "the Way begins and completes the ten thousand kinds of entities by means of [its] featurelessness and namelessness." Second, the namelessness is a necessary feature of the Way, not a deficiency of man or language to be made up one day.

8. In *LZWZLL* 1.49–51, Wang Bi comments on this phrase in a similar manner.

9. This phrase is based on *Laozi* 40.3 and recurs in Wang Bi's writings; cf. Wang Bi on *Laozi* 1.3. See also Han Kangbo on *Zhouyi, Xici*, 7.9.b3ff. See, for the analysis, my *Language, Ontology, and Political Philosophy*, Chapter 2.

Zhang 22 Translation Notes

1. This sentence is quoted in full as Wang Bi's commentary on *Laozi* 73.5.

2. The last phrase does not carry a commentary and is difficult to understand. *Gui* 歸 is regularly used by Wang Bi in two contexts, one the "relating back" or "return" to the "root" or "One," the other All Under Heaven's or the ten thousand kinds of entities' "rendering" themselves to the Sage Ruler. As the context here is that of the Sage applying the "Way of That-which-is-of-itself-what-it-is" in his own action, the second reading is preferable.

Zhang 23 Numbered Text Notes

1. For the reasons I have retained the duplication of 道者 against the opinion of all scholars consulted, cf. note 2 to the translation.

2. 服部悔庵 quotes the 臧疏 with a Wang Bi commentary to this *Laozi* passage: 順教返俗 所爲從於道兼忘衆累與空虛合體謂之同道道則應之. I agree with Hatano Tarō, that this commentary passage does not fit Wang Bi's commentary style.

Zhang 23 Translation Notes

1. Wang Bi quotes this passage verbatim in his commentary on *Laozi* 30.7. There he compares the cyclone and cloudburst with ruling the empire by armed might, which "is by necessity not on the Way" and "quickly finished."

2. The *Huainan zi* quotes the phrase 故從事於道者道者同於道 of the *textus receptus* without the duplication of *daozhe* 道者, a reading reinforced by both Mawangdui manuscripts and preferred by many scholars, including Wei Yuan, Hatano Tarō, and Shima Kuniō. In the extant Wang Bi commentary, there is no direct trace of such a duplication, which seems to have carried over from the Heshang gong text. The Fu Yi edition, which is otherwise closely related to Wang Bi's *Laozi*, offers a very explicit text for the duplicated reading by repeating not only the *congshi yu* 從事於 but adding this also for the *dezhe* 德者 and the *shizhe* 失者, which then gives a different meaning. However, the *zhang* in its entirety

suffers from very uneven transmission, and all scholars have operated with a lot of emendations, as the main text manifestly does not correspond to Wang's commentary. In the two following phrases, 得者同於得 and 失者同於失, we would have a rigid parallel to 道者同於道. Read in this way, the first segment 故從事於道者 ... (That is why, if [the Sage] handles things [in accordance with] the Way, ...) would be the general condition under which the three subsequent sentences operate and in fact could be repeated before each one of them. This reading would require a double proof, namely, a commentary confirmation of the general nature of the first segment (That is why, if [the Sage] handles things [in accordance with] the Way, ...), and second, a statement in text or commentary that made it clear that all three phrases in fact are meaningful under the general condition of the Sage Ruler's running affairs according to the Way. The first part of the commentary for 23.3 provides the first proof, the text 23.6 the second. The transitive translation of *tong* 同 as "makes [them] identical [with]" follows this line of thinking. Within the commentary it is based on the phrase "so that the other entities [all] achieve their true [nature]," which indicates that the Sage's practicing of the Way in his government will have this effect.

3. The phrasing here, 從事謂舉動從事於道者也, is odd, because it actually presupposes that the main text only had 從事, which then is explained with the words following. A repetition of the 從事 itself with the explanation is possible, but it is unique that the entire 從事於道者 should be repeated in a definition. The textual transmission of the 於道者 is solid, but both MWD A and B simply write 從事而 and then start the series 道者同於道 ... (i.e., they do not have the 於道者). I do not know what to make of this, because, in terms of content, the 於道者 certainly fits into Wang Bi's text. Could it be that his text lacked the 於道者, but that he knew it from other copies and indicated in this manner that he agreed with this interpretation?

4. The commentary does not make the object of *de* 得, "attaining," and *shi* 失, "losing," clear. From the explicit parallel with *Laozi* 22.5, I would assume that the object of attaining is the same as there, where it is the "root" or the "true [nature]," which would correspond to the term "Way" in the present *zhang*.

5. The object of "losing" is identified through the parallel with *Laozi* 22.5 There "reduction," *shao* 少, is contrasted with "increase," *duo* 多, reduction having "attaining" *de* 得 as a consequence, and increase being defined as a "delusion," *huo* 惑, caused by one's getting "further away from the root." Although Wang Bi uses a different terminology here, he operates with the same contrast of attaining and losing the root, or the Way, and therefore the object of "losing" has to be transferred here from *zhang* 22.

6. This translation is very unsatisfactory. With 言 "this means" Wang Bi announces a "translation" into a more explicit language in which most of the original textual ingredients are still visible. Nothing of this is the case here. The suggestion by Tao Hongqing to read 隨其所行 for 隨行其所 seems plausible enough, however, that both *Jizhu* and *Yongle dadian* would carry such a text with its obvious illegibility shows that the editors remained faithful to the manuscripts in their hands

rather than changing the text to perhaps make it even more incomprehensible. Furthermore, Tao's emendation immediately leads to the next problem, namely, that 故 becomes superfluous. In this construction it makes little sense. Tao himself noticed this and proposed to eliminate it. The entire *zhang* is transmitted with an extraordinarily high degree of variation, even within the textual family of Wang Bi's *Laozi*. My reading can claim consistency within Wang Bi's thinking but not to have solved all of the problems in this *zhang*.

7. The phrase is the same in *Laozi* 17.5. There the implied subject of the first half clearly is the ruler; the second half the people below him. The phrase stands as a summary statement about the reasons for the changing relations between ruler and subjects as a consequence of the deterioration of the ruler's moral fiber. The terms used in the commentary, *zhong xin* 忠信, appear in a similar sequence in *zhang* 38. I have seen no other option but to confront this phrase directly with that about the Sage who follows the Way in all of his doings, with the consequence that all entities attain their true nature (which for some, like the grass and the dogs in *zhang* 5, means being eaten, while for others, like the cattle and humans in the same *zhang*, means eating), the attainers theirs, and the losers theirs too. If, however, as in the last sentence, the person at the top lacks "credibility" (for this term, see my *Language, Ontology, and Political Philosophy*, Chapter 2), then so will his subjects.

8. The radical change of 下 to 上 is necessitated by the direct parallel with *zhang* 17.5, mentioned in the previous note, and a plethora of statements that impute the loss as well as the attainment of the "true nature" of social entities to the quality of the person at the top, and never the other way around. As it stands, the text is both meaningless in the context and in direct contradiction to well-established assessments of Wang Bi.

Zhang 24 TRANSLATION NOTES

1. The *zhang* has much of the same content as *zhang* 22 but deals not with the Sage Ruler but with a leader who does not keep to the principles outlined there. He does not have to be the ruler as the example of Xi Zhi in 24.3 shows, but the basic relationship is that of one with the many, the "others," the extreme of which is that of the ruler with his subjects. Both Mawangdui manuscripts stress the link between the two *zhang* by putting this *zhang* 24 between *zhang* 21 and 23. The dynamics outlined in both chapters operate only between someone in the top position and his subjects.

2. The term *wu* 物 is taken from 24.3, which makes clear that the "other entities" are going to loathe him, the ruler, if he does the things outlined here.

3. With the exception of the first sentence in this series, the others are all inversions of sentences about the Sage in *Laozi* 22.7, which are "translated" by Wang Bi in his commentaries to *Laozi* 22.1–22.4. My additions in the brackets have been taken from these "translations."

4. The *Zuo zhuan* writes under Duke Cheng, 16th year [cf. J. Legge, *The Chinese Classics: I, The Ch'un Tsew with the Tso Chuen*, 394], that Xi Zhi had "in talks with Duke Xiang of Shan frequently boasted of his exploits. The Viscount of Shen said to the great officers: 'Ji of Wen [= Xi Zhi] will go under! His station is lower than that of seven other people, and he strives to block out his superiors['' merits]. This brings about an accumulation of resentment [against him] and is the root of turmoil. If he increases the resentment [against himself] and treads the steps towards turmoil, how can he remain at [his] position?' The *Book of Xia* (*Shujing* III.iii.5) says: 'How could one [deal with] resentment only when it is [already] apparent! Before it is visible it has to be dealt with.' That [shows] how careful one has to watch [resentment] while it is still small. But now as it is [already] apparent, can something still be done" [to avert disaster? No]. One generation after Wang Bi, Du Yu 杜預 (222–284) comments on this passage: "This means Xi Zhi blatantly praised his own merits, therefore there is the disaster of resentment [already] apparent" (Du Yu, *Chunqiu jingzhuan jijie*, 770, n. 7). In fact, resentment against Xi Zhi and his clan built up to a point that he was killed a year thereafter, although he himself had discouraged his clansmen from preempting the strike against them by a counterattack, with the argument that they owed allegiance to the duke and should not rebel. The *zhang* contains no IPS. The structural writing here only serves to highlight the relationship between the text and the commentary.

5. Obviously, the *Laozi* text itself has no interlocking parallels here, but the commentary picks up the two terms in the text to develop them in parallel fashion, which transforms the subsequent main text into a general statement.

Zhang 25 Numbered Text Notes

1. Shi Falin 釋法琳 (572–640) refers in his *Bianzheng lun* 辨正論 to this passage. The section containing this quotation is transmitted in two different places, in Shi Daoxuan's *Guang Hong ming ji* 廣弘明集, T. 2103, Taishō vol. 52:187a.18ff, and in a separate edition of the *Bianzheng lun*, T. 2110, Taishō vol. 52:537.a.10. The version in the *Guang Hong ming ji* is definitely preferable, not least because it makes it quite clear that it is a summary of Wang Bi's opinion, not a verbatim quotation. It runs (with the deviations of the T.2110 in brackets): 王弼之 [云] 言天地王 [之] 道並不相違故稱法也自然無稱窮極之辭. The subsequent phrase, 道是智慧靈知 [巧] 之號, is in fact Falin's conclusion from Wang Bi's argument, namely, that the Dao is a highest intelligence and sublime insight but remains conditioned by the 自然. Although the passage takes up elements of the Wang Bi commentary, such as the notion of 違, and closely echoes others, such as the 自然者無稱之言窮極之辭也 in 自然無稱窮極之辭, this subsequent phrase is not a part of the summary and thus does not have a basis in Wang Bi's commentary. The reference has been first pointed out by Hong Yixuan 洪頤宣's (1765–1833) *Dushu conglu* (1821) 讀書叢錄, 12.1, quoted by Hatano Tarō as including the phrase 道是智慧靈知 [巧] 之號 as a quotation from Wang Bi. For the above-mentioned reasons, I agree with Hatano Tarō in not accepting the quotation as genuine.

Zhang 25 Translation Notes

1. In his comments on *Lunyu* 7.6 (*Wang Bi ji jiaoshi*, II.624), Wang Bi writes about the Way much in the same manner as here, that it is "vacant without substance" 寂然無體. This use of the character 寂 confirms the *textus receptus* reading, because in fact the characters 宋 and 寂 are interchangeable.

2. The translation of 返化終始不失其常 is uncertain. The split in my translation between 返化 and 終始 in a style strongly based on phrases of four characters such as Wang Bi's is at least very unusual. The expression 返化 has some antecedent in Zhuang Zun, but nothing that would help here. I read it as an allusion to and an interpretation of the term 反/返 further down in 25.8., which there is commented upon as: "It does not follow what it chances upon; its substance 'stands alone' [as the *Laozi* says in 25.2]. That is why [the text] says: 'It stands aloof'" [from change]. In the context there, I see no other way to translate the term *fan* 反/返. Because of this link, I have preferred the reading 返 in 25.8 over another tradition in the same textual family, which reads 反. The term's interpretation by Wang Bi here does not link up with what otherwise is handled with the terminology of 反, 復, and 歸, namely, the "return to" or "relating back to" the That-by-which. The term *chang* 常 is defined by Wang Bi in his commentary on *Laozi* 16.6.

3. The term "grand shape" does not recur in Wang Bi's writings. Wang Bi often uses the term *da* 大 to describe absolute as opposed to relative size. This is the case here.

4. The same formula is used by Wang Bi on *Laozi* 14.3 about the diffuseness of the One.

5. For the difference between *ming* 名 and *cheng* 稱, cf. *LZWZLL* 5.1ff. and my analysis in Chapter 1 of my *Language, Ontology, and Political Philosophy*, 71–78.

6. For the technical use of the term *qu yu* 取於 in Wang Bi, cf. Chapter 1 of my *Language, Ontology, and Political Philosophy*, 69–70.

7. This core phrase of Wang Bi's is also in his *LZWZLL* 5.6.

8. Fu Yi and Fan Yingyuan both read 人亦大 instead of 王亦大. Although Wang Bi quotes 王亦大 in his commentary here, in some rare cases the quotations were adapted to the reading in the superimposed text. Wang Bi's commentary begins with the quotation from the *Xiaojing*, which deals with man as the most exalted being and then defines the king as the highest of men. This argument would seem to support the assumption that Wang Bi's text read 人 here. The purpose of this quotation and the implied argument, however, are different. Wang Bi intends to explain why the king is not "great" but only "also great." 亦大 He is "also" great because Heaven and Earth have given the highest endowment to humans, and he is their lord. He is not intrinsically great but "also great" by this endowment.

9. *Xiaojing zhushu* 孝經註疏, 9.5, p. 1.

10. Hatano Tarō has suggested eliminating 者 after this quotation. Wang Bi, however, does on occasion add 者 in such situations; cf. *LZWZLL* 1.42 所謂 "自古及今, 其名不去" 者也, or Wang Bi on *Laozi* 59.3 故曰 "早復謂之重積德" 者也.

11. The *locus classicus* for the notion that Earth "carries" and Heaven "covers" the ten thousand entities is in *Zhongyong* 1633b and 1634c.

12. The term *wucheng* 無稱, the "designationless," sets the That-which-is-of-itself-what-it-is against the Dao, which is the "greatest among [aspects that can be assigned] designations." Han Kangbo uses the term in Wang Bi's sense in his comments on the *Xici* 上 phrase "the Yi has the Great Ultimate" 易有太極 with the words: "The Taiji is a designation for the designationless, for that which it is impossible to name 太極者無稱之稱不可得而名. It takes the ultimate of entity and goes beyond it to the Great Ultimate" (*Wang Bi ji jiaoshi*, 553). The term *qiongji* 窮極, translated here as "getting to the Ultimate," comes in two fairly different patterns in Wang's work. In Wang Bi on *Laozi* 35.3 and 40.2, and probably 16.12, it clearly is a verb, meaning "to exhaust." In this sense, the Dao is "inexhaustible" 不可窮極. We also find it in the *Liezi* 90, where "the thousand changes and ten thousand transformations [of the changelings 化人] are inexhaustible." In other cases it seems to be a verb with a positive meaning, "to fully exhaust" or "to get to the very end," with the subject being the Dao, such as in Wang Bi on *Laozi* 25.8, where the term 遠 is explained with 遠極也周無所不窮極. "'Getting far' means 'reaching the very end.' It 'travels all around' [as the *Laozi* says in 25.3], and there is no place where it does not reach the absolute end." Finally, it appears again as a verb in expressions such as 窮極虛無, "fully penetrating to the ultimate emptiness and negativity" as the Great Man does in Wang Bi's commentary on *Laozi* 16.12. While these meanings have some variety, the common element seems to be that 窮極 is a verb, and that it refers to getting to some absolute end with something. My translation is based on these two common elements.

13. The same formula in Wang Bi on *Laozi* 37.1.

14. Tao Hongqing has suggested changing this passage to 王所以爲主其主之者一也, but I do not believe this to be necessary. Wang Bi writes in his commentary on *Laozi* 42.1: "The Hundred Families hold on to their [variegated] ambitions, different states have distinct customs, but those of the kings or dukes who attain the One, are [their] lord." The term *unifies* here carries neither the meaning of geographical or mental unification but of establishing the necessary One which, according to Wang Bi, alone is capable of preventing the many by its own noninterference from leaving their natural places.

Zhang 26 Translation Notes

1. In his commentary to the broken top line in the *Zhouyi* hexagram 32 *heng* 恒, Wang Bi deals with the same issue, writing: "Generally speaking, the calm is

the lord over the impetuous, and the securely resting is the master of the mobile. Therefore it is secure rest where the highest situates himself [like the broken line on the top of the hexagram]; and calmness is the way to be able to endure long."

2. The additions in the bracket are induced by the structural position of this phrase as well as the beginning phrase of text 5 to which it refers. For the explanation see the section Structure at the end of this *zhang*.

Zhang 27 NUMBERED TEXT NOTES

1. 常善救物故無棄物 del. Hatano Tarō. There is no commentary by Wang Bi to the phrases 善救物故無棄物. Lu Deming does not give any readings for them. Their contents furthermore are not taken up in the remaining part of the *zhang* or elsewhere in Wang Bi's writings, while the phrases dealing with the Sage's saving other people are taken up elsewhere. There are various statements about manuscripts without these eight characters. Wang Pang 王雱, editor of the 道德眞經集註 of 1070, which has been used here as an important basis for the reconstruction of Wang Bi's *Commentary*, states that there is "one MS which does not have the 8 characters beginning with 常善救物" (4.19a). Hatano Tarō quotes a note on the margin of an "Old handwritten copy of the Heshang gong Commentary to the Daodejing," which says "Wang [Bi's] manuscript does not have the 8 characters beginning with 常善救物." The Mawangdui manuscripts furthermore undermine the reading of the phrases 善救物故無棄物 by providing a strongly truncated version, 物無棄財, a reading supported by two quotations from the *Huainanzi*, namely, 物無棄財 and 物無棄物. These, however, presuppose the 人無棄人 in *Laozi* 27.5, which is given by both the 傅奕古本 and the 范應元本, but not by the Mawangdui manuscripts. There is, on the other hand, the strange statement by Chao Yuezhi (1059–1129) who, in his preface from 1115 to his Wang Bi *Laozi*, printed at the head of the *Guyi congshu* 古逸叢書 edition of Wang Bi's *Laozi Commentary*, claims that Wang Bi "did not know that the phrase '[the Sage] is constantly good at saving other people and for this reason there is no rejection of other people [by him]; he is constantly good at saving other entities and for this reason there is no rejection of other entities by him' in fact occurs only in the Heshang gong [versions] but not in the Old Manuscript[s]; this can be verified from Fu Yi." The Fu Yi "Old Manuscript[s]" as well as Fan Yingyuan, however, contain both phrases, which means that Chao must be referring to a different Fu Yi edition than the one we have. From this statement it would seem that Chao's edition contained the contested phrases. Due to the absence of commentary and the diffuse record of the phrases, I have followed the suggestion of Hatano Tarō and have eliminated the phrases from Wang Bi's *Laozi*. It remains to be noted that the phrase 是謂襲明 also lacks commentary. Standing at the end of an argument, this would fit a practice of Wang Bi's to not comment on the conclusion of an argument.

2. Lu Deming, *Laozi Daodejing yinyi*, 4a, quotes the items 所好; 裕, and 長

from a piece of Wang Bi's *Commentary* that must have been attached to a *Laozi* statement situated in *zhang* 27.4–27.9. It is lost.

Zhang 27 Translation Notes

1. The same terms appear in Wang Bi's commentary on *Laozi* 20.7 about the mental activity of an idiot.

2. Wang Bi repeats this last phrase in varying formulations. Cf. Wang Bi on *Laozi* 17.6: "He [the topmost, identified through cross-references as the Sage] does not set up the other entities by means of a [definite] shape"; Wang Bi on *Laozi* 36.2 interpreting the sentence, "The state's useful instrument cannot prevail by showing it to people," writes: "'Useful instrument' is the instrument useful to the state. If [the ruler] only adapts to the nature of entities and does not rely on physical punishments to regulate the other entities so that the instruments [of government] cannot be perceived, but the entities still each attain their place, then [government truly] is 'the state's useful instrument.'"

3. The last section, "there is no rejecting other people," is quoted verbatim by Wang Bi in his commentary on *Laozi* 49.3.

4. Wang Bi paraphrases this phrase in his commentary on *Laozi* 28.6: "Responsive to [the fact] that their [the people in All Under Heaven's] allotments have dispersed, the Sage [does not cut and trim them but] purposely sets up officials and elders for them. 'Making the good ones into teachers . . .' and 'the not good ones into [their] material . . . ,' changing [in this manner] the[ir] habits and altering the[ir] customs is [his way] of 'returning [them] again to the' One."

5. Wang Bi follows here the interpretation of *zi* 資 given by Zheng Xuan 鄭玄 in his comment on *Xiaojing* 5.1 資於事父以事母而愛同資於事父以事君而敬同, where Zheng writes 資取也. Cf. *Xiaojing zhushu*, 2:2548b.7f. Cf. also Wang's commentary on *Laozi* 49.5 能者與之資者取之.

6. Tao Hongqing and Yi Shunding, followed by Hatano Tarō and Lou Yulie, have suggested inserting 不 before the 以善棄不善也. This would reject the unanimous reading of the two best sources, the 集註本 and the 永樂大殿本, and would prompt a translation of "and do not reject the not good ones by means of their [own] goodness." The good ones, however, are not the Sage but officials installed by him. Within their domain, the not good ones will indeed be rejected and punished; cf. my *Language, Ontology and Political Philosophy*, pp. 190–192.

7. According to Wang Bi's commentary on *Laozi* 28.6, which explicitly refers to this *zhang*, the Sage installs officials and teachers to administer the entities once they have assumed their differentiations. However, the sole purpose of these institutions is to help the entities relate back to the One that is their root. He will therefore avoid the mechanism described by Wang Bi in his commentary on *Laozi* 27.5 where, through the honoring of worthies and the appreciation of rare goods,

the leader makes the people fight for advancement and profit. This context forces the above translation, according to which the Sage neither honors the teachers nor loves their "materials," as both would only constitute the cause for great competition and turmoil.

Zhang 28 Numbered Text Note

1. Shima Kuniō assumes that this last phrase of the *Laozi* with Wang Bi's commentary is in fact the first phrase of the next *zhang*. The evidence is the Pelliot MS 2462, with Yan Shigu's 顏師古 commentary to the 玄言新記明老部, which has this division and the reference to "cutting" in Wang Bi comm. on 29.3. The evidence does not seem convincing to me, because the commentary to 29.3 quite explicitly refers only to the text of *Laozi* 29.3.

Zhang 28 Translation Notes

1. The justification for the logical links in this translation as well as the translation of 28.2, which is parallel to this statement, is in Wang Bi on *Laozi* 41.6; cf. note 3.

2. The 德 here has to be translated as 得. See note 3.

3. Wang Bi links the first sentence with *Laozi* 7 through a direct quotation. A similar passage is in *Laozi* 66. The valley has the lowly position of the hen. Lying low, everything runs into it of its own accord. Similar interpretations are given to the Way in *Laozi* 32.4, which is like the "rivers and seas" into which all rivulets run of their own accord, because they lie low; and to the "big state" in *Laozi* 61.3, which "lowers itself" so that everyone comes running toward it, and which is called "the female of All Under Heaven." With the "not to be separated," *bu li* 不離, of the next sentence of the text, Wang Bi links up with *Laozi* 10.1. "[For a ruler] to keep to the camp, to hold on to the[ir] One, and be able not to be separated from it—ah!" According to the commentary, the "it" in this sentence is the "One." The "to be able," *neng* 能, prompts me to assume that Wang Bi read the *de* 德 as *de* 得, as he so often does. The link with this phrase as well as the explicit mentioning of the One in the commentary on *Laozi* 28.6 is the reason for the insertion of "the One" into the bracket here. According to the commentary to *Laozi* 10.1, the consequence of this ability is that the ten thousand entities will come to him without being called. Wang Bi writes "'To keep to' is like 'stay in.' 'Camp' is the abode of eternal sojourn of human beings. The 'One' is the true [nature] of [the other] human beings. [The sentence] means: If a human being would be able to stay in [his] abode of eternal sojourn, 'hold on to the One' and purify [his] spirit, [so that] he would be able to be permanently 'not separated' from [the abode and the One]—ah, then [indeed] 'the ten thousand kinds of entities [would] submit

[to him] of their own accord as guests'" [as the *Laozi* says in 32.1]. From this it follows that the subject of 爲天下谿 in our text is the person who knows how to be [All Under Heaven's] cock, that is, the Sage, and the consequence of this sentence is that the ten thousand entities will come to him as into a valley. The subject and object of the last sentence are determined by Wang Bi's interpretation further down in the commentary on *Laozi* 28.6, where the Sage, after things have evolved into their specifications 復使歸於一也, makes [the ten thousand entities] "'again return' to the One." The wording 使歸 directly links up with the wording 復歸於嬰兒 in the passage 28.1 under consideration here. The subject of the phrase is thus a person with all of the accoutrements of the Sage, so that Wang's commentary, which explicitly establishes this link, has solid contextual support.

4. Cf. Wang Bi's commentary on *Laozi* 41.7, "It is [the Sage's achievement of being All Under Heaven's] Great Whiteness to be well-nigh black," reads: 知其白守其黑大白然後乃的 "[He who] 'knows that as its [All Under Heaven's] whiteness he [has to] keep [being] its blackness' [as the *Laozi* says in 28.2] will as a consequence achieve [being] the 'Great Whiteness.'"

5. Cf. Wang Bi on *Laozi* 22.6 for a similar definition.

6. Wang Bi does not comment on the word *zu* 足. It appears in the *Laozi* in sentences such as, "He who knows to have enough, will be wealthy" (*Laozi* 33.3).

7. Wang Bi talks here about the "mother that brings about the achievements," *wei gong zhi mu* 爲功之母 mentioned in the end of Wang Bi on *Laozi* 38, p. 247, and in Wang Bi on *Laozi* 39.3. The first passage reads: "That is why if only [the ruler] would obtain the mother bringing about the achievements, then 'the ten thousand kinds of entities [would] come about' 'without their being given orders [by him]'; the ten thousand kinds of affairs [would] persist without [his] laboring. . . . "

8. Wang Bi translates 爲官長 into 爲之立官長. The 爲 seems translated twice, once as 立 and once as 爲之.

9. The "hundred styles of action" 百行 do not appear elsewhere in Wang Bi's work. From uses elsewhere, we can infer that this term refers to the variety of morally different kinds of action rather than to the different professions. The expression *shulei* 殊類 is used by Wang Bi on *Laozi* 58.2 and 59.1. In the latter case, the farmer's "elimination of different varieties" 去其殊類 in his field, and their "reduction to a single one," is used as a model for "regulating men and serving Heaven." It would seem that both terms refer to the development of social hierarchies in society beyond the simple dichotomy of the ruler and the people.

10. *Fen* 分 in Wang Bi's terminology is the particular lot of the individual entity within a prestabilized harmony. In this sense it is identical to *zhen* 眞, the "true nature" of an entity, as used for example in Wang Bi on *Laozi* 5.1. Cf. Wang Bi on *Laozi* 16.6, where it is the result of the ruler's "having lost this [knowledge of the Eternal]" that "entities diverge from [their assigned] stations 物離其分. (For another reading of this passage, see *Wang Bi ji jiaoshi*, 39, note 9.) My reading

is confirmed by the same thought and language in Wang Bi on *Laozi* 5.1, where again as the consequence of a (hypothetical) active interference from Heaven and Earth, the "entities would lose their true" [nature] 物失其眞.

11. Cf. Wang Bi on *Laozi* 32.3 for the entire process of setting up a state administration.

Zhang 29 NUMBERED TEXT NOTE

1. This commentary is not carried by the 永樂大典本. Support for its authenticity is 物有常性而造爲之, in Wang Bi on *Laozi* 29.3.

Zhang 29 TRANSLATION NOTES

1. This phrase is a fine example for the reading strategies informed by a conscious knowledge of the rules for IPS. The phrase stands alone in all transmissions, except the *Wenxuan* commentary quoting *Laozi* as quoted in the *Wenzi* (26/5/7), which adds another parallel phrase on "holding on to" 執. Within a chapter written in IPS, this makes it into a phrase dealing with both chains, that on 取/執 as well as that on 爲, or a *c* phrase, as it is called here. As a consequence of this structural position, 爲 changes meaning and becomes a term encompassing both "interfering with" and "holding on to." Wang Bi's commentary makes this very explicit by unfolding the "it is impossible to interfere . . . " into a double statement about both "interfering" and "holding on to." There is a remote possibility that Wang Bi's text indeed had the second phrase carried by the *Wenxuan* commentary. This has been suggested by Yi Shunding 易順鼎.

2. In his commentary on *Laozi* 20.3, Wang Bi uses the two terms *mi* 迷 and *huo* 惑 for delusion and confusion, with the first referring to beauty and promotion, and the second to glories and desires.

Zhang 30 NUMBERED TEXT NOTES

1. This phrase is one of the few where the reading in Wang Bi's text not only coincides with both 馬王堆 versions but also with the 河上公 version.

2. Evidently, the 傅奕古本 provides a very weak base text here. Both 馬王堆 manuscripts, however, have lacunae. Their size shows that the phrase 大軍之後必有凶年 did not occur, but the surviving fragments contain many phonetic and graphic loans, so that they cannot very well qualify as base text.

Zhang 30 Translation Notes

1. The term 爲治者, "someone actively bringing about order," as the opposite to the 有道者, "someone who has the Way," seems to be a neologism of Wang Bi's.

2. The expression 務欲還反無爲 must be read as strictly parallel to 務欲立功生事 in the preceding sentence. There 務欲 is a verb ("making efforts and desire to") with two objects, 立功 and 生事. In the same manner 還反 and 無爲 must be read as two objects. *Huanfan* 還反 is the action of the Sage in making All Under Heaven "return" or "relate back" to the One described, for example, in *Laozi* 28.1–5 with Wang's *Commentary*.

3. 大軍之後必有凶年 is omitted in MWD A, B, Xiang Er, and Ma Xulun, and by Shima Kuniō, because there is no commentary to the phrase by Wang Bi. For the textual history of this passage, cf. Li Dingsheng and Xu Huijun, eds., *Wenzi yaoquan*, 6 ff.

4. The sudden introduction of an "I", *wu* 吾, into the text here forces a translation such as "someone" or "a person." On the use of this term in the *Laozi*, cf. my *The Craft of a Chinese Commentator*, 127–29.

Zhang 32 Numbered Text Notes

1. The 取善集 quotes this segment of the commentary directly after the 道常無名 of the first text in this *zhang*. As it does not quote the rest of this commentary, there is no reason to assume that it had a different segmentation *Laozi*/Wang Bi here.

2. For this *zhang*, Shima Kuniō has found another commentary in Jiang Siqi's *Daode zhenjing xuande zuanshu* (纂疏) 9.4a–b attributed to Wang Bi: 王弼曰此舉喻言道不居一天下今將在天下法譬之猶川谷之與江海川谷爲末以喻於有名江海是本以喻於無名川谷從何而來從江海而來今日欲歸何處還復歸於江海有名從何而來從無名而來今日攝化衆生欲歸何處還歸於無名河海若無川谷則無以滿川谷若無江海則無以流無名若無有名則無以顯有名若無無名則無以出江海猶 (= 由) 川谷故所以滿無名由有名故以顯. I consider this attribution wrong. Cf. note 6 of the translation.

Zhang 32 Translation Notes

1. The term *chang* 常, "the Eternal," is treated by Wang Bi as a separate noun; cf. Wang Bi on *Laozi* 47.1: "the Ways have a Great Eternal" 道有大常, Wang Bi

on *Laozi* 16.12, "once he . . . attains the Eternal of the entities" 得物之常, and Wang Bi on *Laozi* 52.9, where 常 is defined as "the Eternal of the Way" 道之 常. It is defined separately in Wang Bi on 16.6: "The Eternal as such is neither [inwardly] partial nor manifest [in its preferences]; it has an appearance without either brightness or darkness, and features without either warming or cooling." A similar definition is given in Wang Bi on *Laozi* 55.6.

2. The same two terms, *wu xing* 無形 and *buxi* 不繫, appear with the Way as the subject in Wang Bi's commentary on *Laozi* 21.2 and 21.3.

3. The sudden appearance of *wo* 我, "I," as the subject of this sentence leaves two options. It can be read as a general term for the "subject, e. g., the duke or king," which would be highly unusual, because there seems to be no need for the shift. Or it can be read as a signal of a change of topic. In the next commentary, Wang Bi refers back to *zhang* 28.6, which runs: "Once the unadorned has dispersed, they [the entities] become instruments. Making use of them, the Sage makes officials and elders [for them]." The subject of the action is the Sage. I believe, therefore, that this subject has to be transferred here. There are two supports for this. The expression *ruo* 若 describes in Wang Bi's reading of the *Laozi* a hypothetical subjunctive to be translated "if only," with the implication that it is not the case. Therefore, the dukes and kings at least in the "present" of the *Laozi* and of Wang Bi do not qualify for their potentially positive role. The sentence here under consideration is juxtaposed with a phrase about Heaven and Earth being in harmony. In the understanding of Chinese political philosophy, Heaven and Earth are always in harmony, and thus the parallel must be with an agent who always does what the dukes and kings only should do, namely, the Sage. This engenders another change. The *qi* 其 in the phrase *wo shou qi zhenxing* 我守其眞性 has to refer to the other entities. In his commentary to *Laozi* 3.4, Wang Bi comments on the phrase: "He [the Sage, who is explicitly mentioned as the subject of the phrase in the preceding line] permanently prompts the people to be without knowledge and desires" with the remark: "[That means] he [the Sage] preserves their [the people's] true [essence], *shou qi zhen*" 守其眞, which is the formula repeated here in the commentary on *Laozi* 32.2.

4. *Chunqiu Zuozhuan zhengyi*, 43:2044.b.

5. The 世行道於天下者 is a unanimous tradition. I have followed Tao Hongqing to amend 世 to 也. If 世 were to stand, the phrase would read: "If for generations the Way was practiced in All under Heaven . . ." This reading could claim support from the plural in 32.1 "If only the dukes and kings . . . " which might imply several generations. I have, however, not found an echo of such a thought of a gradual return to the Dao elsewhere in Wang Bi's work. I therefore have followed the trivializing amendment of Tao Hongqing.

6. The 纂疏 gives a further commentary here that it attributes to Wang Bi. This commentary argues for an interdependence of "that which has names" (here the rivulets and streams) and "that which is without name" (here the rivers and the seas). The rivulets come from the rivers and seas and return there; that which has names—the entities—emerges from the nameless and returns there. "Without

that which has names the nameless would have nothing in which to shine forth; without the Nameless that which has names would have nothing from which to emerge." This notion of interdependence of Being and Entity and of circular movement between them is not part of Wang Bi's philosophy, but has been spelled out in greatest detail by Wang Bi's contemporary, Zhong Hui 鐘會, who also was the author of a *Laozi Commentary* preserved in lengthy quotations. For an example of his reading of the *Laozi* in this perspective, cf. my *The Craft of a Chinese Commentator*, 177–255. I assume this commentary to be from the hands of Zhong Hui or someone close to his philosophy. The extant quotations attributed to Zhong Hui known to me do not contain this interesting piece.

Zhang 33 TRANSLATION NOTES

1. Cf. the commentary to text 4 and the note on the structure at the end of this *zhang*. The justification for identifying the subject as the ruler is the next commentary. There Wang Bi speaks of the "evasion" 避 of the other entities as well as of their craftiness, *qiao* 巧. Both are described elsewhere as the product of governmental spying and interference; cf. *LZWZLL* 6.27ff., Wang Bi on *Laozi* 17.4, 18.2, and 65.3. The justification for the bracket "practices the Way" is contained in Wang Bi on *Laozi* 33.4.

2. The term *jiu* 久, "long lasting," from the main text, is explained by Wang Bi through reduplication here as *jiu chang* 久長. I believe this to be different from the use of the two terms in *Laozi* 7.1, where 長 is to be read *zhang*, with the meaning "to excel."

Zhang 34 TRANSLATION NOTES

1. *Wang Bi ji jiaoshi*, 86ff., n.1, points to a passage in *Zhuangzi* 59/22/44 ff., which gives a similar but more elaborate explanation.

2. This is a frequently recurring topic in Wang Bi's thinking; cf. Wang Bi on *Laozi* 1.2; 17.1 and 17.6; 21.3.

3. According to Wang Bi's reading of *Laozi* 1.3, the Way's "subtlety" 妙 can be perceived when the entities are without desires.

Zhang 35 NUMBERED TEXT NOTE

1. Support for 道之出言淡兮其無味也: Wang Bi on *Laozi* 23.1 下章言 道之出言 淡兮其無味也.

Zhang 35 Translation Notes

1. The "if . . . then" reading is based on the commentary here as well as *LZWZLL* 1.31, which also makes this conditional connection explicit by inserting 則.

2. The transmission of 天象, "heavenly images," is stable. The term refers to heavenly bodies such as the sun, moon, and stars. As it does not occur elsewhere in Wang Bi's opus, Hatano Tarō suggested 天下. In such a case, a reference to 天地 in *Laozi* 28.3 would be more probable.

3. Cf. Wang Bi on *Laozi* 16.6.

Zhang 36 Numbered Text Note

1. The selection of the base text here is difficult, because the 集註本 contains a lacuna and a clear scribal error, while the 永樂大典本 is in better shape but has adapted the 翕 to the changed main text 歙. I have opted for the more complete version. All commentators have considered this commentary passage corrupt and have made various, sometimes very radical, suggestions for improvement. I assume the basic argument proffered by Hatano Tarō to be convincing, namely, that the last passage is to illustrate how the ruler might adapt to the nature of violent entities to have them self-destruct. On this assumption I have accepted only one additional emendation beyond the change of 與 to 翕, namely, the change from 改 to 攻. The resulting text is legible and meaningful, although certainly not optimal.

Zhang 37 Numbered Text Notes

1. There is agreement that this passage is corrupt.

2. The 集註本 places this commentary after the first phrase of what is traditionally the first segment of *Laozi* 37.4 無名之樸, however, this piece does not figure in Wang Bi's *Laozi* text.

Zhang 37 Translation Note

1. The same formula in Wang Bi on *Laozi* 25.12.

Zhang 38 Numbered Text Notes

1. This text is quoted only in Fan Yingyuan's 范應元 commentary. Hatano Tarō is alone in accepting it as a genuine piece of Wang Bi's commentary. Although I do not see a directly parallel phrase in the rest of Wang Bi's writings, I agree with Hatano Tarō, because the style of the argumentation resembles that of Wang Bi.

2. The text for the two crucial formulae 無不爲 and 無以爲 is corrupt, even within the textual family to which the Wang Bi *Laozi* belongs. For the person with the superior receipt, Hanfei zi, Yan Zun, Fu Yi, and Fan Yingyuan all read 無不 爲, while both MWD A and B give 無以爲, to be followed by the Heshang gong textual family. Wang Bi's commentary here decides the case by writing 上德之 人 . . . 能有德而無不爲 不求而得 不爲而成, which reproduces the three core elements of the *Laozi* sentence, namely, 上德, 無不爲 and 不爲 (instead of 無爲). Li Shan quotes the Wang Bi edition with the full formula, as I have suggested it here. For the person with the inferior receipt, the Daozang and Wuyingdian editions both write 有以爲, but both Fu Yi and Fan Yingyuan write 無以爲. Both MWD texts leave out this phrase altogether. The Wang Bi commentary writes first 下德 爲之而有以爲. However, Fan Yingyuan quotes Wang Bi here as saying 無以爲. The plausibility of this argument is confirmed by the fact that Wang immediately thereafter explains the meaning of 無以爲. In Wang Bi's view, the *Laozi* first makes a grand distinction between 上德 and 下德. Then he proceeds to outline hierarchy within 下德. At the top comes 上仁, and this is indeed defined in the *Laozi* text here as 爲之而無以爲. I therefore conclude that Wang Bi wrote 爲之而無以爲.

3. The phrase presents difficulties. Directly afterward, Wang Bi quotes hexagram *fu*, "Return," of the *Zhouyi* for the purpose of illustration. We are thus able to extrapolate the meaning of the present phrase from Wang Bi's interpretation there. Commenting on the *tuan* statement there [Lou Yulie, *Wang Bi ji jiaoshi*, I.336], Wang Bi writes: "Thus although Heaven and Earth are great, are richly endowed with the ten thousand entities, thunders roll and winds blow, and ten thousand transformations follow one another, that which calm and supreme negativity is their root. . . . If they had taken an entity as their heart [and not negativity], the different categories [of entities] would not manage to exist simultaneously" 若其 以有爲心 則異類未獲具存矣. The argument that only by not itself being specified is the Dao capable of securing the complete existence to all entities is expressed with a variety of terms. Among them 全 figures prominently; cf. Wang Bi on *Laozi* 25.12, on *Laozi* 40.3, and on *Laozi* 45.6. I therefore suggest amending 免 to 全.

4. The reading 不能舍/捨無以爲體也 does not make sense. The definition that only the Dao is 大, great, in the sense of absolute greatness 大之極, means that the other "great" entities such as Heaven, Earth, and the Ruler are great only insofar as they make use of the Dao. They are restricted, however, in their greatness to one particular aspect, such as Heaven's covering all of the ten thousand kinds of entities but not being able to do what Earth is doing, namely, to "support" them. We have to expect, therefore, a statement marking the difference between

the absolutely great and these minor Great Ones. The Peking University editors of the *Zhongguo zhexue shi jiaoxue ziliao xuanji, Liang Han—Sui Tang shiqi*, 367, n. 2, have noticed the problem. They suggested reading 捨 as 舍, which does not present a problem, but then they suggested understanding this 舍 in the sense of 居住, "to settle in," that is, in exactly the opposite sense the normal reading of 舍/捨 has in Wang Bi, which is "to reject, to abandon." They thus suggested reading 捨無以爲體 as "即以道爲體." While I think that this is unacceptable philologically, the drift of their argument is valid. For my own conjecture, I suggest turning to Han Kangbo 韓康伯. Han Kangbo continues Wang Bi's project of a *Zhouyi* commentary, writing the commentaries for the *Xici* and other wings. In these he makes much use of Wang Bi's concepts and often quotes him. The formula 全無, which I have used for the emendation of 舍無, here comes from Han Kangbo's comments to statements in the *Xici* A. Given the importance of these comments and of the emendation, I will translate the section in full:

Once Yin, then Yang—this is called the Dao 一陰一陽之謂道.

> *What is the Dao? It is a designation for negativity. There is nothing it does not penetrate, nothing that is not based on it. Still one is saying "the Dao is calm and without substance, it is not possible to form an image of it"; [thus] by necessity the usability of Entity is made absolute, and the achievements of negativity shine forth. That is why by arriving at [Xici statements such as] "the spirit is without spatial dimension, the Yi 易 is without substance" the Dao can be perceived. That is why probing the transformations by way of fully penetrating the spirit, and going by the spirit by way of illuminating the Dao [the Zhouyi argues] that although Yin and Yang are distinct, it is the negative One by which they are maintained. In the Yin it is the non-Yin, and the Yin is generated by it, in the Yang it is the non-Yang, and the Yang is completed by it. That is why [the Xici] says: "Once Yin, then Yang . . ." 道者何 无之稱也无不通也无不由 也況之曰道寂然无體不可爲象必有之用極而无之功顯故至乎神无方 而易无體而道可見矣故窮變以盡神因神以明道陰陽雖殊无一以待之 在陰爲无陰陰以之生在陽爲无陽陽以之成故曰一陰一陽也.*

What perpetuates it [the Dao] is the good. What completes it is human nature. Once a humane person makes it visible, he calls it humaneness. Once the knowledgeable makes it visible, he calls it knowledge.

繼之者善也成之者性也仁者見之謂之仁知者見之謂之知

> *Once the humane person takes the Dao as his material by way of making visible his humaneness, and once the knowlegeable takes the Dao as his material by way of making visible his knowledge, each one of them fully lives out his lot 仁者資道以見其仁知者資道以見其知各盡其分.*

The Hundred Families make daily use of it [the Dao] but do not know it [the Dao]. That is why the Dao of the Gentleman is a rarity 百性日用而不知故君子 之道鮮矣.

The Gentleman embodies the Dao by way of making use of it. As [his] humaneness and knowledge in fact are restricted to that which is visible, and as the "Hundred Families" in fact "make daily use of it [the Dao] but do not know it" is it not quite a rarity to embody this Dao? That is why [as the Laozi 1.3 says], "While they [the ten thousand kinds of entities] are [still] constantly without desires, one has something by means of which to perceive its [the Ultimate Principle's] subtlety," and is for the first time in a situation to speak about the Ultimate and to talk about the Absolute. [Mark the difference between Wang Bi and Han Kangbo in assigning a subject to the Laozi phrase] 君子體道以爲用也仁知則滯於所見百性則日用而不知體斯道者不亦鮮矣故常无欲以觀其妙始可以語至而言極也.

[In short, the Dao] is manifest in humaneness and [at the same time] hidden in [its] being used 顯諸仁藏諸用.

It [as the Laozi 34.2 says] "dresses the ten thousand kinds of entities." That is why [the text here] says:" [The Dao] is manifest in humaneness." [At the same time the Hundred Families] "make daily use of it but do not know it." That is why [the text here] says: "[The Dao] is hidden in [its] being used" 衣被萬物故曰顯諸仁日用而不知故曰藏諸用.

It [celebrates] the ten thousand kinds of entities with drumming but does not have the same worries as the Sage 鼓萬物而不與聖人同憂.

The ten thousand kinds of entities are basing themselves on it [the Dao] for [their] transformations; that is why [the text] says: "It [celebrates] the ten thousand kinds of entities with drumming!" Although the Sage [who has been referred to as the Gentleman above] embodies the Dao by making use of it, he is unable to completely have negativity as his substance. That is why, as he is adapting to and penetrating All Under Heaven, there will be traces of his managing activity [as opposed to the Dao which remains hidden.] 萬物由之以化故曰鼓萬物也聖人雖體道以爲用未能全无以爲體故順通天下則有經營之迹也.

It is quite clear that the Sage/Gentleman in this passage makes use of the Dao as do Heaven and Earth, but he cannot fully embody the Dao. Source: *Wang Bi ji jiaoshi*, 541ff. (There is a textual variant in Ruan Yuan, *Shisan jing zhushu*, 66b, for the crucial 全无, namely 至无, but the use of the term 全 in this context is well enough attested).

Zhang 38 Translation Notes

1. The translation for 德 "receipt/capacity" is based on two aspects of the term that are not united in any Western term I could think of. *De* 德 is defined as *de* 得 , "what one gets from the Dao." In this sense, Heaven "receives," *de* 得, from the

Dao the ability to cover all entities. At the same, time what it gets is a capacity, *de* 德, in this case, to cover all entities. I have therefore joined the two terms.

2. The two phrases about ritual and foreknowledge are strictly parallel. The *bo* 薄, "wearing thin," of the first phrase refers to truthfulness and credibility wearing thin; in the same manner, the *hua* 華 of the second phrase must refer to the "ornamenting" of the Way, that is, to its transformation into something external and merely decorative. The term *yu* 愚, "stupid," is read here in the sense Ban Gu uses it in his "Table of Personalities from Former and Recent [Times]" in his *Hanshu*. There, the "stupid," *yuren* 愚人, are at the bottom of his nine-tiered quality scale. The most conspicuous example is the bad last emperor of the Shang dynasty, Zhou 紂. Ban Gu, *Hanshu*, 889.

3. For the identification of the Great Man with the Sage, cf. the translation of *Laozi* 17, note 1.

4. The tradition of defining *de* 德, "the receipt/capacity to act," a term sometimes translated as "power" (A. Waley) or "virtue" (D. C. Lau), as *de* 得, to obtain in the sense of a capacity obtained from the Way, is old. Cf. *Zhuangzi yinde* 30/12/38 (chapter *Tiandi* 天地): "What beings obtain, *de*, to live is called *de* receipt/capacity" 物得以生謂之德; *Hanfei zi* (chapter Jie Lao 解老), 1.136: 德者得身; Jia Yi, *Xinshu* 8.87: "What one obtains, *de*, to be alive is called *de*, receipt/capacity" 所得以生謂之德. Wang Bi repeats the identification in his commentary on *Laozi* 51.2.

5. Both references refer to hexagram *fu*, Return, of the *Zhouyi*. The first quotes from the last sentence of the *tuan* to the hexagram, which runs 復其見天地之心乎; the second comes from a section of the *xiang* for the entire hexagram, which follows immediately thereafter and runs 先王以至日閉關. They read in a translation extrapolated from Wang Bi's *Commentary to the Zhouyi*:

> [To sum up, meaning that this phrase at the end of the *tuan* does not comment on any one of the *guaci* phrases that deal with the hexagram in general:] Return, *fu*—here the heart of Heaven and Earth becomes visible!

Wang Bi's Commentary runs:

> "Return" is an expression for "returning [or relating] back to the root." Heaven and Earth are such that they take the root as their heart. Generally speaking, when movement dies down, there is calm, but calm is not something that is the opposite of movement [but its absence, its negative]. When speech dies down, there is silence, but silence is not something that is the opposite of speech [but its absence, its negative]. In the same sense it is true that, although Heaven and Earth are great, "richly endowed" [as the Xici 上 5 says of the Way] with the ten thousand entities, although thunders roll and winds rage and ten thousand transformations follow one another, the "tranquil" [as the Xici 上 9 says about change] supreme negativity is their root. This is why, when movement [the hexagram's lower trigram, zhen 震, being, according to Shuogua 7 and Xugua 2,

"movement"] dies down "in the midst of Earth" [as the xiang *immediately following says, "Earth" being, according to* Shuogua 4, 9, *and* 11, kun 坤, *the upper trigram of hexagram* fu], *the "heart of Heaven and Earth" indeed "becomes visible." Had they taken a [specific] entity as their heart, the different categories [of entities] would not have managed to exist simultaneously.*

The *Xiang* for the hexagram runs:

When thunder [which according to *Shuogua* 12 is *zhen*, the lower trigram of hexagram *fu*] [comes to] rest in the middle of Earth [i.e., the upper trigram], this is return, *fu*. The former kings closed the passes because of the solstices [so that] the merchants and traders would not travel and the lords would not inspect affairs.

Wang Bi comments:

Fang, "region," "affairs," is [to be read here like] shi 事, *affairs. The arrival of winter [with the solstice] is the return [i.e., the beginning of the reduction] of Yin, the arrival of summer [with the solstice] is the return [i.e., the beginning of the reduction] of Yang. That is why when return is coming about, [everything] arrives at the tranquil great quietude. The former kings were such as to imitate Heaven and Earth in their doings; [on the day of the solstice] when return [to quietude] of movement was coming about, [they were] calm; the return of traveling came about so that [the merchants and traders] stopped, the return of [government] affairs came about so that there was no business attended to" [by the lords].* Wang Bi ji jiaoshi, 336ff. For another translation see Lynn, *The Classic of Changes*, 286 ff.

6. The same formula occurs in Wang Bi on *Laozi* 41.6.

7. A similar formula in *Xunzi* (chapter "On Heaven" 天論, 205ff.: "To complete without interfering, to get without striving this indeed is what I call Heavenly Office" 不爲而成不求而得夫是之謂天職.

8. The "at best" in brackets is inferred from the highest form of someone with "lower capacity," namely, the person with "highest kindliness," who also is said to have "no ulterior motive," while the person in the next category already "has a motive."

9. Wang Bi normally writes 舍, not 捨, often supported by Lu Deming. Cf. Wang Bi on *Laozi* 39.3, 42.1, 49.5, 52.2, 53.2, and 57.4.

10. For the term 興 here, see Wang Bi on *Laozi* 30.7.

11. This argument links up with Wang Bi on *Laozi* 4.1, where Wang Bi deals with Heaven, Earth, and the ruler of men, all of whom have to model themselves after the next higher unit to perfect their own achievement. "That is why even a human being [= ruler] who is knowledgeable about the establishment of order among the ten thousand kinds of entities, but does not proceed in his ordering by

means of the Way of the two principles [Heaven and Earth], will not be able to fully provide [the ten thousand kinds of entities with order]."

12. Extrapolated from Han Kangbo's commentary, *Wang Bi ji jiaoshi*, 542ff., the *Xici* passage, alluded to by Wang Bi above, runs together with Han's commentary, which again echoes Wang Bi's commentary to the *Laozi* 38 passage here:

> [In short, the Dao] is manifest in humaneness, and [at the same time] hidden in [its] being used 顯諸仁藏諸用.
>
> *It [as* Laozi *34.2 says] "dresses the ten thousand kinds of entities." That is why [the text here] says, "[The Dao] is manifest in humaneness." [At the same time the Hundred Families] "make daily use of it, but do not know it" [as the* Xici *says just before this passage]. That is why [the text here] says: "[The Dao] is hidden in [its] being used"* 衣被萬物故曰顯諸仁日用而不知故曰藏諸用.
>
> It [celebrates] the ten thousand kinds of entities with drumming, but does not have the same worries as the Sage 鼓萬物而不與聖人同憂.
>
> *The ten thousand kinds of entities are basing themselves on it [the Way] for [their] transformations; that is why [the text] says: "It [celebrates] the ten thousand kinds of entities with drumming"! Although the Sage embodies the Dao by making use of it, he is unable to completely have negativity as his substance. That is why, as he is adapting to and penetrating All Under Heaven, there will be traces of [his] managing activity* 萬物由之以化故曰鼓萬物也聖人雖體道以爲用未能全無以爲體故順通天下則有經營之跡也.
>
> [But his] blossoming capacity and great achievement are achieved indeed! 盛德大業至矣哉
>
> *It is a fact that that by which he penetrates the entities and orders affairs is altogether based on the Way! [That is,] the mother of the achievement and application of the Sage is in substance the same as the Way. This is the reason why he is able to "achieve" the "blossoming capacity and great achievement"* 夫物之所以通事之所以理莫不由乎道也聖人功用之母體同乎道盛德大業所以能至.
>
> That he richly provides [the ten thousand kinds of entities] is called [his] "great achievement" 富有之謂大業.
>
> *[He] broadly provides, that is why [the text] says: "He richly provides"* 廣大悉備故曰富有.
>
> That he daily renews [himself] is called "blossoming capacity" 日新之謂盛德.
>
> *He embodies change and adapts to transformations, that is why [the text] says: "He daily renews [himself]"* 體化合變故曰日新.

13. The sections on ritual and foreknowledge are parallel in the main text but are treated here quite differently. Given Wang Bi's great obsession with the negative effects of government supervision, as practiced by his own government, it is reasonable to assume that the disproportion in the treatment is not due to unequal textual transmission but to different degrees of interest in the respective topics.

14. The expression 舍己 also occurs in Wang Bi on *Laozi* 5.4 (as in the present passage, along with 任物); it goes back to the *Shangshu*, 4.22b, expression 舍己 從人, which praises Emperor Shun for abandoning ideas of his own and adapting the views of the others. The *Mengzi*, 3B.27下, praises the Emperor with the words "That Great Shun has something great about him is that he is good at agreeing with others, discarding his own [opinions], and following others" 舍己從人 . . .

15. The expression *wei gong zhi mu* 爲功之母, here translated as "the mother bringing about the achievements," is a neologism created by Wang Bi. It also occurs in Wang Bi on *Laozi* 39.3 and in the very end of the *LZWZLL*.

16. In order to establish parallel chains for both lines in passages written in IPS, Wang Bi occasionally has to construct a pseudo-quotation for purposes of symmetry. There is no phrase about the ten thousand kinds of affairs matching that about the *wanwu* 萬物 in the *Laozi*. The phrase is a construct matching its parallel number.

17. While the phrase here seems to link up with *Laozi* 2.4, its main thrust is taken from a statement on the Dao in *Laozi* 34.2, which provides the formula 不辭.

18. This is a further example of a quotation matched with a phantom parallel.

19. The term *congming* 聰明 appears further above in the beginning of the ruler's use of foreknowledge. There it refers to the ruler's "intelligence" and figures in the chain on the left side. From the parallel with the preceding sentence, here it is clear that *congming* must refer to the *shi* 事, the "processes" or "affairs," as opposed to the *wu* 物, the "material things." The rule in parallel style, that the use of the same term in different phrases indicates that they belong to the same chain, does not apply here.

20. The expression *pei tian* 配天, "to match Heaven," occurs in *Laozi* 68.5 in a different form and a very much different context. I see no possibility of transferring the subject that there is said to "match Heaven" meaningfully into the present context. The parallel with the "shapes and names" makes it imperative that this phrase, too, should refer to the specific entities. The key terms *da* 大 and *mei* 美 are used further down in this *zhang* in a parallel construction . . . 本在無爲母在 無名棄本而適其末舍母而用其子功雖大焉必有不濟名雖美焉僞亦必生. This links the achievements, *gong* 功, to the chain about the "shapes," and the "names" to the chain about the "names." The pattern is confirmed by the recurrence of the two terms in this connection further down in this commentary.

21. These two sentences are disturbing. They take up terms from the two

chains, namely, "mother" and "shape." However, as Wang Bi has argued above in this *zhang*, the "mother" is not only the basis for kindliness and righteousness but for ritual and respect as well, and therefore the sentence here must be *pars pro toto*, a frequent occurrence in IPS. The second sentence seems to take up the term *shape* from the left chain, but there the appropriate word would not have been the artisan but the Way. I therefore assume that these two sections deal with a general insight, namely, that that by which the specific shapes and names are cannot be confused with these shapes, because it is the unspecificity of the "That-by-which" that allows it to be the basis of widely different phenomena. For Wang Bi's theories about the origins of evil, see his *LZWZLL* 6.2 ff. and my analysis in my *Language, Ontology, and Political Philosophy*, Chapter 3, pp. 154–155, 165–166, 208–209.

Zhang 39 NUMBERED TEXT NOTE

1. The phrase 萬物得一以生 does not fit Wang Bi's argument, because it deals only with "great" entities able to deal with the entirety of the many. Wang Bi's *Laozi* did not have this phrase. It does not occur in the two Mawangdui manuscripts, which shows that there was a textual tradition without it. It is not in Zhuang Zun's *Laozi*. Traces of its absence have survived the editing of Wang's *Commentary*. The 集註本 for Wang Bi on *Laozi* 39.1 lists only five verbs, all referring to the "great" entities. The verb in later editions such as the 張之象本, which refers to the ten thousand kinds of entities, *mie* 滅, is absent here. In the commentary on *Laozi* 38.2, the 集註本 does carry a reference to the ten thousand kinds of entities, but the term referring to them, 生, is appended at the end and does not correspond to the position that the 萬物 would have had in the sequence. I therefore have deleted this addition.

Zhang 39 TRANSLATION NOTES

1. For the role of the One in controlling the many, cf. my *Language, Ontology, and Political Philosophy*, pp. 121–125. This passage has been much discussed. It is quoted as 各是一物所以爲主 for 各是一物之生所以爲主 in Liu Xiaobiao commenting on *Shishuo xinyu* AA 20a, Huida, *Zhaolun shu*, 413.b.a16, and Tōjō Itsudō. However, Lou Yulie and others have been wrong in changing this reading. They assumed that the *wu* 物 in the beginning refers to the *wanwu* 萬物, while I believe that it refers to the *wu* actually mentioned further down in this *zhang*, such as Heaven and Earth. These, however, are all Ones confronting Manys, and therefore *cheng* 成 must be translated as a transitive verb.

2. This sequence has an interlocking rhyming pattern. The Chinese terms for clear, calm, efficacious, full, and standard rhyme, as do those for being torn

apart, getting into commotion, becoming exhausted, being drained, and being toppled.

3. On Wang Bi's theory of the necessary public posture of the dukes and kings, see my analysis in my *Language, Ontology, and Political Philosophy*, pp. 199–212. These two phrases are quoted in inverse order in Wang Bi on *Laozi* 40.1.

4. Cf. *Zhuangzi yinde* 46/18/11: "The highest fame is to be without fame" 至譽無譽.

Zhang 40 TRANSLATION NOTES

1. The sentence is quoted by Wang Bi on *Laozi* 28.5. The subject there is the Sage. The very complicated translation for 反 here, as "acting by way of the negative opposite," is based on the context both in Wang Bi on *Laozi* 28.5 and here. At its core is the notion that the ruler with his high position and immeasurable wealth has to perform publicly the negative opposite in order to stabilize society and to secure his life and position. For my analysis, cf. the chapter "Wang Bi's Political Philosophy" in my *Language, Ontology, and Political Philosophy*, pp. 199–201.

2. For the formula 有以無爲用, see Wang Bi on *Laozi* 11.2. It is interpreted there as "They all depend on negativity for their usability."

3. The strange formula 動皆之 . . . , "[his] moves all go towards . . . ," is taken from Laozi 50.2, where the moves of those craving the richness of life all go toward the place of death.

4. Cf. Wang Bi on *Laozi* 43.2: "There is nothing that the empty and negative, as well as the soft and the weak do not penetrate."

5. This formula has become a standard of Wang Bi's ontology. Cf. Wang Bi on *Laozi* 1.2: "Generally speaking, Entity all begins in negativity."

Zhang 41 TRANSLATION NOTES

1. Wang Bi comments on *Laozi* 33.4 強行者有志也, "He who powerfully practices [the Way], will have his will," with a quotation from the above *Laozi* 41.1, namely "Practicing it to the utmost of his capacities," while *Laozi* 41.1 here is commented upon with a quotation from *Laozi* 33.4, namely, 有志也. The formula takes up a statement by Confucius in *Lunyu* 7.6, "[I] set my will upon the Way," for which there is a commentary by Wang Bi.

2. The term *dayi zhi dao* 大夷之道, the "Way of bringing about Great Evenness," seems not to occur elsewhere. The identification of *yi* 夷 with *ping* 平, however, makes it into something much more familiar, that is, the *daping zhi dao* 大平之道 or *taiping zhi dao* 太平之道, commonly rendered as "The Way of

Great Peace" as the ultimate ideal of goodness, political stability, and prosperity. The interpretation of this passage of the *Laozi* takes up the argument from *Laozi* 27.4, where the maxims are listed that the Sage follows. The formula *yin wu zhi xing* 因物之性, "to go by the nature of entities," occurs there verbatim.

3. Wang Bi does not have a verbatim quotation from the *Laozi* here to suit his purpose; he thus uses a formula coined by himself in his *Commentary* on *Laozi* 38, where he comments on the sentences "He with the highest receipt/capacity does not make anything of [his] receipt/capacity. That is why he is in possession of the [highest] receipt/capacity" with the words: "The person with highest capacity will make use only of the Way and will not take his capacity to be [any particular] capacity. He does not hold on to anything, and does not make use of anything. That is why it is able to 'possess receipt/capacity' and still 'nothing remains undone.' He does not strive, but still obtains, he does not interfere, but still completes. That is why, although he 'possesses capacity,' he does not have the definition of [someone having a particular] receipt/capacity." The structure of the Sage's being a valley is discussed in Wang Bi on *Laozi* 28.1, although the expression used there is not *gu* 谷 but *qi* 谿.

4. In *Laozi* 28.2, the concluding formula is "will be the rule for All Under Heaven."

5. The expression 廓然無形 occurs in Wang Bi's commentary on *Laozi* 20.4, where the Sage says of himself: "I am vacant, without clues [for others to recognize me], like a baby that has not yet started to smile," on which Wang Bi comments: "This means: I am vacant without a shape that could be named, without a clue that could be taken up, like a baby that is not yet capable of smiling."

6. Wang Bi's definition of *tou* 偷 as *pi* 匹 has puzzled many scholars, including Hattori Nankaku, Usami Shinsui, Ma Xulun, Hatano Tarō, and Lou Yulie. The textual transmission, however, is stable, even including texts from other families. The two terms in fact overlap in one segment. In *Lunyu* 8.2, Confucius is quoted: "When old friends are not neglected by them [the gentlemen], the people will not be mean." The term 偷 is explained in the commentary put together by He Yan, the *Lunyu jijie*, through a combination with a second term as 偷薄, "vulgar," or "mean."

7. The phrase again takes up the words and the argument of *Laozi* 27.4, where the text says: "He who is good at locking [doors] will [do this] without the catch of a lock, and still [the door] cannot be opened. He who is good at tying [strings] will [do this] without a knot, and still [the tie] cannot be opened." The Commentary: "He goes by the other entities' That-which-is-of-itself-what-it-is, and neither sets [them] up nor makes [them] do" [something].

8. Wang Bi uses the term *yu* 渝 with *zhen* 眞 as an object consistently in the sense of "to dirty, to pollute." Cf. his comments on *Laozi* 4.1, 50.2, and 55.3; see also the comment on *Laozi* 70.5.

9. With the expression "to brag," Wang Bi refers to statements about the Sage's not bragging in *Laozi* 22.7, 24.2, and 30.5, all of which use the same term.

10. A change in translation strategy is necessitated here by the change in the grammatical pattern. The next four phrases all deal with "great" phenomena. Although the commentary to this first text of the series still links it directly to the Sage, this is not the case with the rest. The formal parallel has to take precedence over the seeming continuity of the theme of the Sage. The transitive for *fang* 方 as "squaring" is forced by the parallel in *Laozi* 58.7, 8 and 9, where the equivalents of *fang* all have to be translated as transitives.

11. Tao Hongqing suggests here changing 全別 to 分別, which would be well in line with Wang Bi's language and thinking. In this case, the translation would be "does not manage [each and every] detail and specification."

12. The same argument is made by Wang Bi in his *LZWZLL* 1.18.

13. Texts 13 and 14 are quoted in inverted order as a statement by *Laozi* in *Hou Hanshu* 30b, 1070, in a memorial by the famous specialist in heavenly portents, Lang Yi 郎顗. He explains it with *Lunyu* 13.10, according to which Confucius claims that, were he employed, things would be successfully completed after three years. It is interesting to note that quotations like this could be quoted in a fairly trivial manner within the rhetoric of a second-century memorial as general maxims or observations of wisdom to be explained in conjunction with Confucius quotations, without major interest in the context in which they originally appeared.

14. Cf. *Laozi* 35.1: "If [the ruler were to] hold on to the Great Image, [then] All Under Heaven [would] come [to him]." Wang Bi's commentary: "The Great Image is the mother of the heavenly images. It is neither hot nor cold, neither warming nor cooling. That is why it is capable of embracing and penetrating the ten thousand kinds of entities without there being one that is crossed or hurt."

Zhang 42 NUMBERED TEXT NOTES

1. 文選遊天台山賦李善注, 2.25b7, quotes here the following Wang Bi commentary: 王弼曰一數之始而物之極也謂之爲妙有者也欲言有不見其形則非有故謂之妙欲言無物有之以生則非無故謂之有也斯乃無中之有謂文妙有也. As the first phrase is a verbatim quotation from Wang Bi on *Laozi* 39.1, and the term 妙有 does not occur elsewhere in Wang's work and is probably Buddhist, the rest of this text cannot be a part of Wang's commentary. For a translation of this passage, which is still strongly influenced by Wang Bi, see the note 1 to the translation.

2. There is a potential minor conflict here between the *LZWZLL* and the Wang Bi *Laozi* commentary. In the *LZWZLL* 4.25, Wang Bi refers to this passage with the words 明侯王孤寡之義, 而從道一 以宣其始. The 侯王 contrasts with the 王侯, suggested in this passage by the textual family as well as by the commentary expression 得一者王侯主焉.

3. This is one of the rare cases where none of the texts available in Wang Bi's textual family fits his commentary. I have therefore drawn on the 莊遵 text, because Wang Bi in many ways continued an interpretive tradition going back to

this scholar. The option in 傅奕古本 and 范應元本, to write a 我 after 人之所
教, is eliminated by the 人相教 in the commentary. The option to insert a 以 to
make it 人之所以教 is eliminated by the straight object in the parallel 我之教人
in the commentary. The option present in the base text to have a 之 after 亦我教
is eliminated through the commentary's 亦我教人 and the fact that the 教人 is a
well-attested option offered by 馬王堆 A, 傅奕古本, and 范應元本.

Zhang 42 Translation Notes

1. Li Shan's *Commentary to the Wen Xuan* here quotes the first line of Wang
Bi's commentary on *Laozi* 39.1, followed by a disquisition on the Buddhist term
miaoyou 妙有, which is strongly influenced by Wang Bi statements but is not from
Wang Bi's hand.

> Wang Bi says: "The One is the beginning of numbers and the ultimate
> of entities." It is spoken of as something "embryonically existing."
> If one wants to call it existing, [the truth still remains] that one does
> not see its form so that [in this sense] it is not existing. That is why it
> is spoken of as "embryonic." If one wants to call it non-existing, [the
> truth still remains] that the entities are generated on the basis of it so
> that [in this sense] it is not non-existing. That is why it is spoken of
> as "existing." [See also Wang Bi on *Laozi* 6.1 and 14.2.] This [One]
> accordingly is Entity within negativity, and one speaks of it as "embry-
> onically existing."

The particular argument about Entity within negativity is closer to He Yan's argument in his *Wuming lun* 無名論; cf. the translation in my *Language, Ontology,
and Political Philosophy*, pp. 52–53.

2. Lou Yulie interpunctuates the characters 由無乃一一可謂無已謂之一豈
得無言, in my view, correctly, by putting a question mark behind 一可謂無 and
behind 豈得無言. Shima Kuniō puts a stop between 已 and 謂.

3. The argument takes up a similar statement from the *Zhuangzi*, *Zhuangzi
yinde* 5/2/53 ff.: "Heaven and Earth are born simultaneously with me, and the ten
thousand kinds of entities and I are one. As we are already one, do I still manage
to have this [extra thing, the] word ['one']? Having already *called* [it] one, do I still
manage to be without [this other thing, the] word? The One plus the word make
two, two plus one make three. Proceeding from here, even an expert calculator
cannot get to the end of it, much less a plain man. Therefore if we take the step
from nothing to something, we [already] get to three, and how much worse if we
take the step from something to something!" Cf. *Chuang-tzu: The Seven Inner
Chapters and Other Writings from the Book Chuang-tzu*, trans. A. C. Graham,
p. 56. Wang Bi had access to what was probably the only copy of the *Zhuangzi*
available at the time; cf. my *The Craft of a Chinese Commentator*, 12–14. The

basic argument here is that up to the number three, no actual entity is involved, and only from then on the realm of the ten thousand entities begins, while up to the three it is the "realm of the Way," *dao zhi liu* 道之流.

4. The Chinese term for "one" here is *wu* 吾, "I." For the use of this term, cf. *The Craft of a Chinese Commentator*, 126–28.

5. The expression *you xin* 有心 recurs in Wang Bi on *Laozi* 38.2 in the form *you qi xin* 有其心. The context there makes it clear that 有 has to be read not as simply "having" but in a strong sense "holding on to."

6. The passage as transmitted in all existing texts would translate, awkwardly: "The Hundred Families have their [various] ambitions, different states have distinct customs, but what they attain as the One are a king or duke as master." There is no other passage in Wang's surviving writings talking about the states "attaining" a ruler. In this reading, furthermore, the ruler would automatically be the One holding together the place in all of its variety. This, however, was not Wang Bi's idea. For him, the ruler is able to hold the country together only if and as long as he is able to "hold on to the great image," as he says in the *LZWZLL* 1.31. The formula used here is linked to another in *Laozi* 39.2: "As long as the kings and dukes attain the One, they will be the standard for All Under Heaven through it." In *Laozi* 39.4, the point is also made why the terms through which the kings and dukes refer to themselves imply their link to the One.

7. This statement takes up an argument from *Laozi* 22.5 and Wang's commentary here.

8. The link between the previous sentences in this *zhang* and the two remaining ones is not clear and not made explicit by Wang Bi. The *wo* 我 speaking here is evidently the Sage. The link between the two sections must be the last conclusion in the first section. Increasing something reduces it in the sense that someone who goes all out will deviate from his nature and land in misfortune, while someone brutally encroaching upon others and thereby "increasing" will be reduced to coming to no good end.

Zhang 43 Numbered Text Notes

1. Dong Siqing's 集解本 inserts this commentary after *Laozi* 43.3 and ends it with the phrase that I have inserted as the commentary after 43.3.

2. This phrase is only transmitted in the 集解本.

Zhang 44 Translation Notes

1. The term *shen* 身 means both "the body" and one's "person." Here, both meanings apply.

2. The *shu* 孰, "who?," "which?," is read by Wang Bi throughout the *Laozi* as a rhetorical question for which the answer does not have to be spelled out, because it is considered evident. That is why, after three questions with *shu*, the text here can continue with a *shigu* 是故, "that is why."

Zhang 45 Numbered Text Note

1. The 集註本 gives a different commentary here: 學行大成常如玷缺謙則 受益 故其材用 無困弊之時. Shima Kuniō has identified it as being the commentary of Emperor Xuan 玄宗. The 張之象本 text is confirmed by the 陸德明 釋文, which quotes the 不爲 from this commentary and which does not occur in the text offered by the 集註本.

Zhang 45 Translation Notes

1. Commenting on *Laozi* 60.1, "[In] managing a big state [the Sage Ruler acts] is as if he were frying small fish," Wang Bi writes: "[That is] he does not worry. Bustling activity [as in stirring the fish] will cause much damage, [but] if he is calm, then he will keep their true [essence] intact."

2. In his commentary on *Laozi* 72.1, Wang Bi uses the term *qing jing* 清靜, "pure calmness," for the correct behavior of the ruler.

Zhang 46 Translation Notes

1. The language used by Wang Bi here, *xiu qi nei* 修其內, "taking care of internal matters," might indicate that he is not just speaking of the state and international trade but reads the statement about the use of the horses as a metaphor for taking care of one's inner life and striving for material goods outside in a much broader sense. Still, the language of cultivating one's inner life does not appear elsewhere in Wang Bi's work.

2. The expression *ke yu* 可欲, "[things] that might be craved for," occurs in *Laozi* 3.1. There it is a summary expression for social status and material wealth. The three phrases in the beginning of *Laozi* 46.3, therefore, are not just a list but a general statement in the beginning with two particulars to follow.

3. There is no commentary to this section. I assume that the expression "to know how to be satisfied" refers to material goods, leaving the "desire to achieve" with fame or social renown as the probable object. In *Laozi* 44.5, to which Wang Bi refers in his first commentary here, the material goods and social renown are the two unwholesome objects of desire.

Zhang 47 Translation Notes

1. The brackets "only when . . . " are justified by the sequel in 47.2 in light of Wang Bi's commentary on the present text. While a "when" without "only" is still too diffuse, the alternative "only by . . . " would be too harsh, because it would imply that anyone would understand All Under Heaven and the Way of Heaven by simply not going out of doors and by not peeping out of the window. However, as we see from Wang Bi on *Laozi* 49.5, which uses nearly verbatim the same argument as the beginning of his commentary on *Laozi* 47.1, the Sage King will not simply not go out of doors but will actually screen his eyes and plug his ears so as to avoid the blinding and deafening variety of society's affairs around him.

2. Cf. the beginning of the *LZWZLL* and Wang Bi on *Laozi* 49.5, where the terms *zong* 宗, "principle," and *zhu* 主, "master," are inverted: "Things will have their principle, processes will have their master." The term *li* 理 might go back to *Xici* 上, 7.1b7, where *tianxia zhi li* 天下之理 is mentioned.

3. The quotation is not entirely verbatim. It runs 子曰天下何思何慮天下同歸而殊塗一致而百慮 "The Master said: What is [everyone] in All Under Heaven thinking about and cogitating about? As to All Under Heaven—what they lead to is the same, but [they get there] through manifold roads; what they end up in is one and the same, but the cogitations [leading there] are of a hundred [kinds]" *Zhouyi*, 8.3.b8ff. Han Kangbo's commentary to this passage links the One to which all of these thoughts and cogitations eventually lead to Confucius' statement in the *Lunyu* 4.15, that it "is the One by which my [manifold] teachings are threaded through" 吾道一以貫之哉. Wang Bi refers to the same *Xici* passage in the *LZWZLL* 1.16.

4. For the notion of *li* 理, see my *Language, Ontology, and Political Philosophy*, pp. 115–121.

5. Wang Bi quotes this phrase of the *Laozi* in his commentary to the fifth line of hexagram *lin* 臨 in the *Zhouyi, Wang Bi ji jiaoshi*, 313. This is a case where a weak line [person] is in the emperor's position, which is often read by Wang Bi as the best combination. Wang Bi comments: "[Sitting in this position], he does not resent the growth of the strong [line in the second position] but is capable of putting it into his service. To put entities in charge according to their capabilities without contravening them means that the intelligent will go to the utmost of their perspicacity, and those strong in knowledge will do the best in the way of their capability to strategize; [in short, as the *Laozi* 47.4 says of the Sage,] 'without [his] acting on them, he gets [them] completed' and [as the *Xici* 7.8.b1 says of what the Sage in his spirit-like quality "gives" to All Under Heaven] 'without his acting, he makes [them] do the optimum.' This and nothing else is [what the main text calls] 'the [way] appropriate to a great gentleman.'" In the commentary on *Laozi* 38.1, Wang Bi again quotes this phrase to characterize "the person with highest capacity."

Zhang 48 NUMBERED TEXT NOTE

1 The 集註本 text for Wang Bi on *Laozi* 57.1 does not have the 又, but the 張之象本 has. As the text of *Laozi* 48.5 in the 張之象本 does not have this 又, it cannot be argued that the quotation in Wang Bi on 57.1 has been adapted to fit this text, because it does not. Given the presence of the 又, in 傅奕古本, as well as a lacuna accommodating such a character in 馬王堆 B (及其有事也 □ □足 . . .), a lacuna read, however, as a single space by Gao Ming, *Boshu* 57, it is safe to assume that the 張之象本 reading of Wang Bi on 57.1 is preferable and that Wang Bi's *Laozi* read 又不足.

Zhang 48 TRANSLATION NOTE

1. Wang Bi gives, verbatim, the same commentary on *Laozi* 49.1: "As a Sage [I am] without a permanent heart [of my own]. The hearts of the Hundred Families [I] take as [my] heart."

Zhang 49 TRANSLATION NOTES

1. Wang Bi gives, verbatim, the same commentary on *Laozi* 48.4.

2. Wang Bi's commentary to this phrase in *Laozi* 27.5 runs: "The Sage does not establish shapes and names in order to impose restrictions on other entities. He does not create promotions and honors in order to separate and reject the incapable. He 'boosts the ten thousand kinds of entities' That-which-is-of-itself-what-it-is,' [, as the *Laozi* says in 64.9,] but 'does not initiate' [, as the *Laozi* says about the Sage in 2.4]. That is why [the text] says: 'There is no rejecting other people [by him].'"

3. Wang Bi takes his interpretation of the nature of infants from *Laozi* 10 and 55. He comments on the notion of "baby" in *Laozi* 10.2 "[For a ruler] . . . to be able to be like a baby—ah!" with "to be without desires." The term used there is *yinger* 嬰兒. In *Laozi* 55.1, the expression is *chizi* 赤子. The *Laozi* sentence "[a ruler] who has the fullness of capacity in himself is like an infant" is commented upon by Wang Bi: "An infant is without cravings and without desires, and [thus] does not offend the multitude of [other] beings." Among the characteristics of such an infant in the *Laozi* 55.5 is that it achieves "the culmination of harmony." In both cases, the infant is not the model for the people but for the Sage Ruler.

4. There is no commentary by Wang Bi on the *Xici*. The translation of the section has to be adapted to the narrative persona, which is the Sage speaking in the first person, and to the context in which the quotation is used, which is mostly determined by the subsequent sentences. Hatano Tarō and other scholars

refer to Han Kangbo's commentary on the *Xici*, which is seen as being written in the vein of Wang Bi, as well as to Kong Yingda's subcommentary. In my view, the translation extrapolated from Han's commentary and Kong's subcommentary, however, is incompatible with any possible reading of the present context. As the entire passage is both important and difficult, I shall give a full rendering of the Han Kangbo/Kong Yingda version, *Zhouyi zhengyi* 8.79.

[In accordance with] Heaven and Earth, [he] establishes the positions. The Sage completes the capabilities [of the ten thousand entities].

Commentary [Han Kangbo]

The Sage relies on the standard of Heaven and Earth [in establishing the positions] and each of the ten thousand entities completes its capabilities.

Subcommentary [Kong Yingda]

That "Heaven and Earth establish the positions" means that the Sage [,as Han Kangbo says,] "relies on the standard of Heaven and Earth" and "establishes the positions" of worthy and lowly. That "the Sage completes the capabilities" [means] that the Sage goes by the nature created [for the entities] by Heaven and Earth in completing for each of them their capability so that all get [their proper] place [and position].

With others he consults, with spirits he consults. The Hundred Families give [support] to [him as the most] capable.

Commentary [Han Kangbo]

"With others he consults," that is, he deliberates with the multitude in order to determine what is advantageous and what [is] not. "With spirits he consults," that is, he relies on oracle and milfoil stalks to investigate what is auspicious and what [is] not. [As to the former,] he does not fret and brood about, and [still] what is advantageous and what is not will be clear of its own accord. [As to the latter,] he does not labor over investigating and probing, but [still], what is auspicious and what is not will manifest itself of its own accord. As he sorts out the feelings of the ten thousand kinds of entities and penetrates the causes of the obscure and deeply [hidden], the "Hundred Families give [support] to [him as the most] capable"; they "rejoice in promoting [him] without harboring any resentment" [as the Laozi *66 says about All Under Heaven's attitude towards the Sage].*

Subcommentary [Kong Yingda]

This means that, whenever the Sage begins an endeavor, he first consults with the multitude of others in order to determine what is advantageous and what [is] not. He also [questions] the spirits and gods [with] oracle and milfoil stalks in order to find out what is auspicious about it and what [is] not. That is the [meaning of] his "consulting" with "spirits." Accordingly, the Sage first consults with others and with spirits and does not wear himself out with fretting and brooding [about what is advantageous and what is not] as well as investigating and probing [about what is auspicious and what is not]. Quite naturally he is capable of "sorting out the feelings of the ten thousand entities" and he is capable of "penetrating" the principles "of the obscure and deeply" [hidden]. Such being his capability, the Hundred Families in All Under Heaven will accordingly be close to and support [such a] capable man, and they will joyfully promote [him] to be king.

While the reading of the first sentence more or less ties in with Wang Bi's context, two elements in the reading of the second sentence do not. Evidently, there is no reference in Wang Bi to the promotion of the most capable one to be the king, and, second, Kong Yingda eliminates the political reading of Han Kangbo's commentary, which still refers to the ruler's using the intelligence services to ferret out opposition and resentment.

5. This passage is difficult, indeed, because the *Xici* passage preceding it determined some of its vocabulary and content but is not clear either. I have tried to present a consistent—and falsifiable—translation, but I am well aware that the text might be corrupt.

6. The emperor's *mian* hat and the cushions on his ears are described as devices to help him overlook the heterodox and not hear any slanders. Hatano Tarō, II.10ff., has collected many of the standard references to these two contraptions.

7. This quotation from the *Huainanzi* again has to be integrated into the I narrative of this commentary. Wang Niansun, *Dushu zazhi* 14.14., vol. 3, p. 51, has argued that 在智 and 在力 had to be replaced by 任智 and 任力, respectively, in the *Huainanzi*, an argumentation taken up for this quotation by Hatano Tarō and Lou Yulie. There is no manuscript supporting this view, either for the *Huainanzi* or for Wang Bi's *Commentary*. The *Commentary* wording proves that at least in Wang Bi's time, the *Huainanzi* text indeed read 在智 and 在力.

8. The statement goes back to *Lunyu* 12.13, "As to hearing litigation, I am like [= not superior to] others. It has to be brought about that there is no [more] litigation [at all]." No comment by Wang Bi survives. The comment in He Yan's *Lunyu jijie* stresses that things have to be solved before coming to litigation. This is also the way in which Wang Bi quotes this phrase by Kongzi in his commentary to the *Zhouyi* hexagram *song* 訟, *Wang Bi ji jiaoshi*, 249, where he says: "[To bring it about] that there is no litigation depends on taking care of the issues in the formative stage" 無訟在於謀始.

9. This sentence again goes back to *Huainanzi* 14.138.10 ff., directly after the passage quoted verbatim just above: "It is impossible [for a ruler] to get others to have no knowledge, but it is possible [for him] to get others [to the point] of being unable to use their knowledge against him. It is not possible [for him] to get others to have no physical strength, but it is possible to get others [to the point] of being unable to apply their strength against him." The *Jizhu* 集註 transmits a text closer to the *Huainanzi*. This closeness has led Hatano Tarō and Lou Yulie to assume that it has preserved an older reading that originally directly quoted the *Huainanzi*, although the *Jizhu* has minor deviations from the transmitted *Huainanzi*. As Lou correctly remarks, Wang Bi's argument in fact differs from that of the *Huainanzi*, as is evident from Wang's next sentence. The standard text fits very well into the argument, while either the *Jizhu* or the two emendations based on it only do so after changes for which there is neither a textual basis in the various manuscripts, or in the *Huainanzi*. I therefore believe that no change is necessary.

10. The entire passage in the *Zhuangzi* reads: "If the ruler truly cherishes knowledge but is without the Way, then great turmoil in All Under Heaven will result. How do we know that this is the case? It is a fact that if knowledge about

devices like bows, crossbows, nets, and darts becomes too much, then the birds will be in turmoil above; if knowledge about catching devices like fish-hooks, baits, nets, and fish traps becomes too much, then the fishes will be in turmoil in the water; if knowledge about catching devices like traps, snares, nets, and pitfalls becomes too much, the wild animals will be in turmoil in the marshes; if knowledge about dissimulation, slow poisons, innuendoes, [sophistries about] the 'hard' and the 'white' and various rhetorical tricks becomes too much, the customs will be deluded in sophistry. That is why each time if All Under Heaven is in great turmoil, the blame lies with [the ruler's] cherishing knowledge." Cf. R. Wilhelm, *Dschuang Dsi. Das Wahre Buch vom Südlichen Blütenland*, 72.

11. *Lunyu* 4.10: "The Master said: 'The Gentleman is in his relationship with All Under Heaven without preferences and without disdain.'" As there is no comment to this phrase by either Wang Bi himself nor in He Yan's *Lunyu* edition, my translation broadly follows A. Waley, *The Analects of Confucius*, 104, which is based on Zheng Xuan's reading 無適無莫 as 無敵無慕, *Lunyu jijie*, 254. Cf. also *Lunyu zhushu* 2471b, where Kong Yingda defines *shi* 適 as *hou* 厚, "wealthy," and *mo* 莫 as *bo* 薄, "impoverished," and says: "The [passage] means that the Gentleman will in his dealing with the other people in All Under Heaven pick neither the wealthy ones nor those who are impoverished" [but if there are righteous ones, he will associate with them]. Extrapolated from this commentary, the *Lunyu* passage would read: "The Gentleman in his relationships with [people of] All Under Heaven will [prefer] neither the rich nor those who have nothing, but will associate only with those who are righteous." From the use made of the quotation in Wang Bi's commentary here, it is evident that this was not his reading.

12. On the basis of the language used in these two phrases, Tao Hongqing has suggested that the vocabulary of the phrase that it counters should be changed appropriately. The two phrases here talk of "spying out" 察 and "evading" 避, on the one hand, and "going after" 求 and "reciprocating" 應, on the other hand. The passage that this one rejects, "if I were to spy out . . . if I were to spy out," operates with a vocabulary of 察–應 for both segments, that concerning "insight" and that concerning "strength." The suggestion is valid indeed. However, the stylistic figure of a double repetition of 察–應 could be consciously crafted. I have therefore left it in place.

Zhang 50 Translation Notes

1. In *Laozi* 76.1, both the followers of life and of death are mentioned again. Arguing that, while they live, people are soft and weak and at death firm and rigid, the *Laozi* says: "Hardness and violent rigor are the companions of death; suppleness and softness are the companions of life." The conclusion is that those who are firm and rigid will use violence to impose their will, but they will "not win" because, as Wang Bi says, others in their numbers will get together to oppose them and bring them to death.

2. The passage has been much discussed, and various emendations have been proposed. From Wang Bi's commentary it is clear that the two groups of the companions of life and death do not present the problem but the ones alluded to through the comparison with the eagle and the sea turtle, who "can be said to

reside in a realm without death" but, lured by the bait, eventually "enter into the realm where there is no life" by being killed. This, accordingly, is the third group discussed in the text passage under scrutiny here.

3. The two parallel segments dealing with the eagle and the sea turtle, respectively, are written in interlocking style but not integrated into the a/b chain dominating this section. I have therefore indented them.

4. The term *xin* 信, "credibility," here refers to *Laozi* 21.5: "[If] their essence is verily truthful, there is credible [evidence] in them," where "them," according to Wang Bi's commentary, refers to the entities. They thus carry in themselves "credibility" in the sense that the That-by-which of the ten thousand entities is present in them as their true essence. For a more detailed analysis, cf. my *Language, Ontology, and Political Philosophy*, pp. 60–62.

Zhang 51 Numbered Text Notes

1. The 張之象本 here gives a commentary 命并作爵, which is a gloss on a variant 爵/命 and not a commentary, as the editor of the 四庫 edition of this text remarks.

2. From the fragment in the *Chuxue ji*, which directly links up with the transmitted text, we see that originally this commentary segment was much longer, commenting on all of the notions appearing in the text. This is one of the few instances where significant lacunae can be discovered in Wang Bi's transmitted text.

Zhang 51 Translation Notes

1. The rigid parallelism of the first four phrases suggests a staircase structure. The *zhang*, however, operates with the basic division between *dao* and *de*. From Wang Bi's commentary here, we learn that he did not read the parallelism of the four phrases as an indication of their identical grammatical structure. Both the implied subject and the implied object of the phrases change. The *wu* 物, physical entities, and *shi* 勢, here translated as "situations," although they fill exactly the place of the immaterial "processes" *shi* 事, in Wang Bi's and other philosophers' terminology, are thus those that receive their capacity on the basis of the Way. Therefore they appear as a subgroup to *de* 德 in the structural writing of this *zhang*. The structure of the first four sentences of *Laozi* 51 thus is

a   b

b1

b2

This reading is reinforced both by Wang Bi's quotation from this *zhang* in his commentary on *Laozi* 1.2, and from the *Laozi*'s own reduplication of this passage in 10.7 ff. The arrangement suggested here determines the arrangement of the entire *zhang*.

2. Cf. *LZWZLL* 5.1ff., where Wang Bi is developing the theory of heuristic terms.

3. Wang Bi's 道者物之所由 is a nearly verbatim quotation from the *Zhuangzi* 88/31/49 且道者萬物之所由也, but it also is one of his often repeated basic philosophical assumptions.

4. For the identification of *de* 德 with *de* 得, cf. *Laozi* 38, Translation note 1.

5. This is a short form of the phrase in Wang Bi's commentary on *Laozi* 38.1, beginning, where he writes: 何以得德由乎道也 "By means of what does one obtain [one's] receipt/capacity? On the basis indeed of the Way!"

6. The passage is quoted in Wang Bi on *Laozi* 1.2, where the text says:

When there are not [now] names, it is the beginning of the ten thousand kinds of entities.	When there [already] are names, it is the mother of the ten thousand kinds of entities.

Generally speaking, Entity all begins in negativity. That is why it will be

at a time when there are neither the shapes nor names, the beginning of the ten thousand kinds of entities.	*when it comes to a time when there are shapes and names, that which [according to* Laozi *51.3] "lets [the ten thousand kinds of entities] grow, nurtures them, specifies them, and completes them"; [in short,] it will be their mother.*

The condition for the possibility of the existence of the entities is thus the Way; two stages are differentiated—generation, normally called *sheng* 生, and completion, normally called *cheng* 成. It is highly probable that Wang Bi's *Laozi* text did not have the *de* 德 in this sentence at all, as is the case in MWD A and B, Fan Yingyuan, as well as two manuscripts from the Xianger family. Cf. Shima Kuniō, 162. Still, the break after "generates them" remains necessary, and so does the change in the subject and object of the sentence.

7. The same pair of phrases are used in *Laozi* 10.9. The switch in subject after *er* 而 is inferred from Wang Bi's commentary there.

8. There is some doubt about the authenticity of this piece of commentary.

9. Cf. Wang Bi's commentary to the parallel passage in *Laozi* 10.9, which is nearly the same.

Zhang 52 TRANSLATION NOTES

1. Wang Bi consistently maintains that it is the Way that both generates and sustains the ten thousand entities. The term *de*, 德 receipt/capacity, is thus reduced to a noun expressing what the entities "attain" or "get," *de* 得, on the basis of the Way. The argument here is echoed in Wang Bi on *Laozi* 1.2, as well as in the preceding *zhang*.

2. There is an English equivalent term for *ben* 本, namely, "root," but none for *mo* 末 , which denotes the offspring from this root, that is, both stem and branches.

3. Doors, *men* 門, signify in the *Laozi* and in Wang Bi's writing the openings out of which things come. This leaves for the *dui* 兌 the notion of openings through which things enter, in this case, enter the body. In his commentary on *Laozi* 65.3, Wang Bi quotes the above *Laozi* passage. There, the object whose openings and doors are closed, is the "people." Here it corresponds to All Under Heaven. In *Laozi* 56.3, the same passage occurs. The commentary and context there suggest the same reading. I have not found the expression *shi yu* 事欲 elsewhere. *Shi* 事, normally in Wang Bi's writing stands in contrast to *wu* 物, the material objects, as the immaterial processes. Together, the *wu* and *shi* make up the "ten thousand kinds of entities." *Shih* would typically include immaterial but very real things such as social status or renown. The term *shi* recurs in the next commentary as well as in the text of *Laozi* 52.5 separately. Therefore, the *shi yu* must be a "desire for *shi*." As the processes involved here seem to be those of social contention, I have used the term *action*.

4. The ruler is in a position that is "great" 大, but his public stance has to be that of smallness. The term 小, "smallness," is associated with the Dao itself (34.1) but also defines the term *simplicity*, *pu* 樸, in *Laozi* 32.1, the standard term for the Sage Ruler's public stance.

5. The phrase here, 不明察, is the negative form of a false behavior of the ruler mentioned several times in Wang Bi's commentary; cf. 以明察物: "if I were to spy out other entities by means of [my] insight" in Wang Bi on *Laozi* 49.5 or Wang Bi on *Laozi* 18.2 "If he [the ruler] practices tricks and applies his intelligence to spy out cunning and deceit" 行術用明以察姦偽. That is why the term *ming* 明 in this sentence cannot be translated as has been done two lines before.

Zhang 53 TRANSLATION NOTES

1. The only person dealing with "All Under Heaven" in its entirety is the ruler, therefore, the ruler is the implied subject. Grammatically, it is possible that the knowledge to be curbed is that of the ruler himself. But, commenting on *Laozi* 3.2, "That is why the governing [technique] of the Sage consists in emptying their

[the people's] hearts and filling their bellies." Wang Bi writes: "The heart contains knowledge, and the belly food. He empties [that which has] knowledge [the heart] and fills [that which has] no knowledge" [the belly]. The object here clearly is the people, or All Under Heaven, as confirmed by Wang Bi's commentary to the present passage and the next. My translation of *jieran* 介然 is based on this parallel with "emptying."

2. The argument is that the people love the bypaths so much that, even were he able to reduce their knowledge and make them abide by the Great Way, any minute interference from his side would instantly cause their move to the bypaths.

3. This is to illustrate that a single "interference," like having his court tidied up, leads to general social disaster and conflict. That is the cause of the "worry" of the first phrase.

Zhang 54 Translation Notes

1. For the expressions "root" and "stem and branches," see my *The Craft of a Chinese Commentator*, 281–84.

2. The term *bao* 抱 appears in the *Laozi* with two significant objects, *pu* 樸, "the unadorned" or "the simple," in *Laozi* 19.1, and *yi* 一, "the One," in *Laozi* 22.6. As the commentary explains that he "has no craving for having more," the implied object of *bao* might be either one, since they are related.

3. The *Laozi* text here reads 子孫以祭祀不輟, which, verbatim, would translate "the sons and grandsons bring sacrifices without interruption," which is the meaning that most translators have chosen. That translation leaves the *yi* 以 awkwardly unexplained and seems utterly devoid of any visible link to the previous phrases. Wang Bi reads 54.3 as a general statement dealing with the two preceding sentences. "This Way" in his commentary directly refers to the preceding statements. What, then, about the sacrifices? He does not explain the meaning of the expression *ji si* 祭祀 in this commentary. However, in the summary of the *zhang* in his commentary on 54.7, he says 察己以知之不求於外也: "I examine myself by way of cognizing it [All Under Heaven], and I do not strive [for this cognition] on the outside." The chain going from one's own self to the entire world is given in the *zhang*, but there is no counterpart in the text to the expression *cha ji* 察己, "to examine oneself." Thus we have an uncommented on expression 祭祀 in the text, and a term 察己 in the commentary for which there is no text. Both are, it is my contention, the same. The term *ji* 祭 is in fact explained as *cha* 察 in the *Shangshu* 尚書 (*Shangshu*, Chapter 6, *Shangshu dazhuan zhuzi suoyin*, p. 25, line 24) and in the *Chunqiu fanlu*, Chapter 16 (*Chunqiu fanlu zhuzi suoyin*, p. 75, line 13). The latter runs "to sacrifice is to investigate" 祭者察也; it means to investigate the spirits, and this by means of good deeds. Because these good deeds find out about things that cannot be seen or heard, one calls them an "investigation." Wang Bi must have read the *si* 祀 as a variant for *ji* 己. The subsequent

text unfolds from how examining oneself the entire world may be understood and regulated. The expression *cha ji* 察己 also occurs in Wang Bi on *Zhouyi* hexagram *guan* 觀, fifth position: "That is why [I, the ruler,] observe the people's customs by way of examining myself, and, if the Hundred Families commit transgressions, this is due to [me] the single human" 故觀民之俗以察己[之]百姓有罪在于一人 (*Wang Bi ji jiaoshi*, 317).

4. For the other elements such as person, family, and districts, there were always other counterparts. This is not true for All Under Heaven. Wang Bi's commentary tries to solve this weak point in his interpretation by adding two different attributes to All Under Heaven, so that there is a difference between the two. The second sentence of this commentary takes up *Laozi* 73.5 ff.: "It is the Way of Heaven not to struggle but still to be good at winning, not to speak but still to be good at being followed." Wang Bi comments on the second part with the words "That following [his teachings] brings luck, deviating from them, misfortune [is meant by] 'not to speak but still being good at being followed.'" A similar thought is taken up in Wang Bi on *Laozi* 38. Cf. Translation note 5 there, where Wang Bi quotes the *tuan* to hexagram *fu*, "Return," from the *Zhouyi*, that by way of "[the entities'] return" "the heart of Heaven and Earth becomes visible." Accordingly, the commentary here inserts itself into Wang Bi's thinking, so that the suspicions of some commentators listed by Hatano Tarō, that this passage might be spurious do not seem to be well founded.

Zhang 55 TRANSLATION NOTES

1. The "ruler" has been interpolated as the implied subject on the basis of the commentary to the last line of this *zhang* as it appears in *Laozi* 30.7. From this commentary it is clear that the opposite of "him who has the fullness of capacity in himself" and who is like an infant is the violent ruler.

2. The same formula occurs in Wang Bi on *Laozi* 4.1 and 50.2.

3. *Jing* 精, the "essence," is linked by Wang Bi to the true core of entities, which is linked to the Way; cf. Wang Bi on *Laozi* 21.5, where the term *jing* 精 is explained as *zhen jing* 眞精, "true essence."

4. The statement by Wang Bi about the "ancestor of the ten thousand entities" in *LZWZLL* 1.6 uses similar language.

5. In *Laozi* 16.6 there is the verbatim formula: "Having knowledge of [this] Eternal means being enlightened. [But] if he [a ruler] does not know the Eternal, then acting recklessly he brings about a nefarious" [outcome]. Wang Bi comments: "The Eternal [essence of the entities] as such is neither [inwardly] partial nor manifest [in its preferences]; it has an appearance without either brightness or darkness, and features without either warming or cooling. That is why [the text] says: 'Having knowledge of [this] Eternal means being enlightened'"!

6. There is a possibility that the two sections of this *zhang* have direct parallels. The *shi qi* 使氣, "engaging the vital breath," might relate to the infant's muttering all day without getting hoarse, and the *yi sheng* 益生, "having life in excess," might relate to the opposite in the infant with its weakness and softness. However, in the surviving Wang Bi commentary, there is no indication of such a link. Accordingly, the only definite statement possible at this stage is that, from the "but" in text 7 on, the "wrong" attitude is described. While those analogous to the infant "attain the Eternal" and cannot be harmed by others, those described after the "but" will "die young."

7. Wang Bi links this commentary to *Laozi* 42.3: "Those who are violent and brutal will not meet their [natural] death."

8. The same textual passage is in *Laozi* 30.7. There Wang Bi's commentary runs: "'Growing mighty' means a rapid surge of military might. [The expression] is a metaphor for imposing violent [rule] in All Under Heaven by means of soldiers. [As the *Laozi* 23.2 says] 'A cyclone does not outlast a morning, and a cloudburst does not outlast a day.' That is why [the text says that such a] rapid surge [in military might] is by necessity 'not on the Way' and 'quickly finished.'"

Zhang 56 NUMBERED TEXT NOTES

1. From *Laozi* 4.1, it is clear that 挫其銳 belongs with 解其紛 to form a pair. Text and commentary here are cut at the wrong point. I have transferred 挫其銳 from 56.3 to 56.4.

2. 馬王堆 A, 馬王堆 B, and 郭店 A have a different sequence of phrases for *Laozi* 56.3–56.6. Instead of the sequence (here given without the character variants) 塞其兌閉其門挫其銳解其紛和其光同其塵, they write 塞其兌閉其門和其光同其塵挫其銳 (馬王堆 B adds 而) 解其紛.

3. The repetition of the 物物 in Wang Bi on 56.5 and 56.6 excludes the possibility of a scribal error. Read as is, it is a perfectly meaningful text. The 張之象本 seems to have tried to smooth out the unwieldiness of the 物物 and is the later redaction.

Zhang 56 TRANSLATION NOTES

1. The basic confrontation in this *zhang* is again between the "other entities" and him, in charge of them all, the ruler. From phrase 3 on, the text deals with the strategies of the Sage Ruler, the principle of which has been stated in the commentary to 56.1. The phrase *tong qi chen* 同其塵 from text 6 is directly applied to the Sage in Wang Bi on *Laozi* 70.5. The *gui* 貴 of text 10 in the end also occurs in *Laozi* 70.4 in the same context for the Sage as it does here.

2. The same phrase is in *Laozi* 52.3. There *qi* 其 referred to All Under Heaven. Here *qi* 其 refers in an even more general sense to the *wu* 物, "entities," mentioned in Wang's commentary to 56.5 and 56.6.

3. The last two pairs occur also in *Laozi* 4.1, where these sentences are said of the Way itself as a model for the Great Entities, including the Sage Ruler.

Zhang 57 NUMBERED TEXT NOTES

1. This commentary section has marks of corruption. First, while the phrases about the "standards," the "increasing of taboos," and the "multiplication of useful instruments" are all taken up in this *zhang*, the phrase about increasing the people's "knowledge and wit" is not. On the other hand, it might be argued, as I do, that the phrase about an increase in people's knowledge and wit is a summing up and consequence of the two preceding phrases. Second, the *duo* 多 after *hun* 昏 further down is evidently misplaced. It might in fact be the leftover of a phrase dealing with the increase in people's knowledge and wit, if indeed there was such a phrase. Third, the parallels among the three surviving phrases are very irregular. In the next phrase, 多利器欲以強國者也而國愈昏, we have a 者也, which changes the grammar by making the "multiplication of useful instruments" the subject instead of the ruler and making 強 into a main verb instead of a verb subordinated to 愈昏. This 者也 has no parallel in either of the two preceding phrases, although both are otherwise constructed in a parallel fashion. There are three options: either to cut the 者也 in the phrase about the useful instruments, to assume that this is the older reading and add it to the two other phrases (as well as the possibly lost fourth phrase about the people's wit and cunning), or to proceed, as I have done, and add it only to the phrase about "increasing the taboos." I do not add it to the first phrase in this commentary, because I read it as a direct explanation of the last stage of the development outlined here, when eventually standards and luxury goods are being displayed, the robbers multiply, and the last recourse is the military.

2. From Wang Bi's commentary 我之所欲唯無欲 here it is clear that his *Laozi* text cannot have been the 我無欲 given by the 傅奕古本 and the 范應元本. The only available version accommodating the twofold use of 欲 is 馬王堆 B and 郭店 A, which read 我欲不欲. The 不欲, however, in this version does not correspond to Wang Bi's 無欲. I therefore assume that his *Laozi* text combined features from different texts of his textual family. As the core feature marking this text is in fact the 欲, I have taken the text closest to Wang Bi in this respect, namely, the 馬王堆 B, as the base text here. The decision to accept the 之言 rests on the presumed closeness of this Wang Bi *Laozi* phrase with the reading of 馬王堆 B, as well as the fact that the 莊遵 text, which is loosely related to Wang Bi's textual family, also has the 之言. The decision to change the 馬王堆 B 曰, even though it again has support in 郭店 A, to 云 is based on the fact that 云 is common to 莊遵, as well as the 傅奕古本 and the 范應元本.

Zhang 58 NUMBERED TEXT NOTE

1. The expression *dundun* 惇惇 seems to present one of the few cases where Wang Bi's *Commentary* has been adapted to a different reading in the *Laozi* text printed with it. In terms of content, the reading present in Chen Jingyuan's 陳景元 *Zuanwei* 纂微 fits Wang Bi's commentary best.

Zhang 58 TRANSLATION NOTES

1. The term *yao* 妖 only appears once in Wang Bi's *Laozi* Commentary. Wang Bi's standard term for "evil" is *xie* 邪. In his *Commentary on the Zhouyi*, 5.16.a3, Wang Bi talks of the *yaoxie zhi dao* 妖邪之道, the "way of evil." For this reason I have adopted this meaning in the present context.

2. Hattori Nankaku, Hatano Tarō, and Lou Yulie all assume that this commentary segment is corrupt. The thought expressed in my translation as given above does not appear elsewhere in Wang Bi's surviving work. It does, however, fit Wang Bi's thinking. I have therefore made use of it; cf. my *Language, Ontology, and Political Philosophy*, p. 153.

Zhang 59 NUMBERED TEXT NOTE

1. Shima Kuniō and Lou Yulie give an interpunctuation 嗇, 農夫. In Wang Bi's comments such A = B sentences always come with a 也 which is missing here. Wang Bi continues with 農人 and not with 農夫 which makes this reading even more implausible. The phrase following 夫 has all the markers of a general statement of a type introduced by 夫 in the meaning "generally spoken, it is true that . . . " I assume that Wang read 嗇 as meaning "sparing" or "reductive," and based his comment on the standard use of 嗇 for 穡 with the meaning of "harvesting," "gathering in," or "husbandry," which early commentators saw as derived from the meaning of 嗇.

Zhang 59 TRANSLATION NOTES

1. For Wang Bi's notion of the "return," cf. my *Language, Ontology, and Political Philosophy*, pp. 138–143; 177–213.

2. For these terms in another meaning, see the translation of *Laozi* 7.1.

Zhang 60 TRANSLATION NOTES

1. Cf. Wang Bi on *Laozi* 45.6: "Being calm keeps intact the true essence of entities. Bustling activity contravenes the nature of entities."

2. The Commentary inserts the *ze* 則, "then," in both sentences, only to clarify the relationship between the first and second parts. The content remains elusive.

3. *De* 德 is here translated as *de* 得 in the sense of Wang Bi's commentary on *Laozi* 38.2 德者得也.

Zhang 61 NUMBERED TEXT NOTE

1. 馬王堆 A and 馬王堆 B invert these two phrases to 天下之牝天下之郊 也 and 口口口也天下之交也, respectively.

Zhang 61 TRANSLATION NOTES

1. Grammatically, both sentences are linked by a *ze* 則, "then," "as a consequence." The rivers and seas, however, are naturally organized this way, while it takes a conscious effort for a big state to imitate the rivers and seas in projecting a lowly and modest image. Therefore, the two *ze* have to be translated differently.

2. Cf. for a similar thought *Laozi* 28.1 and *Commentary*, as well as *Laozi* 32.4 and *Commentary*. The image of the female is linked to the "lowly position" in the commentary to *Laozi* 6.1.

Zhang 62 TRANSLATION NOTE

1. The same formula in Wang Bi on *Laozi* 51.3 explaining "the Way generates them [the ten thousand entities] and nourishes them: it lets them grow and nurtures them, specifies them and completes them, protects and covers them."

Zhang 63 NUMBERED TEXT NOTE

1. This commentary is only transmitted in the 取善集 but fits Wang Bi's thinking and vocabulary.

Zhang 63 Translation Notes

1. The subject, the Sage Ruler, is introduced here from *Laozi* 2.2 and 2.3, to which the first two statements are linked by the commentary. The passage there runs: "This is why the Sage takes residence in management without interference and practices teaching without words." In Wang Bi's commentary on *Laozi* 17.1, this statement is again quoted for the characterization of the Great Man, *da ren* 大人.

2. This phrase seems to link up with two statements in the *Laozi*. The term *tian dan* 恬淡 occurs only once in the *Laozi*, namely, in *Laozi* 31, for which there is no commentary by Wang Bi and even some tradition for his assuming that the *zhang* is spurious. The phrase there talks about the reluctance of the Gentleman to make use of the military. He "considers quietness and insipidness as the best, and [even] if he is victorious, he will not exult," the text runs there. The particular reference, however, seems to be to *Laozi* 35.3, "The words [however], uttered about the Way indeed are stale; they are without taste!"

3. The phrase does not have a match. Although it clearly refers to the chain on the right about the "big" 大, it therefore assumes a *pars pro toto* role. This has to be reflected in the translation, because the stylistic position of the phrase implies a second, a shadow, phrase: "[even] the Sage only by not acting upon [things] that have already become difficult, is in the end able to take care of difficulties." Wang Bi's commentary proceeds from the assumption of this shadow phrase.

4. The linkage of this phrase with the rest is not clear to me, and Wang Bi's commentary does not provide any guideline. The second part, however, clearly relates to the "difficulty" section, so that, for lack of a better choice, I was forced by default to assign this passage to the chain dealing with "great" things.

5. The phrase again has no match and is a *pars pro toto* construct. The shadow phrase would be: "That is why even the Sage is careful about promises for fear of losing trust."

6. The phrase has no match and fulfills a *pars pro toto* role. It is treated as such by Wang Bi, who supplements the shadow references.

Zhang 64 Numbered Text Notes

1. This text is not transmitted in the 集註本.

2. It is probable that the 集註本 retains some trace of a phrase here that was built in strict parallel to the previous commentary. I am unable, however, to extract from the nonsensical 閒 how this element might have looked.

3. 郭店 A has a *zhang* consisting of the first part of this *zhang* up to 足下. It puts the rest of the modern *zhang* 64 into another *zhang* that starts with 為知者 敗之 and goes to the end. 郭店 C also contains this second *zhang*.

Zhang 64 Translation Notes

1. From this *Xici* passage also comes the identification of the subject of the phrase. The Gentleman mentioned as the subject in the *Xici* passage in fact operates as the model for the Sage Ruler, as his responsibility is the entire society. In order not to confuse terminology, I have inserted the Sage Ruler as the general subject of these sentences. In his *LZWZLL*, Wang Bi develops this thought into a general ontological argument; cf. *LZWZLL* 4.1 ff. The *Laozi* text 64.1 is indirectly quoted in Wang's commentary to *Laozi* 73.8.

2. Although Wang Bi speaks of the "four" statements, he in fact groups them into two pairs through the first sentence of the commentary. The corresponding parts in both pairs, however, are linked again, but this is hard to make visible.

3. The same phrase is in *Laozi* 29.3, where Wang Bi adds a long commentary, the basis of the present commentary as well as of my translation.

Zhang 65 Numbered Text Note

1. All commentators agree that the passage transmitted here in the early (and all available) editions is corrupt. The most systematic attempt at reconstruction has been made by Tao Hongqing, who suggests: 智猶巧也以智巧治國乃所以賊之故謂之賊也. This rearranges some of the linguistic material but does not establish a coherent text. The replacement of *zhi* 治 with *qiao* 巧 fails to pick up the hint in the formula 以智術動民. . . . I agree with Hatano Tarō and Lou Yulie in not following this emendation. In this corrupted passage the notion of *zei* 賊, translated here as "plague," as the antonym of *fu* 福 in the next phrase, was probably explained. The core sentence, however, seems lost. I therefore suggest cutting the entire section as it stands, because the argument links directly to where I begin.

Zhang 65 Translation Notes

1. This passage has to be read in the context of *Laozi* 10, where in fact the Sage Ruler is depicted as operating the *xuan de* 玄德, the capacity coming from That-which-is-Dark, in analogy to the operations described through this term in *Laozi* 51 and Wang Bi's commentary. For the interpretation of the terms *deep* and *distant*, cf. *LZWZLL* 2.24 and 2.26.

2. For this argument about the continued validity of the insights gained by those in old times, who "were good at the Way," see *Laozi* 14.4 and 14.5: "That holding [today] on to the Way of antiquity it is possible [for a Sage Ruler] to regulate occurrences of the present, and that [from these] one [the Sage Ruler] has something by which to cognize the oldest beginning, this [I] call the continuity of

the Way." Wang Bi comments: "The featureless and nameless is the ancestor of the ten thousand kinds of entities. Although the present and antiquity are not the same, although times have changed and customs have changed, there definitely is no one who has not based himself on this [featureless and nameless] by way of completing their regulated order. That is why it 'is possible' [for him] to 'to hold on to the way of antiquity by way of regulating occurrences of the present.' Although high antiquity is far away, its Way still persists. That is why, although one is existing today, it is possible 'by means of this [present-day reality] to cognize the oldest beginning.'"

3. This verbatim repetition of the main text without any explanatory matter must mean that the commentary is corrupt here. We might expect either [lost] explanations to be followed by the [existing] verbatim quotation after a "That is why [the text] says" or [lost] explanations inserted into these verbatim elements.

Zhang 66 Numbered Text Note

1. The Mawangdui texts and the entire textual tradition have an inconsistency here. While the 上 from the 上/下 pair is taken up in the 處之上, the 先 from the 先/後 pair is not, and reappears as 前 in 處之前. The 郭店 A alone is consistent with this point.

Zhang 67 Numbered Text Note

1. The transmission of this first phrase is intriguing. The 傅奕古本 and 范應元本 write 吾大, 馬王堆 B writes 我大, but all old traditions, including the Heshang gong tradition, agree that there is no 道. This is transmitted only in the Daozang edition of the Wang Bi *Commentary*, the 四庫 edition based on the 張之象本 and the 浙江局本. Song texts such as the 集註本 already give a reading 我道 for the *Commentary* of Tang Emperor Mingdi. I therefore assume the 道 to have been introduced into the *Laozi* at this late date.

Zhang 67 Translation Notes

1. The identification of the subject of these sentences as the Sage Ruler is based, first, on Wang Bi's reference in the commentary to text 4 to *Laozi* 7.2. There the Sage "puts his own person in the background" and "disregards his own person," the very terms alluded to in this commentary; second, in the quotation from the *Xici* in the same commentary, the subject of the sentence is again the Sage.

2. The term *bu xiao* 不肖 involves a pun. It means "not like [something else]," but is at the same time a lexeme, which as the opposite of *xian* 賢, "the worthy,"

means "the unworthy." The text plays on both meanings. My brackets try to make the pun explicit.

3. The quotation from the *Xici* is verbatim, with one minor difference against the standard text of the *Zhouyi*. The standard text reads 以爲天下利, while the present text of Wang Bi's commentary reads 爲天下利. The full quotation in the *Xici* runs as follows: "As to setting up objects and bringing them to use and so establishing and completing instruments for the benefit of All Under Heaven, none is greater than the Sage." There is no commentary by Han Kangbo to this passage. It is important that the "greatness" referred to in the first text of *Laozi* 67 also appears in this *Zhouyi* passage.

4. The Commentary here reads 且猶取也. This means *qie* 且 has to be translated as a verb, like *qu* 取.

Zhang 68 Translation Note

1. This commentary section is difficult. Scholars have assumed that the grammatical parallelism between 不爭之德 and 用人之力 would force a translation here for the main text: "This is called the power to use others." However, this parallelism is superficial. The element 不與, on which the 不爭之德, "capacity of not fighting," rests, comes from the second part of the preceding *Laozi* text 善勝敵者不與, while the element 用人, "using others," rests on the first part of the preceding passage 善用人者爲之下. In order to establish symmetry between the two, the above commentary takes up the corresponding element here, namely, 人之力. Once the nonparallel is established, the commentary reads quite comfortably.

Zhang 69 Numbered Text Note

1. After 是謂行無行, both 集註本 and 張之象本 give a curious commentary, 彼遂不止. It has been incorporated into modern editions. As Hatano Tarō has pointed out, this commentary piece seems to have been moved here, verbatim, from the Heshang gong commentary on the same phrase. There, however, it is integrated into a complete sentence 彼遂不止爲天下賊 . . . According to the inherited arrangement, Wang Bi's commentary would resume after 扔無敵 with the words 行謂行陳也, which clearly comments upon the 行無行. I have therefore eliminated this piece and rearranged the segments of the *Laozi* text here to accord with Wang Bi's own indications.

Zhang 69 Translation Notes

1. Wang Bi's commentary to *Laozi* 30.4 reads: "'Get [things] done' is like 'bring order.' [The above phrase] means: someone who is good at using troops will just set his mind on bringing order to troubles and that is it, but he will not by means of military force impose violent [rule] in All Under Heaven."

2. The same argument is made in Wang Bi's comm. on *Laozi* 67.6.

Zhang 70 Numbered Text Note

1. For this segment, the earliest sources for Wang Bi's commentary do not help; they both give 君 in connection with 事. However, Wang Bi refers to this passage in a statement about the *Laozi* in the *LZWZLL* 6.1 言不遠宗事不失主. From this reference it clear that Wang's reading was 事有主. In his comments on *Laozi* 49.5, Wang Bi again uses the pattern of this pair of phrases, saying 物有其宗事有其主. Although here the 言 gave way to the 物, the phrase 事有其主 remains intact. I therefore assume that Wang Bi's commentary has been adapted to a reading that prevailed in other traditions. The surviving commentary readings in the 集註本 and 張之象本 still show the change. The transmitted form is 宗萬物之宗也君萬物之主也. From the repetition of the 宗 in the first segment, a repetion of the 君 in the second segment could be expected. The original 主 was replaced by 君, but not the second 主.

Zhang 70 Translation Notes

1. In his *LZWZLL*, Wang Bi quotes this passage with direct reference to the *Laozi*, saying that the "words [of the *Laozi* text] do not depart from the ancestor, and [his] activities do not lose [sight] of the ruler." Accordingly, the "I" is *Laozi* himself. On the other hand, the *Laozi* elements used by Wang Bi in his commentary here come from passages where the subject is the Sage. The relevant passage in *Laozi* 47.3 runs: "That is why the Sage cognizes without going to [the objects] and gives [the correct] name to [the objects] without looking at [them]. [In short] without his acting [on them], he gets [them] completed." Wang Bi comments on *Laozi* 47.4: "As he is clear about the nature of the entities, he just goes by that [nature] and nothing more. That is why [, as the text says,] even 'without his acting [on them,]' he has them become 'complete'" [themselves]. As the Sage appears in the last phrase of *Laozi* 70 and as, consequently, there is a difference between the "I" and the Sage, we have to assume that, for Wang Bi, Laozi basically belongs to the category of the Sage but remains slightly inferior to *the* Sage, Confucius.

2. These two statements, nearly verbatim, resemble those made in Wang Bi's commentary to *Laozi* 20.3: "The vulgar scholars are beguiled by beauty and pro-

motion, bedazzled by glory and profits." The simple "others" here are the *zhong ren* 衆人 there the "vulgar scholars." On them, cf. my *The Craft of a Chinese Commentator*, 128..

3. For a detailed analysis of the rhetorical structure of these first phrases of *Laozi* 70, cf. my *The Craft of a Chinese Commentator*, 60–72.

4. The full passage of the *Xici* to which Wang Bi refers here runs: "It is a fact that the *Yi* is that by which the Sage pursues to the very end the deep, and investigates the barely existing. Insofar as he [pursues to the very end] the deep, he is able to penetrate the intentions of All Under Heaven. Insofar as he [investigates] the barely existing, he is able to complete the endeavors of All Under Heaven."

Zhang 71 NUMBERED TEXT NOTES

1. The two textual traditions 是以聖人之不病以其病病是以不病, as well as the tradition given here, are in fact both present in the textual family of Wang Bi's *Laozi*, the first in the 馬王堆 manuscripts (which shares it with the 想爾本), the second in 傅奕古本 and the 范應元本 (which shares it with the 河上公 tradition). Due to the generally closer relationship of the Wang Bi *Laozi* to Fu Yi's text, here I have opted for this alternative. This is supported by the commentary, which seems to take up the general statement, not its application by the Sage.

2. This commentary is not transmitted elsewhere. Its content seems authentic.

Zhang 71 TRANSLATION NOTE

1. The subject is identified as the ruler on the basis of the frequent invectives against the use of knowledge as an instrument of governing; cf. *Laozi* 65.3 with commentary, and 10.4 with commentary.

Zhang 72 TRANSLATION NOTES

1. Wang Bi quotes this phrase without the 矣. On the basis of the overwhelming evidence of the close and distant members of his textual family, I have inserted it. Lou Yulie gives an inaccurate punctuation of both the *Laozi* and Wang Bi here.

2. Wang Bi translates the "frugality," *jian* 儉, which is one of the "three treasures" of the Sage in *Laozi* 67, into the notion of "modesty," *qian* 謙; cf. Wang Bi on *Laozi* 69.2.

3. I do not find a direct reference to the term 生 used in this manner. However, in *Laozi* 7.2, the Sage is imitating Heaven and Earth by putting himself into the

background and disregarding his own person. The result for him is described by terms such as 先, he "will come to be to the fore" and 存, "he will persist," while for Heaven and Earth the result is 長久, to "excel and live" [long].

4. The terms *yao* 耀 and *guang* 光 are used together by both the *Laozi* and Wang Bi. According to *Laozi* 58.10, the Sage "enlightens but does not investigate," 光而不耀, which is commented on by Wang Bi: "By means of enlightenment he clears up what has deluded them [the people] but does not by means of his enlightenment shed light on their [the people's] secret hideouts. This is what is said [in *Laozi* 41.3] 'It is the [Sage's] Way of enlightening to be well-nigh dark.'"

Zhang 73 Numbered Text Notes

1. Shima Kuniō, p. 209, has argued that the segment 是以聖人猶難之 was not part of the *Laozi* in the Han dynasty but was included in the text before the Tang. The argument has received additional support from the two Mawangdui manuscripts, neither of which has the passage. On the other hand, the evidence for this passage's being in Wang Bi's *Laozi* is solid. The quotation in Zhang Zhan's *Liezi zhu* includes a reference to the Sage, and Lu Deming gives the pronunciation of two terms from the passage about the Sage.

2. This commentary is not transmitted in the 集註本.

Zhang 73 Translation Notes

1. 孰 *shu* is a rhetorical question for which the answer is supposed to be evident; cf. my *The Craft of a Chinese Commentator*, 314, note 29. Wang Bi in fact makes this clear by providing the implied answer in the Commentary: the Sage.

2. The Sage "practices teaching without words." [*Laozi* 2.3] The particulars of this teaching are dealt with in *Laozi* 42, where Wang Bi comments on the *Laozi* phrase: "What other people teach, I also teach other people" (42.2) with the words "My teaching of other people does not consist in forcing them to follow, but in making use of [their] That-which-is-of-itself-what-it-is. [I] take up their highest ordering principle [and teach that,] following it, they will necessarily enjoy luck, [while] deviating from it, they will necessarily suffer misfortune. That is why other people's teaching each other to deviate from it [with the result] that they necessarily draw their own misfortune upon themselves, is like my teaching them not to deviate from it [which will necessarily bring them luck and thus positively teach them the same lesson others will teach negatively]." The phrase after "following it . . ." is nearly the same as the present comment.

3. Similar arguments are made by Wang Bi in *LZWZLL* 4.1 ff., and in his comments on *Laozi* 64.1ff.

Zhang 74 Numbered Text Note

1. The indications in the commentary here are too scanty to permit decision between the 傅奕古本 version and the decidedly more elegant 馬王堆 version. I have opted for the text generally closer to Wang Bi's *Laozi*.

Zhang 74 Translation Notes

1. The use of *wu* 吾 in the sense of "one" occurs in classical authors such as the *Mengzi*. A fine example is Mengzi's discussion with Xuan of Qi (*Mengzi* 3/1A/7) 老吾老以及人之老幼吾幼以及人之幼, "treating the elders in one's [family with the reverence due to] elders so that [this treatment] shall be extended to the elders of others, and treating the young in one's [family with the kindness due to the] young so that [this treatment] shall be extended to the young of others—and All Under Heaven will go round in [one's] palm" is a fine example of this use. In the same passage, *wu* 吾 is also used by both King and *Mengzi* for themselves. The current translations of this *Laozi* passage all assume that the "who" in the last section of this Wang Bi text refers to those committing the crimes, "who would dare to do" in the sense of "who would dare to commit them." This reading suffers from a lack of linkage to the following section, which says that such personal execution of villains by the ruler will end up hurting the ruler himself, and that he should leave the killing to the spontaneous action of those resenting deviation and the absence of humaneness.

2. The image of the Great Carpenter seems to refer to Heaven in the same sense as the image of the Great Authority in *Laozi* 72.1 and is read by Wang Bi as a reference to Heaven. From the commentary here it is clear that the executions are to be handled by the good people who go along and espouse humaneness. These people then are the counterpart to Heaven.

Zhang 75 Numbered Text Note

1. In the 集註本, this comment is followed by another statement: 疑此非老子之所作: "probably this has not been written by Laozi." In Dong Sijing's 董思靖 道德眞經集解 the same statement is quoted as: 此章疑非老子所作: "this *zhang* probably has not been written by Laozi." It is improbable that the statement is from Wang Bi's hand. He gives a commentary to the chapter and reads it in a manner quite compatible with statements elsewhere in the *Laozi* and his commentary.

Zhang 75 Translation Notes

1. From the commentary to this statement, which speaks of people becoming "wicked," 僻, it is clear that the standard reading for *ji* 饑, namely, "hungry" or "starving," does not apply. According to the *Mozi* 5/5/10, "if the five grains are not harvested, one calls it *ji.*" The term denotes the causes of famine more than famine itself.

2. Dong Siqing's *Dao De zhenjing jijie* adds a note here that is not transmitted elsewhere: "Wang Bi says: This *zhang* has probably not been written by Laozi." The zhang has suffered much from the bluntness with which some textual traditions have put the blame for all social distress and upheaval on the ruler. From Wang Bi's commentary not only to this *zhang* it seems clear that his text followed the most radical line, transmitted today in Fu Yi's "Old MS."

Zhang 76 Numbered Text Note

1. Fu Yi and the other members of the textual family read for the main text instead of *mie* 滅, "will go under," *bu sheng* 不勝, " will not win." As the *zhang* deals with the relationship between death and *qiang* 強 in its double meaning, this "will not win" definitely is inferior to the ruler's "going under." Wang Bi's commentary stresses that a ruler who uses violence to establish his hegemony in All Under Heaven will be "loathed by the other entities," which means that they will get together to make an end of him. This reading is again confirmed by a very old variant transmitted by Zhang Zhan in his *Liezi Commentary*, whose reading I have adopted. This in turn forces us into the unusual step of accepting the reading *mie* for the main text, although it is transmitted only in early texts quoting the *Laozi*, such as the *Huainanzi* and the *Wenzi*, but not in a single surviving text edition, including the MWD manuscripts.

Zhang 76 Translation Notes

1. The term *qiang* 強 denotes violence in the sense of both aggressive and unyielding. It is used in this *zhang* in both senses; for the dead, the aspect is the unyielding rigor; further down for the military, it is aggressive violence.

2. Fu Yi does not have *wan wu* 萬物 here; neither does Zhuang Zun. However, Fan Yingyuan and the two MWD manuscripts all have it. There is thus no basis for a decision. The *wanwu* here stand in contrast to the trees and grasses, and therefore must be the animate nature, not the ten thousand kinds of entities, as usual.

Zhang 77 Numbered Text Note

1. The reconstruction of Wang Bi's *Laozi* text is difficult here. I have opted for the 傅奕古本 as a base text for the following reasons. 孰能損有餘 以奉不足 於天下者 is taken up in the commentary with the "translation" 唯能處盈而全 虛 損有以補無 和光同塵. The core phrase here seems to be 損有以補無, which corresponds best to the 傅奕古本 version. The 損, which is absent in the two Mawangdui manuscripts, is necessitated by the commentary 損有.. and present in 莊遵. The alternative offered by the 范應元本 to write 以奉天下 does not accommodate the 無 in 補無 in the commentary phrase, which the 不足於天下 seems to do. The alternative 天 for 天下 in the Mawangdui manuscripts does not seem viable, because Heaven could hardly be considered in need of supplement. The alternative 有道者 offered by the 馬王堆 B (又道者) and the 范應元本 is not supported by the commentary's 唯其 道也, which has to be inverted to 其唯道 也 to accommodate an existing textual version. From the commentary it follows that the 者 after 道 in the text cannot be read as a reference to a person's having achieved the Dao, but refers just to the Dao itself. With the 和光同塵, Wang Bi refers back to *Laozi* 4 where the subject under discussion is the Dao not the Sage. That is also why the emendation proposed by Tōjō Itsudō to change 道 to 有道 者 cannot be accepted.

Zhang 77 Translation Notes

1. The same quote occurs for the Sage in Wang Bi on *Laozi* 5.2, and the same identification of the Sage and the Great Man is made in Wang Bi on *Laozi* 17.1.

2. These two statements about the Sage also occur in *Laozi* 2.4.

3. Two options are offered by the textual tradition for the translation of both text and commentary here. In one, the Way itself is spoken of, and the Sage then imitates it. This would presume a reading of "only the Way." In the other, "he who has the Way" is spoken of. Wang Bi refers to the 唯道者乎 of the text with a 唯道 乎, which seems to indicate that he read "only the Way." The statements repeated in Wang's commentary refer in one case, *Laozi* 56.5 and 55.6, to the Sage and in the other, *Laozi* 4.1, to the Way, so that from this cross-reference, no conclusions can be drawn. Furthermore, the grand language in the beginning of the commentary to 77.2 would seem to better befit the Dao than the Sage. Interestingly enough, the pair of phrases about the Sage in 77.2, also occurring in *Laozi* 2.4, have a different function there. In 2.4 the second phrase "[the particular] achievements come about without his installing" [himself in them] is a general one summing up a preceding pair, one element of which is the phrase: "the Sage acts, but does not presume" [upon the other entities], while in 77.2 the two together form an equal pair.

Zhang 78 Numbered Text Note

1. This commentary is not transmitted in the 集註本.

Zhang 78 Translation Note

1. In his commentary on *Laozi* 13.5, Wang Bi writes about the Sage 無以易 其身, which in part is a verbatim quotation from the last phrase of the *Laozi* text above. The *zhi* 之 at the end of *Laozi* 78.1 technically refers to water, but through the identification of the Sage Ruler with the water's characteristic, it also refers to him himself. The meaning of the term 易 in the sense of "alter" or even "deform" is inferred from Wang Bi on *Laozi* 13.6, where a parallelism is established between 易 and 損, "to detract from" or "to alter." The two even appear as a binomial in this commentary. In the same sense it appears in Wang Bi on *Laozi* 17.6. Because of the "wordless" teaching of the Sage, "there is no other entity that can alter his words, [his] words by necessity are being followed." Translators such as Chan, Lau, and Henricks have rendered it "to replace." I see no other passage in the *Laozi* to justify this rendering.

Zhang 79 Translation Notes

1. This refers to *Laozi* 63.2: "With regard to big and small, many and few [resentments], [he] reciprocates for the resentment by means of [his] receipt/capacity." Wang Bi's commentary: "If there is a small resentment, it is not worth reciprocating. If it is a big resentment, then it is a case where All Under Heaven desires the execution [of the culprit]. [His] going along with what All Under Heaven agrees on is [meant by] 'receipt/capacity.'" The Sage, in other words, does not reciprocate.

2. These two phrases were considered important enough by Wang Bi to be included in the *Laozi*'s core program, as outlined in *LZWZLL* 2.44.

3. The sparseness and partially bad transmission of the commentary in the *zhang* make an extrapolative reading well-nigh impossible.

Zhang 80 Numbered Text Note

1. The segment 至治之極 民各 is carried only by the 傅奕古本 and the 范 應元本. Wang Bi uses the expression 治之極 on two occasions in his *Laozi* commentary, on *Laozi* 63.1 以無爲爲居 以不言爲教 以恬淡爲味 治之極也, and on *Laozi* 58.3 言誰知善治之極乎. On both occasions, it may well refer to an

expression of the *Laozi* itself. The only place where such an expression occurs is in the segment above. I therefore have opted for accepting it as part of Wang Bi's *Laozi*.

Zhang 80 TRANSLATION NOTES

1. For an explanation of this "return to antiquity," see note 2 below.

2. The allusion in the first commentary to a "return to antiquity," which is not explicitly mentioned in the *Laozi* text, is explained through the context in which the "knotted cords" appear in the *Xici*. I have, therefore, from Wang Bi's perspective, included this *Xici* reference in brackets in the main text, because Wang Bi doubtlessly assumed that the *Laozi* was referring to this passage.

Zhang 81 NUMBERED TEXT NOTE

1. The existing text/commentary arrangement is not satisfactory. First, the sequence is irregular. The two parallel phrases about beautified words both receive a commentary, the next commentary comes after one pair, uncommented on altogether, and the first phrase of a third pair. The standard would seem to be that the first in each pair has a commentary, while the second is explained by implication as being merely the inversion. I have thus rearranged the transmitted sequence where the commentary 本在樸也 comes after the *Laozi* phrase 美言不信 to insert it after the next phrase 知者不博. The second problem is that the commentary "the absolute is in the One" does not tie in with either the phrase it follows or any other phrase in that section. The MWD B has preserved a reading for the transmitted phrase 善者不辯, which is 善者不多; this must have been in Wang's text, and the commentary must have followed this sentence, which also settles the rest. The relationship between the three pairs is the next problem. As they are three, and there is no other parallel group of three sentences or pairs, they break down in IPS, into two plus one, the one being the general statement. The only pair, plus commentary, qualifying for a generalization of the other two is the one about the person "doing good." Again, the MWD B provides a text that puts this sentence at the end of the three pairs. The MWD A is fragmentary at this place, but from the surviving bits, it is clear that it had the same sequence as MWD B.

Bibliography

Balazs, Etienne, and Yves Hervouet, eds. *A Sung Bibliography (Bibliographie der Sung)*. Hong Kong: Chinese University Press, 1978.

Ban Gu 班固. *Hanshu* 漢書. 12 vols. Peking: Zhonghua Press, 1964.

Beijing daxue zhexue xi Zhongguo zhexueshi jiaoyanshi 北京大學哲學系中國哲學史教研室 ed. *Zhongguo zhexue shi jiaoxue ziliao xuanji* 中國哲學史教學資料選輯. Peking: Zhonghua Press, 1981–82.

Benn, Charles. "Taoism As Ideology in the Reign of Emperor Hsüan-tsung (712–755)." Ph.D. diss., University of Michigan, 1977.

Boltz, Judith. *A Survey of Taoist Literature, Tenth to Seventeenth Century*. China Research Monograph 32. Berkeley: University of California Press, 1987.

Boltz, William G. "The *Lao Tzu* Text that Wang Pi and Ho-shang Kung Never Saw." *Bulletin of the School of Oriental and African Studies* 48:5 (1985): 493–501.

———. "The Religious and Philosophical Significance of the 'Hsiang Erh' *Lao-Tzu* in the Light of the Ma-Wang-Tui Silk Manuscripts." *Bulletin of the School of Oriental and African Studies* 45 (1982):95–117.

———. "Textual Criticism and the Ma Wang tui *Lao tzu*." *HJAS* 44:1 (1984):185–224.

Bumbacher, Stephan P. *The Fragments of the Daoxue zhuan*. Frankfurt/M: Peter Lang, 2000.

Chan, Wing-tsit. *The Way of Lao-tzu*. Indianapolis and New York: Bobbs-Merrill, 1963.

Chang, Chung-yue. "The Metaphysics of Wang Pi," Ph.D. diss., University of Pennsylvania, 1979.

———. "Wang Pi on the Mind." *Journal of Chinese Philosophy* 9 (1982):77–105.

Chao Gongwu 晁公武. *Junzhai dushu zhi jiaozheng* 郡齋讀書志校證. Edited by Sun Meng 孫猛. Shanghai: Shanghai guji Press, 1990.

Chao Yiduan 晁貽端, ed. *Chao shi congshu* 晁氏叢書. Liuan: Daixuelou, 1826–1832.

Chao Yuezhi 晁說之. "Fuzhi ji 鄜畤記." In *Ji Tangzi Laozi Daode jing zhu* 集唐字老子道德經注, p. 1.

———. *Songshan Jingyu sheng ji* 嵩山景迂生集, in Chao Yiduan 晁貽端, ed. *Chao shi congshu* 晁氏叢書.

———. *Songshan wenji* 嵩山文集, in *Sibu congkan* 四部叢刊. Shanghai: Commercial Press, n.d.

———. "Ti xieben *Laozi* hou 題寫本老子後." In *id. Songshan Jingyu sheng ji*, ch. 18, p. 7b–8a.

———. "Wang Bi Laozi Daode jing ji 王弼道德眞經記," in *Daode zhen jing zhu*, appendix.

Chen Jingyuan 陳景元. *Daode zhen jing zangshi zuanwei pian* 道德眞經藏室纂微篇. In *Zhengtong Daozang*, Schipper 714.

Chen Qiyou 陳奇猷, ed. *Hanfeizi jishi* 韓非子集釋. 2 vols. Peking: Zhonghua Press, 1962. Cf. Liao. *The Complete Works of Han Fei Tzu*.

Chen Shixiang 陳世驤. "'Xiang Er' Laozi Daojing Dunhuang canjuan lunzheng '想爾' 老子道德經敦煌殘卷論證." *Tsing Hua Journal of Chinese Studies* 1: 2 (1957):41–62.

Chen Zhensun 陳振孫. *Zhizhai shulu jieti* 直齋書錄解題. Shanghai: Shanghai guji Press, 1987.

Cheng Rong 程榮, ed. *Han Wei congshu* 漢魏叢書. Shanghai: Commercial Press, 1925.

Cherniak, Susan. "Book Culture and Textual Transmission in Sung China." *HJAS* 54:1 (1994):5–125.

Chunqiu fanlu zhuzi suoyin 春秋繁露逐字索引. Edited by D. C. Lau. Hong Kong: Commercial Press, 1994.

Chunqiu Zuozhuan zhengyi 春秋左傳正義. In *Shisan jing zhushu*, vol. 2, edited by Ruan Yuan.

Congshu jicheng 叢書集成 *chubian* 初編. Edited by Wang Yunwu 王雲五. Shanghai: Commercial Press, 1936.

Couvreur, Séraphin. *'Li Ki,' ou mémoires sur les bienséances et les cérémonies. Texte Chinois avec une double traduction en Français et en Latin*. 2 vols. Repr. Paris: Belles Lettres, 1950.

Daode zhen jing jizhu. See Wang Pang.

Daode zhen jing zhu 道德眞經註. With commentary by Wang Bi. In *Zhengtong Daozang*, Schipper 690.

Demiéville, Paul M. *Choix d'Études Sinologiques (1921–1970)*. Leiden: E. J. Brill, 1973.

———. "Notes additionelles sur les éditions imprimées du Canon Bouddhique."

In Paul Pelliot. *Les Débuts de l'Imprimerie en Chine*. Paris: Maisonneuve, 1953. 121–38.

———. "Langue et littérature chinoises. Résumé des cours de 1946–1947." *Annuaire du Collège de France* 47 (1947):151–57. Repr. under the title "Le vocabulaire philosophique chinois, I; Tchouang-tseu, ch. II," in id., *Choix d'Études Sinologiques (1921–1970)*, 49–55.

Dong Sijing 董思靖. *Daode zhen jing jijie* 道德眞經集解. In *Zhengtong Daozang*, Schipper 705.

Dong Zhongshu. See *Chunqiu fanlu zhuzi soyin*.

Du Guangting 杜光庭. *Daode zhen jing guangshengyi* 道德眞經廣聖義. In *Zhengtong Daozang*, Schipper 725.

Du Yu 杜預. *Chunqiu jingzhuan jijie* 春秋經傳集解. 2 vols. Shanghai: Shanghai guji Press, 1988.

Duyvendak, Jan J. L. "The Dreams of the Emperor Hsuan Tsung." In *India Antiqua*, edited by Kern Institute, 102–08. Leiden: E. J. Brill, 1947.

Edgren, Soren. "Southern Song Printing at Hangzhou." *Bulletin of the Museum of Far Eastern Antiquities* 61 (1989):1–212.

Erkes, E. *Ho-shang-kung's Commentary on the Lao-tse*. Ascona: Artibus Asiae, 1950.

Ershier zi 二十二子. Zhejiang: Zhejiang shuju, 1875, reprint Shanghai: Shanghai guji Press, 1986.

Fa Lin 法琳. *Bianzheng lun* 辯正論, vol. 52. Ed. Taishō, T. 2110, 489–550. Main parts are also in Shi Daoxuan. *Guang Hong ming ji*. In *Taishō shinshū daizōkyō*. Tōkyō 1928–1934, vol. 52, T. 2103, ch. 13, p. 175–187.

Fan Ye 范曄. *Hou Han shu* 後漢書. Peking: Zhonghua Press, 1965.

Fan Yingyuan 范應元. *Laozi Daode jing guben jizhu* 老子道德經古本集註. In *Xu Guyi congshu* 續古逸叢書. Yangzhou: Jiangsu Guangling guji Press, 1994. Also reprinted in Yan Lingfeng 嚴靈峯, ed. *Wuqiubeizhai Laozi jicheng* 無求備齋老子集成, Coll. 1. Taipei: Yiwen Press, 1965.

Fang Xuanling 房玄齡. *Jinshu* 晉書. 10 vols. Peking: Zhonghua Press, 1974.

Fu Yi 傅奕. *Daode jing guben pian* 道德經古本篇. In *Zhengtong Daozang*, Schipper 665.

Gao Ming 高明. *Boshu Laozi jiaozhu* 帛書老子校注. Peking: Zhonghua Press, 1996.

Graham, Angus C. *Chuang-tzu: The Seven Inner Chapters and Other Writings from the Book Chuang-tzu*. London: Allen & Unwin, 1981.

———. *Later Mohist Logic, Ethics, and Science*. Hong Kong: Chinese University Press, 1978.

Guang Hong ming ji 廣弘明集. Edited by Shi Daoxuan 釋道宣. In *Taishō shinshū Daizōkyō*, vol. 52, T. 2103, 97–361.

Guanyin zi 關尹子. In *Sibu beiyao* 四部備要. Peking: Zhonghua Press, n.d.

Guo Xiang 郭象, comm. *Nanhua zhen jing zhu* 南華眞經注. In *Xu Guyi congshu* 續古逸叢書. Peking: Zhonghua Press, 1994.

Guo Zhongshu 郭忠恕. *Hanjian* 汗簡. Edited by Li Ling 李零 and Liu Xinguang 劉新光. Peking: Zhonghua Press, 1983.

Harbsmeier, Christopher. *Language and Logic*. In *Science and Civilization in China*, vol. VII.1, edited by Joseph Needham, Cambridge: Cambridge University Press, 1998.

Hanfeizi 韓非子. Cf. Chen Qiyou. *Hanfeizi jishi*. Cf. Liao. *The Complete Works of Han Fei Tzu*.

Hatano Tarō 波多野太郎. *Rōshi Ō chū kōsei* 老子王注校正. *Yokohama shiritsu daigaku kiyō* 橫濱市立大學紀要, Series A-2, No. 8 (1952); Series A-3, No. 15 (1953); Series A-8, No. 27 (1954).

He Yan 何晏, ed. *Lunyu jijie* 論語集解. In *Sibu beiyao*. Peking: Zhonghua, n.d.

Henricks, Robert G. "Examining the Chapter Divisions in the Lao-Tzu." *Bulletin of the School of Oriental and African Studies* XLV:3 (1982):501–24.

———. "Examining the Ma-Wang-Tui Silk Texts of the Lao-Tzu, with Special Note of Their Differences from the Wang Pi Text." *T'oung Pao* LXV:4–5 (1979):166–98.

———. "The Ma-Wang-Tui Texts of the Lao-Tzu and Lines of Textual Transmission." *Chinese Culture* XXVI:2 (June 1985):29–43.

———. "A Note on the Question of Chapter Divisions in the Ma-Wang-Tui Manuscripts of the Lao-Tzu." *Early China* 4 (1978–1979): 49–51.

Heshang gong 河上公. *Daode zhen jing zhu* 道德眞經注. In *Zhengtong Daozang*, Schipper 682. Cf. E. Erkes, trans. *Ho-shang-kung's Commentary on the Lao-tse*.

Heshang gong. See Zheng Chenghai and Wang Qia.

Huainanzi. 淮南子. In *Sibu beiyao*. Peking: Zhonghua, n.d.

Huainanzi zhuzi suoyin 淮難子逐字索引. (*A Concordance to the Huainanzi*). Edited by D. C. Lau. Hong Kong: Commercial Press, 1992.

Huang Zhuo 黃焯. *Jingdian shiwen huijiao* 經典釋文彙校. Peking: Zhonghua Press, 1980.

Huang Zongxi 黃宗羲. *(Zengbu) Song Yuan xue'an* (增補) 宋元學案. In *Sibu beiyao*. Peking: Zhonghua, n.d.

Hui Lin 慧琳. *Yiqie jing yinyi* 一切經音義, *Taishō Shinshū Daizōkyō*. Vol. 54, T.2128. Tōkyō 1929–1934.

Huida 惠達. *Zhaolun shu* 肇論疏. In *Zokuzōkyō* 續藏經, vol. 150. Taipei: Hsinwen-feng, 1976, 833–96.

Hung, William. "A Bibliographical Controversy at the T'ang Court A.D. 719." *HJAS* 20:1:2 (1957):74–134.

Illich, Ivan. *Im Weinberg der Texte*. Munich: Luchterhand, 1989.

Ji Tangzi Laozi Daode jing zhu 集唐字老子道德經注. In *Guyi congshu*. Peking: Zhonghua Press, 1990.

Ji Yun 紀昀. "Laozi Daode jing tiyao 老子道德經提要" vol. 1055. In Wenyuange Siku quanshu. Taipei: Taiwan Shangwu, 1983–99.

Jiao Hong 焦竑. *Guoshi jingji zhi* 國史經籍志. In *Yueyatang congshu* 粤雅堂叢書. Taipei: Hualian, 1965.

———. *Laozi yi* 老子翼. In *Zhengtong Daozang*, Schipper 1486. Repr. in Yan Lingfeng, ed. *Wuqiubeizhai Laozi jicheng*.

Jia Yi 賈誼. *Xinshu* 新書. In *Sibu beiyao*. Peking: Zhonghua, n.d.

Jingmenshi bowuguan 荊門市博物館, ed. *Guodian Chu mu zhujian* 郭店楚墓竹簡. Peking: Wenwu, 1998.

Jinshu. See Fang Xuanling.

Jiu Tangshu 舊唐書. See Liu Xu 劉昫.

Kandel, Barbara. *Taiping jing. The Origin and Transmission of the "Scripture on General Welfare": The History of an Unofficial Text*. Hamburg: Gesellschaft für die Natur- und Völkerkunde Ostasiens, Mitteilungen No. 75, 1979.

———. *Wen tzu: Ein Beitrag zur Problematik und zum Verständnis eines taoistischen Textes*. Berne: Lang, 1974.

Kitahara Mineki 北原峰樹, ed. *Rōshi Ō Hitsu chū sakuin* 老子王弼注索引. Hokyushū: Hokyushū Chūgoku shōten, 1987.

Laozi Daode jing 老子道德經. Ed. Wenyuange Siku quanshu, Taipei: Taiwan Shangwu, 1982–99. vol. 1055.

Lau, D. C. *Chinese Classics, Tao Te Ching*. Hong Kong: Chinese University Press, 1982.

Legge, James. *The Chinese Classics: Chun Tsew with Tso Chuen*. Repr. Hong Kong: Hong Kong University Press, 1960.

———. *The Chinese Classics: The Works of Mencius*. Repr. Hong Kong: Hong Kong University Press, 1960.

Liu Chongsheng 劉充升. "Daode zhen jing qushan ji xu 道德眞經取善集序," in Li Lin. *Daode zhen jing qushan ji*.

Li Dingsheng 李定生 and Xu Huijun 徐慧君, eds. *Wenzi yaoquan* 文子要詮. Shanghai: Fudan daxue Press, l988.

Li Fang 李昉 et al., eds. *Wenyuan yinghua* 文苑英華. Peking: Zhonghua Press, 1982.

Li Lin 李霖. *Daode zhen jing qushan ji* 道德眞經取善集. In *Zhengtong Daozang*, Schipper 718.

Li Qiao 李翹. *Laozi guzhu* 老子古註. Fenxiaoguan Press, 1929.

Li Shan 李善, comm. *Wenxuan Li Shan zhu* 文選李善註. 4 vols. In *Sibu beiyao*. Cf. also *Liuchen zhu Wenxuan*.

Li Shuchang 黎庶昌, ed. *Guyi congshu* 古逸叢書. 3 vols. Yangzhou: Jiangsu Guangling guji Press, 1990.

———. "Ke Guyi congshu xu 刻古逸叢書序." In *id., Guyi congshu*, 1/1a–2a.

Liang Jiong 梁迥. "Houxu 後序." In *Daode zhen jing jizhu*, in *Zhengtong Daozang*, Schipper, 706.

Liao, Wen-kuei. *The Complete Works of Han Fei Tzu. A Classic of Chinese Legalism*. 2 vols. London: Probsthain, 1939.

Lin, Paul J. *A Translation of Lao Tzu's Tao Te Ching and Wang Pi's Commentary*. Michigan Papers in Chinese Studies No. 30. Ann Arbor: Center for Chinese Studies, University of Michigan, 1977.

Liu Baonan 劉寶楠. *Lunyu zhengyi* 論語正義. In *Zhuzi jicheng*. Peking: Zhonghua Press, 1954, vol. 1.

Liu Dabin 劉大彬. *Maoshan zhi* 茅山誌. In *Zhengtong Daozang*, Schipper 304.

Liu Guojun 劉國鈞. "Laozi Wang Bi zhu jiaoji 老子王弼注校記." *Tushuguanxue jikan* 8:1 (1934):91–116.

Liu Shao 劉邵. *Renwu zhi* 人物志. Edited by. W. Bauer (Bao Wugang 鮑吾剛) as *Renwu zhi yinde* 人物志引得. San Francisco: Chinese Materials Center, 1974.

Liu Weiyong 劉惟永. *Daode zhen jing jiyi* 道德眞經集義. In *Zhengtong Daozang*, Schipper 724.

———. *Daode zhen jing jiyi dazhi* 道德眞經集義大旨. In *Zhengtong Daozang*, Schipper 723.

Liu Xiaobiao 劉孝標, comm. *Shishuo xinyu zhu* 世說新語注. Comm. to Liu Yiqing. *Shishuo xinyu*.

Liu Xu 劉昫. *Jiu Tangshu* 舊唐書. 16 vols. Peking: Zhonghua Press, 1975.

Liu Yiqing 劉義慶. *Shishuo xinyu* 世說新語. Shanghai: Shanghai guji Press, 1982. Cf. also Yu Jiaxi, *Shishuo xinyu jianshu*.

Liuchen zhu Wenxuan 六臣註文選. 2 vols. In *Sibu congkan*. Peking: Zhonghua Press, n.d.

Lou Yulie 樓宇烈, ed. *Wang Bi ji jiaoshi* 王弼集校釋. 2 vols. Peking: Zhonghua Press, 1980.

Lu Deming 陸德明. *Jingdian shiwen* 經典釋文. 3 vols. Shanghai: Shanghai guji Press 1985.

———. *Laozi Daodejing yinyi* 老子道德經音義. In *id., Jingdian shiwen*.

Lu Xisheng 陸希聲. *Daode zhen jing zhuan* 道德眞經傳. In *Zhengtong Daozang*, Schipper 685.

Lunyu jijie. See He Yan.

Lunyu yinde 論語引得. Harvard-Yenching Institute Sinological Index Series. Supplement No. 16. Repr. Taipei: Ch'eng-wen, 1966.

Lunyu zhushu 論語註疏. In *Shisan jing zhushu*, edited by Ruan Yuan.

Lynn, Richard J., trans. *The Classic of Changes: A New Translation of the I Ching As Interpreted By Wang Bi.* New York: Columbia University Press, 1994.

———. *The Classic of the Way and Virtue: A New Translation of the* Tao-te ching *of Laozi As Interpreted by Wang Bi.* New York: Columbia University Press, 1999.

Ma Duanlin 馬端臨. *Wenxian tongkao* 文獻通考. In *Sibu congkan.* Peking: Zhonghua, n.d.

Ma Xulun 馬敘倫. *Laozi jiaogu* 老子校詁. 3 vols. Repr., Peking: Zhonghua Press, 1974.

Mao shi zhengyi 毛詩正義. In *Shisan jing zhushu*, edited by Ruan Yuan.

Mather, Richard. "K'ou Ch'ien-chih and the Taoist Theocracy at the Northern Wei Court (425–451)." In *Facets of Taoism*, edited by H. Welch and A. Seidel, New Haven, Yale University Press, 102–122.

———, trans. *Shih-shuo Hsin-yu. A New Account of Tales of the World.* Minneapolis: Minnesota University Press, 1976.

Mawangdui Hanmu boshu zhengli xiaozu 馬王堆漢墓帛書整理小組. "Laozi jiaben yiben Fu Yi ben duizhao biao 老子甲本乙本傅奕本對照表." In *Mawangdui Hanmu boshu Laozi*, edited by Mawangdui Hanmu boshu zhengli xiaozu, Peking: Wenwu, 1976, 65–94.

———. *Mawangdui Hanmu boshu* 馬王堆漢墓帛書. Vols. 1 and 2. Peking: Wenwu Press, 1974.

———. *Mawangdui Hanmu boshu Laozi* 馬王堆漢墓帛書老子. Peking: Wenwu, 1976.

———. "Mawangdui Hanmu chutu *Laozi* shiwen 馬王堆漢墓出土老子釋文." *Wenwu* 文物 11 (1974):8–20.

Mengzi yinde 孟子引得. Harvard-Yenching Institute Sinological Index Series. Supplement No. 17. Taipei: Ch'eng-wen, 1966.

Mozi yinde 默子引得. Harvard-Yenching Institute Sinological Index Series. Supplement No. 21. Tōkyō: Tōyō bunko, 1961.

Mugitani Kuniō 麥谷邦夫. "'Rōshi Sōji shū' ni tsuite '老子想爾注' について." *Tōhō gakuhō* 57 (March 1985):75–107.

Nan Qi shu 南齊書. Cf. Xiao Zixian.

Nanhua zhenjing zhu. See Guo Xiang.

Ouyang Xiu 歐陽修 and Song Qi 宋祁. *Xin Tangshu* 新唐書. 20 vols. Peking: Zhonghua Press, 1975.

Pei Songzhi 裴松之, comm. *Sanguo zhi zhu* 三國志注. Commentary to Chen Shou, *Sanguo zhi*. Peking: Zhonghua Press, 1962.

Pelliot, Paul. *Les Débuts de l'Imprimerie en Chine*. Paris: Adrien-Maisonneuve, 1953.

Peng Hao 彭浩. *Guodian Chu jian "Laozi" jiaodu* 郭店楚簡〈老子〉校讀. Wuhan: Hubei renmin, 2000.

Peng Si 彭耜. *Daode zhen jing jizhu* 道德眞經集註. In *Zhengtong Daozang*, Schipper 707.

———. *Daode zhen jing jizhu shiwen* 道德眞經集註釋文. In *Zhengtong Daozang*, Schipper 708.

———. *Daode zhen jing jizhu zashuo* 道德眞經集註雜說. In *Zhengtong Daozang*, Schipper 709.

Peterson, Willard J. "Making Connections: 'Commentary on the Attached Verbalizations' of the Book of Change." *Harvard Journal of Asiatic Studies* 42:1 (1982):67–116.

Poon, Ming-sun. "Books and Publishing in Sung China (960–1279)." Ph.D. diss. University of Chicago, 1979.

Qian Zeng 錢曾. *Dushu minqiu ji* 讀書敏求記. In *Congshu jicheng chubian*, vol. 0049.

Qiang Siqi 強思齊. *Daode zhen jing xuande zuanshu* 道德眞經玄德纂疏. *Zhengtong Daozang* Schipper 711.

Qu Wanli 屈萬里. *Han shijing Zhouyi canzi jizheng* 漢石經周易殘字集證. Zhongyang yanjiuyuan lishi yuyan yanjiusuo zhuankan, 46 中央研究院歷史語言研究所專刊, 46. Taipei: Zhongyang yanjiuyuan lishi yuyan yanjiusuo, 1961.

Rao Zongyi 饒宗頤. *Laozi Xiang Er zhu jiaozheng* 老子想爾注校證. Shanghai: Shanghai guji Press, 1991.

———. "Laozi Xiang Er zhu xulun 老子想爾注續論." In *Fukui Hakushi shōju kinen Tōyō shisō ronshū* 福井博士頌壽記念東洋思想論集, edited by Fukui hakushi shōju kinen rombunshū kankōkai 福井博士頌壽記念論文集刊行會. Tōkyō: Fukui hakushi shōji kinen rombunshū kankōkai, 1960, 1155–71.

———. "Wu jianheng er nian Suo Dan xieben Daode jing canjuan kaozheng (jian lun Heshang gong ben yuanliu) 吳建衡二年索紞寫本道德經殘卷考證 (兼論河上公本源流). The Su Tan Manuscript Fragment of the Tao-Te Ching (A.D. 270)." *Journal of Oriental Studies* 2:1 (1955):1–71.

Roth, Harold D. *The Textual History of the Huai-nan tzu*. Ann Arbor: Association for Asian Studies Monograph 46, 1992.

Ruan Yuan 阮元, ed. *Shisan jing zhushu* 十三經注疏. 2 vols. Peking: Zhonghua Press, 1987.

Rump, Ariane, in coll. with Wing-tsit Chan, trans. *Commentary on the "Lao-tzu" by Wang Pi*. Monographs of the Society for Asian and Comparative Philosophy, No. 6. Honolulu: University Press of Hawaii, 1979.

Seidel, Anna K. *La Divinisation du Lao Tseu dans le Taoisme des Han*. Publications de l'École Française d'Extrême Orient LXXI. Paris: École Française d'Extrême-Orient, 1969.

————. "The Image of the Perfect Ruler in Early Taoist Messianism: Lao-Tzu and Li Hung." *History of Religions* 9:2–3 (1969/1970):216–47.

Shangshu dazhuan zhuzi suoyin 尙書大傳逐字索引. Edited by D. C. Lau. Hong Kong: Commercial Press, 1994.

Shangshu 尙書. See Ruan Yuan, ed. *Shisan jing zhushu*.

Shi Daoxuan 釋道宣. Cf. *Guang Hong ming ji*.

Shi Falin 釋法琳. *Bianzheng lun* 辯正論, vol. 52. *Taishō Shinshū Daizōkyō*, T. 2110, and in *Guang Hong ming ji*.

Shima Kuniō 島邦男. *Rōshi Kōsei* 老子校正. Tokyo: Kyukoshōin, 1973.

Sima Qian 司馬遷. *Shiji* 史記. 10 vols. Peking: Zhonghua Press, 1973.

Strickmann, Michael. "The Longest Taoist Scripture." *History of Religions* 17: 3–4 (1978):331–354.

Su Yu 蘇與. *Chunqiu fanlu yizheng* 春秋繁露義證. Peking: Zhonghua Press, 1992.

Sun Kuang 孫鑛. *Wang Bi zhu Laozi* 王弼注老子. In *Wuqiubeizhai Laozi jicheng*, first selection, edited by Yan Lingfeng.

Takeuchi Yoshiō 武內義雄. *Rōshi genshi* 老子原始. Tōkyō: Shimize Kobundō, 1926. Repr., Tōkyō: Kobundō, 1967.

————. *Rōshi no kenkyū* 老子の研究. Tōkyō: Kaizōsha, 1927.

Tao Hongqing 陶鴻慶. *Du Laozi zhaji* 讀老子札記. In *Tao Hongqing Laozi Wang Bi zhu kanwu buzheng*, edited by Yan Lingfeng. Taipei: Wuqiubeizhai, 1957.

————. "Laozi Wang Bi zhu kanwu 老子王弼注勘誤." In *Tao Hongqing Laozi Wang Bi zhu kanwu buzheng*, edited by Yan Lingfeng. Taipei: Wuqiubeizhai, 1957.

Tōjō Itsudō 東條一堂. *Rōshi Ō chū hyōshiki* 老子王註標識. In *Wuqiubeizhai Laozi jicheng*, edited by Yan Lingfeng.

Tongxuan zhenjing zhu 通玄眞經註. *Moxi zi* 默希子 comm. In *Zhengtong Daozang*, Schipper 746.

Tongxuan zhenjing zuanyi 通玄眞經續義. In *Zhengtong Daozang*, Schipper 748.

Tuo Tuo 脫脫 *et al. Songshi* 宋史. Peking: Zhonghua Press, 1977.

Twitchett, Denis. *Printing and Publishing in Medieval China*. New York: F. Beil, 1983.

Usami Shinsui 宇佐美灊水. *Rōshi dōtoku shinkyō—Ō chū Rōshi dōtoku kyō* 老子道德眞經王注老子道德經. In *Wuqiubeizhai Laozi jicheng*, edited by Yan Lingfeng.

Van der Loon, Piet. *Taoist Books in the Libraries of the Sung Period*. Oxford Oriental Institute, Monograph 7. London: Ithaca Press, 1984.

Wagner, Lothar. "Art As an Instrument for Political Legitimation during the Tang: The Small Script and The Legitimation Seal." *Oriens Extremus* 40:2 (1997).

Wagner, Rudolf G. *The Craft of a Chinese Commentator: Wang Bi on the Laozi*. Albany: State University of New York Press, 2000.

———. "Die Fragen Hui-yüan's an Kumârajiva." Ph.D. diss., University of Munich, 1969.

———. "Die Unhandlichkeit des Konfuzius." In *Weisheit. Archäologie der literarischen Kommunikation III*, edited by A. Assmann, 455–64. Munich: Fink Verlag, 1991.

———. "Exploring the Common Ground: Buddhist Commentaries on the Taoist Classic *Laozi*." In *Commentaries—Kommentare*, edited by Glenn Most. Göttingen: Vandenhoeck & Ruprecht, 1999, 95–120.

———. *Language, Ontology, and Political Philosophy in China: Wang Bi's Scholarly Exploration of the Dark (Xuanxue)*. Albany: State University of New York Press, 2003.

———. "Lebensstil und Drogen im chinesischen Mittelalter." *T'oung Pao* 59 (1973):79–178.

———. "The Impact of Conceptions of Rhetoric and Style upon the Formation of Early *Laozi* Editions: Evidence from Guodian, Mawangdui, and the Wang Bi *Laozi*." *Transactions of the International Conference of Eastern Studies* No. XLIV (1999): 32–56.

———. "The Wang Bi Recension of the *Laozi*." *Early China* 14 (1989):27–54.

———. "Wang Bi: 'The Structure of the *Laozi*'s Subtle Pointers' (*Laozi weizhi lilüe*)." *T'oung Pao* LXXII (1986):92–129.

Waley, Arthur. *The Analects of Confucius*. London: Allen & Unwin, 1938.

Wang Baoxuan 王葆玹. "Shilun Guodian Chu jian gepian de zhuanzuo shidai jiqi beijing—jian lun Guodian Baoshan Chumu de shidai wenti 試論郭店楚簡各篇的撰作時代及其背景——兼論郭店及包山楚墓的時代問題," *Zhexue yanjiu* 20 (1989):366–90.

———. "'Wuxing da yi' suo yin Wang Bi 'Zhouyi da yan lun' yiwen kaoshi '五行大義' 所引王弼 '周易大演論' 佚文考試." *Zhexue yanjiu* 8 (1983):67–74.

———. "Zenyang renshi Wang Bi de bentilun 怎樣認識王弼的本體論." *Wen shi zhe* 3 (1985):17–19. Repr. in *Zhongguo zhexue shi* 6 (1985):57–59.

———. *Zhengshi xuanxue* 正始玄學. Jinan: Qi Lu Press, 1987.

Wang Bi 王弼. *Laozi Daode jing zhu* 老子道德經注. In *id. Wang Bi ji jiaoshi*, vol. 1, edited by Lou Yulie, 1–193.

———. *Laozi weizhi lilüe* 老子微旨例略. In *Zhengtong Daozang*, Schipper 1255.

———. "Laozi zhilüe 老子指略." In *Zhongguo lidai zhexue wenxuan, Liang Han Sui Tang bian*, edited by Zhongguo Kexueyuan zhexue yanjiusuo, Zhongguo zhexueshi zu and Peking daxue zheshi jiaoyanshi, 308–323.

———. "Laozi zhilüe 老子指略." In *Wang Bi ji jiaoshi*, vol. 1, edited by Lou Yulie, 195–210.

———. *Laozi zhu* 老子注, under the title *Ji Tangzi Laozi Daode jing zhu* 集唐字老子道德經注. In *Guyi congshu*. Cf. P. Lin, *A Translation of Lao Tzu's Tao Te Ching and Wang Bi's Commentary*; cf. A. Rump with Wing-tsit Chan, *Commentary on the "Lao-tzu" by Wang Bi*.

———. "Lunyu shiyi 論語釋疑." In *Wang Bi ji jiaoshi*, vol. 2, edited by Lou Yulie, 621–637.

———. "Lunyu shiyi 論語釋疑," in Ma Guohan 馬國翰, ed., *Yuhan shanfang jiyishu* 玉函山房輯逸書. Kyōto: Chūban, 1980, vol. 3, 1769–75.

———. "Zhouyi lüeli 周易略例." In *Wang Bi ji jiaoshi*, vol. 2, edited by Lou Yulie, 591–620.

———. "Zhouyi lüeli 周易略例." In *Zhouyi Wang Han zhu*, ch. 10. In *Sibu beiyao*. Peking: Zhonghua, n.d.

———. "Zhouyi zhu 周易註." In *Wang Bi ji jiaoshi*, edited by Lou Yulie, vol. 1, p. 211; vol. 2, p. 590. Also as *Zhouyi Wang Han zhu*. In *Sibu beiyao*. Cf. Richard J. Lynn, trans. *The Classic of Changes*.

Wang Deyou 王德有, ed. and trans. *Laozi zhigui quanyi* 老子旨歸全譯. Chengdu: Bashu Press, 1992.

Wang Huai 王淮. "Wang Bi zhi Laoxue 王弼之老學." M.A. thesis, Taiwan National University, 1975.

Wang Niansun 王念孫. *Dushu zazhi* 讀書雜志. 3 vols. Shanghai: Commercial Press, 1933.

Wang Pang 王雱. *Daode zhen jing jizhu* 道德眞經集註. In *Zhengtong Daozang*, Schipper 706.

Wang Pu 王溥. *Tang huiyao* 唐會要. 2 vols. Peking: Zhonghua Press, 1990.

Wang Qia 王卡, ed. *Laozi Daode jing Heshang gong zhangju* 老子道德經河上公章句. Peking: Zhonghua Press, 1993.

Wang Qinruo 王欽若 et al., eds. *Cefu yuangui* 冊府元龜. Peking: Zhonghua Press, 1960.

Wang Weicheng 王維誠. "Wei Wang Bi zhuan *Laozi zhilüe* yiwen zhi faxian 魏王弼撰老子指略佚文之發見." (Peking daxue) *Guoxue jikan* 7:3 (1951):367–376.

Wang Xianqian 王先謙, ed. *Xunzi jijie* 荀子集解. 2 vols. Peking: Zhonghua Press, 1988.

Wang Yinglin 王應麟. *Yuhai* 玉海. Taipei: Hualin Press, 1964 (repr. of 1337 ed.).

Wang Zhongmin 王重民. *Laozi kao* 老子考. Peking: Zhonghua shuguan xiehui, 1927.

Wei Yuan 魏源. *Laozi benyi* 老子本義. In *Zhuzi jicheng* 諸子集成, Shanghai: Shanghai shudian, 1986, vol. 3.

Wei Zheng 魏徵. *Suishu* 隋書. 6 vols. Peking: Zhonghua Press, 1973.

Welch, H., and A. Seidel, eds. *Facets of Taoism.* New Haven, Conn.: Yale University Press, 1979.

Wenzi yaoquan 文子要詮. See Li Dingsheng and Xu Huijun, eds., id. *Wenzi yaoquan.*

Wenzi zhuzi suoyin 文子逐字索引. (A Concordance to the Wenzi). Edited by D. C. Lau. Hong Kong: Commercial Press, 1992.

Wilhelm, Richard. *Dschuang Dsi. Das Wahre Buch vom Südlichen Blütenland.* Jena: Eugen Diederichs, 1920.

Xi Kang 嵇康, with commentary by Dai Mingyang. "Yangsheng lun 養生論." In *Xi Kang ji jiaozhu.* Peking, Renmin wenxue Press, 1962, 143–160.

———, with commentary by Dai Mingyang 戴明揚. In *id., Xi Kang ji jiaozhu* 嵇康集校注. Peking: Renmin wexue Press, 1962.

Xia Song 夏竦. *Guwen sisheng yun* 古文四聲韻. Peking: Zhonghua, 1983.

Xiang Er. See Rao Zongyi.

Xiao Zixian 蕭子顯. *Nan Qi shu* 南齊書. 3 vols. Peking: Zhonghua Press, 1972.

Xiaojing zhushu 孝經注疏. In *Sibu beiyao.* Peking: Zhonghua, n.d.

Xie Shouhao 謝守灝. *Hunyuan shengji* 混元聖記. In *Zhengtong Daozang,* Schipper 770.

Xin Tangshu 新唐書. See Ouyang Xiu and Song Qi.

Xing Shou 邢璹. "Zhouyi lüeli zhu 周易略例注." In *Han Wei congshu* 漢魏叢書, edited by Cheng Rong 程榮, Shanghai: Commercial Press, 1975.

Xiong Ke 熊克. "Ke fu song 克伏誦." In *id. Daode zhen jing zhu.* In *Zhengtong Daozang,* Schipper 690; also in *Laozi Daode jing,* in *Wenyuange Siku quanshu,* Taipei: Taiwan Shangwu, 1982–99, vol. 1055, 185a–185b.

Xu Dachun 徐大椿. *Daode jing zhu* 道德經注. In *Xu Lingtai xiansheng yishu* 徐靈胎先生遺書, Wuxuan: no publ., 1860–90, vol. 12.

Xu Jian 徐堅. *Chuxue ji* 初學記. 3 vols. Peking: Zhonghua Press, 1989.

Yan Lingfeng 嚴靈峯. *Lao Zhuang yanjiu* 老莊研究. Hong Kong: Yazhou Press, 1959. Rev. ed., Taipei: Zhonghua Press, 1966.

———. *Laozi weizhi lilüe* 老子微旨例略. Taipei: Wuqiubeizhai, 1956.

———. (ed). *Wuqiubeizhai Laozi jicheng* 無求備齋老子集成. Taipei: Yiwen Press, 1965.

———. *Tao Hongqing Laozi "Wang Bi zhu kanwu" buzheng* 陶鴻慶《老子王弼注勘誤》補正. Taipei: Wuqinbeizhai, 1957.

Yan Shigu. *Xuanyan xinji ming Lao bu* P 2462. Paris: Bibliothèque Nationale.

Yang Bojun 楊伯峻, ed. *Liezi jishi* 列子集釋. Peking: Zhonghua Press, 1985.

Yao Nai 姚鼐. *Laozi zhangyi* 老子章義. Taipei: Guangwen Press, 1975.

Yao Shixue 姚氏學. *Bu Sanguo yiwenzhi* 補三國藝文志. In *Shiyuan congshu* 適園叢書. Shanghai, 1913–16.

Yu Jiaxi 余嘉錫. "Hanshi san kao 寒石散考." In *Yu Jiaxi lunxue zazhu* 余嘉錫論學雜著. Peking: Zhonghua Press, 1963, vol. 1, 181–226.

———. *Shishuo xinyu jianshu* 世說新語箋疏. Shanghai: Shanghai guji Press, 1989.

Zhan Ying 詹鍈, ed. *Wenxin diaolong yizheng* 文心雕龍義證. 3 vols. Shanghai: Shanghai guji Press, 1989.

Zhang Junfang 張君房. *Yunji qiqian* 雲笈七籤. ed. *Zhengtong Daozang*, Schipper 1032.

Zhang Zhan 張湛. *Liezi zhu* 列子注. See Yang Bojun, *Liezi jishi*.

Zhao Xibian 趙希弁. *Zhaode xiansheng junzhai dushu houzhi* 昭德先生郡齋讀書後志. In *Sibu congkan*. Peking: Zhonghua, n.d.

Zhao Xueshi (Bingwen) 趙學士 (秉文). *Daode zhen jing jijie* 道德眞經集解. In *Zhengtong Daozang*, Schipper 695.

Zheng Chenghai 鄭成海. *Laozi Heshang gong zhu jiaoli* 老子河上公注斠理. Taipei: Zhonghua Press, 1971.

Zheng Qiao 鄭樵. *Tongzhilüe* 通志略. In *Sibu beiyao*. Peking: Zhonghua, n.d.

Zheng Xuan 鄭玄. *Xiaojing zhushu*. See *Xiaojing zhushu*.

———. *Zhouli zhushu* 周禮註疏. In *id. Shisan jing zhushu*, edited by Ruan Yuan, 631–94.

Zhengtong Daozang 正統道藏, 60 boxes, Taipei: Yiwen, 1963.

Zhongguo kexueyuan zhexue yanjiusuo, Zhongguo kexueyuan zhexue yanjiusuo Zhongguo zhexueshi zu 中國科學院哲學研究所, 中國哲學史組 and Peking daxue zhexueshi jiaoyanshi 北京大學哲學史教研室, ed. *Zhongguo lidai zhexue wenxuan* 中國歷代哲學文選, *Liang Han Sui Tang bian* 兩漢隨唐編. Peking: Zhonghua Press, 1963.

Zhongyong 中庸. *Shisan jing zhushu*, edited by Ruan Yuan, 1625–1636.

Zhou Zhongfu 周中孚. *Zhengtang dushuji* 鄭堂讀書記. Repr., Peking: Shangwu Press, 1959.

Zhouyi Wang Han zhu 周易王韓注. In *Sibu beiyao*. Peking: Zhonghua, n.d.

Zhouyi yinde 周易引得. Harvard-Yenching Institute Sinological Index Series No. 10, Repr. Taipei: Ch'eng-wen, 1966.

Zhuang (Yan) Zun 莊(嚴)尊. *Daode zhenjing zhigui* 道德眞經指歸. In *Zhengtong Daozang*, Schipper 693.

———, "Junping shuo er jing mu 君平說二經目," In *id. Laozi zhigui quanyi*, edited by Wang Deyou, 131.

Zhuangzi yinde 莊子引得. *A Concordance to Chuang Tzu*. Harvard-Yenching Institute Sinological Index, Series Supplement No. 20. Cambridge: Harvard University Press, 1956.

Index

513